An INTRODUCTION to UK POLITICS

Joanie Willett & Arianna Giovannini

An INTRODUCTION to UK POLITICS
Place, Pluralism, and Identities

1 Oliver's Yard
55 City Road
London EC1Y 1SP

2455 Teller Road
Thousand Oaks,
California 91320

Unit No 323-333, Third Floor, F-Block
International Trade Tower
Nehru Place, New Delhi – 110 019

8 Marina View Suite 43-053
Asia Square Tower 1
Singapore 018960

Editor: Andrew Malvern
Assistant editor: Daniel Price
Production editor: Martin Fox
Copyeditor: William Baginsky
Proofreader: Derek Markham
Indexer: Silvia Benvenuto
Marketing manager: Fauzia Eastwood
Cover design: Francis Kenney
Typeset by: C&M Digitals (P) Ltd, Chennai, India

Editorial arrangement and Introduction © Joanie Willett and Arianna Giovannini 2024

Chapters 1 and 5 © Joanie Willett 2024
Chapters 2 and 6 © Arianna Giovannini 2024
Chapter 3 © Amina Easat-Daas and Simon Stevens 2024
Chapter 4 © Frederick Harry Pitts and Lorena Lombardozzi 2024
Chapter 7 © Judith Sijstermans 2024
Chapter 8 © Rosie Campbell 2024
Chapter 9 © Steven Harkins 2024
Chapter 10 © Thomas Caygill 2024
Chapter 11 © Patrick Diamond 2024
Chapter 12 © Kate Alexander-Shaw 2024
Chapter 13 © Clare Saunders 2024
Chapter 14 © Ben Whitham 2024

Apart from any fair dealing for the purposes of research, private study, or criticism or review, as permitted under the Copyright, Designs and Patents Act, 1988, this publication may not be reproduced, stored or transmitted in any form, or by any means, without the prior permission in writing of the publisher, or in the case of reprographic reproduction, in accordance with the terms of licences issued by the Copyright Licensing Agency. Enquiries concerning reproduction outside those terms should be sent to the publisher.

Library of Congress Control Number: 2023944527

British Library Cataloguing in Publication data

A catalogue record for this book is available from the British Library

ISBN 978-1-5296-0290-6
ISBN 978-1-5296-0289-0 (pbk)

Praise for *An Introduction to UK Politics*

This is a very rare kind of book. It provides an introduction to British politics while at the same time challenging a number of dominant assumptions and exploring the emergence of new pressures. At its core is an emphasis on pluralism and power. The interwoven nature of modern British governance – in relation to ideas, processes and institutions – is laid bare in an account of a changing polity which is as sophisticated as it is subtle, and as engaging as it is accessible.

Matthew Flinders, Professor of Politics, University of Sheffield and Vice President of the Political Studies Association of the United Kingdom

A comprehensive and fascinating look at key topics in British politics today. Weaving together theory, empirical analysis and expert contributions, this is both clearly written and thought-provoking. A must read for all British politics students.

Laura Richards-Gray, Lecturer in British Politics, Birkbeck University of London

This book goes beyond the study of political institutions, portraying a 'diverse array of voices' and how these perspectives shape the UK's political system. This inclusive approach to the study of politics helps us understand the UK as a multinational state (how it got here and where it might be going) and it provides a hard-hitting account of the challenges facing citizens and decision-makers today. This is a different kind of textbook which comes highly recommended.

Lynn Bennie, Lecturer in Politics, University of Aberdeen

This book offers a stimulating and accessible introduction to the ideas, identities, and institutions that shape our politics today. It will be an invaluable resource to students seeking to navigate the complex and rapidly changing politics of the United Kingdom.

Richard Hayton, Associate Professor of Politics, University of Leeds

An Introduction to UK Politics provides a solid introduction to the institutions of UK governance, whilst also being rooted in 'everyday' political lives. Up to date, and with attention to theoretical concepts, it will be of real benefit to students who want to know how UK politics really works.

Daniel Gover, Senior Lecturer in British Politics, Queen Mary University of London

This book brings a fresh and original perspective to the changing panorama of British politics. Unlike the more traditional institution-focused textbooks, this new Introduction engages with the fragmentary and sometimes contradictory elements of British politics in a sharp and stimulating fashion.

Cillian McGrattan, Lecturer in Politics, Ulster University

This is a fascinating and highly original introduction to the study of contemporary British politics. By focusing on the concept of pluralism, the authors succeed in drawing together both traditional and novel perspectives on what British politics is all about. Students who read this book will learn not only to understand contemporary political institutions, actors and issues, but to situate them in a broader story of what it means to do politics in a multinational, multicultural, multidimensional modern state.

James Strong, Senior Lecturer in British Politics, Queen Mary University of London

This innovative and intellectually stimulating textbook provides a highly relevant approach to the study of British politics. It enhances our understanding of the UK's political system by reference to important contemporary themes, such as pluralism, historical legacy, identity and inequality.

Geoff Horn, Lecturer in Politics, Newcastle University

Contents

Online resources	xiii
About the editors and contributors	xv
Preface	xvii
Acknowledgements	xxiii
An introduction to politics in the UK	1
Joanie Willett and Arianna Giovannini	

Part I Foundations — 15

1. Power, pluralism and politics in the UK — 17
   Joanie Willett

2. The UK as a multi-national state: Contested histories, state formation and constitutional settlement — 33
   Arianna Giovannini

3. The global history of the UK: Colonialism and decolonisation — 53
   Amina Easat-Daas and Simon Stevens

4. Class and gender as structural inequalities in the UK: The politics of production and social reproduction — 73
   Frederick Harry Pitts and Lorena Lombardozzi

Part II Institutions — 95

5. Creating political change: From the (informal) politics of the everyday to formal politics — 97
   Joanie Willett

6. Devolution, sub-national governance and inequalities — 115
   Arianna Giovannini

7. Do British political parties reflect British pluralism? — 139
   Judith Sijstermans

8. Elections, referendums and public opinion — 159
   Rosie Campbell

9. Place, pluralism and the media: Who tells us about political affairs? — 185
   Steven Harkins

10. The legislature — 205
    Thomas Caygill

11. The executive — 225
    Patrick Diamond

Part III Big questions   **245**

12   An economy for all?   247
     Kate Alexander-Shaw

13   UK environment and climate change politics   273
     Clare Saunders

14   Britain in the world   293
     Ben Whitham

References   313
Index   347

Extended contents

Online resources	xiii
About the editors and contributors	xv
Preface	xvii
Acknowledgements	xxiii

An introduction to politics in the UK   1
Joanie Willett and Arianna Giovannini

Introduction	1
The UK as a multi-national state	3
Regional (in)equalities	5
Politics and identities in the UK	5
The UK and the legacy of colonialism	7
Structural inequalities	8
Institutions in UK politics	11
Conclusion	13

Part I Foundations   15

1 Power, pluralism and politics in the UK   17
Joanie Willett

Introduction	18
Assemblage, power and UK politics	20
Political representation in the UK	22
What is pluralism?	24
Governance, multiculturalism and diversity	28
Conclusion	30

2 The UK as a multi-national state: Contested histories, state formation and constitutional settlement   33
Arianna Giovannini

Introduction	34
What's in a flag?	35
The historical roots of the UK and the process of state-building	39
The UK constitutional settlement	45
Conclusion	50

3 The global history of the UK: Colonialism and decolonisation   53
Amina Easat-Daas and Simon Stevens

Introduction	54
Key terms and context	55
The state of nature and political order	60

'Doing politics' for the postwar migrant	63
Minority representation: From exclusion to reproducing elitism	65
Conclusion	69

4 Class and gender as structural inequalities in the UK: The politics of production and social reproduction — 73
Frederick Harry Pitts and Lorena Lombardozzi

Introduction	74
This chapter: Bringing work back in	75
Class, labour and structural inequalities	79
Social reproduction, class and gender	80
Pluralism and predistribution	88
Policy: Fair pay agreements	91
Conclusion	91

Part II Institutions — 95

5 Creating political change: From the (informal) politics of the everyday to formal politics — 97
Joanie Willett

Introduction	98
Governance	99
Everyday politics and cultural norms	103
Social capital: Strong, pluralist local democracy	111
Conclusion	113

6 Devolution, sub-national governance and inequalities — 115
Arianna Giovannini

Introduction	116
Framing and key concepts: What is devolution?	116
Local government in the UK	118
Devolution in the UK	123
Conclusion	136

7 Do British political parties reflect British pluralism? — 139
Judith Sijstermans

Introduction	140
Inside British political parties: The three faces of the political party	141
The British political party system	150
The (waning?) importance of British political parties	152
Conclusion	157

8 Elections, referendums and public opinion — 159
Rosie Campbell

Introduction	160
What is 'public opinion'?	160
The thermostatic model of public opinion	163
Measuring British public opinion	164
Voting behaviour	166

The 2019 British general election in historical context	168
General elections	178
Conclusion	181

9 Place, pluralism and the media: Who tells us about political affairs? — 185
Steven Harkins

Introduction	186
Journalism in the UK: A forum for plural political debate?	187
Closing down the debate: The news media as an extension of corporate and state power	190
The news industry in the UK	192
Conclusion	201

10 The legislature — 205
Thomas Caygill

Introduction	206
Context	208
Core functions	209
External relations	220
Conclusion	223

11 The executive — 225
Patrick Diamond

Introduction	226
The traditional debate: Cabinet versus prime ministerial government	228
The core executive	229
Challenge to the core executive (1): Policy networks	234
Challenge to the core executive (2): The multi-level polity and devolution	236
Challenge to the core executive (3): Individual citizens	237
Challenge to the core executive (4): The dysfunctional centre	239
Conclusion	242

Part III Big questions — 245

12 An economy for all? — 247
Kate Alexander-Shaw

Introduction	248
The UK economy today	250
Economic policy in the UK: The difference that politics makes	257
Towards an economy for all: Thinking about economic change	265
Conclusion	269

13 UK environment and climate change politics — 273
Clare Saunders

Introduction	274
Focusing the chapter	277
The dynamic nature of political and lifestyle activism: From splinter groups to government interlocuters	278
Policy-makers' dilemma: The scientific construction of environmental knowledge	283

	Post-politics and the undermining of pluralism	287
	Conclusion	289
14	**Britain in the world**	**293**
	Ben Whitham	
	Chapter overview	294
	Introduction	294
	Britain's role(s) and place(s) in the world	298
	Institutions, trends and controversies in British foreign policy	303
	Conclusion	311

References	313
Index	347

Online resources

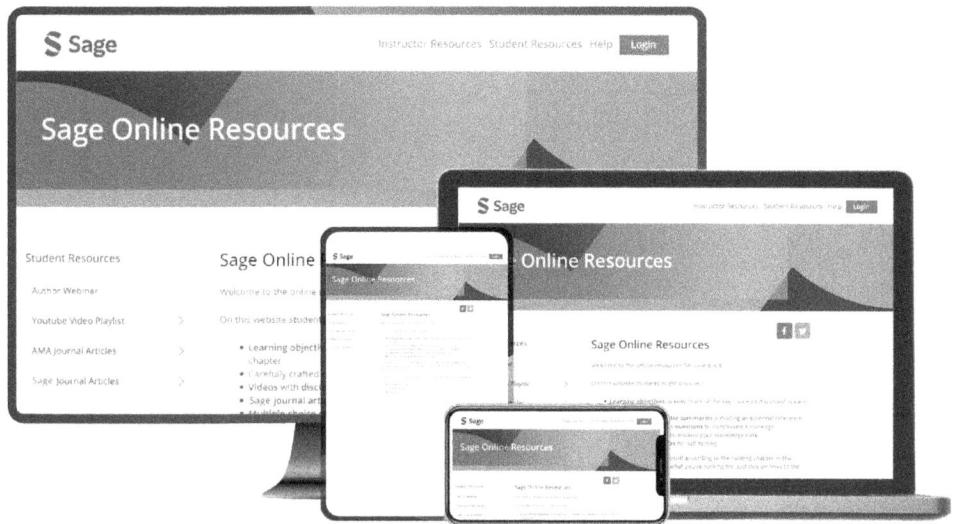

An Introduction to UK Politics is supported by a wealth of online resources for lecturers to use with students to support teaching, which are available at:
https://study.sagepub.com/Willett1e.

For lecturers

Teaching guides outline the key coverage in each chapter and provide suggested activities/examples to use in class or for assignments.

PowerPoint decks designed for use in lectures can be downloaded and customised for use in your own presentations. They feature figures and tables from the book, and the key themes and theories from the chapters.

About the editors and contributors

Editors

Joanie Willett is Associate Professor in Politics with the University of Exeter. Joanie's research looks at the entangled relationships between people, how we organise our communities, and our environments. She publishes on local government, identity politics, and economic development.

Arianna Giovannini is Professor of Political Sociology in the Department of Economics, Society and Politics at the University of Urbino (Italy). Until 2023, she was Associate Professor/Reader in Local Politics & Public Policy at De Montfort University, Leicester. Arianna's research interests focus on territorial politics, multilevel governance, devolution and regional inequalities in the UK.

Contributors

Kate Alexander-Shaw is a research officer in the European Institute at the London School of Economics and Political Science. She specialises in British and comparative political economy, with a particular interest in the politics of economic ideas.

Rosie Campbell is Professor of Politics and Director of the Global Institute for Women's Leadership at King's College London. She has written widely on British political behaviour and has presented eight episodes of BBC Radio 4's *Analysis* on British politics and elections.

Thomas Caygill is a senior lecturer in Politics at Nottingham Trent University and specialises in parliamentary politics. His current focus is on how parliaments can build capacity in order to increase their influence in the policy-making process.

Patrick Diamond is Professor of Public Policy and Director of the Mile End Institute at Queen Mary, University of London. He is a former Head of Policy Planning in 10 Downing Street and Government Special Adviser.

Amina Easat-Daas is a senior lecturer in politics. Her research interests include the study of Muslim political participation, French and Belgian politics, gendered Islamophobia and countering Islamophobia through the arts. Her monograph is entitled 'Muslim Women's Political Participation in France and Belgium'.

Steven Harkins is a lecturer in journalism studies at the University of Stirling. His research interests focus on the relationships between politics, journalism and society and his previous research has focused on communicating poverty, inequality and environmental issues.

Lorena Lombardozzi is a senior lecturer in Economics at the School of Social Sciences & Global Studies in the Faculty of Arts and Social Sciences at the Open University.

Frederick Harry Pitts is a senior lecturer in Politics at the Department of Humanities & Social Sciences on the University of Exeter's Cornwall Campus in his hometown of Penryn.

Clare Saunders is Professor in Environmental Politics in the Department of Humanities and Social Sciences, Cornwall, University of Exeter. She publishes widely on green politics in journals such as *Environmental Politics & Society* and *Natural Resources*.

Judith Sijstermans is a lecturer in the Politics and International Relations department at the University of Aberdeen, where she researches independence-seeking political parties in the UK and comparatively across Europe.

Simon Stevens is a senior lecturer in political philosophy/political thought. He specialises in methods in political philosophy, specifically focusing on storytelling and fictional narratives. He has also written on hostile architecture and homelessness. He is currently writing a political theory textbook that aims to transform, decolonise and diversify the curriculum, and won the 2022 Political Studies Association Bernard Crick Prize for Outstanding Teaching.

Ben Whitham is a lecturer in International Relations at SOAS, University of London. His research interests include the historical and contemporary roles of British foreign and security policies in the production of global inequalities. He is the co-author (with Andrew Heywood) of *Global Politics* (Bloomsbury, 2023).

Preface

We have designed this volume to be an essential textbook for first, second and third year university courses that focus on politics in the UK. Our chapters have been carefully curated to form the basis of required readings and seminar discussion and our innovative approach will help to frame modules in a way that is interesting and engaging and draws on our experiences of student needs when examining politics in the UK.

Why this book?

When presented with the question of 'What does UK politics mean to you?' students routinely tend to frame their answers in terms of national politics played out in Westminster. This perspective is reflected in most undergraduate teaching resources, which emphasise the national level institutions of government. Having taught UK politics for many years, we felt that different approaches can help to better understand the complexities of the subject and we trialled some of our thoughts in the classroom. The idea of this book stems from these reflections. We seek to adopt a pluralistic approach, arguing that 'what happens in Westminster' is only a part of the complex and intersecting processes, relations, (hi)stories and practices that underpin UK politics.

Thus, we present a critical assessment of the UK political system that looks at whether, how and why power is or should be dispersed throughout different levels of governance as well as civil society, rather than simply accept that political authority is concentrated in the working of the central state. Our experience in the classroom and more broadly in academia tells us that there is a need for a textbook which reflects the whole breadth of politics in the UK and emphasises the ways that contribution to political life happens – and *should* happen – not just in London, but in our communities, towns, villages and cities in our everyday lives.

Taking a networked approach based on Deleuzian assemblages, we show that individuals, governmental and non-governmental institutions, organisations, businesses and pressure groups are all key political actors. They devise formal and informal campaigns situated, operating with and interacting at different levels across the country. Our aim is for students to feel that the body politic is something that we *all* have the capacity to shape and that we are all a part of, rather than something that is remote and inaccessible. We want students to see politics as something that is 'done by us all', and not 'on us'. That is why we use the concept of 'the politics of the everyday' as a driving principle that shapes the authors' analysis across the book. Ultimately, this allows us to introduce UK politics in an accessible way to students, and as a subject that they can actively engage in, rather than simply focusing on distant and far away processes and practices that only elites can access and influence.

To achieve this, we have organised our textbook around the central question of '*How plural is politics in the UK?*' As well as reflecting our pressing concerns about the diversity and accessibility of different forms of political engagement in the UK today, this question operates as a way to analyse and explore the many different aspects of political engagement that thread across the UK and weave UK politics together.

Overall, this textbook approaches UK politics as an analytical lens rather than a descriptive introduction. We show the way that the past folds into and informs the present to create the identities and cultures in which our politics and government happen, and which exposes some of the tensions and fracture lines that may lead to further changes in the future. This enables us to consider the central role that identities and inequalities play in contemporary UK politics, which is not yet reflected in the current range of undergraduate textbooks. It also means that our textbook provides a dynamic analysis, offering an action-focused, problem-based and engaging introduction to the topic.

We take equality, inclusion and diversity as a guiding principle, not just in terms of the subject matter of this book, but also for what concerns the crafting of its contents. Our editorial team and chapter contributors bring many different perspectives to this publication, which informs our analyses and the aspects of politics that we consider to be important. We are from a range of different class, career, national and cultural backgrounds, and are based in universities reflective of the different types of institutions which exist in the UK today.

What's in this book

Our textbook is the first designed to represent UK society today – shifting the focus from static institutions to how UK politics is changing across different sectors of society. We argue that society in the UK has evolved rapidly over the past years and these changes have created a fluid and dynamic political landscape. This is illustrated by events like the 2016 vote to leave the European Union or the 2014 Scottish independence referendum, as well as by broad and long-lasting dynamics such as political re-alignment, and movements like Black Lives Matter and Extinction Rebellion. The importance of identity politics and the UK's changing relationship with the world as well as with its constituent nations underscore the need for teaching resources that can explore and reflect the shifting interplay between culture, society and government in the UK. To cover all this, the textbook is organised in three sections.

Part I lays the foundation for a pluralist interpretation of UK politics and provides a set of framing chapters that offer an account of what it means to study UK politics from a pluralist perspective, and some of the inequalities which thread the UK.

In Part II we cover key structures, concepts and institutions that form the heart of UK politics such as power, community politics, territorial politics and devolution, the legislature, executive, political parties and the media.

In Part III we examine some of the big questions in the contemporary UK: socioeconomic inequalities, the green agenda and the UK's relationship with the rest of the world.

Our chapter structure follows the themes traditionally taught on UK politics courses, but the content is very different, reflecting our central question of how plural UK politics is, considering how society in the UK is 'assembled' and the relationship that this has with formal and informal politics.

The Introductory chapter provides an overview of how to approach the study of politics in the UK, giving readers a sense of (some of) the different kinds of identities and analyses which underpin politics in the UK.

Chapter 1 argues that UK politics needs to be understood as being made up of a diverse array of political actors, from everyday people through to those working in the machinery of central government. The chapter asks *why* pluralism matters for a liberal democratic government and considers pluralism as a descriptive and normative tool which has utility for well-functioning liberal democracies. We also cover the ways that histories impact on the degree to which ideas and knowledge resonate and gain traction, and how this affects the flows of information, people and ideas between assembled parts of the UK political system.

Chapter 2 takes a critical look at how the UK as we know it today has come together over time as a multi-national state and the impact these processes of 'assemblage' have on the territorial and constitutional settlement of the country. The chapter first considers what a nation-state is, and what makes a state 'multi-national'. Second, and drawing on this, the chapter offers an overview of the specific dynamics of territorial distinctiveness across the nations of the UK, and it concludes by evaluating the constitutional settlement that has emerged from the long path of incremental unification that characterises our country.

Chapter 3 addresses the racial contract, examining the way in which the obligations between the state and individuals are bound by conceptions of race. We look at what is meant by colonialism and the ideas (or myths) that were employed to justify and legitimise it. We also examine postcolonial migration to Britain, and the ways in which it brought many formerly colonised people to the UK. Next, we consider multiculturalism and the ways in which diverse communities live in Britain, how this shapes British politics. This includes how racialised postcolonial migrants to Britain engage with and are represented in the British political arena.

Chapter 4 examines structural inequalities as they relate to the relationship with work in the present-day UK, through the prism of class and gender as intersecting forms of identification relevant to UK politics. We use 'social reproduction' to illuminate the struggles over the value of 'key' or 'essential' work, and assess the proposals put forward by UK political parties and other actors to ameliorate these inequalities. We consider different distributive and 'predistributive' policies to address relevant structural inequalities, and the meaning of 'pluralism' in the context of industrial relations as the 'politics of work'.

In Chapter 5 you will learn that policy change is complex, involving many different individuals, pressure groups, organisations and political actors, even if these are different in size and in their ability to produce change. By examining everyday politics and cultural norms we see that political change often grows out of cultural change. The micropolitics of everyday activities and living one's authentic self create new structures and norms to which policy has to respond. We use the concepts of social capital and pluralism to see how strong, pluralist democracies rely on an active and vibrant civil society, participating in formal and informal community place-shaping.

Chapter 6 looks at the process of devolution in the UK and at the state of sub-national governance across the country, linking these debates to issues concerning regional inequalities. First, the chapter considers what is (and what is not) devolution and how this policy agenda fits within the UK constitutional setting. Second, it draws on this to assess the asymmetric character of the process of devolution and how it is evolving in each of the four component nations of the UK. It concludes with a critical reflection on the democratic and socioeconomic inequalities that stem from these dynamics.

Chapter 7 shows that political parties are neither the exclusive domain of the elite nor entirely democratised bodies. Political parties are an accumulation of parts, which sometimes fit together seamlessly and sometimes rub one another up the wrong way. The chapter will help students to identify political parties' internal sub-groups, including the role played by party members, party staff and elected representatives. We explore how political parties can reflect dimensions of difference in the UK, including territorial and ideological diversity, and learn how political parties organise political competition in the UK. Finally, the chapter considers whether political parties remain essential to British democracy.

Chapter 8 focuses on elections and referendums. These are infrequent opportunities for citizens to express our preferences and hold our elected representatives to account. In this chapter we consider theories of elite and mass opinion formation to understand how the political representation of our interests, beliefs and values works, or doesn't work, in practice. We explore the relationships between values and party choice and how these have changed over time. Finally, we examine the Scottish and EU referendums, considering how they have altered the relationships we have with the political parties and the way we understand public opinion in the UK.

Chapter 9 looks at how the news media have a critical public service role in a democratic society. We show that ideally journalism will offer a platform for a wide range of ideas to be debated, which will help inform the public on political affairs. We examine whether the news media enhances or restricts pluralism in the UK political system, and we see that news coverage of political affairs in the UK is limited and hampered by systemic problems, but it is an essential part of the democratic system, and the democratic system would be worse off without the news industry.

Chapter 10 will help students to reflect upon the extent to which the UK Parliament meets our modern pluralistic values, understand the ways in which citizens can access and influence the institution, and identify areas where the UK Parliament can be reformed to resolve some of its limitations. The chapter shows that the UK Parliament has developed over the centuries and historical institutionalism acts as a drag on reform. Enhancements have been made in the quality of petitioning and the engagement activities of select committees but progress is slow. Government dominance remains a challenge and parliamentary sovereignty means government sovereignty through parliamentary majorities.

Chapter 11 focuses empirically on the premierships of recent UK prime ministers, notably David Cameron, Theresa May, Boris Johnson and Liz Truss. The chapter addresses how far the experience of governing from 10 Downing Street can be understood from the perspective of the core executive literature, conceiving of the prime minister as reliant on other actors and institutions in central government. It is also necessary to consider how the UK executive manages relationships with civil society and citizens considering recent events. The chapter considers the limitations of academic perspectives such as the core executive approach given recent developments in UK politics and policymaking.

Chapter 12 looks at the policy models that have shaped the UK's economy into what it is today. It considers the balance of interests in the UK economy, how economic and political resources are distributed, and the extent to which the United Kingdom can claim to have an economy for all. It provides an overview of some key trends in the UK economy and a sense of the different economic policy models that have been applied by successive UK governments. We consider whether politics can change economic outcomes, and why there may be constraints on it doing so.

Chapter 13 explores the ways in which UK environment and climate politics is a dynamic assemblage through the case study of veganism and the related animal movement. We see why a range of differentiated environmental organisations exist and how political and lifestyle activism interact. You will examine the pathways through which environmental knowledge is constructed, assembled, contested and sometimes used to inform UK environmental policy. You will also learn about the range of related political views held between and among vegans and environmentalists and explore how these energy flows shape environmental knowledge.

Chapter 14 takes us through the significance of the Brexit referendum and the contested foreign policy narrative of 'Global Britain.' We look at the relationship between public opinion and foreign policy, and the extent to which these have or have not been shaped by pluralistic influences. The chapter demonstrates that, from the history of the British Empire to Brexit and beyond, issues of foreign policy – how the British state acts beyond its territorially defined borders – have always been messily and inextricably intertwined with social issues within those borders.

How to use the book

Our textbook has a series of features to support student learning and ensure that students can engage with the topics covered in an interactive manner. These include:

- **Need to know**: This boxed section signposts students to some of the foundational knowledges around each topic, and where they should go to look into this topic in more depth (e.g. government websites).
- **Case studies**: Our case studies showcase differing perspectives on the same event, supporting and encouraging students to interpret the familiar through different positionalities.
- **Theory**: In our theory boxes, we feature different concepts in action, exploring how to employ these concepts, and how they help us to interpret particular worlds.
- **Spotlight on research boxes** across chapters are intended to spark debate and critical thinking by showcasing the latest seminal or controversial publications.
- **Annotated reading lists** provide students with a way in to some of the key wider literature.

Acknowledgements

Editing and putting together this book has been an exciting journey. We are hugely indebted to Andrew Malvern at Sage who, from day one, with his constant enthusiasm, support and professional advice has been just the best commissioning editor any author could hope to work with. Daniel Price at Sage has also been a constant source of support and professional help. Daniel has fantastic interpersonal skills and was able to keep us to schedule (ish) in a beautifully gentle but firm way. We are extremely grateful to both. We would also like to thank the reviewers for their extremely useful comments on the initial book proposal and draft chapters, and who helped us improve its content and final shape. Of course, thanks are also due to the fantastic contributors to the book who, with their diverse, original and timely analyses have brought to life the ideas and aims we proposed as editors. We hope students and instructors will find this book valuable and use it as a springboard to promote the study of UK politics from a new angle.

Joanie Willett, St Austell, Cornwall

Arianna Giovannini, Sheffield

August 2023

An introduction to politics in the UK

Joanie Willett and Arianna Giovannini

> **Learning objectives**
>
> After reading this chapter you should be able to:
>
> - Have an overview of how to approach the study of politics in the UK
> - Understand (some of) the different kinds of identities which underpin politics in the UK
> - Identify a range of of analytical lenses through which to construct your own knowledge about politics in the UK
> - Understand how the different political institutions in the UK fit together

Introduction

The aim of this introductory chapter is to set the framework that guides this book and present some of the key concepts, ideologies and issues that underpin the analysis developed in its chapters. This will allow you to make the most of the book's contents and understand how to use it as a learning resource that will help you to build your own knowledge of UK politics.

Before you begin working through this chapter, we want you to ask yourself a question. Is there anything on which all people in the United Kingdom can agree? Have you got an example of something that is often considered to be a universally held value, which on reflection very much is not?

Joanie's example is about university education. From one standpoint, we imagine this to be something to which everybody aspires, and which all parents encourage and support their children to do. Joanie's experience is very different and she remembers the note of panic in her mother's voice when she told her, aged 24, that she planned to go to university. Her mother was apparently more horrified than when Joanie had told her that she was having a baby nearly nine years previously. Her mother's objections were on religious grounds, but there are many other reasons why some people throughout the UK feel that something as apparently universally good as a higher education is not for people like them.

Why are we telling you this? To make the point that there are many different *UKs* and that we cannot make the assumption that the one that we inhabit is anything like the same as the one that other people experience. Instead, and as we will discuss in more depth in the chapters to follow, the UK is assembled from *many* different experiences, assumptions and expectations. This is why this book is tied together by the question *How plural is politics in the UK?* This is another way of asking the extent to which the many different experiences, cultures, beliefs and meanings held by people in the UK are represented, listened to and heard in the various machineries which makes up UK politics and government.

We talk about what we mean by 'assembled' and the relationship between this perspective and pluralism in the next chapter. This offers us a way of approaching UK politics which looks at power as something which is dispersed throughout the political system. In this book, we want to get away from the idea that politics and power in the UK are clustered around the Parliament in Westminster, London. Instead, we want to focus on how people everywhere, across the country, are important in understanding and shaping UK politics. This is why we open the book with a discussion about the different identities which make up the UK, before talking about institutions only later. In our view, political institutions rely on people to give them meaning and purpose.

In other words, rather than being the most important part of UK politics, we look at our political institutions as an expression of how we are currently choosing to organise ourselves in the UK. For us in this book, looking at how the UK is assembled helps us to retain this focus on people. Furthermore, we also argue that we cannot understand politics in the UK – its structures, infrastructures, debating points and issues – unless we also get to grips with the diversity that characterises the UK, understanding the many different 'UKs' that people inhabit and perceive through their lived experiences. Over the next few pages we will introduce you to some of the foundational principles of the UK that are necessary to hit the ground running, before we start with in-depth analyses of specific issues, processes and insitutions in the following chatpers. These principles include: i) a view of the UK as a multi-national state and that this is still reflected in its regional diversity and inequalities today; ii) an understanding of the UK as a nation-state with a history of colonising large parts of the world – a contested 'heritage' that still has a huge impact on our polity today; iii) an acknowledgment that, despite being a developed country, the UK still has many structural inequalities which affect the life-chances and ability of people to participate in political processes and procedures. After we have unpacked these points, we will provide an overview of some of the institutions which make up the UK political system, looking at how they connect together. We will close by explaining some theoretical approaches through which you might like to make your own analyses of UK politics. In this way, we hope that the book will become a useful resource for you, enabling all students to develop a critical and interactive understanding of politics in the UK.

Need to know: What is the UK?

One of the things which both unites and divides us relates to what we actually call this polity that most of us are living in right now. Do we call ourselves the United Kingdom? Great Britain? Great Britain and Northern Ireland? England? This is what we often called the UK before 1997, when we began to understand that we had been naming the entire polity by one of its constituency nations. You might still have the experience of going overseas and having people refer to you as coming from England, even if you actually are from one of the other UK nations. Some of the university modules that you are encountering will make some sort of reference to politics in the UK, but there will still be others which are entitled something like 'British Politics'. However, just like knowing the British Isles as 'England' was clearly wrong, carrying all kinds of colonial linguistic legacies as it overlooked Northern Ireland, Scotland, Wales and Cornwall; so too 'Britain' leaves out Northern Ireland. Therefore, if we are to use a way of naming which accurately reflects the land mass governed by the Parliament in Westminster, London (with support of the Parliaments in Scotland and Wales, and the Northern Ireland Assembly), we need to use the term 'United Kingdom of Great Britain and Northern Ireland' and 'UK' as a shorthand for it. Yes, this is complicated and perhaps a bit confusing, but it also reflects the complexities that underpin the UK as a multi-national state (for a full discussion, see Chapter 2).

The UK as a multi-national state

Understanding the nature of the UK as a multi-national state is essential to capture how its constitution and territorial settlement have evolved over time, and the extent to which power is dispersed across and within the official constituent nations (England, Scotland, Wales and Northern Ireland) of the country. In Chapter 2 we discuss this in detail, providing a full explanation of key concepts as well as the historical path through which the UK has come together.

For now, it is important to note that the process that led to the creation of the UK as we know it today was underpinned by a series of conquests, annexations, unions and separations of constituent nations over several hundred years. The UK has been united into one sovereign nation-state, but the histories, cultures, values and identities of Scotland, Wales, Northern Ireland and England (and also Cornwall and English regions with a stronger sense of distinctiveness) have not been eradicated. As a result, throughout this process, feelings, demands and struggles for more autonomy and even self-determination have kept bubbling under the surface, and have at times emerged in different forms, including armed and violent episodes. For example, while for a time Ireland was part of the UK, the 1916 Easter Rising saw the beginning of the end of UK rule over most of the island of Ireland. For Scotland and Wales, key moments that expressed a desire for more autonomy were the 1997 devolution referendums which introduced a Parliament in Scotland and an Assembly in Wales (now a Parliament). We should also remember that in 2014, despite strong opposition from the government in London, Scotland held an independence referendum. While the pro-independence camp lost its battle in the end, almost 85 per cent of the Scottish population went to the polls, thus showing that they cared about the future of their nation. And a year later, the Scottish National Party (SNP) banked an astounding victory at the general election, taking 56 of an available 59 seats – abruptly transforming it from a 'minority party' on the UK stage to one with a major impact on the country's politics (Rose and Shepard, 2016).

Why do people in the UK's constituent nations campaign for autonomy or even independence? In his seminal book *The Break-Up of Britain* (1977), Tom Nairn argues that this is because after the end of the Empire, civic nationalism has replaced class as people seek to have their interests heard and needs met. Furthermore, highlighting the relationships of conquest (and domination) between England and the other nations of the UK, Michael Hechter (1975) used the term 'internal colonialism' to characterise socioeconomic and political dynamics across the union. At the bottom line is a sense that the UK is not very good at ensuring that the benefits of the country's wealth are fairly distributed throughout all its nations – signalling an issue with the allocation of power within and away from the central state and the government in London.

Indeed, this issue is not limited to the so-called Celtic nations. The centrifugal effects of late capitalism, pooling resources towards the major cities (Martin et al., 2016) combined with a continual tendency in the UK towards centralising decision-making in London, contributed to the development of a 'geography of discontent' (McCann, 2018) in the so-called 'red wall' areas in the North of England and the Midlands. Despite being traditionally Labour, voters switched to the Conservatives in the 2019 general election, allowing Boris Johnson and his party to win. Indeed, the 'levelling up' agenda heralded during the election campaign and initiated by Johnson once in government was aimed precisely at trying to even out some of these regional inequalities (Giovannini, 2021a; Tomaney and Pike, 2020).

The UK is not alone in being a multi-national state cut across by cultural, historical, economic and political differences. Many nation-states globally are more or less (un)easy alliances of different nations, brought together by conquest or pragmatism. For example, if we look at mainland Europe, just as the UK has a secessionist movement in Scotland, the Catalans and Basques have parties that campaign for them to become independent from Spain, and demands for Corsican independence from France have led to many political struggles. Many nations within multi-national states also have their own distinctive language. In the Netherlands (never Holland, for the same reason that the UK is not England) the Frysians speak a very different language from the Dutch. Slovenia is comprised of three different cultural and linguistic-facing communities, leaning towards each of Italy, Austria and Croatia. In Italy, there are parts of the country like South-Tyrol where, in some areas, most of the population speak German as their first language and barely know Italian as they were annexed to the country from Austria after the Second World War. The importance of language as a cultural marker is so intense that linguistic justice is a central plank of the European Free Alliance, the European political party which represents regional and national autonomy and independence movements in the EU Parliament. In the UK, speakers of minority languages (including in Wales, Northern Ireland and Scotland) have had to endure discrimination for keeping their native tongue.

The point that we want to make here is that there is nothing 'natural' about the nation. Nations, their myths, memories and symbols are (re)interpretations of older or sometimes even invented traditions, in order to achieve particular ends and outcomes (Hobsbawm and Ranger, 2014; Smith, 1991). Indeed, Linda Colley, in her seminal book *Britons: Forging the Nation* (2009), provides us with a wonderful overview of how Britain was invented. What this also shows us is that nations and nation-states (including the UK) are in a constant state of adaptation and flux, rather than being fixed entities.

Regional (in)equalities

Looking at territorial diversity also introduces questions of (un)equal opportunities, life chances and societal and economic outcomes of people in different parts of the UK. The UK is one of the most regionally unequal nations in the developed world, containing both some of the poorest parts of Europe (such as Northern Ireland, Cornwall, West Wales and the Valleys), as well as some of the richest parts of Europe (Raikes et al., 2019). The so-called North/South divide within England also provides a language which connotes the different kinds of lives experienced by people in the North, and those in the South (Giovannini and Rose, 2020). However, regional inequalities go much further than the economic questions which we have introduced here, and we will explore this in greater depth in Chapter 6. They also extend to how politics in the UK is imagined.

An exercise that you might like to try is to make an internet search of images for politics in the UK. Then ask yourself how many of these images (beyond flags) depict something beyond London, the Parliament in Westminster, and the various political actors that participate in Westminster politics. These kinds of imaginaries construct a story which says that politics in the UK is all about what happens in one small part of the country (i.e. in and around its capital). If we were to stick only to these depictions, we would hardly know that other parts of the UK exist, or what they are. And yet, regional inequalities, a sense of being 'left behind', needing 'levelling up', or greater political decentralisation have all, in various guises, been a mainstay of UK politics since at least the late 1990s (Giovannini, 2021a; Willett et al., 2019). Regions might be less visible than nations – but they keep occupying a hefty part of the UK policy agenda. In this book, when we ask how plural the UK is, we are also asking about the extent to which different regions of the UK are represented in political debates, regional inequalities are visible, and people from the regions are active participants in a pluralist politics in the UK.

Politics and identities in the UK

Sometimes it can be tempting to imagine identity as a monolithic entity – identity just *is*: it's the essence of a thing, that people hold and that ties a group of people together (Parekh, 2008). To unpick this, it is useful to start with Benedict Anderson's (1991) assertion that national identities are *imagined*. In other words, the political community of the nation is so large that we cannot possibly know everyone within it. So the actual community is constructed in our minds around various myths and memories and symbolism, which creates a sense of belonging around shared stories, values and vernacular that work as invisible ties that bind specific groups of people together. We will come back to stories a little bit later but for politics, a sense of 'we-ness' is really important. People need to feel that the nation-state caters for and provides fair representation to their political community if the concept of the 'nation' is to inspire their loyalty and therefore their consent to government (Bryant, 2010). But what exactly is the identity that we collect around in the UK? This is difficult to pinpoint, precisely because, for example, a person can feel at the same time British and Scottish, or English and British, Cornish and British, or even Yorkshire, English and British. This is the point. Identities are fluid, multiple, overlapping and ever changing.

The identities underpinning politics in the UK have territorial connotations, but also other key dimensions. For hundreds of years the inhabitants of this collection of nations have been engaging in conversations and geopolitical positioning amongst themselves and in their interactions and imaginaries of other nations beyond what would come to be known as Britain and the United Kingdom. UK identities have often been framed in terms of being part of western civilisation. Before we talk about colonialism and its impact, it is important to note the very idea of western civilisation is an ideologically created construct which in itself generates an artificial separation between European knowledge, polities, ideas, and cultures, and those of the rest of the world (MacSweeny, 2023), or more specifically, the 'East' or the Orient (see also Said, 2003).

Debates about contemporary UK identities have been framed as 'culture wars' since at least the early 2000s. In their book *Culture Wars, the Media and the British Left*, James Curran et al. (2005) traced the shifts in identities within the UK that have led to the profound political changes which happened over the decades since the 1970s. Part of the argument here is that the relationship between evolving identities in the UK and politics is tangled and co-evolutionary. We could ask ourselves questions about the extent to which the political consensus in the UK has altered because our politicians have taken a leadership role in setting out a policy agenda and convincing people to follow them. Or perhaps our political leaders have had to follow a continually evolving thread of identities, experiences, beliefs, attitudes and aspirations amongst people in many different parts of the UK. Regardless of the influences on popular culture, what we have seen over the decades since the 1970s is a set of identities built on a greater sense of individualism rather than the collectivism which underpinned the previous post-Second World War consensus.

Note here the term 'consensus'. By this we are making the explicit point that identities in the UK are multiple rather than singular. There *is* no single, collective UK under which the public assembles. Instead, we are made up of a multiplicity (or plurality) of experiences that shape our individual sense of self – and therefore the identities in the polity which we are part of and help to create. The point about consensus is that it provides a kind of thread or an 'ish' which resonates enough with our experiences to be able to follow even if it does not fully reflect our identities. This is where the politics of pluralism is important and we will look at this in more depth in Chapter 1.

For some analysts, it is the *lack* of pluralism in the UK, combined with some fundamental changes about so called 'British values', which underpinned the vote to leave the European Union in the 2016 referendum (Ashcroft and Bevir, 2016; Goodwin, 2023). We look at this in greater depth in Chapter 5, but the idea that there is a tangled interrelationship between people's sense of identity and the political choices (see also Dorling and Tomlinson, 2020) that we make is an interesting one, and one to which analysts and students of politics in the UK need to be much more alert. This is why the first part of the book focuses on the structural and identity-related issues which underpin politics and pluralism in the contemporary UK.

The UK and the legacy of colonialism

One of the recurrent themes in UK politics is immigration. In public debates, the language around this issue shifts from refugees, asylum seekers, economic migrants, 'deserving' and 'undeserving' immigrants, people smugglers and, more recently, people trying to cross the Channel in small, overcrowded, unseaworthy boats (Blinder and Allen, 2016). In each instance the language about migrants shifts, with words designed to raise different emotional responses (e.g. see Ahmed, 2004). However, we cannot understand attitudes towards immigration in the UK without also understanding the UK's history of colonialism.

Although the sun may have set on the British Empire in the aftermath of the Second World War (Ferguson, 2004), its impact on society and politics in the UK has been enormous. In fact, Satthnam Sanghera makes the argument in his book *Empireland* that it is impossible to understand the UK right now without also understanding the long impact of colonialism. We will look at this in more depth in Chapter 3. However, the empire provided the British people with both a sense of pride and national superiority, and also a racialised doctrine which allowed for the brutal treatment and even genocide of 'native' peoples (Elkins, 2022; Lawson, 2014).

To understand this more fully, we need to think of the long effects of culture and memory. People who were educated in the UK in the 1950s are likely to have encountered experiences similar to those related by Richard Evans in an article in the *New Statesman* in July 2020. With the trigger warning that some of his education taught extremely offensive and dehumanising language around people of colour, he wrote:

> ... when I was a child in the early 1950s, much of the world map displayed on the classroom wall was still painted pink, depicting the 'British Empire, on which the sun never sets'. I learned to read from a primer called 'Little Black Sambo' about a Tamil boy and his parents Black Mumbo and Black Jumbo.

He went on to share some of the many ways in which extremely offensive racist attitudes and symbolism were learned and shared as part of the fabric of everyday life in the UK. We are not making the claim here that all older people are racist. Society and people evolve. What we want to highlight is how attitudes and values are embedded into cultural norms, as in the offensive education example above, and how such attitudes and values can have an extremely long reach through the generations.

For individuals and their families from formerly colonised lands, this had an enormous impact on the kinds of lives which they lived. The 'no blacks, no dogs, no Irish' signs showcased in some venues made it extremely difficult for people from colonised lands, invited to take part in the post-Second World War reconstruction of the UK, to get housing, work, or access to basic services. Andrea Levy's award-winning book *Small Island* (Levy, 2014), drawing on the experiences of her mother when she moved to the UK from Jamaica, really brings this to life. But the violence and racism experienced by people of colour was utterly appalling and completely dehumanising. This is well documented by scholars such as Paul Gilroy (2002) in his book *Ain't no Black in the Union Jack* and Robbie Shilliam's (2018) *Race and the Undeserving Poor*.

Whilst we might like to imagine that there have been improvements in societal attitudes in the intervening decades, and certainly legal instruments such as the 2010 *Equality Act* and those which went before it, have gone a long way towards making overt discrimination illegal. However, there is still significant structural racism and underlying racist attitudes. If anything, it is now manifest in more 'sophisticated' and subtle ways (Showunmi and Tomlin, 2022). The Windrush scandal is a clear example of this. The Empire Windrush was a ship carrying migrants from the Carribean, invited to the UK to help to fill a labour shortage in the late 1940s. As Levy (2014) documents, many of these immigrants already thought of themselves as British, but there was also the understanding that they and their descendants would of course be formally British citizens, able to live and work in the UK indefinitely. However, under the 'hostile environment' to immigration from 2012, many Windrush generation migrants and their descendants found themselves deported – sometimes to countries in which they had never lived or visited and had no networks at all (Gentleman, 2019). The point that we are trying to make here is that the legacy of colonialism still affects the UK, particularly with regard to race and racism.

Structural inequalities

We should not imagine that structural inequalities in the UK founded on dehumanisation are limited to people of colour and immigration. For example, when in 1869 J.S. Mill published his book *The Subjection of Women* calling for women in the UK to have the vote, one of the charges that he had to make was that women were not (as was commonly believed) an inferior species of human to men. Mary Wollestonecraft (2009 [1792]) made some similar arguments in the 1790s. She was writing at a time when married women were literally, legally considered to be the property of their husbands. This was not something that would change in law for many decades. In living memory of when Wollestonecroft had been writing, between 1541 and 1743 thousands of (mostly) women were legally killed on accusations of being witches. As Marianne Hester wrote in 1996, this was part of a deepening patriarchal move towards the control of women. Although women often played a role in shaping politics, from social campaigners such as Emily Hobhouse to the vigorous activism for votes for women by the Pankhursts and their supporters, this was played out over a time when the options available to women were severely limited. In her book *Testament to Youth*, first published in 1933, social activist and journalist Vera Britain recalled how before the First World War, even for a woman of her class and privilege, going to university or even travelling unaccompanied was extremely difficult. The social disruption of the war meant that she was able to do what would have been unthinkable before – earn her own money and make her own choices. Although options for women have improved enormously over the intervening decades (Gottleib and Toye, 2013), the structural exclusions which women experience are still very much present although they have shifted and morphed (Evans, 2015).

The Equality Act 2010 covers discrimination on the basis of gender, sexual orientation, age, disability, religion, race and ethnicity. The fact that so many groups in society require legislation in order to be protected against discrimination is telling and links tightly to the thread at the heart of this book. The fact that people with so many different experiences are structurally excluded from enjoying life to the fullest in the UK raises important issues around pluralism in UK politics and the degree to which different people are able to participate in setting or influencing the political agenda. In the following chapters, we seek to weave many different experiences throughout our examples and case studies. In Chapter 4, we link structural inequalities to work, which also helps to make visible class – one aspect of discrimination *not* covered by the Equality Act, which nevertheless has had an enormous impact on life chances and opportunity. It also affects the kind of voice that people have in the political landscape (McGarvey, 2018). The changing nature of work helped to create and perpetuate economic and societal inequalities which are very much part of the fabric of the contemporary UK (e.g. see Hobsbawm, 1999). One of the interesting things for us to do as political analysts is to explore just how our politics is (or is not) evolving over time in response to the structural inequalities which we see, and further, what the machinery of government needs to do in order to keep up with and better reflect these changes.

Theory box: Political analysis

In the next chapter we will introduce you to the concept of the assemblage, which will be the main lens through which we examine politics in the UK. However, we strongly encourage you to always ask yourselves the question 'What angle is this claim about UK politics coming from?' The claim that we are making right now is coming from a post-structural perspective which holds that all 'truth' is subjective and, therefore, dependent on one's viewpoint.

Space does not permit us to go much beyond the key positions, but books such as Freeden and Stears' (2013) *The Oxford Handbook for Political Ideologies* and Barbara Goodwin's (2016) *Using Political Ideas* are excellent starting points for you to get a deeper understanding about what different analytical frameworks look at and show. It can also be really valuable to examine the same set of ideas through a number of different ideological lenses to help to get a more well-rounded understanding of a topic. There are many different intersections between the ideologies which we list below.

Some key ideological positions include:

- *Conservatism*: Not necessarily to be conflated with the Conservative Party (both Margaret Thatcher and Liz Truss were very radical prime ministers), conservative beliefs emphasise the importance of incremental change. It is a pragmatic doctrine focusing

(Continued)

on 'what works now', and 'how can this be adapted to work better' rather than following normative ideas about abstract notions of the 'good' society.
- *Liberalism*: Liberalism *is* concerned about core notions of the good society. Considered to be extremely radical at the time of its inception from the late 1600s onwards (alongside the rise of modernity and enlightenment thought), varieties of liberalism privilege the universal ideas of liberty, natural rights, individualism, progress and welfare. At times liberals can favour welfare systems which more libertarian versions feel is at odds with individual freedom, so like many analytical perspectives, it is a very broad church.
- *Social democracy*: In general, social democracy is a kind of fusion between liberal ideas of freedom and rights, and more socialist perspectives about the value of collective action in order to overcome the inequalities and exploitation inherent in free-market capitalism and more economically libertarian ideas.
- *Anarchism*: Often imagined predominantly as being about the abolition of hierarchical forms of government such as states, this can be considered problematic by anarchists who identify with more left-leaning, collective action types of anarchism who do not want to be associated with the extreme liberal individualism of, for example, free-market varieties. At its core, anarchism is about self-organised and adaptive types of societies.
- *Economic libertarianism*: Economic libertarianism has been a theme of the global economy of the latter part of the 20th century, following the belief that a free market is the best form of distributive mechanism, and that economic rationales should be applied to political questions.
- *Nationalism*: Nationalism foregrounds an emphasis on the needs of the nation. Often it is associated with the far right and a sense of ethnic exclusivity around who 'belongs' within the nation. However, it is also often used as a means of making visible a group of people bounded by territory and a common sense of belonging (e.g. through shared culture, beliefs, religion or language), who are experiencing or perceiving various types of experiences (such as the impact of colonialism).
- *Populism*: Populism centres a discourse on the divide between 'out of touch' elites who hold positions of power and 'ordinary people', and seeks to reverse this. In some regards it is an extreme form of liberalism in its emphasis on popular sovereignty. However, it also risks becoming a 'tyranny of the majority' which has serious issues regarding the inclusion of minorities.
- *Feminism*: Feminism exposes the spaces in which patriarchal structures and knowledge dominate the private and political sphere. As with all ideologies, there are many different forms of feminism, which argue that gender is still an extremely important societal cleavage through which women are disadvantaged and, as such, it should be mobilised and politicised to establish full equality.
- *Green theories*: Green theories cover a very wide range of different ideological positions which all foreground the relationship between people and the natural environment and the political solutions which could improve this relationship. They range from deep green perspectives which place ecologies as paramount and call for radical lifestyle changes, to ecological modernisation perspectives which ask what kinds of technological solutions can enable climate adaptation without significant lifestyle changes.

- *Decolonisation*: Decolonisation explores and exposes the impact that colonialism and decolonisation has had, and continues to have on people of colour, inclusion, discrimination and life chances. It seeks ideas and policies which can ameliorate historic and contemporary injustice and seeks to ensure that people of colour are equally visible throughout the public sphere.

Institutions in UK politics

In this last part of our introductory chapter, we want to give you a brief overview of the institutions that you will encounter later on in this book, so you can see roughly how they all fit together and support each other. We claim that in order to understand the institutions of politics in the UK, we first need to understand the people and our histories through which these institutions came in to being. In short, political institutions, including the buildings, practices and knowledge of the Parliaments in Westminster, the long-standing practice of voting and emerging institutions around social media use are created, constructed, and maintained by us, the people. As the 2016 referendum vote to leave the European Union and the UK's subsequent departure at the end of 2019 show us, we only join and maintain our institutions if 'we' choose to.

The people

Without the experiences, attitudes, values and beliefs of 'ordinary' people living across the United Kingdom, we would not have a UK politics! As voting and non-voting members of the public, some of us choose to organise into clubs, associations, membership organisations, or even political groups. As we will see in Chapter 5, these all have the role of shaping our communities in some way or alerting us to things we care about and that affect our lives which need to be changed. This might be something that we get involved in at a local level, or it might be something that takes us to a national or a UK-wide platform. Qualifying citizens, over the age of 18, also choose our governments at all levels.

Local government

Local government acts as a really important bridge between localities, communities and different levels of government. They are run by councillors who are chosen at regular elections and include county and unitary authorities, non-metropolitan district councils, metropolitan district councils, and town and parish councils. Not every area is served by every type of council, and London is different again with the Greater London Authority as the first tier, and 33 boroughs plus the London Corporation below it. We will explore this complex landscape more fully in Chapter 6.

Local government follows strategies and funding set by central government and is responsible for implementing government policy and delivering a wide range of services (Barnett et al., 2021). However, local government sometimes struggles to do this, especially since the introduction of austerity measures that have led to increasing and severe budget cuts over more than a decade (Barnett et al., 2021). In recent years, the growing constraints under which local government operates have led some to argue that councils should take a lot more control over local decision-making (e.g. see APSE, 2021). In England, these calls are connected with the ongoing 'devolution agenda', which involves the creation of 'combined authorities' (i.e. groups of two or more councils that collaborate and take collective decisions across council boundaries) led by a directly elected Metro Mayor. Where they exist (and they are by no means universal) town and parish councils are the level of government which should be the easiest for people to interact with because they are literally the closest to where people live their lives (Willett and Cruxon, 2019).

Parliaments

We use parliaments as a plural here to include the devolved institutions in Scotland, Wales and the Northern Ireland Assembly alongside the Parliament in Westminster. Devolved institutions are (at least in principle) still subordinated to the UK Parliament but have direct power over so-called 'devolved matters' (i.e. the specific policy areas for which Westminster has transferred power to them). In theory, Westminster should not get involved in these areas (Syed et al., 2023) but, due to the principle of parliamentary sovereignty which guides the UK constitution, it still retains the authority to take back any competence it has transferred to the devolved parliaments. Parliamentary decisions are made by representatives (members), chosen by the people during election cycles. We hope that by the time that you encounter Chapters 11 and 12 you will see that parliaments in general, and the Westminster Parliament in particular, are just some (very important) parts of a *much* bigger system of UK politics. We would of course, encourage you to reflect on the different feedback loops between parliaments and the public, and the degree to which it reflects the different kinds of lives of people in the UK.

Political parties

Political parties are organised groups of people which actively seek to bring about changes in their communities by competing in elections and seeking to win power and get into public office. Party members operate at all levels of government, including town and parish councils; district, county and unitary councils; and all parliaments and the Northern Ireland Assembly. Some members of the Scottish, Welsh and UK Parliaments were previously councillors, as they learned their craft in the practice of politics. Political parties play an important role in linking together public opinion and different levels of government (Pattie and Johnston, 2016). We will look at the feedback-loops between party policy, public opinion and government in Chapter 7. However, political parties will consult a range of different individuals and organisations when setting out their agendas for government.

Elections and referendums

Elections play a vital role in UK representative democracy. This means that every few years qualifying citizens aged 18 and over, are invited to vote in an election to decide who they would like to represent them. Occasionally, on contentious or big topics, the public is invited to decide what should happen through a referendum, or a vote on a single issue (such as the Brexit referendum in 2016, or the Scottish Independence referendum in 2014). Elections and referendums are one way in which people can feed their opinions, attitudes and beliefs into government policy. In elections, voters can choose which political party they would like to run government at whichever level is being targeted – national or local. We will look at this in more depth in Chapter 8.

The media

For democracy to work well, it is important that people are able to be informed about what is happening locally and nationally. Ideally, following a balance of the evidence, the public can then make up their minds about what they think about key topics. The media are important in sharing this kind of information and include TV, radio, print, online and social media reporting. There is a debate about the level to which the media shape or are shaped by public opinion. However, the different types of media in the UK play a vital role in sharing information around people, organisations and government. They can expose us to people who experience very different versions of the UK to ourselves, discuss policy solutions... and demonise or 'other' particular groups of people. We look at the role of the media in Chapter 9.

Conclusion

So what do we take from this chapter. The first thing is that the UK is built on many different inequalities. Many of these have foundations in the colonial histories of England – one of the constituent nations of the UK. Many of the United Kingdom's nations experience social, economic, and historically, political inequalities compared to England. Even within England, where you live has a huge impact on your life chances and how well you are able to participate in UK politics. Culturally too, there are many groups in UK society who historically have been excluded from political participation on the basis of class, gender, sexual orientation, disability and, of course, ethnic background. This latter relates to Britain's colonial histories, the exploitations that this entailed, and the cultural meanings which enabled colonial abuses to be maintained. History matters. 'Living memory' puts those of us who are younger in touch with the cultures in which those of us who are older were raised. But to analyse the question of how plural UK politics is, you will need to consider your own analytical tools, and in this chapter we have outlined some of these and the key institutions that you will want to think about. However, as you work your way through this book, we want you to feel that UK politics is something that we *all* have the capacity to shape, from our communities, towns, villages, cities, nations and everyday lives. We hope that you will feel better equipped to navigate the various different spaces through which individuals, institutions and organisations help to make and shape politics.

Key take-home points

- The UK is a multinational state.
- There are many different inequalities within the UK. Some are cultural and some are regional (territorial).
- Culture has deep roots and long-term impact – which is why things which happened a long time ago still matter today.
- There are many different analytical perspectives through which to examine politics in the UK. We provide a basic outline above.
- We also identify some key institutions in UK politics.

Part I
Foundations

1 Power, pluralism and politics in the UK... 17
2 The UK as a multi-national state: Contested histories, state
  formation and constitutional settlement.. 33
3 The global history of the UK: Colonialism and decolonisation..................... 53
4 Class and gender as structural inequalities in the UK: The politics
  of production and social reproduction... 73

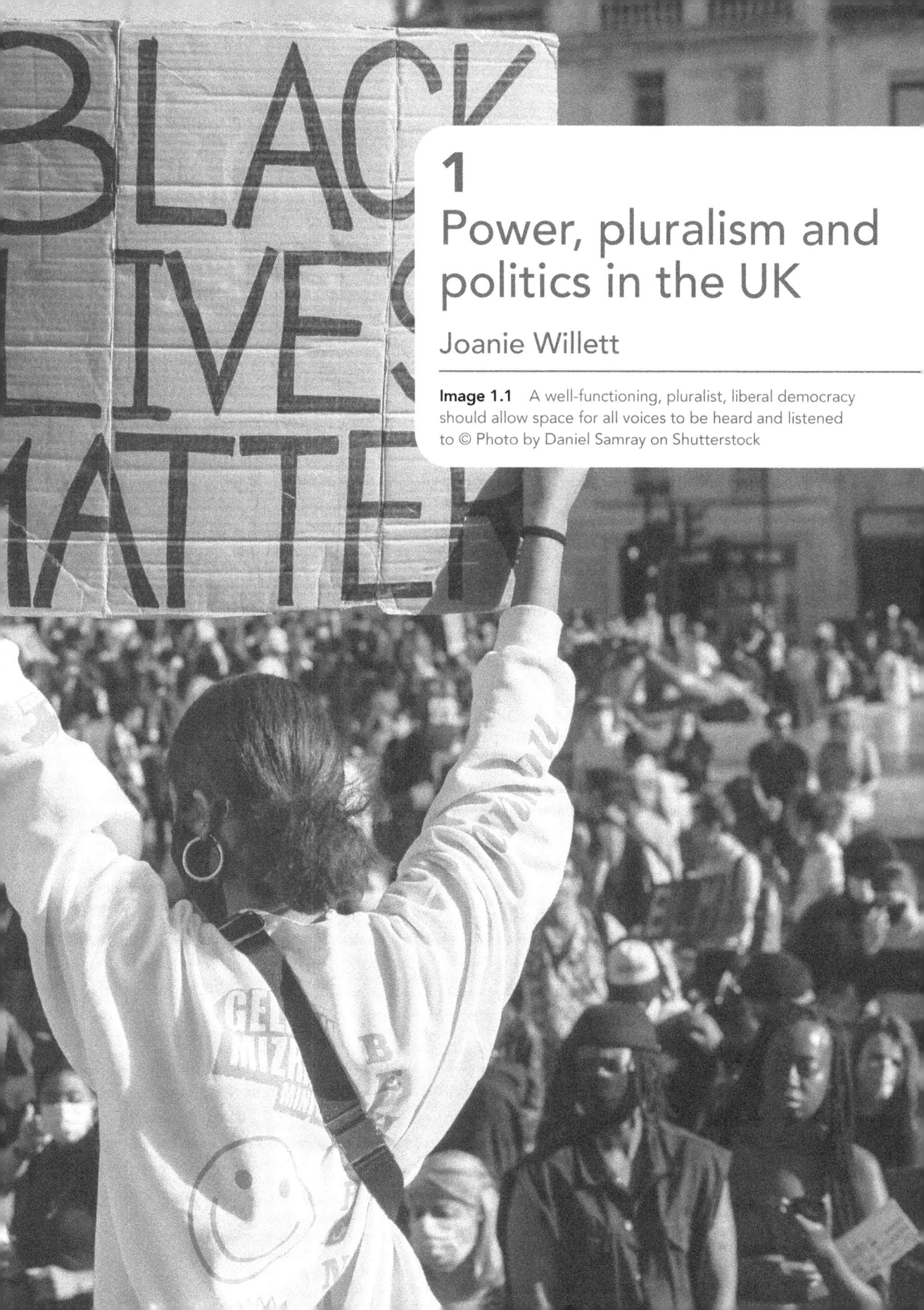

1
Power, pluralism and politics in the UK

Joanie Willett

Image 1.1 A well-functioning, pluralist, liberal democracy should allow space for all voices to be heard and listened to © Photo by Daniel Samray on Shutterstock

Learning objectives

After reading this chapter you should be able to:

- Understand how to read and interpret this book
- Discuss the importance of pluralism for a well-functioning liberal democracy
- Explore what we mean by the argument that British politics needs to be understood as being an assemblage of political actors
- Appreciate how this book will help you to consider how plural British politics actually is

Introduction

In the early summer of 2020 it still felt like the world had shut down. We hadn't yet come to terms with the 'new normal' of Covid lockdowns, and suddenly some of us, furloughed or having to lead much quieter lives because of the pandemic, had much more time on our hands to listen and think. We were also realising that people of colour in the UK were being disproportionately impacted by Covid, both as those who caught the disease, but also as those more likely to die by it. Against this backdrop and following the trigger of the killing of George Floyd as he was arrested by US police in Minneola, Minnesota, the Black Lives Matter (BLM) movement erupted back onto the political landscape with major protests in cities such as London, Birmingham, Bristol, Liverpool and Hull. The movement began in 2013, also in America, following the trial in Florida for the killing of Trayvon Martin in 2012 and a chapter was opened in the UK in 2015, in Nottingham. Patricia Francis (2021) argues that there was something about the 'quiet' of the pandemic which allowed George Floyd's death to resonate, reverberate and catch hold to produce the shifts that it has in UK politics and popular culture, in a way that, for instance, the 2016 protests marking the anniversary of London's Mark Duggan's killing did not. Online slogans spread into the offline world, onto placards and t-shirts, facilitated by a range of offline community groups and organisations (Ruiz, 2022). Iconic moments such as the toppling of the statue of slave trader Edward Colston in Bristol (Hayes et al., 2022; Nasar, 2020) helped to cement BLM in the popular imaginary, focusing attention on the structural injustices and systemic violence experienced by people of colour (in the UK and globally). Instead, BLM made visible the ideologies, histories and power dynamics of colonialism that underpin the categories, analyses and knowledge through which we come to learn about the world (Archer et al., 2022; Parsons., 2022; Yusoff., 2018), and which sit subtly beneath the surface, underpinning racialised inequalities.

In calling for mainstream attention to Black subjectivities (Davies, 2022), the Black Lives Matter movement in the UK responded to a situation whereby the marginalisation of Black voices and the systemic racism that facilitated this marginalisation, were (and are) deeply embedded in recent and distant UK histories. Authors such as Paul Gilroy in *Ain't No Black in the Union Jack* (2002) and Robbie Shilliam in *Race and the Undeserving Poor* (2018) document the overt and subtle, physical and emotional abuses that people of colour experienced. Many of us know that migrants to a postwar UK struggled to find accommodation due to the infamous signs 'no dogs, no blacks, no Irish', and in part this is built on a historical, colonial legacy whereby people from colonised lands were able to be treated by colonisers as sub-human, inhuman and therefore as targets of abuse.

Ray Moxham (2003) in his book *Tea* documents the way that these attitudes and the appalling treatment that they facilitated, are folded in to iconic symbols of Britishness, such as the hot beverage, tea. Rashmi Paun (2022), in a blog with inclusivity think tank *British Future*, discussed his experiences of being both a student, and a refugee in 1960s Britain. His experiences highlight the ways that structural racism damages the ability of people of colour to contribute to UK politics in the ways that they might want to and are skilled to do. Sadly, this shouldn't have been surprising given that we also know how in the postwar years, overt racism was a political platform which literally won elections. For example, MP Enoch Powell's 1968 'Rivers of Blood' speech arguably helped the Conservative Party to win the 1970 general election, forcing an unwilling and liberal party leadership into a manifesto which promised tighter controls on immigration (Peele, 2018). Although Powell was exiled to the back benches by the parliamentary party, his vehement criticism of mass immigration touched a grass-roots nerve and has become symbolic of the way that racism sought to push people of colour out of the public sphere. At some times this has been overt, by literally banning such groups from the public space; but it can also be covert and subtle, such as maintaining norms and values that make it harder for marginalised groups to participate fully, or even to exist and flourish.

As we will see later in this chapter, this kind of structural exclusion matters to liberal democracy, and therefore to the study of UK politics. They impact on the extent to which excluded groups are able to participate in assembled civil society and political debate, contributing to discussions about how the UK should evolve and adapt to contemporary challenges. In this book, politics in the UK is not only a study of institutions, it is also a study of civil society, history and culture, and the way that various groups of people seek to shape our institutions and polity.

The point that we are making in this chapter is that a well-functioning liberal democracy should provide space for all the different groupings within society to operate, be heard and listened to. Put another way, this chapter will argue that good politics and good policy need to come from a plurality of voices – or many voices. For us in this book, pluralism is not just an abstract and difficult concept to grasp. Instead, it reflects the way that policy is developed with, and by, people with a diverse range of experience and experiences. We see pluralism as essential for a flourishing and equitable politics. This is because there is no one, singular UK culture, or one, singular UK experience. Instead, politics in the UK is assembled out of many, many different groupings and experiences, values and histories. In our example above, we discussed assembled differences in terms of race and ethnicity. In this book, you will also encounter (some of) the many different experiences in the UK, formulated in terms of gender, class, sexuality, nation or region.

What we hope to show through the example (above) of Black Lives Matter, and also considering feminism and the LGBTQ+ movement, is that a pluralist democratic politics does not have to be about state power alone. Instead, it includes the everyday politics and multiple stories out of which UK society is assembled and UK politics emerges. Our examination into pluralism considers it as both a descriptive tool and a normative goal. Pluralism is both a moral imperative and a device which has utility for well-functioning, flourishing, liberal democracies which are able to adapt to the physical and natural environments and challenges put before them. This brings us to the question of power. The version of pluralism that we use in this book borrows from a conceptualisation of power that views it as 'rhizomatic', or radically dispersed throughout society, culture and economy, as opposed to one-directional and hierarchical. We begin by asking what pluralism is and why it matters. This takes us to William Connolly's (2005) version of pluralism, and for us in this book, the language around how the UK is assembled. From here we ask the question about what an assemblage *is* and how it works for us in our analysis of and understanding about UK politics. Finally, we address the language that we attach to contemporary analyses of pluralism.

Assemblage, power and UK politics

This section discusses what we mean when we talk about how the UK is assembled. Analyses about how 'things' are assembled are used in academic disciplines far beyond the social and political sciences, wherever scholars have needed to describe highly complex systems involving many different actors, institutions, practices, objects, meanings, organisms, patterns and places. It also helps analysts to see the ways in which the assembled fabric of our communities does (or doesn't) connect with other things, structures, infrastructures, economies, polities, meanings and experiences (e.g. see Bajpai et al., 2020; Willett, 2021).

The assembled parts that make up human communities are complex and entangled. Drawing on the seminal philosophy of Deleuze and Guattari (2004), Delanda (2016) describes in his work the ways in which our environments, institutions, practices, beliefs, symbols and histories are often symbiotic, needing each other in order to be able to function. If we were to apply this to the study of politics, we can see how the idea of a parliament – whether in Westminster, Stormont, Cardiff, or Holyrood – does not make sense without a public, or a people. Equally, a political party presupposes that there is both a people to vote for it, and an organising body in which once returned elected persons can participate. But there is no ideal type of 'organising body'. It just so happens that in the UK we have a parliament, which appears in the way that it does because of complex histories over an extended period of time (about which, more in the chapters to follow).

Over recent centuries UK political institutions have evolved around general principles of liberal democracy, but even other liberal democratic governments globally have different structures and systems to those that we have in the UK. The point is that there is no one, perfect kind of political institution. Our institutions evolve over time in an entangled interaction between the many different actors, actions, relationships, meanings and flows of information over a period of centuries. Jane Bennett in her book *Vibrant Matter* (2010) adds an additional layer to this. She incorporates the natural environment and the non-human into our anthropocentric political assemblages, reminding us about the symbiotic relationships that we have between ourselves and the natural environments in which we live (see also Lemke, 2021). We shape it, and it shapes us, but we couldn't exist without it (although the natural and physical environment clearly could exist without us!).

We need to understand which groups of our assembled UK are structurally advantaged in making their voices heard, which are disadvantaged, and how we can improve this balance. One of the things that an assemblage does for the study of politics in general – and UK politics in particular – is that it reminds us that there is no singular 'essence' of a thing (see Connolly, 2005). For example, there is no single ideal type of government structure. Instead, the ideas and meanings that are assembled around the institutions of local and national governance, their interrelationships with civil society, businesses, campaign and lobby groups, voluntary associations and environments are all in a constant process of evolution. Even institutions which appear to be relatively stable, are changing in many different ways, sometimes large and sometimes microscopic.

Each of these organisations or institutions which are connected with government in some way are also an assemblage, formed from and connected to many other assemblages. Some of these connections and flows of energy will be affected by deep historical legacies and differences in the meanings and attitudes that they attach to the same objects and things. Sometimes interpersonal/organisational relationships can have an enabling effect which builds energy, and at other times these relationships can be draining, which dissipates enthusiasm, willingness and capacity. For the study of politics in the UK, this means that we will be able to understand it a lot better, if we consider the interactions of a rich constellation of political actors – including local and national campaign groups, industry champions, unions, social movements, businesses, various levels of government and organisations.

It is important to note that this is a theory of *change* rather than stasis. No assemblage will remain long in its current shape but will evolve, connecting with different assemblages and abandoning others. We mentioned earlier about race and racism in the UK, and how racist attitudes were used at times to win elections. From this, we come to understand that at one point these kinds of beliefs were pretty central to UK assemblages. What the Black Lives Matter movement and others like and before it have done is to try to push these attitudes outside of UK assemblages and make them no part of it. Although there is still a long way to go in the UK (Parsons, 2022), the overt 'no blacks, no dogs, no Irish' type of discrimination described by Gilroy is a thing of the past.

However, racism is so far from pushed outside that the Vote Leave campaign for Brexit was able to use it to mobilise the right-wing populist vote (Durrheim et al., 2018). Vote Leave had to be more subtle about it than Enoch Powell. This highlights the fact that shifting attitudes mean that racism has no overt and open place in our public sphere, even if some people still hold these views privately. We know that the institutions, relationships, values and knowledge which make up UK politics are also changing – sometimes very rapidly. Drawing on social scientist Bruno Latour (2005), this means that rather than study the *object* of UK politics, we need to understand better the processes, mechanisms and flows of information through which these changes occur. Exploring UK politics through a theory of change helps us to better comprehend, and even predict, some of these changes.

Finally, analysing UK politics in this way provides us with a different way of looking at power which helps us to understand how political power does not have to be focused on parliamentary processes, but is also dispersed throughout civil society. Traditionally, power in politics is imagined along the lines of Robert Dahl's (1957) ability to get someone to do something that they would not otherwise do. It is a mechanical, one-directional flow from the power-full, to the power-less. It has what Stephen Lukes (2021) calls 'the three faces of power' – decision-making, non-decision-making (agenda setting), and ideological power which influences peoples' desires, thoughts, and beliefs. One of the contributions of post-structuralism, seeking to expose, explore and dismantle social, political and cultural structures and the workings of power is to re-cast power as something that is shared throughout the political system. For example, Michel Foucault (1998) tells us that even the people that we imagine as 'power-less' are able to find spaces to access power. For example, there is a power in resistance. To illustrate, Foucault tells us that in forming a resistance, counter-cultural and marginalised ideas become more deeply dispersed (and therefore known about) throughout society. Consequently, whilst we might *imagine* that power is 'held' and exercised by some, another way to think about it is that there are many possible sites of power. Part of the skill of doing politics is about being able to observe, harness and utilise these sites of dispersed, systemic power.

Deleuze and Guattari (2004) use the biological metaphors of the tree root versus the rhizome to help to visualise systemic power. They observe how although big, heavy, and strong, tree roots are relatively easy to dismantle if you have the correct tools and enough force. This is because all of the power and life force comes from one central node. Rhizomes, on the other hand, papery thin and tangled though their roots may be, have the benefit of having *no* central node. Instead, power is dispersed throughout the system. Consequently even though the root can be broken apart using only my fingertips, and I can dig the bulk of the rhizome root out of the ground with relative ease, if I leave any part of the root in the ground, it will have the power and capacity to regenerate and grow, and the plant will start again. To imagine UK politics as only being about the parliamentary system is to liken the parliamentary machinery to Deleuze and Guattari's metaphorical tree root with its single site of power. Instead, we might prefer to imagine UK politics as rhizomatic, dispersed throughout society and into the everyday lives of the inhabitants of these isles – all of whom contribute in some way to how our political system and its cultural underpinnings develop. Power in UK politics can be observed and harnessed at a local, individual and everyday level as well as through our formal political institutions.

Political representation in the UK

Because it is so central to liberal democracy, the concept of political representation is really important. The starting point for us is the normative claim that politics in the UK *should* contain a fair representation of the diverse population of the UK, but empirically, in practice, it often doesn't. Durose et al. (2013) describe it as a polity dominated by middle-aged white men. This is an issue which is shared with the devolved parliaments, and referring to Northern Ireland, Galligan (2013) reminds us that a lack of representative voices in government is a problem for democratic accountability. In short, if governments are not making policy which reflects the needs of all citizens, this affects the legitimacy of government.

Moreover, political representatives with intersecting identities are able to show greater empathy with persons from a wider cross-section of the community, following a much broader policy agenda (Tatari and Mencutek, 2015).

As we began to see in our example of Black Lives Matter above, there undeniably *are* (many) spaces in which diverse voices have been and are, ignored at best, or pushed out and derided at worst. For just a moment, we are going to take representation in the parliament at Westminster (through Members of Parliament) as a proxy measure for diversity amongst some of the most visible political actors in the UK. We would want to note that in the 40 years following the end of the Second World War, when many persons from lands that Britain had colonised answered the invitation to help in postwar reconstruction, there were no Members of Parliament of colour in Westminster at all. Postwar migrants and their descendants were for decades entirely unrepresented amongst people who were supposed to represent the interests and experiences of people in the UK. Unbelievably, this means that there were more non-white MPs in the 40 years between 1892 and 1932 than there were in the next 55 years. In 1987, Diane Abbott, Paul Boateng, Bernie Grant and Keith Vaz were the first (Labour) MPs of colour since Shapurji Saklatvala, the Member of Parliament for Battersea North, standing for the Communist Party of Great Britain and of Indian Parsi heritage, was elected in 1922.

In fact, if political representation in Westminster is our proxy for diversity, the UK Parliament as an institution has a long history of being extremely unequal. The first ever female MP to take her seat was Nancy (Viscountess) Astor in 1919, standing for Plymouth Sutton (Constance Markievicz, elected in 1918 for Sinn Féin did not take her seat). However, in the 101 years since Markievicz's election and the 2019 general election, there have only been a grand total of 552 female MPs. To put this into perspective, the total number of female MPs over this 101-year period would not fill the 650 seats in the House of Commons. In fact, 220 of this total figure of 552 were elected to Westminster in 2019 where, in making up only 34 per cent of the total number of MPs, they are considerably fewer than the proportion of women in the general population.

We can see similar issues in the UK in terms of class. Parliamentary data uses attendance at a fee-paying school as a proxy for class. Ninety-three per cent of the population did *not* attend a fee-paying school but went to either a comprehensive or state-funded grammar school. According to the 2019 *Elitist Britain* report by the Sutton Trust and the Social Mobility Commission (2019), the 7 per cent of Britons who went to a fee-paying school occupy 39 per cent of the top positions in public life. This is a severe under-representation of persons who attended state schools. Actually, 65 per cent of judges, 59 per cent of Civil Service permanent secretaries, 57 per cent of the House of Lords and 52 per cent of diplomats were privately educated, as were 43 per cent of the most influential news editors and broadcasters. In this context, the 2019 Parliament doesn't look *quite* so bad. Only (only!) 29 per cent of parliamentarians were educated privately (Sutton Trust and Social Mobility Commission, 2019). This is over four times higher than the electorate that they represent and means that few MPs will have had any personal experience of the desperation of destitution and decisions about whether to 'heat or eat'.

Image 1.2 The UK is assembled out of a rich diversity of different groups of people, who bring a wide range of different experiences and perspectives

Photo by David Fowler on Shutterstock

The examples above are an illustration of the difficulties experienced by the wider population in accessing and being represented by parliamentary assemblages. This lack of representation means that a wide variety (or plurality) of voices struggle to be heard in UK national politics. In other words, this translates to a physical lack of pluralism across a range of different measures, at the heart of our parliamentary democracy. But why does this matter? In the next section we are going to explore what pluralism is, and why it is desirable.

What is pluralism?

Pluralism literally means a diversity of lifestyles and norms (cultural), values and ethics (moral) and political choices (political) (Heywood, 2015). When we talked about Black Lives Matter earlier in this chapter, largely we discussed cultural pluralism. In the previous section, we talked more about political pluralism, and the ability of different groups to alter political processes. Moral pluralism is a little more complex. Here, we ask about whether our polity and civil society can accommodate different values and ethics. Whilst we are comfortable, for example, with the idea that persons with different ethical values derived from religious or spiritual beliefs can co-exist within UK society and politics, we are less certain about pluralism that threatens a core value of liberal democracy.

Theory box: John Locke, liberal democracy, and the importance of pluralism

Liberal, democratic governments are based on the concepts of popular consent and legitimacy. This Theory box explains what we mean by them, how they came to be considered important, and in brief how they impact on UK politics.

Liberal democracy as a form of government is a product of the modern era. By this we mean that there is a tangled (inter-) relationship between enlightenment thinking; the rise of science as a means of understanding our world; capitalism as an overarching economic framework; the industrialisation of the labour market; and an interest in individual rights, freedoms, and the ability to hold decision-makers to account.

One of the early important figures of enlightenment who thought about how government should be run was John Locke (1632–1704). Locke's views on government were impacted by his experience of political instability during the English Civil War (1642–1651) and the restoration of the monarchy in 1660. In 1689 Locke published his *Two Treatises on Government* in which he provided a moral basis for, and outline of, a type of government in which sovereignty resided in citizens rather than in the monarch. By this we mean that the purpose of government is to protect the natural rights of citizens, and government only governs through the popular consent of the *people*. Locke talks about the importance of being able to 'cashier one's governors', or to be able to hold those with authority to account for their actions. Unlike in systems where sovereignty resides in a monarch, or king (such as that advocated by Locke's contemporary Thomas Hobbes), Locke introduces a form of government whereby the legitimacy of government rests on the consent of citizens, for whom their life, liberty and property is protected.

Locke also introduced other principles to government that we will find familiar – such as the 'separation of powers' between the principal arms of government of the Legislature, the Executive and the Judiciary, ensuring that no part of government would get too strong. It is important to note that whilst these ideas seem normal to those accustomed to Western politics now, they were considered as radical in UK politics right up to the early 1800s. Other key theorists included Jean-Jacques Rousseau, Thomas Paine and Mary Wollstonecraft, and Enlightenment thinking underpinned the American War of Independence (1775–1783) and the revolution in France (1789–1799). Both nations initiated governments expressly founded on these principles. The UK had a more incremental journey towards adopting Enlightenment principles in government, and we can still see echoes of this – for example, in the way that we do not have a complete separation of powers.

As we see in the chapter, contemporary pluralism is still founded on the premise that government needs to protect the rights and freedoms of the public if it is to retain its legitimacy and popular consent. Key differences relate to who the public is imagined to be, and how they are incorporated into assembled processes of governance.

Pluralism can also be normative or descriptive. When making a normative claim, we are saying that something *should* be more plural, representing a more diverse cross-section of society. If we are making a descriptive claim, we are asking how diverse something that we observe actually *is*. As a concept, it can be traced back to the early foundations of liberal democracy, as put forward by John Locke (1632–1704) (see Theory box above). Whilst liberal democracies are generally agreed that political pluralism is good and important, cultural and moral pluralism are more contentious because some conservatives argue that government relies on a unity of values to bind people together and through which to steer a policy middle ground. From this position, too broad a range of cultural and moral diversity threatens good governance. Echoing Modood (2000), the problem with this argument is that there *is* no one, singular, unifying, essential UK identity. Instead, we are assembled from a range of positions and experiences which complicate a unified identity. Sometimes, groups feel that their particular interests and needs are unheard, which can lead to them taking drastic forms of resistance in an attempt to make themselves more visible. For some analysts, this was at the core of the Leave vote in the Brexit referendum (Ashcroft and Bevir, 2021). To deal with similar situations better, we need to embrace pluralism, the multiple identities out of which Britain is assembled, and its rich diversity of voices at a local, cultural and political level (Ashcroft and Bevir, 2016).

Above, we have a number of different claims arguing for cultural and moral pluralism within UK politics. Modood's and Ashcroft and Bevir's claims rest on the descriptive argument that culture and society just don't function any other way. Norman and Kymlica's (2000) argument is more normative – that minorities should have a right to be heard. Another normative argument for pluralism can be found in the utilitarianism of philosopher J.S. Mill. For Mill in *On Liberty* (2008 [1859]), cultural, political and moral diversity encourages us to question, adapt and update the things that we think that we know, which means that we challenge our beliefs. In turn, this means that the things that we 'know' are founded on reason rather than belief, meaning that we make better decisions. Consequently, there is a utility in following the principles of pluralism.

The key differences between a pluralism based on rights and one based on utility is that rights-based perspectives represent a moral rule which should be followed at all times. It is a 'first principle', which means that it should determine all future actions. 'Utility' refers to a moral rule which is right because of the *consequences* of following that rule. A popular way of showcasing these differences is by asking the question 'Is it OK to tell a lie?' If our moral choices are based on first principles, and a first principle is that lying is bad, then it is never OK to lie. But if by telling a lie, I am able to stop a worse thing happening, then under the principle of utility, telling a lie is OK because the *consequences* of the action are beneficial.

To bring this back to pluralism, a question that we have to ask ourselves as political analysts is about whether pluralism is good because it conforms to certain liberal ethical values, or whether pluralism is good because it helps us to make better and more informed choices. For example, if my decisions are made with full regard for the diversity of experiences of citizens in the assembled UK, then I am making decisions based on a more accurate interpretation of the assembled political landscape. Therefore, my decisions will be better able to help the UK evolve and adapt to our changing world (Montpetit, 2016).

As a concept, pluralism has a rich and highly developed history, rooted in disagreement over the precise meaning and applicability of the term (Lassman, 2011). Tocqueville's (1835) *Democracy in America* is often cited for its insights into the varied ways in which different perspectives were able to be aired and heard in the America that he witnessed on his travels. Adcock and Vail (2012) provide us with an in-depth history of its journey from 1950/1960s liberal interest group pluralism, where scholars such as Robert Dahl argued that not all people choose to actively engage in politics, but that organisations and political groupings have the legitimacy to speak for those that choose not to engage (see also Chambers and Carver, 2008). The 1970s and 1980s saw a neo-corporatist analysis of the structural barriers in unequal access to power. Following the end of the Cold War and the collapse of the Soviet Union, 1989 to the 1990s saw the concept return to liberal pluralism, with the key difference that this time the emphasis was on voluntary associations rather than on interest groups, including on the value of the autonomy of collective non-state actors.

Robert Putnam's (2000) *Bowling Alone* is a good example of this perspective, and his work is explored in more depth in Chapter 5. Whilst Putnam provides us with an empirical analysis, the conceptual architecture offered by William Connolly's (2005) *Pluralism* reworks its ontological underpinnings (see Spotlight on research below). Pluralism goes from a conservative theory of order and the status quo to a radical discussion of the nature of political activity (Chambers and Carver, 2008) and how politics is assembled. In creating a rhizomatic pluralism to which everyone can contribute, Connolly provides a rich, dense conceptual architecture through which to examine pluralism in contemporary politics.

Spotlight on research: William Connolly's pluralism

William Connolly's contribution to our understanding of pluralism has been rich and varied. In the 1990s his work addressed questions around identity, difference and the problem of the 'other'. For example, in his works *Identity/Difference* (1991) and *The Ethos of Pluralization* (1995), he explores the tensions between the need to draw boundaries around identities, and the risk that this takes. For example, identities are important for movements in order to help them to become visible and increase their ability to create political change, but this also creates divisions, which sustains cruelty and violence.

Connolly's solution was to explore the complex adaptive assemblages of Deleuze and Guattari. The assemblage *has* no fixed and rigid boundaries. Things, ideas, structures and institutions are merely collected around other ideas, concepts, structures or institutions. These collections are fluid and constantly evolving. This means that ideas, concepts, structures, things and institutions that are connected (either within assemblages or outside of them) have the capacity to *affect* (see Chapter 5), impact or shape other things, ideas, concepts, etc. This kind of pluralism is a radical democracy because the scope for political change lies right the way across assembled political actors and civil society, incorporating memory (Connolly, 2002) and also, the environment (Connolly, 2017). In fact, one of the interesting questions posed by Connolly is 'What is the limit of political actors?' So, in *Facing the Planetary: Entangled Humanism and the Politics of Swarming* (Connolly, 2017), through the concept of affective assemblages, Connolly asks about the degree to which our politics is a more-than-human entanglement with our environments.

Connolly's evolutionary perspective also adds to pluralism a sense of the deep interrelationship between the past and the politics of what we will become, our future. In this sense, politics is about much more than the present. It includes how we think about our pasts, how these stories reflect the diverse range of experiences of citizens within the assembled UK, and the flow of ideas and knowledge between the different parts of the political system.

We also need to understand the ways that the emotional responses behind our stories are used politically (Ahmed, 2004) to generate further spaces for political change. These histories also play a crucial role in the development of what Connolly (2008) calls 'resonance machines', self-sustaining feedback loops between assembled parts of our political system, creating and amplifying stories, flows of information and knowledge, and path dependencies and stasis.

If we were to trace pluralism's journey using the example of Black Lives Matter, set out in the Introduction, we might have begun with organisations and political groupings associated with (better) representing people of colour within UK politics (neo-corporatist and later, liberal). Putnam's version of pluralism would have added the day-to-day activities of people of colour within our communities (what we might also call place-shaping), and how this feeds back through from local to national politics. Connolly's pluralism would include the histories, values and beliefs through which people of colour have navigated their worlds, the formal and informal structures that this has created and which affect the conditions for possibility – or the ability of people of colour to flourish and achieve their human potential. It would draw connectivities and temporal reverberations between the knowledge and emotive responses engendered by colonialism and would showcase how the assembled 'UK' incorporates a myriad of different stories and experiences which have been overtly or covertly affectively impacted by the global assemblage of colonialism, to which it is tightly connected.

This version of pluralism might then showcase the many different spaces that people of colour – both in the UK and also by those embedded in other, connected assemblages (e.g. the US or Haiti) – have organised and resisted racial inequalities and injustices. We would see how resistance in the micro-politics of the everyday reverberates into the macro-politics of national and even international processes, affecting and shaping attitudes, values, beliefs and emotional linguistic attachments. In other words, an assembled pluralism allows us to see the entangled messiness of political change, and the ways in which ordinary people are also a part of creating political change.

Governance, multiculturalism and diversity

Over recent years, scholarly debate and discussion about pluralism as a concept has waned. However, the liberal democratic belief in plural politics, ensuring that many different voices are heard and contribute to political decisions, remains as a strong thread throughout UK politics. We think this makes our central question of 'How plural is UK politics?' such a resonant one. Moreover, we have tended to replace the word 'pluralism' with other words which discuss concepts that signify aspects of pluralism. We will discuss the three most important ones briefly, here. These are governance, multiculturalism and diversity. This is not to say that they have replaced the importance of pluralism as a concept. On the contrary, they signify three important elements of a well-functioning pluralist society.

'Governance' as a concept is designed to better reflect the multiplicity of different actors who contribute to 'government' (Bevir, 2012a). 'Government' tends to imply a singularity and a central power source and invites mechanical metaphors around things like the 'levers' of power. As we have started to allude to above and will see in much greater detail throughout the book, whilst government might be *a* central node, visible as a decision-making, and sometimes as an executive, body implementing these decisions, a multiplicity of non-governmental organisations and individuals feed in to both policy decisions and implementation.

More accurately, drawing on Connolly's (2005) version of pluralism here, policy and government are an assembled network of civil society organisations and Putnam-style associations that describe pluralism within government processes (Husband and Ireland, 2022). For political analysts, part of the challenge is to understand where and how power and decision-making lie in governance networks. For example, is local government moving to a more decentralised, 'devolved' form, or does an analysis of power, networks and decision-making lead us to the conclusion that UK local government is still, essentially, an outreach office of Whitehall? (Hambleton and Sweeting, 2004).

Multiculturalism gained traction as a concept in the 1990s and argued that there was no single, essentialised way of being British (Modood, 2000). Instead, political identities are fluid – adapting, evolving, and growing over time – and reflect broader local and global changes that the individuals living in these isles experience. In this context, ensuring that assembled constellations around what 'Britishness' means reflect the different cultural backgrounds of the peoples of the UK is important. Minority and immigrant cultures have a right to be respected and defended as part of this process. Scholars such as Modood (2000), Gilroy (2002) and Parekh (2008) show how over time persons from minority cultures combine aspects of an individual's cultural heritage with elements of the dominant culture which they choose to adopt, developing 'hybrid' cultures.

More recently, the language around pluralism has adapted again and now clusters around the concept of 'diversity'. This broadens the concept of multiculturalism to include diversity around gender, class, sexuality, disability, as well as ethnicity. An interesting development here relates to the use by scholars of racial diversity of the term 'decolonising' to describe and explore the historical and structural processes, practices and meanings rooted in colonialism and imperialism through which racial inequalities have been maintained and sustained into the contemporary UK (Parsons, 2022; Saini and Begum, 2020). Part of the response to this has come through what has been termed as the 'culture wars' (Curran et al., 2018), whereby some have found it more difficult to keep pace with the ways in which contemporary UK societies and identities have changed over time. In some cases this has resulted in a defensive backlash, which attempts to challenge recent changes and assert a more unified (as opposed to plural) sense of UK identity.

Need to know: Culture wars

Ashcroft and Bevir (2021) discuss the belief that the result of the Brexit referendum reflected the degree to which some people in UK politics felt left out or unheard by mainstream political debates. Sometimes, this is discussed as part of the 'culture wars' whereby

(Continued)

cultural change is happening so rapidly that it is difficult or disorientating for people to keep pace with (e.g. over race, gender and sexuality). In some respects, it is an updating of the former term 'political correctness' and frequently divides society into imagined (and often inaccurate) binary opposites between conservatives and progressives, old and young, and rural and urban. At times, the level of 'debate' is of such toxicity that it actually inhibits the pluralist discussion of the diverse range of positions out of which the UK is assembled.

Conclusion

The central question of this book asks how plural UK politics is. This chapter sets out to introduce this question, making the argument that a well-functioning liberal democracy should provide the space for all of the different groupings within society to operate, be heard and listened to. Put another way, good politics and good policy need to come from a plurality of voices – or many voices. We have seen that whilst some people fear that too much pluralism will harm the unity of identity that assists government, from other perspectives to deny the rich diversity of experiences, positions, attitudes and beliefs that exist within the nation-state creates more problems than it solves. Moreover, it is also an inaccurate reflection of the UK that we live in, which is a rich tapestry of assembled difference. For politics and policy, there is a utility in embracing this difference and the many views and perspectives available for solving problems. It means that we continually question and update beliefs and knowledge, which in turn helps to enable the UK to evolve and adapt more effectively to global problems.

For us in this book, examining how the contemporary UK is assembled helps to enable us to explore and understand the diversity underpinning society and on which UK politics is based. To adapt Visit Glasgow's slogan, 'People make the UK' and this book aims to explore in detail how people make politics. We show that individuals, governmental and non-governmental institutions, organisations, businesses and pressure groups are all key political actors, devising formal and informal campaigns situated, operating and interacting at different levels across the country. But this also has a temporal element. The politics that we have now has grown out of and in response to the structures, attitudes, values and beliefs out of which 'the UK' was assembled in the past – or in various different pasts. Whilst we are not determined by our assembled histories, an understanding of these histories can help to explain some actions, attitudes, values and beliefs in the present. In this book, we argue that politics is threaded throughout the assembled UK, and that rather than being separate from a distant political centre we are all intricately and intimately a part of and connected to UK politics and the UK's political system. The everyday and our everyday activities, interests and involvement play a really important role in shaping the political system through which our civil society is organised. This means that politics is 'rhizomatic', something that (if we should choose) we can all be actively engaged in rather than distant from.

Key take-home points

- The UK is assembled out of people with many different experiences, beliefs and values.
- A well-functioning liberal democracy needs the space for all groups in society to be heard and listened to.
- Exploring many different perspectives helps us to adapt and evolve as a society.
- Individuals, governmental and non-governmental institutions, organisations, businesses and pressure groups are all key political actors, operating and interacting at different levels across the UK.
- Politics in the UK is threaded throughout our communities amongst the formal and informal identities and everyday interests that we are a part of.

Annotated reading list

Ashcroft, R. and Bevir, M. (2021) Brexit and the myth of British national identity. *British Politics*, 16, 117–132.

This journal article presents a useful discussion of pluralism in the UK post Brexit. It argues that British national identities have been inherently plural since the post-imperial renegotiation. However, being bound to the binary between universalism and particularism, contemporary UK political parties are ill-suited to be able to address this pluralism. As a consequence, the authors claim that many sections of UK society feel that they are ignored and not listened to, which in turn has led to a widespread feeling of alienation amongst the broader population. The authors argue that the idea of a shared UK national identity is a myth, and adherence to it is destabilising our politics. Instead, we need to better understand and debate the identities and communities out of which the assembled 'UK' is composed. As well as providing their own diagnosis, the authors invite us to reflect on the enmeshed relationships between pluralism, representation, identities, consent and government, and to consider how this changes over time.

Connolly, W. (2005) *Pluralism*. Durham: Duke University Press.

The version of pluralism put forward here fuses identity and politics, arguing for deeply plural political identities, social and personal lives. For Connolly, pluralism goes far beyond the interaction between the government and organised interest groups. Instead, it extends to the private sphere and acceptance of the plurality of people's attitudes, beliefs and values. He talks about how societal 'threats' are used in an attempt to impose singular narratives about 'who we are'. Connolly develops what he calls 'multi-dimensional pluralism' to connote the expansion of diversity (plurality) in multiple dimensions of individual, social and political life. Connolly takes pluralism as far as asking whether it needs to be limited to human actors, but whether there are ways of incorporating the non-human. For persons interested in exploring these ideas further, Jane Bennett's book *Vibrant Matter* (2010), (Durham: Duke University Press) may be of interest.

Putnam, R. (2000) *Bowling Alone: The Collapse and Revival of American Community.* London: Simon Schuster.

In this seminal book, Putnam explores the importance of an active civil society for ensuring that we have a vibrant, pluralist liberal democracy. Part of what Putnam encourages us to reflect on is that the relationship between 'the people' and governments is much more than merely a two-way dialogue but extends towards ensuring that communities are organised. Putnam provides us with a way of imagining the polity as active vs passive and that it is through activity that we are better able to shape our local, national and global communities. Empirically, Putnam observes that the ways that people live their lives in late capitalism means that we have become atomised, fragmented and detached from our communities. For Putnam, this impacts on the ability of people to be able to shape our worlds – or in other words, impacts on the plurality of our politics.

2
The UK as a multi-national state

Contested histories, state formation and constitutional settlement

Arianna Giovannini

Image 2.1 British identity is complex and diverse
© Photo by Andrei_Diachenko on Shutterstock

Learning objectives

After reading this chapter, you should be able to:

- Understand key concepts and theories that help explain state-formation processes
- Understand how the UK has come together as a multi-national state through incremental unification, and why this matters for its political system
- Critically assess the UK constitutional settlement, its origins and contemporary challenges
- Understand why in the UK power tends to be concentrated in the centre and the implications this has on current political dynamics, as well as for a pluralistic account of UK politics

Introduction

This chapter takes a critical look at how the UK, as we know it today, has come together over time as a multi-national state and the impact these processes of 'assemblage' have on the politics of the country. To achieve this, it considers what a nation-state is and what makes a state 'multi-national', it assesses the specific dynamics of territorial distinctiveness across the nations of the UK, and it evaluates the constitutional settlement that has emerged from the long path of incremental unification that characterises the country.

Before we begin, it is important to clarify a few key concepts. First: what is a nation-state? And what makes a state, like the UK, *multi*-national? In a broad sense, the concept of nation-state underlines the relationship between the two composing parts of this hyphenated term. The state refers to a political organisation that has sovereignty within its territorial borders and in relation to other states, exercised through a set of permanent institutions (like parliament, government, etc.; see Haywood, 2000). The nation refers, broadly, to the people who live within the geographical borders of a state and is thus defined as a political community whose members share some common traits (e.g. language, culture, history, traditions, ethnicity, religion, etc.). These traits bind them together and make them feel part of the same group, with a sense of attachment to a clearly demarcated territory (see Gibernau, 1996; Haywood, 2000). Nations are 'imagined' (because members of nations do not all know each other, for obvious reasons), and the political community of the nation is very powerful, shaping people's political, territorial, and cultural identity in a profound way, and thus impacting their political behaviour (Anderson, 1983; Billig, 1995).

Nation-states are meaningful political units both on a domestic and an international dimension. From a world order perspective, the nation-state is a territorially bounded sovereign polity based on the principle of state sovereignty, first articulated in the Treaty of Westphalia (1648), which recognises the right of states to govern without external interference. However, from a domestic angle – i.e. looking within the boundaries of a nation-state – the concept becomes a bit more complex.

From this internal perspective, in principle, the nation-state should bind state *and* national sovereignty (i.e. the right of nations and their communities to govern themselves). Indeed, we often tend to think that there is some sort of natural relationship between these two notions, and that the nation and the state always coincide. When this happens, we have coherent nation-states, where government institutions are uniform and represent a cohesive people, sharing similar traditions and cultural norms across the whole country, and a limited degree of 'internal diversity'. Yet, especially in the context of a globalised world, it is difficult to find fully coherent nation-states, as most countries in the world contain more than one national group. Perhaps Japan is an example that gets closest to the idea of a coherent nation-state, as it has widely shared culture, history and language, represented by a set of institutions protected by the constitution, which operate within clearly demarcated borders – although some small elements of diversity persist.

However, a nation is not always necessarily a state, and a state is not always necessarily a single nation. Some nations are 'stateless' – for example, if they are included within the borders of a state that does not cater for their historical, cultural or economic distinctiveness, and dismisses or seeks to repress them (Keating, 2005). Often, stateless nations seek to achieve self-determination (i.e. the right to govern themselves) through secession or independence. Conversely, some states include more than one nation: we call these multi-national states (Keating, 1999). In essence, this means that a country has a set of institutions (the state) that must account for, accommodate and represent more than one political community (i.e. nations, each with its own distinctive history, culture, language, ethnicity or religion) within its territorial boundaries. The depth and degree of this 'internal diversity' directly affects the political dynamics of the country in question and can generate or ease tensions between its different component nations and the state (Elias and Tronconi, 2011; Hepburn, 2009).

The United Kingdom of Great Britain and Northern Ireland, as its composite name suggests, belongs to this category. It is a multi-national state with a set of permanent political institutions (mostly based in London, at Westminster and Whitehall; see Chapter 6). These, however, preside over four distinct nations (i.e. England, Northern Ireland, Scotland and Wales), each with its own cultural, political, economic and identity characteristics. To recognise this, since 1997, these areas (with the exception of England) have their own devolved parliaments. This multi-level arrangement has profound repercussions on the politics of the UK, especially concerning power distribution and pluralism. And yet, this aspect is often overlooked/underplayed by traditional accounts that tend to focus primarily on the role of Westminster and Whitehall as the undisputed 'core institutions' of the state that define the UK political system.

The main aim of this chapter is to challenge the idea of the UK as a monolithic state, where all power rests in the centre, and explore through an analysis of the process of unification the idea of the UK as an assemblage of nations and histories that extend far beyond London. It will offer a reading that, we hope, will allow you to grasp the importance of the territorial diversity that characterises the UK and its constituent nations, and critically assess contemporary political events through this lens. To unpack these complexities, we start by looking at the UK flag.

What's in a flag?

Flags are compelling political emblems: despite being just a piece of cloth, they are powerful symbols that represent and unify a country and give a sense of belonging to its people.

Simple acts such as flying the national flag at sports events or hanging it outside one's door are far from being just mundane – they offer people a shorthand way to show (and feel) that they are members of a distinct political community (Billig, 1995), thus acting as identity markers. For example, many of you will have attended or followed on the TV Olympic games events and will have experienced, either live or through the screen, the adrenaline rush that comes from being part of the community that supports 'Team GB'. On such occasions, waving the UK flag is a political act: you do not just back a player or a team; you show that you belong to and support *your* country 'against others'. And yet, you will have also noticed that on other types of sports events – such as international football games like the World Cup – there is no UK flag to fly: instead, you will wave the English, Scottish or Welsh colours, depending on which political community you feel part of. This is a very British catch. On the one hand, the Union Flag seeks to represent the UK as a unified political community, and yet, on the other hand, on some occasions members of the component nations of the UK feel compelled to stand behind their respective flags. This demonstrates the diversity, multiplicity and interchangeability of the political identities that underpin the UK as a multi-national state.

The 'making' of the Union Flag reflects the history of the country and how it has come into being over time, as well as the controversies that underpin these processes. The first clue is in the name: the *Union* Flag underlines both the process of unification through which the UK has emerged, and the aspiration to provide a unifying symbol for its component nations. Indeed, like the multi-national state it symbolically represents, the Union Flag is a made of different, overlapping and intersecting elements. It consists of three heraldic crosses. The cross of St George represents England – as the Kingdom of England was the first political unit around which the UK was created. The cross of St Andrew represents Scotland and was combined with the St George's cross in 1606 to mark the 'union of the crowns' following the accession of James VI of Scotland to the throne of the Kingdom of England, which eventually led to a full union between Scotland and England in 1707. Finally, there is the cross of St Patrick, which represents, at least initially, Ireland after the Act of Union of Ireland with the Kingdom of Great Britain (i.e. England (plus Wales) and Scotland) sealed in 1801.

Interestingly, the Welsh dragon does not appear on the Union Flag. This absence is telling: the official reason is that by 1606, when the first Union Flag was created, Wales had already been united with England, thus ceasing to exist as a separate nation. As explained in more detail later on in this chapter, Scotland maintained a degree of its status as a nation with its distinctive identity in the process of union with England that culminated in the 1707 Act – symbolised by the addition of the cross of St Andrew on the one of St George. Wales, however, was assimilated into England and lost, at least on the surface, its status as a nation, with a consequent 'suppression' of its identity markers (language as the most obvious one) – symbolised by the absence of the dragon in the Union Flag. The case of Ireland is more complex (as discussed in this chapter and in Chapter 6). In 1801 the union between Ireland and Great Britain came into force, creating the United Kingdom of Great Britain and Ireland – symbolised by the addition of the cross of St Patrick onto the 1606 version of the Union Flag. But by the early 1920s turbulence started to surface, eventually leading to the formation of the Republic of Ireland (1937) – a separate nation-state in its own right – while Northern Ireland continued to be part of the UK. These developments remain unaccounted for in the

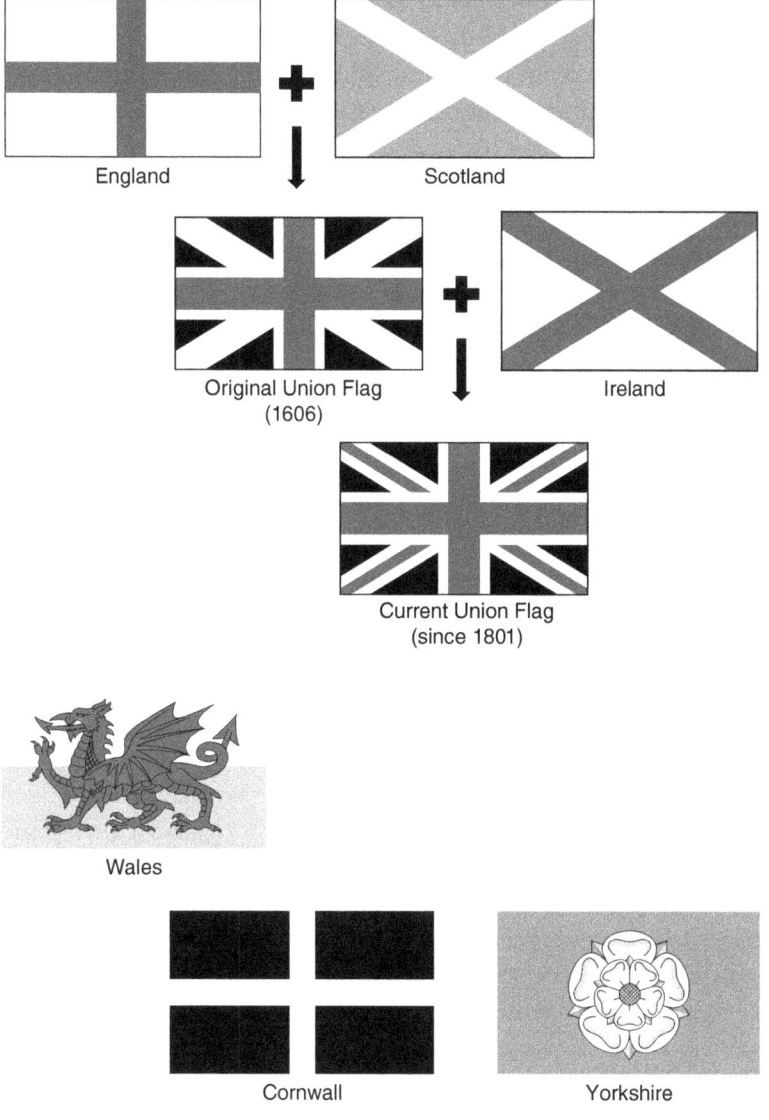

Figure 2.1 The making of the Union Flag

current version of the Union Flag – perhaps unintentionally symbolising how the 'Irish and Northern Irish Questions' are still not fully addressed.

There are also other identities that remain unaccounted for in the Union Flag. With its focus on the main, official nations of the UK, the flag does not include, for example, the small nations (such as Cornwall) and regions (like Yorkshire, or even Wessex) that are part of England but have no official political representation through directly elected bodies. Interestingly, these areas have their own flags and political movements (such as Mebyon Kernow in Cornwall, the Yorkshire Party and the Wessex Regionalists) that seek recognition for their national and regional identity within England.

This overview shows how the Union Flag can be seen, essentially, as an assemblage of different national (hi)stories that reflect, symbolically, both how the UK has come into being, and the complexity of the multiple identities present within the country. The Union Flag might represent an attempt at bringing together the UK nations under the banner of a 'collective identity' – and yet, it is remarkable that, unlike most other countries, there is no adjective that captures this in full. The term 'British' is often used to this end, but it disregards Northern Ireland as if the UK included only Great Britain. As Rose (1982: 11) notes, 'no one speaks of the *UKes* as a nation'. Interestingly, the same does not apply to Scotland, Wales or Ireland, which seem to have a more clearly defined sense of their 'national self'.

The dominant role of England in the process of unification had a double effect in terms of territorial identities. On the one hand, England worked as the 'other' against which the national identity and distinctiveness of Scotland, Wales and Ireland were shaped after the union and, at times, mobilised to promote autonomy or secession claims (see Chapter 6). On the other, however, it also shielded England from putting into question the role of its national identity in the politics of the country. It was only with the inception of devolution from 1997 that debates about Englishness and its political significance started to surface.

Within this context, Britishness emerged as an overarching identity that, for a long time, helped 'stitch together' the idiosyncrasies that underpin the UK state, its composing nations and their national identities (Colley, 1992, 2014; Kumar, 2009). Yet, while this allowed Scotland, Wales and Northern Ireland to retain dual identities (e.g. Scottish and British), the same did not apply to England, where British and English were long understood as synonyms, or 'fused identities' (Kumar, 2009). Only in recent times, polls and academic studies have underlined the growth of 'Englishness' and its political magnitude (see Henderson and Wyn Jones, 2021; Kenny, 2014, 2016). Furthermore, within England itself, regions and small nations with their own identity (such as Yorkshire and Cornwall) have started to become more vocal (Giovannini, 2016; Willett and Giovannini, 2014). The fall of the British Empire and the process of devolution were key factors in this process (Colley, 1992, 2014; Kumar, 2009), stimulating the (re)emergence of single national identities, especially across Great Britain, leading to associated territorial tensions that have shaken up the UK state by challenging its constitutional settlement (see Chapter 6). The process of constitutional reform which led to the introduction of devolution to Scotland, Wales and Northern Ireland in 1997 was aimed at addressing these issues. And yet, as the case of the Scottish independence referendum held in 2014 suggests, devolution has not 'killed nationalism stone dead' as hoped by its architects in the 1990s. A sense of belonging to distinct national (and in the case of Northern Ireland religious) communities still persists across the UK.

But what are the roots of the deep-seated territorial diversity that make up the UK? In the next section, we take a closer look at historical processes that help tackle this question.

Spotlight on research: Political Englishness

Within the academic literature, there is an abundance of excellent studies assessing the role of territorial and national identity in Scotland, Wales and Northern Ireland. Much of this work was prompted by the inception of devolution, which conveyed the attention of scholars on the parts of the UK that gained new directly elected institutions in 1997. Yet much less has been said about the role of political identity in England. Ailsa Henderson and Richard Wyn Jones' book *Englishness: The Political Force Transforming Britain* is an excellent account that bridges this gap in the literature.

Taking the Brexit referendum as their starting point, the authors argue that before that event English nationalism did not have clear political connotation and was mobilised only by very small fringes. Yet they contend that Brexit has been a momentous event that has brought English nationalism under the spotlight, especially in connection with the attitudes of Leave voters.

Henderson and Wyn Jones develop a fascinating analysis that helps to extend our understanding of Englishness and its growing political significance, drawing on data from the Future of England Survey (i.e. a specially commissioned public attitudes survey programme exploring the political implications of English identity). In this way, they show that English nationalism is not growing in contraposition to Britishness; instead, it emerges from the combination of a sense of grievance about England's place within the United Kingdom with a commitment to a particular vision of Britain's past, present and future. Thus, they conclude that English nationalism has a Janus-faced nature which is key to understanding its political magnitude and potential, as well as the ways in which it is impacting on UK politics.

This is a great study, extremely well evidenced and compelling. As a side note, though, by focusing on England as a nation, it does not look at local expressions of identity within it. Thus, to get the full picture, we suggest combining its reading with other studies such as Bernard Deacon's (2007) *Cornwall: A Concise History* or Dave Russell's (2004) *Looking North: Northern England and the National Imagination*, or Robert Colls and Bill Lancaster's (1992) *Geordies: The Roots of English Regionalism*.

The historical roots of the UK and the process of state-building

As discussed so far, the UK as we know it today is not a uniform nation-state: it has come together through incremental processes of assemblage of previously autonomous or separate nations, each with its own history, culture, heritage and even language. In this section, we dig deeper into these histories and reflect critically on how they continue to shape the present, arguing that understanding how the UK state was formed is crucial to appreciate how it evolved, as well as to grasp the constitutional settlement that characterises the country. To support the analysis, we will draw on the concepts of union and unitary state, based on Rokkan and Urwin's (1982) typology of state formation, as well as on Mitchell's (2006, 2009) take on these (see Theory box below).

Theory box: Rokkan and Urwin's state formation typology

In their seminal book *The Politics of Territorial Identity: Studies in European Regionalism* (1982), Stein Rokkan and Derek Urwin develop a typology (i.e. a classification based on models) that helps to explain and understand state-building processes in Western Europe. Rokkan and Urwin's work distinguish between unitary and union state models (as well as between mechanical and organic federalism), and define them as follows:

- *Unitary state*: A unitary state is built up around an unambiguous political centre which enjoys economic dominance and pursues administrative standardisation, with a single source of power and authority and in which central government *delegates*, but does not relinquish, some authority to sub-national units and channels policy decisions down to them for implementation. Thus, all areas of the state are treated in the same way, and all the institutions are under the direct control of the centre (Rokkan and Urwin, 1982). Thus, this model accounts for state-building processes that lead to the creation of countries with a strong concentration of power in the centre. Rokkan and Urwin included countries like France, Denmark, Sweden and Finland in this model.
- *Union state*: In a union state, incorporation of at least parts of its territory has been achieved through personal dynastic union (e.g. by treaty or marriage). Integration is less than perfect. While administrative standardisation prevails over most of the territory, in some areas pre-union rights and institutional architectures survive and preserve a degree of regional autonomy (Rokkan and Urwin, 1982). Thus, this model accounts for state-building processes that lead to the creation of countries where power is more dispersed: there is a centre, but this retains only some powers, while others are passed down to sub-state political units of government. Rokkan and Urwin included countries like the Netherlands, Spain and the UK in this model.

Rokkan and Urwin used this typology to classify most western European countries and placed the UK within the union state model. They argue that the process of incremental unification that led to the creation of the state generated an 'uneven union', with a clear political centre (symbolised by the parliament in London) which, however, left a degree of autonomy to its 'peripheries' and did not eradicate in full their distinctiveness. In this way, they sought to convey the idea of the UK as a composite state made of different units, able to preserve characteristics of distinctiveness, rather than being blended into a fully homogenous whole – in other words, an assemblage.

Yet, for a long time, the UK was traditionally defined by others (including, most notably, in the Royal Commission on the Constitution of 1979) as a unitary state – emphasising the parliamentary supremacy of Westminster as the key principle of the UK uncodified constitution. This interpretation rested on the view that in the UK power is centralised around its sovereign parliament and strong government, and, thus, can be seen as unitary (Keating, 1999; Mitchell, 2009).

Reflecting critically on Rokkan and Urwin's work, James Mitchell (2006, 2009) has challenged traditional orthodoxies, arguing that – especially since the inception of devolution – the UK is neither a union nor a unitary state, but a *state of unions*. He presents this concept as a subset of the union state model that 'acknowledges the varieties and legacies of each union that contributed to the creation and subsequent development of the UK' (Mitchell, 2006: 155) – thus highlighting how the UK territorial constitutional settlement is informed by the histories of each composing nation of the country and is still in flux.

To understand these processes, we have to start by looking at England, as it played a central role in the path that led to the formation of the UK. Indeed, it was through its expansion that the union was achieved; and, for this reason, England is often seen as the UK state's core. England developed through the expansion of Wessex and it became unified (almost as a prototypical nation-state) far earlier than any other European country, around the 1st century – adopting a system of government that was substantially uniform (Bogdanor, 2001). In this process, distinctive nations present within England, like Cornwall, were gradually 'absorbed into the mainstream of English life' (Rowse, 1941). As a result, as Mitchell (2009: 6) notes, essentially 'England was created as a unitary state and this had considerable implications for the UK', in particular because 'the territorial pattern set by state formation in England lasted' – with 'the myth of parliamentary sovereignty' as its most important legacy. This, in essence, laid the institutional foundations of what came to be the United Kingdom and its constitutional setting.

Over time, Wales, Scotland and Ireland were joined to England – although by very different means. Wales was, in effect, annexed to England through a process of conquests. This incorporation was formalised through two Acts of Parliament (the Laws in Wales Acts of 1535 and 1542), which extended English law to Wales, established English as the official language, and more broadly set the details of the assimilation of Wales into England. For example (unlike Scotland, as we will discuss next), Wales could not maintain any distinctive, pre-union institution that could help preserve its memory of independent statehood (Bogdanor, 2001; Mitchell, 2009). For government purposes, Wales came to be treated as if it was part of England (Bogdanor, 2001).

Image 2.2 London County Hall, former seat of the London County Council and its successor, the Greater London Council, which was abolished in 1986 by Thatcher's government. Today it is the site of tourist attractions and two hotels.

© Photo by A.B.G. on Shutterstock

And yet, this process of assimilation was never complete: Welsh distinctiveness found expression in different forms and did not disappear. In particular, as Mitchell (2009: 8) notes, it was 'religion and language, rather than the apparatus of the state, that made Wales different' and allowed it to maintain some degree of cultural identity and a sense of Welshness. So in the absence of distinctive Welsh institutions, it was left to activists, writers and poets to preserve the memory and everyday narrative of national belonging.

At political level Wales could return 26 MPs to the parliament, but beyond that power firmly rested in London. Paraphrasing Gladstone, until the end of the 19th century the distinction between England and Wales was totally unknown to the UK constitution. It was only from the 20th century onwards that some form of administrative devolution started to be pursued in Wales. By 1945, 15 government departments with offices in Wales were established, and in 1965 the Welsh Office was created. From the 1970s the articulation of political demands for Welsh autonomy started to emerge and were mobilised – but they were more concerned with the preservation of a culture and way of life which were perceived to be under threat, rather than with political independence (Bogdanor, 2001). In Chapter 6 we will discuss in greater depth this process and how it is connected with Welsh devolution. For now, it is important to note that the initial union of England and Wales was characterised by political centralisation and uniformity, with England playing a dominant role, thus resembling the key characteristics of a union state.

Despite many attempts, Scotland was never conquered by England. It became constitutionally linked to England in 1603 through the so-called Union of the Crowns, when James VI of Scotland succeeded to the English throne, becoming James I of England. This process, though, did not lead to the creation of a new state or nation. It was a purely dynastic union, and Scotland (as well as England, by then including Wales) maintained their separate political institutions, including their own parliaments. The political union between Scotland and England came into being only in 1707, with the ratification of the Act of Union by both nations. This provided for the creation of the Kingdom of Great Britain – i.e. a new state, with its own *sovereign* parliament, as England's and Scotland's parliaments were dissolved. Yet, despite being formally a new institution, the parliament of the Kingdom of Great Britain was based at Westminster and took on the characteristics of the English parliament (Bogdanor, 2001). At the same time, though, pre-existing nations were not eradicated (Mitchell, 2009). Scotland could keep a set of institutions that proved key in sustaining its national identity and in protecting its national interest – such as the Kirk (the Church of Scotland, which back then was much more at the centre of Scottish national life than the parliament), and its own legal system (Bogdanor, 2001).

As a result, on the one hand, the terms of the Union allowed Scotland to reconcile its national identity with membership of the wider UK for a very long time (see Chapter 6). On the other hand, by this point, the political interests of Scotland, like Wales, could only be represented at state level by a small number of MPs (45) sitting in the new sovereign parliament dominated (in terms of size and geographical location) by England, which continued to maintain a strong political ascendancy in the Kingdom of Great Britain (Keating, 2021; Mitchell, 2009). The tensions between these two dynamics remained dormant for a long time – notably, as long as Scottish institutions continued to be perceived as sufficient to protect and represent its national interest. Over time, changes in politics and society (such as secularisation and the decline of the role of the Church in favour of the state) altered this tacit balance, signalling that the terms of the union had started to become obsolete (Mitchell, 2009). This, eventually, led to the mobilisation and politicisation of Scottish national identity, especially from the 1970s onward (see Chapter 6). On balance, this reconstruction of the process of union between Scotland and England (plus Wales) did not lead to full assimilation: integration under the new state was less than perfect, and pre-Union architectures could survive and served to preserve national distinctiveness. In this respect, it seems to be more attuned with the union state model (see Theory box above). And yet, the supremacy of Westminster remained as a key feature of the UK constitution, suggesting the presence of a residual element of the unitary state.

The history of the relationship between Ireland, England and the broader UK has deep roots, is extremely complex and is characterised by a tight connection between religious and political divides. Since the Middle Ages, various attempts were made by the English to conquer and subjugate Ireland, and by the early 17th century Ireland had become subordinate to England. After that, various exclusionary and sectarian processes, including the plantation of the province of Ulster by Protestants, mostly from Scotland, led to marginalisation of the Catholic population of Ireland from its political life (e.g. by excluding it from parliament, as happened in 1692, and depriving them of the right to vote in 1727). As a result, as Bogdanor (2001: 16) notes, 'in Ireland the King and the English state were associated not with local aspirations, but with alien Protestant settlers, and the Catholic majority came to develop a separatist ideology'. This had deep repercussions on the relationship between the state and the nation(s): the Irish parliament, unlike the Scottish one, was at the centre of the nation's political life, but in Ireland the state and the official political nation were essentially Protestant in character as the Catholics were excluded from parliament and could not vote. In 1782 the Irish parliament gained co-ordinate powers to those of Westminster, but it kept representing only the Protestant side of Irish society.

Eventually, in 1800, Acts were passed by the parliaments of the Kingdom of Great Britain and Ireland, providing for the union between the two countries under one parliament (Westminster), thus leading to the creation of the United Kingdom of Great Britain and Ireland. Despite the pledges made during the negotiations that led to the 1800 Acts of Union, the government in London did not end political discrimination against Catholics that was creating growing tensions across the country. Thus, Ireland's religious divisions remained unresolved: this fracture continued to define the politics of the country and eventually led to the dissolution of the initial union. In the 19th and 20th century open resistance to the union started to emerge taking political and violent forms (for a full discussion, see Colley, 1992, 2014).

At the turn of the 20th century, the UK state's response to this upsurge was a series of Acts aimed at introducing Home Rule (i.e. giving Ireland a degree of autonomy and self-government, while remaining within the UK; see Chapter 6). These, however, did not succeed and pressures for the creation of an independent Irish republic continued to mount across the Catholic population, leading to the Irish War of Independence that sparked in 1919. After prolonged conflict, in 1921 the union with Ireland was dissolved through the Anglo-Irish

Treaty: Ireland was granted the status of 'dominion' as the Irish Free State (which eventually became the Republic of Ireland in 1949) with its own independent parliament. However, the six counties that today comprise Northern Ireland opted out and remained part of the United Kingdom under the terms of the 1800 Act of Union. The United Kingdom of Great Britain and Northern Ireland was thus created, and Northern Ireland was given a devolved parliament that lasted, amidst many troubles and suspensions, until 1972 (see Chapter 6). This new arrangement, however, did not resolve religious fractures: Northern Ireland was predominantly Protestant, but a Catholic minority was present too. The Protestant majority were in favour of remaining with the UK, while the Catholic minority held the opposite view and continued to be marginalised from political life. From the late 1960s onwards, these frictions again took violent form and the so-called 'Troubles' began, the conflict lasting for about 30 years (for a full account see, e.g. McKittrick and McVea, 2012). Only in 1998, with the Belfast Agreement, the peace process in Northern Ireland started finally to be addressed – although, as many would argue, it was never settled in full (see Chapter 6). Overall, the processes through which Ireland, and then Northern Ireland were joined to the United Kingdom of Great Britain are complex and make it difficult to fit neatly within the union or unitary state models, not least because the process of creating a single state was incomplete. Mitchell (2009: 11) comments that 'there never was a serious effort to integrate Ireland with the rest of the [UK] state; it was treated more as a colony than an integral part' and, afterwards, 'Northern Ireland's integration in the union remained imperfect'. Perhaps this suggests the case of Ireland/Northern Ireland is closer to the union state model but it is also true that the UK state used its power from the top-down on many occasions, including through coercion, to deal with the 'Irish and Northern Irish Questions'.

This overview of how the United Kingdom of Great Britain and Northern Ireland was created helps us to understand how history has shaped, and is still shaping, power dynamics across the country. As we have seen, the UK has come together incrementally through the expansion of England by means of conquests, treaties, negotiations and, sometimes, suppression. This is a very important point to note because, in practice, it means that England played a key role in the creation of the UK state – and this put it at the core of the union, in terms of power and ability to shape the political system. Some scholars have gone as far as describing this process as one of 'internal colonialism', arguing that the English core has come to dominate and treat the other parts of the UK as its peripheries, thus generating political and economic inequalities (Hechter, 1975).

The idea of the UK as a unitary state helps to capture the centralisation of power that has characterised the process of state formation, albeit that it tends to focus disproportionately on the English polity (Mitchell, 2009). And yet, as we have seen, it is also important to remember that, in this process, each of the nations of the UK followed a specific path, suggesting that the concept of the union state, too, can help to grasp such complexity. The inception of devolution from 1997 has complicated things further: in practice, this process of constitutional reform has seen the (re)creation of directly elected parliaments in Scotland, Wales and Northern Ireland, with varying degrees of direct or executive powers, but not in England. In the wake of these changes, it is now difficult to describe the UK purely as a unitary state as, despite the presence of a supreme parliament in Westminster, power is now in practice dispersed and three of the four nations of the UK have autonomy on certain policy areas. In academic debates, a new orthodoxy that sees the UK as a union state has emerged to acknowledge the changes introduced by devolution. However, paradoxically, this view does not account for England (which lacks its own parliament), as well as the sub-national and regional identities within it (which do not have any devolved institutional 'anchor' to represent them). The debate is thus still open.

Despite this, we hope that what has become clear through the discussion in this chapter is that the process that led to the creation of the UK was not a straightforward one. The country we know today came about through the intersection of distinct histories and events and the union involved a number of parties, each with its own historical roots, claims, issues and distinctive relations with the state. Indeed, as we have seen, England started off as a prototypical unitary state. Wales was incorporated into England, and thus the new union also took the form of a unitary state, while the union with Scotland and Northern Ireland was more in line with the union state model, as (albeit for very different reasons and in different forms) each was allowed to maintain a degree of autonomy. To address this important point, Mitchell (1997, 2006, 2010) suggests that it is useful to think of the UK not as a single union (and thus as a unitary or union state) but as consisting of a number of unions, each with a different legacy shaping its political path – or, as he puts it, as a 'state of unions'.

The state that has emerged from these complex processes is, as Jeffery and Wincott (2006) put it, 'unusually lopsided'. To understand this character of the UK state in greater depth, in the next section we will look at the constitutional settlement that has emerged from the process of union, looking at the key principles that guide the UK constitution.

The UK constitutional settlement

So far in this chapter, you have learnt about how the UK has come together through a process of amalgamation that, while giving rise to a new state, has also allowed each nation to maintain some degree of distinctiveness, albeit in very different forms. The union has worked as a 'glue', keeping together the different parts of the UK multi-national assemblage, despite tensions between autonomy claims in some parts of the country and the dominant role that England played from the start – but it has had to 'adapt' to contain these forces. To understand how these potentially divergent ambitions have been 'managed', it is important to examine the constitutional settlement that underpins the union, looking at the key characteristics of the UK constitution.

As explained in the previous section, the UK was created through ordinary acts of parliament (Bogdanor, 2001), rather than by a constitutional document as is the case for many western liberal democracies. Besides, unlike most western countries, the UK did not experience a revolution or defeat in a war that led to the birth of a new state. Therefore, it never had cause to consolidate its constitution into a single document; instead, statutes, conventions, treaties, and acts of parliament were, and still are, at the basis of the UK constitution. Thus, in many respects, much like the union, we can see the UK constitution as an assemblage that has evolved over time and is still in flux.

Need to know: Different types of constitutions

A constitution is a key component of any state, as it acts as the rulebook for a political system. A constitution 'sets out the fundamental principles by which the state is governed. It describes the main institutions of the state, and defines the relationship between these institutions (for example, between the executive, legislature and judiciary). It places limits on the exercise of power, and sets out the rights and duties of citizens' (Constitution Unit, online).

Most countries have their rulebooks codified in a single document: we call these written or codified constitutions. This type of constitution contains fundamental law that is superior to ordinary acts of parliament – it is, therefore, the ultimate source of legal authority. For this reason, they are more difficult to amend. In countries adopting this system, constitutional change can only be approved via 'special measures', such as a referendum or a super-majority in parliament, or sometimes both. For instance, in Italy constitutional amendments require a double vote in both chambers of the parliament with a majority of two-thirds; if in the second vote an absolute majority is obtained, the proposal can be put to the public via a referendum.

Other countries have their constitution written in different documents such as statutes, conventions, judicial decisions and treaties. These, however, are not codified and brought together into a single 'rulebook': thus, we call this type of constitution uncodified. (Referring to them as 'unwritten' is technically incorrect as they are written, but in a number of documents rather than in just one.) In countries adopting this system, amending the constitution is relatively easy, and can be done through ordinary law. The UK, Israel and New Zealand are among the few countries in the world with an uncodified constitution.

Countries might opt for codified or uncodified constitutions for various reasons. Typically, codified constitutions emerge following a specific 'critical juncture', when the rules by which a country is governed need to be changed – such as revolution (France, in 1791), regime change (post-Soviet Russia), war (Italy, after World War II) or the attainment of independence (India, in 1947) (Bogdanor, Khaitan and Vogenaure, 2007). The UK never had such a 'constitutional moment' (ibidem): therefore, it could be argued that it never had reason to codify its constitution.

The UK has an uncodified constitution, and this has important consequences on how the state works and power is distributed across the country. In the absence of a single rulebook, some key principles have emerged to guide the work of political institutions. The Westminster model has often been used as a frame of reference to explain and describe the UK political system.

Need to know: The Westminster model

The Westminster model is shorthand for a framework that has been traditionally employed to explain and describe the UK political system. Although first outlined by Bagehot in the 1860s in *The English Constitution*, the Westminster Model gained particular traction through the work of Arend Lijphart, captured in the book *Patterns of Democracy* (2012). Lijphart sought to classify countries and their political systems based on whether they have the characteristic of 'consensus democracies' (which usually have a written constitution and where power is dispersed across different levels of government) or 'majoritarian democracies' (which usually have a flexible constitution and a concentration of power in the centre). For Lijphart, the UK's Westminster model provided the prime example of a majoritarian democracy. This model is based on several principles, summarised in the table below. Parliamentary sovereignty provides the guiding principle of the Westminster model to highlight the central and supreme role of parliament in the working of the UK constitution and political system.

While still widely acknowledged as a useful framework for understanding how institutions and power function in the UK, the Westminster model has also been criticised for having become 'obsolete', and not able to grasp the most recent developments in UK politics, such as the introduction of devolution, which challenges the supremacy of Westminster, or the limits of the 'core executive' model (see Chapter 11), or the fact that in recent times coalition or weak governments have emerged from general elections. For a debate on different views on the Westminster model, see the Annotated reading list at the end of this chapter.

Key principles of the Westminster model	
Constitution	Uncodified and flexible; constitutional reform does not require special procedures, just ordinary acts of parliament
Parliament	Sovereign – Westminster has supreme legislative authority, no other body can overturn its legislation; bi-cameral system (House of Commons, elected and House of Lords, unelected)
Government	Dominant ('core executive'), backed by a majority in the House of Commons and advised by the civil service; ministers are accountable to parliament, but the two bodies are essentially fused
Judiciary	Administers justice by interpreting the law when its meaning is in dispute. Courts cannot challenge constitutional legislation
State and power distribution	The state is conceived as unitary, with concentration of power at the centre. Local government is weak and does not have constitutional protection. Government offices (e.g. Scottish Office, Welsh Office) represent the nations of the UK at the centre, and the centre in the nations
Electoral system	Simple plurality (or first past the post), almost invariably delivers stable majority governments; single party governments are the norm; regular free elections ensure representatives are accountable to the public
Party system	Characterised by two parties competing to hold government (minority parties exist, but due to the electoral system they do not stand many chances to get elected/into government)

As we have seen, throughout the various stages of the process of union, representation in a common and supreme parliament for the four previously independent nations of the UK was achieved, acting as a key binding element. Since then, the principle of the supremacy of Westminster has emerged as the guiding value of the UK constitution, and it implies that power is centralised in one supreme and omnicompetent parliament (Bogdanor, 2001: 1). However, as previously discussed, Westminster had begun as the English Parliament and the constitution of the UK has been marked, since its inception, by the predominance of the institutions of the English state. Political power is thus centralised around a supreme institution that, in theory, should equally represent all the four nations of the UK but, in practice, tacitly accepts and mirrors the dominant role of one of them. This has obvious repercussions on the constitutional settlement of the UK, which tends to be tilted towards England, thus potentially limiting its pluralistic remit.

In addition, it is interesting to note that the absence of a codified rulebook means that some institutions lack constitutional protection. This, again, has significant repercussions on the balance of power within the UK. In particular, sub-state governance (i.e. the networks of formal and informal institutions that operate at a territorial level below the state) is overtly subordinated to the centre and subject to its decisions. In practice, this means that other levels of government (such as local government in England or the devolved administrations in Scotland, Wales and Northern Ireland – see Chapter 6) do not have *full* autonomy. Instead, (at least in principle) the supremacy of Westminster means that their powers could be repealed, or they could even be dissolved altogether, through a simple act of parliament. This is another critical element of centralisation that is inscribed in the UK constitution, with the potential to limit its pluralism.

This arrangement is in contrast with what happens in most countries with a written constitution. In states like Italy or Spain, for example, there are sections of the constitution that deal explicitly with the powers and remits of local and regional government, providing full details of the policy areas on which they have autonomy, or even direct legislative powers, and those that remain competence of the central state. This constitutional protection matters, because in practice it means that neither parliament or central government can unilaterally repeal sub-national governments' authority, or even reform them. Any such change would require a long process of constitutional amendment (see Need to know above). In the UK, constitutional change requires only the majority sufficient to pass an act in parliament, and that makes a big difference – leaving a lot of discretion in the hands of the centre regarding the fate of sub-state institutions. There have been cases, such as the abolition of the Greater London Council in 1986 where an entire layer of local government was single-handedly eradicated by parliament (see Case study box). This would be unthinkable in a country with a written constitution.

Case study: The Greater London Council

Can you imagine a huge capital city like London not having its own local council, able to make decisions over its governance and service delivery? That seems absurd, right? Yet, for a period of time, Greater London (i.e. the area that covers the city of London and the 32 London boroughs) was without its own local council. In 1985 The Greater London Council (GLC) was dissolved by the Local Government Act 1985, and from 1986 it ceased to exist. This matters, because the GLC was responsible for a series of services, such as waste disposal, transport and planning that directly affect the life of local communities.

The decision to disband the GLC was taken by Margaret Thatcher's government, and it required just an ordinary act of parliament to be enacted. For the Conservative government of the time, the abolition of the GLC was based on an economic rationale and was presented to the public as a means to cut the excessive costs incurred by the council. Critics, however, argued that getting rid of the GLC was a political choice: the council embraced 'municipal socialism' and promoted progressive policies that were in stark contrast with the neoliberal approach of Thatcher's government. In practice, the GLC's powers were transferred to a myriad of smaller borough authorities, central government departments and unelected boards, thereby removing a crucial element of local democracy (as well as scrutiny and accountability) – leaving London as the only capital city in the western world without an elected council to represent it as a whole.

In any case, it is remarkable that such an important institution could be disbanded without consultation or appeal – showing the degree of power that the UK constitution gives to the centre at the expense of sub-state levels of government.

As the union evolved over time, the inconsistencies of these arrangements started to emerge. From the late 1960s, tensions and demands for further autonomy coming from Scotland and Wales challenged the centralised nature of the state. The response was the creation of a Royal Commission on the Constitution (also known as the Kilbrandon Commission, after the name of its chair), which was set up in 1969. The main recommendations in the Commission's final report included the introduction of devolution for Scotland, Wales and Northern Ireland, and a form of regional decentralisation for England. It took almost 30 years, and a failed referendum in Scotland and Wales in 1979, before a constitutional reform introduced devolution to these nations (but not to England) in 1997 (see Chapter 6).

For the purpose of our discussion here, it is important to reflect on the impact that devolution had on the UK constitution. The key point to note is that the very principle of devolution puts into question the authority of Westminster and central government in some respects. Even though, formally, Westminster remains sovereign, the creation of devolved, directly elected parliaments in Scotland, Wales and Northern Ireland (but not in England) challenge its supremacy in practice. These institutions provide new, direct points of political representation for their respective national communities that have now taken root and would be very difficult to disband single-handedly by the government in London without popular consent.

Thus, on the one hand, it could be argued that devolution has brought in an additional element of pluralism to the UK constitution, as it has given (at least some) political recognition to the distinctiveness of Scotland, Wales and Northern Ireland. On the other hand, however, it also seeks to reconcile two principles that seem hardly compatible – that is, the parliamentary supremacy of Westminster and the grant of autonomy on domestic policy to Scotland, Wales and Northern Ireland (Bogdanor, 2001). In this way, devolution could put under strain the constitutional settlement that underpins the union.

In sum, the UK constitution has long been characterised by concentration of power in the centre. However, over time, some adjustments in a more pluralistic sense have been made through devolution. Yet, the asymmetric system that has emerged from this is still in flux, and often marked by tensions between centralising logics and autonomy demands.

Such tensions are difficult to settle, and at times have even brought about direct challenges to the union, as in the case of the 2014 Scottish independence referendum or calls for the reunification of Northern Ireland with the Republic of Ireland in the wake of Brexit.

To address these issues and preserve the union, some have suggested that the UK should become a federal state, introducing a codified constitution that clearly sets the division of power between different levels of government. This, however, would be a very time-consuming and onerous process, as it would entail reconsideration and reorganisation of the many thousands of documents that make up the current uncodified constitution. It would also risk creating an imbalanced federation as, being far bigger than the other nations, England could end up dominating the overall federal arrangement. Furthermore, this would not resolve the issue of overcentralisation that persists in England (see Chapter 6), or the lack of recognition of territorial differences and autonomy claims within England itself (e.g. in regard to small nations like Cornwall, or regions with a stronger sense of identity like Yorkshire). Others have proposed constitutional reform including the abolition of the House of Lords and its replacement with a 'chamber of the nations and the regions', so as to have a representative body sitting at Westminster that would be directly catering for territorial diversity across the country. Although discussed in political manifestos of the Labour party in recent general elections (e.g. in 2019), such options still seem to lack the cross-party support that would be required for them to come to fruition. Finally, some have also argued that the current system is fine as it is: the flexibility brought in by an uncodified constitution allows for incremental adjustments without compromising the union and, despite some glitches, the Westminster model still works. Yet, recent events, such as the 2014 Scottish independence referendum, seem to suggest that there are limits to this interpretation.

Conclusion

In this chapter we have explored the idea of the UK as a multi-national state, looking at how it came together over time through the process of union. We have placed particular emphasis on the idea of the UK as an assemblage, as it includes diverse nations with their own roots and legacies that have persisted over time. This has impacted on the process of state formation and power dynamics: for a time, the main approach of the state has been that of pushing for amalgamation of national histories, promoting a centralised form of government and seeking to develop a sense of Britishness as an overarching, binding identity.

However, national (and, indeed, sub-national) differences did not disappear. The introduction of devolution in 1997 has, in many respects, reflected this through the (re)creation of national parliaments in Scotland, Wales and Northern Ireland, dispersing power away from the centre. On the one hand, it could be argued that devolution has brought a welcome element of pluralism to the UK constitution, as it has given (at least some) political recognition to the distinctiveness of Scotland, Wales and Northern Ireland. On the other hand, by seeking to reconcile the parliamentary supremacy of Westminster and the grant of autonomy to Scotland, Wales and Northern Ireland, devolution also poses a challenge to the key principles of the UK constitution, which, for this reason and in the wake of other external shocks such as Brexit, is still in flux.

Key take-home points

- The UK is a multi-national state that has come together through an incremental process of amalgamation.
- Through this process, the central state has established its authority through the principle of parliamentary sovereignty that guides the UK's uncodified constitution.
- However, each nation of the UK has maintained its distinctiveness, and this has shaped (and is still shaping) the territorial constitution of the UK.

Annotated reading list

Anderson, B. (1983) *Imagined Communities: Reflections on the Origin and Spread of Nationalism.* London: Verso.

This text is a classic, and it's a must read for anyone who is interested in nationalism! While many books have been written about nationalism as a political movement, Anderson offers a different take, focusing on the personal and cultural feeling of belonging to a nation through the concept of 'imagined communities'.

Billig, M. (1995) *Banal Nationalism.* London: Sage.

This is another fantastic book that takes an unorthodox approach to the study of nationalism by focusing on the everyday, less visible forms of nationalism that are constantly flagged through routine symbols and habits of language. Although banal, they are extremely powerful. Truly compelling reading!

Keating, M. (2021) *State and Nation in the United Kingdom: The Fractured Union.* Oxford: Oxford University Press.

Michael Keating is one of the leading experts on territorial politics in the UK. He's also a prolific writer, and it was very hard to choose one book among the wide range of publications he has produced! In the end, I went for this text because in many respects it brings together a lot of the thinking developed in other works. It really helps to understand the idiosyncrasies that underpin the union, and how recent events, such as Brexit or demands for independence or further devolution, put into question its stability.

Colley, L. (2014) *Acts of Union and Disunion.* London: Profile Books.

This is a wonderful book that really helps to understand, as the title suggests, what has held the UK together over time, and what might be dividing it. Colley's work has also been used as the basis of a great BBC Radio 4 programme of the same name, that can be downloaded from BBC Sounds at www.bbc.co.uk/programmes/b03pn0vv

Russell, M. and Serban, R. (2022) Why it Is indeed time for the Westminster model to be retired from comparative politics. *Government and Opposition*, 57(2), 370–384.

Flinders, M., Judge, D., Rhodes, R. and Vatter, A. (2022) Stretched but not snapped: A response to Russell and Serban on retiring the 'Westminster model'. *Government and Opposition*, 57(2), 353–369.

These two articles engage with a critical debate over the Westminster model, and the extent to which it is still a useful concept to understand the UK political system. While Russell and Serban argue that the Westminster model is 'a concept stretched beyond repair' and therefore should 'be retired', Flinders, Judge, Rhodes and Vatter disagree and contend that the concept is 'stretched but not snapped'. I'll leave it to you to decide which argument you find more convincing.

Russell, M., White, H. and James, L. (2023) *Rebuilding and Renewing the Constitution: Options for Reform*. London: The Constitution Unit and Institute for Government. www.ucl.ac.uk/constitution-unit/news/2023/jul/new-report-rebuilding-and-renewing-constitution

This is a great report that explores and presents the latest developments in the debate on the future of the UK constitution, including a set of reforms available to political parties to strengthen the UK's constitution and institutions.

3
The global history of the UK

Colonialism and decolonisation

Amina Easat-Daas and Simon Stevens

Image 3.1 This photograph shows a protester from the 2018 protests in Whitehall London in support of those impacted by the Windrush affair. The sign reads "Migrants built our country, what do you do for us?" © Photo by David Mbiyu on Shutterstock

Learning objectives

After reading this chapter, you should be able to:

- Understand the racial contract: Through the consideration of Charles W. Mills' work, the chapter examines the way in which the obligations between the state and individuals (which have typically previously been thought of through the social contract and as racially neutral) are in fact bound by conceptions of race
- Discuss colonialism and civilising burdens: The chapter also looks at what is meant by colonialism and the ideas (or myths) that were employed to justify and legitimise its existence
- Explore postcolonial migration to the UK: Here, the chapter explores what happened after colonialism formally ended and the ways in which it brought many formerly colonised people to the UK
- Discuss multiculturalism: A consideration of the ways in which diverse communities live in Britain, and how this shapes UK politics
- Understand political participation by minorities: Finally, the chapter reviews the ways in which racialised postcolonial migrants to the UK engage with and are represented in the political arena

Introduction

Imagine arriving to a place that presented itself to the world as engaged in a 'civilising mission', of ordering the world around a social contract and sovereignty, which involved your native land. Imagine finding yourself within a discourse about people from 'other places' – and people of colour in particular – which was exclusionary, exploitative and brutal. Imagine being told one ought to be proud of this country.

This is the cultural landscape in which postwar migrants to the UK from formerly colonised lands (including the so called Windrush generation), and people of colour in general found themselves. The dehumanisation of formerly colonised peoples was echoed in the often-cruel treatment of postwar migrants to the UK and was underscored in an explicitly racist social, cultural and political discourse which attempted to effectively exclude migrants and their UK-born descendants from the political sphere.

This chapter explores the many assembled threads about what this means and has meant for people of colour in the UK as they navigated systemic racism, other intersecting structural inequalities around class and gender, and how this has affected pluralism in the UK. The chapter begins by outlining the theoretical basis and ideas around the long-standing impact of British colonialism on the UK political arena. The chapter continues with a consideration of what this has meant for participation in informal political activity in the UK by racialised postcolonial communities, and also their participation in UK formal politics in government, through the use of case studies and quantitative data. These include looking at participation by racialised women in UK trade union activism and also the wide-reaching ramifications of the Windrush affair. The chapter also considers the ways in which migrant communities have challenged and continue to challenge exclusion from many spheres of cultural, economic and political life in the UK, taking pertinent examples such as intersectional feminist work. We also explore the importance of national myths and folk heroes binding the assembled polity together, and the ways that the legacy of colonisation persist in these stories. We also consider the persistence of quasi-eugenic ideas of race apparent in historical narratives around 'civilising burdens' and contemporary discourse around *racialised alterity*. We show that beginning with the level of cultural memorialisation, people of colour are still not fully included into mainstream UK political and cultural life: but still carve a space for themselves.

Key terms and context

Since this chapter deals with topical but sometimes contentious themes, here we outline these terms and define the principal understandings of the terms in the literature and for this chapter.

Colonialism

With regard to colonialism, put most simply, it is the act of one country taking over or dominating another. Colonialism typically comprises economic control and exploitation, but in addition it is also legitimised by wanting to be perceived as powerful and an alleged self-professed 'moral obligation' by the coloniser to colonise – evident in Rudyard Kipling's 'The White Man's Burden' (1899), or the state-sanctioned *Mission civilsatrice* (Civilising Mission) apparent in the French context.

In this chapter we recognise the often-violent ways in which colonialism is initiated and maintained. That is to say, colonialism did not accidentally come about; rather, it was an intentioned and violent process. French thinker Jean-Paul Sartre, writing in *Portrait of the Coloniser and the Colonised* defines colonialism as a 'conquest occurred through violence, overexploitation and oppression' and states that its maintenance requires 'continued violence' (Sartre, cited in Memmi, 1974: 20).

This violence and conquest were legitimised through racist tropes that allege the (racial) superiority of the coloniser over the colonised. Memmi argues that racism is normalised in the context of normalisation: '… colonial racism is so spontaneously incorporated in even the most trivial acts and words, that it seems to constitute one of the fundamental patterns of the colonialist personality' (Memmi, 1974: 114). Colonial racism permeates every aspect of interaction between the coloniser and the colonised that according to Memmi, it is founded upon three central ideological tenets: a presumed cultural difference (or arguably perceived cultural superiority) that is maximised for the coloniser and seen as absolute fact (Memmi, 1974). In this chapter we argue that this colonial racism persists and shapes the everyday lived political experiences of racialised postcolonial migrants in the UK.

These ideas were cited to legitimise control over the colonised in their indigenous lands. Sartre writes: 'Colonialism denies human rights to human beings whom it has subdued by violence and keeps them by force in a state of misery and ignorance that Marx would rightly call subhuman (Sartre in Memmi, 1974: 20). Other prominent postcolonial thinkers such as Antonio Gramsci and Homi Bhabha have described this state of the colonised as the 'subaltern', perhaps most notably in the seminal essay by Gayatri Chakravorty Spivak's 'Can the Subaltern Speak?' (1988). The creation of the subaltern as a colonial underclass was central in maintaining colonial domination.

Postcolonialism

If this is the simplified and brief basis of colonialism, what then is the postcolonial? Most simply, *postcolonialism* refers to the period following the decline of the colonial power and control, typically marked by the physical retreating of the coloniser from the geographically colonised space to allow for the formation of new governance in the once colonised lands. Postcolonial thought or ideas, led by thinkers such as Said, Spivak and Bhabha, typically frames the colonial as a defined and complete period. In contrast, decolonial is comparatively more focused on the ongoing legacies of the colonial (Asher and Ramamurthy, 2020). However, Bhambra (2014) argues that both come from the same tradition of rethinking and contesting global assumptions that come from the world order established by European colonisers.

Postcolonial scholars, such as francophone Afro-Caribbean psychiatrist and political philosopher Frantz Fanon, generally agree that the end of empire only came about when the violence of colonialism was met with an even greater resistance. Fanon puts it that '… the mass of the country have never ceased to think about the problem of their liberation except in terms of violence, in terms of taking back the land from the foreigners, in terms of national struggle, and of armed insurrection' (Fanon, 1961: 126–127). In short, based on Fanon's arguments here, we can argue that decolonisation would only come about with violence and force, and not benevolence by the coloniser.

Nevertheless, this physical decolonial retreat did not automatically result in the retrenchment of colonial ideas and hierarchies imposed under colonial rule. Ideas, like colonial racism as described by Memmi, persist even after self-determination has been achieved. Furthermore, these ideas are bi-directional; in short colonialism affects both the coloniser and the colonised long after so-called independence has been granted. As Fanon wrote on the internalisation of colonial ideas by (some) formerly colonised peoples: 'This is because the native intellectual has thrown himself greedily upon Western culture … when a minimum nucleus of security crystallises in their psyche, the native intellectual will try to make European culture his own. He will not be content' (Fanon, 1961: 218). In popular culture, debates around 'decolonising one's mind' or adopting critical perspectives of ideas that have historically been normalised by colonialism are evident in emerging and ongoing discussions around LGBTQ+ communities in the Indian subcontinent (and how their presence was only demonised or made problematic via the introduction of colonialism and the imported ideas it brought about sexuality). Or around colourism – whereby the colonially instilled preference for proximity to whiteness is normalised across a range of formerly colonised groups, resulting in a booming global skin whitening industry. Here we see the colonised psyche (as Fanon would describe it) questioning colonial norms and legacies.

Postcolonialism also signified the reimagining of the formerly colonised by the colonialists, meaning that the colonisers were forced to reconsider the ways in which they thought about those who were colonised. Often this meant (reluctantly) moving from a reductive framing of the colonised as savage and in need of civilisation, to free and independent individuals or even equals. Postcolonial scholar and Palestinian Christian Edward Said wrote in his seminal book *Orientalism*: 'The signs of Oriental claims for political independence were everywhere … the Orient now appeared to constitute a challenge, not just to the West in general, but to the West's spirit, knowledge and imperium' (Said, 1978: 268). In short, the privilege that colonialism afforded the coloniser as discussed by Memmi was now under threat. Imagined hierarchies of colonial superiority now had to be rethought and reconfigured; the possibility that the once colonised could now be equals was now an apparent and uncomfortable reality for many in the metropole.

Postcolonial migration firmly brought colonial racisms to within the geographical borders of former colonial powers. Whilst this migration was desired as part of postwar national rebuilding programmes (think of the Windrush generation for example) particularly in Western Europe, the end of the 'myth of return' has made enduring ethnically diverse communities in former imperial nations a reality. The myth of return was the notion that postcolonial migrants would return to their ethnic homelands once the postwar reconstruction of the metropole was complete. Instead, migrant workers tended to seek out family reunification and settle in former colonising countries like the UK or France giving rise to ethnically diverse postcolonial nations. This diversity is often described as *multiculturalism*, but what do we mean by this term and why is the notion regularly the centre of political debate and controversy?

Image 3.2 Image taken from the May 2018 anti-Windrush deportations protests in London. The protester holds two signs, which read "Deport treasonous May" and "We was British b4 [before] invited here, after d [the] donkey work and insults, we don't belong here? 'Hell no'" Similar signs can be seen held by protesters in the background of the image.

© Photo by David Mbiyu on Shutterstock

Multiculturalism

The term multiculturalism and its move to common usage is a relatively novel phenomenon and put most simply it describes cultural pluralism within a given national context which of course varies from one context to another (Wieviorka, 1998).

> **Case study: Windrush**
>
> The Windrush generation takes its name from one of the first ships which brought Afro-Caribbeans to the UK between 1948 and 1973 during the postwar period. Many of these migrants were part of the British Commonwealth and as such had the right to settle and work in the UK. As a result, many Afro-Caribbean migrants worked in the postwar reconstruction of the nation and particularly in the NHS. Since 2017 it has emerged, however, that many of the Windrush generation, who were Commonwealth citizens, were wrongly detained, their rights and access to services curbed, and worse still many were deported to the Caribbean. Although the UK government has pledged to rectify these injustices, UK policies and normative attitudes that allowed the Windrush affair to happen, such as the 'hostile environment' policies and broader structural and interpersonal racism are still very much part of the UK political and everyday landscape.

Former colonial powers, particularly in Western Europe, have repeatedly decried multiculturalism, argued that it has failed, but what does this mean? In the UK multiculturalism has been criticised as encouraging fragmentation and segregation, and that rather than encouraging integration it has fetishised difference (Modood, 2005). Additionally, Modood argues that multiculturalism should be rooted out in favour of promoting values of freedom and democracy (Modood, 2008) – as if somehow cultural difference was exclusive to these ideas. Garner (2010) outlines the way in which discussions around multiculturalism in the UK have come to signify clichéd code around the place of Islam and Muslims in Britain, integration and segregation and the UK's declining place in the world (Garner, 2010), arguably especially pertinent in the postcolonial period.

Racism

Understandings of multiculturalism essentialise and racialise communities. *Racism* presumes an inherent difference between peoples, often based on visible external markers, such as the colour of one's skin. However, we argue here instead that 'race' as a concept remains a socially constructed phenomenon rather than one of 'scientific' merit. Notions of race and racism were central in legitimising and maintaining colonialism. Racism continues to shape the everyday lives of racially marked individuals in every aspect and to varying degrees. In this chapter we examine this in relation to postcolonial politics and political participation by racialised Britons.

Essentialisation of peoples based on their real or presumed ethnic difference, or *racialisation*, is understood to be a key factor in shaping racism. Whilst this is relatively easily understood in explicitly marked peoples, racialisation also functions through perceived difference and imaginaries. For example, in 2019, the UK-based all party parliamentary group (APPG) on British Muslims put forward a definition of Islamophobia based on expert testimonies, stating 'Islamophobia is rooted in racism and is a type of racism that targets expressions of Muslimness or perceived Muslimness' (APPG on British Muslims, 2019: 11). The definition centres on the racialisation of real or perceived Muslimness (including people, places and practices) to better understand the way in which this particular form of racism functions. Additionally, this definition highlights the ways in which racialisation goes beyond obvious skin colour and can be used to group and often malign ethnically diverse groups through their imagined difference. Thinking back to Memmi's criticism of racism within the colonial context, we see a continuation of similar ideas around race and racialisation existing today within the postcolonial period.

Political participation

Finally, this chapter focuses on *political participation*. Here we define this as action intended to influence the state, representatives of the state and political outcomes. Political activity exists both within formal and informal structures; formal examples might include standing as a member of parliament, local councillor, voting or lobbying your local parliamentarian. Conversely, examples of informal political participation might include community and grass roots organising or attending protests and demonstrations. We draw on Martiniello's (2005) work with postcolonial racialised migrants to Belgium and also Easat-Daas (2020) to understand the nature of political participation as a diverse practice that is shaped, motivated or constrained by personal internal factors (such as preference) but also external features such as structural racism and systemic exclusion. This chapter focuses on both formal and informal political participation by postcolonial racialised communities in the UK and although we recognise that political activity exists within legal and illegal parameters, the remit of this chapter means that we look at legal political activity primarily.

Contradictions of an empire

> There was a growing contradiction within the British Empire – liberty and colonisation ...

The idea that race is biological is common, but if we consider it carefully, this can be challenged. There is no cluster of genes that universally groups white, brown or black people. The social view of race differs from society to society. In his book, *Race and Class in the Ruins of Empire*, Akala gives an insightful example of this (2018). He talks about his experiences visiting family in Jamaica. His mother is Jamaican, and his father is Scottish. When in Jamaica, he is treated differently – as if he is wealthy by virtue of living in the UK. In Jamaica, Akala feels like he experienced a sort of white privilege. Yet in the UK, he is brown and suffers discrimination because of it. This difference in Akala's colour is socially constructed.

During the Enlightenment, European thinkers theorised race in order to explain the world around them, but this led to false, biological essentialism – the idea that race fixes traits and characteristics – and colonial ideas of supremacy. Immanuel Kant, a renowned political philosopher for his work on autonomy and morality, theorised racial hierarchies in terms of cognitive abilities (Mills, 2017). British philosopher John Stuart Mill championed freedom of speech and liberty at home (2008 [1859]), yet in colonial India he did not because he thought India was not mature enough as a society. Whilst in the UK censorship was rolling back, in colonial India increasing censorship resulted in newspapers being closed down (Bally, 2007).

The issue that drove political thinkers to distraction was that the UK had a tension within its Empire. The UK itself was becoming increasingly liberal, and with that, political consent and freedom of speech was given greater focus. But how can an empire reconcile colonisation with growing liberal ideas at home? Myth-making provided one answer to these internal contradictions – the UK as a civilising light, bringing political order and progress to the world. The idea that race was rigid, and different races had differing traits and capacities followed on from this. Consent was not required of the colonised if it was decided for them, that it was for their own good.

The foundations were already set for this supremacist, civilising narrative in an aspect of social contract theory. Social contract theory justified political power, but it could also justify colonialism and a particular view of colonised peoples that continued when migrants came to the UK. How? Let's look at this in more detail.

The state of nature and political order

To reconcile contradiction, politics in the UK was infused with a narrative of bringing order and progress to colonial territories. During colonisation, this justified taking territory by framing the colonial identity as savage and infantile. This framing was so deep, it would have continuing effects when postwar migrants came to the 'motherland'. Migrants had been fed a narrative of being part of the Commonwealth, but when they came to the UK, they faced racist attitudes built from this framing of them.

Social contract theory starts with a state of nature and political philosopher Thomas Hobbes' war of all against all (1985 [1651]). Hobbes' concern was, as Michel Foucault interprets it, overcoming *conquest* (2004). Hobbes was living in a time of civil war, where the foundational idea of what gave a ruler authority – divine right to rule – was contested. He therefore sought a resolution which enabled whoever won the civil war to justify their legitimacy so the country would not simply fall back into conflict.

One issue with conquest is that victory through force of arms does not legitimise the authority of the conquerors to the subjugated. The Levellers and the Diggers, groups who fought against the monarchy in the English civil war claimed that they were not rebelling against monarchic power, but that they were continuing a war that went all the way back to the Norman conquest of 1066 (Foucault, 2004). In other words, the fact of conquest made any subsequent power that was established illegitimate.

If colonial conquest made states illegitimate, then ultimately every form of authority was threatened; can any dynasty or ruling class trace their history without having to confront bloodshed and theft? Hobbes therefore sought a hypothetical solution to erase such historical objections. Nothing, for Hobbes, could be worse than a situation in which political authority was claimed by multiple forces. Civil war threatened everything: order, art, civilisation itself. The sooner it ended, the better. Ensuring it never resurfaced was the ultimate goal. The challenge was clear: once war was done, how to get those who lost to accept the legitimacy of the victor?

In response, Hobbes asked a simple question: would one *will* a singular, political authority to exist if it did not? And, in case we are too hasty to answer, Hobbes wanted to detail what life would look like without that singular political authority. And so the state of nature, as a reflection of civil war, was posited as the only alternative to the sovereign state. It was a reflection, because it had the same issue – a lack of a single, sovereign power.

The depiction of a state of nature is familiar to almost everyone, even if the term is not, because of how popularised it has been in pop culture and politics today. From *The Lord of the Flies* (Golding, 1997 [1954]) to *The Walking Dead* (Darabont, 2010–2022) a simple claim is stated: to avoid the anarchy of a lawless society we must establish political order, and for political order we require a singular entity that has the sole power to make laws, and a monopoly on violence to enforce them. The alchemy that Hobbes mixes in is through his description of how consent enters the equation. We do not make a pact with a sovereign power to establish sovereign power; that cannot be possible. One cannot will something into existence through making a social contract with something that already exists. The social contract then, the theoretical mechanism on which political legitimacy is founded and political relations formalised, is a pact *between us*.

I am afraid of you because I cannot know for sure you will not take what I have. You are afraid of me for the same reason. Humans are creatures of motion: moving towards what they want. At some point they will collide, and when that happens there is no power to prevent and manage conflict in a state of nature.

For Hobbes, the key is human vulnerability. No matter how powerful we might be as individuals or as small groups, there is never a power so huge it can be sure it will never be threatened. This breeds anxiety from those precariously holding power, and ambition from those who do not. The solution is to create an absolute monster who can terrify each of us into obedience. This is what establishes relations of trust between us – a position where power is as unequal as possible, like a parent punishing two children for fighting. The nation-state is born.

Hobbes called this beast *Leviathan*. It is overwhelming because it has the monopoly to inflict violence. And if we rebel against it, because the social contract is made between the people it rules over, we are not betraying the sovereign, we are betraying everyone else: each other. Violent resistance, when sovereignty is theorised in this way, condemns those who use it, through the mere act of it. We are breaking the terms of the contract and threatening to pull everyone back into a state of anarchy. This sovereign state does not only put an end to conflict, but political violence establishes political peace, meaning arts and culture can flourish. Anything without a sovereign model of government then, by definition, is a cultureless, backward, barbaric place.

John Locke re-theorised the state of nature as something a little less catastrophic, which meant that we could demand more of the sovereign than simply existing (1988 [1689]). He thought there was a theory of property innate to humankind, and he explained it by thinking of an apple tree. Fruit on a branch belongs to everyone and no one when a tree sits in the middle of unclaimed land. But the act of picking the apple suddenly changes this. Locke was trying to say that when we mix labour with something held in common, no matter how small that labour is, something becomes *owned*. This is his first theory of property, and it is present in a primeval state of nature. Why leave this state then if it is not that bad?

The answer is often that it *can* be and so a state of nature is to live without security guaranteed. Eventually someone will steal, which will provoke a reaction, that in turn will cause a larger fallout, and so on. In the state of nature the issue is that everyone is judge, jury and executioner. We need a sovereign to solely enact this role, to keep order, when people wrong each other. But as Locke says, no one would show their neck to the lion in order to save them from polecats. We would only enter into a social contract willingly if what we had in the first place was upheld, otherwise we are at the mercy of the very thing we conjured for our own protection. Hence, the beginning of a proto form of 'rights' against a government, instilled in a theory of property.

So, Locke disagreed with Hobbes about the severity of a state of nature, but in principle agreed that the sovereign model of government, achieved through the social contract, was what maintains political order. In doing so, Locke's theory aligned with *Terra Nullius* (Pateman and Mills, 2007). This was a European idea that claimed that if land was empty, it was open for settlement. As Locke put agricultural work and industry as the only form of labour that formalised property ownership, indigenous tribes became invisible and their claims on land empty. They did not cultivate or labour within the narrow confines of Locke's theory, so the land was free for the taking, and the people on it largely irrelevant. When Europeans saw other, different forms of political organisation, they therefore did not see order. They saw a warlike, primitive, state of nature in *need* of ordering. This became their civilising 'burden'.

This criticism of social contract theory can be found in Charles Mills' book *The Racial Contract* (1997). He argued that European social contract theory framed indigenous peoples as disordered and warlike, never really settling land, because settling land meant agriculture, industry and trade.

A key quotation is:

> The establishment of Society thus implies the denial that a society already existed; the creation of society requires the intervention of white men, who are thereby positioned as already sociopolitical beings. White men who are (definitionally) already part of society encounter nonwhites who are not, who are 'savage' residents of the state of nature characterised in terms of wilderness, jungle, wasteland. (Mills, 1997: 13)

So, we return to our question above: how does one explain society in the UK becoming increasingly liberty-centric, protecting property rights and slowly but surely expanding the democratic franchise to its citizens, whilst maintaining its colonial hold? The answer is because the social contract placed a lens over indigenous societies as typifying the state of nature European societies had lifted themselves out of. Africa, North America, Australia and so on were this 'savage, jungle, wasteland': pre-political societies in need of being pulled out of their own state of nature.

Before rights comes the need for the political institutions to secure them. Consent therefore did not include the so-called 'native'. Only once they had been educated and civilised could they consent; and once that had been achieved, then surely they would be thankful for being pulled out of 'wilderness' and into 'civilised order'. *Hypothetical* consent could therefore be twisted to justify imperialism.

The social contract, for Mills, was not a device for inclusion, but exclusion of brown, black and indigenous peoples: hence, his renaming of it as the *racial contract*. This 'contract' ideology and the ideology of Terra Nullius – empty land – did not retreat in a decolonial era, though the geographical boundaries did. Indeed, posthumously published, Mills explored the famous *Lord of the Rings* as representing the anxiety of former empires amidst decolonisation: grand bastions of civilisation, slowly but inevitably surrounded by a multitude horde of orcs – brown and complete with working-class phrases, no less (2022). Politics in the UK had for so long been presented as a nation that engaged in political *ordering*, and in doing so, infantilised peoples within these territories as 'savages' in need of it. This perspective was so embedded, it would shape racist attitudes and barriers to postwar migrants.

Thus, a complete disconnect occurred. People from colonial and former colonial territories arriving in the UK often felt themselves coming to the 'motherland'. They had lived under imperial rule and now sought opportunity at the heart of it. Akala writes that many migrants from the West Indies kept portraits of the Queen in their homes, and when they came to the UK, they expected to be welcomed as fellow citizens (2018). They had paid tax to the Empire for years after all. But what they were met with was a narrative that they were parasites, draining jobs and resources away from native English people. The horde descending upon Middle-Earth.

To face the UK narrative of civilising political order, and then to find barriers to being part of it, was the lot of postwar migrants. Understanding the complexity of this is difficult because it requires the telling of an entire theoretical tradition first. The story of the racial contract is not mainstream thought. Bolstered by fighting the evil of Nazism, British national identity took on a mythic, invincible presentation. Society had been saved; the *social* contract upheld. The UK was the saviour. The white, English working class were weaponised as a line of defence against naysayers. How could postwar migrants engage with this narrative? How the country was run could invite critique, but the country itself, and the vision of it as the land of liberty, was sacrosanct. Yet disengagement for an othered group was dangerous, and simply confirmed existing prejudices against them, as apolitical and uncivilised.

'Doing politics' for the postwar migrant

This political othering inevitably meant postwar migrants did not see themselves as citizens able to make claims on a national government, as a social contract narrative suggested. Rather, they had to fix problems themselves – politics was local and grass roots to them.

Political behaviour

Postwar migrants *were* politically active: they just carved their own spaces for it. They had theory for their politics: they just did not have the opportunity to publish it in academic tomes or speak from lofty platforms. Here, we can take note of Patricia Hill Collins' *Black Feminist Thought* (2000 [1990]). Her own experience when studying for a PhD in the USA was to note a real lack of published work written by Black women. There can only be one conclusion. Either Black women did not have a theory of power or the political, or they did and because of exclusion from academia and conventional politics, it had simply manifested in other spaces. She asserted the latter. As such, we are opened to the idea of studying 'music, literature, daily conversations and everyday behaviour' (2000: 252 [1990]) as areas of political expression. This theory explains how excluded communities think of politics, and what doing politics is, differently.

Image 3.3 Image taken from the Nottingham-based Black Lives Matter protests in June 2020. The protester's placard reads "Solidarity with the Windrush Generation" and highlights the local contextual nuance that the global Black Lives Matter protests took on across the globe.

© Photo by James Ivor Wadlow on Shutterstock

The point of focusing on the social contract tradition has been to show that how politics is framed, and set up to exclude, runs deep. Social contract ideas gave people the idea that government only existed from consent. This shaped people's ideas of politics – representation from a national government. But from a postwar migrant perspective, this could not make sense. The idea that the sovereign state was a pact to which one consented was a theory, but to migrants it was a myth. This was confirmed on their arrival to the UK. For such people, the local therefore became their main political site, and, importantly, a mindset of not relying upon the state to provide for you but sorting out issues within your own community.

Spotlight on research: Behaviour as theory?

Lester K. Spence has echoed Collins' claim, arguing that studying behaviour, or praxis, enables us to read 'political theoretical responses from actors' that are 'far less individualized, less Andro-centric, and less elitist' (2020: 551, 565). Studying behaviour as a form of political theory is something that is now theorised a lot more. Jonathan Floyd's recent *normative behaviourism* creates two criteria for people expressing satisfaction with a political system: low levels of crime and civil insurrection. Is this a good metric, or does it leave the political dissatisfaction of migrants, often struggling to make ends meet and politically disempowered, unheard?

Within state-provided education, the children of postwar migrants faced racist attitudes from their own teachers. The top schools and universities were not accessible to them. Akala explains that as a result parents set up Saturday schools to ensure their children received the education they needed (2018). Embedded in a community and taking action to fix injustices – injustices often caused or condoned by a national political centre – became politics. Many years later, the deportation of the Windrush generation, and the local resistance this faced, speaks to this continued feeling.

UK politics for postwar migrants, ironically, was about forming their own order. It is this action that we look at next.

Minority representation: From exclusion to reproducing elitism

Against this theoretical background, what are the lived political experiences of racialised postcolonial peoples in the UK today, and in particular how do these experiences, when coupled with the coexisting legacies of British colonialism, impact the ways in which racialised postcolonial minorities engage with and participate in UK politics?

Case study: Engagement across the political spectrum

Perhaps the most visible examples of participation in politics by racialised communities include the first British Asian Prime Minister, British Indian Hindu, Oxford and Stanford educated Rishi Sunak. Similarly, the first British Asian Muslim to hold the post of Scottish First Minister, Pakistani Glaswegian Muslim Hamza Yousaf of the Scottish National Party (who is also simultaneously the youngest and first British Asian Muslim to hold this post) is another clear example of racialised communities succeeding in the most senior levels of British politics. Across the UK bicameral parliament, the British postcolonial diaspora occupies a notable role, such as the noteworthy example of Baroness Sayeeda Warsi, a peer in the House of Lords and former co-chair of the Tory party and former shadow minister for Communities and Social Cohesion – coincidentally the first Muslim (woman) to serve as a cabinet minister. Similarly, Labour MP for Hackney North and Stoke Newington since 1987, Diane Abbott of British Afro-Caribbean heritage highlights the ethnic diversity among the postcolonial diaspora active in formal national level politics in the UK. This list is just a very small selection of ethnic minority parliamentarians active in UK politics. However, organisations like Operation Black Vote provide a more comprehensive and regularly updated list of minorities in UK representative politics.

This small sample of racialised British postcolonial migrants and their diverse engagement across the political spectrum in the elite levels of representative UK politics underlines the hugely varied political affiliations of ethnic minorities in UK politics. In short, those with heritage from former British colonies participate in representative politics at the national level across the political left and right wing, in the upper and lower houses of parliament and increasingly hold politically significant roles. Similarly, the above examples showcase the diversity – in terms of religion, ethnicity, education and political roles, within and between racialised political representatives in the UK. So, upon reflecting on these direct and prominent examples from across the UK political spectrum, it might be argued that minorities have performed as well as non-marginalised groups in UK society. However, when considering political representation by all, questions around elitism, socioeconomic status and privilege become pertinent. Put alternatively, if we take the case of Rishi Sunak, we might ask whether his educational career, the knowledge and networks he gained as a result of these experiences shaped the likelihood of his becoming Prime Minister? Here, we begin to think about the multifaceted identities held by individuals – no one person can be reduced to a singular identity, be that as a racialised person, or more simply a vegan or meat eater, as someone who plays sport or someone who doesn't, to offer but a few varied and seemingly meaningless possibilities. In terms of the academic literature, when we talk about the multifaceted identities of racialised individuals we use the term 'Intersectionality' – we talk about this more later in the chapter.

Beyond the explicit anecdotal examples, empirical statistical evidence shows that around 13 per cent of the UK population is from an ethnic minority background and following the 2019 general election only 66 ethnic minority MPs were elected, or 10 per cent of the overall parliament (Uberoi and Burton, 2022). This disparity (between 13 per cent ethnic minority population and 10 per cent actual representation) demonstrates an underrepresentation of non-white communities in UK national politics. In the House of Lords, ethnic minority representation is poorer still, with only 7.3 per cent of all peers coming from an ethnic minority background (Uberoi and Burton, 2022). However, this gap in representation is comparatively less stark than seen in other European nations – for example, in France, despite a 15 per cent ethnic minority population, only 1.8 per cent of the French lower parliamentary chamber is made up of ethnic minority representatives (Murray, 2016). Ethnic monitoring statistics are approximations in the French context since there is no official reporting/census in the country. Furthermore, under the national rhetoric of egalitarianism, the French national imagination centres arguably flawed ideas of colour blindness. In the UK context (and more broadly speaking) ethnic minority representatives tend to be more likely to be affiliated with left-wing parties (Uberoi and Burton, 2023; Vidal and Bourtel, 2005). So, thinking back to the earlier examples of postcolonial minorities who have secured representative roles in the elite rungs of UK politics, when we look at the statistical (or quantitative) data, we see the picture is not so clear. Further, the evidence indicates that racialised postcolonial communities do not fare so well in formal representative politics at the national level in the UK and further afield.

Looking at local governance in the UK, ethnic minority representation is closer to proportional with 4.5 per cent ethnic minority representation in Holyrood compared to 4 per cent non-white population in Scotland. Similarly, in Wales where the national ethnic minority population is 5.9 per cent, representation in the Senedd is currently 5 per cent (Uberoi and Burton, 2023). However, conversely in Northern Ireland, although there is a 3 per cent non-white population, there are no ethnic minority representatives in the Northern Ireland Assembly (Uberoi and Burton, 2023).

There is significant contextual variance in ethnic minority representation at the local level, but overall, 1,235 of a possible 7,306 local representative roles are held by ethnic minorities (OBV, 2019: 4). Again, and perhaps even more noticeable than at the national level, ethnic minority councillors tend to be on the left of the political spectrum, with 84 per cent Labour, 11 per cent Conservative, 3 per cent Liberal Democrat and 2 per cent other (OBV, 2019: 4).

We tend to find that in areas with larger ethnic minority constituencies there are more likely to be non-white elected local officials – for example, in Slough Borough Council 69 per cent of local elected representatives are from ethnic minority backgrounds compared to only 54.3 per cent ethnic minority share of the wider local population (Uberoi and Burton, 2023: 13). This is contrasted with the Central Bedfordshire council where in spite of 6.1 per cent of the overall population being from an ethnic minority background, there are no minority representatives in local governance (Uberoi and Burton, 2023: 13) – clearly local context matters in shaping minority representation.

These differences in formal ethnic minority representation between the national and local levels then beg the question, why do these disparities exist? Sobolewska and Begum (2020) argue that generally, minority representation tends to be poorer overall at the local level when compared to the national level. This discrepancy exists because the mainstream parties see greater rewards for self-portrayal as diverse at the high-profile national level and since local politics tends to be lower profile, the comparative incentives to have diverse representation are lessened and therefore less desirable for political parties (Sobelewska and Begum, 2020). Additionally, our own research (Easat-Daas, 2020) indicates that although grassroots activism tends to be higher among racialised women, parties often rely on minority candidates to win seats for the local and national levels in ethnic minority dominant constituencies. Party rationale tends to be that ethnic minority constituents will vote for ethnic minority candidates. This is known as 'ethnic minority vote seeking' (Vidal and Bourtel, 2005).

Once in office, these candidates tend to find that their presence is tokenistic rather than meaningful (Easat-Daas, 2020). For example, in our own research we found that minority candidates elected in minority-heavy constituencies tended to find that they weren't able to engage in projects that mattered to them. Alternatively, those who had voted for them were either relegated to more 'behind the scenes' roles or given roles and responsibilities that outwardly correlated with stereotypes about their identities. For example, women would work in teams or hold positions specific to their identities as women instead of being able to pursue political roles associated with finance or the green agenda for example (Easat-Daas, 2020).

For many ethnic minority political representatives, tokenism and instrumentalisation of their presence in politics can dissuade them from participating in formal political office. These candidates tend to find that their presence is tokenistic rather than being meaningful to them and wider politics (Easat-Daas, 2020). In our work with Muslim women who participate in both formal and informal politics in Belgium and in France, being instrumentalised or being included only to encourage the support of ethnic minority voters was described as barrier or limit to participation in politics (Easat-Daas, 2020).

Similarly, in the same study we found that beyond instrumentalisation of minority candidates, Muslim women who were active in French politics argued that in order to succeed in politics they needed to negate the complexities of their own multifaceted and intersectional identities, stating that they need to be 'more royal than the king' (Easat-Daas, 2020: 147). This meant that the women interviewed felt that they needed to perform publicly and be more French than their French counterparts in order to be accepted. This then meant that those who participated in the study felt that they had to modify and change their outward perceivable appearances and behaviour so that they would be accepted in politics. This included, for example, removing their headscarves for their political engagements (this is particularly pertinent in this case, given the long-standing and ongoing French fixation with Muslim women's dress). This notion recalls Erving Goffman's (1956) work on performativity and begs the question, do racialised postcolonial minorities need to 'perform' certain accepted identities in order to succeed in UK politics?

Based on these case studies and the broader quantitative data, it is evident that racialised groups participate and succeed in formal UK politics, but does this fully illustrate the wider picture? How, for example, are racialised postcolonial communities limited from participating in UK politics? In addition to tokenism and the associated instrumentalisation of ethnic minorities in representative politics, increased ethnic minority membership or even representation at the local and national level is not uncommonly met with calls of 'entryism' (Fielding and Geddes, 1998). This is the idea that ethnic minorities only participate in formal politics as part of a sinister plot to 'take over' – this narrative of demographic and ideological threat fits into broader contemporary racist ideas that circulate (Law et al., 2020). Similarly, being accused of entryism can serve to dissuade ethnic minorities from participating in formal politics.

These calls tend to result in minorities feeling excluded from mainstream formal politics and as such push ethnic minorities to find alternative means and modes of participating in politics and having their voices and political claims heard. For example, empirical research with British Muslims highlighted that there are in fact a variety of self-fashioned and self-appointed representative bodies in existence (O'Toole et al., 2013). Such organisations vary in nature, size and scope and include groups such as the career-centred British Islamic Medical Association (BIMA) or creative arts-based endeavours like the Muslim Arts and Culture Festival (MAC Fest) among countless others. These organisations represent and publicly showcase a certain vision of Muslimness to wider society, whilst also generating space for individuals with shared interests and identities to come together. However, this then begs the question as to which groups carry legitimacy and why, whilst also highlighting potential limits in representative potential of any self-appointed group. In the UK the answers to these questions are not always clear, although arguably all of these groups carry some representative potential, not least for their direct members (rather than always representing the wider community). In contrast in nearby Belgium, for example, all recognised faith groups have an elected representative body that acts as an interlocutor between sections of racialised communities and the state. This in turn can provide a bridge between ethnic minority informal organising and the formal political arena. Nonetheless, in spite of state-enforced formation of such organisations we must continue to question the extent to which this might facilitate the creation of a 'good immigrant' narrative by outsiders. In short, does involvement by the state in such organisations generate a narrative of what constitutes an acceptable migrant/ethnic minority person in the UK and consequently also create ideas around what is deemed to be 'bad' or unacceptable for racialised minorities in the UK?

Spotlight on research: British South Asian women and trade unions

During the 1970s, South Asian women's groups dramatically changed UK trade union activism (Anitha et al., 2018). Compelled to mobilise on account of the intersectional prejudices that they faced in the labour force, both as women and as South Asian postcolonial migrants to the UK, these women, including Jayaben Desai, led grassroots activism. Collectively, this challenged colonial notions framing South Asians as cheap workers who would not take their statutory breaks, and South Asian women in particular as submissive 'easy targets'. This moment marks a turning point and unsettles the British postcolonial imagination about ethnic minorities and gendered stereotypes. Nonetheless, this example highlights the ways in which ethnic minorities have been forced to politically mobilise through informal channels in ways that might differ from the dominant white mainstream.

This example also highlights the way in which the British South Asian women cited above occupied and held multifaceted identities, as British, as women, as having South Asian heritage. As discussed earlier, this hybridity of identity also describes an intersectional identity. Influential black feminist and American legal scholar, Kimberlé Crenshaw first hypothesised about *intersectionality* in the 1990s in relation to her black women clients, who she argued were at a disadvantage because of their gender and existing structures rooted in sexism and misogyny. Additionally, they were also being disadvantaged by their black identities given the wide-reaching anti-black racism in the US and globally (Crenshaw, 1991). Those writing on gender and race since have continued to expand and add to Crenshaw's work on intersectionality; for example, in this case returning to the example of British South Asian women's trade unions in the UK in the 1970s, their intersectional experiences (of discrimination) spurred their political engagement.

In the political sciences there is growing focus on and celebration of participatory governance as a comparatively new way of doing politics. However, upon examining British colonialism, postcolonialism and ethnic minority participation in UK politics we question the extent to which this has long been the dominant way of functioning, due to necessity, for postcolonial migrants to the UK and as such what can be learnt from their experiences.

Conclusion

Politics involves ideas on how we should live together and how we ought to organise ourselves collectively. Politics, therefore, cannot avoid being imbued with theory, ideas and answers to this question.

In this chapter, we have examined social contract theory, and the rejoinder – racial contract theory – to help explain political discrimination and othering. The social contract tradition is not just an idea of political consent but embedded ideas on what political order was, and what it was not. What it was not was anarchy – or a state of nature. To European thinkers and politicians, the state of nature looked like non-European societies. Social contract theory did not cause imperialism, but it reflects ideas which did empower and justify colonisation. These ideas became political and culturally entrenched, and postwar migrants were faced with this. Bringers of order, and those who needed ordering, echoed notions of white supremacy which were hard to eradicate, especially when the UK itself had just helped defeat the Nazis. Criticising the UK in such a context was challenging.

Postwar migrants arriving in the UK were seen as a dangerous multitude that would threaten 'civilised society' in the UK. They came from the very places that had been colonised on the justification of political infantilism through myths like the civilising burden. They had been framed as pre-political and under-developed, lacking culture or civilisation. Nonetheless, migrant communities arriving in postwar UK soon realised that being political meant that they had to work together locally rather than petition or elect a sympathetic government. Put alternatively, in the early postwar period postcolonial migrants to the UK began their political engagement through grassroots level politics. Thinking back to our earlier consideration of noteworthy racialised UK parliamentarians, postcolonial migrants and their descendants have a remarkable level of engagement in UK politics.

We looked at some examples of this through the examination of ethnic minority participation and representation in formal and informal politics to highlight the range of context-driven specificities that shape this. Although there are at present a growing number of high-profile postcolonial ethnic minorities in significant political roles, further probing reveals the intersecting costs and rewards, or driving and limiting factors shaping minority participation and representation in the postcolonial political arena. This analysis raised further questions: are minorities foregrounded to make political parties appear to be champions of diversity? Put another way, is visible minority presence in politics merely tokenistic? How do dominant groups perceive this diversity, is entryism genuinely shaping politics in the UK? Furthermore, a closer look at the statistical evidence underlines the continued underrepresentation of minorities in UK politics on the whole. We argued that these potential constraints, coupled with legacies of colonial racisms (and intersecting sexisms) have historically pushed minorities to mobilise through informal channels and suggest that perhaps here more can be learnt about the wider and evolving nature of participation in UK politics across diverse UK society.

Key take-home points

- Race, racism and empire have shaped and influenced society and politics in the UK today and continue to do so.
- The British Empire was built on myths which infantilised colonised peoples and constructed the coloniser as saviour. This myth has become entrenched and persists to inform the ways in which postcolonial migrants in the UK are thought of in the present day.

- British postcolonial migrants often began their political engagement in the UK at the grassroots level. However, many postcolonial migrants now occupy senior roles in UK politics. Probing of the latter, however, raises questions of intersectionality, representation and tokenism.

Annotated reading list

Crenshaw, K. (1991) Mapping the margins: Intersectionality, identity politics, and violence against women of color. *Stanford Law Review*, 43(6), 1241–1299.

Crenshaw's seminal article examines the multiplicity and hybridity of identity, and helps us understand the ways in which intersecting identities often signal multiple and intersecting disadvantage.

Fanon, F. (2004 [1961]) *The Wretched of the Earth*. New York: Grove Press.

Fanon's book is a vital piece in post-colonial theory that makes a case for violent resistance. He explores colonisation from an existentialist view – decolonisation is not just about independence, territories or land, but a need to unburden oneself from its psychological scars.

Pateman, C. and Mills, C. (2007) *Contract and Domination*. Cambridge: Polity.

Charles Mills is a non-ideal theorist who takes on the social contract tradition to argue that it has been a theoretical system of exclusion, rather than consent and inclusion. He teams up with Carole Pateman in *Contract and Domination* (2007) to compare their work on the social contract. Whereas Mills theorised how it excluded based on race, Pateman's earlier work (which influenced Mills), looked at how it did this in relation to gender.

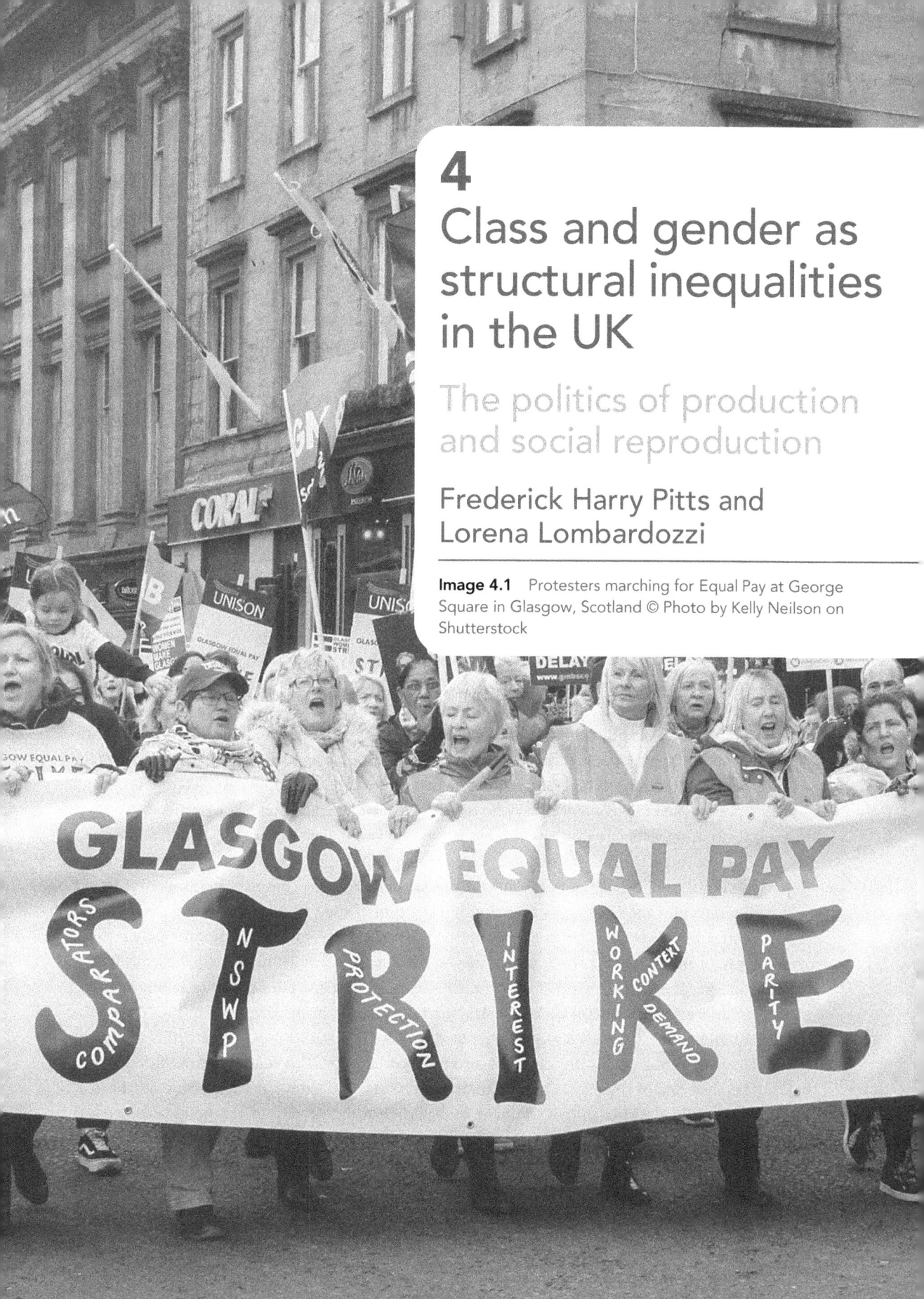

4
Class and gender as structural inequalities in the UK

The politics of production and social reproduction

Frederick Harry Pitts and Lorena Lombardozzi

Image 4.1 Protesters marching for Equal Pay at George Square in Glasgow, Scotland © Photo by Kelly Neilson on Shutterstock

Learning objectives

After reading this chapter, you should be able to:

- Analyse structural inequalities as they relate to the relationship with work in the present-day UK, specifically through the prism of class and gender as intersecting forms of identification relevant to UK politics
- Explore the potential use of the concept of 'social reproduction' in illuminating the struggles over the value of 'key' or 'essential' work – such as that found in the care sector – in the context of the Covid-19 pandemic and its aftermath as a defining moment in UK politics
- Assess the proposals put forward by UK political parties and other actors, you will gain a better grasp of the relative capacity of different distributive and 'predistributive' policies to address relevant structural inequalities
- Understand the meaning of 'pluralism' in the context of industrial relations as the 'politics of work'. From a UK perspective, Fair Pay Agreements will be considered as an example of how this approach plays out in practice

Introduction

Structural inequalities are differences in wealth, status and opportunity that relate to underpinning barriers to accessing wealth, resources and property. Possibly the most important of these material conditions concerns the relationship of different groups to the means of production, or in other words the capacity to produce the goods and services sold on the market as commodities. The central inequality that characterises a capitalist society such as the UK and the rest of world today is that between the owners of the means of production – business owners, investors and others – and those who depend for their livelihood on being recruited to operate them or on someone who is – in other words, the vast majority of people. Structural inequalities, in this sense, are understood not as a simple unhappy accident of processes of capital accumulation, but rather as the outcome of class as a relation constitutive to capitalist society itself. Whilst the employment relationship is a central site in which this inequality is worked through, it does not exhaust the salience of class as an issue, and class is not the only relevant way of understanding these inequalities. In this chapter, we define structural inequalities as 'intersectional', meaning that they cut across class, gender and ethnicity or racialised identity.

Indeed, much discussion about structural inequalities in the UK today centres on a series of interconnecting categories of difference, exclusion, stratification and identification along lines of gender, class and ethnicity or racialised identity. This matters to politics not least because one of the effects of structural inequalities is to limit the capacity people have to devote time and cognitive bandwidth to participating actively in the political process to defend their voice and interests. More broadly, it constrains their ability to help their communities and workplaces through informal groups and civil society organisations like trade unions and others. Material worsening in work and economic life, and the relative capacity of different political parties and actors to effectively respond to these shifts, have been seen as one of the determining factors underpinning electoral realignments in and around the Brexit years.

In short, these realignments saw traditional working-class voters increasingly move away from the Labour Party and its focus on conventional programmes of economic redistribution to respond instead to the cultural and emotional politics of status and belonging offered by UKIP and later the Conservative Party as their electoral offer adopted a right-wing populist stance; here, a sharpening divide between the voting habits of graduates and non-graduates takes on a profound significance (Cutts et al., 2020). Many UK studies have evidenced the limited character of a traditional social democratic policy toolbox of redistribution to attract voters suffering from an increasing sense of insecurity and declining status in the context of industrial change (Antonucci et al., 2017; Gingrich, 2019).

These studies find this apprehension of future hardship to be especially felt by working-class voters whose skilled labour had guaranteed them a reasonable degree of material comfort prior to the onset of various economic processes seen to devalue their work. This apprehension attracted voters to the promise that their social status would be shored up by a populist politics attuned to substitute sources of pride and belonging such as national or ethnic identity. Hence, the substantial shifts from Labour to the Conservatives in the so-called 'Red Wall' that fell with Boris Johnson's hard Brexit platform in the 2019 general election. One of the crucial questions confronting UK politics in the period that followed these upheavals is whether the arrival of direct hardship for a broader swathe of the population in the context of rising inflation and stagnant real wages will mean a return to stronger material redistributive preferences on the part of some of these voters (Curtis, 2022), or whether they will seek other forms of redress, for instance at the level of the workplace.

This chapter: Bringing work back in

Over the same period as these electoral shifts, the academic and political appreciation of the intersecting character of structural inequalities has become more sophisticated. The long-standing struggle to redress social, economic and political imbalances in wealth and power along lines of gender and ethnicity or racialised identity has been augmented by a greater focus on inequalities of access to assets and housing along lines of age, disabilities and youth. This has seen the proposal of new political subjectivities and dividing lines, especially on the left, that go beyond traditional class affinities and no longer sustain a durable connection with identities forged in the workplace or around the employment relationship (Cruddas et al., 2021; Pitts et al., 2022; Thompson et al., 2022). For some of these commentators, class in particular is an increasingly meaningless framework insofar as the category of working class remains confined to an association with older skilled and manual workers, with younger service workers persistently codified as 'middle class'. This means also that class has all but become a 'proxy for age' in the terms used by pollsters and opinion-formers. At the same time, age has become 'one of the key modalities through which class is lived' and through which young people 'become aware of their actual class position'. Age represents just one 'fracture' that makes it more difficult to understand 'class interests' as coherent across individuals and groups, with younger people earning less, bearing more debt, having fewer job opportunities, and facing more barriers to home ownership than generations past (Milburn, 2019: 21–23).

For some, the proliferation of such arguments among the Labour Party as it turned leftwards in recent years represented a historical break with the party's traditional base, a rejection of the centrality of labour–capital conflict to overall political struggle, and the challenge to any integration of an identifiable 'labour interest' in the state by means of the electoral system (Cruddas, 2021a). This is seen as reflecting an increasingly distribution-focused approach to inequalities focused on more fairly sharing the fruits of the surplus society produces, rather than redressing the imbalances of power and voice that bake in inequalities to the way that surplus is produced in the first place. This has political and policy ramifications insofar as it encourages an agenda that some commentators see as seeking to remedy inequalities only by redistributing slices of an ever-shrinking fiscal pie to ameliorate and compensate for the negative consequences of de-industrialisation, globalisation and technological change (Lind, 2020).

These can be associated with the rise of neoliberal policies in countries like the UK – so-called 'neoliberalism', a key concept for understanding many of the phenomena discussed in this chapter. Neoliberalism here is defined as a particular stage of capitalism which started at the end of the 1970s in the UK and USA with Margaret Thatcher and Ronald Reagan. It is also associated with an ideology which identifies in free market competition the defining rule of human–capital relations and see in the free-market mechanisms the most efficient way of regulating society. As a result, the role of state policies in shaping and regulating production, consumption and distribution of resources is reduced to a minimum, public investment and industrial policies declines and privatization became pervasive. It is argued that this particular mode of capitalism has favoured the interest of the private capital and financial classes (Duménil and Lévy, 2005).

Neoliberalism, as well as processes of de-industrialisation, globalisation and technological change, have seen many advanced capitalist democracies seek comparative advantage in the provision of services as a response to a more interconnected global market where manufacturing is cheaply and easily located in countries further back in the path of economic development to exploit their cheaper cost of labour. Technological shifts were seen to support investment in graduate skills to populate high-value knowledge sector jobs, downscaling and devaluing the contribution of traditional industrial trades and occupations to overall growth. However, the reality of the rise of services as a proportion of the economy is instead represented in a vast preponderance of poorly paid precarious roles in low-value sectors with a human element, such as retail, hospitality, cleaning and care. In a context where productivity gains through technical processes are hard to achieve, this lopsided economy offers little basis for incentivising the investment in skills, innovation and industrial upgrading needed for durable and inclusive economic growth.

This lack of economic dynamism depletes the fiscal resources available to the state to compensate the 'losers' of these shifts as was initially the case in the nineties and noughties and leaves available to the UK limited capacity to satisfy the competing demands of the different players in the distributional battles raging on picket lines and elsewhere today.

The contest over a dwindling surplus thus becomes ever sharper – the generational rift being a possible example of this. But for commentators who point to the constraints of this 'distributionist' bias in the analysis and mitigation of structural inequalities (e.g. see Hagglund, 2019; Pitts, 2022c), what is needed is a return to the politics of production and, we add here, the politics of *social reproduction*.

Whilst there are considerable merits in the focus on new forms of political identification around age and asset ownership, then, this strategic and analytical turn takes place against a backdrop of industrial change and shifts in working life that are important in broader structural inequalities. In this context, a complementary focus on class as a constitutive relation of difference, exclusion, classification and identification based on work and the employment relationship has often been lacking from political discourse and policymaking. Through an intersectional approach to structural inequalities, this chapter explores the relevance of class to contemporary UK politics and in turn the continuingly central role played by work and employment in defining class dynamics today.

We argue that structural inequalities cannot be understood without some sense of the relationship of individuals and groups to a set of social and material processes focused on work of one kind or another. *Production* is the process whereby workers are employed in the creation of commodified goods and services. *Social reproduction* is the process whereby human subjects and their bodies are made and cared for. *Valorisation* is the process whereby these activities are valued in terms of their monetary social worth and the wealth they generate realised in the form of wages or profits. The relationship to production, social reproduction and patterns of value extraction from labour, we suggest, are core aspects of structural inequalities in the context of the UK's political economy. It follows that opening up new paths for struggle over value and the (re)valuation of work and workers represents a vital way of redressing wider structural inequalities.

In particular, we focus on how spheres of employment like care work epitomise contemporary contests over social and economic value forged in the context of the pandemic, and which today take on greater political significance for the recognition of the role of care work beyond the market, and in the market through industrial disputes and strike action. The pandemic saw many poorly paid, precarious and predominantly female job categories recoded as 'key' or 'essential' work – cleaning, retail, hospitality, health and, crucially, care, whether childcare, adult social care or care for the elderly or vulnerable (Winton and Howcroft, 2020). Of these, some 60 per cent were women compared to 43 per cent in non-key industries (Farquharson et al., 2020).

Despite the rhetorical (re)valuation of these forms of work, and their celebration through so-called 'clap for carers' on UK doorsteps over the first phase of the pandemic, workers involved in them tended to face a much greater degree of risk in the context of Covid-19 with little in the way of recompense or recognition thereafter (Lucio and McBride, 2020). The social construction of the skills on which they depend – frequently seen as involving physical or emotional aspects that come naturally as an extension of domestic activities and thus require little training or reward – underpins relatively meagre financial returns, especially for the women who take on the lion's share of such jobs (Cockburn, 1983). As we shall see, theories of social reproduction help explain why, and how, structural inequalities emerge around this intersection of skill, gender and pay, expanding our understanding of class in turn.

We explore, later in the chapter, the policy proposals parties are putting forward to resolve the long- and short-term causes of this discontent. In particular, we consider the proposal of 'Fair Pay Agreements' specifically matched to the challenges of work in the care industry. This would emulate the implementation of a similar piece of legislation by the Labour Party in New Zealand and would be rolled out first in the care sector before being applied economy-wide. Such agreements operate through a petition of workers in a given sector – conducted by an organisation such as a union, perhaps – which then establishes the basis for negotiations with the employer side in that industry about setting certain basic standards around pay and conditions. In an age of inflationary pressures, this would enable workers to command pay rises more in line with sharp increases in the cost of living and address the pervasive intersectional inequalities that characterise sectors like care.

Parties are coming around to the importance of addressing these issues not least because the politics of work is intimately intertwined with the fortunes of pluralism in UK politics. The experience of workplace change, economic transformation and de-industrialisation undoubtedly has a cultural dimension, expressed in the upheavals of Brexit and populism. The roots of this can be traced back at least as far the unravelling of the postwar social and industrial compromise, for which populism of both right and left represents a kind of nostalgia (Steenvorden and Harteveld, 2018). Pluralism, understood in an industrial relations sense, means a system of representing the competing interests of workers, bosses and states through largely autonomous forms of association and bargaining independent of government and not exclusive of other forms of representation emerging alongside or as an alternative (Schmitter, 1974). The so-called 'death of consensus' (Tinline, 2022) that came with the collapse of the postwar compromise and the onset of de-industrialisation and globalisation, however, went hand in hand with the destruction of these mechanisms for channelling grievances and mediating social conflicts and antagonisms. The fractious terrain that remains is the one that contemporary UK politicians on all sides of the spectrum must find ways to articulate across in order to construct electoral coalitions.

However, rather than the particular implications of this for political behaviour narrowly conceived, our focus in this chapter will be on the material underpinnings of structural inequalities and how they translate into the everyday politics of the current regime of production and reproduction. We explore the material factors at the heart of structural inequalities through the conceptual framework of social reproduction theory, which reframes work outwards from the sphere of production alone to the various locations and practices through which human bodies, values and institutions are produced and reproduced more widely. Through the case studies used of care work in and out of the Covid-19 pandemic, the chapter continues to broaden out the conceptualisation of class to include the gendered and racialised divisions of labour around which the vast majority of socially reproductive forms of work and labour are organised in capitalist societies. The chapter closes by considering a pluralist politics of work based on 'predistribution' as a potential response to the weakness of the redistributive welfare state in responding to structural inequalities in the era of neo-liberalism. Predistribution – granting workers power to command better pay and conditions at the coalface of production rather than after in the welfare and benefits system – recognises that, just as structural inequalities are shaped through the relationship with work, the way to confront those inequalities is through the relationship with work as well.

Class, labour and structural inequalities

Inspired by Marxist analysis, 20th-century critical social science tended to confront structural inequalities by foregrounding material and economic dynamics and seeing social and political dynamics as following from them. However, as society changed with de-industrialisation, globalisation and the waning of the traditional workers movement, there was a widespread academic aversion to the conceptualisation of the working class as a political actor with a privileged perspective on broader societal transformation. Social scientists instead devoted themselves to how processes of identification, subjectivication and domination occur, at a microscopic level, through the interplay of words, symbols and practices. As inequalities sharpened and gained in visibility with the acceleration of de-industrialisation, globalisation and the crises that followed, however, there was a backlash against this aversion to material conceptualisations of class divides as they relate to the relations of production. In particular, critics point to how an analytical focus on language and identity has entailed a neglect of material aspects of workplace life and the material outcomes of power inequality (Prichard and Mir, 2010).

Whilst class has cultural dimensions that do not necessarily reduce to structural inequalities of a material or economic character, in this chapter we set these aside to focus on the relationship of class inequalities with work, the workplace and working lives (see also Pitts, 2022a, 2022b). As 'a central part of man's [sic] experience in acting on the world and reproducing the economy', work and the employment relationship possess 'a privileged insight' as regards any 'theoretical or political challenge to the system', as well as playing a vital part in meeting the 'fundamental material and social needs of human life' (Thompson, 1989: 242; 1990: 100; Thompson and Smith, 2001: 56–57). The relationship with work is thus an important part of explaining structural inequalities. However, it is important to keep in focus the broader array of 'forms of domination through which labour is subjugated to capital', and the fact that the workplace and the labour process itself are not the only location in which structural inequalities are created and reproduced within a broader array of processes of valorisation (Rowlinson and Hassard, 1994; Spencer, 2000). Moreover, there is no necessary connection between the experience of work and political subjectivity, each maintaining a relative autonomy that is mediated by various institutional forms and social forces (Thompson, 1989). The workplace does not directly structure the character of wider class politics or formal politics, not least because 'different sections of the working class have different, even antagonistic, interests whose resolution will be a political question irreducible to the 'science' of 'political economy'' and contingent on a host of extraeconomic conditions (Cressey and Macinnes, 1980: 20–29).

One of the most influential founding approaches to the study of this relationship derives from the work of Karl Marx, which situates dynamics in the sphere of production within a wider context. As set out in his masterwork *Capital* (Marx, 1976), for Marx, the historical and logical precondition of capitalist society rests in the separation of one class from the means of subsisting independently of the sale of their *labour power* – meaning not labour itself but the potential capacity to labour when applied to means of production. Meanwhile, the means of production necessary to actualise this potential to labour are concentrated in the hands of another class. Where the former class reproduces itself through selling their labour power, the latter reproduces itself by buying that labour power and consuming it in the 'hidden abode' of production in the production of commodities for exchange in pursuit of expanded value and profit in the market, expressed in money. Meanwhile, those dependent on disposing of the one commodity they own – labour power – live through acquiring commodities on the market with the wage they are paid as the price of that labour power. In this way, these antagonistic social relations generalise money and commodity exchange as the structuring principle not only of production but also of subsistence and thus life itself in capitalist society – in other words, of social reproduction.

As well as providing a basis to expand our understanding of class to include a broader variety of social antagonisms not only in the 'hidden abode' of production but beyond and behind it, this also challenges the way in which inequalities are talked about and acted upon in contemporary politics. Inequality is often bemoaned as a consequence of capitalism, but it is also one of its conditions. Inequalities do not arise only because the surplus generated in the production of commodities is shared out or distributed unfairly. Rather, the organisation of how goods and services are produced for profit presupposes a society wherein there is an inequality between those who live through selling or reproducing labour power and those who live by acquiring it and putting it to work. Each depends on the other: the worker on the boss and the boss and the worker.

But within this dependence, conflicts arise at every level. For their employment, workers in the UK and worldwide must compete against other workers in labour markets that are 'gendered, racialised, and also nationalised' (Bonefeld, 2016: 34). Because of these intersectional differentiations, class inequality 'structur[es] the lives of different individuals in different ways', establishing often contradictory identities and positions both across groups and as a 'fracture-line' running through individuals themselves (Gunn, 1987), including with reference to other aspects like ethnicity or racialised identity and gender. This brings us to the concept of social reproduction contained within Marx's account of the social constitution of class society and the category of labour power.

Social reproduction, class and gender

Building on the foundations provided by Marx, theories of social reproduction (see Lombardozzi and Pitts, 2020; Pitts, 2022a; Pitts et al., 2017) conceptualise the intersectional character of structural inequalities in the context of a classed, gendered and racialised division of caring labour. This perspective conceives of this caring labour as central to the reproduction not only of the bodies and selves of workers in capitalist societies, but of those societies more broadly (see Theory box below). As such, within social reproduction approaches there is a subtle distinction between, on the one hand, conceptualisations that locate 'the domain where lives are sustained and reproduced' (Zechner and Hansen, 2015) within a narrower frame of reference relating to the domestic sphere and the gender division of paid and unpaid labour around which it is organised, including the exploitation of migrants and people of colour within these dynamics (Fraser, 2016) and, on the other, conceptualisations that stress instead social reproduction as the totality of relationships within which life and society themselves are generated and reproduced, and which therefore brings in moments outside both the home and the workplace such as the state and other institutions (Bhattacharya, 2017). The framework of social reproduction helps us to make explicit the dynamics of material exploitation visible through paid (productive), informal and unpaid (reproductive) work performed by women in capitalistic social relations. While one approach emphasises that patterns of work asymmetries between men and women are centred within the family and the domestic division of labour, the other emphasises that public norms within the community and institutions also contribute to shape and reproduce social reproduction outcomes, namely gender inequality, for instance through austerity in care and social services, discrimination in the workplace, but also through the disinvestments in infrastructures which limit the mobility and access to assistance of the most vulnerable.

Across both of these complementary strands, social reproduction approaches foreground the activities that biologically and socially reproduce human life. This includes 'the provision of food, clothing, shelter, basic safety, and health care, along with the development and transmission of knowledge, social values, and cultural practices and the construction of individual and collective identities' (Bezanson and Luxton, 2006: 3). This centres on 'extensive, undervalued, and largely invisible' work occurring in communities, schools, hospitals, religious and civil society organisations (Bezanson, 2006: 175). This typically rests on waged and unwaged formal and informal work that disproportionately rests upon the exploitation of the paid and unpaid labour of women, migrants and racialised subjects in a global division of labour (Yeates, 2012). The value of the labour of care workers and others is determined by the wage they are able to command for living, with most forced to lower their 'standard of necessity' to a minimum, and to rely on other sources of income to survive (Zanoni, 2019). The variability and indeterminacy of the value of labour in this context makes social reproduction a key site of class struggles, expansively conceived. In this sense, a social reproduction framework strategically locates class struggle at the intersection of the workplace and other spheres, incorporating, for instance, the fight for access to resources such as clean water, health services or education, and the rethinking of the articulation between class struggles and gender, ethnicity or racialised identity and geography.

This strand of thought has known a new impetus over the years of social and economic crisis since 2008, in which the ramifications of the global financial crisis have been reconceptualised as a 'crisis of social reproduction' or 'crisis of care' sparked by the severed link between the wage and subsistence and simultaneous cutbacks in the welfare state (Fraser, 2016). Such analyses suggest that the limits of labour's commodification have been breached, the link between the wage and the reproduction of the means of living has been broken, and the reproduction of ourselves as healthy, productive human beings is inadequately guaranteed in the context of an economy that cannot provide jobs for all with a wage to match. In the wake of the retrenchment of the welfare state under austerity, empirical studies informed by the concept of social reproduction examined struggles over domestic reproduction.

Studies of the period of austerity following the Great Recession (Bayliss et al., 2017) show that women were the first to be cut off from the wage–subsistence relationship with additional and indirect risks of segregation, subordination and dependence on asymmetrical income relations. These have produced consequences crucial to our understanding of the sources of structural inequality in the UK. These include the disinvestment in care and the absence of collective services provided by the state or civil-society institutions, as well as commodified services employing migrant, racialised and female wage labourers to perform reproductive tasks (Ferguson, 2017).

As for the broader crisis of social reproduction, a range of subsequent phenomena or threats that have since reared their heads, whether climate catastrophe, pandemic or the risk of technological unemployment, have only served to worsen the bleak prospectus.

Social reproduction perspectives present a historical account of how this crisis came to be in the intersecting paths of structural inequalities around class and gender (Fraser, 2016; Lombardozzi, 2020). With the rise of the welfare state in western countries pro-worker legislation has abolished child labour and initiated the first pension systems allowing people to retire when old. As a result, the adult male became the figure at the core of the market labour force. In this period the working class intensified its collective progressive political projects advocating for better working conditions. Yet, this momentum of political emancipation has somehow crystallised a gendered division of labour within and outside the household. During that time, women had the exclusive duty of supporting the family by being responsible for food preparation, cleaning, childcare, elderly care, and so on. However, feminist movements – with the support of social democratic parties – started to fight to promote adequate rights within the family, including abortion and divorce, but also have been effective in advocating for more and better public services provision for childcare and elderly care. These services have socialised, at least in part, the burden of the reproductive work into society. Furthermore, it increased the possibility for women to access paid jobs which contributed to the fulfilment of women's intellectual, economic and political aspirations (Lombardozzi, 2020).

However, in the 1980s, as Thatcherism took hold via successive Conservative governments, the UK saw the rise of neoliberal policies, putting these achievements in danger. A series of reforms based on privatisation and disinvestment in social policies eroded the working-class livelihoods, including women's material and socio-political emancipation. Male wages declined in real terms and were no longer sufficient to maintain living standards. As a result, women have been pushed into the labour market to meet households' material needs with humble jobs in hospitality or the care sector. Yet women have often been exposed to exploitative working conditions, precarious contracts and part-time work (Boyer et al., 2017). For instance, social services in the health and care sector are mostly performed by migrant women and women of colour, often on zero-hours contracts, wages which are barely at the legal minimum wage and exhausting working rota. They are often victims of patriarchal dynamics in the workplace, which put them easily at risk of losing their jobs with disastrous consequences in terms of income and basic needs such as housing, health and food. The underlying structural conditions that enable such scenarios is the perpetuation of a neoliberal model which over the past four decades has dismantled social protection, deregulated work contracts, and curtailed wages, thus losing ground with the cost of living.

Women who cannot access public support and cannot afford private care services are forced to remain at home or engage in part-time jobs. In some circumstances, women come together and organise to pay for shared home-based childcare, and private nursery and elderly care homes have become increasingly rare and unaffordable. Therefore, the most vulnerable segments of society to tackle the care crisis are poor women, both as producers and consumers of such care services. Women in poor contexts face unprecedented pressure to balance and meet the expectation of the market and society for them to deliver productive labour and reproductive work. As a result, women struggle with mental health due to stress and anxiety, which slows down their socioeconomic mobility and political participation. Indeed, working for fewer hours translates into smaller pensions and social insurance. Moreover, these dynamics put women in a condition of segregation, subordination and dependence on male partners based on asymmetrical income relations (Bayliss et al., 2017).

Overall, then, theories of social reproduction crack upon the concept of class and its connection with work to include a broader array of intersecting inequalities and struggles over value and recognition. For Zechner and Hansen (2015), 'struggles around social reproduction allow for a renegotiation around what is considered work, or what is valued as such'. This renegotiation of the historically and socially specific separation between production and social reproduction helps illuminate a multiplicity of forms of inequality and domination beyond the traditional class relation. Thus, production and social reproduction do not take place in the economic and the social spheres respectively but are both fields of labour conflict and class struggle, criss-crossed by the gendered and racialised divisions of labour on which they rest (Dinerstein and Pitts, 2018). In times of crisis such as our own, the 'contradiction between the needs of the workers and the needs of capital that lives at the core of the problem of social reproduction cannot be more vivid. This is not a political, economic or social issue but it is about the reproduction of human "life"' (Dinerstein, 2002: 14).

Theory box: Social reproduction

This chapter is based in part on the concept of *social reproduction*. This theory box explains what we mean by the term, how it came to be considered important, and in brief, its potential relevance for UK politics. We define social reproduction as the sphere or process through which human subjects, bodies and lives are made and remade. In other words, it refers to the various kinds of work, paid and unpaid, through which workers, households, communities and institutions subsist and survive.

In a context such as the UK where advanced neoliberal capitalism has marketised and commodified the whole set of conditions for social reproduction, and increasingly monetised services such as education, health and care, the concept of social reproduction helps us make visible those pockets of work, cooperation and solidarity outside the market. It theoretically legitimises the time and value of all aspects of reproductive work and it invites us to acknowledge it in the understanding and evaluation of policy solutions. Also, it helps us to identify the

(Continued)

unevenness of the impact of policies which fail to take into account social reproduction. Such impacts are exemplified in social inequalities along the lines of gender, ethnicity or racialised identity and class. For these reasons, social reproduction is a concept that can be easily applied to the context of the UK and explain the contemporary UK politics of work.

The Covid-19 pandemic exposed the centrality of various forms of so-called 'key', 'critical' or 'essential' work for the way that society sustains itself. Many of these occupations and sectors have a role in social reproduction of human life, labour and livelihoods more broadly: care, health, education and so on. However, the association of these roles with women within a gender division of labour, and in particular the assumption that the activities they involve rest not upon learned skill but a natural capacity to care, underpin a rhetorical and material undervaluation of their worth and status.

The pandemic saw various manifestations of a new political valorisation of these forms of work, with the 'clap for carers' and other events. But the translation of this into better pay or conditions after the pandemic has not arrived. Greater remuneration or security at work was made all the more difficult to achieve due to spiralling inflation, even as the rising cost of living chipped away at real wages and exacerbated an underlying crisis of social reproduction.

The concept of social reproduction thus helps illuminate the industrial conflicts that have opened up as unions representing such workers have sought to lay claim to the real value of their labour in the wake of the Covid-19 pandemic.

Case study: Care work in crisis

The Covid-19 pandemic both highlighted and hardened the important socially reproductive role played by fields like health and care work in the contemporary economy. This reflected and extended underlying shifts. Just as, when societies get richer, a greater share of household income is spent on labour-intensive services like restaurants and hospitality, a society in which people live for longer means an expansion of care services. Such lines of work are largely immune to productivity-raising technologies and are at the mercy of demographic dynamics that increase demand, and thus will more likely see expansion rather than elimination of jobs in the years to come. Much of this work will be distributed across class, gender and racialised lines.

At the same time, the Covid-19 pandemic highlighted and helped redefine the importance of 'essential' work and workers in fields such as health, care, transportation and more, primarily through the rhetorical valorisation of these roles in the public and political imagination during the pandemic. The lack of seasonal migrant workers has put at risk entire food supply chains and made essential commodities unaffordable or prone to being wasted. However, as the pandemic has waned, the moral and ethical assessment of the worth of these industries and professions has failed to pass over into material gains. The condition of vulnerability of care workers has seen a peak during the recent Covid-19 pandemic. A wide range of feminist scholars have documented the multidimensional social and care crisis that emerged as a result (see the 2021 Special Issue of *Feminist Economics* including Stevano et al., 2021).

There is a consensus that Covid-19 has contributed to a reconfiguration of the meaning and organisation of work. Indeed, it has questioned the validity of the classifications of low-skill jobs, identifiable with the professions of care workers, teachers and nurses as low-value producing in opposition to apparently high-skill jobs such as in financial and legal services which have been for a long time considered high-value producing. In the context of Covid-19 so called low-skilled workers were in reality recognised as essential for the maintenance of society. These jobs are highly segregated, as they tend to see a concentration of women, migrants, and ethnic minorities.

In terms of organisation of work, the 'stay at home' policy has intensified the burden of reproductive work within the household, but it has also shown the heterogeneity of conditions in which UK households have had to cope with such a care burden. While reproductive work remained highly gendered, it was also performed in very diverse conditions depending on class. Asset-based inequality was visible in terms of space gaps which worsened the risk of contagion of the virus, but also in terms of domestic facilities and infrastructure such as internet and devices which were indispensable for home schooling and work. As a result of the conditions for essential workers both outside the household due to lack of safety at work and in the household, Black, Asian, Latino and other ethnic minorities have been disproportionately affected by Covid-19. From this perspective, Covid-19 has also amplified an already disempowered condition of this segment of society.

A stark example of the marketisation of social reproduction is also visible in the hybrid space between the market, the household and the state, namely through the activities of the so-called third sector. In the UK and across Europe and the US, the volunteering and community sector has indeed helped marginal communities, minorities and migrants to meet essential needs such as shelter and food (Lombardozzi, 2023). Food banks and community kitchens, very often led by women of colour from the same communities which struggle to access resources to redistribute, have not only provided warm meals and primary care to people in need, but also helped them reconnect with a thin welfare system which increasingly neglects such social reality due to financial cuts coupled with racialised and classist forms of institutionalised discrimination (Lombardozzi, 2023).

Spiralling and unregulated inflation has sharpened the underlying process by which rates of pay have become increasingly incapable of keeping pace with the cost of living. This has led unionised workers in these fields to enter into dispute and industrial action in order to materially realise their worth in the form of better remuneration. Dwindling growth and productivity in the UK have intensified the struggle between employers and employees, with firms attempting to introduce modernisation and efficiency drives as workers feel the pinch on the pound in their pocket. Since the early 1990s the UK median wage decoupled from productivity growth (see Figure 4.1) and the gap has widened in recent years. Though less than in the USA or Germany, this has produced a more rancorous industrial relations context in the UK.

Elsewhere, there are many more non-unionised workers for whom organisation and representation through established industrial relations actors is unfeasible, inaccessible or unaffordable. In sectors such as care, a proliferation of fragmented small businesses and highly localised, personalised forms of managerial contracts obstruct the capacity of workers to unionise and collectively bargain for better pay and conditions. The obstacles to organising intersect with the imbalances of power represented in the prevalence of migrant women and women of

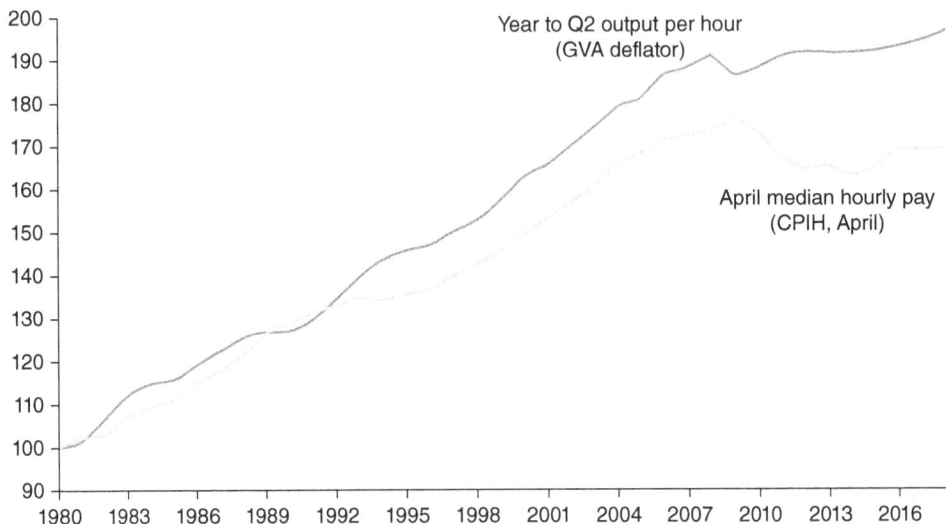

Figure 4.1 Indices of real terms median pay and labour productivity, 1980=100: UK

Source: Whittaker, M. (2020) Dead-end relationship? Exploring the link between productivity and workers' living standards. RF analysis of ONS, National data. https://www.resolutionfoundation.org/publications/dead-end-relationship/ © Resolution Foundation 2020

colour in the care workforce. The gig economy, under the motto of flexibility, has in reality normalised a bundle of casual and non-permanent work which leaves the new working poor with very little job security. These workers are tied to platforms which contribute to the fragmentation of their voices and disenfranchise their social protection. While some of these workers are very visible because they wear uniform, care workers are hidden in households and have a lot of difficulties organising and making their working conditions known (Woodcock and Graham, 2019). Platform and gig workers are among those whose 'undervalued' social contribution became temporarily clear during the pandemic but who have not seen due recognition or remuneration of that value in the period that followed – indeed, there is evidence that the initial hit from the pandemic saw around half of gig workers lose their jobs and the rest suffer a two-thirds cut in income (Inversi et al., 2020).

For workers who find themselves operating in the wild-west-like regulatory environment of low-wage UK depicted in exposés like James Bloodworth's *Hired* (2019), redressing these inequalities will require specific policies and institutional remedies. The lack of recourse to collective solutions to poor pay and conditions is made all the more problematic because of the fundamental undervaluing of fields like care work as something that is unskilled, innate and natural – especially for women workers who are constructed as biologically and emotionally predisposed to perform and give care to others without it being a skill acquired through learning and practice-like skills traditionally constructed as being the preserve of male workers.

These tendencies to privatise and individualise care responsibilities through the marketisation of social reproduction have been exacerbated by a race to the bottom in wages and working conditions as government cuts reduced local council budgets, with tenders awarded to the lowest bidder meaning that care services are provided on the cheap. This also intensifies the labour involved as care workers are disciplined into dealing with care recipients as quickly and efficiently as possible, in spite of human need. This combination of defunding and labour transformation causes what some refer to as a 'crisis of care' in societies like the UK, within a broader global division of care labour that is both gendered and racialised.

The pandemic saw a more coherent politics of work emerge in the context of a profound social and economic crisis. As the pandemic exposed the differentiated experiences of work many people face in the labour market, specifically those who find themselves in a state of precariousness owing to the patchy application of benefits and protection, many governments in Europe implemented policy responses in the wake of Covid-19 that rendered working life more secure for the period of the pandemic. These included job retention schemes, expanded benefit provision, minimum income guarantees, targeted cash transfers and assistance with household expenses. These measures limited the impact of the crisis on income levels and inequality to some extent. Whilst these policy initiatives were gradually wound down as the pandemic waned, some EU states sought to try to extend rights and benefits to formerly excluded groups of workers as part of the recovery that followed. This incorporates a much stronger defence of universality in the provision of benefits and protection, escaping the conditionality that has characterised welfare systems over the past decade or more.

More profoundly, however, the compensatory politics of redistribution through which the political centre ground has sought to ameliorate structural inequalities for decades has been called into question by declining growth. The long downturn prohibits the vast systems of tax credits and so on that were possible in the nineties and noughties, and politically residualises the welfare state into a service seen as being for the poor but paid for by the rich. Even were it practical in the circumstances, a policy agenda based on compensating and redistributing can sometimes obstruct the development of a politics of production addressed to creating a fairer and more just economy prior to the fruits of growth being shared out.

Spotlight on research: Universal basic income

One of the controversial topics on the crisis of social reproduction and structural inequalities is the potential role of universal basic income for women's empowerment and for the strengthening of security and voice in reproductive work (Dinerstein and Pitts, 2018; Lombardozzi, 2020; Lombardozzi and Pitts, 2020). While some recognise the support that UBI can provide, others adopt a more cautious approach as monetary redistributive transfers cannot tackle the constitutive character of inequalities in capitalist society and the shortfalls of 'predistributive' power that maintain them. On the one hand existing research observes that in parallel with the withdrawal of the welfare state and the weakening of unions, economic growth has been centred on financialisation and services, which has led to de-industrialisation in poorer areas of the country. As a solution to the resulting decline of share of labour income, individualised and monetised solutions are proposed. However, researchers have found that the marketised logic governing such interventions propagates,

(Continued)

rather than mitigates, structural inequalities. Take, for instance, research on the role of volunteering in addressing the weakening of social reproduction services related to care. Lombardozzi (2023) untangles the gendered and racialised relations within volunteering communities and analyses how the state is enabling a marketisation, class stratification and racialisation of social care services. The alternative, as argued in this chapter, is predistributive and progressive fiscal policies to tackle structural inequalities at their root.

Pluralism and predistribition

Whilst class is a negative category of social domination, its connection with work, employment and economic life brings together individuals in such a way as to enable them to contest the terms on which their labour is valued and their status recognised at the level of the state. In this way, class struggle moves 'in and against' the state to achieve legal and regulatory gains through the conditions of 'political integration' it offers the working class and the 'labour interest' (Clarke, 1992: 136; Cruddas, 2021a). The regulation and valuation of labour power also acts as a space within which struggles to contest structural inequalities are granted 'room to move' (Gunn, 1987: 63; Marx, 1976: 198). There is no class society without struggle at its core and the state is a form within which this central antagonism is mediated, temporarily reconciled and given a platform to play out in an organised, coordinated and regulated fashion. This dimension became particularly important as the pandemic passed into the heated industrial relations context of the post-pandemic period.

As became clear in the immediate aftermath of the pandemic, the bold claims being made about the revaluation of undervalued labour performed by those newly classified as 'key workers' would ultimately be settled not automatically or by dint of the generosity of the state, but through struggle, organisation and legal and workplace mobilisation. The world of work became a story of strikes and industrial strife over material remuneration in recognition of the moral worth and social value of many of the groups of workers who had been lauded as 'essential' during the tentative industrial compromise that characterised the early stages of Covid-19. Politics, however, has largely been incapable of accommodating the demands

Image 4.2 A nurse returns from their shift at Watford General hospital as local residents clap their hands for carers and key workers.

© Photo by Eric Johnson Photography on Shutterstock

of the undervalued socially reproductive labourers of our society owing to an absence of institutional frameworks and parliamentary willpower to do so.

This calls for a re-creation of pluralist industrial relations institutions and frameworks for bargaining over the value of labour (Ackers, 2020; Heery, 2016). The postwar period having represented the highpoint of pluralist industrial relations in the UK, the seventies saw a more state-driven corporatist model pass over into the neoliberal assault on worker organisations in the eighties, with little reconstruction since (see Panitch, 1986). What was lost in this transition was the focus of pluralist industrial relations approaches on a particular assessment of the character of structural inequalities in capitalist society, as noted by Cruddas (2021b):

> Pluralist labour relations traditions stress the inevitability of workplace conflict given the plurality of interests within complex social systems such as the firm. Such interest groups, including management and workers, represent conflicting sites of authority over the organisation and regulation of employment. The management of such conflict is key to both the success of the enterprise and the wider economy. Emphasis is placed on methods to efficiently represent these legitimate, competing interests. Unions and collective bargaining express the collective voice of the workers and can serve to regulate conflict and counteract the unilateral, over-mighty rule of the employer and achieve just outcomes.

The absence of pluralist frameworks of contestation and negotiation over the terms and conditions of care and care work in the UK is indicative of a wider problem. Collective bargaining is the traditional mechanism for balancing labour and employer interests at work. It remains the central means for doing so, with even centre-right think tank the Institute for Fiscal Studies recognising that addressing income inequality requires some form of mediation at work (Giupponi and Machin, 2022). Yet the latest statistics on trade union membership show that in 2021, just one in four people in the private sector were covered by a collective agreement (BEIS/ONS, 2021). Whilst it is untenable to simply call for a return to widespread unionisation and frameworks of traditional sectoral or collective bargaining – which would require a more fundamental political and economic reset than the lifetime of a single government would allow – the wave of industrial unrest at the time of writing has witnessed a return to serious policy thinking about potential practical solutions in the political sphere.

In this sense, refocusing the conversation on structural inequalities like class and gender back to work, the employment relationship and the connection with production has important political and policy consequences. As we discussed at the beginning of this chapter, scholars and policymakers alike attempt to analyse and address structural inequalities through a focus on distribution – in other words, how the fruits of production are shared rather than a more fundamental reconfiguration of the architecture of work and economic life through a focus on production – and, we might add, social reproduction. In particular, the extremely popular analyses of Thomas Piketty represented what one critic labels 'a paradigmatic example of a social democratic critique of neoliberal capitalism', in that the policy programme that flowed from its diagnosis of capitalism's ills 'centred on redistribution' rather than the character and organisation of work itself (Hagglund, 2019).

The policy expressions of this distributionist approach, especially on the technocratic political centre ground in countries like the UK, have long tended to rest on the assumption that capitalism would generate levels of growth capable of facilitating redistribution of the proceeds. For instance, as Cruddas (2021a) describes, on entering office in the 1990s, New Labour was confronted by an economy experiencing the consequences of de-industrialisation and global competition, including a decline in real wages and disposable income. Rather than employment regulation and an extension of collective bargaining, tweaks to the tax system were seen as sufficient to support workers in a service-based economy. Globalisation and financialisation were expected to deliver economic dividends that could then be redistributed to workers as benefits and tax credits to compensate them for wider effects on the economy, and buttress low wages. These assumptions took a long time to meet the cold hard reality of economic and political upheavals, where now the UK faces very little growth at all with which to satisfy competing redistributive demands.

Across this landscape policymakers have largely left untrodden the path of what was briefly called 'predistribution' as a response to structural inequalities – in other words, the attempt to improve working life at the coalface by granting workers the power and capacity to lay claim to value in and prior to production, without waiting for ameliorative cash transfers from the state after the fact. As Cruddas notes (2021b), this briefly popular policy perspective touched upon 'fundamental design questions in the nature of modern capitalism' and challenging its 'associated degradations' at source rather than tinkering around its edges with 'remedial cash transfers'. However, the path was not taken, and the focus remained on 'how you chop up the proceeds of growth rather than redesigning the system itself'.

A preoccupation with these fashionable distributional alternatives left untouched the foundations of the increasingly insecure labour market and unrewarding workplace that emerged in the long post-crisis period. With the wage–labour relationship weakened by unemployment and the crash exacerbating low growth, this era of austerity populism had appeared to sharpen distributional conflicts, including along generational lines. These conditions helped incubate a national–populist backlash. Centre-left policymakers responded by once again returning to the proposal of policies focused on the provision of cash transfers to address or mitigate the perceived ill effects of capitalist economics. As policymakers attempted to work with a more difficult fiscal picture, left and right alike threw themselves into politically prioritising distributional conflicts between warring parties rather than a common attempt to address pay and conditions at work.

With an emptied-out system of industrial relations depriving the economy of any countervailing power capable of commanding gains from below, Lind argues (2020: 122–124), policymakers on left and right alike were left with little choice but to attempt to 'co-opt alienated populist voters' with impossible and ineffective 'after-tax redistribution schemes'. Purporting to iron out contradictions produced by the neoliberal era, rather than fundamentally confronting the underlying relations of work and production, these would simply seek to 'reconcile voters to an unchanged economic order'. The cost-of-living crisis throws this impasse into stark relief. Workers possess limited bargaining power to eke out wage increases in line with inflation, and the state faces limited capacity to find new ways to dish out a shrinking economic slush fund.

However, new measures being proposed by mainstream parties show that there is a growing political consensus that the untrodden path of 'predistribution' might well be a useful starting point to addressing structural inequalities as they relate to production (and social reproduction), and in particular the role of predominantly women workers in industries like care.

Policy: Fair pay agreements

The Labour Party has proposed fair pay agreements (FPAs) as a policy instrument that would specifically benefit sectors like care where collective bargaining arrangements are not in force (Pakes and Pitts, 2022). Tentatively outlined in Labour's Employment Rights Green Paper (Labour Party, 2021), FPAs promise to improve private sector pay and conditions against a backdrop of low union membership and the untenability of reviving full collective bargaining in many sectors of the contemporary economy. This mimics the agenda of the recent Labour government in New Zealand, where FPAs anchored a broader set of reforms to enable workers to lay claim to value.

The process of negotiating an FPA is instigated by gaining the support of either 1,000 employers or 10 per cent of the workforce in a given sector, whichever is less. Once negotiations between unions and employer representatives commence, FPAs have as their mandatory end result a minimum pay floor below which people cannot fall. It is also mandatory to discuss, if not agree, a series of other non-pay terms and conditions. Agreements are confirmed through a vote of employees and employers in a given sector.

Initially, in the UK version proposed by the Labour Party, FPAs will be geared towards priority areas to be determined by the state. Social care is one such area. Care is typical of a sector where the tendering process compels firms to compete on cost, causing a race to the bottom, run on the basis of forcing down worker pay and conditions. From this foundation, the aim is that eventually FPAs roll out across the economy as a whole, incentivising investment in skills and productivity rather than cost-cutting.

Advocates suggest that such a policy would broker discussion and debate between labour, capital and the state in order to further enable workers to contest the terms on which their work is valued. At the international level, the principle of sectoral bargaining (to which FPAs bear a resemblance) has received support from the OECD (OECD, 2019), suggesting that industrial or occupational agreements produce higher wages, better conditions and improved productivity when compared to those struck at a workplace-by-workplace level.

A crucial point is that, whilst FPAs would open up the potential for unions to organise to a much greater extent in the care sector, these agreements would not necessarily depend on widespread unionisation – for many reasons difficult in the care industry – to be effective. In so doing they may hold the potential of re-creating pluralist forms of contestation and negotiation in a greenfield area pivotal to many contemporary social, economic and political challenges.

Conclusion

Measures such as FPAs present a possible alternative to the neoliberal emptying out of pluralist architectures in the wake of the unravelling of the postwar social and industrial compromise, which has eroded the capacity of workers to exert countervailing power to the force of employers and the state to dictate the terms on which they produce and socially produce themselves, others and the world around them. In turn, this has reshaped the constitutive relations that define structural inequalities in capitalist societies. The conflicts around the politics of work in the UK exhibit the consequences of a political economy that since the 1980s has become more unequal at the same time as it has become less dynamic. The top 10 per cent has steadily acquired more than 30 per cent of the wealth in society (see Figure 4.2). This trend is situated in an economic context where the UK has observed a decline in foreign direct investment projects due to a combination of factors including the pandemic and Brexit and has relatively modest domestic investment in fixed capital formation (Ernst and Young, 2023).

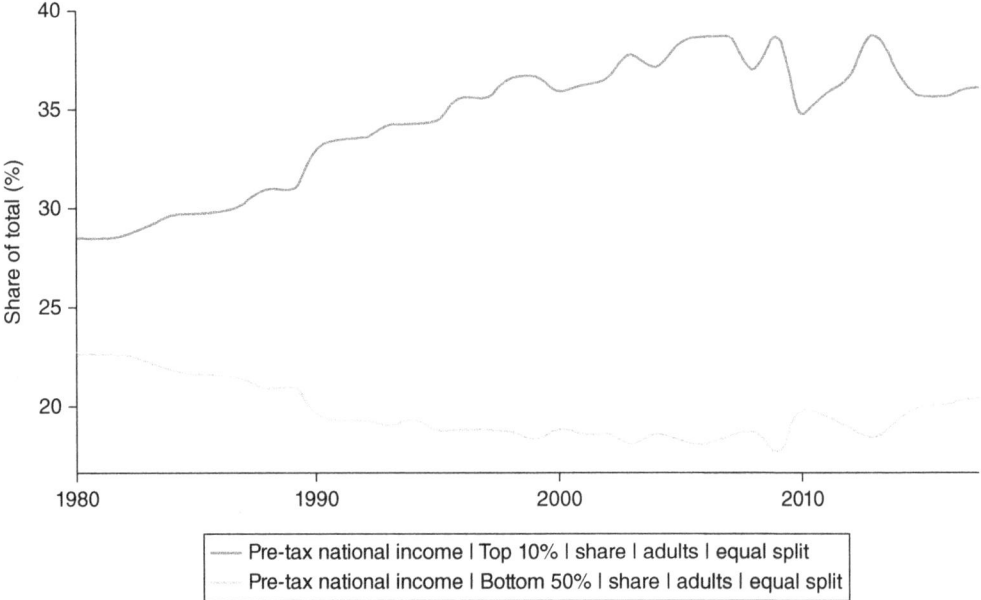

Figure 4.2 Income inequality

Source: WID, used under a CC BY 4.0 Deed license

A reinvigoration of pluralist architectures of bargaining may well help channel and mediate conflicts towards a new kind of political economy, but the form and content of the institutions through which this is achieved will likely have to be much different to those that characterised earlier periods. This will require the openness and flexibility to enable classed, gendered and racialised subjects to contest the terms of social reproduction up and down, from the bottom to the top of society.

Responding to the issues raised in this chapter, attempts to increase wages are undoubtedly an important part of the struggle for the recognition of the value of the labour of care workers and others. The economic obstruction of channels for social and political processes of recognition and valuation means that the struggle for recognition can take ever more vexed and unpredictable forms – as witnessed in the populist politics of grievance that have characterised the last decade. This means that new institutional mediation and forms of association are necessary. As we have shown here using the case study of women workers and the care sector, one way in which this can be taken forward is through a re-envisioning of the role of trade unions in the economy to increase the power, voice and political participation of workers at the coalface of contemporary production and social reproduction. Granting workers bargaining power, as well as new forms of countervailing power in the political sphere, would intervene in how the structurally unequal cake is baked and not simply how it is cut and sliced.

Key take-home points

- At a time when it is largely assumed that processes of political identification bear no relation to the workplace, the employment relationship and the spheres of production and reproduction are vital sites for understanding structural inequalities around class and gender. The politics of work is important for analyses of populism and also the pandemic.
- As a socially constitutive element of capitalist society, class intersects with gender. A key area in which this intersectionality becomes clear is in all those sectors and activities where 'labour power' – the capacity to labour – is reproduced in society. This has implications for how we understand structural inequalities.
- The neoliberal era of capitalism has fundamentally challenged the capacity of the welfare state to address structural inequalities. Since the 1980s care services have been rapidly monetised and privatised, which has increased the burden on women for reproductive work and increased racialised inequalities.
- Reproductive work includes all the paid and unpaid work that is performed in the household and in the community to maintain life. The Covid-19 pandemic has magnified a 'crisis of social reproduction' and highlighted the essential role of care in capitalism.
- The differential valuation of different kinds of labour in the context of a cost-of-living crisis has compelled a wave of industrial conflicts over wages and conditions. As a pluralist response to these conflicts, fair pay agreements can offer a useful starting point to address structural inequalities based on the valuation of different forms of labour.
- The capacity of the redistributive welfare state to address structural inequalities having been limited by political and economic change, 'predistributive' policies that grant power and voice to workers can help offset the consequences of de-industrialisation and financialisation.

Annotated reading list

Lombardozzi, L. and Pitts, F.H. (2020) Social form, social reproduction and social policy: Basic income, basic services, basic infrastructure. *Capital & Class*, 44(4), 573–594.

This article untangles the contradictions of universal basic income as a distributive re-envisioning of the welfare state in response to the crisis of social reproduction.

Stevano, S., Mezzadri, A., Lombardozzi, L. and Bargawi, H. (2021) Hidden abodes in plain sight: The social reproduction of households and labour in the Covid-19 pandemic. *Feminist Economics*, 27(1–2), 271–287.

This article highlights the interconnections between domestic institutions and labour markets in the context of the Covid-19 pandemic, also including a Global South perspective.

Thompson, P., Pitts, F.H., Ingold, J. and Cruddas, J. (2022) Class composition, Labour's strategy and the politics of work. *Political Quarterly*, 93(1), 142–149.

This article considers contemporary debates about class in UK politics, surveying attempts on the left to displace traditional class differences onto other indices such as age.

Part II
Institutions

5 Creating political change: From the (informal) politics of the everyday to formal politics 97
6 Devolution, sub-national governance and inequalities 115
7 Do British political parties reflect British pluralism? 139
8 Elections, referendums and public opinion 159
9 Place, pluralism and the media: Who tells us about political affairs? 185
10 The legislature 205
11 The executive 225

5
Creating political change

From the (informal) politics of the everyday to formal politics

Joanie Willett

Image 5.1 Everyone is involved in shaping political norms, as part of our everyday lives © Photo by AlanMorris on Shutterstock

Learning objectives

After reading this chapter, you should be able to:

- Understand the difference between governance and government
- Understand that policy change is complex, involving many different individuals, pressure groups, organisations and political actors – both now and in the past. This decentralises power
- Discuss the relationship between everyday politics and cultural norms. you will see how political change often grows out of cultural change and that everyday activities create new structures and norms to which policy has to respond
- Understand that strong, pluralist democracies rely on social capital – active and vibrant civil society participation in formal and informal community place-shaping
- Outline the many different ways that people are able to create change in the UK, both individually and collectively. You should also have a better understanding of the relationship between change and power and the degree to which some individuals or groups are able to effect more change than others

Introduction

This chapter is about political change. Perhaps one of the most obvious ways that we visualise this is by parliaments in Westminster, Holyrood, Cardiff and Stormont making decisions to make new laws, adapt old ones or implement strategies to take UK nations in directions that governments and voters feel are important. For example, in December 2022 the Welsh Parliament updated its Net Zero Wales carbon reduction strategic plan to get Wales Net Zero by 2050. This didn't happen purely because members of the Welsh Senedd decided in a linear, top-down way that carbon reduction is an important policy area. Neither were they being solely influenced by global governance norms such as those around the United Nations Climate Conferences (the COP meetings) and/or the G7 meetings of the leaders of the richest nations. They were also responding to calls and campaigns from wider civil society, including the groups and individuals who gathered in Cardiff in November 2022 to call for climate justice (BBC, 2022). Parliamentarians are not the only actors in policymaking, and we are going to see in this chapter how the landscape around political change is much more complex, interactive and accessible to persons who are not politicians than this. Policy change involves a plurality of different individuals, groups and organisations right the way through the body politic.

We will see in this chapter that there are complex feedback loops between the attitudes, values and beliefs that we hold and share as part of our everyday lives, the pursuit of the things that matter to us, and the policies which become codified in our formal political institutions. In some respects, they are inseparable. We will explore how political norm-making extends right the way through civil society, into the things that we do in our everyday lives.

This shapes the values on which local and national policy is based and governments are elected. In other words, we are making the argument that representative democracy relies on an active civil society, which shares its needs and concerns with political representatives in many different ways, from engaging in the political process to creating and shaping societal norms.

The chapter is structured around three of five key take-home points. The first is around *governance*. Here, we show that policy change is complex, involving many different individuals, pressure groups, organisations and political actors. This activity has an important *temporal* element too as political ideas are historically contextualised and produced. Previous formal and informal political activity directly affects how present-day campaigns are received. It also highlights that power is not only contained in government bodies but is dispersed throughout society.

Our second take-home point relates to *everyday politics and cultural norms*. Here we will explore the ways that our interests and daily activities can become entry points into political campaigning. We will use the concept of affect to discuss the ways that political change often grows out of cultural change, and everyday activities can end up creating new structures and norms to which policy has to respond. This helps us to visualise how political change not only comes from formal campaigning at a local or national level, but extends to norm-making and norm-shaping, which happen at the level of everyday activities in which people participate.

In the third section, we will explore *the role of social capital in developing a strong pluralist society*. We will define what social capital is and explore the close link between it and the concept of pluralism. Drawing on Robert Putnam's seminal work in *Bowling Alone* (2000), we consider the role that a vibrant and active civil society has on formal and informal community place-shaping and thereby on local and national democracy.

A thread running through this chapter brings us to our fourth take-home point, that *there are many different ways of engaging in political participation in the UK*, formally and informally. However, we will also observe that social and cultural norms and inequalities of power can inhibit the impact that we might have.

Finally, relating to our fifth take-home point, we ask how plural the UK is from the perspectives outlined above. This concluding section will make the argument that whilst there are many different ways that individuals and groups can shape our civil society, we need to understand more about the extent to which different individuals and groups are able to be heard and listened to.

Governance

Governance is a word that you will often hear during your political studies. We define it here and consider the different organisations and institutions, meanings, values and ideas that constitute governance in the UK. To understand its complexity, we will present governance as an assemblage. Next, we look at pressure groups, exploring the role that they have in helping to shape UK governance, the connections between pressure groups and members of the public, and the tools and methods they might use. Finally, we examine the role of local governance in creating political change.

Usually we end defining governance against government. Briefly, 'government' refers to circumstances in which the state is the most important actor for making decisions and implementing policy. However, in Chapter 1 we set out the conceptual background that argues that although the state and the government are important actors, there are also many other organisations which feed in to how a country is managed and run. Central government might be the space where (final) decisions, or laws, are made, but many other individuals and organisations throughout civil society contribute to government decisions (Bevir, 2012a; Considine, 2002; Pierre and Peters, 2020; Stoker, 1998). We describe the complex and dynamic policy networks of pressure groups, public–private partnerships, business interests, media, NGOs and charities that input into government decisions as 'governance'. Governance actors all help to shape the environment within which government is able to act.

Case study: Plastic pollution, policy and time

In autumn 2017 BBC broadcaster David Attenborough's *Blue Planet* TV series lit a touch paper about plastic pollution in the world's oceans. A cascade of national and local media, pressure groups, NGOs, charities and the general public began to campaign against single-use plastics. Member of the Scottish Parliament Kate Forbes started the 'Final Straw' campaign, working with businesses to end their use of disposable plastics (Hopkins, 2018). Such was the wave of popular feeling, 'affective economy' or 'resonance machine' about the topic (see Theory box below) that institutions such as the Church of England and the late Queen supported the measure, and giant multinational corporations such as McDonalds banned plastic straws. In reporting this, the *New York Times* noted that the UK had 'turned against' plastic (Tsang, 2018). However, the policy process moves more slowly than civil society. The deliberative nature of UK policy meant that it would be 18 months before a ban would be announced (Harvey, 2019) and a further 18 months before that ban would come into force (Friends of the Earth, 2020). In all, it would take three years from the emergence of a broad civil society consensus about plastic and the enactment of this consensus in law.

Formal and informal governance institutions reflect the culture out of which they were formed (Thomson, 2019). Key questions about governance ask whether government is in control of shaping governance processes or is sidelined by the networks of governance (Sorensen and Torfing, 2007), and what the connections are between governance, people and community organising (Wills, 2023). This reminds us of debates about power that we first encountered in Chapter 1, namely, that the 'new localism' that has grown out of a resurgence of populism has helped to create powerful local networks that sustain significant pressure on government actors (Katz and Nowak, 2018).

In short, the concept of governance overlays with the type of pluralist radical democracy that we considered in Chapter 1, and the 'assembled interconnectivities' of Connolly's

(2005) pluralism. The concept of the assemblage adds much here to our understanding of the networks of governance, offering explanations and examinations of the ways in which ideas, cultural attitudes, values and meanings transfer (see Ahmed, 2004) or flow between and amongst connected actors. To illustrate, if we were to take the example of plastic pollution in the text box above, we would spot the development of a 'governance regime' of media, scientists, civil society, pressure groups, NGOs and charities. This is also an 'assemblage' (see Chapter 1) of actors, which is bound together around a particular campaign issue, and as such has the capacity to affect or impact each other in many different ways. For example, journalists covering plastic pollution will also readily 'plug in' or connect to assembled networks around the wider media, being able to share information back and forth through these connections. Consequently, media assemblages will have access to knowledge about emerging cultures and norms around the plastic pollution governance assemblage, and governance assemblages can share the 'affective economies' creating a sense of shared values with the wider media. The concept of the assemblage helps us to understand the impact of histories, legacies and meanings that create the cultural environments in which actors within assemblages operate. Examining policymaking and governance in this way helps us to understand and appreciate the complex and tangled connections, meanings and relationships that form the policy process.

Pressure groups

There are many pressure groups, covering many different topics. They operate at a range of different levels of government/governance. They work in different ways and request a variety of forms of engagement from the public. Some encourage volunteers to join them or ask for donations to support their campaigns and their day-to-day running costs. Some urge supporters to contact local or national elected representatives, become involved in community action, or help to raise awareness through connecting with schools, businesses or community events (Grant, 2000; Watts, 2007). The balance of supporter involvement varies between groups. For example, at the time of writing the Wildlife Fund for Nature encourages participation largely through fundraising. Supporters are asked to donate money, become a member or adopt an animal. From the money raised, the pressure group will campaign and take part in conservation efforts on their supporters' behalf. Supporters are not asked to be actively involved. Some pressure groups such as the Royal Institution of Chartered Surveyors are industry associations, campaigning on behalf of members to help to create the kind of environment in which the industry can flourish. Within the academic discipline of politics, our learned society, the Political Studies Association, also acts as a pressure group helping to create and maintain vibrant conditions for the study of politics.

Pressure groups vary in size. The Royal Institution of Chartered Surveyors, which claims to have 134,000 'highly qualified trainees and professionals' and 'offices in every significant financial market' (RICS, 2023) is significantly larger, wealthier, has more staff, and therefore has more capacity to make its voice heard than the tiny local group, Beach Guardian. Beach Guardian is staffed entirely by volunteers and driven by the energy of its founders (Beach Guardian, 2023). Therefore, RICS and its assembled members have much more capacity to be able to shape the cultural and political agenda in the UK. However, and as discussed in Chapter 1, power does not necessarily operate mechanically. Small as Beach Guardian is, they are able to collaborate with other, related organisations to increase their visibility and campaigning power. As we will discuss in more depth later in this chapter, particular campaigns or organisations can be amplified by wider cultural interest in their topic. This can mean that specific topics can 'resonate' with the discourses, symbolism, meanings and ideas in the campaign, amplifying their message disproportionately to their size. This does not mean that, for example, a 'reduce plastics' message from small social movements will necessarily outweigh the monied heft of the International Association of Oil and Gas Producers. However, highly interconnected assembled networks of local, national and global campaigners can have an incredible impact, as evidenced by the local, national and global shifts such as the campaign to end slavery in the 19th century, the introduction of votes for women and equality for LGBTQ+ people.

Pressure groups also vary in the means through which they seek change, and the terrain used. For example, the Rivers Trust released a report in 2021 which sought to directly impact government policy, launching at an event which included members of parliament who were involved in Parliament's Environmental Audit Committee and the Department for Environment, Food and Rural Affairs (Defra). This pressure group sought to directly influence central government. Indirectly, they might also work with public bodies such as Natural England and the Environment Agency, which both advise central government and help to deliver its environmental and conservation objectives and policies. Working with or trying to have an impact on public bodies like this, in their advisory capacity, can be another way of trying to reach and impact central government policy. The Scottish Environment Protection Agency, Natural Resources Wales, the Northern Ireland Environment Agency, and NatureScot are key equivalents in the UK's other nations with devolved governments. Campaigners living in Northern Ireland, Scotland or Wales will have the additional option of interacting with their devolved governments and will make decisions about the appropriate level of government to target for particular campaigns and issues (Cairney, 2014).

Local governance and political change

Does this mean that the various other tiers of government are less important for policy-building? Not at all. Despite the hollowing out of local government over successive decades (Institute for Government, 2022), the centre still needs local government in order to receive information about the specific needs and requirements of localities around Britain. In England and the devolved governments, environmental legislation and regulations might be decided at a parliamentary or assembly level; however, they are implemented through the various county, unitary or borough, town and parish councils. Alongside planning *how* to implement government policy, these tiers of government also act as conduits of knowledge and information back up to larger scales of governance. This means that engaging with local government can be an important space for pressure groups of all sizes when trying to bring about policy change in the UK. Of course, through education and expanding the local volunteer base, pressure groups can amplify the number of people willing and able to work with local policymakers.

What practical steps might a campaigner undertake if they have decided that they want to work closely with devolved, local or national government? As an individual, they might write an email to their councillor or parliamentary representative, or visit them in their office. But it is very difficult to persuade them to change their minds and actions on their own. Therefore, it can be more efficient (and sociable) to join with other campaigners – by seeking out, connecting with and participating in pressure groups that are already working in their area of interest, or by starting their own campaign, telling people about the problem and what they can do about it, and encouraging behavioural change. It is also noteworthy how whilst the parliaments in, Holyrood, Cardiff or Westminster and the assembly in Stormont might be constructed as the most important political institutions in UK governance, they are not necessarily the ones where as individuals we can have the most impact or that are the most accessible. In some respects this is where the smallest tiers of government, the town and parish councils if we are lucky enough to have them in our community, are actually the most important 'spaces of opportunity' as we try to make the changes in our localities that we feel are necessary.

Town and parish councils are interesting but frequently overlooked in terms of scholarship and popular culture due to an emphasis on informal, rather than formal, local political participation (e.g. setting up campaign groups to improve local water quality rather than focusing on working with various levels of local councils). Often this is because town and parish councils are characterised and imagined in very uncomplimentary ways as being old fashioned or 'cliquey', with little impetus to address community wants and needs (Willett and Cruxon, 2019). However, between 2010 and 2020 local government funding was cut by 63 per cent in real terms (Institute for Government, 2022), and so local authorities have sought to divest themselves of some obligations by asking town and parish councils to take on additional responsibilities. This was facilitated by the Localism Act 2011, which allowed suitably qualified councils to manage additional local amenities (Wills, 2016). For some campaigners, engaging with town and parish councils can be an important way of addressing a topic locally. If we take our example around water quality and the environment, towns and parishes have a considerable interest in ensuring that the natural environment in their locality is clean and well managed. Additionally, some localities have taken proactive steps to make themselves more inclusive, representative and accessible to a wider proportion of the population. The 'Flatpack Democracy' (MacFadyen, 2017) 'takeover' of Frome Town Council is one example. In 2011 an organised group of independent (i.e. not aligned to a political party) councillors took 10 of the 17 council seats. Through a programme of civic pride and non-adversarial politics, they had increased voter engagement by 75 per cent between 2007 and 2011 (Burnett and Nunes, 2021). The idea behind this kind of initiative is about creating the kinds of spaces where individuals and pressure groups can get involved and make changes locally, with and through town and parish councils.

Everyday politics and cultural norms

In this section we draw connections between the cultural norms and political change. One of the arguments that threads through this chapter is that we contribute to political changes through the things that we do in our everyday lives. But is this a rather optimistic assumption?

> **Need to know: Cultural change – a process or an event?**
>
> Many of us who have been involved in political campaigning will feel disheartened sometimes that change does not happen quickly enough. Indeed, it was over 136 years following publication of Mary Wollestonecraft's Vindication *on the Rights of Women* in 1792 that women got the vote on the same terms as men (in 1928), which must have been incredibly frustrating for Suffragettes. The Committee for Womens Suffrage was formed in Manchester in 1867 and, frustrated by the slow pace of change, Emmeline Pankhurst began the group that would become known as the Suffragettes in 1903. Nearly a hundred years after getting the vote, women are still not treated equally to men. They tend to be paid less (Sneider et al., 2021) and were more vulnerable during the Covid-19 pandemic (Smith et al., 2021). There are many different factors which impact on the length of the process leading to legislative change. Flinders and Lowery (2023) argue that there were four important factors in the 25-year campaign to end tax on menstrual products: 1) the issue-attention cycle; 2) the balance between domestic pressures and international obligations; 3) trying to appease campaigners with a degree of incremental change; 4) co-option of the topic by a campaign which touched a UK-wide nerve (the campaign to leave the EU). We might add emerging global norms to the kinds of influences that affect policy change. The point is that the actual policy change is the final moment of an often (very) long process.

Until this point, we have been making the assumption that ultimately, political campaigners, at what-ever level and scale, seek to bring about policy changes. Here we will talk a lot about the role of cultural 'norms' in policy questions. By this we mean the informal cultural rules to which people in a particular culture tend to conform, impacting individual action and social interaction (Hechter and Opp, 2001). Marmor (2009) describes norms as 'social conventions', which regulate behaviour. Group behavioural norms operate on many different scales, from small subcultures to the international community and might be enforced through mechanisms varying from informal rules upheld by varying levels of social stigmatisation, through to formal rules created by government and upheld in law (see Marmor, 2009). For example, in the UK there was never a law stating that it was illegal to have a child outside of marriage. However, the social stigma attached to being an unmarried mother (or the family of one) was so great that without significant family support it was extremely difficult for unmarried mothers to get adequate work or housing (Page, 2015). Therefore, the real threat of cultural exclusion acted as a regulatory mechanism for behaviour. This also meant that many unmarried women had to go to extreme lengths in the event of pregnancy, which had wider societal ripples of implications and affects. Chapter 4 explored the ways in which cultural norms and their associated rules of behaviour create structural exclusions which make it much harder for some groups to engage in civil society and (help to) create the changes that they need.

Some societal norms are deemed so abhorrent and troubling to a given culture that they are criminialised and sanctioned by the state. A frequently given example of this is murder, which is considered so contrary to societal norms that it is illegal globally. However, deviance from norms is culturally produced and some state-sanctioned norms change over time (Anderson, 2017; Foucault, 1995). A good example here relates to homosexuality, which in the UK was illegal until 1967. Now, because of the extent to which culture has changed, this seems absurd. Foucault discusses the impact of societal norms and conventions as a 'technique on the self', through which individuals come to self-regulate behaviours. In fact, he makes the claim that in industrial societies, the state is able to extend its reach into an individual's everyday life through the ways in which people self-regulate their behaviours according to real or imagined societal norms and conventions. This is not always a bad thing, and means that the state can encourage necessary changes to societal norms. However, at other times individuals may wish to challenge dominant norms, and Foucault argues that it is in this realm of the everyday that this kind of power can be resisted (Foucault, 1998). In other words, the micropolitics of everyday life are a crucial space for shaping societal attitudes and the larger governance apparatus which rests on them.

The fact that norms change is important for politics because it means that culture and politics are tightly interrelated. Political activity can shift the norms on which our formal and informal societal rules are based, and our rules that have been formalised by government (our laws) can shift our attitudes. For example when smoking in indoor public spaces was banned across the UK by mid-2007, there had been some scepticism that the public would consent to such measures (and so uphold the rule); however, in the event 97 per cent of premises complied with the law, prompting a significant shift in societal norms around smoking (Davis, 2007). This means that culture (and 'lifestyle') is an intensely political space, in many different ways, which we will explore in more depth below. For example, Haenfler (2019) discusses the abstinence campaigns in the US as being a 'lifestyle movement', whereby activists sought to influence wider cultural change by encouraging people to adopt a different lifestyle. This encourages us to consider whether cultural change creates, or is shaped by, policy, or whether the interaction between policy and culture is more entangled than this, involving norm making, and norm shaping, in our everyday lives. This brings us back to micropolitics. Next, we are going to look at both sides of this coin. Firstly, we will explore the ways in which individuals can become politicised through everyday activities that one might not associate with politics. Finally, we will consider the micropolitics of creating cultural and behaviour change in more depth.

From the everyday to political activism

Whilst we might not imagine our everyday activities to be political, our everyday experiences can be deeply politicising in ways that might surprise us, and even if we don't consider ourselves to be politically minded. For example, surfers are not well known for their political activism. In fact, more frequently they are imagined as self-regarding hedonistic thrill-seekers, known for partying hard, and dominated by an obsession with wave-riding (Wheaton, 2006). However, in the 1980s and 1990s, some surfers in North Cornwall were sick of the raw sewage being routinely released into the seas, near their local breaks. Sewage made surfing quite unpleasant, and many surfers got very unwell. Water companies were privatised in 1989, and in 1991, the Urban Wastewater Treatment Directive provided a legislative framework through

106 • Institutions

Image 5.2 Sometimes, our leisure pursuits and interests alert us to important issues that we feel need to be changed. Surfers Against Sewage are a good example of this, taking a local issue, building a UK-wide network, and working with government at all levels to change policy.

© Photo by JMundy on Shutterstock

which a campaign group could shape, influence and drive efforts to clean up the seas. The pressure group Surfers Against Sewage was born against this backdrop, and an apolitical pass-time led to a highly successful UK-wide campaign organisation.

Perhaps we could construe this issue as only relevant to the Cornish surfing community rather than having a UK-wide appeal. However, it is a wider environmental problem that also affects many other water users, in many other parts of the world, with whom Surfers Against Sewage (SAS) were able to join forces.

Wheaton (2006) describes this as being in the framework of identity-based politics, where through a common interest, passtime or identification, surfers and national and transnational activists were able to join forces to amplify and globalise their call for ocean pollution reduction measures, creating meaningful policy changes at a national and international level. Something else that is interesting in this everyday politics story is the way that the organisation has been able to broaden its identity-based appal and expand its supporter base. In other words, SAS campaigners have been able to assemble surfers in Cornwall and connect them with a much bigger group of assembled water users in the UK and overseas.

Through such collective action and building of shared meanings, values and goals, and being connected to each other, they have been able to amplify their impacts significantly. Another way of describing these processes would be 'hegemony', a Gramscian term describing coalitions building around shared goals or identities (Hall, 2017; Williams, 2019). For example, SAS's Safer Seas and Rivers app is used by recreational swimmers, kayakers and paddle-boarders, drawing other water-users into key campaigns, raising awareness and mobilising political activity around water quality. By starting up the Protect Our Waves all party parliamentary group, SAS folded parliamentarians into this assemblage, raising awareness and driving the Westminster parliamentary agenda that grew into the 2022 Environment Act (which replaced environmental legislation that was lost when the UK left the European Union). Surfers Against Sewage demonstrate how from apparently very local origins around a local lifestyle problem (and their head office is still in North Cornwall), connecting with wider identity politics movements, a person or group can still find themselves trying to shape policy at the heart of central government.

What does this tell us? Sometimes, our activities, hobbies, and passtimes provide us with a unique position through which to view the world and the things in it that are important. Would an elected representative from an urban area know that ocean pollution was an issue that matters? Possibly not. The different perspectives through which we view the world, and the different experiences that our everyday activities provide us with, help to enrich the terrain about the things that matter. Furthermore, *because* our activities matter so deeply to us, we are more energised to campaign for them, amplifying our efforts further, assembling the networks, connections and broader cultural environment that recognise a problem and support efforts to find solutions. Following Connolly's (2005) version of pluralism (see Chapter 1), this also helps create and shape the values system within which movements to create political change operate. Next, we will look at culture and political change in more depth. The Theory box below will help you to understand the psychological processes underpinning this movement.

Theory box: What is affect?

Affect has its roots in the atomism of Ancient Greece and comes to us through philosophers such as Spinoza (*Ethics*, 1996 [1677]) and Deleuze and Guattari (2004) (*A Thousand Plateaus*). Quite literally, it refers to the impact that things have on other things. When a body collides with another body, it changes it, altering its course of action. This change might be minimal or it might be profound, disproportionate to the size of the initial impact. Here it is useful to think of affective impact as (potentially) amplificatory. Some things can act as a kind of 'trampoline', amplifying the impact and creating large and widespread affects (Connolly, 2002). If we think of this in terms of ideas, sometimes the affective impact of a thought, meaning, word or sentence resonates (see Connolly, 2008) with the collective mood at the time, acting as a trigger or catalyst for a much bigger change – such as David Attenborough's *Blue Planet*, and the campaign against plastic pollution. Other times, words, ideas and actions literally 'fall on closed ears'. By the time that the point of amplificatory resonance occurs, campaigners (in this instance about single use plastics) may have been trying to affect public opinion and culture for many years, in a cultural environment which accepted the increasing disposability of consumer products.

This introduces us to the temporal aspect of affect, and the impact of memory. Borrowing from the philosopher Henri Bergson (2004), our perceptions of things that we encounter are overlaid – or cloaked – by previous memories, knowledge and ideas. In the example that we have been working with, our attitudes towards plastic are overlaid by a symbolic cultural repertoire whereby using single-use plastics is a normal part of life, embedded in everyday practices. We might say that it has become part of an 'affective economy' whereby mutually reinforcing ideas, values, practices, institutions and capital economies further disperse these embedded knowledge and practices (Clough, 2010).

Sometimes disparate values, meanings and concepts can be joined together through shared collective meanings. As Sarah Ahmed (2004) illustrates with regard to migration, this

(Continued)

can create stories whereby unease with immigration can transfer to a narrative whereby the 'nation' is being penetrated or invaded. Both of these words carry their own affective repertoires of meaning, which through the perpetual movement of the affective economy that it is a part of, facilitates the overall discourse to slide into a desire or need to 'protect' the nation which has become constructed as under threat. New affective feedback loops become created which help to reproduce, adapt and amplify these narratives (Boler and Davis, 2018). Connolly (2008) calls these amplificatory affective economies 'resonance machines' (see Case study above).

The difficulty that campaigners face is that on an individual and collective level, affective economies of meaning are deeply culturally embedded (Feola, 2016). Ideas are much more likely to resonate and amplify if people who receive campaign messages are familiar with and agree with the messages that they receive. Conversely, ideas which are very different to my own embedded cultural economies are going to be much more difficult for me to receive and will take time before a campaign might eventually be able to find or build a point of resonance through which I might be happy to change my thoughts and behaviour.

Cultural change and micropolitics

Is telling my story a political act? Gabriel (2016) would say, yes. Firstly, culture never stays the same, but is fluid and mobile, adapting to a range of political, socio-cultural and economic factors. Consequently, telling stories about diverse lives and lived experiences can challenge stereotypes, prejudice and discrimination, and contribute to more egalitarian knowledge, practices and policy. It also introduces us more fully to the micropolitics of governance assemblages that we explored above, and which shape, and are shaped by, policy. In short, the way that we choose to live our lives is a deeply political act which contributes to how an identity, value or practice is perceived by the wider community. Over time this helps to create an affective landscape whereby practices and attitudes that once seemed 'different' become normalised, sometimes producing significant attitudinal and cultural shifts.

For example, Fish et al. (2018) discuss how important it was for members of the LGBTQ+ community to be able to live their authentic lives in order to make the enormous societal attitudinal changes required for the transformation from criminalised other to fully participating members of the wider community. This was not just about the relationship between visibility and wider acceptability, it was also about how making oneself visible can facilitate building or expanding the social bonds, friendships and/or networks which could galvanise collective action and the capacity of campaigners around LGBTQ+ issues (Fish et al., 2018). The concept of affect (see Theory box above) helps us to understand how this shapes and changes attitudinal norms and values, providing spaces and feedback loops for newly visible lifestyles to reverberate and entangle with wider culture (see also Connolly, 2005). Fish et al. (2018) believe that for the LGBTQ+ community, this micro-political activity was as effective, if not more, than what they call the 'iconic' activism of high-profile events, creating the cultural changes through which 'iconic' activism could gain more affective purchase, capturing the public imagination.

Whilst such cultural, micropolitical shifts can be exciting, some people can also experience them as frightening, and can find that they have become culturally 'left behind' as societal attitudes, values and norms have shifted over time. This can be bewildering for people as they find that ideas that were once considered mainstream are no longer acceptable. Ford and Goodwin (2014) attribute this sense of dislocation to the rise of the UK Independence Party (UKIP), whereby *resistance* to cultural change created its own political movement. For some political analysts the feeling of being left behind from mainstream political culture underpinned the vote to leave the European Union in 2016 (Ashcroft and Bevir, 2021). Dorling and Tomlinson (2020) go a step further, arguing that the vote to Leave was a last gasp of misplaced nostalgia for the British Empire. One of the interesting things about Dorling and Tomlinson's argument is that they suggest that the (highly selective) meanings, knowledge and institutions around empire, which although an inaccurate reading of the present, provided a sense of certainty in an uncertain world. The salience of phrases such as 'take back control' in the Leave campaign (Cutts et al., 2017) hints to us how discombobulating and fearful it can be to find oneself newly on the outside of mainstream culture.

In many respects, this takes us back to the importance of a radical pluralist society in order to try to ensure that all sections of the polity feel listened to and heard. This becomes a complicated set of debates, ranging from the position taken by Ashcroft and Bevir (2016), which argues that the UK needs to embrace more effectively the diversity of cultures out of which Britain is assembled, to that taken by Goodwin (2023). Sometimes, these polar opposite perspectives intersect around the claim that 'important parts of UK civil society are feeling unseen and unheard', by out-of-touch political elites. Goodwin describes a conservative position which feels that the liberal elite dominating so-called 'progressive' identity politics *also* overlooks its unease at the rapid pace of societal change. Their response is conversely to call for *less* pluralism as a means of slowing societal change to a more manageable rate.

It is important to also recognise that micropolitics can be (and is) a tool through which central government can seek to create the types of cultural changes that it feels are desirable. For example, as prime minister, David Cameron introduced a 'Nudge Unit' (now called the Behavioural Insights Team) to try to shape people's attitudes and behaviours towards those that are more conducive to a cohesive society (John, 2013). For some scholars, this raises questions about the extent of state control on the lives of the individual (Cromby and Willis, 2014). However (and as we have a hint at from our Brexit example above), creating cultural change is not as simple and straightforward as some of our examples might seem, and we turn to this in the next section.

Creating cultural change

A key problem for movements trying to create the kinds of cultural shifts required to initiate the types of political changes that they feel are important is what we call the 'value–attitude gap'. We explore this below, asking how the concept of the assemblage can better help us to understand the social processes underpinning political change. This helps us to understand that creating change is not just about pulling certain mechanical levers to induce people to act and think differently, but is much more complex, involving the wider cultural context within which people are situated.

Quite literally, the value–attitude gap shows us that it is not enough to simply 'educate' people about a particular set of abuses, issues or problems, because people do not always (or often) act in accordance with the knowledge that they have obtained and the beliefs and values that they hold dear (Lucas et al., 2008; Peattie and Peattie, 2009). One way of closing this gap is to try to create a consumer culture whereby 'good' behaviours are constructed as being a choice which was connected to an assembled affective constellation of meanings around affluence or status, encouraging the selection of 'good' choices as a means to signify 'status' (Hurth, 2010). This introduces us to the idea that behaviour is not simply something that the individual does in isolation, but it is culturally produced with reference to other people in our worlds, and in relation to our 'feelings' about something. In other words, an individual's behaviour is part of an affective economy that is sustained and reinforced by the meanings that we attach to things and ideas, in the cultural assemblages in which we participate. The problem with Hurth's (2010) approach in terms of a pluralist politics of the everyday is that to construct a set of symbolic meanings which connect 'good' choices with wealth and status means that favourable choices carry a cost premium, taking them out of reach of those who have to be more cost conscious. Consequently, this is not a policy or campaign option which is widely inclusive.

Affect – or people's feelings, attitudes and emotions – is a useful tool in order to shape (or 'nudge') individual and cultural everyday choices, in order to change societal norms by trying to fuse particular behaviours with particular emotional responses. For example, mobilising fear can be a useful campaign strategy, although relying too heavily on this can paralyse people into inaction, and too little does not induce any behaviour change at all (Van Cappellen et al., 2018). Connecting desired behavioural changes with positive affects can also be a useful tool (O'Donnel, 2017). However, chiming with some of the literature about pressure groups and everyday politics, some of the strongest and more long-lasting behavioural changes happen when they are internalised and embedded into an individual's lifestyle, engendering a stronger emotional investment to the practice (Burke et al., 2018). In other words, and echoing Gabriel (2016) and Fish et al. (2018), in order to create a long-lasting cultural shift, behavioural change needs to be culturally embedded in one's lifestyle, situating these practices within a supportive cultural milieu of sympathetic symbolic meanings, beliefs and values.

In short, the people that an individual is around, and the kinds of experiences, attitudes, institutions and processes that they encounter, has a significant effect on the way that people are able to embed new practices and lifestyles into their worlds. Being located within a mutually supportive network or environment helps individuals to co-create and 'activate' new sets of values, exploring how to fit new norms within their lives, learn and gain fluency with new affective languages around the cultural change with which they are involved (Hackney et al., 2021; West et al., 2021; Willett et al., 2022).

Case study: Feedback loops between culture and politics

In this re-telling of the sustainable clothing story, we see the centre of gravity, or mobilising force, beginning with a constellation of charities and NGO's – organised bodies of people that coalesce around an issue or a topic that matters to them. These assembled UK-based and international bodies were then able to act as national and international pressure groups on government and business. They also responded to a consumer desire for clothing suppliers attuned to their ethical values, developing what Deleuze and Guattari (2004) would call a 'line of flight' – a connected-but-different set of ideas around which people, institutions, values, practices and objects assemble and coalesce. In the next phase, sustainable clothing assemblages evolved and adapted, spotting a space of opportunity around central government interest (represented by Defra), which is then able to incorporate much of the wider clothing industry in the UK.

Government interest provided significant 'life-force' to sustainable clothing campaigns, when in 2018 the House of Commons Environmental Audit Committee took an interest, launching its Fixing fashion: Clothing consumption and sustainability inquiry. This drew together fashion companies (Asda and Boohoo), industry bodies (the British Retail Consortium and the Institution of Mechanical Engineers), NGO's (Fashion Revolution, Friends of the Earth, and Facebook-based Waste Not, Want Not), as well as academics studying many different aspects of the problem.

This time, however, the knowledge discussed spilled back out into popular culture through the conduit of the media, once again dispersing knowledge around the hidden side of the fashion industry. Many different news outlets, from broadsheets, to tabloids, to television watch out for parliamentary inquiries that will resonate with their readers. During the Inquiry, news interest kept the story 'live' in popular attention. For example, presenter Stacy Dooley reinvigorated her TV work around fashion's 'dirty secrets', reaching an even wider audience than she had previously. This kept the affective economy (see Ahmed, 2004) around sustainable clothing mobile, active and alive, dispersing knowledge and practices far more broadly. Sustained media interest indicates that culturally the issue continues to resonate, and although we don't know the extent to which people have put into practice the issues that they are hearing, it does mean that the ideas are still available to act as a catalyst or trigger for wider change.

However, the decision of Theresa May's Conservative government not to implement the recommendations from the *Fixing Fashion* report (such as the 1p per item 'fast fashion tax') might indicate that she felt that there was not sufficient impetus amongst her supporter-base to create formal rules around the topic. However, public interest and pressure group campaigning *have* managed to keep the topic on the agenda of various government organisations, highlighting both the importance of governance for creating change, but also the importance of public pressure and everyday norm and culture building over issues which matter.

Social capital: Strong, pluralist local democracy

So far, our emphasis in this chapter has been on exploring what political change is and the spaces through which individuals and groups can create change in our assembled communities. In the closing pages we are going to reflect a little on the utility of a strong, pluralist, local democracy – or why strong citizen engagement in our localities matters. By this, of course, we are not only thinking about people being part of local councils, we are also thinking about how people are mobilised through their experiences to try to make some important changes in their community to help to make it work better.

Spotlight on research: Robert Putnam and social capital

The predominant way of discussing many of the questions that we have been addressing in this chapter is through the concept of social capital, which Robert Putnam develops in *Bowling Alone* (2000). Putnam argues that civic participation – being part of community groups and organisations (including the apparently non-political sports clubs indicated in the book title) facilitates regular interaction and norms of reciprocity with other people which in turn make individuals more empathetic, tolerant and less cynical. They build trust and trustworthiness between us, which in turn 'greases the wheels to allow communities to advance smoothly' (Putnam, 2000: 288). This trust makes social and business transactions less costly as then you don't have to employ enforcement mechanisms. The social capital that we develop through our networks and interactions 'serve as conduits for the flow of helpful information that facilitates achieving our goal' (p. 281), optimising the other kinds of capital (i.e. human and financial) that we have in our communities. On the flip side, *not* being part of trust-bonded social networks means that people *don't* get involved in their communities, and therefore become apathetic, failing to build cohesive societal norms. In short, Putnam is arguing that being a part of groups and associations is important not only for the political health of our communities but also for our economic health. This latter insight was extremely popular in economic development studies in the early 2000s in particular (e.g. Atterton, 2007).

In making these claims about the utility of community participation for our politics, Putnam was picking up a baton that originated in Tocqueville's *Democracy in America* (1840). Tocqueville was noting through observations that participation in civic associations is a cornerstone of democracy and democratic engagement, developing people and communities through reciprocal action. Later scholars have asked the question of whether participation in our communities really *does* improve political participation. On the one hand, it can improve the skills that can help in more effective political participation (Freise and Hallmann, 2014; Gutmann, 1998). However, there is also the risk that persons who join community associations are more likely to be politically minded themselves, and therefore it would be *expected* that more vigorous and lively community associations, and a vibrant participatory democracy would be connected (Fung, 2003; Van Ingen and van der Meer, 2016). Indeed, using longitudinal data from the British Household Survey, Binder (2021) finds that there is a correlation.

Not entirely dissimilar to our Surfers Against Sewage example (Wheaton, 2006), Binder also finds that being part of organisational activity can *create* political interest amongst the previously uninterested, depending on the type of associational membership and activity.

We start to see that when Binder (2021) talks about political engagement, he is referring to support for political *parties* rather than making political changes more broadly, so is following a narrower definition of politics than the one that we explore here. But he also finds a link between *type* of associational membership and political party support. Environmental and sports groups seem to be the most likely types of groups that foster political inclinations amongst members. Interestingly, for those of us interested in improving engagement in party politics, Binder's research shows that encouraging people to be part of associations as ways of learning about politics in general, is not the answer to increasing political participation, but instead emphasis should be placed on the personal benefits of association membership, such as individual well-being. In other words, we can't think of creating civic participation and community associations as mechanistic tools to increase political participation. Instead, participation needs to come from feeling invested enough in one's community, such as we see in our Surfers Against Sewage example.

Conclusion

Over the course of this chapter we have come to see that making political change is about *much* more than campaigning for devolved or central government to make new laws. The UK is a representative democracy, but our political representatives need to be provided with information about the many different UKs that people inhabit, and the hopes and concerns and fears that impact us individually or collectively. We might share this information through actively campaigning, or we might share it through the micropolitics of our daily lives and living our authentic selves. We have seen that there is a tight interrelationship between cultural norms (which are basically informal rules) and the laws and regulations to which we are bound formally. In fact, there are (or should be) deep feedback loops between UK culture and government policy. In other words, participating in our communities is vital for a vibrant, pluralist democracy because it creates conduits through which we can share information about the places in which we live and disperse cultural norms, meanings, practices and values. We learned how social groups based around activities and interests might not appear to be political, but they can provide an entry point through which individuals might collectively pursue some form of change. These groups can also be where we learn informally about politics and being political.

Moreover, it is through community groups and community concerns that we can see the things that need changing within our localities, and how we might work with local government and governance institutions in order to make these changes happen. In fact, we learn that the politics of the everyday and the politics in our localities is every bit as important as the politics that plays out on a UK-wide basis. We can also see that the impact of the things that we do at whichever level we operate at can sometimes have a significant and disproportionate impact on politics throughout our communities. In other words, there are lots of potential spaces in which individuals consciously or subconsciously shape the communities of which we are all a part, even if we might not see the fruits of our efforts for some time. Of course, we can better effect political change as part of organised interest, pressure or campaign groups, and some groupings are bigger or more powerful than others. So technically, there are many *potential* spaces around which a vibrant pluralist democracy can exist in the UK. But sometimes cultural norms and political and economic power can create structural exclusions which make it much harder for some individuals and groups to impact policy (see Chapter 4).

Key take-home points

- Making political change is about much more than campaigning for new laws.
- Political change includes changing attitudes, norms and values.
- Our communities help to shape our attitudes, norms and values.
- By being part of communities, we see things that we would like to change.
- It is easier to make change as part of organised groups although we also contribute to political discourse through the micropolitics of living our authentic selves.

Annotated reading list

Gabriel, D. (2016) Blogging while black, British and female: A critical study on discursive activism. *Information, Communication and Society*, 19(11), 1622–1635.

This paper beautifully illustrates the relationships between lifestyle, visibility and culture that we discussed above. Gabriel discusses the ways that Black British women have been able to use blogging as a way of making their marginalised experiences visible and creating powerful counter-narratives that challenge gendered and racialised stereotypes. It encourages us to reflect on the ways in which living one's authentic self is also a political act, and actively sharing our lives helps to disperse important counter-knowledge further.

Beaumont, C. (2017) What do women want? Housewives associations, activism and changing representations of women in the 1950s. *Women's History Review*, 26(1), 147–162.

I love this paper and was really sad not to have been able to include it in the chapter. Keeping with the theme of 'what actually *is* political', Beaumont looks at housewives' associations. There are many useful threads here but the one that I want to emphasise is about the ways that a group that is often imagined as being highly apolitical, clearly was not! Read this piece with Putnam in mind and consider the importance and significance of organising as an interest group to developing social capital, make issues visible and bring about political change in many different spheres.

Thomson, J. (2019) *Abortion Law and Political Institutions: Explaining Policy Resistance*. London: Palgrave Macmillan.

A beautiful examination of (gendered) institutions of multi-level governance, told through a gripping case study of abortion law in Northern Ireland. Thomson highlights for us that governance structures are never objective and value free but are always culturally contextualised.

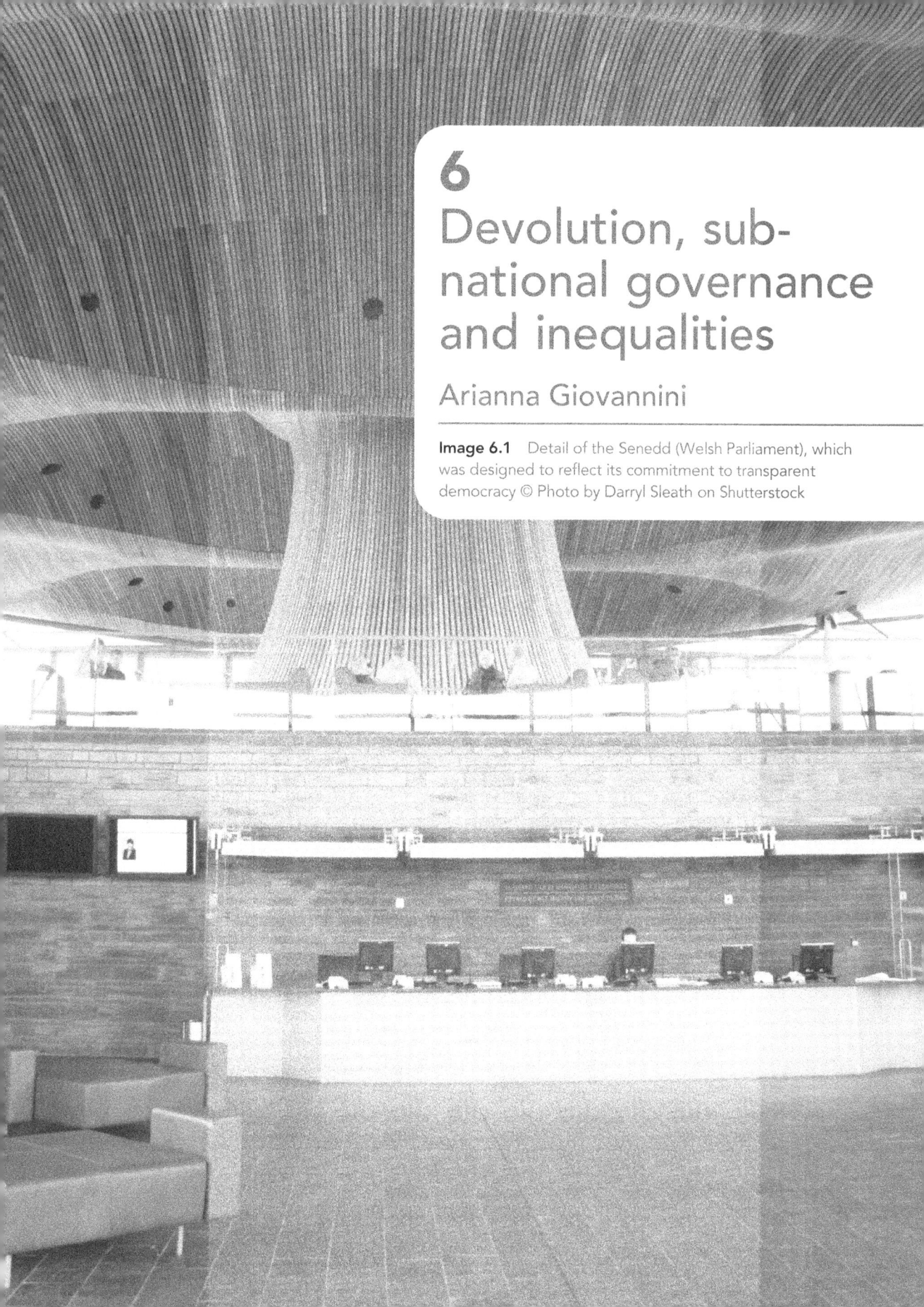

6
Devolution, sub-national governance and inequalities

Arianna Giovannini

Image 6.1 Detail of the Senedd (Welsh Parliament), which was designed to reflect its commitment to transparent democracy © Photo by Darryl Sleath on Shutterstock

Learning objectives

After reading this chapter, you should be able to:

- Have an understanding of key concepts and theories that help explain devolution and centre-periphery relations in the UK
- Have an overview of how local government and devolution have developed across the UK nations and regions
- Have a critical understanding of how centralisation of power impacts on democratic and socioeconomic inequalities, and the implications this has on current political dynamics

Introduction

This chapter takes a critical look at the process of devolution in the UK and at the state of sub-national governance across the country, linking these debates to issues concerning democratic and socioeconomic inequalities. Building on the content of Chapter 2, this will help you to understand the complex nature of multi-level governance in the UK and how this impacts on disparities between (and within) its nations and regions. To achieve this, the chapter considers what devolution is and how it fits within the UK constitutional setting as well as the wider system of multi-level governance; it draws on this to assess the state of local government across the UK and how devolution is evolving in each of the four UK nations; and it concludes with a critical reflection on the democratic and socioeconomic inequalities that stem from these dynamics.

Framing and key concepts: What is devolution?

Before we start our analysis, it is useful to clarify the key concepts as well as the broader context that frames this chapter's discussion. As explained in Chapter 2, the UK's uncodified constitution, with the supremacy of the Westminster parliament as its key principle, tends to produce a model of government where power is highly concentrated at the centre. For a long time, it was the central state that took the main strategic policy decisions that affected the whole country, especially for what concerned matters of 'high politics' such as foreign affairs or the economy (Bulpitt, 2008). In this context, sub-national bodies such as local and regional governments enjoyed some degree of autonomy as the central state offloaded territorial matters ('low politics' in Bulpitt's terms – i.e. local matters that were considered to be less important and thus left to 'the peripheries') to local elites. But from the 1970s onwards local autonomy has been incrementally eroded, re-centralising powers and leaving local authorities mainly to play the role of implementing on the ground policy decisions taken in London by the central state and delivering key services (Barnett et al., 2021). The inception of devolution from the 1990s onwards has (re)opened a debate on sub-national governance and has challenged this settlement in a profound way by altering the vertical distribution of power between the centre and new territorial institutions that have been created in the four nations of the UK.

But what exactly is devolution? And how does it work in the UK? Devolution can be described as a process whereby the UK Parliament (Westminster) transfers *some* of its powers to other representative bodies that operate at a territorial level below the central state (i.e. devolved parliaments in Scotland, Wales and Northern Ireland, and regional bodies in England). These institutions, however, remain subordinated to the parliament in London. Thus, through devolution Westminster does not relinquish its supremacy and maintains (at least in theory) the ability to unilaterally take back the competences it has passed down to national or regional bodies (Bogdanor, 2001; Torrance, 2022a).

Devolution can take many forms, depending on the power and resources transferred from the centre:

- *Administrative devolution* is the process by which the centre continues to take strategic decisions on policy matters, with devolved/local bodies taking on responsibilities for their implementation. In practice, administrative devolution involves the transfer of some responsibilities to territorial departments of the same government (Torrance, 2022a), with the aim of improving the effectiveness and efficiency of the territorial administration of the state but the main frameworks and standards remain, however, set by the centre.
- *Executive devolution* is the process by which power is transferred from the centre to enable policy decisions to be made by an elected executive at devolved level. In this case, the devolved bodies have, typically, only secondary legislation powers on devolved matters, while primary legislation remains a preserve of the centre.
- *Legislative devolution* is the process by which the centre transfers power to make direct law on a set of specific devolved matters to directly elected devolved institutions. The range of powers transferred is still set by the centre but devolved bodies have autonomy (in terms of legislation and implementation) over these.
- *Fiscal devolution* is the process by which the centre transfers taxing and spending powers on specific matters to directly elected devolved institutions. The degree of fiscal devolution will depend on the number of resources passed down from the centre and the autonomy in managing such resources given to devolved bodies.

In the UK, there is a system of 'asymmetric devolution', which means that devolved institutions across the country's four nations have been granted different forms of devolution, holding different degrees of autonomy, clout and resources. As we will discuss in more detail later in this chapter, since 1997 Scotland has gained legislative devolution, with the ability to raise its own taxation. In the same year, Wales gained executive devolution, but this changed to legislative devolution from 2007. From 1998, Northern Ireland also gained legislative devolution, although its devolved assembly has been suspended, with Westminster exercising direct rule on several occasions. Of the four nations of the UK, England is alone in having only a weak form of decentralisation. (For a full account of these processes, see Torrance, 2022a).

For now, it is important to note that the inception of devolution has created a very diversified system of power distribution across the UK nations. Devolving power, or adopting an asymmetric system of power distribution, is not unusual in other countries across Europe. For example, Italy and Spain have asymmetric regional governments (i.e. they are organised respectively into 20 and 17 regions, but not all of them have the same powers and responsibilities), while Germany has a fully federal system (organised into 16 *länders*, i.e. regional states). What makes the UK system stand out is the fact that it lacks a codified constitution (see Chapter 2), and this has repercussions on how power is dispersed across different levels of government. In Italy and Spain, as well as in Germany, the powers and resources available to devolved institutions or federal states are enshrined in the constitution and are therefore protected. This means, first, that the autonomy granted to regional governments cannot be reversed or taken back unilaterally by the central state or by an act of parliament, as is the case in the UK. Any such measure would require a complex process of constitutional reform to be passed. Second, and related to this, the presence of a codified constitution also helps to define and enact the respective scope of central and devolved institutions. Therefore, there is a clear *division* of powers between central and devolved/regional governments/states, and the authority of each of these is *coordinated* and *shared*. This is not the case in the UK: in the absence of a codified constitution, parliamentary sovereignty works as the main guiding principle. Thus, powers are simply *transferred* from the centre to devolved institutions, while supreme authority remains a preserve of Westminster. This means that, ultimately, devolved institutions are a mere product of statute and (at least in theory) devolution is a reversible process (Torrance, 2022a).

This overview helps us to understand the broad meaning and role of devolution in the UK political system, and in the rest of the chapter we will delve into the details of how these processes have developed in the four UK nations. But before we do this, it is important to remember that multi-level governance (see Need to know below) in this country also includes other levels beyond the devolved institutions and the central state. In the next section, we focus on this, starting with local government.

Local government in the UK

Despite rarely being at the centre of public attention, local government plays a vital role in our lives providing key services as well as a crucial democratic role. In England, Scotland and Wales, councils are responsible for functions such as social care, schools, housing, planning and waste collection. In Northern Ireland local government's remit is a bit more limited and councils provide some neighbourhood services such as waste collection and street cleaning but are not responsible for social care or education.

Local government is also the tier of government that operates closer to citizens and is thus the first point of contact between communities and political institutions (Wilson and Game, 2011). And yet few people know or understand in full how local government works and what it is responsible for. One reason that helps explain this is that in the UK multi-level governance, and within it local governance, is very complex (Giovannini, 2021b).

Need to know: Government, governance and multi-level governance

In common parlance, it is easy to use the terms government and governance interchangeably. Yet they have very different meanings. In broad terms, it can be argued that both government and governance refer to processes of decision-making that affect the policy cycle and impact on people's lives. However, the main difference between them is that government denotes the decision-making process through formal institutions while governance concerns decision-making by multiple actors that operate in networks, and thus involves both formal and informal institutions.

Today, in its day-to-day operation, it is very common for any government to get involved in and develop relationships with a wide range of actors to make policy decisions – this is why governance has become 'the new normal'. For example, the UK government might want to implement a new policy on net-zero, but to achieve (and implement) this it is not enough just to make an agreement between the relevant ministers and departments in London. Environmental policy affects all levels of government, so devolved administrations as well as local councils will have to be involved. But there will also be pressure and interest groups, as well as local community organisations, that will want to have a say on the matter. Furthermore, there will be supranational institutions (such as the G7 or the EU) which will have set agendas on climate change that the UK government will need to consider. Bringing together the views of all these bodies and groups is important for the democratic process, but also for ensuring that decisions taken by the government can be effectively implemented. Thus, to make a decision on net-zero, the government will have to develop formal and informal discussions, open negotiation tables and relations with a wide range of actors within and beyond formal institutions – navigating across multiple levels of authority. This is one key aspect of what we mean by governance – and it also helps to explain why the concepts of government and governance are deeply entangled and can often be confused.

In this chapter, we are particularly concerned with power relations that involve actors operating at different territorial levels. Indeed, within a state, authority – understood as the power to make legitimate and binding decisions – is often dispersed from the centre both upwards (e.g. towards supra-national organisations, like the European Union) and downwards (e.g. towards sub-state, regional and local bodies; Hooghe and Marks, 2003). We call these processes of power dispersal within and beyond the central state 'multi-level governance'. In the context of our discussion on devolution, we focus on multi-level governance *within* the UK – that is, the power relations and decision-making processes that involve and affect central government, devolved institutions, local government bodies and the myriad of actors and formal and informal institutions that operate around these tiers.

For example, if you live in Liverpool, you will be represented by local councillors elected in your ward, but you will also have a directly elected city mayor who leads the council, and a directly elected metro mayor who is at the head of the Liverpool City Region Combined

Authority (i.e. a group of six councils cooperating in the development and delivery of a devolution deal – more on this later). However, if you live in the town of St. Austell, Cornwall, you will have neither a metro mayor nor a mayor, but you will be represented locally by your town council and by councillors elected in your ward sitting on Cornwall Council. However, if you are based in Scotland, irrespective of the city or town where you live, you will only have a unitary council catering for local needs, operating below the devolved Scottish parliament. Quite complicated, right?

It is legitimate to ask why this is the case. The first point to consider is that centre–local relations in the UK are intrinsically lopsided: this, as explained in Chapter 2, is due to the nature of the Westminster model and the principle of parliamentary sovereignty, which allows for power to be hoarded at the centre without any constitutional status or protection to local authorities (Barnett et al., 2021). In this context, in short, local government is a mere 'creature of statute' (Wilson and Game, 2011). As a result, council's powers, responsibilities and resources could all be radically changed, and local government could even be abolished altogether by the government of the day by simply taking the necessary legislation through parliament. As we saw in Chapter 2 when we looked at the abolition of the Greater London Council, this has happened in the past.

In any case, being a 'creature of statute' also implies that councils can only do what the law allows them to. Thus, the levers to define the exercise of the responsibilities that local government has to carry out in its day-to-day operation are firmly in the hands of central government (Wilson and Game, 2011). As a result, the relationship between the centre and the local level is not one between equal parties: the centre holds all the cards while local government is subordinated to it in its activities, operations and funding (Barnett et al., 2021). This is at odds with what happens in most European countries, where local government has constitutional protection and its scope is defined, broadly, by the principles of 'local self-government' and subsidiarity. Indeed, within the EU, the Council of Europe's *European Charter of Local Self-Government* commits to 'guaranteeing the political, administrative and financial independence of local authorities (…) [and it] provides that the principle of local self-government shall be recognised in domestic legislation and, where practicable, in the constitution' of the signatory member states (Council of Europe, 1985). Considering this stark difference, it is perhaps unsurprising that the UK features towards the bottom (42nd out of 57 countries) of the EU Commission's local autonomy index (Ladner et al., 2021).

In addition, the lack of a codified constitution and local authorities' subordinated role mean that reforms to the architecture of local government are the result of an incremental process of changes that have amplified the complexity of local institutions' structures. Indeed, local government is organised in different ways within and across the four nations of the UK.

In Scotland, Wales and Northern Ireland there is only one level of principal authorities, namely unitary councils (32 in Scotland and 22 in Wales) and district councils (11 in Northern Ireland). In Scotland and Wales there are also non-principal councils (i.e. community councils) that operate at the level below unitary councils, while Northern Ireland does not have (and has never had) non-principal councils (Sandford, 2022). It should be noted that, since the inception of devolution in 1997, local government is a devolved matter, and its 'management' is therefore under the direct responsibility of the devolved administrations.

On the one hand, this means that local authorities are not tied to the subordinated relationship to Westminster that we have described above. On the other hand, however, some commentators have highlighted how, paradoxically, devolution has reproduced the centralisation instincts of Westminster in the devolved nations. According to this interpretation, while substantial political power has been transferred to parliaments in Scotland, Wales and Northern Ireland, these bodies have not passed it down further to councils and have instead kept a strong hold over their newly acquired competencies, thus constraining local government's autonomy (McGarvey, 2020).

In England the situation is even more complex as the structures of local government vary from area to area. Overall, as of 2023, in England there are 317 principal councils. These can include either two tiers of local government (i.e. non-metropolitan county and district councils, with responsibility for statutory services split between them) or a single tier structure (i.e. metropolitan district councils and unitary councils, responsible for all services in their area). Furthermore, some areas have an additional tier of non-principal councils (i.e. parish and town councils), which typically focus on activities such as managing parks, allotments, footpaths, community centres and other local amenities. Finally, London has the Greater London Authority as its first tier, and 32 boroughs plus the London Corporation below it. Figure 6.1 offers a visual representation of these differences in the structures of local government.

In addition, internal governance for local councils can follow different models. In England, most local authorities are run by the leader of the council and a cabinet, both selected from councillors of the majority party or a coalition of parties in cases of no overall control. Other authorities, however, use a committee system. In this case, decision-making is delegated to committees of councillors from all parties with specific policy briefs, but budgetary decisions still need the support of a majority across the council (Paun et al., 2019). Furthermore, 16 local authorities in England (such as Liverpool, Leicester and Doncaster) have transferred council leadership powers to executive mayors. In some cases, however, these new institutions have not taken root. For example, in May 2022, through a referendum, Bristol residents voted to abolish their directly elected mayor and revert back to the committee system from 2024. In July 2022, Liverpool City Council also voted to abolish their mayor and returned to the leader and cabinet model from May 2023. Since 2014, another type of mayor, known as 'metro mayors', have been introduced in some areas. Metro mayors lead Combined Authorities (CAs, i.e. groups of two or more councils that work together) and exercise strategic economic and public service functions in partnership with leaders of the councils in the CA. The establishment of these new roles is connected with the form of devolution in place in England (i.e. 'devolution deals') and we will look at this in more detail later on in this chapter.

In Scotland and Wales, unitary councils are led by a council leader and a cabinet elected by the council itself. In Northern Ireland, councils typically use a committee system of governance and are led by a chairperson (or mayor) chosen by the council for a one-year term. There are no directly elected mayors in these parts of the UK: the legislation on directly elected mayors applies both to England and Wales, but there are currently no directly elected mayors in Wales. Scotland and Northern Ireland have no legislative power to introduce mayors (Sandford, 2023a).

122 • Institutions

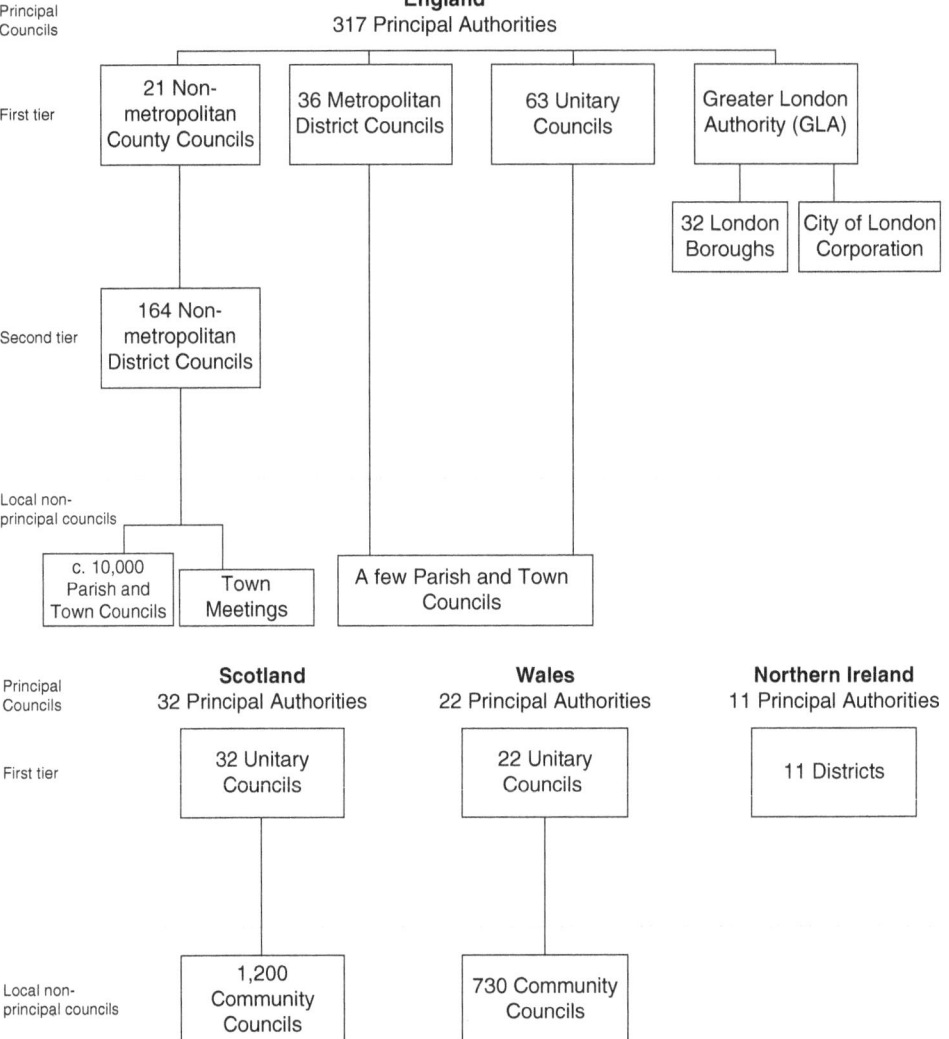

Figure 6.1 Local government structures in the UK

And there is more! Differences to the structures of local government also concern the way in which councils are elected (including timing of the elections and electoral systems) and, crucially, their funding. Space does not allow us to cover all these dimensions here, but the Annotated reading list at the end of this chapter suggests useful sources to consult to get an in-depth explanation of all aspects of local government functioning.

Overall, this overview shows that the differences that characterise how local government works across the UK are many and complex. This could be seen as resembling an assemblage – however, contrary to the use of this concept that we adopt in this book (see Chapter 1), in practice what emerges from these diverse arrangements is a disconnected whole, where the various 'pieces' that make up local and sub-national governance in the UK remain disjointed, and power remains unequally dispersed. In the next section, we dig deeper into this, looking at another key dimension of multi-level governance in the UK: devolution.

Case study: The chewing gum task force

Let's face it: it's so annoying to step on chewing gum left on the curb! But who is responsible for addressing the problem and clamp down on anti-social littering, removing discarded chewing gum and their unsightly stains from our town centres? The Chewing Gum Task Force, of course! Yes, that's right: in 2021, central government set up this body to provide funding to councils to prevent and mitigate chewing gum litter. However, this is a centrally controlled fund and local authorities have to compete for access to it.

The Chewing Gum Task Force is just one of many examples that illustrate how central government can keep a strong hold over local government funding and autonomy. In 2020, the Department for Transport (DfT) launched a call for councils who wanted to erect a new traffic sign to display on roads with high populations of hedgehogs, badgers, otters or other small animals. Four councils applied but were denied permission because they did not provide sufficient evidence. More recently, the government set up competitive funds to help councils invest in benches, bulb planting and bat boxes (Levelling Up Parks Fund), public toilets (Changing Places Fund) and tree-planting (Local Authority Treescapes Fund). In 2023, the government published a prospectus (as part of the Levelling Up Parks Fund) inviting local authorities to register their interest to get a chess table and four seats. The funding available is £2,500, and government specified that they 'are not expecting local authorities to provide chess sets but they may choose to do so'.

Applying for competitive funding (that may or may not be successful) is extremely time- and resource-consuming for local authorities that are already strapped for cash and personnel since the inception of austerity in 2010. Furthermore, even if successful, councils have to deal with many small pots of money over which they have no discretion.

These examples might seem trivial and perhaps even funny, but they do raise important questions about centre–local relations and the degree of centralisation that characterises our country. Is central government involvement and control really needed for this type of (clearly local) projects? Or should local authorities have more autonomy over decisions that directly affect the communities they serve?

I'll leave it to you to reflect upon these questions, discuss them in class with your peers, and decide what position you agree with and why.

Devolution in the UK

As a university student, you might have noticed that if you are from and live in Scotland and you chose to study at a Scottish university, the Scottish government will cover the cost of your tuition fees. But if you are from and live in England, and you decide to study at any university across the UK, you will have to pay a rather hefty fee, and the government will not cover this for you. Why is this the case? The answer is devolution. Education is a devolved matter and this means that the Scottish Parliament has the power to pass primary legislation on it, which might (as it does in this case) create policy that diverges from what happens in other parts of the UK.

We have already discussed in the opening of the chapter what devolution means as a concept and clarified that the process of devolution in the UK is asymmetric. In this section we will look at how this arrangement works in practice by looking at cases in Scotland, Wales, Northern Ireland and England. As explained in Chapter 2, understanding the contemporary 'territorial constitution' of the UK and the process of devolution that underpins it requires keeping in mind how the union has come together incrementally over time, also acknowledging the legacies and distinctiveness that each nation kept or lost throughout this process. This section draws on this approach, with particular attention to the tensions relating to the management and distribution of power between central government in London and the nations of the UK, arguing that the centre–periphery cleavage (see Theory box below) played a key role in shaping the path towards devolution in the four nations of the UK. This will help us to show that, much like the union, devolution is a process: it is ongoing and in flux, and this has important repercussions on how the UK is held together and functions as an assemblage.

Theory box: The centre–periphery cleavage

As explained in Chapter 7, there are political cleavages that define our society and help us to understand political competition and behaviour. A 'cleavage' can be defined as a historically determined social or cultural symbolic line that divides citizens within a society into groups with differing political interests, resulting in political conflict among these groups (Bartolini and Mair, 1990).

Specifically, the centre–periphery cleavage, as defined by Lipset and Rokkan (1967), marks the division between elites in the central administrative areas of a country (typically in and around the capital, where economic and political power tends to be concentrated) and those in peripheral areas (that, due to lack of key political and economic levers, usually tend to be put in a relationship of dependence by and with the centre). Thus, the 'defining line' that divides people into groups in this case is a territorial one. Indeed, according to Lipset and Rokkan (1967), this fault line has its roots in the creation of modern nation-states, and its depth depends on the extent to which nation-state processes that involved incremental unification of pre-existing, distinct political units were successful (or not) in assimilating their cultural, historical and political differences. When areas labelled as 'peripheries' have maintained a degree of (cultural, social, economic or political) distinctiveness and their own territorial identity but perceive that these are not fairly recognised by the centre, they might start to make claims for further autonomy or even independence, leading to the mobilisation and politicisation of the centre–periphery cleavage, often led by regionalist, nationalist or separatist parties.

The centre–periphery cleavage is very helpful not just to understand how territorial belonging and identity can shape political behaviour, but also to grasp how territorial distribution of power can shape political relations between different parts of a country, especially when looking at multi-national states or states that include regions with their own distinctive characteristics.

Many countries across the world have experienced this type of process. For example, within Europe, in Spain, Catalonia has a range of nationalist and separatist parties that are actively mobilising the centre–periphery cleavage on economic and cultural grounds. They have played a key role in the process that has led to the extension of autonomy and in the recognition of the status of 'nationality' to Catalonia, and some of them are also actively campaigning for full independence. In Italy, regionalist parties like the Northern League actively politicised the centre–periphery cleavage, also on economic and cultural grounds, although, unlike the Catalan case, the aim is not independence from Italy but further fiscal and political autonomy for regions like Veneto and Lombardy (for a full account, see Giovannini and Vampa, 2020). In the UK, as we will discuss in greater depth in this chapter, Scotland and Wales have their own parties (the Scottish National Party and Plaid Cymru) whose raison d'être revolves around demands for full independence, mostly on political and cultural grounds. In many respects, devolution can be seen as a response from the central state to pressures arising from the centre–periphery cleavage, in an attempt to provide more autonomy to its nations without breaking the union.

Scotland

As explained in Chapter 2, Scotland was the last nation to join the UK through the 1707 Act of Union. As we have seen, Scotland was never fully assimilated into England or the UK and was able to maintain a set of institutions that allowed it to preserve a distinctive sense of national and political identity (Mitchell, 2009). In the early days of the union, institutions like the Scottish Church played a key role in this sense. Later on, the creation of a Scottish Office in 1885 marked another important step. Indeed, the Scottish Office 'had both a symbolic and a substantive function. Symbolically, it represented the recognition by government at the centre that Scotland was different. Substantively, it developed a considerable range of responsibilities' (Michell, 2009:17). This made it difficult for the parliament in Westminster to hold the Scottish Office to account (Bogdanor, 2001), and the Scottish Office stimulated rather than satisfied the appetite for autonomy in the nation, as 'it made Scottish government at once more Scottish and less subject to parliamentary control' (Miller, 1981). Crucially, by granting a degree of administrative autonomy to Scotland over its domestic affairs, London's government avoided for a time the politicisation of the centre–periphery cleavage, as institutions like the Scottish Office catered for its distinctiveness.

From the 1960s onwards, however, the situation started to change as a new political actor – the Scottish National Party, the SNP – began to mobilise and politicise the territorial cleavage. The SNP was created in the 1930s, but it had no electoral influence until the 1960s (Lynch, 2013). In 1967 the party unexpectedly won a by-election in Hamilton, at the expense of Labour. This was a momentous event: it pushed Scotland's constitutional status onto the national agenda (Mitchell, 2009), attracting the attention of (and generating anxiety across) central government, led by Labour at the time.

From there onwards, the SNP went through a period of electoral 'boom and bust' (Lynch, 2013). Nevertheless, its strategy became more targeted and effective. The politicisation and mobilisation of the centre–periphery cleavage became more explicit, especially through the 'It's Scotland's oil' campaign, which stressed how the government in London was gaining the economic benefits of the tax wealth brought by North Sea oil, while Scotland was exploited and was losing out on its own resources. In time, this allowed the SNP to gain more consensus and win more seats in parliament.

As a response to the fears generated by this 'nationalist wave', the government set up a Royal Commission on the Constitution (known as the Kilbrandon Commission). This reported in 1973 setting out proposals for devolved assemblies, with different powers, to Scotland and Wales, but not for England. In the case of Scotland, the Commission acknowledged the presence of a widening territorial fracture and growing support for autonomy, and it identified devolution as an 'appropriate means of recognising Scotland's national identity and of giving expression to its national consciousness' (Kilbrandon, 1973, cited in Mitchell, 2009: 113).

Meanwhile, the SNP made further headway, winning a record 11 seats while holding second place in 35 of Labour's 41 seats in the second general election held in 1974 (Lynch, 2013). This result prompted the Labour party in government to act on the recommendations of the Kilbrandon Commission on devolution: the Scotland Act passed in 1978 and a post-legislative referendum held the year after. The referendum results proved controversial: 52 per cent of those voting supported the creation of a devolved assembly, but due to the so-called '40 per cent rule' (which required that 40 per cent of the Scottish electorate – not just of those who voted – support devolution for the Act to come into force) devolution could not go ahead. This led to a vote of no confidence in the Labour government, which was defeated at a general election in May 1979. The Scotland Act was promptly repealed a month later by Margaret Thatcher's new Conservative government.

Despite this defeat, devolution did not disappear from public debate. The presence of a Conservative government at Westminster, which Scotland had not voted for, fuelled new divisions. Scotland started to perceive itself as ruled by a distant government that did not represent its interests and treated it like a 'test bed' for controversial policies (such as the infamous 'poll tax'), thus leading to a further widening of the centre–periphery cleavage. Devolution started to be seen as a necessary measure to restore democratic legitimacy by parties across the political spectrum – except for the SNP, which politicised to the extreme the territorial cleavage, calling for independence, and the Conservatives who remained averse to devolution.

The setting up of the Scottish Constitutional Convention in 1987 was an important step too. Comprising representatives from political parties in Scotland (except the SNP and the Conservatives), local authorities, churches and voluntary organisations, the Convention's work helped shape both the details of a new proposal for devolution for Scotland (summarised in its final report *Scotland's Parliament, Scotland's Right*, 1995) and gather civil society consensus around it.

By the 1990s, the mood within the Labour party had changed, and there was now widespread awareness that making devolution happen was essential both for the party to maintain its support in its stronghold in Scotland and, in the words of the Shadow Secretary of State for Scotland, to 'kill nationalism stone dead'. According to one interpretation, the Labour party did not commit to devolution because it genuinely believed in the need to give political representation to Scottish identity but purely for strategic and electoral reasons. In any case, the policy was a key element of Labour's 1997 general election manifesto and, after a landslide victory, once back in power the party began a process of constitutional reform with devolution at its core (Giovannini, 2022).

A second referendum on Scottish (and Welsh) devolution was held in May 1997, but this time the vote preceded the passage of a dedicated act in Parliament, and there was no 40 per cent rule. The result saw 74 per cent support for the creation of a Scottish Parliament and 64 per cent for granting tax-varying powers to the new institution. Shortly after, the Scotland Act 1997 passed legislative powers on all matters (such as local government, education, health, housing, agriculture and fisheries) not reserved at Westminster, as well as tax varying ones, to the new Scottish Parliament at Holyrood).

Since its inception, devolution has been characterised by elements of continuity with the past, as it built on a system of distinctive institutions that had been in place for a long time (Mitchell, 2009), while also bringing in change, as it has transformed in a most profound way the political dynamics and power relations within Scotland and between Scotland and the rest of the UK.

One of the main achievements of devolution has been in terms of representative democracy (Mitchell, 2009: 141), as it helped to restore the legitimacy that was missing during the years of Conservative government in the 1980s and 1990s. But devolution also helped enhance the Scottish dimension to politics, providing space for the emergence of a political system that does not reflect Westminster's traditional two-party dynamics. Within a few years of Holyrood's inauguration, much against the hope of devolution's architects, Labour was replaced by the SNP as the main political force and lost control of the devolved parliament in its third election. Since then, the SNP has led Scotland's government, making a huge leap from niche to majority party (McAngus, 2016) by proving its worth in government and by developing an agenda that mixes nationalism and social-democratic values with a distinctive Scottish focus, building an image as a party that stands up for Scottish interests. While in 1997 devolution was conceived as a 'project of containment' of the centre–periphery cleavage, assuming that granting Scotland a conspicuous degree of autonomy would be enough to keep the UK together, the electoral growth of the SNP and the loss of support for Labour created the impetus to use devolved powers in a different way (i.e. as a springboard for independence), thus threatening the future of the union.

This is what happened in 2014 when the SNP called for and held an independence referendum. Even though, in the end, the No camp won, this was a momentous event. First, it allowed Scotland to get 'devo max' (i.e. to further increase its devolved powers). Second, it showed how devolution is becoming entrenched: even though it operates under the principle of parliamentary sovereignty, it would be extremely hard to reverse the autonomy granted to Scotland without generating turbulence. Third, the referendum sent waves across the UK, raising awareness in other parts of the country of the value of devolution. It is no coincidence that the day after the results were announced, the prime minister David Cameron announced that more devolution would be granted not just to Scotland, but also to the other nations of the UK, including England.

Much has happened since the 'Indy Ref' in Scotland. While firmly rooted, devolution continues to evolve and the role of Scotland within the union is still in flux. Several questions remain open. Events such as Brexit and the Coronavirus pandemic have re-ignited debates about the relationship between Scotland and the UK. Scotland did not vote for Brexit but had to leave the EU nonetheless as a result of the UK-wide balance of votes, leading to questions about the democratic legitimacy of a process that does not match 'Scotland's will'. Furthermore, attempts by the UK government to restrict the exercise of legislative powers of the devolved government in the aftermath of Brexit (e.g. as in the case of the Internal Market Bill), created disquiet across the Scottish political class and society. The management of the pandemic, especially in its first phase, with central government adopting a top–down command and control approach that sidelined the Scottish government, was also negatively received. All these factors fuelled new calls for independence. Although these have not materialised, the examples above indicate that the centre–periphery cleavage still plays a key role in post-devolution Scotland. Finally, after decades of success, the SNP fortunes have started to falter, especially due to the involvement of key political figures (including the former first minister Nicola Sturgeon) in a series of financial and political scandals in 2023. While this has dealt a heavy blow to the independence cause, it also offers the possibility for democratic change and renewal within the devolved system.

Wales

The way in which Wales joined the union shaped its path to devolution. The fact that, as explained in Chapter 2, Wales was essentially assimilated into England meant that it never had formal institutional arrangements that helped preserve its distinctiveness. Yet Welsh identity and nationalism were not swept away but had to find different forms of representation.

Welsh nationalism developed in a defensive way, against the imposition of English dominance brought in by the union. In this context, language emerged from the start as a key element of Welsh distinctiveness and became intimately related to the idea of Welsh national identity. But language had a territorial dimension that restricted its appeal only to some parts of the nation. Indeed, the way Welsh identity was associated with language affected constitutional preferences across the population and undermined the notion that Welsh was a uniform political entity (Mitchell, 2009: 143). As such, the territorial cleavage that characterised Wales was less sharp than in the Scottish case, and it took longer to be fully mobilised and politicised.

It is no coincidence that the Welsh Office was created much later (in 1964) and had less power than its Scottish counterpart, reflecting the different stages of development of a sense of national distinctiveness in the two nations. Nonetheless, the Welsh Office provided an all-Wales focus that had not previously existed (Mitchell, 2009). Indeed, the inception of administrative devolution in Wales played a significant role in fostering the growth and political relevance of Welsh identity – slowly, but steadily, undermining the 'myth of assimilation to England' (Mitchell, 2009: 144). Like Scotland, Wales had a nationalist party (Plaid Cymru, the Party of Wales) that from the 1960s mobilised the centre–periphery cleavage on cultural/linguistic grounds but this focus limited its political appeal to predominantly Welsh-speaking areas, like north-west Wales.

The combination of all these factors influenced central government views on Welsh autonomy and the type of devolution that was offered in the Wales Act 1978 (i.e. a limited form of executive devolution). At the pre-legislative referendum held in 1979, linguistic divisions within Wales impacted voting behaviour: a narrow majority of Welsh speakers voted for devolution, but a wide majority of non-Welsh speakers rejected it (Evans and Trystan, 1999, cited in Mitchell, 2009). The result was a meagre 20 per cent of support for devolution, while 80 per cent voted against it. As in Scotland, the Wales Act 1978 was repealed by the Conservative government elected in 1979 (Foulkes et al., 1983).

In the following years, as in Scotland, increased support for devolution across Wales stemmed from a growing sense of disenchantment towards a Conservative government in London that was perceived as distant and dismissive of Wales as a political entity and enjoyed relatively low levels of electoral support in the nation, fuelling the notion of a democratic deficit (Torrance, 2023). A campaign for a Welsh Assembly was launched in 1987, following the example of Scotland. But what really made a difference was that, in the long term, the centre–periphery cleavage (represented, up until this point, by Plaid Cymru) aligned with the class cleavage (see Chapter 7) represented by Labour. In this way, by the 1990s, defensive nationalism had given way to positive campaigning for devolution (Mitchell, 2009).

By the time of the second devolution referendum in 1997, the mood across Welsh society and political class had changed and this was reflected in the results. This time, 50.3 per cent of voters supported devolution, with a gap between the Yes and No camps of only 6,721 votes (Torrance, 2023). This was a wafer-thin victory, but compared with the results of 1979 the swing in favour of devolution was much greater in Wales than in Scotland. A Welsh Assembly was created, but only executive powers were transferred to it by Westminster, thus granting it only secondary legislation powers. The Assembly also operated on a 'conferred' (rather than 'reserved' as in Scotland) model of devolution, meaning that it was able to pass secondary legislation only on specific areas (such as agriculture, fisheries, education and housing) explicitly listed by Westminster. The then Secretary of State Ron Davies famously described Welsh devolution as 'a process, not an event'. Indeed, this has been borne out by developments in Welsh devolution since its inception (Senedd Cymru, online).

The National Assembly for Wales was inaugurated in May 1999. However, it soon became clear that its structure as a single corporate body responsible for executive and scrutiny function was problematic and slowed down its activity. This prompted the creation of a series of Commissions to review the powers and functioning of the Assembly, leading to an incremental growth of its powers. The Wales Act 2006 provided for the legal separation of the executive and legislature as individual legal entities, and it also devolved primary law-making powers to Wales. In 2011, a third devolution referendum was held in Wales, on whether full primary legislation powers should be extended to the National Assembly in those areas over which it had responsibility. Sixty-three per cent of voters supported this, suggesting that devolution had started to take root in Wales. The Wales Act 2014 granted new financial powers to Wales. The Wales Act 2017 established the National Assembly on a new constitutional basis, making it a permanent part of the UK constitution, and it also introduced a shift from the 'conferred powers model' to the 'reserved powers model' of devolution. Finally, through the Senedd and Elections (Wales) Act 2020, the National Assembly was recognised as a fully fledged parliament. The Assembly changed its name on 6 May 2020 to Senedd Cymru or Welsh Parliament to reflect its new constitutional status as a law-making and tax-setting parliament.

This short overview shows how devolution might have started on a slower track in Wales compared to Scotland, but once established it steadily evolved, leading to a constitutional leap. The history of Wales' relation to the UK, and England in particular, played a key role in this process and shaped the development of a Welsh political system along very different lines to Scotland's. Notwithstanding swings in its support base, Labour has remained the largest political party in Wales since the creation of the Welsh Parliament and, as of 2023, all Welsh first ministers have been Labour. Despite its strong historical links with England, since the inception of devolution Welsh Labour has internalised the centre–periphery cleavage and put the Welsh dimension of politics at its core. Plaid Cymru never managed to develop the momentum and widespread support of the SNP, possibly due to its focus on the cultural dimension of the centre–periphery cleavage that made its appeal territorially limited. Nonetheless, the party has always had a presence in the Welsh Assembly, maintaining a share of seats above 20 per cent in all its elections (except 2011).

Devolution in Wales, still remains 'a process' and, as in Scotland, is still in flux. Here, too, recent events such as Brexit and the Covid-19 pandemic have created turbulence within the political system and in the relationships with central government. However, Labour's (and the first minister's) ability to focus on the Welsh dimension of these 'crises' has helped maintain stability in support of devolution.

Northern Ireland

As explained in Chapter 2, Ireland joined the union in 1800, after a long process of incremental, forced subordination to England. The cleavage that has long defined the power relations between the two nations is religious/ethnic, intersecting with the territorial dimension: a deep fault-line between Catholic and Protestant communities is rooted in and has always shaped the political dynamics between England/the UK and Ireland/Northern Ireland. While many attempts were made by the UK government to put a lid on these tensions, these never worked in full.

As discussed in Chapter 2, the peace process in Northern Ireland took a long time to be addressed, and devolution was used as a means to find a solution to it. Attempts to develop a system of 'home rule' at the beginning of the 20th century intersected with religious conflicts. Eventually, they led to the creation of a Northern Ireland parliament (Stormont) in 1921, but this was a Protestant-controlled institution, which fostered segregation between communities, thus fuelling rather than help bridging the religious and territorial cleavage. In the wake of the Troubles (see Chapter 2), Stormont was first suspended and then abolished.

In 1998, the peace process took a key turn with the Belfast Agreement (also known as the Good Friday Agreement). Among its many provisions, passed via two referendums held both in Northern Ireland and the Republic of Ireland, the Agreement involved the creation of a devolved assembly with primary legislation powers, which officially came into being in December 1999. This time, clear measures were taken for Stormont to address sectarianism and segregation between political communities, putting power-sharing at the core of the new settlement. The single transferable vote (STV) system was chosen to maximise representation. Elected assembly members also had to designate their status (as Protestant, Catholic or Other). Provisions were made for all decisions within the Northern Ireland Assembly to be taken on a cross-community basis (through 'parallel consent' or 'weighted majority') to avoid biases for or against any group. The roles of first minister and deputy first minister were also designed to be 'co-equal' and interdependent (i.e. if one resigns, the other is required to do the same).

Image 6.2 One of the 'Peace Walls' in Belfast, Northern Ireland that were built to separate and 'keep peace' between nationalist Catholic and unionist Protestant areas of the city. There are over 20 miles of 'Peace Walls' across Northern Ireland.

© Photo by meunierd on Shutterstock

As such, the Good Friday Agreement sought, at least in its principles, to set a more pluralist distribution of power across Northern Ireland, catering for the diversity of its communities. Surely, the fact that in recent years the DUP and Sinn Féin (the main parties in Northern Ireland, representing, respectively, the Protestant and Catholic communities – see Chapter 7) have been in government together at Stormont can be seen as a positive step forward in the peace process. However, despite all good intentions, the religious cleavage between Protestants and Catholics has not disappeared. Since its (re)opening in 1998, Stormont has operated intermittently, and has been suspended five times, often as a result of tensions between the DUP and Sinn Féin and the communities they respectively represent. Several recent events have challenged in new ways the peace process and devolution in Northern Ireland.

For example, in 2016 the majority of the Northern Ireland electorate voted to remain in the EU, whilst the rest of the UK (with the exception of Scotland) voted for Brexit, generating tensions across the political system. First, this prompted Sinn Féin to call for a border poll on the reunification of Ireland, and although no referendum has been held this has reignited debates that many hoped had been addressed by the Belfast Agreement. Second, since

Northern Ireland is the only part of the UK that shares a land border with another EU country, the exit of the UK from the EU could have led to the re-introduction of a hard border between Northern Ireland and Ireland, as was the case during the Troubles. Both practically and symbolically, this would have been a huge setback, undoing the provisions for free movement set by the Belfast Agreement. Indeed, the so-called Northern Ireland Protocol, which sought to overcome the issue by setting a border in the Irish Sea/at Northern Ireland ports became a sticking point in the Brexit negotiations. Similarly, the Windsor Framework, which was set in 2023 to adjusts the operation of the Northern Ireland Protocol and help to address both issues concerning its troubled implementation and political concerns especially from the Ulster Unionists, has not put an end to controversies (Whitten and Phinnemore, 2023). Indeed, as of autumn 2023, debates over the Framework are still a key factor in the refusal of the Democratic Unionist Party to allow the operation of the Northern Ireland Assembly, and put an end to the ongoing suspension of devolved government in Northern Ireland. In short, Brexit reopened old sectarian fractures and set a range of challenges to the stability of Stormont, and perhaps also to the future of the Union.

On the positive side, shifts in traditional political allegiances – marked by the decline in support for unionist parties registered in the 2017 and 2022 Northern Ireland Assembly elections, to the benefit of non-sectarian actors like the Alliance Party – suggests that old religious cleavages might be changing, and that the polity is no longer just about unionism vs nationalism (Tonge, 2020). However, it remains to be seen 'whether Alliance can continue to grow as a centre party, reshape a binary divide and create new civic space, less predicated upon the old conflict model' (Tonge, 2020: 466).

Spotlight on research: Feminist institutionalism

Feminist institutionalism is an approach that seeks to identify and assess gender bias and the gendered nature of institutional rules, thus shedding light on how gender norms operate within institutions and how institutional processes construct, maintain or challenge gender power dynamics, unpacking a key dimension of the relationship between gender and power. This approach offers an extremely important perspective from which we can analyse the process of devolution in the UK, which is worth taking into account. As such, in this box my aim is to bring your attention not just to one piece of work, but to various research contributions that help bridge this gap (but keep in mind these are just some examples – I will leave it to you to use these as a springboard to explore the field in greater depth).

For instance, Mackay and McAllister's (2012) article *Feminising British politics: Six lessons from devolution in Scotland and Wales* assesses the contrast between the levels of women's representation in the House of Commons, the Scottish Parliament and the National Assembly for Wales between 1999 and 2012, drawing lessons across political jurisdictions on what can be done to improve gender equality. Jennifer Thompson's book *Abortion Laws and Political Institutions* (2019) is a great piece of research that offers key insights into feminist institutional theory around issues of gender, multi-level governance and devolution, using the case of abortion politics in Northern Ireland.

More broadly, Joni Lowenduski's *Feminising Politics* (2005) is a classic account that provides a compelling, comprehensive analysis of how institutions, processes and procedures are affected by the changing numbers of women in politics, exploring what is at stake when we try to achieve gender equality in public office, and drawing out the ways in which the constraints and possibilities for political action are gendered. The website of the Feminism and Institutionalism International Network (FIIN, a body of feminist scholars from over 50 countries who study political institutions through a gender lens) provides links to the most up-to-date research in this field (https://femfiin.org).

England

England is the only nation of the UK that does not enjoy any form of political devolution. Again, its role in the process of formation of the union helps explain this. As discussed in Chapter 2, England was considered to be 'the core' of the union and almost a synonym for 'Britain'. As such, for a long time, its political and constitutional role was not put into question, especially because all the main institutions of power (i.e. Westminster and Whitehall) were based within it, in London.

This, however, does not mean that England does not have its own internal divisions and territorial tensions. England, too, was formed through processes of incremental expansion and annexation of previously autonomous units. To the present day, England includes small nations, like Cornwall, and historical counties, like Yorkshire, or broader regions like the north of England, each with its own distinctive cultural, economic and political traits. It is also worth noting that, within England itself, the main seats of power are all located in just one specific area (i.e. the south-east) and, more specifically, London, giving rise to centre–periphery dynamics captured by the notion of a north–south divide (Giovannini and Rose, 2020), as well as between the south and areas like Cornwall. And yet, in England, the centre–periphery cleavage has never been fully politicised as in Scotland and Wales. For example, for a long time, the Labour party was the main political actor concerned with the issue of addressing the north–south divide. As such, the class cleavage (see Chapter 7) kept playing a key role in centre–periphery dynamics, somehow absorbing the territorial dimension (Giovannini, 2016). Regionalist parties have emerged in the north and in Cornwall (e.g. the Yorkshire Party or Mebyon Kernow), but they remain small and unable to compete on the national stage (Giovannini, 2016).

Featherstone (2009) suggests that the Empire played an important role in displacing metaphors and manifestations of centre and periphery within England, as it drew attention to an outward, global dimension of power. However, a series of events – such as the end of the Empire, the nationalist waves of the 1960s and 1970s in Scotland and Wales, and the eventual inception of devolution in 1997 – have opened new debates not only about who the English are but also on the role and place of England within the union (Bryant, 2003; Morgan, 2002).

Thus, the so-called 'English Question' (Hazell, 2006) took longer to be brought to the fore. Dealing with political devolution in England is a particularly difficult task due to perceptions that dispersing power away from the core component of the union could have the potential of weakening what holds the UK together. This perhaps helps explain why devolution in England has been linked to economic motifs rather than democratic or identity drivers as in the case of the other nations of the UK.

Even though debates on English devolution emerged, especially within the Labour party from the 1960s onwards, England was not included in the process of constitutional reform that sought to introduce devolution to Scotland and Wales in the 1970s. No equivalent of the Scottish or Welsh Office was ever set up for England, and only in 1994 were the Government Offices for the Regions (GOs) set up to deliver government policies and programmes in areas like regeneration, housing, public health, education and skills across England's nine administrative regions.

In 1997, the newly elected Labour government included England in its programme of constitutional reform. But the only part of England that was granted devolved powers in the short term was Greater London, where an assembly led by a directly elected mayor was created in 2000. There were also plans to create elected assemblies in other English regions, but these were swiftly abandoned after a failed referendum held in the north-east in 2004 (see Giovannini, 2022; Willett and Giovannini, 2014). In the end, English regions were granted only a limited form of administrative decentralisation through the creation of Regional Development Agencies. From there onwards, political devolution for England was essentially shelved (Giovannini, 2022) and the focus shifted towards policy strategies that could help address economic inequalities between the north and the south of England, with little concern about issues of identity, regional distinctiveness and democratic representation (Giovannini, 2016, 2018).

It took a decade after the north-east referendum before a new agenda for English devolution started to take shape, this time under the coalition and then Conservative governments, from 2010 onwards. In the wake of the Scottish independence referendum, as previously explained, the prime minister David Cameron pledged to deliver more devolution to all the UK nations. But again, the plan for England focused mainly on bridging regional inequalities: between 2010 and 2018, the Northern Powerhouse (see Berry and Giovannini, 2018) was the main strategy that sought to use devolution to rebalance the economy; from 2019 onwards, the 'Levelling Up' agenda has taken its place, but essentially it still seeks to achieve similar aims (Tomaney and Pike, 2020).

Crucially, the form of devolution that has been developed since the 2010s is still very limited and substantially different from those granted to the other UK nations (for a full discussion, see Sandford, 2023b). First, it is based on 'devolution deals' – that is, partnership agreements between central government and local council leaders within newly established combined authorities (CAs) – groups of two or more councils that collaborate and take collective decisions across council boundaries, some of which are led by directly elected 'metro mayors'. Second, devolution is a competitive process, and local authorities have to submit bids to the government to be granted a deal. Third, all the new institutions that revolve around devolution deals (such as CAs and metro mayors, as well as other bodies like Local Enterprise Partnerships) were set up without any substantial public consultations or referendums. Fourth, devolution does not cover all parts of England, but only a selected few (i.e. currently only 11 devolution deals are in place, ten led by a metro mayor; see Figure 6.2), thus creating disparities between deal 'haves and have nots' (Giovannini, 2018). As such, devolution in England is a top–down, disconnected project that does not benefit all people and places in the same way and takes the form of a patchwork of ad hoc deals – crucially, due to the nature of centre–local relations in England explained earlier on, with the terms and conditions of these still set, for the most part, by the centre (Giovannini, 2021b; Barnett et al., 2021).

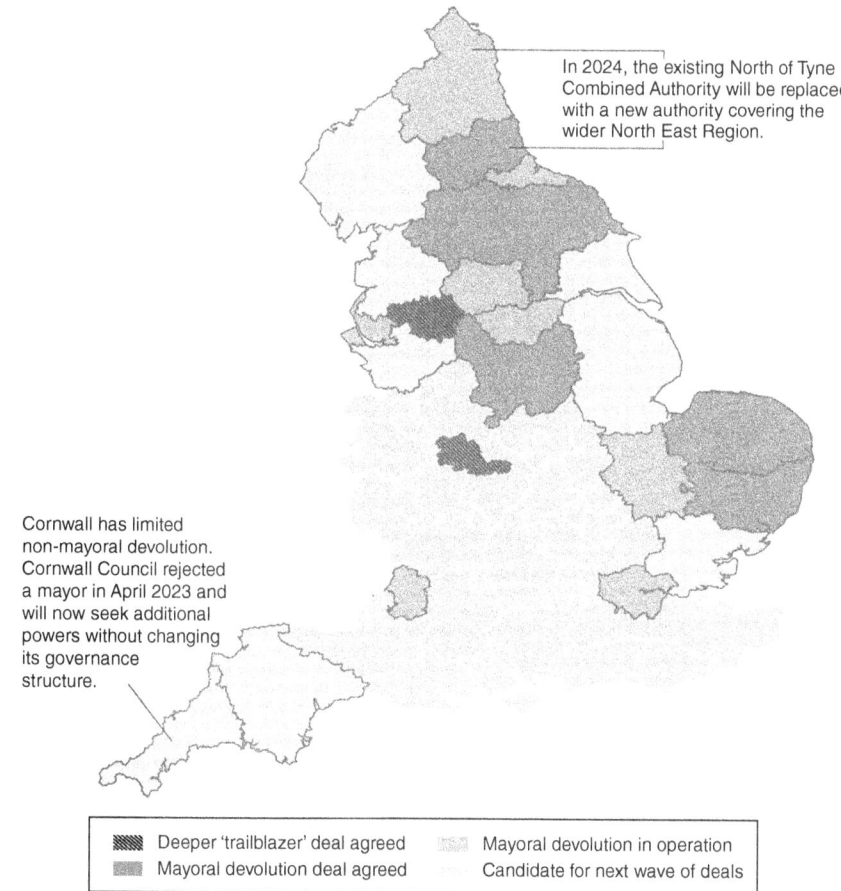

Figure 6.2 Devolution deals in England: Existing and proposed

Source: Institute for Government, available at: https://www.instituteforgovernment.org.uk/explainer/english-devolution

Most importantly, the devolution strategies developed so far have not addressed in full the 'English Question', as England remains highly centralised in the context of a devolved UK. In addition, recent research has shown that regional inequalities in England continue to grow, suggesting that devolution has not (yet, at least) achieved its intended main aim of rebalancing the economy (Raikes et al., 2019; UK 2070 Commission, 2020). According to some, the two issues are connected: England is the most regionally unequal country in the developed world, and over-centralisation is the root cause of these disparities (Raikes et al., 2019; Webb et al., 2021). Following this interpretation, only a substantial revision of centre–local relations in England underpinned by an inclusive process of devolution for all areas, coupled with a reform of central government, could help address both regional inequalities and the growing democratic deficit that stems from them – perhaps also by recognising the importance of regional identities (Giovannini, 2021). However, such overhaul of the system would require a long-term, cross-party commitment able to last beyond the duration of one parliament. To date, no political party has sought to take up this challenge.

Conclusion

In this chapter we have explored the complexities of sub-national governance in the UK, looking in particular at relationships between central and local government, as well as at the asymmetric process of devolution in the UK. What we hope has become clear throughout the analysis is that where power lies and how it is territorially distributed matters, and impacts on pluralism. The programme of devolution introduced from 1997 should have helped (re-)establish spatial justice and achieve a more equal economy as well as better democratic representation through territorially based institutions.

However, the lack of a codified constitution in the UK has favoured the development of a system of multi-level governance that is asymmetric and is producing different outcomes in different parts of the country. Local government remains strongly subordinated to the centre, especially in England but also in the devolved nations. Meanwhile, devolution is taking divergent trajectories in the four nations of the UK, often fuelled by the politicisation of territorial cleavages, leading some to argue that it might lead to an 'ever looser union' (Mitchell, 2009).

Dedication

This chapter is dedicated to the late Craig McAngus who, despite his young age, was one of the sharpest analysts of territorial politics in the UK. I wish he was still here to comment on this contribution, and tell me off for having omitted 'some veeery important details' with his quick wit, unique sense of humour and infectious laugh.

Key take-home points

- Devolution implies the transfer of powers from Westminster to elected bodies operating at a level below the central state, but leaving intact (at least in theory) parliamentary supremacy.

- Sub-national governance in the UK is complex: local government as well as devolution take different forms in each of the UK nations.
- Acknowledging how each nation has joined the UK and the importance of centre–periphery cleavages help us to understand how devolution has emerged and evolved.
- How power is territorially distributed matters and impacts on pluralism.

Annotated reading list

Sandford, M. (2022) *Local Government in England: Structures*. House of Commons Library Briefing 07104 https://researchbriefings.files.parliament.uk/documents/SN07104/SN07104.pdf

Barnett, N., Giovannini, A. and Griggs, S. (2021) *Local Government in England – 40 Years of Decline*. Unlock Democracy. https://static1.squarespace.com/static/5bd057c434c4e2d8eb0434e6/t/60796c249a89215efe3cd382/1618570303662/Local+Government+in+England+-+40+Years+of+Decline.pdf

Local government in England is a very complicated affair! These two reports will help you clarify and make sense of the complexities of its structures, the way in which it is funded and the roots of its subordinate relationship with the centre. More broadly, if you have questions or doubts about any aspect of local government in England, consult Mark Sandford's reports on the House of Commons Library website (https://commonslibrary.parliament.uk/authors/mark-sandford): he's a true local government guru!

Raikes, L., Giovannini, A. and Getzer, B. (2019) *Divided and Connected: Regional Inequalities in the North, the UK and the Developed World*. London: IPPR. www.ippr.org/publications/state-of-the-north-2019

This report was one of the first publications that uncovered and assessed the connection between regional inequalities and over-centralisation of power, and it is very useful to understand why devolution, especially in England, is both essential and difficult to achieve.

Hayward, K. (2020) Why it is impossible for Brexit Britain to 'take back control' in Northern Ireland. *Territory, Politics, Governance*, 8(2), 273–278.

Hayward, K. (2021) 'Flexible and imaginative': The EU's accommodation of Northern Ireland in the UK–EU Withdrawal Agreement. *International Studies*, 58(2), 201–218.

These are two great articles that help us understand how Brexit is posing new challenges to the peace process as well as devolution in Northern Ireland.

Cheung, A., Paun, A. and Valsamidis, L. (2019) *Devolution at 20*. London: Institute for Government. www.instituteforgovernment.org.uk/publication/devolution-20

This is a great report that provides a full overview of how devolution has evolved across the UK nations since its inception, assessing its main achievements and the challenges ahead.

7
Do British political parties reflect British pluralism?

Judith Sijstermans

Image 7.1 Political parties in Scotland compete for last minute attention at the polling places on election day
© Photo by Iscotlanda Photography on Shutterstock

Learning objectives

After reading this chapter you should be able to:

- Identify political parties' internal sub-groups, including the role played by party members, party staff, and elected representatives
- Understand how political parties can reflect dimensions of difference in the UK, including territorial and ideological diversity
- Learn how political parties organise political competition in the UK
- Consider whether political parties remain essential to British democracy

Introduction

On the eve of 18 September 2014, political parties were out in full force in Scotland. Among them was the Scottish National Party, whose political party members were actively knocking on doors and spreading pro-independence materials in local areas and urban centres. They came together in campaign hubs, usually festooned in the bold colours and logo of their campaign – white and blue, 'Yes Scotland', echoing the Scottish flag (the saltire). Their cars, windows and t-shirts were often emblazoned with the same logo. Online, they had been promoting independence for months on Facebook and Twitter. SNP staff worked behind the scenes, organising members' activities and coordinating with staff in the campaigning group of Yes Scotland. In front of dozens of cameras set up outside the Scottish Parliament building, the SNP's representatives explained the party's claims for independence, speaking to a wide audience in the UK and globally.

Political parties and the individuals invested in them – activists, staff, politicians – were crucial to the referendum on Scottish independence. In a wider sense, political parties have long been mobilizing, motivating actors in the UK's greatest political debates. Political parties are also *transformed by* the UK's great political moments.

In the wake of defeat in the 2014 Scottish independence referendum, the Scottish National Party's membership swelled from just over 20,000 members to almost 120,000 in 2016 (Bennie et al., 2021). The party's leader stepped down and a new SNP leader, and Scottish First Minister, Nicola Sturgeon took the helm in 2014. At the same time, and in the years to follow, the Conservative and Unionist Party was challenged by the UK Independence Party (UKIP), which pushed for the vote to withdraw the UK from the European Union in 2016.

Amid this period of change, the UK's usual democratic processes continued. Political parties including the Conservatives, SNP and UKIP competed in 2015, 2017 and 2019 UK Parliament elections, 2016 Scottish Parliament, Welsh Assembly and London Mayoral elections, and local council elections throughout this period. Political parties, acting within these diverse legislative and public service institutions, are crucial actors in the UK's democratic decision-making process. Political parties structure the more ordinary functioning of the UK's democracy and contest its moments of big decision-making.

This chapter pushes back against popular perceptions of political parties as unitary, monolithic, and often elitist, bodies. While political parties contain elite politicians and supply these politicians as representatives to the UK's legislatures, there are many other aspects of political party life. Political parties include pluralist party members and politicians and generate varied ideas that can transform British political life. In their competition for electoral support, parties are incentivised to reflect different sectors of people and opinions in the UK.

In this chapter, we first explore the complex inner life of political parties through the idea of the 'three faces' of the political party. Then, we look at the parties' roles externally: how party interactions with one another shape political competition. We conclude by considering parties' contributions (or lack thereof) to British democracy.

Need to know: Which are the UK's political parties?

- *Conservative and Unionist Party*: Colloquially referred to as 'Tories', this party was founded in 1834. Its policy priorities are free markets, a limited role for the state in the economy and conserving traditional social values.
- *Labour Party*: The Labour Party was founded in 1900, growing out of the trade union movement. Its policy priorities are workers' rights, the role of the government in addressing socioeconomic inequality, and progressive social values.
- *Liberal Democrats*: Colloquially known as 'Lib Dems', this party was a merger between the Liberal Party and the Social Democratic Party in 1988. It is a centrist party with a focus on civil liberties, environmentalism and social justice.
- *Scottish National Party (SNP)*: Founded in 1934, the Scottish National Party is the main political in the Scottish nationalist movement. The party promotes Scottish independence and a wider social democratic policy platform.
- *Democratic Unionist Party (DUP)*: The DUP is a Northern Irish party established in 1971. The party's main objective is to keep Northern Ireland in the UK. It also places a strong emphasis on traditional conservative social values.
- *Sinn Féin*: Sinn Féin was founded in 1905 to promote Irish republicanism. Its policy priorities include promoting social equality, economic justice and Irish reunification.
- *Plaid Cymru*: Plaid Cymru (the Party of Wales), established in 1925, emphasises economic development, social justice and environmental sustainability in the context of an independent Wales.
- *Green Party of England and Wales*: The Green Party of England and Wales is a political party founded in 1990. It promotes policies that address climate change, the protection of natural resources, and creation of a fairer society.

Inside British political parties: The three faces of the political party

Political parties are often referred to by using shortcuts or general terms. For example, people might say 'the Tories' launched a policy programme, or 'Labour' are the architects of devolution. Leaders may also be referred to in this kind of shorthand. For example, people might often say that 'Boris Johnson' responded to the Covid pandemic. These discursive shortcuts make each party and leader sound like a singular body. However, each political party is made up of sub-groups of individuals and individuals who play specific roles. Collective action, such as a party manifesto, is negotiated between these sub-groups and individuals. Specific individuals like the prime minister (PM) may have specific powers to speak for their party, but even the PM is chosen and held accountable by their political party.

To reflect the internal pluralism of political parties, Richard Katz and Peter Mair (1993) created the idea of the 'three faces' of political party organisation. Those faces are the party on the ground, the party in central office and the party in public office. These three faces of the party sometimes compete for power. For example, party members on the ground might seek to influence decisions made by parliamentarians. The different faces of the party may also work together, for example with party staff providing crucial support for parliamentarians and party members to mobilise during electoral campaigns.

In this section, I briefly describe each aspect or 'face' of political party organisation and illustrate these faces using cases from British political parties. As I do so, you will start to understand political parties beyond the common shortcuts we use and to see them as complex, multi-layered and pluralist organisations.

The party on the ground (and online)

The 'party on the ground' can be understood as party members as well as a more 'loosely' defined group of 'the core of regular activists, financial supporters, and even loyal voters, whether or not they are formally enrolled as party members' (Katz and Mair, 1993: 597). As society has changed, this group can also include individuals who primarily affiliate with the party digitally – for example, as online followers or cyber-members (see Spotlight on research below).

In British politics, the party on the ground is most easily illustrated by groups of party activists roaming the streets of their local town, usually clad in distinctive party colours – for example, the red of the Labour Party, the green of the Green Party. Party activists take part in canvassing (i.e. knocking on doors to talk to voters and identify supporters), leafleting (i.e. distributing party materials) or representing their party in public spaces (e.g. stalls at local markets). In the modern age, party activists usually snap pictures of these activities and post them on their X (Twitter), Facebook and Instagram pages.

Party members and activists are the party's face on the ground and online. They provide the political party with legitimacy by showing that they have popular support. Members provide considerable voluntary people power during elections as well as funds through donations or membership fees. Activists are the party's 'foot soldiers' and 'free human capital' (Bale et al., 2019; Seyd and Whiteley, 2004: 361). Activists provide free campaign labour, fund the party through donations, provide legitimacy and give the party a foundation in civil society (Heidar, 2006: 304).

One illustration of the role of party activists is the community organising 'experiment' in the Labour Party between 2010 and 2015. A certain sector of the Labour Party sought to bring the party back to a local community level in order 'to unleash the potential of local party branches to act as vehicles for local political campaigns that would reconnect the party to the public and local civil society organisations' (Scott and Wills, 2017: 125). This organising was driven by the party, including the hiring of a local organiser in specific areas, but enabled by ordinary members and supporters. One of the main roles of local organisers in Cardiff and Southampton was to build capacity among party members through working side by side with them and delivering structured training. Scott and Wills' (2017) in-depth analysis also highlights the way that local Labour campaigning in Cardiff allowed the Labour Party to engage 50 new people including those in civil society. In this sense, the cooperation of party staff and the party 'on the ground' helped to expand the party's reach in the area.

The UK's first past the post (FPTP) system, which rewards an overall winner rather than proportional winners, means that British political parties need to work harder to convert electoral support into parliamentary seats, as smaller proportions of votes are not reflected in Parliament as well. One effect of this FPTP system is that political parties have to focus their campaigning on key constituencies.

The case of the UK Independence Party (UKIP) illustrates the challenges of mobilising and training members for smaller parties. Researchers who spoke with UKIP activists after the 2015 general election found that a lack of knowledge and resources about ground campaigns hindered the party's strategy (Cutts et al., 2017: 72). Surveys also found that most UKIP members reported being active in the party to a very limited extent (Whiteley et al., 2021). This may have been particularly affected by how new UKIP is organisationally and shows the advantages that the more established parties may have in the British political system.

Importantly, party membership is not fully equivalent with party activism. Many members do not engage actively with their party. Research has found that in UK political parties, in a survey of the 2015 and 2017 elections, 36.2 per cent of members spent no time campaigning. In the 2017 election, 59.9 per cent of party members did less than five hours work for the party (Bale et al., 2020). With an increase in online communications, some party member activities have changed towards some lighter touch online activities such as 'liking' Facebook posts or retweeting party material.

These lighter touch activities might require less input from members or supporters themselves but the online sharing of material has been shown to be effective in changing electoral results. For example, in the aftermath of the 2017 election, the Labour Party's surprising success was attributed in part to their success in engaging with voters and supporters online by employing a positive message (Dorey, 2017; Gerbaudo et al., 2019). Crucially, social media success 'facilitates' local activism by spreading information and news at the local level (Dorey, 2017: 316). My work in Belgium shows that political parties with a strong digital platform may see online and in-person activism as two sides of one coin rather than an either-or (Sijstermans, 2021). Research into the Labour, Liberal Democrat and Conservative parties shows that Twitter followers are 'loyal' in that they only follow MPs from one party on Twitter (Bartlett et al., 2013). This shows a similarity between online following and more formal forms of party affiliation.

The nature of party membership and political parties may be more fundamentally altered by the rise of what Paolo Gerbaudo (2018) has called 'the digital party'. The classical digital political party is solely organised online; some examples of digital parties include Italy's Five

Star Movement and various European Pirate parties. However, parties can also adopt certain digital organisational tools such as *Nationbuilder*, *Consul* and *Loomio*. These online platforms help parties seek member input. While the UK does not have any prominent *fully* digital parties, parties such as the Labour Party and the SNP have sought out online tools as a way to engage with supporters (Dommett et al., 2021a).

Party members are activists, but they are also co-creators of the party through party democracy. Intra-party democracy, sometimes abbreviated to IPD, has been split into two main types: (1) assembly IPD, in which decisions are made through meetings, and (2) plebiscitary IPD, in which all members are given power through a ballot (Poguntke et al., 2016).

One key plebiscitary moment for political parties is the leadership election. Prior to the 1970s, in the Labour and Conservative parties, MPs were the only ones allowed to choose party leaders. But since then, leadership elections have democratised and all parties in the UK allow members to have a vote on the party's next leader. This means that leadership elections are often a space for members to express dissatisfaction or set the future direction of the party.

For example, in the Scottish National Party leadership election in 2023, the party faced a choice between continuity (in Humza Yousaf's candidature) and change (in Kate Forbes and Ash Denham's candidatures) (Sijstermans, 2023). This forced the party, which had long been led by a small group of representatives, to consider alternative ideological factions in the party, including Forbes' more conservative economics and Denham's more conservative social policies. While Yousaf won the election, Forbes won a significant part of the vote which showed members' dissatisfaction with the status quo. On the other hand, the Conservative Party first has a series of votes for MPs to select candidates, which means that Conservative leadership elections are much more a reflection of parliamentarians than members (Booth et al., 2023; Jeffery et al., 2018).

Another visible type of intra-party democracy in political parties is the party conference, which can be seen as a form of assembly democracy in which party members come together to discuss policy and strategy decisions. While party conferences allow members to *discuss* these issues, their *decision-making* power is less clear. For example, in both the Conservative Party and Labour Party the leadership have a chance to overrule the decisions of party conferences (Pettitt, 2013). While they provide a space for talking, party conferences are not necessarily bottom-up spaces. In a comparative study including the UK Labour Party, scholars concluded that conferences are 'increasingly stage-managed with careful selection of speakers and orchestration of decision-making' (Faucher-King and Treille, 2003: 71).

Intra-party democracy also has an online component. When the internet first became more widespread in the late 1990s, scholars saw a potential for increased democratisation of party decision-making but found that this did not occur in practice (Gibson and Ward, 1999; Margolis et al., 1997). Green parties across Europe are seen as having a high level of intra-party democracy and digital savvy (Datts and Gerl, 2023). This has been seen in the UK as well, where the Green Party has sought digital expertise to expand its reach with supporters and to help with its messaging. This was in stark contrast to the Conservative Party which initially saw this as less important due to the smaller proportion of its support base online (Dommett et al., 2021a).

When political parties evolve ideologically, members and party representatives may form sub-groups, called 'factions', to promote their ideological stances in the political party. For example, in the Conservative Party, the European Research Group (ERG) emerged to oppose the UK's involvement in the EU and European Convention on Human Rights. Factions may compete or cooperate with one another to influence party decisions, but they may also sometimes contribute to the potential break-up of existing political parties (Boucek, 2009). However, the ERG did not seek to break-up the Conservative Party despite accusations that it was acting as a 'party within a party'; instead, the Group sought to influence Conservative policy (Murray and Armstrong, 2022).

Factions have different organisational goals. For example, in the Labour Party, alongside the election of Jeremy Corbyn as leader, a political activist group called Momentum was created. Momentum, according to its own website, 'is a socialist and anti-racist organisation committed to a fundamental and irreversible shift in wealth and power to the working class in all its diversity.' While its aims refer to roots in the grassroots, Momentum was also directed by party elites and was seen by some as an electoral vehicle for Corbyn (Watts and Bale, 2019: 101). Factions may thus be both grassroots and directed by key and powerful individuals within political parties, and party factions reflect individuals' disputes over power.

Momentum may also have played a part in a surprising statistic on party members that emerged from the Labour Party. Like parties across the world, mainstream British parties have seen declining membership numbers and disengagement from remaining members (Seyd and Whiteley, 2004). A 2022 briefing from the UK Parliament showed that most parties' membership numbers had either decreased or stagnated in the last 20 years, with the notable outlier of the Labour Party. Momentum's campaigning network was one contributor to an almost doubling of Labour Party membership between 2012 and 2017.

Regardless of absolute numbers, as highlighted in the Spotlight on research box and in this section more widely, party membership may not only be falling but also evolving. Members' activities and forms of affiliation to the party are taking on many different forms including more amorphous concepts of supporters such as online followers, news audiences and 'cyber-members' (Scarrow, 2015). In their study of the 2010 general election, Fisher et al. (2014) found that non-member supporters of the Labour, Conservative and Liberal Democrat parties did approximately two-thirds as many campaigning activities as members, providing a significant contribution.

While the nature of political party membership has changed significantly over time, political parties are built on the ground. The interconnections between members and supporters of political parties – whether in person or online – create an important foundation for political parties' campaigns, ideologies and organisational structures.

Spotlight on research: Beyond party members

Susan Scarrow's *Beyond Party Members* (2015) is a pivotal work on political parties which goes beyond the common narrative (the party member is a dying breed) towards a more

(Continued)

nuanced understanding of party membership. She explains that parties always varied in their interest in and recruitment of party members. Furthermore, Scarrow introduces the concept of 'multi-speed' membership which recognises that formal, traditional membership is no longer the only form of affiliation between party supporters and their preferred political party.

In the multi-speed membership framework, Scarrow identifies different categories of party supporter: the traditional member, activists, sustainers, cyber-members, followers, electors, light members and the news audience. These categories often overlap – for example, many activists will be traditional members and some online followers will also be traditional members. Multi-speed membership aligns well with the pluralist approach of this book by recognising that political parties provide different opportunities to different types of supporters. It also recognises that for political parties it is often more important what party supporters *do* (campaign, share information, vote, etc.) than whether they are formal members.

The development of different forms of affiliation to political parties may foster more pluralist political parties by allowing parties to consider a wider range of supporters' views. Parties' wider reach may potentially also strengthen their ability to play a role in democratically linking voters with the instruments of government. As such, Scarrow's approach highlights a more nuanced, and ultimately more optimistic, view of the future of political parties.

The party in central office

Party activists and party representatives are by their very nature visible to the public. They speak for the party either 'on the ground' or in the media or legislature. The party in central office is initially less immediately noticeable – as the name suggests, they may be squirreled away in offices. However, central staff are crucial to managing the activities of both activists and representatives.

The central office is understood, however, to comprise two main parts. The first is a party executive committee or committees which usually represent both elected representatives and the party on the ground. The second is central party staff, who serve the needs of the party and are paid to do so. While this second group may be seen as 'the servant of the national executive', in this section, we first consider how staff are 'more assertive' than this description suggests (Katz and Mair, 1993: 599). Second, this section considers how people become part of the central office and whether this limits or reflects pluralism in the UK.

Katz and Mair note that the party in central office is often conflated both with the party in public office and with the party on the ground. In the case of the former, the party in central office is seen as simply the staff of, or assistants of, elected members. And in the case of the latter, staff in central office simply serve the organisational and administrative needs of a membership organisation. This lack of centrality and difficulty in distinguishing the party in central office has meant that scholars of political parties have focused less on this aspect in their studies.

However, political party staff members' impact on parties' decisions is significant. Party staff are involved in policy development, communications management and organising tasks, in addition to the administrative, legal and financial responsibilities of political parties. In my own research, I have spoken to over a hundred political party members, staff and representatives in the UK, Belgium, France and Spain. I have found that political party staff across these contexts do a variety of work. This work includes drafting party manifestos, writing party press releases, and writing and designing communications on social media. Harmel (2018) found that the manifesto process varied significantly across parties but usually involved input from staff, representatives and members. Staff working on these types of documents may have leeway to shape policy messages and details. This type of work often happens quickly and in ad hoc ways, which means that staff who work for the party full-time are likely to take significant responsibility in comparison to members (who are voluntary) and parliamentarians (who have legislative and constituency tasks).

For example, one parliamentary staffer wrote about the challenges of the job which required wearing many hats. They explained: 'As a caseworker, I worked on complex cases for people at imminent risk of homelessness and deportation, as a secretary, I triaged hundreds of emails and meeting requests each week, and as a researcher, I met with interest groups, worked on Parliamentary speeches at short notice and helped to scrutinise legislation' (Kulig, 2023).

Given their powers in the party in terms of policy and strategy development and their inside knowledge of political parties, it matters *who* is a political party staffer. The demographics of this group is not well known or documented across the UK's political parties. This lack of visibility reflects their position in the *backstage* of the party. Furthermore, a party's parliamentary staff are often recruited in an ad hoc manner, with each parliamentarian in charge of their own office staff.

While they are relatively less visible and well understood than party members and parliamentarians, staff are not any less important as they act like the hinge between the members and the party, and the parliamentarians and the party and the public.

The party in public office: Westminster and beyond

Throughout this chapter, you have seen mention of *party representatives*. Political representatives are individuals who are elected to represent the interests and preferences of a specific constituency within a political system. In our political system, these people (unless elected as Independents) also represent the views of a specific political party.

Mair and Katz (2002) have argued that parliamentarians have increasingly become the most powerful actors in political parties. Parliamentary groups are often the recipients of funding and staffers, which allows a significant amount of control over the party's direction. Parliamentarians are also the beneficiaries of increasing political professionalisation and media attention, and they are able to capitalise on social media by growing their own personal profile and following within political parties. For example, SNP MP Mhairi Black saw her profile and popularity increase significantly after her maiden speech in the House of Commons went viral online, allowing her progressive views and straightforward style to significantly shape how voters saw the SNP as a party (BBC News, 2015b).

In a book that takes the reader inside the UK Parliament, Emma Crewe (2015) reveals the different roles and experiences that parliamentarians go through. Among these are legislating and taking part in parliamentary scrutiny and serving their constituents. However, parliamentarians also keep an eye on political party dynamics. For example, they develop friendships and rivalries within their party. They also face consequences for disagreeing with or diverging from their party (often through the process of political party 'whipping'), sometimes placing them 'between a rock and a hard place ... caught between the demands of constituency and party' (Allen, 2016: 948).

The demands of political parties may sometimes be out of sync with the interests or demands of parliamentarians. And given parliamentarians' growing power in the political party, MPs may push back against their leaders. For example, Conservative parliamentarians voted against their own party's government during Brexit negotiations. Repeated votes rejected agreements negotiated by the UK government led by Conservative prime minister and leader Theresa May, including one in January 2019 in which 118 Conservative MPs voted against her proposal. Whether they voted against May depended on their ideological leanings and could be predicted, in one way, by whether they were a member of the European Research Group (ERG) (Roe-Crines et al., 2021) discussed earlier in this chapter. This example also shows that, like members of political parties, parliamentarians sometimes disagree with one another and develop different intra-party groupings.

Sometimes, ideological differences between the party and the parliamentarian can be so serious that the parliamentarian chooses to leave the party (when they join another party, we often call this *defecting*). Sometimes this can also lead to the creation of a new party – for example, in the case of Change UK, which was a short-lived political party formed by members of the Labour, Conservative and Liberal Democrat Parties based on differences of opinion on Brexit. Parliamentarians' ability to start a new political party if their preferences differ significantly from the rest of their party again shows the power that they have in the political party system.

In the UK, political parties have representatives at multiple territorial levels: in local government, devolved legislatures (the Scottish Parliament, Welsh Parliament (*Senedd Cymru* in Welsh), Northern Ireland Assembly), and the UK Parliament (House of Commons, House of Lords). These different legislative arenas, or *venues*, mean that parliamentarians may develop their profile at different levels. For example, Scottish Conservative leader Ruth Davidson, who led from 2011 to 2019, took advantage of being established in the Scottish unionist arena to grow her profile during the 2014 Scottish independence referendum. She also sought to emphasise her position at a distance from the UK-wide Conservatives as a strategic choice (Torrance, 2020). Parliamentarians may also 'shop' legislation to different venues to pass certain policy goals such as tobacco and alcohol regulations (Cairney, 2007; Holden and Hawkins, 2013). This 'venue shopping' means that they will look to pass a policy in different Parliaments around the UK.

Parliamentarians don't have equal powers or abilities in different parts of the UK. As James Mitchell wrote, 'The absence of devolution in England (other than the London Assembly), Scottish legislative devolution, the Welsh Assembly without primary legislative powers, and the consociational institutions of Northern Ireland, reflect and entrench long established asymmetries' (Mitchell, 2010: 86). These asymmetries are also constantly in flux. For example, since Mitchell wrote, the Welsh National Assembly gained primary legislative powers after a series of reforms put in place formally through the Government of Wales Act 2006.

On the other hand, members of the Northern Ireland Assembly have often been stopped from doing legislative work by political gridlock. Given the differences between religious and political communities in Northern Ireland, the Northern Ireland Assembly was set up to ensure balance through a system called consociationalism. This system includes a requirement that the First and Deputy First Ministers have equal power and that one is from a nationalist party and the other is from a unionist party. When these two sides of the political spectrum cannot agree with one another, the Northern Ireland Assembly may be suspended. This has happened on numerous occasions including two very long periods, from October 2002 to May 2007 and from January 2017 to January 2020. Republican and pro-Irish unity party Sinn Féin won seven of Northern Ireland's 18 seats in the UK Parliament but has a long-standing policy of not taking up seats in said UK Parliament. As such, parliamentarians in Norhern Ireland might at times be less empowered than others in the UK's legislatures.

Parliamentarians in the House of Lords, on the other hand, are not elected but instead appointed to these roles through several different processes. Two that are relevant to our chapter are the appointment of peers through political party lists and resignation honours lists from outgoing prime ministers. Given these processes, it is important to note that not all political parties have members in the House of Lords. The Scottish National Party and Sinn Féin choose not to send members to the House of Lords as part of their political stance against it, and the Labour Party has sent limited numbers of nominations. Smaller parties that haven't had many or any parliamentarians are also excluded from these spaces.

The House of Lords appointment process thus reinforces the power of those political parties that were successful. For example, during the Brexit process, the House of Lords regularly voted in favour of measures to remain in or connected to the European Union. This reflected the time period in which many peers were appointed, particularly the power of Liberal Democrat peers, which reflected their previous successes. Given this form of appointment rather than election, the House of Lords' power is often debated and criticised. This is one of the democratic issues we will discuss towards the conclusion of this chapter.

Parliamentarians, despite their various levels of power and arenas, often provide the substance to the UK's ideological and political debates through their appearances in legislatures and in the media. In the third section, we will explore how political parties compete with one another and define two key dynamics of competition that are important in the UK.

Theory box: Political cleavage theory

Political parties' competition with one another is one of their key functions, which allows political debate to happen among voters and parliamentarians. To understand political competition, we consider the political cleavages that define society and the differences between political parties. The concept of political cleavages was first conceptualised by

(Continued)

Lipset and Rokkan (1967) who identified four main cleavages: centre–periphery, church–state, urban–rural, and class. The last division addresses the political differences and conflict that are driven by economic differences and inequalities. This economic difference is often understood to underpin the division between parties on the 'left' (social democratic, labour) and those on the 'right' (conservative, liberal).

Society has changed significantly since 1967. People are more educated, more urban and more diverse with governing systems immeasurably more complex. Big changes include more globalisation, individualisation and interconnection (e.g. through the internet). As such, left–right cleavages underpinned by traditional social class have become less important in determining people's political choices. This process is called *dealignment* because it has created a mismatch between specific political parties and specific social interest groups. In addition to *dealignment*, voters have *realigned* themselves along different lines of cleavage.

Scholars such as Hooghe and Marks (2018), Inglehart (1981), Kitschelt (1988) and Kriesi (1998) have explored the development of new values in political parties. New cultural issues that are important in politics include sexuality, immigration and European integration. This new political cleavage has often been identified as having two sides: the GAL (green, alternative, libertarian) and the TAN (traditionalist, authoritarian, nationalist).

The British political party system

In the first part of this chapter, we looked at the internal differences within political parties. In the second part, we look at the relationships *between* political parties in the UK. These relationships shape the nature of political competition by allowing voters to choose a party that might best fit their political opinions. From there, the political parties seek to represent those interests, find compromise where necessary, and, if in opposition, hold those in charge accountable.

Perhaps the best illustration of this competitive role of political parties is the Westminster Parliament chamber. The chamber is designed with two sets of seating facing one another in an oppositional design. In fact, the story is that the government and opposition benches are 'two sword lengths' apart to ensure that legislators couldn't take political competition to a more violent level. The traditional British system of political parties focuses on two contrasting groups – on one side the government, on the other side the 'official' Opposition. In practice, these roles have been taken up by the Conservative Party and the Labour Party with the roles changing hands between the two. This two-party set-up affects the allocation of speaking time and media attention on different political actors. For example, the 'Leader of the Opposition' has a significant role in beginning the questioning of the prime minister at Prime Minister's Question Time (PMQs) every week.

However, the British party system's competitive field is more plural than this. One important role is that of the 'third party' in the UK Parliament, which has been predominantly held by the Liberal Party or Liberal Democrats since 1945. Since 2015, it changed hands to the SNP. In the 2010, 2015, 2017 and 2019 general elections, there were respectively 7, 9, 8 and 10 political parties with MPs elected. The competitive field of the UK party system is thus more plural than it seems on the surface.

In the next sections, we explore two key dimensions of competition in British politics: the left–right dimension and the territorial dimension.

From the left, from the right

The most common form of political cleavage is the class cleavage, which (as noted above) underpins the common heuristics that place a party to 'the left' or 'the right'. The terms, which have been used since the French Revolution, provide a 'cognitive map of political and ideological relationships' (Arian and Shamir, 1983: 139). Parties are usually separated into 'left' and 'right' based on their positions on economics and key social issues. Economically, the key dynamics at play are parties' stance on economic redistribution, justice and organisation. Socially, key dynamics include parties' stance on gender and LGBTQIA+ rights, migration and multiculturalism, and the environment.

Surridge (2018) shows that from 1992 to 2017, Conservative voters were more 'right-wing' on the 'left–right' than Labour voters, confirming the split between the parties and showing that voters vote based on this dimension of politics. However, these findings were not uniform over time, with parties' voters coming closer together around 2005 for example. This shows that party positions and voters' perceptions of those positions can change over time, cued by a variety of factors.

Political parties may also contain multitudes, with certain representatives identifying as more to the 'left' or 'right' than their political party stands. For example, after their defeat in the 2010 general election and with a relatively open approach under Ed Miliband, numerous actors in the UK Labour Party began to form different factions to advocate for different futures for the party. The most well known of these were Blue Labour and *The Purple Book* (Beech and Hickson, 2014). These groups pushed forward alternative ideological directions for the party, including for Blue Labour the idea of a less centrally driven state and thus, in part, less left wing.

Furthermore, whether a party is understood to be to the left or right is to some extent part of political discourse and identification. It is part of 'labelling for self- and party identification on the one hand as well as of vetoing and rejecting others' cues on the other hand' (Arian and Shamir, 1983: 140). In this sense, it is possible to reject parties by arguing that they are too far to the 'right' or 'left' for your liking. For example, in Scotland, the SNP is sometimes called 'Tartan Tories' by their opponents to illustrate the belief that their economic policies are conservative and right wing. Some people saw the success of Kate Forbes' leadership campaign in the 2023 leadership elections as a vindication of this label (Elliards, 2023).

As such, while the language of left and right is used across the world, where someone stands substantially affects how they might position parties on this cognitive map.

The centre–periphery divide

We started this chapter with a discussion of the way that the different parts of the Scottish National Party mobilised around the 2014 independence referendum. While this referendum was the most visible and well known, there are numerous forms of territorial conflict in the

UK. Territorial conflict is caused by the divide in ideologies and policies between the 'centre' and the 'periphery.' Those in the periphery 'oppose centralization of authority in the central state and favour various forms of decentralization and cultural defence' (Marks and Wilson, 2000: 438). Peripheral political actors can be those who advocate for specific regions, such as Scottish and Welsh nationalists, as well as political movements that advocate for groups that are 'territorially dispersed' such as farmers.

In the UK, peripheral political parties are usually those defending certain regions. These are sometimes called sub-state nationalist parties or ethno-regionalist political parties (Dandoy, 2010; Hepburn, 2009). These include bigger parties such as the SNP, Plaid Cymru and Sinn Féin, which have been associated with the promotion of more power for and separation of Scotland, Wales and Northern Ireland respectively. However, other parties also make claims for greater powers for their region, including Mebyon Kernow in Cornwall and the Yorkshire Party in Yorkshire.

Devolved institutions have given political parties in Scotland, Wales and Northern Ireland more distinctive patterns of political competition. For example, in Scotland, the SNP has sought to take on a social democratic and left-wing positioning while promoting Scottish independence, putting them in direct competition with the Scottish Labour Party for voters on the left. This has set up a different focus of political competition in Scotland which led to specific challenges for the Scottish Labour Party, which struggled to find a clear position on the centre–periphery issue (Bennett et al., 2021).

In England, too, different political actors have sought to articulate the need for further decentralisation of power. This has particularly come in the form of local politicians from UK-wide political parties developing local centres of power and demands, enabled by the creation of mayoral combined authorities. For example, Andy Burnham, the Labour mayor of the Greater Manchester metropolitan area, sought to promote more decision-making power for Manchester during the Covid pandemic. Burnham employed not only left-wing language but arguments against the centre when he claimed that the UK Government was 'bullying' Manchester into accepting insufficient funding to support businesses (Nurse, 2020).

Political parties, and their dominant actors, thus are key proponents of the policy and ideological positions in the UK through their legislative roles but also extra-parliamentary messaging and engagement with voters. These cleavages, as set out by Lipset and Rokkan (1967), are not mutually exclusive but rather overlapping and allow parties to differentiate themselves from one another to attract support.

The (waning?) importance of British political parties

Political parties have been described as 'ubiquitous' (Dalton et al., 2011: 4) and 'an unavoidable part of democracy' (Stokes, 1999: 263). In traditional understandings of democracy, the political party is a vital institution. However, as the world changes so does the role of political parties. The competitive party system, the policy issues under debate by those parties and the internal workings of parties have all been challenged. This is as true in the United Kingdom as in other parts of the world.

In recent decades, the British political party system has shown increasing changeability. In 2010 the Conservative Party went into coalition with the Liberal Democrats and in 2017 the Conservative Party required the support of the Democratic Unionist Party to rule. These events were a significant departure from post-1945 British politics, which saw until 2010 exclusively one party in government. The same period marked the rise and establishment of the SNP in power at the Scottish level, first in minority government in 2007, then governing with an overall majority in 2011. They even became the third largest party in the UK Parliament in 2015.

Image 7.2 Activists raise placards with party slogans at a Labour Party rally in Leeds ahead of election day.
© Photo by Victoria M Gardner on Shutterstock

UKIP also rose during this time, peaking in popularity during the 2014 European elections and the 2016 Brexit vote. On the other side of the political spectrum, the Green Party of England and Wales elected its first MP in 2010 and continued to see unprecedented successes in the general election in 2015 and local elections in 2019. The combined votes for these two parties led to an unprecedented proportion of votes for parties outside of Labour, the Lib Dems and the Conservatives. In fact, in 2015 UKIP and the Green Party had five million votes collectively, which resulted in only two elected MPs. This inequality in the link between votes and representation also put pressure on the electoral institutions of the UK (House of Commons, 2015).

For the traditionally dominant parties, Labour and Conservative, these electoral challenges have been exacerbated by post-Brexit divisions. Scholars have found that Brexit led to long-lasting polarisation between different identity groups (Hobolt et al., 2021). This resulted in a changing electoral map. Labour consolidated its hold in Remain-voting urban areas while the Conservative party encroached into the traditionally Labour areas in the north of England (Fieldhouse and Bailey, 2023). This changing electoral landscape highlighted the evolving nature of party politics in the aftermath of Brexit, with new fault lines challenging traditional party loyalties. As a result, both major parties have had to redefine their policies and messaging to adjust in a new political landscape.

As discussed above, political parties have been adjusting to a rapidly changing internal world, including adapting to the role that digital media and communications now play. Social media and digital platforms have changed how members and supporters promote their political party to the outside world, and they also provide a new way for parties to collect more information about and solicit the opinions of their members. These changes have occurred in parallel to a long-term decrease in political party membership in the UK and across the world. The UK has also seen the growth of social movements, particularly around climate activism. In 2019, particularly, the UK saw Extinction Rebellion protests in London that resulted in thousands of arrests, and thousands of young people joined school strikes for climate action (Ares and Bolton, 2020).

All these dynamics mean that political parties in the UK's political system are no longer as stable or as dominant as they once were. New political party and social movement challengers can set the tone of political competition and policy priorities. Furthermore, challenges within political parties, including allegations of bullying and unrepresentativeness alongside a growth in populist rhetoric, have eroded trust in political parties. In this section we explore these critical challenges and opportunities for British political parties of the 21st century.

Parties' role in democracy

In his seminal work on political parties, Giovanni Sartori (1976) emphasised that political parties are crucial to democracies. In democracies, they aggregate and allow diverse interests to *participate* in politics and help to divide (*partition*) those interests in a competitive system. In other words, political parties provide an opportunity for individuals to take part in their country's decision-making processes: through grassroots membership, parliamentary representation or electoral support. They allow wide representation of interests. Political parties also separate parliament into the 'government' and 'opposition' where different party groupings carry out functions of democracy such as holding the government accountable, electing prime ministers and scrutinising proposed legislation. They thus facilitate compromise between those different interests.

Even as Sartori wrote about the important functions of the political party in the 1970s, political scholars began to write about the decline of political parties, in the UK and across the world. Webb (1995: 302–303) outlined two main dimensions of this supposed decline: the fall in parties' legitimacy due to public apathy and distrust, and the decline in parties' organisational strength such as reduced funding or activist base. Cross-national polling on public images of political parties showed that distrust and dissatisfaction with political parties is a 'general pattern across the Western democracies' (Dalton and Weldon, 2005: 947). Smith identified this in the UK as a 'growing dissonance between the elite practice of politics through parties and the way politics is experienced by citizens' (2014: 102).

Ideas for democratic change in the UK have long been proposed by political parties and electoral campaigners. For example, the Electoral Reform Society (ERS) was founded in 1884 and was supported by MPs from both the Conservatives and Labour. At founding and still today, ERS's aim is to promote proportional representation. This would end the first past the post (FPTP) electoral system. FPTP means that voters only vote for one candidate and the candidate with the most votes wins, meaning that all other votes cast in that constituency are not represented. Some call this a 'winner takes all' system. In another electoral system, such as the alternative vote system proposed in a 2011 referendum in the UK, voters can rank candidates and thus have their preferences considered.

In Wales, Scotland and London, and at European Parliament level, proportional representation elections have been put in place, showing some shifts in electoral systems despite the 'conventional wisdom' that electoral systems are stubbornly stable (Dunleavy and Margetts, 2001: 296). However, at a UK-wide level, the vote to move towards proportional representation was defeated in 2011 and electoral reform remains unlikely. In part, this is due to the assumption that elections to the House of Commons are 'primary' elections while elections at other levels can be seen as 'secondary' and thus can be reformed. Furthermore, the Conservative Party continues to push against electoral reform while the Labour Party was long split on the issue, showing that existing political parties can maintain political institutions (Flinders, 2010).

As such, while Sartori argued that institutionally political parties were essential to democracy, in the UK the reality of political parties as representative bodies that allow people to *take part* has long been criticised. While activists have sought institutional changes in the UK's democratic system and devolution has led to more proportional and decentralised parties, this has not yet been realised uniformly across the country.

Party as community

Political parties have been described as families in two senses. First, scholars use the term 'party family' which groups different types of parties together in terms of their origins, ideology and transnational links – for example, social democratic parties or Christian democratic parties (Mair and Mudde, 1998). In this sense, members and representatives of political parties may find a sense of commonality and community that crosses national boundaries. This sense of transnational community has been particularly revealed by the creation of 'party groups' in the European Parliament and associated 'European political parties' which allow representatives elected in the European Union's member states to legislate and cooperate.

Second, political parties are often described as families by those inside of them. For example, party members might describe being in a party as being part of a 'big family' that provides them with a community, and activism serves as a tool to foster this type of community (Albertazzi, 2016; Sijstermans, 2021). A strong community- and membership-driven party is now less likely to exist. As the studies cited above show, the nature of political party affiliation is changing, with fewer people choosing to be party members and with members and supporters choosing different types of affiliation, such as social media support. Some scholars argue that those parties still maintaining a wider membership organisation are more likely to be populist and radical right-wing parties (Albertazzi and van Kessel, 2021; Heinisch and Mazzoleni, 2016). These two 'family' functions – within the party and between states – mean that the political party could have a continuing and important role in building political societies.

However, political parties in the UK have shown signs of being a sometimes bullying, corrupt and harmful family. For example, in a difficult time for Conservative prime minister Liz Truss, Conservative whips were accused of 'clear bullying' to secure support from backbench MPs for her prime ministership (BBC News, 20 October 2022). Bullying allegations have been levelled at MPs in relation to different groups of people – for example, ministers bullying civil servants, MPs threatening and intimidating and even blackmailing one another, and politicians turning a blind eye to sexual assault or harassment in their midst (Krook, 2018). The political party can facilitate such behaviour, for example in the case of the Conservative whips' behaviour in October 2022. The political party can also sanction bad behaviour through actions such as suspending or expelling individuals from a party, as was the case with an SNP MP who was suspended for two days over a sexual advance on a staff member (BBC News, 14 June 2022).

As such, political parties may still have an important role in bringing together people who believe in a certain ideology and through campaigning and social activities, creating a political family. However, like other types of families, these families have faced significant challenges and posed risks for their members.

Not that important? Not that special?

As these discussions may suggest, there is some sense that political parties are no longer as important or special as they were once meant to be. This particularly manifests itself in the sense that political parties are no longer the *exclusive* voices of the ordinary person in the political arena.

In recent years, other forms of political organising have emerged that have challenged or altered the role of the political party. Chief among these is the emergence of strong social movements, such as Extinction Rebellion (XR) in relation to climate change. One case study of XR showed that the movement aimed its communications at voters and prospective parliamentarians – for example, by holding climate hustings in different constituencies (Rhodes, 2019). However, this does not mean that social movements will replace political parties entirely. In fact, movements sometimes become political parties, such as the Green parties that emerged in Europe (McAdam and Tarrow, 2010).

On the other hand, political movements may also take hold within existing political parties. For example, certain individuals in the Conservative Party have embraced environmental politics and issues such as Conservative Lord Zac Goldsmith who became Minister of State for Overseas Territories, Commonwealth, Energy, Climate and Environment. The relationship between social movements and political parties may also occur at the level of the 'rank and file'. For example, researchers showed that supporters of far-right social movement Britain First (BF) and political party UKIP often overlapped. Interestingly, when UKIP's electoral support faltered after the Brexit referendum, the BF social movement sought to take on electoral politics themselves (Davidson and Berezin, 2018).

As Britain First indicates, another challenge to political parties across the world and in the UK is the rise of populist political forces, which have been characterised by setting up an oppositional relationship between the 'ordinary' people and the 'corrupt' elite (Mudde, 2004). Populism can be seen in the rhetoric and ideologies of individual leaders, political parties or social movements. Many political parties have *benefited from* using populist messaging and not all of these parties are on the radical right wing. Some scholars argue that Plaid Cymru and the Scottish National Party have also engaged in these types of discourse, for example in combating the policy of economic austerity (Massetti, 2018). However, while political parties often use this language, paradoxically populist rhetoric often undermines the legitimacy of political parties themselves as it presents traditional politics as corrupt.

This feeling of disconnection and alienation may be particularly strong in young people in the UK. Young people tend to vote less, in part due to feelings of alienation from politics and a frustration with the bad behaviour of politicians. Researchers asked young people about their feelings towards political parties and politicians. Only 17 per cent of respondents expressed positive dispositions towards these actors, while 81 per cent felt negatively about them (Henn and Foard, 2012. Sloam (2007: 565) explained:

> Young people are interested in politics, but not in the political process, though their interest is not matched by a deep understanding of how things work. This hampers debate and discussion of the issues, but also acts as a barrier to participation in conventional politics and adds to the feeling of powerlessness and disconnection from the political process.

Conclusion

This chapter has provided you with the tools to understand political parties deeply, even as they continually evolve. As we showed in the first section, political parties can be internally understood in different ways: the party on the ground, the party's central office staff and the party's public representatives. Within each of these groupings, we may see ideological and strategic factions and collaboration occur. When looking at the relationship between political parties, you've learned about the concept of political *cleavages* which separate parties and structure political competition – from left to right, centre to periphery and niche to mainstream. Finally, we have concluded this chapter by critically recognising both the importance and the challenges of political parties in our complex and continuously changing democracy.

From this chapter, it may become clear to you that political parties are neither the exclusive domain of the elite nor entirely democratised bodies. Political parties are an accumulation of parts, which sometimes fit together seamlessly and sometimes rub one another the wrong way. To add to this complexity, at times the UK's political parties have been essential to driving political change – for example, the role of UKIP in pushing forward Brexit, the role of the Scottish National Party in advocating for Scottish independence – but in other cases, political parties may be faltering, with lower membership numbers, or become less important given the rise of social movements working on salient contemporary issues. The future of political parties remains uncertain as different forces such as populism, the dominance of social media and political apathy grow.

Key take-home points

- Political parties are composed of different individuals and sub-groups, such as supporters, members and activists ('on the ground'), staff in the central office and public representatives.

- Different constitutive elements of parties negotiate to develop the collective party position and sometimes disagree with one another.
- Parties are fundamental to democracy because they channel different interests into the institutions of government, where they compete and seek compromises.
- Political parties continue to face many challenges, including the growth of non-partisan social movements, decreasing membership, and public discontent and distrust in party politics driven partly by the growth in populist rhetoric.

Annotated reading list

Crewe, E. (2015) *The House of Commons: An Anthropoloy of MPs at Work*. London: Bloomsbury.

In this book, Emma Crewe takes the reader inside the Houses of Parliament. In this exploration of the way that Parliament works, she shows how MPs relate to and work with their own party members and mentors. Crewe also shows how they deal with personal enmities and friendships with MPs in other political parties. Crewe's book is particularly appealing in the way that it transcends the idea that MPs' behaviours and relationships are always rational. Instead, Crewe recognises that politics and how individual politicians act is also about emotion.

The book also includes fun insider details – for example, MPs sit in the Tea Room along party lines, except for the Welsh table which includes 'Labour miscreants'. These more intimate portraits of British politicians show that, although many will say, 'You're all the same', the experience of representatives inside of political parties is diverse. And furthermore, the relationships between MPs within parties and across parties are more complex than the binary and oppositional images of the Westminster Parliament allow for.

Thompson, L. (2018) Understanding third parties at Westminster: The SNP in the 2015 parliament. Politics, 38(4), 443–457.

Thompson, L. (2020) *The End of the Small Party? Change UK and the Challenges of Parliamentary Politics*. Manchester: Manchester University Press.

Change UK was a political party formed of defecting politicians from various parties who were dissatisfied with the way that Brexit was being handled. While it may have been a flash in the pan, Thompson's analysis shows how challenging it is for politicians to step away from their parties and why being a small party in Westminster is quite so difficult.

8
Elections, referendums and public opinion

Rosie Campbell

Image 8.1 The elephant and the rider © Photo by Happy Together on Shutterstock

Learning objectives

After reading this chapter you should be able to:

- Understand how participating in referendums and elections relates to everyday politics
- Explore theories of elite and mass opinion formation
- Examine the relationship between values and party choice
- Understand the role that recent referendums have played in shaping public opinion
- Learn the best practices in surveys of public opinion

Introduction

Elections and referendums are not everyday activities, although they have been occurring more often recently, with the Scottish and EU referendums and three general elections taking place since 2014. Nonetheless, they are infrequent opportunities for citizens to express our preferences and hold our elected representatives to account. And yet, as we have explored throughout this book, how we relate to formal political processes and institutions is shaped by our everyday interactions and experiences. It is pretty apparent that how we feel about specific political parties and politicians is shaped by the media we consume and the conversations we have with others, but it's sometimes less obvious to us how our beliefs, values and opinions are shaped by our environments. Chapter 5 outlined the impact that group membership has on our engagement with politics; in this chapter we explore how our lived experiences translate into our choices at the ballot box.

In this chapter we will consider theories of elite and mass opinion formation to understand how the political representation of our interests, beliefs and values works, or doesn't work, in practice. We will explore the relationships between values and party choice and how these have changed over time. Finally, we will examine the Scottish and EU referendums considering how they have altered the relationships we have with the political parties and the way we understand public opinion in the UK.

What is 'public opinion'?

To understand how our everyday experiences shape how we vote in elections we need to start by thinking about how our values and opinions are formed. Put another way, 'Where does public opinion come from?' Intuitively we tend to assume public opinion is something that exists independently of politicians. Sometimes, however, in reality the divisions we experience between groups in society are deliberately exaggerated by politicians who are trying to 'mobilise their base' and by media outlets seeking to hook in readers with provocative stories. Arguably, this is largely currently the case in the UK when it comes to the issues typically described as constituting the 'culture wars' or 'cancel culture'. Research undertaken by the Policy Institute at King's College London, with the polling company Ipsos, found that 47 per cent of their respondents in 2020 had never heard of cancel culture, but this figure had halved by 2022.

At the same time the number of news stories on the topic had risen exponentially, driven at least in part by politicians actively pushing the narrative (see Duffy, 2022). Alternatively, sometimes as society changes public opinion moves first and breaks through to transform the debate among political elites. There is good reason to think this was the case with our attitudes to gay rights and women's rights, where our beliefs about relationships and family structures have changed at a pace that has outstripped the legal and policy agendas of our elected politicians. For example, same-sex marriage was only legal in the UK in 2014 but a majority of the British public supported the right since the mid-2000s (Clements and Field, 2014). This leads us to an important political question: which came first public or elite opinion?

In common with many either/or questions, the answer is probably a bit of both. To understand why, let's consider a classic account of opinion formation. The American political scientist Philip Converse's work stands out as having made a significant impact on the way we tackle this question. Building on the analysis of earlier scholars, Converse viewed public opinion as an amalgamation of our individual views (Converse, 1964) – that is, opinions are formed inside our own heads and public opinion is their aggregation. From this perspective individuals process the information they receive through political experiences and media sources and it is through the evaluation of this material that our opinions are formed. For public opinion to have a meaningful existence outside of elite influence our individual responses to political polling questions should reflect a rational system of evaluation that guides our answers. Converse set out to establish the extent to which this was the case by assessing whether voters had coherent sets of opinions that together formed a political ideology. He analysed multiple responses to survey questions and concluded that most Americans in the 1950s did not have logically structured opinions but instead gave random sets of answers to questions. In fact, he argued that the overwhelming majority of Americans had 'nonattitudes' that were inconsistent and based on little factual information, making them vulnerable to persuasion from politicians who would not serve their best interests. Converse, therefore, was very much of the view that public opinion is largely elite driven rather than something that exists 'out there', independent of the messages being transmitted by politicians. This is a very troubling account of opinion formation from the perspective of representative democracy, which assumes that elected representatives act on behalf of citizens and are held accountable for failure to do so at the ballot box. If we citizens are not paying attention, have little information or interest in politics then how can we hold politicians to account?

Theory box: Moral Foundations Theory (MFT)

This theory provides an account of the underlying processes that support our political preferences. Jonathan Haidt outlines moral foundations theory in his influential book *The Righteous Mind: Why Good People Are Divided by Politics and Religion* (Haidt, 2012). Building on the Nobel prize winning work of Amos Tversky and Daniel Kahneman, Haidt claims that our verbalised opinions often reflect a post-hoc rationalisation of unconscious and instinctive processes (Tversky and Kahneman, 1974) – that is, the feeling comes first and the rationalisation second. Haidt uses a metaphor of the elephant and the rider to illustrate his point. He argues that rather than evaluating our policy preferences using

(Continued)

conscious rational (the rider) cost–benefit analysis to work out where we sit on an issue, instead we intuit (the elephant) how we feel about the issue morally, is it right or wrong, and then we come up with a rational argument to support our case after we've already determined our position. The elephant is really in charge.

Haidt argues that the moral foundations on which we build our opinions are influenced by culture. Thus, whilst we might believe that our rational conscious minds rule over our opinions, they are largely driven by unconscious processes shaped by our lived experience embedded in established moral cultures. This is a very brief precis of moral foundations theory, and I would strongly recommend reading *The Righteous Mind*. However, the key message for us here is that, much as we might believe that our opinions are truly our own and that we have come to hold them through rational consideration of the evidence, it is very likely that our journey has been influenced by the values espoused by those around, and before, us.

Using the US ideological liberal/conservative political spectrum to categorise political opinion, Haidt claims that these two groups rely on different sets of moral foundations (Graham et al., 2009). Haidt and colleagues found that liberals most often endorse and use harm/care (this is the dislike of the suffering of others) and fairness/reciprocity (this is our sense of justice) moral intuitions, whilst conservatives use five equally, harm/care, fairness/reciprocity, ingroup/loyalty (patriotism and prioritising the group before yourself), authority/respect (deference to leaders or elders) and purity/sanctity (avoiding contamination both physical and spiritual). Whilst concerns about group loyalty, respect for authority and the sacred play an important role in explaining how conservatives respond to political issues, these foundations are of little consequence to liberals. This is potentially why liberals and conservatives in the contemporary US so often speak past each other; they are relying on different criteria to intuit the rightness or wrongness of any given government policy or programme.

Critics of MFT point to the lack of a coherent theoretical account of why these specific foundations should have come to dominate human morality (Curry, 2019), a point that is conceded by some MFT proponents (Graham et al., 2013). Whether the specific operationalisation of the theory is correct or not, MFT is an intriguing account of how we come to hold our values and why we sometimes feel so vociferously that we are right and others are wrong. In contemporary British society political polarisation appears to have deepened since the Brexit referendum. Understanding public opinion as a division between those who are right and those who are on the wrong side of an issue loses sight of the underlying explanations for these diversions:

> If you really want to change someone's mind on a moral or political matter, you'll need to see things from that person's angle as well as your own. And if you do truly see it the other person's way – deeply and intuitively – you might even find your own mind opening in response. Empathy is an antidote to righteousness, although it's very difficult to empathize across a moral divide. (Haidt, 2012: 49)

If Converse was right, then perhaps rather than worrying too much about what we actually think about political issues we would be better off focusing on how political parties attempt to persuade us to support them and their preferences. From this perspective a top–down, elite focused analysis of the political issues of the day and the drivers of our electoral behaviour seems warranted. However, whilst for many of us our political opinions do not follow the same tight ideological lines as many elected politicians, and other members of political elites, that does not mean that they are entirely unstructured or 'random'. Studies of public opinion that focus at the mass or aggregate level, rather than on individuals, find more consistency and logical patterns and trends. From this perspective we should think about public opinion as a thermostat that indicates whether the general public would like a little more, or less, government intervention on key issues (Soroka and Wlezien, 2009). The fact that on any one issue we might not have full information, respond accurately to political knowledge questions or have sets of ideas that can be neatly described as left wing/right wing or liberal/conservative does not mean that as a collective there is no such thing as informed or meaningful public opinion. Phew! Perhaps representative democracy might just work – at least better than the alternatives:

> Many forms of Government have been tried, and will be tried in this world of sin and woe. No one pretends that democracy is perfect or all-wise. Indeed it has been said that democracy is the worst form of Government except for all those other forms that have been tried from time to time. (Winston Churchill, 11 November 1947)

The thermostatic model of public opinion

The thermostatic model of public opinion moves away from testing individual voters' political knowledge, or the consistency of our preferences, and instead looks at trends in our collective attitudes. On the basis that where we express random 'nonattitudes' in opinion surveys these will cancel each other out, as my random selection of an answer will be cancelled out by your random selection of another response option to the same question. The responses that are non-random (informed by some information, experience or understanding!) will aggregate together into a trend that moves over time. This trend doesn't need to be generated by in-depth policy knowledge, it can be based on our responses to meaningful cues, such as experiences of public services, in schools and hospitals for example, and the information we receive from media and our social networks. For any specific policy area there need only be a sufficient number of people paying attention to these cues for public opinion to send a signal of our preferences to our elected politicians.

> Shifts in the policy temperature tend to be correlated with thermostatic shifts in public opinion. This is equivalent to a control that switches on when there is 'too much' and switches off when there is 'too little'. (Jennings, 2009: 850)

Another way of describing this aggregate or mass level way of understanding how public opinion reacts to and informs governments is as an error correction model. In the long run the trends in public opinion in a democracy should mirror those of government policy; when they get out of sync, there may be a delay, but if opinion informs vote choice then political parties have an incentive and should realign to public opinion to attempt to win elections. Will Jennings and Peter John demonstrate a relationship of this kind between public opinion about the most important problem facing the country and the issues the government chose to focus on in

Queen's Speeches between 1960 and 2001, although the level of responsiveness, and the duration of the lag, vary by issue and over time (Jennings and John, 2009). An aggregate approach to understanding public opinion is thus more useful than focusing on our individual preferences. Although these are of course important, at the mass level we can see that public opinion does inform government policy – that is, public opinion sends a meaningful signal that over time influences party policy platforms. The relationship does, however, go in both directions. Governments and parties can also lead public opinion, as evidenced in the growth of the 'culture war' narrative. In sum, we can rest assured that public opinion exists, not as a summation of our individual rational evaluations of government's success or failure in every policy domain, but as a collective trend that responds to, and directs, political parties' programmes. After this deviation into the world of where our opinions come from let us return to the matter at hand – UK politics. How can we use the theoretical concepts and empirical insights from the study of public opinion formation to better understand public opinion in contemporary Britain?

Measuring British public opinion

We've devoted a fair bit of time to theorising public opinion but what about measuring it in the UK today? Simply reading off our preferences from an opinion poll might not give political parties all the information they need to be responsive (Johns, 2019). Rob Johns cites polling conducted in the early 2000s which found that many Conservative party policy ideas were popular, unless they were attributed to the Conservative party. This is because Labour supporters, for example, were less keen on the very same policies if they knew that they were being proposed by the Conservatives. (This is an example of the elephant leading the rider we learnt about from moral foundations theory.) Thus, simply tracking the public's policy preferences can give too little information to a party trying to reach beyond its core supporters. One way to better understand what the polls are telling us is to complement them with qualitative research, usually through focus groups. Focus groups can help us explore how issues, and survey questions themselves, are understood by participants. Political parties typically employ focus groups alongside opinion polls to gain further insight, and to shape questions asked in surveys.

Another issue is how polling questions are phrased. When we know little about a subject, and/or aren't very interested in it, we are more likely to simply respond 'yes' to a 'yes/no' question. (This is in keeping with Converse's identification of 'nonattitudes'.) Johns uses the example of a survey experiment where British respondents were asked two different versions of the same question: 'Individuals are more to blame than social conditions for crime in this country' and 'Social conditions are more to blame than individuals for crime in this country'. Sixty per cent agreed with the first statement and 57 per cent with the second (Johns, 2019: 4). These issues, and other elements of survey design, such as question order effects, influence how reliable polls are as measures of public opinion. Researchers have devoted a great deal of energy into assessing these survey effects and recommending best practice to avoid leading questions and biased results. Reputable polling companies in the UK are members of the British Polling Council, a voluntary association that sets rules around transparency and methodology. Even so, the most trustworthy sources of data on public opinion in Britain are the large publicly funded social surveys such as the British Election Study and the British Social Attitudes Survey.

The British Election Study (BES) series (which began in 1964) is the most reliable source specifically on electoral behaviour in the UK. The BES methodology is essential to obtaining a clear picture of how the nation votes because it contains a face-to-face random probability sample (the gold standard of survey research) which reduces response and selection bias, although it does not eliminate them. The surveyors return to the randomly selected respondent's residential address up to five times, at different times of day, in order to try and obtain an interview with the respondent and the survey also includes a validated voter measure where the team literally check the electoral register, not for party of vote, but for turnout. In recent years the BES has also included a very large online sample to supplement the smaller random sample. The majority of the studies that I am citing in this chapter make use of BES data.

Another measurement issue is a subject we have touched on already, ideological scales. Converse used a Liberal/Conservative axis to analyse the extent to which American citizens express coherent opinions. One way to measure our political attitudes that is widely used is simply to ask whether we're on the left or the right of the politics, which is a unidimensional approach comparable to the one employed by Converse. Researchers in the UK, however, have often used at least two scales to attempt to measure how our attitudes are organised: liberal/authoritarian and socialist/laissez faire to distinguish between economic and social attitudes (Evans et al.,1996) (see Figure 8.1).

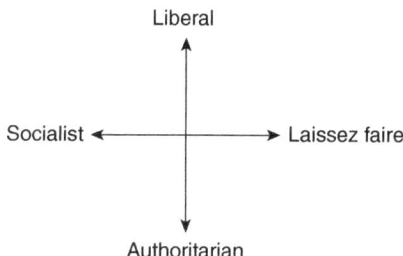

Figure 8.1 An example of two-dimensional political attitudes

There are numerous ways to try to identify where our attitudes fit in political space. We could start with thinking about a simple spectrum of left to right (or liberal/conservative if you are American). This approach is often used in studies of public opinion, but it relies on us all sharing an understanding of what we mean by left- and right-wing attitudes. In the UK most emphasis has been placed on economic attitudes so left wing would represent socialist views that support higher levels of taxation and public spending (and historically state ownership of national industries) and right wing the laissez faire perspective that government intervention in the economy should be minimal. One difficulty with this approach is that it is not obvious how we should categorise attitudes towards social issues. In the US the liberal/conservative scale often merges these two sets of values, so that minimal state intervention in the economy is also associated with authoritarian attitudes about how society should be organised – supporting the death penalty for example. This elision of different sets of values partially explains why Converse failed to find a consistent pattern in American public opinion in the 1950s (Feldman, 1988).

I've listed survey questions from the British Election Study series that are commonly used to measure these two dimensions of political attitudes (see Table 8.1). The questions are sometimes worded so that a positive answer would give a left-wing response and sometimes a right-wing response to ensure that respondents who tick 'agree' to all, for example, do not bias the results. Can you identify which questions belong with which scale, socialist/laissez faire or liberal/authoritarian? (Answers at the end of this chapter.) Once you've done this, have a look at the two-dimensional representation of these attitudes (Figure 8.1). Where would you place yourself?

Table 8.1 Measuring socialist/laissez faire and liberal/authoritarian values

	Socialist/Laissez faire	Liberal/Authoritarian
Ordinary working people get their fair share of the nation's wealth		
There is one law for the rich and one for the poor		
Young people today don't have enough respect for traditional British values		
Censorship of films and magazines is necessary to uphold moral standards		
There is no need for strong trade unions to protect working conditions and wages		
Private enterprise is the best way to solve Britain's economic problems		
Major public services and industries ought to be in state ownership		
The government's responsibility is to provide a job for everyone who wants one		
People should be allowed to organise public protests against the government		
People in Britain should be more tolerant of those who lead unconventional lives		
For some crimes, the death penalty is the most appropriate sentence		
People who break the law should be given stiffer sentences		

In addition to these to aspects of our political attitudes, researchers in the UK have also put increasing emphasis on our globalist or cosmopolitan versus nationalist values. Globalist/nationalist attitudes can be measured by looking at how we feel about issues such as immigration. If you would like to see where researchers would place you in three-dimensional political space across economic, social and nationalist axes then the electoral calculus website has a great tool (www.electoralcalculus.co.uk/survey3d.html).

We will see how important distinguishing between these different aspects of our political beliefs and values has become when we discuss voting behaviour and the Brexit referendum later in this chapter.

Voting behaviour

Partisan and class alignment

No introduction to British electoral politics would be complete without a discussion of partisan and class alignment, and subsequent dealignment. Philip Converse, who we met earlier, was part of the behavioural revolution in political science in the 1950s and 1960s, when researchers moved from a focus on formal–legal political institutions to individual and group action using scientific methods of observation and analysis. The behavioural revolution had a profound impact on the study of elections and voting behaviour. Leading revolutionaries Angus Campbell, Philip Converse, Warren Miller and Donald E. Stokes published a groundbreaking book *The American Voter* in 1960 (Campbell et al., 1960).

Image 8.2 Election Day
© Photo by Rawpixel.com on Shutterstock

The overarching theme of *The American Voter* is the role of partisan identification in vote choice. The authors argued that rather than making a rational calculation at election time, regarding which candidate or party would be best equipped to take office, most voters instead consistently voted for the same party election after election because their evaluations of the current context were shaped by long-term psychological attachments. They claimed that voters develop a partisan identification through childhood and adult socialisation, whereby individuals are exposed to the party preferences of those around them in their families, communities, institutions and workplaces and acquire a stable attachment to a party. Short-term influences were thought to play only a minimal role because individuals were believed, in general, to be incapable of making an election-by-election choice because they lacked the tools necessary to evaluate the wealth of information available to them. Instead, information would be filtered through a psychological framework that gave precedence to issues perceived to be important to the individual because they were of the type that were discussed around them in their community.

David Butler and Donald Stokes extended this behavioural approach, developed by Campbell et al. to British voting behaviour (Butler and Stokes, 1974). In the British context the partisan identification model was expanded to encompass occupational class. The model developed by Butler and Stokes became the foundational text of British voting behaviour. In common with the Michigan model, Butler and Stokes assumed that most people had little knowledge about politics and that their beliefs were formed in the main by socialisation processes. Butler and Stokes founded the British Election Study (BES) to test their theories and found that voters failed to respond to the questions in a consistent way over the years in which they were surveyed. However, three-quarters of the respondents felt a strong affiliation to a political party, without any demonstrable link to the left–right scale. Therefore, parental class and party were believed to have a direct influence on voters' partisan identification. As in the Michigan model, party identification was understood to be a long-term factor explaining voting decisions and political attitudes seen as a consequence, not a cause, of party loyalty. Actual vote choice in any given election could be affected by short-term factors, but these were underplayed. The model suggested that electoral change occurred as part of a gradual process of demographic change rather than resulting from the specific issues at play during any given election campaign. The founders of the study of psephology (voting behaviour) in Britain considered class to be the pre-eminent factor shaping British election results because there was such a strong and stable relationship between social class and partisan identification with approximately two-thirds of middle-class voters supporting the Conservative party and roughly the same proportion of working-class voters supporting Labour:

> Class is the basis of British party politics; all else is embellishment and detail. (Pulzer, 1967)

Pulzer might have been right in 1967 but since then much ink has been used contesting the extent to which social class still predominates. It is widely accepted that since the 1970s a process of partisan and class dealignment has taken place – that is, the old stable party allegiances and predictable relationship between social class and party support have broken down. The extent of this dealignment was hotly debated into the 1990s but trends since then have confirmed that the old alignments have weakened to the point that class is now a much weaker predictor of party support.

It is important to understand the historical context that has shaped how we vote, what the parties offer at election time, and of course how we study and explain voting behaviour to help us situate the factors that influence our vote choices today. However, bear in mind that was a very rapid summary of a vast field. If you would like to know more about trends in voting behaviour over time take a look at the suggestions in the Annotated reading list at the end of this chapter.

The 2019 British general election in historical context

In this section we are going to bring together everything we have learnt about public opinion and the history of voting behaviour in Britain using a case study of the 2019 general election, situated in historical context. We will consider the role that the Scottish and Brexit referendums played in shaping the 2019 results. Our goal here is to explore how our lived experiences translate into our choices at the ballot box.

The contemporary UK has a multi-level system of governance with policymaking distributed across the devolved parliaments and assemblies and elections taking place at the local, regional and national level. We are focusing on the 2019 general election as an illustration here, using examples of how the party system varies within different localities of the UK. However, if you are interested in studying this topic further, I strongly recommend that you read more about elections at different levels within the UK (see the Annotated reading list at the end of this chapter).

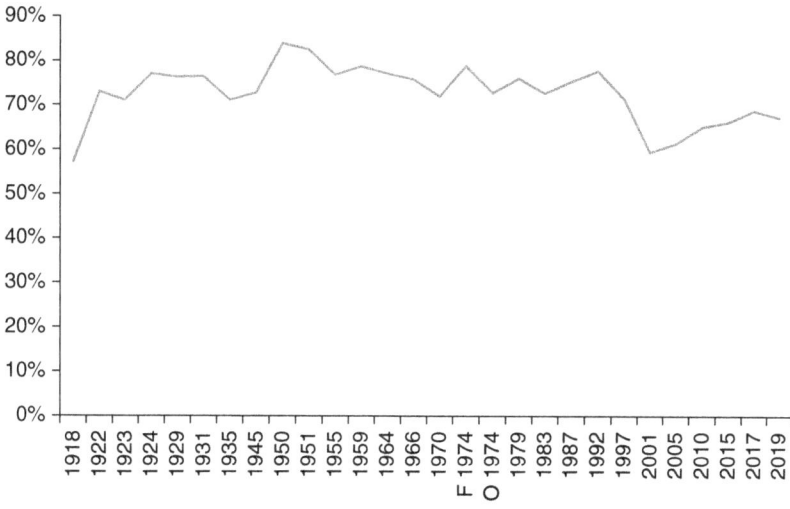

Figure 8.2 Turnout in general elections

Source: Cracknell, R., Uberoi, E. and Burton, M. (2023) UK Election Statistics: 1918–2023, *A Long Century of Elections*. House of Commons Library. Contains Parliamentary information licensed under the Open Parliament Licence v3.0

So, what happened in 2019? On the face of it we might think that the 2019 British general election was business as usual. Overall, 67 per cent of registered electors turned out to vote, not far off the average of 73 per cent and in keeping with the gradual increase since the nadir of the 2001 election, when turnout reached its lowest level since 1918 (see Figure 8.2). The two largest national parties together (Conservative and Labour) secured nearly 76 per cent of votes cast. The Conservative party secured nearly 47 per cent of the vote (the highest for any party since 1979) giving them 365 of the 650 seats in the House of Commons. This translated into a working majority of 80 MPs in the House of Commons for Boris Johnson's government. This is what is supposed to happen in a majoritarian electoral system like ours, majority government and a two-party system. But if we dig a little deeper, we can see that British elections have changed beyond recognition from the time Butler and Stokes were writing.

A multiparty system

When looking at the national picture of Westminster party vote share over time (see Figure 8.3) it certainly makes no sense to talk about the British party system as having just two 'main' parties. We can see that there was a period between 1983 and 2010 when the Liberal Democrats had peaks of support, very close in share of votes to the Labour party, and that support for the SNP and Plaid Cymru had grown over time.

A two-party focus makes even less sense when we consider regional patterns of party support and look beyond general elections. One feature of partisan dealignment has been the rise of third parties, particularly the SNP in Scotland and to a lesser, but still significant, extent Plaid Cymru in Wales. In 2019 the SNP won 48 of the 59 seats in Scotland and took

45 per cent of the Scottish vote. This is a continuation of the dominance of the SNP over the electoral landscape in Scotland since the Scottish independence referendum in 2014. Although a majority of Scots (55.3%) voted 'no', against independence, the closeness of the result and the intensity of the debate led to a realignment in Scottish politics with attitudes towards an independent Scotland becoming the most significant division in public opinion translating into party support for the SNP.

This change manifested itself in Westminster when British politics radically altered overnight after the 2015 general election when the SNP went from holding six of the Scottish Westminster seats to 56 (all but three) and the Labour party, which secured 41 Scottish seats in 2010, returned just one MP in Scotland. The old party loyalties that had shaped British politics and given us an approximately uniform swing at general elections, which had been gradually eroding, were swept away in Scotland. Since the Brexit referendum in 2016 the centrality of attitudes to Scottish independence was moderated somewhat by attitudes towards Britain's relationship with the EU. A majority of voters in every local authority area in Scotland voted to remain in the EU and as the SNP supported remain in the referendum, this firmed up support among pro-Scottish independence remainers, but lost them support from Scots who wanted to leave the EU.

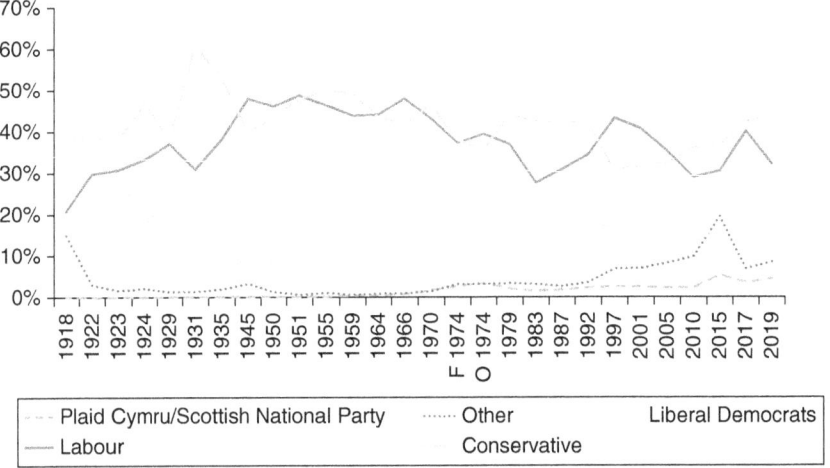

Figure 8.3 UK general election party vote share 1918–2019

Source: Cracknell, R., Uberoi, E. and Burton, M. (2023) UK Election Statistics: 1918–2023, *A Long Century of Elections*. House of Commons Library. Contains Parliamentary information licensed under the Open Parliament Licence v3.0

The growth in support for the SNP in Scotland is part of a trend whereby place-based identity has become increasingly important in British elections. General election results have always looked very different inside Northern Ireland than the rest of Britain, but other national, regional and local identities have grown in terms of their electoral impact. Where we live and the specific economic and social circumstances we find ourselves in of course have a profound relationship with the way we understand political issues, magnified by Britain's centralised political system and geographic economic inequality. In contemporary

Britain there is an interaction between place-based identity and social class that has become critical to how we vote.

Social class and place

To understand this place–class identity and its impact, let us first return to consider the role that social class plays in British politics, historically the predominant force shaping our relationships with the political parties. The declining role of class as an explanatory factor at election times started with structural changes in the British economy, emerging after the Second World War and taking hold in the 1970s and 1980s, which resulted in fewer working-class jobs in manual industry and growth in the service sector. As the working class, traditionally defined, shrunk, the Labour party needed to reach into the expanding middle class to have a chance of securing an electoral majority. New Labour, under the leadership of Tony Blair, led a shift towards the ideological centre of politics to attract middle-class voters and the party recruited more middle-class candidates to stand for election (Heath, 2015). At the same time many of the institutions that brought working-class communities together, which were tied to the Labour party, faced declining membership, such as trade unions and working men's clubs. These social changes resulted partially from forces of globalisation that made the manual production of goods in Britain less economically attractive, but they were also the consequence of policies enacted by the Conservative government, such as the sale of council houses to their residents. These trends led to a gradual class dealignment whereby working-class voters felt less strongly attached to the Labour party. The most immediate consequence was a decline in voter turnout among working-class communities (Heath, 2018).

This disaffection with Labour did not immediately manifest itself in fewer Labour seats returned to the House of Commons because many of the working-class constituencies in the midlands and the north of England, where turnout declined, had vast historic majorities for the party (the so called 'red wall' of historic support for Labour). Thus, Labour could afford to lose a lot of votes before the seats were in danger. However, the growing psychological detachment from the Labour party provided fertile ground for other parties to make an appeal to working-class voters and to seize these constituencies. The seismic changes did not take place at Westminster until 2019, but the historic foundation of Labour party identification had begun to crumble long before.

That Labour's foothold in its traditional heartland of post-industrial working-class communities was loosening became evident in the 2017 election when the party lost Stoke-on-Trent South, a seat the party had held since its creation, to the Conservatives. Likewise in 2017, the Conservatives lost Kensington, the wealthiest parliamentary constituency in the UK, to the Labour party. These seats changing hands illustrates that the old linkage between class, place and party was eroding. Two members of the 2019 British Election Study Team Geoffrey Evans and Jon Mellon (2020) outline what happened. They demonstrate that in 2015 there was an 18-point gap between the Conservative/Labour lead for middle-class voters compared to working-class voters – that is, the Conservatives did better among the middle class, but by 2017 the Conservatives actually had a lead of 9 percentage points among working-class voters which grew to 19 points in 2019, whilst the

Conservative lead among the middle class remained at 10 points. They break the British electorate into four classes: professional and managerial 'middle class'; routine white collar 'intermediate class'; self-employed or small business 'own account' class; and 'working class' composed of semi-routine, routine and supervisory workers. Evans and Mellon found that voters they had classified as own account or working class were most likely to support the Conservatives in 2019, whilst the other classes were more likely to support Labour. They concluded that 'British class politics is not disappearing, it is realigning. Owners and workers on one side, the professional, managerial and administrative middle classes on the other.' This is a seismic shift in the relationship between class and party of vote in Britain that led to the Conservative party breaking through the 'red wall' to gain seats held for generations by the Labour party.

How did the Conservative party increase its support so dramatically among working-class voters? The critical factor in leading to this realignment was the Brexit referendum in 2016 and the political antecedents of it. There is a strong association between leave support and hostility towards Britain's membership of the EU, obviously, and for many voters anti-EU sentiment stems from an association between EU membership and immigration, a linkage that was reinforced by Nigel Farage through UKIP and then the Brexit party. However, researchers have found that liberal/authoritarian attitudes are also a strong predictor of Brexit support, especially among voters in working-class communities, whereas remain support is associated with positive feelings about EU membership, lower salience of immigration or positive support for greater immigration and liberal attitudes. In 2019 the Conservative party had the ingredients to sweep up leave voters: a leader, in the shape of Boris Johnson, who was a leading figure in the Brexit campaign, who shifted the party towards a hard Brexit, giving the Conservatives the opportunity to take the mantle as the party of leave from the Brexit party. At the same time Johnson campaigned on a 'levelling up' agenda designed to address regional inequalities in England. This strategy was highly successful in recruiting working-class leave voters to support the Conservative party because in 2019 voters sorted themselves into two camps – leave/Conservative and remain/the rest. A key element of the Conservative party's success was scooping up a huge proportion of leave voters, whilst remain voters were more dispersed across the other parties in mainland UK.

The interaction between social class, place and values that has become such a pivotal fault line in UK politics is beautifully illustrated by Will Jennings and Gerry Stoker in their article 'The bifurcation of politics: Two Englands' (Jennings and Stoker, 2016). They show how our values are shaped by the moral cultures we experience through our communities, as we have understood through moral foundations theory. They argue that 'two Englands' have emerged, with two different moral outlooks. The first is cosmopolitan and liberal and embraces immigration and diversity and is prevalent in urban affluent areas that have benefitted from globalisation. The second is more inward looking, traditional and relatively illiberal, and more prevalent in what Jennings and Stoker describe as the economic backwaters of England. These divergent perspectives on politics shaped the Brexit referendum outcome, and the electoral geography of the UK post 2019.

Values

Figure 8.4 is from an article published by UK in a Changing Europe, a research network funded by the Economic and Social Research Council bringing together academic research on Britain's relationship with the EU. They illustrate that leave and remain voters were not divided by economic values but that leave voters were considerably more authoritarian in their values than remain voters. Values have come to be seen as much more important in explaining our voting decisions since Brexit. In the period of growing class and partisan dealignment researchers shifted their focus onto *valence explanations* for our party of vote (Clarke et al., 2004) – that is, without a strong psychological attachment to a party, voters

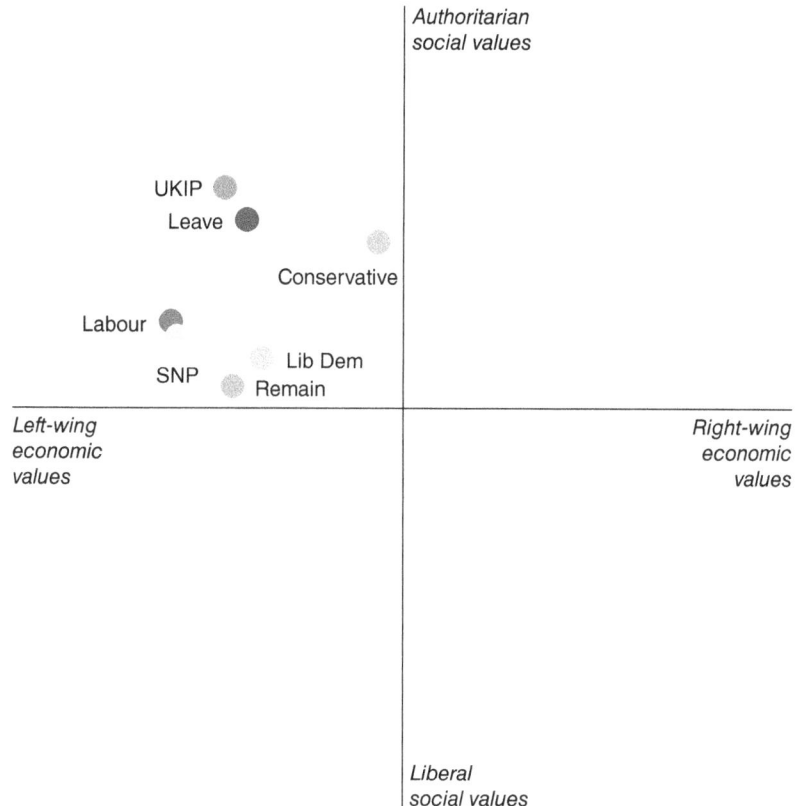

Figure 8.4 The values of leave and remain voters differ more for social issues than economic ones. Position of the average voter in the value space, by political party in 2015 and referendum vote in 2016.

Source: Surridge, P. (2021) Brexit, British politics and values. UK in a Changing Europe. https://ukandeu.ac.uk/long-read/brexit-british-politics-and-values

placed greater emphasis on the competence to govern of parties and their leaders. The 'valence' approach to understanding British general elections was set out by the 2001 to 2010 BES team, which showed how values and attitudinal differences became less important explanations of election outcomes in the New Labour period when there was less ideological difference between the two largest parties than during the 1970s and 1980s. The Brexit referendum and subsequent elections have led researchers to pay more attention to values and values change.

We have seen massive generational values change, with multiple causes. The new social movements of the 1960s and 1970s influentially campaigned for civil rights, women's rights and gay rights, transforming our societies. Greater numbers of young people have entered higher education, and having a degree has long been associated with liberal values. Globalisation has increased trade and competition with the rest of the world, reshaping our economies and societies. For those with the qualifications and lifestyles that can take advantage of the opportunities of globalisation these changes have been understood as positive, but for people living in communities that have become more economically deprived there is a sense that globalisation has 'left many behind'. Thus, the forces that have seen a surge in liberal values have not exerted themselves equally across the country and generations. The growing significance of liberal/authoritarian attitudes is accompanied by the role our global/nationalist attitudes play with an association with more authoritarian and more nationalist attitudes underlying support for Brexit.

The 2019 European election

Prior to the 2019 general election voters went to the polls for the final European election before Britain left the EU. The proportional electoral system combined with the propensity for voters to cast protest votes to punish large parties, especially incumbents, in second-order elections (elections viewed as less important by voters) (Hix and Marsh, 2007) meant the party system was much more fragmented than in the 2019 general election. Although the Brexit Party, Liberal Democrats and Greens also stood in the general election, they captured many more votes in the European election, coming in first, second and fourth respectively. Motivated by the second-order (or given Britain's pending exit from the EU, third-order) nature of the election, voters were free to choose a party closest to their ideological, attitudinal or policy preferences, without the encumbrance of rating competence to govern, or fear that a vote for a smaller party would benefit their least preferred party by dividing the vote. The difference in party support in these two elections, in the same year, shows the critical role that the nature of the election and the electoral system play in shaping our vote choice.

Other social characteristics

As the role social class plays in shaping our relationship with political parties has declined, other social characteristics have become more important, such as our age or generation, our gender and our experience of education.

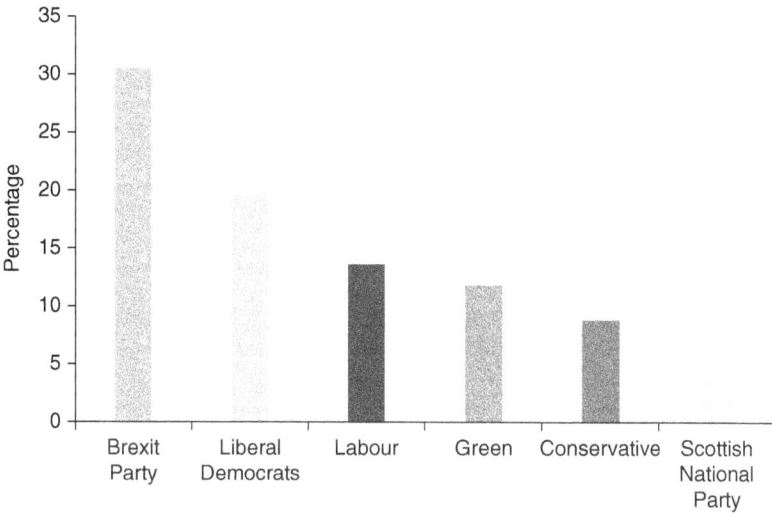

Figure 8.5 Party of vote in the UK in 2019 European elections

Source: Fella, S., Uberoi, E. and Cracknell, R. (2019) *European Parliament Elections 2019: Results and Analysis.* https://commonslibrary.parliament.uk/research-briefings/cbp-8600 Contains Parliamentary information licensed under the Open Parliament Licence v3.0

Age and generation

One the most profound social background characteristics shaping how we vote is now age, or generation. An age or life cycle effect is one where our preferences change as we get older. Historically, older voters were more likely to support the Conservatives and researchers argued that this was because older people were more likely to have property and investments, for example, and therefore had an interest in lower taxation. A generation effect is one where an event, or zeitgeist, influences the preferences of a generation that sticks with them throughout their lives. It is possibly too soon to tell whether the emergence of age as a predominant force in electoral politics is an age or life cycle or generational trend.

We've already discussed the massive generational shift in liberal values that has taken place over the last 50 years and how this has manifested itself in a politics that is divided along cosmopolitan/nativist or liberal/authoritarian lines. The 'two Englands' described by Jennings and Stoker (2016) are delineated by place, income, education and generation, with younger generations much more liberal than those they are replacing. There has long been a tendency for older voters to be greater supporters of the Conservative party, but this effect has been magnified as liberal values and attitudes to immigration have come to play a more important role shaping party of vote (Fieldhouse et al., 2019). Figure 8.6 illustrates the pattern whereby younger voters, under 45, were more likely to support the Labour party whilst older voters where more likely to vote Conservative in 2019. In 2017 many commentators argued that age was the new dividing line in British politics and the trend was very much still in evidence in 2019 (McDonnell and Curtis, 2019), although the tipping point lowered as the Conservative party secured more votes from people in their forties in 2019 than in 2017.

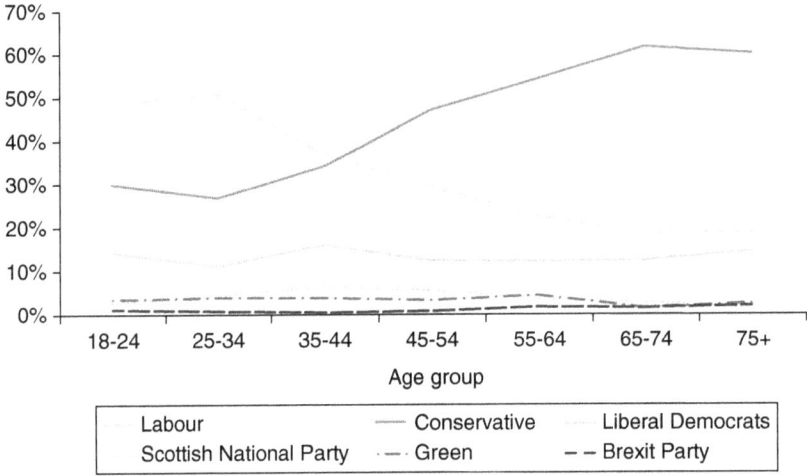

Figure 8.6 Age group and party of vote in the 2019 general election

Data source: The 2019 British Election Study Post-Election Random Probability Survey (version 1.1.1). Fieldhouse, E., Green, J., Evans, G., Prosser, C., de Geus, R., Bailey, J., Schmitt, H., van der Eijk, C., Mellon, J. (2022). British Election Study, 2019: Post-Election Random Probability Survey. [data collection]. UK Data Service. SN: 8875, DOI: 10.5255/UKDA-SN-8875-1

Gender and generation

Our gender is an aspect of our lived experience that may influence our political attitudes and our voting behaviour. We live in a society where, despite massive change, traditional gender roles still play a role in shaping our lives. Women continue to undertake more unpaid caring work, particularly for children, than men and as a result women are more likely to be employed in part-time, lower paid and precarious work. Women are also more often employed in the public sector. These gender differences can lead men and women, on average, to prioritise different political issues. For example, women more often raise healthcare and education as the most important issues facing the country whereas men more often list the economy, taxation and relations with the European Union (Campbell, 2012).

Historically, gender played only a marginal role in predicting party of vote. Women during the post Second World War period were slightly more likely to vote Conservative than men but this gap declined over time and was not statistically significant from the 1970s. The 2017 general election was a critical turning point for the relationship between gender and voting behaviour in Britain. Prior to 2017 a greater proportion of women voted for the Conservative party than men in almost every general election since 1945 (see Figure 8.7). However, in the 2017 and 2019 elections for the first-time women were more likely to vote Labour than men, and men were greater supporters of the Conservative party (Campbell and Shorrocks, 2021). This overall gender gap was driven by younger women being considerably more likely to vote for the Labour party than younger men. In 2017 the gender gap can be accounted for by younger women's greater concerns about the economy (Sanders and Shorrocks, 2019), and in 2019 younger women's hostility to Brexit seems to have been a factor driving them towards Labour (Campbell and Shorrocks, 2021). Thus, the generational difference in party support, widely reported in the media and academic research, has a significant gender dimension.

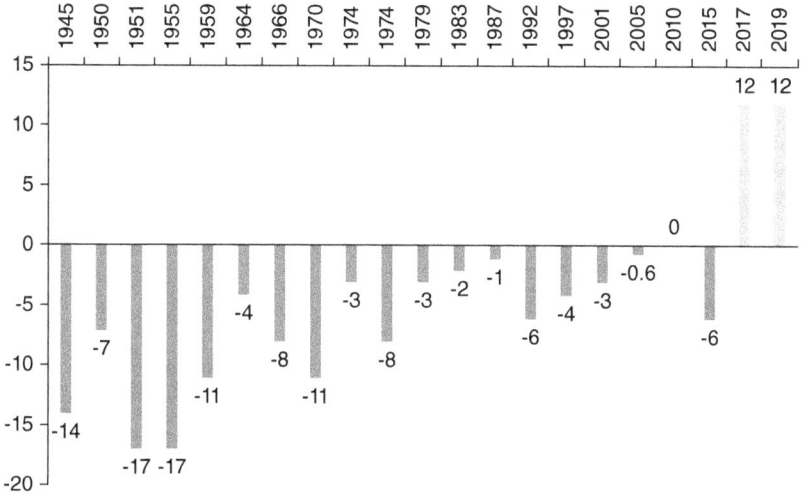

Figure 8.7 The British two-party gender gap, 1945–2019

Source: Gallup Polls, 1945–59; British Election Study, 1964–2019. Adapted from Norris, P. Gender: A gender-generation gap? In G.Evans and P. Norris (eds) *Critical Elections: British Parties and Voters in Long-Term Perspective*. London: Sage, pp. 146–163. The gender gap is calculated as the difference in the Con-Lab lead for women and men

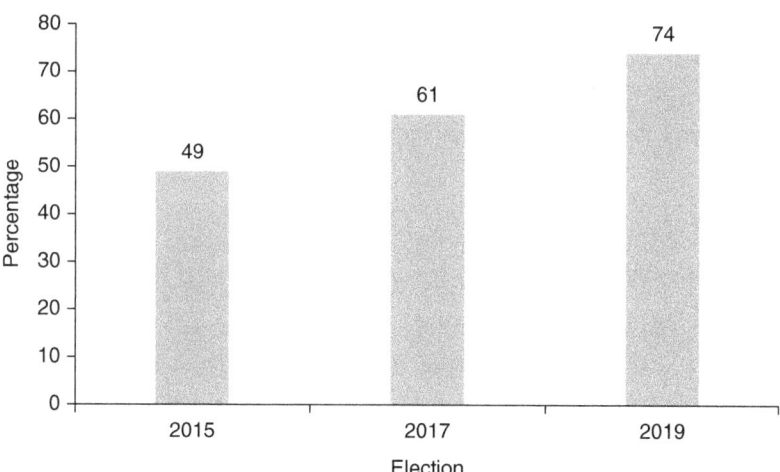

Figure 8.8 Percentage of respondents to the BES without qualifications who supported the Conservatives, among those who voted for either of the major parties

Source: Fieldhouse, E.A., Evans, G., Green, J., Mellon, J. and Prosser, C. (2021) Volatility, realignment and electoral shocks: Brexit and the UK general election of 2019, p. 8. SSRN: https://ssrn.com/abstract=3764477 or http://dx.doi.org/10.2139/ssrn.3764477. Adapted under a CC-BY license.

The role that our education plays in shaping our attitudes and preferences also interacts with generation. There has been a huge increase in the proportion of students attending higher education institutions. In the early 1960s about 4 per cent of school leavers went on to university (Mayhew et al., 2004). By 2022 37.5 per cent of 18-year-olds took up a university place (Bolton, 2023). Holding a university degree has long been associated with having more liberal values and with many more people now attending university this partially explains the generational divide in values. Holding a university degree has now become a strong predictor of vote choice, with a growing association between having no educational qualifications and supporting the Conservative party and those with university degrees supporting Labour (see Figure 8.8).

Spotlight on research: Brexitland

Sobolewska and Ford's (2020) *Brexitland: Identity, Diversity and the Reshaping of British Politics* does a tremendous job of analysing and explaining the long-term social and demographic changes that have transformed British politics. Sobolewska and Ford illustrate the trends that have led to greater polarisation of public opinion in the UK and to the emergence of 'Brexitland'. The expansion of higher education and increasing ethnic diversity have had twin effects on different sectors of society. Those with a university education are well placed to reap the economic rewards delivered by a more diverse society, pushing those on the winning side of globalisation in the UK towards more liberal and globalist values. At the same time citizens who have not benefited from the expansion of higher education more often see immigration and globalisation as a threat to their standards of living and national way of life. Sobolewska and Ford demonstrate how these forces have shaped more than our attitudes, they have had a profound effect on our identities and our understanding of what it means to be British, or English. They illustrate how the political parties have responded to this changed electoral landscape and how the Conservative party shifted to a more nationalistic and Eurosceptic stance to appeal to disaffected Labour voters.

Need to know: Who can vote, for what, where and how

The choice among political parties available to us at the ballot box in Britain is shaped by the nature of the specific electoral contest: the geographic area it covers, the electoral system in operation and the political moment in which it takes place. Voters in Britain are faced with quite a different array of contenders dependent on these factors.

General elections

In Britain a general election must be held within five years of the first meeting of the current Parliament, with an additional 25 working days for an election campaign (Haddon, 2022). The 2019 general election was held on the 12th of December 2019 and Parliament first met

Table 8.2 Eligible voters in UK elections

Election type	Voting age	British citizens	British Overseas Voters	Resident Irish citizens	Resident qualifying Commonwealth citizens	Citizens of other countries	Convict prisoners detained in prison
Who can vote in UK election?							
UK Parliamentary election	18	Yes	Yes	Yes	Yes	No	No
England							
Police and crime commissioner	18	Yes	No	Yes	Yes	Resident EU citizens	No
Elected mayors	18	Yes	No	Yes	Yes	Resident EU citizens	No
Council and parish council	18	Yes	No	Yes	Yes	Resident EU citizens	No
Scotland							
Scottish Parliament	16	Yes	No	Yes	Yes	Anyone legally resident	Sentence of 12 months or less
Council and Community Council	16	Yes	No	Yes	Yes	Anyone legally resident	Sentence of 12 months or less
National parks authority	16	Yes	No	Yes	Yes	Anyone legally resident	Sentence of 12 months or less
Wales							
Senedd cymru	16	Yes	No	Yes	Yes	Anyone legally resident	No
Council and community council	18*	Yes	No	Yes	Yes	Resident EU citizens	No
Police and crime commissioner	18	Yes	No	Yes	Yes	Resident EU citizens	No
Northern Ireland							
Northern Ireland Assembly	18	Yes	No	Yes	Yes	Resident EU citizens	No
Council	18	Yes	No	Yes	Yes	Resident EU citizens	No

* The provisions allowing those aged 16 and 17 and all qualifying foreign nationals to vote in local elections will take effect at local elections in May 2022

Source: Johnston, N. (2022) Who Can Vote in UK Elections? Research Briefing cbp-8985. House of Commons Library. https://commonslibrary.parliament.uk/research-briefings/cbp-8985 Contains Parliamentary information licensed under the Open Parliament Licence v3.0

five days later on the 17th. This meant, therefore, that Parliament had to be dissolved, and an election called, by the 17th of December 2024; the election was required to take place by January 2025. Most British citizens aged over 18 (on the day of the election) and resident within the UK, are entitled to vote in general elections and to do so we must be registered to vote.[1] British citizens who reside outside of the UK can participate in the ballot if they have been registered to vote within the last 15 years. Irish citizens and citizens of Commonwealth countries, who are living in the UK and have leave to enter or remain in the UK or who don't require that leave, are all entitled to vote. Convicted prisoners who are detained in prison are excluded from the electoral franchise for general elections (Johnston, 2022).

Table 8.2 shows the variation across British elections in terms of who can, and cannot, participate. In Scotland's elections prisoners with a sentence of 12 months or less are entitled to vote. In elections to the Welsh Parliament, the Senedd Cymru, the qualifying age to vote is 16 not 18. These variations demonstrate that there is not a static unifying consensus regarding who should be entitled to vote. Instead, the pattern reflects a history of contestation that has translated everyday actions into formal rules of inclusion.

At British general elections we elect individual members of parliament to represent our electoral (geographic) constituency to the House of Commons, using a majoritarian, first-past-the-post (FPTP), electoral system. This method is sometimes referred to as 'winner takes all' and that neatly sums it up at the constituency level, where the candidate who secures the most votes is successful, even if they are ahead by just one vote. The advantage of this system is that it is very simple to understand and manage. Some argue that it has the additional bonus of making strong governments more likely, as FPTP tends to inflate the number of seats gained by a political party compared to the proportion of votes cast, avoiding political stalemate in the legislature. On the negative side there are a lot of 'wasted' votes in a winner-takes-all electoral system.

Historically British general elections have been the most politically consequential, first order elections, though this has changed through devolution. The centralised Westminster model of politics, still remains as an overarching structure with ultimate decision-making power residing in Parliament, but the Scottish Parliament, Senedd Cymru and Northern Ireland Assembly (when it is sitting) now also play a critical role in our electoral landscape. The relative powers of local government have varied over time, but local elections are often described as second order because of the dominance of the national Westminster government. There are four different electoral systems in use in the UK, first-past-the-post, the additional member system, the single transferable vote and the alternative vote. For a full explanation of how each of these systems work see the House of Commons Library briefing on voting systems in the UK https://commonslibrary.parliament.uk/research-briefings/sn04458/ (see Table 8.3).

Table 8.3 Electoral systems used in the UK

Voting System	Used for
First-past-the-post	House of Commons
	Local elections in England and Wales
	Mayoral elections in England
	Police and crime commissioners in England and Wales
	Scottish National Park authorities

---

[1] If you are not already on the electoral register you can do so online here https://www.gov.uk/register-to-vote

Voting System	Used for
Additional member system	Scottish Parliament
	Senedd Cymru
	London Assembly
Single transferable vote	Northern Ireland Assembly
	Local elections in Northern Ireland and Scotland
Alternative vote	Expected hereditary peers in the House of Lords
	Scottish Crofting Commission elections

Source: Johnston, Neil. 2023. 'Voting systems in the UK.' London: House of Commons Library. Licensed under the Open Parliament Licence v3.0.

Conclusion

In this chapter we have explored how our everyday experiences shape our attitudes, beliefs and values and how in turn they influence how we cast our votes. The underlying values that inform our political preferences are moulded by our interactions with our communities, be these the places where we have grown up, studied for a degree or started a new job. Our values are also affected by the generation we belong to and the norms and expectations about how society should be organised or changed. There is often a logical consistency underlying our preferences, despite what some of the classic accounts of political behaviour argued, but we are also driven by the elephant (our unconscious biases and predispositions) to support the policies espoused by our preferred political parties even if they might not be in our own 'best' interests.

In the UK there has been a profound shift in how our everyday lives influence our voting behaviour or, to use the academic parlance, new cleavages have emerged. As society has changed, with the decline of manual industry, social class has ceased to be such a reliable predictor of party support, and age and generation have become a much better predictor of how we vote. However, class still matters, but it interacts with place and education, generating a more complex relationship between socioeconomic status and party support than was the case in the 1950s and 1960s, when the majority of working-class voters supported Labour and middle-class voters the Conservatives. Now, younger people, those with university degrees and people living in urban areas are the most likely to be Labour supporters.

Key take-home points

- Social class used to be a key electoral cleavage shaping party support and electoral outcomes in the UK.
- Age and education have overtaken class to become more powerful predictors of which party we will support at election time.
- Class still matters but the linkage between class, place and education is key to the new electoral geography of the UK.

Table 8.4 Measuring socialist/laissez faire and liberal/authoritarian values: Answers

	Socialist/Laissez Faire	Liberal/Authoritarian
Ordinary working people get their fair share of the nation's wealth	x	
There is one law for the rich and one for the poor	x	
Young people today don't have enough respect for traditional British values		x
Censorship of films and magazines is necessary to uphold moral standards		x
There is no need for strong trade unions to protect working conditions and wages	x	
Private enterprise is the best way to solve Britain's economic problems	x	
Major public services and industries ought to be in state ownership	x	
Govt's responsibility to provide a job for everyone who wants one	x	
People should be allowed to organise public protests against the government		x
People in Britain should be more tolerant of those who lead unconventional lives		x
For some crimes, the death penalty is the most appropriate sentence		x
People who break the law should be given stiffer sentences		x

Annotated reading list

Bale, T. and Webb, P. (2021) *The Modern British Party System*. Oxford: Oxford University Press.

This book provides a comprehensive account of the changing British electoral and party landscape, bringing together empirical studies of specific elections with theoretical accounts of political change. It is an excellent resource to take a deeper dive into the issues we have covered in this chapter.

Cowley, P. and Ford, R. (eds) (2019) *Sex, Lies and Politics: The Secret Influences That Drive Our Political Choices*. Hull: Biteback Publishing.

A highly informative and entertaining source of information on public opinion and voting behaviour. I strongly recommend that you read this book if you are going to do further study on this topic. It contains short chapters from leading researchers in the field that are an excellent gateway into the academic literature. After finishing the book, read some of the articles cited in your favourite chapters.

Denver, D. and Johns, R. (2021) *Elections and Voters in Britain.* London: Palgrave Macmillan.

This book will give you a thorough introduction to electoral systems and voting behaviour in Brtain.

Fieldhouse, E., Green, J., Evans, G., Mellon, J., Prosser, C., Schmitt, H. and van der Eijk, C. (2019) *Electoral Shocks: The Volatile Voter in a Turbulent World.* Oxford: Oxford University Press.

This book is the most recent in the series of books written by the British Election Study teams.

Ford, R., Bale, T., Jennings, W. and Surridge, P. (2021) The British General Election of 2019. London: Palgrave MacMillan.

This book is part of another long-running series on British elections. This series focuses more on the campaign itself than the British election study books and is an 'everything you need to know' about the election.

Sobolewska, M. and Ford, R. (2020) *Brexitland: Identity, Diversity and the Reshaping of British Politics.* Cambridge: Cambridge University Press.

This award-winning book is a must read for understanding contemporary British electoral politics.

9
Place, pluralism and the media
Who tells us about political affairs?

Steven Harkins

Image 9.1 Keir Starmer, the leader of the Labour Party, getting his message across at the Party Conference
© Photo by Rupert Rivett on Shutterstock

> ### Learning objectives
>
> After reading this chapter, you should be able to:
>
> - Understand how the news media have a critical public service role in a democratic society
> - Explore how, ideally, journalism will offer a platform for a wide range of ideas to be debated, which will help inform the public on political affairs
> - Examine whether the news media enhances or restricts pluralism in the UK political system
> - Discuss journalism studies research and case studies as illustrative examples of the complex interaction between politics and journalism in the UK

Introduction

The news media play a crucial role in providing information that influences the functioning of the UK's complex democratic system. One of the central concerns of this book is examining the extent of pluralism within the UK political system. Any analysis of this would be incomplete without a sustained and critical examination of the role that the news media play in expanding or restricting debates about political affairs. One of the dominant normative claims about the role of journalism in a modern democracy is that journalists are responsible for informing and educating citizens. Furthermore, they are expected to hold powerful elites to account on behalf of the public by exposing abuses of power. They are also expected to adhere to professional norms of objectivity while performing these important social roles. This challenge is difficult when journalists report on political affairs because of the contentious nature of political reporting. Professional journalists are increasingly facing accusations of bias from unhappy news consumers from across the political spectrum.

The chapter begins by looking at a range of studies that make a case for journalism as an active forum for opening up debates on political affairs from a wide range of perspectives. It also looks at the evidence that the news industry closes debate down and only reflects the narrow interests of powerful elite voices. This is seen differently according to regulations and news-gathering practices that differ across broadcast, print and digital platforms and each of these will be examined in turn. Examples of reporting political affairs on each of these platforms are analysed throughout the following discussion before examining some specific case studies around major political events, such as the 2014 Scottish independence referendum and the 2016 referendum on EU membership. The chapter finishes with some observations about news coverage of the 2019 general election and how the news media landscape expanded or restricted pluralistic debate. Before examining these case studies, a broad theoretical overview of how journalism can open and close discussions about political affairs is essential.

> ### Need to know: Pluralism and the news media
>
> - The relationship between the media and political power is the subject of intense debate.
> - At one end of the spectrum, the press is conceptualised as a liberal institution providing a forum for debate and holding power to account. This positive and self-justifying

- view of the press is rarely supported by empirical research into the role of the press. Nevertheless, there are certainly examples of the press performing this role, and in the 'post-truth' era, it is worth having these ideals even if the reality often falls short.
- At the other end of the spectrum, the press is seen as an extension of corporate and political power. While there is evidence to support this view, there are exceptions that prove the limitations of this view of the relationship between the media and the political system in the UK.
- These contrasting views are best used to ask critical questions about the media's role while accepting that no grand theory will apply to such a complex and ever-changing relationship.

Journalism in the UK: A forum for plural political debate?

Any discussion about pluralism in the UK political system would be incomplete without examining its relationship with journalism. This section outlines two clear arguments about the relationship between the news media and political affairs within the UK. Firstly, the chapter examines the concept of the 'fourth estate' in detail by looking at the evidence that journalism offers a pluralistic forum for political debate that encourages a wide range of voices to debate political issues within the UK. Secondly, the chapter examines the evidence that the news media play a role in restricting discussion and echoing the interests of powerful political and corporate actors. While neither of these positions gives a comprehensive overview of the relationship between journalism and politics in the UK, they provide a theoretical basis to help us ask critical questions about how these systems interact. For example, suppose we see journalism as an extension of state or corporate power. In that case, we might ask questions about ownership, political influence and censorship of stories that might embarrass those in power. Alternatively, if we see journalism as a public service that gives a voice to the voiceless and holds power to account, then we might look for evidence of the news media performing these functions. These questions are at the heart of this volume on pluralism in the UK's political system. Does journalism provide a platform for debate amongst a wide range of actors? Or does journalism restrict discussion to the narrow interests of elite actors? We look at the evidence of both of these views beginning with an examination of the power of the news media to widen political debates.

Widening the debate: Journalism, politics and the fourth estate

Journalism is distinct from other forms of communication because of its 'ambition to inform an audience of political developments to enable people to make democratic choices about the world in which they live and work' (Conboy, 2011: 126). Journalism arguably has a wide range of functions within a democratic society, such as informing the public, holding power to account and giving a voice to the voiceless. Connolly's (2005) work on pluralism in politics offered an account that understands democracy as a site of wide participation and contestation. The news media play a key role in this process through providing information and representation to a wide range of disparate groups. Journalism as a forum for political debate is central to liberal notions of the role of the press, which should be free from government control in a democracy. The important role journalism plays within a democratic system has been described as the 'fourth estate', a shorthand term that reflects what emerged from the work of classic liberal theorists such as J.S. Mill (Thompson, 1995). This described an understanding of journalism as a forum for public debate, independent from state control and a watchdog that holds power to account.

Need to know: The fourth estate

Although historians have disputed this origin, Thomas Carlyle attributed the term 'fourth estate' to Edmund Burke. Carlyle described how Burke gestured to the gallery in the House of Commons, arguing that the fourth estate was more powerful than the other three. The idea of journalism as one of the important powers within a democratic system has had an enduring appeal, particularly amongst journalists themselves.

In practice, this means that regardless of the constitutional arrangements of a particular society, genuine political power and influence lies with the news media and the relationship with its audience (Hampton, 2008). Hampton's definition of the role of the fourth estate is 'to promote discussion and "educate readers", or to "represent" them by publicizing abuses' (Hampton, 2008: 3). As Harcup has argued, the 'fourth estate' has become a term to describe the 'quasi-constitutional role of "watchdog" on the workings of government' (Harcup, 2022: 7).

As a way of understanding the role of the press, the 'fourth estate' is a powerful idea that conceptualises journalism as an essential part of the democratic system within the UK. The idea that the news media helps to inform the public, scrutinise the government and provide a platform for expressing public opinion (Curran and Seaton, 2003: 346) is normatively understood as characterising the relationship between the UK's political system and the news industry. Indeed, political reporting has been described as forming the 'prime function' of journalism. One of the most critical developments in the relationship between journalism and politics was the establishment of the lobby system in 1885, which formalised communication between the government and senior reporters. A significant advantage of lobby journalism is that journalists get privileged access to policymakers, allowing them to inform the public by reporting on the government's actions. Political correspondents need to walk a tightrope of maintaining access to elite figures while also holding them to account. The BBC's Andrew Marr describes how political journalism often involves building up close relationships with sources and then betraying them: 'The cynical but professional answer is to have a range of good sources, with more always under cultivation, so that when one is blown, there are others to fall back on' (Marr, 2005: 184).

Marr's description is the epitome of 'fourth estate' journalism, where the news media hold power to account on behalf of the public. There are plenty of examples of this type of adversarial political reporting in the UK. Amelia Gentleman's diligent reporting on the Windrush scandal highlighted historical injustices that devastated the lives of British citizens who were illegally detained by immigration authorities, denied legal rights by the Home Office and threatened with deportation from the UK (Gentleman, 2019). The *Guardian* journalist's reporting led to the resignation of Home Secretary Amber Rudd in 2018 and provided a textbook example of journalists holding power to account on behalf of ordinary citizens (BBC News, 2018). The series of scandals that brought down prime minister Boris Johnson was another example of the 'fourth estate' in action. Pippa Crerar reported on lockdown parties in the *Daily Mirror* and highlighted a series of scandals involving the UK Government. In 2023 Nadhim Zahawi was sacked as chairman of the Conservative party because of detailed reporting on his tax affairs by journalists (Crerar, 2023). These examples show the news industry in the UK operating independently from government control in a way that reflects the liberal democratic system of a free press.

Image 9.2 Allegra Stratton leans on a podium and shares a joke with her colleagues about a party taking place during Covid restrictions (the 'partygate' scandal). This was caught on camera, during a press conference rehearsal that was filmed. Stratton moved from the newsroom to become the Downing Street Press Secretary, in a newly expanded role that was designed to include US-style daily televised press briefings. In becoming the Government's communications adviser from her previous roles at the BBC and ITV, Stratton demonstrates the close relationship between politics and the media. She resigned in December 2021 after the footage emerged. It was reported that the Conservative government invested £2.6m on modelling the Downing Street Press room to be used for the briefings, shown in the photograph, but all plans for the televised briefings have since been scrapped.

Source: Photo by ITV News

Conboy highlights that this is only a partial view of one facet of the complex functions of journalism. Still, political reporting led to the historical establishment of a consistent relationship between newspapers and their readers (Conboy, 2011). This type of media system has been described by scholars as a liberal or north Atlantic system which is characterised as having a popular print market, a highly professionalised news industry and low levels of state power over the media (Brüggemann et al., 2014). Nevertheless, the idea of a truly free and independent press representing the people and holding power to account is favoured by organisations working within the news industry for self-serving reasons. While there is evidence of the existence of this type of journalism, this understanding of the role of the media is often invoked by journalists and editors when they have been subjected to scrutiny for unethical behaviour and misdemeanours. The UK press leans on these noble notions of their role whenever they are in trouble – examples such as the Leveson Inquiry saw news organisations invoke the 'fourth estate' as a defence of their trade. However, analysis of this system has found that 'the vital function of independent and critical political reporting is being progressively undermined to the ultimate benefit of those in power' (Barnett and Gaber, 2001: 1). The next section examines the way that the news media restricts discussions about politics in the UK to the narrow confines of elite interests.

Closing down the debate: The news media as an extension of corporate and state power

This section examines the constraints on journalism in the UK with a clear focus on the influence of the state and the market. This critical examination views the media as an extension of corporate and state power. Herman and Chomsky's propaganda model proposes that news passes through a series of filters that remove any reporting that challenges the interests of elite actors (Chomsky and Herman, 1995). This section focuses on the first three of these filters, which are ownership, advertising and sources. Unlike the liberal theory of the press, which sees an independent media in opposition to political power, the propaganda model sees a close relationship between the press and powerful elites.

News sources and professional networks

Although the state does not have direct control over the news media in the UK and comparative studies of media systems regard its power and influence as relatively low (Hallin and Mancini, 2004), there are key linkages and networks between politics and journalism which have been described as a 'revolving door' that links the two professions. Examples of prominent politicians who have worked in journalism include former prime minister Boris Johnson and Michael Gove. After leaving politics, the former Chancellor of the Exchequer George Osborne became the editor of the *London Evening Standard* between 2017 and 2020. The spotlight was shone on these networks between politics and journalism in early 2023 when it was reported that BBC chairman Richard Sharp had facilitated a loan for the then prime minister Boris Johnson (Abdul, 2023). Sharp was responsible for upholding and protecting the BBC's independence and his relationship with Boris Johnson led to accusations of a conflict of interest from Labour MPs, and he eventually had to resign from the role. Furthermore, when the Commons committee report recommended a 90-day suspension for Boris Johnson for misleading Parliament over the Partygate scandal, he was hired the next day as a columnist for *the Daily Mail*.

Under these high-level examples of political and journalistic networks there are special advisers to government that are often hired directly from media organisations. For students interested in a career in politics, journalism is another profession worth considering, even as a way into politics. The close network between politics and journalism raises questions about the independence of the news media in the UK. Stuart Hall's seminal research into the relationship between the media and elite sources of information found that journalists often repeat the definitions of elite sources of information such as politicians (Hall et al.,

2013: 60 [1978]). Journalists may not work entirely in collusion with these sources, but they do need to work with them in order to maintain access to important information (Cottle, 2003). So, journalists are seen from this perspective as having a 'clubbish symbiosis' with political elites that develops from having a group of people with similar educational backgrounds and coming from the same social class (Conboy, 2011: 127). Indeed, a pair of studies in 2016 found that only 11 per cent of journalists were from working-class backgrounds and the industry is made up of 94 per cent white and 86 per cent university-educated individuals (Martinson, 2018).

Herbert Gans described the relationship between sources and journalists as a dance where the source is in the lead (Gans, 1980). Journalism scholars have a keen interest in sourcing relationships because of 'the persistence of sourcing patterns that privilege a small set of powerful social actors' (Carlson, 2009: 538). The news media's overreliance on elite political sources of information is accompanied by a lack of engagement with sources of news from marginalised communities. The idea that journalism exists to 'give a voice to the voiceless' does not always withstand scrutiny. Pulitzer Prize-winning reporter Katherine Boo describes how 'reporters like me, who work in stigmatised communities, field routine requests to find a "better victim" or choose a more sympathetic, articulate, even photogenic source' (Boo, 2016). News practices that exclude marginalised communities have more to do with market pressures than the relationship between journalism and political elites.

Lost advertising revenue and the concentration of ownership

One of the biggest constraints on journalistic output comes from the market. While public service broadcasters are somewhat insulated from this influence, the majority of news organisations are businesses which are driven by a profit motive. In the current market, journalists are under pressure to produce more content with fewer resources. This makes their news even more reliant on information from elite organisations with well-established public relations teams. Studies have shown that the quality and independence of the UK news media output has been badly affected by its reliance on material from public relations material produced by corporations seeking to skew the news in favour of their interests (Allan, 2010; Lewis et al., 2008). This means that: 'The practical pressures of constantly working against the clock and the professional demands of impartiality and objectivity combine to produce a systematically structured over-accessing to the media of those in powerful and privileged institutional positions' (Hall et al., 2013: 61 [1978]).

These problems have gotten significantly worse following the digital revolution. Fewer newsroom staff and an increased volume of news production mean that material produced outside of the newsroom is being increasingly relied upon and there has been a subsequent reduction in fact checking and quality due to these pressures and constraints (Davies, 2009). These institutional pressures drive an overreliance on source material from elite organisations and actors. Overall, the news industry is structured in a way that favours elite perspectives from the state and corporate actors. This is exacerbated by the concentration of ownership within the UK news market. Three companies have a controlling stake in 71 per cent of the news industry in the UK (Media Reform Coalition, 2021). In Boris Johnson's first year as prime minister, he had regular meetings with billionaire press owners and their representatives, including 40 meetings with Rupert Murdoch's News Corp (Ponsford, 2021). Using elements of Herman and Chomsky's propaganda model, this section has highlighted how constraints on the news industry from the market and the concentration of ownership have amplified elite perspectives and narrowed the window of political debate in the UK.

The news industry in the UK

Formal outlines of the UK news industry focus on the differences between print, broadcast and digital. Each platform has unique challenges and different forms of regulation and needs a separate discussion. However, media convergence has merged all of these platforms into the digital space, blurring the boundaries between print, broadcast and digital. For example, in 2020, the *Times*, the UK's newspaper of record, launched its own radio station. Mainstream news platforms have an increasing digital presence, and audio-visual delivery is becoming of paramount importance for growing a digital audience of news consumers. Furthermore, the news environment has been fundamentally disrupted by social media, which has reshaped traditional power dynamics and delivered a more pluralistic political culture accompanied by issues such as increased political partisanship through echo chambers and a worrying rise in misinformation.

Nevertheless, differences in style and regulation mean that different issues shape political coverage across the UK media landscape. Broadcast journalism sits at the heart of political coverage in the United Kingdom. The BBC's status as a public broadcaster funded through a TV licence gives it an essential role in news coverage of political affairs.

Broadcast

Broadcast journalism in the UK is regulated by Ofcom, an organisation with a broad remit which includes TV, radio and on-demand digital content. Broadcast news is more tightly regulated than the

Image 9.3 Social media platforms play a critical role in contemporary political communication.

Source: @FCDOGovUK on twitter.com

print industry in the UK. As a public service broadcaster, the BBC is important in delivering news to a broad audience in the UK. The BBC is funded through a TV licence fee which frees it from the commercial pressures of other news outlets. As a public service broadcaster, the BBC's mission statement reflects the 'fourth estate' view of journalism outlined earlier in the chapter: 'to act in the public interest, serving all audiences through the provision of impartial, high-quality and distinctive output and services which inform, educate and entertain' (BBC, 2023a).

The BBC plays a critical agenda-setting role in the UK news environment, with Radio 4's *Today* programme often setting the news agenda for other outlets. Channel 4, another public broadcaster in the UK that follows a slightly different model because they are funded through advertising, also plays a key role in influencing the national conversation on particular issues. The UK government announced plans to sell the TV channel in 2021. However, an announcement in January 2023 by UK Culture Secretary Michelle Donelan suggested that the UK government has put these plans on hold. ITV News and Sky News have also established themselves as long-standing parts of the UK's broadcast news infrastructure. The launch of GB News in June 2021 added a new broadcast news option to the UK news landscape. The defining feature of GB News was that it launched as a partisan right-wing channel which critics have likened to a British version of Fox News in the US (Lewis, 2021). Petley highlights the complex challenge that Ofcom faces in trying to regulate this new organisation:

> A major problem here is that when Ofcom comes to make judgments on the 'due impartiality' of the two new channels' programming, it will have to do so in a highly politically charged environment ravaged by the culture wars. Here the idea that the BBC is 'left-wing' or a propaganda organ of the 'liberal metropolitan elite' is loudly proclaimed daily by newspapers with political and economic axes to grind. (Barnett and Petley, 2021:34)

The launch of this new channel raises questions about whether broadcasters should be allowed to emulate the 'hyper-partisan' journalism of the UK print market or 'whether their journalistic output should adhere to the well-entrenched values of impartiality and accuracy' (Barnett and Petley, 2021: 35). One of the justifications for launching channels such as GB News is that they provide balance to an overly liberal BBC (Barnett and Petley, 2021). This criticism shows the difficult position the BBC finds itself in as it is criticised from multiple perspectives. The left accuses it of being too close to the government and, therefore, neglectful of its role as a watchdog on state power.

In terms of news reporting, Ofcom guidelines state that 'news, in whatever form, must be reported with due accuracy and presented with due impartiality' (Ofcom, 2023). The regulator's position on this is relatively nuanced, with a clear argument:

> 'Due' is an important qualification to the concept of impartiality. Impartiality itself means not favouring one side over another. 'Due' means adequate or appropriate to the subject and nature of the programme. So 'due impartiality' does not mean an equal division of time has to be given to every view, or that every argument and every facet of every argument has to be represented. (Ofcom, 2023)

The BBC argues that its commitment to impartiality goes beyond the parameters set out by Ofcom. They define impartiality as 'reflecting all sides of arguments and not favouring any side' (BBC, 2023b). Analysis of the BBC's flagship political programme *Question Time* shows an even spread of appearances across the political system (Burton-Cartledge, 2012; Collins, 2018). *Question Time* gives an illustrative example of the BBC's quantitative approach to ensuring impartiality. Guests from the two main parties make the most appearances on the programme. The weighting of guest appearances is neatly balanced between the UK's two major political parties. This balance of debate between the Conservative party and the Labour party is at the heart of the BBC's attempts to achieve a sense of impartiality throughout its political coverage. Having the main political parties dominate coverage of political affairs reflects much of the journalism studies literature, which shows that official political actors dominate the news.

With this even-handed framing of elite political debate, the programme makers could be accused of invoking the concept of objectivity as a 'strategic ritual'. Tuchman's influential newsroom research study found that journalists engage in the 'strategic ritual' of objectivity and argues that they use it to create the illusion of impartiality, while its primary purpose is to protect them from professional criticism. One of the critical features of this objective ritual is the practice of presenting conflicting possibilities. Tuchman describes how this means that 'newspapermen regard the statement 'X' said 'A' as 'fact', even if 'A' is false (Tuchman, 1972). So, when Donald Trump made false statements about the 2020 US election being stolen, the news media repeated the false claims as part of the story and this practice can serve to amplify these false claims.

Theory box: Objectivity as a strategic ritual

Gaye Tuchman's research critically examines the concept of journalistic objectivity by focusing on the form, content and inter-organisational relationships within the newsroom. Tuchman showed how objectivity is used defensively in order to protect journalists from criticism and to make a claim of producing objective news. To appear objective, journalists will claim that they have:

- Presented conflicting possibilities related to truth-claims
- Presented supplementary evidence to support a 'fact'
- Used quotation marks to indicate that the reporter is not making a truth-claim
- Presented the most 'material facts' first
- Carefully separated 'facts' from opinions

Tuchman (1972) argues that 'Although such procedures may provide demonstrable evidence of an attempt to obtain objectivity, they cannot be said to provide objectivity' (676). She argues that there is a discrepancy between the procedures used to produce objective reporting and the news itself. Although news is a subjective product which has been produced through a process of editorial selection, the most common defence used by journalists when they are subjected to criticism is that news is objective.

The problems associated with this type of reporting are exacerbated by the establishment of 'news values' in journalism. Galtung and Ruge's seminal study into what makes news found that elite nations and persons were one of the key features of news coverage of events (Galtung and Ruge, 1965). Harcup and O'Neil's follow-up studies supported elite actors having news value, and anything concerning the 'power elite' was a key determinant of what made the news (Harcup and O'Neil, 2001, 2017). So, the strategic ritual of objectivity combines with news values to create a situation where false statements by political elites are spread through the news media using practices that are supposed to adhere to objective and impartial news coverage.

Quoting both sides of an issue of political controversy can also lead to a situation where expert voices are balanced with partisan lobbyists with a specific agenda. Think tanks with opaque sources of funding supply experts to appear on the BBC to offer opinions on a wide range of topics. Organisations such as the Institute of Economic Affairs (IEA) and the Adam Smith Institute (ASI) have developed close links with the media and politicians in order to promote free-market policies and cuts to state expenditure (Cockett, 1994). On setting up the ASI, Madsen Pirie described how it helped to have 'people in the media who broadly shared our agenda' (Pirie, 2012: 50). Supplying experts funded by various industry-affiliated interest groups has become part of the political and media landscape and has been effective in causing doubt over a range of environmental and public health issues, including climate change (Oreskes and Conway, 2010). The presentation of conflicting possibilities can also lead to a binary form of balance where expert voices compete with lobbyists from industry, creating doubt about public policy issues. Think tanks operating from 55 Tufton Street in London were subjected to scrutiny during the short-lived Liz Truss administration because of their close ties to her administration (Fenwick, 2022).

Following the safe strategy outlined by Tuchman allowed the BBC to follow a regime of objectivity that interprets balance as a binary between the two main opposition parties. One exception to this balance between the main political parties in broadcast journalism is the ever-increasing reliance on vox pops (public opinion polls).

Research has shown that vox pops play an essential role in broadcast coverage of political news. Broadcast journalists use them to add opinions to otherwise impartial news bulletins. Research has found that broadcast journalists do not balance these vox pops in the same way they balance political sources because most vox pops in news bulletins only quote one point of view (Beckers et al., 2018). Mosey argues that the frequent use of vox pops 'squeeze out the space for analysis' (Mosey, 2016). This is an interesting observation when considering Glasser's argument that 'objective reporting is biased against independent thinking' because 'it emasculates the intellect by treating it as a disinterested spectator' (Glasser, n.d.). This perceived lack of analysis returns to the central question of whether balancing political debate between the two main parties satisfies demands for pluralistic news coverage. The practice is understandable given the limitations of the first-past-the-post voting system, which is used to decide the winner in UK general elections. The need for this 'objective' type of defensive framing has increased over time as news broadcasters face allegations of bias on an almost permanent basis (Ford et al., 2021). The need to tread carefully around issues of impartiality is not something that causes a problem for print journalists in the UK, and this will be examined in the next section.

Spotlight on research: News values

Harcup and O'Neill's (2017) article 'What is news? News values revisited (again)' tackles one of the central questions at the heart of journalism studies. A consistent finding has been a continued focus on the importance of elite actors, which means that political leaders and heads of state have 'news value' because of their elite status. This can create a problem for journalists when these elite actors are dishonest because their statements will be reported regardless of their veracity.

The article builds on previous research in the field and updates it by examining the impact of the digital age on contemporary news values. The attention economy means that news organisations have a keen interest in developing news with a high degree of shareability. Digital analytics show that the most popular stories shared on social media are rarely stories about the power elite, which may signal a shift in the status given to political news.

Print journalism

Print journalism has been on a global decline for decades, and the UK is no exception to this trend. The critical funding source underpinning the print industry is advertising revenue, and the emergence of the digital information landscape has drastically reduced the value of print advertising. The Covid-19 pandemic and subsequent lockdown threatened to finish off the ailing print journalism industry. Media commentator Roy Greenslade argued that:

> Coronavirus is destroying newsprint newspapers across Britain, delivering the coup de grace to businesses that were already in the process of dying. There will not be a post-pandemic 'old media' recovery because it seems inconceivable that publishers, already struggling to fund journalism, will return to the previous status quo.
> (Greenslade, 2020)

Scholars have repeated these predictions about the death of legacy media over the last two decades, but the picture is more complicated than Greenslade's analysis suggests. Print circulation has been in steady decline for decades, but there has been a corresponding increase in online readership. The problem for the news industry is that online audiences are accessing the news for free (Edge, 2022). The dilemma for online newspapers is whether to keep their product free and reach a potentially much bigger audience attractive to advertisers or introduce a paywall system to gain revenue from digital subscribers.

Newspapers in the United Kingdom are self-regulated through the Independent Press Standards Organisation (IPSO). This system of self-regulation has been the source of historical scandals and debates about journalism ethics. The most recent events involved the Leveson Inquiry triggered by the phone hacking scandal, which emerged in 2007 following jail sentences handed out to Glen Mulcaire and Clive Goodman after they pleaded guilty to intercepting voicemails. These arrests marked the beginning of a more comprehensive police inquiry that ended with the closure of the *News of the World*. The scandal touched the heart of Downing Street as Andy Coulson, the then prime minister David Cameron's head of communications, was jailed for his involvement in the scandal (BBC News, 25 June 2014). The scandal led to the closure of the Press Complaints Commission in 2014, which IPSO replaced.

One of the key differences between print and broadcast journalism is the partisanship displayed by UK newspapers. For example, during the 2019 general election, the Conservative party received endorsements from the *Daily Express*, the *Daily Mail*, the *Daily Telegraph*, the *Sun* and the *Times*. The *Daily Mirror* and the *Guardian* offered qualified support for the Labour Party. These newspapers argue that their partisan stances are a careful representation of the views of their readers. However, as Conboy highlights, the UK press is 'more associated with the innate bias of wealthy owners and their corporate priorities than with any specific party affiliation' (Conboy, 2011: 129). Critics of pluralism in UK journalism can point to the concentration of ownership in print journalism as convincing evidence to support this view. Three companies (Reach PLC, News UK and Daily Mail Group) own 90 per cent of the UK's newspapers (Media Reform Coalition, 2021). This concentration of ownership and the need to align with the partisan values of their owners could be a solid basis for discounting print journalism as an agent of pluralism in the UK political system. Nevertheless, some of the most prominent examples of 'fourth estate' journalism have come from the national newsroom, with newspapers holding political actors to account. However, the local press has suffered from a serious decline in recent decades. Clark notes that:

> The provincial press played a vital part in the democratic process in local communities in the past and still could fulfil that role, though the link between local communities and local government has been eroded in recent decades as coverage of local politics in the local press has declined. (Clark, 2018: 190)

Local newspapers have suffered from declining sales, and their content has become more closely aligned with the business interests of their owners. One study into sourcing practices in local newspapers in the UK found that: 'Too frequently the result is bland, banal copy at best; or free advertising and propaganda at worst. All these trends are a serious threat to local democracy, the public interest, public trust, the local public sphere, and the standards of journalism (O'Neill, 2008: 498).

The decline in local print journalism coverage of political affairs has coincided with the rise in some locally focused digital platforms, which are attempting to fill the void left by the decline in the local press (Harte et al., 2018). In the latest news consumption survey from Ofcom, only 32 per cent of people are getting their news from print journalism whereas 49 per cent of people access news through social media. This fundamental shift in how consumers access news means that the digital landscape needs closer examination.

Digital news

The emergence of the contemporary digital landscape has led to a spectacular realignment of the news industry. The impact of this has not been entirely positive. According to the 'Veracity Index', journalism is one of the least trusted professions. Only politicians, government ministers, advertising executives and estate agents were less trusted than journalists in the 2022 version of the Ipsos poll that ranks how well each profession is trusted (Ipsos, 2022). Furthermore, people are actively avoiding the news for a range of different reasons. The *Reuters Institute Digital News Report 2022* shows that news avoidance has almost doubled since 2016 because of 'too much news about politics and Covid-19' (Newman, 2022: 62).

One of the key developments in the emergence of digital news coverage has been the speed of news gathering and delivery. Social media use by journalists led to embarrassment for mainstream journalists during the 2019 general election campaign. With only three days to go until polling, the BBC's political editor Laura Kuenssberg tweeted that a Labour party activist had punched Health Secretary Matt Hancock's adviser. ITV's political editor Robert Peston repeated the allegation, describing how the adviser had been 'Whacked in the face'. These tweets were read by a large audience and drove push notifications to alert the public to the unfolding events. Video footage from the event showed that the punch had never happened. Still, the impact distracted the news cycle from a serious story about NHS underperformance only to be dominated by a story that did not happen. Still, it was spread through social media by traditional broadcast journalists (Ford et al., 2021: 335–337). This is just one incident that has led observers to worry that political affairs are now being conducted in a 'post-truth' or 'post-fact' era driven by digital technology. Pomerantsev describes how this works in practice:

> By the time a fact-checker has caught a lie, thousands more have been created, and the sheer volume of 'disinformation cascades' makes unreality unstoppable. All that matters is that the lie is clickable, and what determines that is how it feeds into people's existing prejudices. Algorithms developed by companies such as Google and Facebook are based around your previous searches and clicks, so with every search and every click you find your own biases confirmed. Social media, now the primary news source for most Americans, leads us into echo chambers of similar-minded people, feeding us only the things that make us feel better, whether they are true or not. (Pomerantsev, 2016)

Instead of ushering in a new, fast age of enlightenment, the digital news era seems to be plagued with problems in informing and representing a wider audience on political affairs. Nevertheless, despite the uneasy relationship between traditional journalism and social media, there have been positive developments on the digital front.

In Scotland, *The Ferret* is a digital investigative journalism organisation that focuses on holding power to account in the interests of their readers, who are also subscribers in a digital model that cuts out the influence of traditional advertising revenue. *The Ferret* was the first news organisation in Scotland to sign up to the regulator IMPRESS, and this was the only regulator that fully implemented the recommendations of the Leveson Inquiry. *The Ferret* has won awards for tackling stories focused on the environment and human rights, and its creation has been driven by some of the weaknesses caused by the traditional legacy media business model: '*The Ferret* is a response to three perceived crises: a democratic crisis facing Scotland, an economic crisis which is shrinking the nation's media and an ethical crisis which is damaging trust in its journalism' (Price, 2017: 1348).

This is not the only organisation in the UK to be producing this type of active, cooperative, subscriber-led investigative journalism. The *Bristol Cable* has a similar model to the *Ferret*. The future sustainability of these organisations has yet to be seen, but these are positive examples of how pluralist political participation can happen on digital news platforms in a positive way. The digital space has also allowed for new forms of media and political participation. On the right, digital publishers such as *Breitbart* London and *Guido Fawkes* and on the left, organisations such as *Novara Media* and the *Canary* were actively campaigning during the 2019 general election (McDowell-Naylor et al., 2022). The *Guido Fawkes* blog takes a more traditional approach to its news coverage with lobby correspondents in Westminster. Meanwhile, *Novara Media* was closely aligned with Jeremy Corbyn and enjoyed insider access to his campaign team (McDowell-Naylor et al., 2022).

Echo chambers

When the news industry is accused of favouring elite perspectives it invariably points to the existence of market forces. The continued existence of news organisations means that they have successfully developed a product that has a big enough audience to sustain it. This means at a certain level they are giving people what they want – rather than setting the news agenda they are reflecting the interests of their readers. In the digital age it is common for people to point to political polarisation and the existence of echo chambers where people select their news based on their already existing beliefs. A review of the research literature on this topic found that politically partisan echo chambers were small in scale and had less influence than is assumed in debates around policy. Nevertheless, the level of interest in news and self-selection of partisan news was seen as having a role in shaping news and media use (Ross Arguedas et al., 2022).

The digital revolution is not the only factor shifting the dynamics of news coverage of political affairs in the UK. The use of referendums to settle major constitutional issues gives some insight into the limits of debate within the impartial coverage under a first-past-the-post regime. However, the next section will argue that the two referendums on Scotland and the EU disrupted these dynamics in interesting ways.

Case study: The impact of direct democracy in the UK

The binary balance of broadcast journalism was given a serious challenge by the Scottish independence referendum of 2014. The unpopularity of the Conservative party in Scotland meant that the Labour party dominated Scottish politics for decades. However, a long spell in government combined with unpopular policies such as the invasion of Iraq in 2003 had eroded the power base of the Labour party, which meant that the Scottish National Party (SNP) was able to steadily increase its vote share until it eventually managed to win control of the devolved Scottish Parliament in 2007 through a minority administration. This laid the foundations for it to gain a majority in 2011 and hold a referendum on

(Continued)

Scotland's constitutional future. The 2014 campaign opened a unique problem for the BBC. The traditional both sides balance of the media between Labour and the Conservative party has been disrupted by a new axis of 'yes' and 'no'.

The referendum put the Conservative party and the Labour party on the same side of the constitutional debate and reshaped the Scottish political and media landscape for the next decade. The 'No' vote won the referendum, with 55 per cent of the voters deciding to stay in the union. Still, the referendum's impact dominated Scottish politics for the next decade. Scottish voters punished the Labour party following the referendum campaign. Lynch notes that the Labour party was the 'main political casualty of the referendum' – although he notes that the party had been declining in Scotland since 2007 (Lynch, 2019). The Conservative party regained momentum by finding a new relevance with the Scottish electorate as defenders of the union, gaining seats in national and devolved elections and becoming the opposition party in the Scottish Parliament. Despite losing the referendum, the SNP won almost half of the Scottish vote in the 2015 general election and took 56 of the 59 seats at Westminster (Johns and Mitchell, 2016). The aftermath of the defeat in the referendum saw 'yes' voters providing a surge of new members, money and campaigning resources for the SNP (Lynch, 2019).

The impact on the Scottish media landscape was also evident. During the referendum, there were protests by supporters of Scottish nationalism at the BBC headquarters in Glasgow (BBC News, 2014). In print journalism, the Scottish press was almost universally against Scottish independence. The exception was the *Sunday Herald*, which decided to support the independence cause. Supporting independence led to it being the only Scottish title to increase sales following the referendum (BBC News, 2015a). The popularity of the defeated 'yes' voters cause also led to the launch of a new print newspaper in 2014. The *National* newspaper was launched in the context of drastically declining readership across the industry and has remained viable while also adding a Sunday version in 2018. Furthermore, as broadcast journalists shifted their focus from balancing the main political parties to equally balancing the 'yes' and 'no' sides, the coverage patterns shifted. The 'no' side was most often represented by elite official sources, fitting the standard pattern for political journalism. However, the 'yes' side was most commonly represented by 'non-elite official' and 'unofficial' sources (Dekavalla and Jelen-Sanchez, 2016). Indeed: 'The unprecedented engagement of ordinary citizens and grassroots campaign groups in the democratic process made the Scottish independence referendum distinctive from other referendums and elections in the UK' (Dekavalla and Jelen-Sanchez, 2017: 449).

This was a clear example of direct democracy changing the news coverage of a key political event in the UK. The balance of voices shifted considerably towards unofficial sources in a pattern which was repeated during the EU referendum of 2016. This time the opposing sides were 'Remain' and 'Leave'. Once again, the shifting sands of electoral interest were evident in the 2017 general election.

> The 2017 election hammered perhaps the final nail into the coffin of the class politics we had become so used to. As Labour flourished in middle-class remain areas, so too

did the Conservatives increase their vote share in working-class, Leave-leaning, constituencies. Both parties – particularly, but not only when it comes to Brexit – now resemble fragile coalitions whose stability is far from certain. (Evans and Menon, 2017: 119)

As with the example from Scotland, the EU referendum shifted the debate. The liberal centrist consensus had dominated UK politics for decades by conducting political debate within a system of 'shades of difference within a broad consensus' (Evans and Menon, 2017: 68). This consensus was firmly rejected by a large proportion of the electorate as coming from a 'centrist elite' that did not represent their interests. This was significant enough to win the referendum and see the UK leave the EU.

While the Scottish independence referendum reconstructed and reinvigorated the Scottish political and news environment, the EU referendum had the same impact in the wider UK. The voter disengagement that was picked up in general election studies was not evident in news coverage of the EU referendum. Tolson highlights how the post-Brexit public sphere put some elements of the political elite in an 'unstable position' while other politicians found themselves 'mimicking voters in their use of populist forms of rhetoric' (Tolson, 2019: 430). Taken together, these two referendums highlighted a pluralist deficit in mainstream coverage of political affairs.

The propositions of 'yes', 'no', 'leave' and 'remain' elicited much stronger reactions amongst the British public than the stale prospect of choosing between the Labour party or the Conservative party. It was the instrument of direct democracy that brought these passions to the fore, raising questions about other issues that the UK public is passionate about that do not fit the usual binary impartial balance between two leading parties. More importantly, these case studies showed there was a large constituency of 'yes' voters and 'leave' voters who were not part of the mainstream media coverage of politics prior to these two votes. These examples run counter to the claim that the news media offer a platform for a wide range of viewpoints when such significant groups were excluded from the debate because of a news industry that is organised around the political party system.

Conclusion

This chapter began by outlining two contrasting perspectives on whether the news media open up a space for plural debates about the political system in the UK or whether they close down this debate alongside the narrow interest of elite groups. The regulatory regimes of broadcast and print journalism have shaped the output of various news organisations. With its tight impartiality rules, broadcast journalism has sought to create balance across the political spectrum. However, as the two referendum case studies show, this does not necessarily reflect the opinions or interests of the broader electorate. Equally, partisan newspapers claim to represent the political opinions of their readers, but there is strong evidence that they also pursue their own agenda, which is driven by ownership and commercial considerations. The digital news space has opened up a more comprehensive platform for disparate news organisations to communicate their message. However, this has also coincided with a lack of trust in the media and active 'news avoidance' practices amongst audiences. Voter input into news coverage of political affairs is often decontextualised through vox pops and limited engagement with the issues at hand. Examining the 2001 general election, journalism scholars found that these constructions of the audience played a role in driving long-established practices that favoured elite voices over voters' interests (Brookes and Wahl-Jorgensen, 2004).

The reliance on elite sources of information also highlights a democratic deficit in UK journalism that stops short of providing the representative ideal. Hackett argues that achieving a truly pluralist media that serves the public interest would require 'regulatory and legislative initiatives, such as subsidies and media ownership ceilings' (Hackett, 2005: 95). These changes might challenge systemic problems within the UK news media that limit pluralism and the voices that are heard speaking about political affairs. This chapter has outlined the problems that regimes of impartiality in broadcast news have limited debates about political affairs. It has highlighted the ways that print and digital media have also reflected elite perspectives and been used to spread 'fake news' about political affairs. Nevertheless, there is hope that digital platforms such as the *Ferret* and the *Bristol Cable* are able to engage with their audiences and subscribers in new ways that reflect the critical role that the news media plays in a democratic system such as the UK.

There is also the consistent watchdog role of the press that has been evidenced throughout the political chaos of recent years. Most recently, Amelia Gentleman's work highlighting the injustices of the Windrush scandal and Pippa Crerar's dogged reporting of the UK government breaking their own rules during the Covid-19 pandemic. At the time of writing, investigative journalists looking into the Conservative party chairman's tax affairs led to his sacking by prime minister Rishi Sunak. So, there is evidence of journalists performing that public service role of holding power to account. However, one of the key lessons of the eventful last few years in UK politics is that journalists and politicians are not broadly aware of what the people want.

The narrow scope of coverage of political affairs that neatly aligns with quantitative vote shares does not offer a detailed representation of people's views. This is evidenced by the way that both of the UK's recent constitutional referendums have reshaped elements of the British political and media landscape. News coverage of political affairs in the UK is limited and hampered by systemic problems, but it is an essential part of the democratic system, and the democratic system would be worse off without the news industry.

Key take-home points

- Research into news coverage of political affairs can provide evidence that the news media open up debate. However, there is also research that suggests that the news media reflect the interests of elite actors.
- Broadcast news is tightly regulated by Ofcom in terms of impartiality. Research has suggested that professional routines in journalism that aim for objective news coverage often fail to produce truly objective news.

- Print journalism is self-regulated and, therefore, free to pursue partisan interests. Concerns about the concentration of ownership raise questions about the ability of print journalism to act in the public interest. Nevertheless, some of the best examples of public service journalism have been produced by reporters working in print.
- The digital space has provided both opportunities and threats to the idea of pluralistic political coverage of political affairs. The rise in fake news and partisan political organisations has changed the media landscape, and even traditional journalists have spread misinformation on social media.
- The digital space has also allowed space for some genuine subscriber-oriented news organisations to develop, such as the *Bristol Cable* and the *Ferret* in Scotland.
- Political news is often mediated through the interests of the two main political parties in the UK. This was disrupted by constitutional referendums in 2014 and 2016, raising questions about how well the news media reflected a wide range of opinions prior to these polls.

Annotated reading list

Lewis, J., Williams, A. and Franklin, B. (2008) A compromised fourth estate? *Journalism Studies*, 9(1), 1–20.

This article questions the role of the British press and a 'fourth estate'. The claim that the media has an independent position that holds power to account is brought into question by analysing the output of the contemporary newsroom in the face of consistent cuts to staffing and increased workloads. The study finds that contemporary newsrooms increasingly rely on pre-packaged material from public relations organisations. This has led to mainstream journalism resembling an extension of the advertising industry rather than a genuinely independent part of the pluralistic democratic system within the UK.

Gentleman, A. (2019) *The Windrush Betrayal: Exposing the Hostile Environment.* London: Guardian Faber.

This book charts Amelia Gentleman's investigation into the Windrush scandal that saw people who arrived in the UK at a young age deported to countries they had never visited. Gentleman's dogged reporting led to the resignation of home secretary Amber Rudd (Gentleman, 2019) and is an example of the notable exception to the problems with journalism that have been highlighted throughout this chapter.

10
The legislature

Thomas Caygill

Image 10.1 The Palace of Westminster (aka the Houses of Parliament) © Photo by Mistervlad on Shutterstock

Learning objectives

After reading this chapter you should be able to:

- Reflect upon the extent to which the UK Parliament meets our modern pluralistic values
- Identify ways in which citizens can access and influence the institution
- Identify areas where the UK Parliament can be reformed to resolve some of its limitations

Introduction

The UK Parliament sits at the heart of our liberal democracy. It is an old institution with a long history and sometimes that history, along with its customs and traditions, holds the institution back from reforming and evolving in an era defined by critical citizens who are seeking easier and impactful ways to bring about change in society. The aim of this chapter is to be a critical friend of the institution and assess the extent to which it is fit for purpose from the perspective of our modern pluralistic political system. By the end of this chapter, we hope that students will feel better equipped to navigate the UK Parliament both in terms of understanding its role in the British polity but also in terms of the many access points citizens can use to influence the institution.

Need to know: Structure of parliament

In this chapter we map out the various functions of the UK Parliament with respect to their contribution to our pluralistic democracy. Students will need to know: that the UK Parliament comprises two Houses of Parliament (House of Commons and House of Lords); that the House of Commons has primacy as the elected House; that the House of Lords is unelected (and for the most part is an appointed chamber); and that the primary roles of parliament are to represent the public, hold the government to account on behalf of the public and pass and shape laws.

In the broadest sense, we can define legislatures as bodies 'created to approve measures that will form the law of the land' (Norton, 2013: 1). The definition focuses on the law-making function as the main role of a legislature. Indeed, the etymological root of the word legislature means law proposer or carrier. However, there are many different local names for legislatures. In the UK we use the term 'parliament', which presents different connotations such as debate, deliberation and accountability, rather than simply law making.

Winston Churchill famously said that 'we shape our buildings and our buildings shape us' (UK Parliament, 2023) and in no place is this truer than the UK Parliament – from the structure of the House of Commons and the House of Lords through to the overall imposing gothic architecture of the Palace of Westminster itself – they all shape how our parliament and how our politics operates.

In 1547, Edward VI (son of Henry VIII) handed St Stephen's Chapel over to the House of Commons for their use. While this might seem inconsequential, it has huge ramifications for our politics. The chapel was set out with members of the congregation sat facing each other, so Members of Parliament (MPs) sat on opposite sides of the chapel facing each other. This is an example of how a random fluke of history has impacted the layout of our parliamentary chambers to this day. If they had been given another room with a different seating plan (e.g. in a semi-circular design as in the Scottish and Welsh Parliaments), perhaps our politics would be less adversarial.

Image 10.2 The semi-circular debating chamber of the Scottish Parliament
© Photo by Fotokon on Shutterstock

Historical institutionalism (see Theory box below) would argue that this is path dependency, this decision to sit in St Stephen's Chapel, which has seen the House of Commons set on a path throughout its history. There have been two times when we have had an opportunity to alter the seating arrangements in the House of Commons. The first was in 1834 when the Palace of Westminster burnt down, and St Stephen's Chapel was destroyed. The second opportunity was in 1943 following the destruction of the Victorian House of Commons Chamber during the blitz. On both occasions the opportunity was not seized. What this tells us is that history matters in Westminster.

Theory box: Historical institutionalism

To understand why parliament behaves the way that it does, we need to understand the broader context in which it operates. As noted above, the historical development of parliament is an important part of its norms and values – and these continue to shape how it functions. Historical institutionalism is a useful theory in helping us to explain how this long history influences and impacts on the behaviour of the institution today. March and Olsen (1989) have emphasised the role of norms and values within institutions, such as parliaments, in explaining how the actors within them behave. They argue that institutions are 'collections of standard operating procedures and structures that define and defend values, norms, interests, identities and beliefs' (March and Olsen, 1989: 17). These ideas

(Continued)

are fundamental to the theory of historical institutionalism. Institutions therefore provide a framework of rules to structure the political game (Kelso, 2009). However, it is important to note that institutions themselves do not cause particular events to occur but do provide structure through which interactions in the institution take place which do influence political outcomes (Thelen and Steinmo, 1992). In addition, while institutions can shape political behaviour, they are also the outcome of political behaviour, strategy, conflict and choice (Thelen and Steinmo, 1992). The theory therefore views political actors as rule followers (March and Olsen, 1984; Simon, 1985). The idea of path dependency is key to this theory and has been used to explain the trajectory of not just public policy but the trajectory of the institution itself when it comes to change (Kelso, 2009). As noted earlier in the chapter in relation to the physical set-up of the Commons and Lords' chambers, despite a number of opportunities for change, they haven't been taken up – hence for a historical institutionalist they are path dependent. Pierson (2000: 253) explains 'the farther into a process we are, the harder it becomes to shift from one path to another'. This helps to explain the institutional continuity of the UK Parliament, where much of the focus is on evolutionary change as opposed to revolution. It is not impossible to change the institution, just that it will require a great deal of political pressure to push parliament off its path dependency. For instance, the substantive reforms we saw to House of Commons select committees was a response to the 2009 MPs' expenses scandal. For most substantive reform, we can draw a line back to great political pressure somewhere in its vicinity. There are a number of norms and values associated with Westminster, picked up throughout its history. These include parliamentary sovereignty (or effectively executive sovereignty given single party majority governments), ministerial responsibility and strong party government (strong party loyalties and a strong whipping system).

Context

Before we go on to critically assess the UK Parliament and its place in our pluralistic and liberal democracy, we do need to place it into more context. In order to understand and assess the UK Parliament, we need to acknowledge that it does much more than just legislate.

The challenge is that a number of academics (Blondel, 1970; Mezey, 1979; Polsby, 1975) judge legislatures on their legislative power. Law making may be a function which legislatures have in common but the system of power in which they operate has huge consequences. For instance, the UK Parliament operates in a system of fused powers. By fused powers we mean that the executive is drawn from and sits in the legislature. In general elections, we elect MPs and thus a parliament, once the final results are known, then a government is appointed based upon who can command the confidence of the House of Commons. This allows the executive to dominate parliament through its majority in the House of Commons. In separation of powers systems (such as the US), the executive and legislatures are elected separately and members of the executive branch cannot sit in the legislature (unlike in the UK where ministers are expected to be parliamentarians). This means that the executive cannot dominate the legislature and that the legislature has more capacity to shape law.

Norton (2013) argues that the UK Parliament is a policy-influencing legislature and in fact most legislatures (or parliaments) in fused power systems are. Parliament itself does not seek to generate policy, rather it scrutinises and assents to policy brought before it by the government (Norton, 2013). In the US, Congress does seek to generate policy and indeed is the main initiator of it, because the executive branch is separate. For the vast majority of its history the UK Parliament has never been a policymaking body. For centuries parliament has looked to the executive (first the monarch and then the monarch's government) to bring forward proposals for it to assent to.

While a number of academics focus on legislative scrutiny (and power) when making judgements about legislatures, the functions of scrutiny of government (holding the executive to account) and representation (representing the views of the public) are incredibly important in fused powers systems where parliaments are the only connection between the citizenry and the executive. All three functions must be assessed in order to fully appreciate the impact and influence of the UK Parliament.

Core functions

In assessing how pluralistic the UK Parliament is we must address the core functions that we expect the institution to undertake. In this section we will address scrutiny of government, legislative scrutiny and representation.

Scrutiny of government

Accountability is central to the British political system and also to parliament's relationship with the executive. Accountability can be viewed firstly as a relationship and secondly as a relationship involving power and control (Barlow and Paun, 2013). Principal–agent theory provides important insights into accountability, and in particular how the actors in our parliament are expected to interact with each other.

> ### Theory box: Principal–agent theory
>
> Accountability requires a specification of who is accountable to whom. This is where principal–agent theory steps in. In this theory, an agent is an actor who is called upon to undertake an action on behalf of someone else. The agent is the actor doing the task and the principal is the person delegating tasks (Gailmard, 2014). In the example of the UK Parliament, the ultimate principal is the UK electorate (i.e. those eligible and registered to vote in UK elections). In our representative democracy, the electorate delegate decision-making power to parliament (via MPs and elections) because it is not possible for the entire population to make decisions on every issue. Parliament, or rather MPs, then become the agents of the electorate. The relationship means that MPs are accountable to the public and thus the public have power over (and can incentivise) MPs as the public can remove them via the ballot box at general elections. In addition, legislatures are reactive bodies at best, so parliament delegates day-to-day governing to the executive (hence why the prime minister is appointed based upon who can command the confidence of the House of Commons (i.e. the principal).

As Beetham (2006) notes, there is not one single relationship but rather a series of relationships. MPs are accountable to the electorate and ministers are accountable to parliament (Scarparo, 2008). This is a key example of how scrutiny and accountability as well as the relationship between government, parliament and the public is assembled. This is a symbiotic relationship between ministers, MPs and the wider electorate. From a pluralistic perspective, this set of relationships is designed to ensure that the government and parliament remain in touch with the views and expectations of the public. It is through scrutiny that accountability can be achieved.

Questions

One of the more familiar mechanisms through which scrutiny is undertaken and accountability is delivered is through parliamentary questions. These questions are of two main types: oral and written.

Oral questions are the first item of business in both Houses of Parliament between Monday and Thursday each week when the Houses are sitting. In the House of Commons, these questions are departmental in nature and are on a rota with each government department (and its ministers) being before the House once a month. Each question time session lasts one hour. Larger government departments (e.g. HM Treasury) get a full hour of questions, whereas smaller departments (e.g. Cabinet Office) only receive 30 minutes – meaning that there is some doubling up during the one-hour sessions.

Much criticism is levelled against Prime Minister's Questions (PMQs) in particular. Research by the Hansard Society suggests that PMQs can in fact turn people off parliament – participants in focus groups have described the event as noisy, childish and dishonest (Hansard Society, 2014). Research by Bates et al. (2014) also highlights the variability in the quality of answers from the prime minister – with Brown and Thatcher performing poorly here in terms of the fullness of their answers (i.e. providing the requested information and/or making their view on the topic clear). Because PMQs is high stakes and the most viewed piece of parliamentary activity, it is incredibly partisan. Departmental questions are less partisan and are able to extract more detailed information from ministers in comparison to PMQs (Bates et al., 2018).

From a pluralistic perspective, there is scope for public involvement in the process. MPs will often use question time to ask questions on behalf of their constituents. Question time is one of the mechanisms through which the views and concerns of the public can be raised (Norton, 2013). Interest groups will also regularly contact MPs in the run-up to question time to offer suggestions in terms of questions they should ask (Watts, 2007).

Case study: People's questions

In 2015, Jeremy Corbyn (then leader of the Labour Party) was praised for introducing an element of crowdsourcing of questions for PMQs. Following a request for ideas, Corbyn received over 40,000 suggestions and put a handful of those questions to then prime minister, David

Cameron, who also praised the consensual nature of Corbyn's approach, although David Cameron reportedly said this made PMQs exchanges easier for him.

> I have a question from Steven, who works for a housing association. He says that the cut in rents will mean that the company that he works for will lose 150 jobs by next March because of the loss of funding for that housing association to carry on with its repairs. Down the line, that will mean worse conditions, worse maintenance, fewer people working there, and a greater problem for people living in those properties. Does the Prime Minister not think it is time to reconsider the question of the funding of the administration of housing, as well as, of course, the massive gap of 100,000 units a year between what is needed and what is being built? HC Deb 16 September 2015, c.1038.

The practice didn't last long but this exercise does show that PMQs could be more pluralistic.

Question time in the House of Lords is not departmental in nature and has only 30 minutes allocated to it on each day's sitting (Monday–Thursday). As it is not departmental in nature, this means that questions on any topic can be asked. The main benefit of Lords' question time is that supplementary questions are not just allowed but encouraged. Only four questions are asked, leaving eight minutes per question (Norton, 2013). Ministers therefore have to be well briefed and can be pinned down by peers in a way not possible in the House of Commons. From an effectiveness perspective, there is more opportunity here to get information from ministers, and interest groups do approach peers with issues to raise (Norton, 2013; Watts, 2007).

Written questions are also utilised in both Houses of Parliament as well. They tend to be more extensively used in the House of Commons (Lilly et al., 2021) to seek information in more detailed form than is possible on the floor of the House (Norton, 2013). As with oral questions, interest groups will email MPs and peers with suggestions of what questions they might want to ask on their behalf, if they were so inclined (Watts, 2007). MPs will also do this on behalf of constituents.

Debates

Debates are the oldest forum through which both Houses of Parliament can scrutinise the government and hold it to account. This section will analyse the extent to which debates in Parliament reflect the interests of citizens.

We start with opposition day debates. There are 20 opposition days in each parliamentary year (also referred to as a 'session' – they are typically 12 months in length but can run for longer) and the topics for such debates are selected by opposition parties. Opposition day debates are important in handing opposition parties control of the parliamentary agenda, meaning a wider variety of issues can be raised on the floor of the House of Commons.

The Backbench Business Committee adds an element of pluralism to the agenda-setting role of MPs in that the concerns of both constituents, interest groups and wider civil society can be raised for debate. The committee was established as part of the Wright Reforms (see Need to know below) following the 2009 expenses scandal in an attempt to 'rebuild the House' following the damage done to its reputation. The committee is cross party and MPs are encouraged to put their proposals in front of the committee in a *Dragon's Den* style pitch. Their criteria for granting backbench time are outlined by Crewe (2015):

- Topicality
- Importance of the subject
- Breadth of interest (support from Select Committees, campaign groups, constituents and others; likelihood of securing debate via government or opposition motions?)

There are also adjournment debates which take place at the end of each day's sitting in the House of Commons for 30 minutes, which gives MPs a chance to raise local and constituency issues. This is an important part of the process – and while the mechanisms discussed here are perhaps insufficient for the constituents concerned (e.g. debates rarely lead to a substantive policy change), they can be effective when used together or in succession.

While there are numerous routes for debates in the House of Commons, there are fewer routes in the House of Lords. According to Norton (2013), debates occupy over 20 per cent of the time of the House of Lords. Unlike the House of Commons, the Lords has had a dedicated day of debate on a Thursday, since 2005–2006, allowing for five hours of debate. The topics for these debates are determined by the party groups (including crossbenchers). Several days are also allocated to backbench peers to select topics by ballot (Norton, 2013). The expertise of the Lords often means that those taking part in debates have experience in the area concerned, which often means that important but non-partisan issues of concern to groups outside of parliament can be raised and discussed (Norton, 2013).

Select committees

Select committees are considered to be the jewel in the crown of the mechanisms available for parliament to undertake scrutiny, due to their permanence, expertise and bi-partisan nature. Select committees are cross-party groups of MPs who scrutinise government and policy.

Our focus here will be on investigative select committees. Select committees are essential for good democracy in the UK and have many significant advantages over the floor of the House of Commons. They pursue issues in detail and are a direct route through which individual voters along with pressure groups can not only help shape the agenda but also shape scrutiny.

Major changes to the way select committees were appointed occurred in 2010 following the MPs' expenses scandal. These reforms have strengthened select committees and secured their independence from government and have provided an important sense of legitimacy for committee chairs, who are now viewed as powerful senior MPs both in the House of Commons chamber and in the media (Geddes, 2020).

> **Need to know: The Wright reforms**
>
> Select committees in the House of Commons were reformed in 2010. Following the MPs' expenses scandal in 2009, the then Labour government tasked Tony Wright MP (hence the

name Wright Reforms) with chairing the Reform of the House of Commons Committee in order to improve the reputation of the House. The Committee recommended the creation of the Backbench Business Committee (discussed earlier in this chapter) as well as a series of reforms designed to strengthen the select committee system. The reforms focused on removing the power of the party whips from appointing committee chairs and committee members, thus reducing the power of the government. Instead the whole House of Commons would elect committee chairs and parliamentary parties would hold internal ballots to appoint select committee members (House of Commons Reform Committee, 2009).

Select committees provide an important avenue to a more pluralistic parliament. As they set their own agendas, they are able to undertake inquiries (see Figure 10.1 for an overview of the inquiry process) and hold evidence sessions on any subject within their remit. Suggestions for scrutiny come from the chair, committee members as well as interest groups and wider civic society. This shows the importance of the public and civic society making their views known, whether through campaigning, writing to MPs or supporting petitions.

While undertaking inquiries, select committees also request written evidence as well as sending out invitations for oral evidence. The calls for written evidence are open to anyone – you do not have to be an expert to submit evidence to a committee inquiry and frequently select committees are keen to hear from the public about how policy is affecting them (Geddes, 2023). Geddes (2017) notes the importance of evidence from a committee perspective, as it is fundamental for detailed scrutiny, builds expertise and presents an opportunity for select committees to engage with the public. That being said, who gives oral evidence is determined by the committee themselves and, while attempts have been made to expand the diversity of witnesses, Geddes (2017) found that the pool of witnesses on which select committees rely does not reflect the UK population and raises important questions over how representative scrutiny actually is.

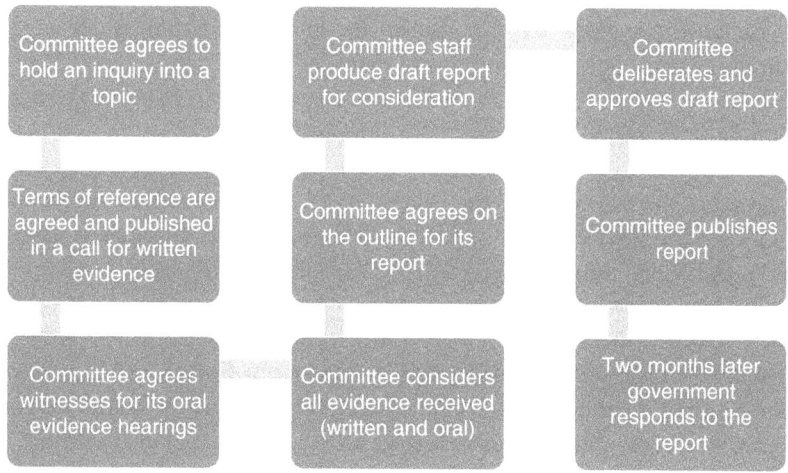

Figure 10.1 Select committee inquiry process

Select committees have also been innovative in the ways they engage with the public and wider civic society. In 2019, six House of Commons select committees commissioned a citizen's assembly on climate change (UK Parliament, 2020). A citizen's assembly comprises a representative group of citizens selected at random to deliberate and make recommendations on a particular issue. The Climate Assembly UK was tasked with providing recommendations on how the UK can achieve its net-zero targets by 2050. The Assembly's 108 members of the public from across the UK were guided through the process by a team of facilitators. Elstub et al. (2021) studied the work of the Assembly and argued that it 'was a highly valuable process that enabled a diverse group of UK citizens to engage in parliamentary scrutiny of government on climate policy in an informed and meaningful manner' (Elstub et al., 2021: 3). The difference between a citizens assembly and normal calls for written evidence is that members of an assembly are actively selected to participate as representative of the population at large and to be fully deliberative, whereas individuals submitting written evidence are self-selecting.

An important question to ask in addition to how pluralistic select committees are is how much impact they make. Seminal research by Benton and Russell (2013) found that they could be more impactful but challenged claims that they were ignored by government. While the success rate of recommendations is below 50 per cent, given the large number of reports published by committees each year this amounts to hundreds of recommendations being acted upon each year.

The work of House of Lords select committees forms another important way through which parliament scrutinises the government and contributes to the policymaking process. The House of Lords select committee system is intended to complement the work of House of Commons select committees (Russell, 2013). Membership is negotiated via the party whips and replicates the party balance in the chamber (Russell, 2013). However, this is less concerning from a Lords perspective because peers are appointed for life and as a result the whipping system is weaker than in the Commons, and peers feel less compelled to vote along party lines. Select committees do, however, operate in a similar way to those in the House of Commons, their powers are the same and they can undertake any inquiry they choose to. As with committees in the Commons, they provide an important access point for civic society to make written submissions and present oral evidence. As the select committees cut across policy areas, they tend to tackle more strategic, longer-term issues.

Select committees provide an opportunity for groups and individuals not normally involved in the policymaking process to have their say.

Legislative scrutiny

As we discussed at the beginning of the chapter, the UK Parliament is a policy influencing legislature (Norton, 1990) rather than a policymaking legislature. This means that it tends to amend and reject policy from the government rather than introduce its own.

House of Commons

The vast majority of legislation considered by the House of Commons originates from the government. In the UK Parliament this dominance over the House of Commons comes from Standing Order 14 – 'government business shall have precedence at every sitting' (House of Commons, 2021). Of course this leads to control of the House and of the legislative process as well, at least in terms of initiation. Dominance in the other parts of the process in the House of Commons comes from its governing majority. Table 10.1 describes the process bills go through when being scrutinised by the House of Commons.

Table 10.1 Legislative process in the House of Commons

Stage	Explanation
First reading	This is purely a formality in which the title of a bill is read out in the House of Commons.
Second reading	This is a debate on the principles of a bill. Typically bills receive a six-hour debate. These debates are opened and closed by ministers and opposition parties have an opportunity to set out their position on the measure. Following the debate the bill will face its first division (vote).
Programme motions	These detail the number of remaining days the House has to scrutinise the legislation. They are drafted by the government and usually pass, giving the government control of the passage of the bill.
Committee stage	This will usually be to a public bill committee although committee stage can take place on the floor of the House (known as committee of the whole House), which allows all MPs to participate in debates. Committee stage is designed to allow for line-by-line scrutiny of a bill.
Report stage	This is an opportunity for all MPs to consider the bill and further amendments, although amendments which were rejected at committee stage cannot be tabled again at report stage unless the government brings them forward.
Third reading	This is a final debate on the bill and is limited to what is in the bill (as the House has just had chance to debate what ought to be in the bill through committee and report stages). Once the bill has passed third reading, it goes to the House of Lords.

Need to know: Public bill committees

Public bill committees are designed to undertake line by line scrutiny of the bills presented to them. However, they rarely have time (as set out in the programme motion) to do so properly (Fox and Korris, 2010). Indeed public bill committees frequently 'run out of time' in the House of Commons. These public bill committees were established in 2006. A key feature is that they can take oral evidence from external witnesses. Fox and Korris (2010) note that the introduction of evidence sessions has increased the quality and quantity of information available to committee members. While select committees have support staff, public bill committees have no such support, so this ability to collect evidence gives them more scope to request amendments to the bill. However, research by Levy (2014) has noted that the use of programme motions and the subsequent timetabling of legislation through committee does not give MPs the opportunity to digest and fully reflect upon that evidence. Thompson (2014) has noted that MPs are more likely to table their own amendments to issues related to the evidence they have heard and cite that evidence to support the case for the amendment. In theory, from a pluralist perspective, there should be an important opportunity for civil society, particularly in the form of interest groups, to present their case for or against legislation. However, in practice this opportunity is limited by government majorities on public bill committees.

(Continued)

While this presents a positive view of public bill committees, it is against a backdrop of government control (party whips still appoint these committees). Despite these recent reforms, research by Thompson (2013) acknowledges that while committees appear to be working much harder than before and spending more time engaging in scrutiny and debating a larger number of amendments, all this work is not producing a material gain for the committees themselves. Amendments tabled by government backbenchers and by the opposition are much less likely to be successful and ministers are making far fewer assurances and undertakings to go away and look at issues in more detail (Thompson, 2013).

Case study: Public reading stage

There have been attempts in the past to establish greater public participation and involvement in the legislative process. A 'public reading' stage was piloted in 2012 on the Children and Families Bill, where the public were encouraged to comment on the Parliament website as the bill was making its way through the legislative process (Leston-Bandeira and Thompson, 2017). Over a thousand comments were submitted. However, research found that despite the impressive response, there was no tangible impact on the legislative process itself due to a lack of proper integration (Leston-Bandeira and Thompson, 2017).

House of Lords

Legislation passes through both Houses using the same framework but how they are dealt with in practice is different.

As in the House of Commons, the first reading is relatively formal with the title of the bill read out. While there is a debate at second reading on the principles of the bill, the House is constrained by the Salisbury–Addison Convention, which states that the House of Lords will not vote down a government bill mentioned in an election manifesto. Peers arguably save their fire for the committee stage of the legislative process, which in contrast to the House of Commons is for the most part undertaken on the floor of the House. This means that every peer has the opportunity to take part in line-by-line scrutiny. The most notable difference between the House of Lords and House of Commons is that there is no concept of programming legislation (i.e. there are no programme motions). So while a bill can 'run out of time' in the House of Commons, this cannot happen in the House of Lords. This is for two reasons. The first is that since 1999 there has been no overall government majority in the House of Lords and secondly, the whipping system is much weaker because, as mentioned earlier, peers are appointed for life. The government therefore has to take the views of the opposition and the non-partisan crossbench peers into account (Russell, 2013). This means that committee stage in the House of Lords takes days as the Lords are keen to ensure they deliver true line-by-line scrutiny (Norton, 2013; Russell, 2013). This provides another handy route for pressure groups to influence the policymaking process. Often pressure groups will target certain peers and MPs simultaneously in order to get them to sponsor amendments in both Houses (Watts, 2007); if an amendment fails in the House of Commons they know there is a second chance in the Lords.

Following committee stage the bill moves onto report stage and third reading. In each of these debates, there are further opportunities for amendments to be tabled and made; however, amendments in the latter stage are supposed to only be technical in nature and focus on tidying up the legislation.

Pre- and post-legislative scrutiny

The introduction of pre-legislative scrutiny in the late 1990s provided further opportunities for civil society to influence policymaking. Pre-legislative scrutiny is the scrutiny of draft bills before the bill has entered the formal legislative process (Smookler, 2006). This type of scrutiny is undertaken by select committees. The government of the day has proven willing to accept the recommendations of pre-legislative scrutiny in shaping the bill it eventually presents to parliament for approval (Fox and Korris, 2010). Watts (2007) notes the importance of pre-legislative scrutiny as an access point for interest groups when the committees call for written evidence and invite witnesses to give oral evidence. The introduction of post-legislative scrutiny in 2008 also provides additional avenues to influence public policy. Post-legislative scrutiny is the examination of legislation after it has entered onto the statute books and allows the select committee system to assess what has and has not worked with acts of parliament and make recommendations on their operation (Caygill, 2019). It is a useful route again for interest groups and civil society more widely to reflect on how the legislation is working/affecting them and for them to present their case to parliament. The challenge with these two additional rounds of scrutiny is that not all legislation receives it due to lack of capacity. While there is evidence of impact with regard to pre- and post-legislative scrutiny, they are not used to their full potential.

There are perhaps more opportunities for civil society to engage in the legislative process than we first imagine, but there are still challenges in terms of how this operates in practice. The public reading stage pilots were not properly integrated and despite public bill committees taking evidence, the government controls public bill committees to such an extent it can easily defeat amendments it doesn't like. The House of Lords provides greater opportunity for influencing the process; however, there are questions of access. Bigger groups are likely to have their own public affairs staff who liaise with peers, and smaller groups can't afford professional lobbying.

Spotlight on research: Executive dominance?

The journal article by Russell et al. (2016) 'Does the executive dominate the Westminster legislative process? Six reasons for doubt' presents a useful critique of the over-exaggeration of the government's dominance of the legislative process in the House of Commons. They present key arguments highlighting that the government's success and opposition's failure is overstated, that Parliament influences the process at other policy stages and that there is influence to be had after the legislative process is complete. This article lifts the lid on the influence that parliament can have on policymaking which is not always noticeable at first glance.

Representation

Representation is a contested concept with multiple definitions. Pitkin (1967) maintains that in order to understand the concept of representation, we must consider the different ways in which it is used. These different uses of representation provide us with a different perspective of the concept. Representation also matters from a pluralist perspective: if a society is to be truly pluralist then different groups in society need a voice and ideally an equal one.

Descriptive representation is concerned with the composition of a legislative assembly and the extent to which the institution reflects society. For instance, a descriptively representative House of Commons would ensure that the total number of women MPs and minority ethnic MPs was proportional to the population as a whole. In order to achieve greater descriptive representation of women in the House of Commons the Labour Party has used all-women shortlists, whereby in certain constituencies only women can stand to be the MP. This has enhanced women's reputation within the Labour Party and in the 2019 Parliament, just over 50 per cent of Labour MPs are women. The implication is that a legislature cannot be truly representative unless it is able to think, feel, reason and act like the population. Representatives from different backgrounds have different perspectives and represent different experiences – the argument is that if a group is marginalised from the legislature by not being physically present through a representative likeness then their views, perspectives and experiences cannot be represented correctly.

Substantive representation is the physical act of representation (Pitkin, 1967) whereby your MP can represent your interests, beliefs and ideology. It is less about the socioeconomic background of the MP and more about how they represent the views of their constituents on particular issues. For instance, if you write to your local MP about foodbanks and they either ask a parliamentary question or write to a minister about the issue, they are substantively representing you. While it doesn't guarantee it, there is an argument that better descriptive representation can lead to better substantive representation if it means that different groups in society (e.g. women, ethnic minorities) are having their experiences and perspectives represented by MPs acting for them. Celis and Childs (2020) note that 'when women are well represented in representative democracies, the formal political agenda is recalibrated away from the political representation of men and their interests'. However, we should be wary of suggesting that groups in society all think, feel and experience the same set of circumstances. As Celis and Childs (2020) note, representation is much more complex than this.

This focus on substantive representation raises two other modes of substantive representation, particularly from the British perspective. We often talk of MPs as being trustees or delegates. The delegate model requires that representatives follow their constituents' preferences, while the trustee model requires representatives to follow their own judgment. In the 21st century, it is generally accepted that MPs tend to stand somewhere in the middle of these two models.

From the perspective of pluralism, we would expect that a diverse range of voices to be present in our national legislature to ensure that the demands, expectations and challenges faced by groups in society are represented on the floor of both Houses and are included on the political agenda.

Descriptive and substantive representation in the House of Commons

From the perspective of gender, in the House of Commons men still outnumber women on a scale of nearly two to one. In 2019 the highest ever proportion of women ever was elected to the House of Commons (220 women MPs), which represents 34 per cent of the total number of MPs (Cracknell and Tunnicliffe, 2022). This is despite over 50 per cent of the total UK population self-identifying as female. While progress has been made, thanks in part to the introduction of all-women shortlists by Labour and the priority (or A) list by the Conservative Party (Kelly and White, 2016), there is still a lot of progress to make before we reach parity.

There is a similar story in terms of the descriptive representation of people with minority ethnic backgrounds in the UK. In 2019 65 MPs were elected from a minority ethnic background (defined as all people who do not identify with a 'white' ethnic group in Great Britain), 10 per cent of the total of the House. While there was substantive progress on the previous election (a 25% increase), in order to reach parity with society (18%), the House of Commons would need to elect another 52 MPs from minority ethnic backgrounds.

In her report *The Good Parliament*, Childs (2016) argues that an inclusive, effective and representative legislature is more than just increasing the diversity of members, it also requires their equal and effective participation. This highlights a point made earlier that on its own descriptive representation is not enough, the institution needs to be inclusive of marginalised groups. This links in with historical institutionalism to some degree. The current Palace of Westminster and many of our political customs and traditions pre-date the liberal democratic era and the era of women's and minority ethnic representation and as such the path dependency (noted in the Theory box on historical institutionalism earlier in this chapter) has meant that these customs and traditions (such as the adversarial nature of our politics) have continued despite our politics having become more inclusive and diverse.

Substantive representation has a number of important dynamics. As noted above, it is connected to descriptive representation to ensure that a wide variety of viewpoints from different groups and within different groups in society are shared but there is also a territorial perspective to this representation too (Judge and Partos, 2018). This is why MPs in the House of Commons straddle both trustee and delegate models of representation. The delegate model means MPs relate mostly to their constituencies whereas the trustee model enables them to act for or on behalf of other groups in society to which they either belong or empathise.

Descriptive and substantive representation in the House of Lords

In January 2022 there were 226 female members and 554 male members of the House. Women therefore made up 29 per cent of the House of Lords (House of Lords Library, 2022) in comparison to 34 per cent of MPs. In terms of minority ethnic members of the House of Lords, they only made up 7.3 per cent of the membership in comparison to 10 per cent in the House of Commons (Uberoi and Burton, 2023). This is against the backdrop of peers being appointed rather than elected, so prime ministers could focus more on diversifying the House of Lords' membership if they chose to.

When it comes to substantive representation, the House of Lords' role is different to that of the House of Commons. The House of Lords does not have a representative function in the geographical sense. However, it does fulfil an expressive function (Norton, 2013). The House of Lords can bring issues onto the political agenda in a way which is not always possible in the House of Commons. MPs can be wary of debating and discussing issues which may not be popular or are controversial with their constituents or which are not partisan in nature (Norton, 2013). One of those issues is assisted dying. Peers are more independently minded than MPs and are freer to raise, represent and express issues.

Overall, there is clearly more work that needs to be done in terms of representation to reach our pluralistic goals of having a political system in which all groups in society have a say and a stake. More work needs to be done to improve descriptive representation in order to ensure that the views of different groups (and within different groups) are heard on the floor of both Houses of Parliament. Part of this will involve reforming Parliament as an institution in order to make it more welcoming to marginalised groups in particular. Childs (2016) outlines 43 recommendations to help us build a Good Parliament, from clarifying what constitutes unprofessional and unacceptable behaviour in the Chamber, to trialing a new layout for the House of Commons.

External relations

Parliament isn't just about its internal functions as the way in which it reaches out has changed, as has the constitutional structure of the UK, meaning that the UK Parliament is no longer the only legislature in the UK. It is these external relations which the chapter will analyse now.

Petitions

While petitioning has been a feature of parliamentary activity for many centuries, in 2015 it became possible for the public to petition the House of Commons and government electronically through the collaborative e-petitions system (Caygill and Griffiths, 2018).

Stoker (2006) argues that petitioning is a low commitment and a fairly low-key type of participation. The rise in petitioning is often against the backdrop of the decline in more conventional forms of participating, such as contacting your local MP. Hay (2007) argues that there has been a change in the mode of participation, from convention to unconventional means. This decline in conventional participation is explained by Norris (1999a) as a rise of 'critical citizens' who 'adhere strongly to democratic values but who find the existing structures of representative government … to be wanting' (Caygill and Griffiths 2018; Norris, 1999a: 3). Hay (2007) argues that these critical citizens are better educated and less deferential than previous generations. This tied in with a greater access to information via the internet means that Parliament (as well as MPs) have to work harder in order to meet the expectations of these critical citizens.

The Petitions Committee meets each week in order to consider all petitions which have received over 100,000 signatures as well as petitions which have received a response from the government (after they have reached 10,000 signatures). The committee has a dedicated slot on Mondays in Westminster Hall for up to a three-hour debate. Petitions reaching 100,000 signatures will usually be debated and this means that the public can put issues directly on to the parliamentary agenda. However, the debates cannot force the government to take action.

From a pluralistic perspective, the system provides an exciting opportunity for parliament to better engage with citizens and provide equal access too. However, if the system is engaging with citizens from socioeconomic groups that are already well represented and engaged (such as older generations, men and people from the middle classes) then the impact of this engagement will be marginal. Secondly, the public's understanding of the petitions system is low (Caygill and Griffiths, 2018). This is problematic if the public come in with high expectations and do not receive the outcome which they ultimately desire. Only a small proportion of petitions reach the 10,000-signature threshold for a government response and even fewer reach the 100,000 threshold required for a debate.

From the perspective of pluralism, the process is more open, transparent and accessible but for petitions to support us further in our pluralistic goals, we need to ensure a wider variety of people are engaging with the system.

Devolution

Following devolution in the 1990s the UK Parliament was no longer the only legislature in the UK. From a pluralistic perspective, you would perhaps expect there to have been substantive changes in Westminster's procedures to support a structured relationship between our legislatures. Indeed, as the McKay Commission, on the consequences of devolution for the House of Commons, noted, the legislatures of the UK should form a legislative partnership and be viewed as co-legislatures for their territories (Silk, 2018). However, Norton (2013) notes that only minimal adjustments have been made to practices and procedures in Westminster to reflect devolution, which is in line with expectations from the perspective of historical institutionalism.

These devolved legislatures are an important fixture of the political landscape. The constitutional principle of parliamentary sovereignty (at Westminster) means the UK Parliament views the devolved legislatures in Edinburgh, Cardiff and Belfast as subordinate legislatures rather than partners.

Norton (2013) notes that the UK Parliament has been slow to adapt to devolution and has not tried to stamp its own authority on devolved relations and exploit the gap which currently exists in both the governmental and parliamentary frameworks. The introduction of the Sewel Convention in the 1990s provided an opportunity for better inter-parliamentary relations but the opportunity was not seized. The Sewel Convention (as written in the Scotland Act 2016 and Wales Act 2017) states that the UK Parliament 'will not normally legislate with regard to devolved matters without the consent' of the respective devolved legislature (Scotland Act 2016, s2; Wales Act 2017, s2). When the UK Parliament wishes to legislate on matters which are devolved, legislative consent motions (LCMs) are required from the devolved legislatures. Where a devolved legislature refuses to pass an LCM, there is no recourse, and they cannot enforce their decision – effectively allowing the UK Government to push the legislation through the UK Parliament regardless. This is in keeping with the concept of parliamentary sovereignty, but it is not in the true spirit of devolution.

> **Case study: The Sewel Convention and the Internal Market Bill**
>
> The Internal Market Bill was one of the few Brexit-related pieces of legislation which fell under the scope of the Sewel Convention. The bill was designed to avoid barriers to trade being created between the constituent parts of the UK (England, Scotland, Wales and Northern Ireland), after the return of powers from the EU to both the UK government and devolved administrations. The UK government stated that the legislation was required to ensure the continued functioning of the UK's internal market. Both the Scottish and Welsh Parliaments withheld consent to this bill on the basis that they felt it was a 'powergrab' by Westminster which undermined devolution. Regardless, the bill still passed in the UK Parliament (Paun et al., 2018).

However, there have been recent attempts, led by the Lord Speaker to develop an interparliamentary forum to facilitate dialogue and cooperation between the devolved legislatures and Westminster (UK Parliament, 2022a). While this forum is not embedded into procedures it may prove to be a wedge which opens the door further to more structured interparliamentary relations. Indeed a recent report by Evans and Silk (2023) through the Study of Parliament Group has argued that the interparliamentary forum should develop into a formal body. Evans and Silk argue that the body should become a force for improving communication and understanding of the devolution settlements and the respective roles of the devolved legislatures within all parliamentary bodies, alongside providing a forum for discussion of wider issues of concern across the UK (Evans and Silk, 2023).

All party parliamentary groups

All party parliamentary groups (APPGs) are non-partisan groups of parliamentarians who seek to further the interests of a particular concern, whether that is related to policy or particular countries and regions (Thomas and Frier, 2018). Although they have 'parliamentary' in the title, they have no official status within Parliament (Office of the Parliamentary Commissioner for Standards, 2023). They are an important vehicle for interest groups in particular to campaign within the institution alongside members. These APPGs are run for and by members of both Houses and often involve interest groups in their administration and activities.

As of the 11 January 2023 there were 623 subject groups covering issues from weddings to motor neurone disease. Alongside these subject groups there are 140 country-specific groups (Office of the Parliamentary Commissioner for Standards, 2023). Thomas and Frier (2018) note that these APPGs vary greatly in terms of the level of activity they undertake. Some will meet only a couple of times a year to celebrate certain occasions (e.g. national holidays for the country-specific groups) while others will hold regular meetings and events in order to exchange information with key stakeholders and government officials (Thomas and Frier, 2018). These groups give members and interest groups the chance to develop policy, focus opinion and ultimately to influence ministers (Besly and Goldsmith, 2019).

However, opinion is divided over the relationship between APPGs and lobbying. Many of these APPGs are externally funded and this brings a degree of risk with it. Indeed, in an unusual joint letter on 11 January 2023, both the Speaker of the House of Commons and the Lords Speaker wrote to the House of Commons Committee on Standards to highlight their concern about how easily APPGs are set up and the need for more regulation of their activities (House of Commons Committee on Standards, 2023). The concern stems from the Westminster accounts, published by Sky News following an investigation into donations in Westminster. Sky News found that £20m had been donated to APPGs in just over three years (Coates, 2023).

There is a benefit that needs to be balanced against the challenges APPGs present, particularly in terms of how they can be abused. It is important that interest groups have access to parliamentarians as they have an important expressive function. This is vital as we strive for a pluralistic democracy and legislature. However, money is nearly always key to pressure group activity and the better resourced groups have more opportunities to influence.

Conclusion

The UK Parliament is an institution which has been shaped by centuries of history. This analysis of how pluralistic the institution at the heart of our democracy is shows a mixed picture. The institution has been able to move with the times, including the creation of the collaborative e-petitions system as well as innovative ways in which select committees are reaching out beyond Westminster. However, there are other areas where progress has been slow. The legislative process provides a useful landscape in which civic society, especially interest groups, can influence and shape public policy – from pre-legislative scrutiny through to public bill committees in the House of Commons, as well as opportunities the unique position of the House of Lords provides. However, government dominance in the process and our wider adversarial political processes limit the impact which can be made. Despite technological advances, meaning MPs are more responsive to the concerns of their constituents, slow progress on the diversity of MPs undermines representation, with some groups still marginalised. Finally, the inability of Westminster to reform in order to operate in our devolved political system, where power is dispersed, shows there is still much progress to be made if the true ideals of pluralism are to be achieved. Historical institutionalism has a lot to answer for.

Key take-home points

- The UK Parliament has developed over the centuries and historical institutionalism acts as a drag on reform.

- Enhancements have been made in the quality of petitioning and the engagement activities of select committees but progress is slow.
- Government dominance remains a challenge and parliamentary sovereignty in reality means government sovereignty through parliamentary majorities.

Annotated reading list

Geddes, M. (2020) *Dramas at Westminster: Select Committees and the Quest for Accountability*. Manchester: Manchester University Press.

This is an in-depth evaluation of the House of Commons select committee system from analysis of the accountability function of committees to the different styles of chairmanship and types of MPs who sit on committees. Given the important avenue which select committees provide for increased public engagement and in turn pluralism, it is a must read to fully understand how the committee system operates.

Leston-Bandeira, C. and Thompson, L. (2017) Integrating the view of the public into the formal legislative process: Public reading stage in the UK House of Commons. *The Journal of Legislative Studies*, 23(4), 508–528.

Leston-Bandeira and Thompson's study provides an unparalleled analysis of an attempt by the UK Parliament to improve access for and engagement of civic society in the shaping of public policy. The lack of integration with the wider legislative process identifies the challenges of achieving reform in Westminster.

11
The executive

Patrick Diamond

Image 11.1 Number Ten Downing Street: The heart of the UK core executive © Photo by Andy Wasley on Shutterstock

Learning objectives

After reading this chapter you should be able to:

- Understand the main theories of the core executive and their application to the workings of central government in UK politics
- Examine the role of key actors at the centre from the prime minister and cabinet ministers to the civil service in Whitehall
- Consider how different conceptions of power shape our understanding of the functioning of the British state

Introduction

Many influential debates in UK politics revolve around the critical question of where power lies in the UK polity and policymaking system. In the past, this discourse was moulded by the set of ideas known as 'the British political tradition' (BPT), a framework of beliefs and practices handed down from previous generations that influenced how we understand the operations of our political system (Birch, 1964). The BPT has continued to shape our analysis of the UK executive, particularly in conceiving the exercise of power as fundamentally centralising, elitist and top–down. The notion of the 'Westminster model' has reinforced that approach, viewing politics and power as hermetically sealed within the institutions of the central state (Richards and Smith, 2016). According to the BPT and the Westminster model, our approach to the executive should focus on the location of power at the centre of government. In the past, the key question was whether power ultimately resides with the prime minister, or the ministers that collectively comprise the cabinet in UK government.

The debate about the 'cabinet versus prime ministerial government' dominated the study of the UK executive throughout the postwar era. While scholars of the political system raised salient questions about the changing balance of prime ministerial power within the state, that approach is no longer adequate as an analytical framework for understanding how the executive operates in Britain. This chapter seeks to address that gap, focusing initially on the idea of the core executive and changing conceptions of power (Smith, 1999). It begins by surveying the main accounts of the UK executive and how we should understand its role in

Need to know: The role of key actors in central government and the executive, in particular ministers, civil servants and advisers

Central government in the UK is organised so that secretaries of state are the political heads of government departments. They are supported not only by the civil service but junior ministers, as well as parliamentary private secretaries, political advisers, temporary appointees and independent experts. The chapter will examine how the functions and powers of the UK executive are related to the concept of accountability and the idea of citizenship.

contemporary politics and policymaking. The chapter provides an overview of the core executive concept while applying it to understand the functioning of central government in contemporary British society. The discussion addresses major challenges that have emerged subsequently, namely:

- The importance of pluralistic policy networks throughout the UK
- The development of the multi-level polity and devolution
- The changing relationship between the executive and individual citizens
- The increasingly dysfunctional nature of the core executive in an era of 'perma-crisis'

Need to know: What is the UK executive?

The UK executive comprises institutions at the centre of the UK state that are responsible for overseeing the formation and implementation of the public policies and regulations that govern society. Through the machinery of government which includes key central departments and agencies, the executive enforces the will of the governing party that has a working majority in the House of Commons. The executive, which traditionally dominates the UK political system, is predominantly located in Whitehall and Westminster, yet has to manage inter-governmental relations with devolved and local authorities.

The chapter argues that after decades of fragmentation and growing discord between key actors in central government, the UK executive no longer offers a governing framework that other countries could or should replicate. The erosion of the traditional model of government, in particular the perceived decline of the 'Rolls Royce' civil service over several decades, has been striking.

Moreover, the chapter seeks to bring citizens and civil society 'back in' to our understanding of government's functioning at the centre. It examines the extent to which the diverse range of voices and cultures that now comprise UK society are reflected in the workings of the executive and the central state. A pluralistic understanding of power is required to address the way in which the executive is located within a cluster of networks and relationships that exist both inside and beyond the state, shaping the perceived legitimacy of the policymaking process.

The paradox of UK governance is that the commitment to top–down decision-making in a 'power-hoarding' polity has continued among political elites despite the fracturing of control that arises as the result of a more complex and diffuse policymaking environment (Cairney, 2018). As Paul Cairney (2018) highlights, the policy process in Britain is shaped by friction between two contrasting narratives: the 'Westminster model' emphasising the authoritative power and legitimacy of the central state, and the 'complex government' story which highlights the dispersal of power to a multitude of actors and agencies.

Cairney's argument goes to the heart of a key conundrum in UK politics and policymaking. On the one hand, the executive and ministers portray themselves as fully controlling the governing machinery. On the other hand, their capacity to shape the outcomes of the policymaking process has eroded. The governance context reflects the reality of far greater complexity in policymaking. So many policy problems in contemporary society are overlapping and multidimensional (such that it is not always clear which department or agency is responsible for resolving them), while the challenge of responding effectively is greater in the light of the dispersal of decision-making authority in a multi-level polity.

Such complexity is also the result of sustained efforts by the UK executive to relate directly to citizens, not least by incorporating new communications technologies and social media platforms into the policy process. The chapter will consider how far mechanisms such as submission of online petitions to the prime minister's office in 10 Downing Street and organising debates around them in the House of Commons enables citizens to participate more directly in shaping the policy agenda of UK government, even if major power inequalities persist.

> ### Theory box: How power shapes the UK executive
>
> The focus of this chapter is how power shapes the operation of the executive in the UK. The chapter will examine the networks and relationships both within the centre of government, and between the central state and the multitude of sub-national devolved institutions, frontline service delivery organisations, civil society actors and citizens. Attention is paid to how concepts of power enable us to address the nature of inter-governmental and citizen-centred relations within, and beyond, the UK executive.

The traditional debate: Cabinet versus prime ministerial government

Our starting point is to understand the workings of the UK executive. The 'cabinet versus prime ministerial government' debate shaped much of this analysis. Yet the resulting scholarship – elaborated by academics such as George Jones and practitioners such as the former Labour cabinet minister Richard Crossman, focusing on the prime minister's power relative to the cabinet – proved inadequate for several reasons (Dunleavy and Rhodes, 1990). Ultimately, the debate was irresolvable since power has always waxed and waned depending on the individual personality of the prime minister. Moreover, the leader's authority is shaped by the political circumstances facing the government of the day. If there was military conflict or a major geopolitical crisis, for example, prime ministers may become more influential within their administration (Diamond, 2014). The structural context determined the extent to which cabinet ministers were powerful in comparison to the prime minister.

- The chapter will focus empirically on the premierships of recent UK prime ministers, notably David Cameron, Theresa May, Boris Johnson and Liz Truss.
- The chapter addresses how far the experience of governing from 10 Downing Street can be understood from the perspective of the core executive, conceiving the prime

minister as reliant on other actors and institutions in central government. It is also necessary to consider how the UK executive manages relationships with civil society and citizens considering recent events, notably the Covid-19 pandemic.
- The approach stems from a conception of power that conceives political power in the UK as pluralistic, fluid and dispersed rather than wholly concentrated at the centre.
- The chapter considers the limitations of the core executive approach as an academic perspective given recent developments in UK politics and policymaking.

Fundamentally, the 'cabinet versus prime ministerial government' debate focused narrowly on the central institutions of the state, reflecting the tacit assumptions of the Westminster model and the primacy of the centralised and unitary state. As such, power was conceived as a 'zero-sum game' in which the centre dominates decision-making. Such an approach was consistent with Dahl's (1957) conception of power as 'the ability to get an individual to do something they would not otherwise do'. There was less acknowledgement that the executive's capacity to implement policies increasingly relied on the cooperation of interest groups, street-level bureaucrats, citizens and communities beyond the formal boundaries of the state. There was little scope within 'the prime minister versus cabinet' debate to address the changing realities of the multi-level polity which increasingly shaped the UK political system after devolution to Scotland, Wales, Northern Ireland alongside the English city-regions in the late 1990s.

The core executive

In acknowledging the limitations of past approaches to the study of UK government at the centre, an alternative concept of the 'core executive' was developed (Dunleavy and Rhodes, 1990; Smith, 1999). The core executive understood UK central government as a policymaking territory that incorporated a range of institutions and actors, not merely the prime minister and cabinet. The political scientists Dunleavy and Rhodes (1990: 15) defined the core executive as 'those organizations and structures which primarily serve to pull together and integrate central government policies, or act as final arbiters within the executive of conflicts between different elements of the government machine'. The framework drew on previous approaches that focused on the 'core executive territory': the organisations and actors in central government that are involved in policymaking. The literature on the core executive established a 'new orthodoxy' in the study of UK government and became increasingly 'dominant' across the discipline (Elgie, 2011: 74; Marinetto, 2003). The concept of the 'core executive' reflected alterations in central government that have occurred since the late 1970s (Dorey, 2020; Smith, 1999).

The core executive referred primarily to key institutions at the centre, notably 10 Downing Street, the Cabinet Office, the Treasury and Whitehall departments. The concept focused on critical actors in central government, notably ministers, political advisers, as well as officials and civil servants. Figure 11.1 depicts the UK core executive as a series of concentric circles: the core is 10 Downing Street and the Cabinet Office where the prime minister is located; next come the Treasury and the Foreign Office, among the most influential departments of state.

Beyond the core executive but connected to it there are other government departments across Whitehall. Finally, there are agencies and non-departmental public bodies that implement policies and provide services directly to citizens.

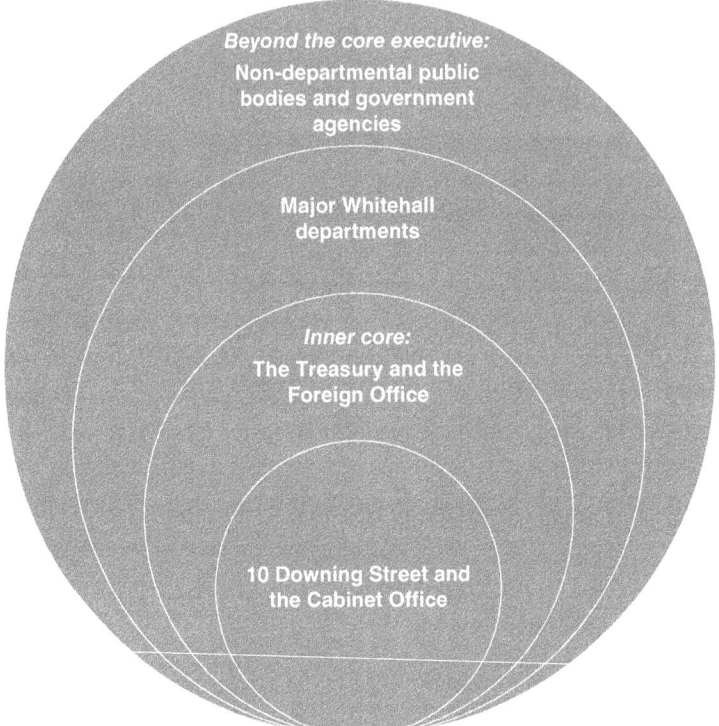

Figure 11.1 The core executive and wider relationships in UK government

The main assumption of the core executive framework was that power is not physically located within the office of the prime minister or cabinet. Nor is power a 'zero-sum game' in which one set of actors retains power at the expense of the other. Instead, actors and institutions have to work together to secure their policy goals. Not only does the prime minister rely on the support and loyalty of cabinet colleagues. Ministers depend on civil servants to provide robust and objective policy advice. Politicians rely on officials to implement policies, translating intentions into delivery on the ground. Instead of controlling civil servants, ministers depend on their cooperation, their ethic of public service and their willingness to 'speak truth to power'.

As such, the core executive approach conceives power not as an object, but as networks and relationships shaping the interaction between institutions and actors in central government. The proposition that the governing process is about mutual dependency among actors rests on a more sophisticated conception of power than previous approaches. Practical examples gleaned from the premierships of David Cameron, Theresa May, Boris Johnson and Liz Truss are discussed below in order to address the nature of power relations at the heart of the core executive.

The core executive acknowledges that prime ministers are influential actors with power resources at their disposal, notably the right to 'hire and fire' ministers. They can direct the machinery of Number 10 Downing Street to enforce the prime minister's will, staffed by special advisers and political aides who seek to exert policymaking influence across Whitehall. For example, Boris Johnson (prime minister from 2019 to 2022) employed Dominic Cummings as his chief strategist, enabling Cummings to determine the policy direction of the government and challenge the influence of the civil service. In the early 2000s, it was argued that the UK prime minister was becoming increasingly 'presidential', using institutional power resources to control the government's agenda (Foley, 2000). The style of governing in central government had altered: it was said that Tony Blair (prime minister from 1997 to 2007) practised a form of 'sofa government' with informal meetings in his Number 10 'den' where formal minutes were rarely taken.

Furthermore, within the core executive approach, departmental secretaries of state were judged to be significant players. Such ministers were able to draw on the vast resources of their department, in particular the policymaking and delivery capacity afforded by the civil service. Ministers' importance was reinforced by their accountability to the House of Commons for all of the actions undertaken by their department, a fundamental principle of the British constitution (Richards and Smith, 2016). Consequently, all major decisions, particularly relating to the use of public expenditure, had to be agreed by ministers. This notion of accountability reinforced the centralisation of UK government. Ministers are less likely to devolve decisions to frontline actors in local authorities and public services if politicians at the centre inevitably get the blame when things go wrong. There are currently over 150 ministers and parliamentary private secretaries of whom around 25 are members of cabinet. It is this 'payroll' vote that helps to ensure that any government is able to get legislation through the House of Commons.

Yet it is important to acknowledge that the agency of prime ministers and departmental ministers in Whitehall is inherently constrained. The growing dispersal of power in the UK creates additional veto-points and checks on executive prerogative, as the debate over Brexit following the 2016 referendum on EU membership illustrated. During the Coalition government under David Cameron (2010–2015), the realities of prime ministerial interdependence were stark. Within a two-party coalition, Cameron relied on the support of ministers from another party, compelled to allocate cabinet positions to the Liberal Democrats. Cameron's team sought to create structures, notably 'the Quad' (at which senior ministers from both the Conservative and Liberal Democrat parties met weekly to take decisions) to maintain cabinet support.

In the case of Theresa May (prime minister from 2016 to 2019), she began to lose the support of ministers after the disastrous result of the 2017 general election. Her authority was already eroding because Conservative MPs believed the prime minister was mishandling negotiations over Britain's exit from the European Union, while she lacked charisma and popular appeal. The Conservative party expected to decisively win the 2017 election but was deprived of its overall majority. May's position in the aftermath of the election became untenable (Shipman, 2017). Her relationship with the Chancellor of the Exchequer, Philip Hammond, grew particularly fractious, illustrating the importance of the prime minister maintaining a collegial relationship with whoever occupies the Treasury. Meanwhile, recent prime ministers have had to deal with more assertive first ministers in Scotland and Wales given the nature of devolved government.

As such, it is clear that the capacity of ministers, including prime ministers, to achieve their objectives depends on how skilfully they use the resources at their disposal, notably formal prerogative and appointment powers, legislation, influencing ability, departmental capacity, media profile and so on. It is recognised that the prime minister's powers are not absolute. They have to identify strategies and deploy resources to achieve their aims in politics and policymaking.

The limitations on prime ministerial power are illuminated by Boris Johnson's tenure. Controversy over events taking place in 10 Downing Street, including apparent breaches of Covid-19 lockdown rules in 2020–2021, led to the withdrawal of support by Johnson's cabinet, culminating in over 50 ministerial resignations during a 48-hour period in July 2022. The situation meant the prime minister's inevitable resignation that summer. Johnson was then succeeded by his former foreign secretary, Liz Truss (prime minister from September to October 2022).

Yet Truss too quickly ran into difficulties, as she was also unable to maintain the support of ministers. Truss fell out with her chancellor, Kwasi Kwarteng, over the government's fiscal strategy. Kwarteng's so-called 'mini-budget' panicked financial markets, promising unfunded tax cuts that threatened the stability of the public finances. The Treasury itself offered half-hearted support, not least because Kwarteng had dismissed the permanent secretary, Tom Scholar, and refused to allow the Office for Budgetary Responsibility (OBR) to independently assess the government's fiscal plans. Kwarteng was then sacked by Truss in an ineffectual attempt to avoid blame. Conservative MPs reacted angrily to the government's loss of economic credibility alongside voters' dismay at rising interest rates stoked by decisions in Kwarteng's budget. Truss resigned as prime minister after less than two months in Downing Street. Seemingly out of her depth and lacking political experience, she was replaced by the former chancellor of the exchequer, Rishi Sunak.

The experience of recent prime ministers endorses key assumptions in the core executive literature, underlining the prime minister's dependency on other actors in the core executive, notably cabinet ministers, parliamentarians and the civil service. The collective loyalty of the cabinet to the prime minister is of pivotal importance. Similarly, a departmental minister who no longer has the confidence of Number 10 is unlikely to survive long in office. Ministers can thwart the prime minister's views where they disagree over policy. Yet if they do so repeatedly, that minister runs the risk of being reshuffled or removed from the government. Similarly, politicians who repeatedly undermine or threaten civil servants endanger their own position since officials will no longer offer their full support. As Smith (1999: 1) reiterates: 'The political process [in central government] is about exchanging resources'. Rather than asserting hierarchical command, interdependent political and bureaucratic actors (both ministers and civil servants) at the centre of government negotiate with one another to achieve their goals. Instead of a chain of command, policymaking in Whitehall is a collaborative process that requires the cooperation of ministers, officials and advisers.

For that reason, ministers, including prime ministers, depend on the advice and support afforded by civil servants. The reciprocal bond between politicians and bureaucrats is a fundamental axiom of UK government. Indeed, 'In Britain's executive-dominated system, many major policy decisions are determined by their interaction' (Wilson and Barker, 2003: 349). The core executive framework acknowledges the mutual dependency between ministers and civil servants. It foresees a bargain or exchange relationship where the functioning of the core executive relies on ministers and civil servants working closely together. There is a clear division of responsibility in which ministers set the overall direction of their department and take decisions based on robust advice from civil servants. Civil servants agree to serve ministers while 'speaking truth to power' in return for permanent contracts and anonymity, upholding the Northcote-Trevelyan Report (1854) principles of appointment on merit and neutrality. Officials rely on ministers to defend the actions of civil servants in the media and parliament. As such, UK central government and the core executive functions on the basis that 'officials advise while ministers decide'.

That said, the relationship between ministers and civil servants has evolved considerably over the last 40 years. From the early 1980s under the Thatcher administrations, politicians were becoming increasingly frustrated with the civil service. A popular complaint was that officials lacked robust understanding of frontline implementation and delivery. Ministers sought 'hands on' civil servants who could manage public bureaucracies and secure results. As a result, politicians have repeatedly threatened to impose reforms that restructure the administrative class. There has been tacit politicisation of civil service appointments, particularly under the Thatcher governments, where officials judged to be ideologically sympathetic to the administration were appointed to key positions. It was believed that small-c conservative civil servants were preventing the administration from pursuing radical economic reforms. In the last decade, demands for reform have intensified: in 2023, the former Cabinet Office minister, Francis Maude, was appointed to conduct a review of the effectiveness and accountability of the civil service. There were particular pressures to bring in more political appointees.

In practice, however, ministers avoided reforms that involved radically overhauling the Whitehall machinery, not least because politicians rely on the enthusiasm and goodwill of the civil service. Most ministers in government have a positive view of their own officials. It is recognised that by international standards, the permanent bureaucracy of the UK is a 'Rolls-Royce' service

Image 11.2 'Whitehall: the headquarters of the UK civil service
© Photo by Tupungato on Shutterstock

that delivers for ministers. The mutual loyalty that, by and large, still prevails between officials and ministers in the UK state militates against rewriting the 'public service bargain' (Richards and Smith, 2016).

Taken as a whole, the conceptual framework of the core executive has succeeded in highlighting prescient issues in UK government. It has served to illuminate key challenges within the administrative process, notably the problem of joining up government, which has become increasingly fragmented, characterised by policy 'silos' that fall between departmental boundaries (Ling, 2002). In complex policy fields such as improving educational and health outcomes for young children, it was difficult for governments to make progress as the issues were not 'owned' by any particular department. At the same time, the literature highlighted the power relationships at work between ministers and officials in the 'court politics' of central government.

That said, the core executive approach was largely concerned with relationships at the centre of the UK state. As the balance of the polity began to shift following devolution and the emergence of multi-level governance, that approach became less analytically credible, not least because it ignored the importance of networks and actors beyond central government. Moreover, the core executive framework downplayed the extent to which governing at the centre relied on reconciling contradictory forces. The executive had the capacity to impose decisions from the centre reflecting key tenets of the Westminster model. The Westminster model offers a coherent account of where power lies in UK government, while it provides normative justification for untrammelled executive power, promising decisive leadership in the national interest. The Westminster model focuses on, 'the notion of an indivisible state elite ruling in the national interest and accountable via parliament to the electorate' (Richards and Smith, 2016: 501). Yet the Westminster model is no longer a reflection of empirical reality. It is a 'legitimating myth' that guides politics and policymaking (Rhodes, 2007; Richards and Smith, 2015). The model is used to justify the centralisation of power, framing public expectations of government's role: invariably, citizens blame politicians in central government when policies fail since the Westminster model has taught them that ministers are in charge.

Nonetheless, the conception of power at the heart of the Westminster model is misleading. The core executive has to negotiate a complex environment in which there are barriers and obstacles to policymaking from the centre (Cairney, 2018). While the executive can strive to impose decisions, it is compelled to acknowledge the dispersed and fragmented nature of power in the UK. As such, the main assumptions of the core executive literature should be revisited. The remaining sections of this chapter elaborate theoretical and empirical challenges to the core executive approach.

Challenge to the core executive (1): Policy networks

The first challenge to the core executive is the role of policy networks and their influence in the policymaking and implementation process. The UK executive acknowledged that its capacity to pursue a governing agenda while achieving policy reforms relies on relations with a multitude of policy networks and policymaking bodies that are not directly controlled by the central state. To implement policies, central government has to secure the commitment and consent of frontline delivery organisations and stakeholders. These actors comprise civil society institutions, pressure groups, non-governmental organisations (NGOs), as well as frontline delivery bodies. Policy networks are the multitude of actors and stakeholders that define a policy sector.

The UK governing process cannot be conceived as a top–down, linear system where central government takes decisions as a tight-knit elite and then pulls a set of bureaucratic levers. More than 40 years ago, the American policy analysts Pressman and Wildavksy (1984) observed that implementing public policies required the involvement of a long and complex chain of actors and institutions (Mazey and Richardson, 2021). It was recognised that a centralised and mechanistic approach to policymaking was more likely to lead to policy failure or at the very least, diminished expectations where policies do not achieve their intended goals. Instead, effective policymaking requires the executive to secure the cooperation and trust of a multiplicity of organisations beyond Whitehall and Westminster. In the UK state, an impositional 'policy style' is likely to prove ineffectual (Richardson, 2018). Radical policy changes and more ambitious policy goals require the agreement of a multitude of stakeholders (Lindblom, 1959).

The reality of policy networks means that governments have to achieve their policy goals through the process of 'meta-governance'. The idea of meta-governance alludes to how the state builds capacity to steer policymaking in the face of continuing fragmentation and complexity. The regulatory bodies created by central government to direct the provision of public utilities, namely water, gas, telecoms and electricity, are a notable example. Regulation is used to protect the public interest and to prevent private sector companies from exploiting consumers where the state does not provide services itself. The fact that so much policy activity is undertaken by the private and voluntary/not-for-profit sector in the UK requires governments to work with diverse networks to achieve their objectives (Sorenson and Torfing, 2017). As Sorenson and Torfing (2017: 829) have written, ministers aim 'to influence the network, while recognising that it needs a certain degree of autonomy to define its purpose and objectives'. Even ministers with formal powers and access to financial resources cannot command policy networks.

At the same time, governments use their capacities in attempting to steer non-state actors. As such, policy networks operate 'in the shadow of hierarchy' (Fawcett, 2014: 114). Meta-governance refers to 'the tools, strategies and relationships used by governments to help govern … from regulation and legislation to behavioural change' (Bell and Hindmoor, 2009: 2). Governments adopt mechanisms such as targets, performance management, inspection and regulation to control policy outcomes. Yet governments have to tread warily, not least because they are never able to fully control a policy network. The executive relies on cooperation with stakeholders to achieve central government's objectives. Recent administrations have emphasised the importance of the non-governmental sector and civil society, underlined by the Cameron government's concept of 'the Big Society'. The 'Big Society' stressed that public goods from care homes to recreational facilities could be delivered as effectively by non-state actors and civil associations. There were limits to how far central government could achieve effective policy outcomes, even if the centre was reluctant to accept any diminution of its role given the ongoing influence of the Westminster model.

Challenge to the core executive (2): The multi-level polity and devolution

The significance of policy networks for the core executive relates closely to the impact of devolution on the UK state. In the aftermath of the constitutional reforms of the late 1990s, the UK was increasingly subject to 'multi-level governance'. Rather than policy decisions being taken at the centre, policymaking occurs across multiple tiers of government: central, regional and local. Actors and institutions at the centre must cooperate with a variety of decision makers: from national parliaments in Wales, Scotland and Northern Ireland to directly elected mayors in English city regions. This point is demonstrated by how the Johnson administration responded to the Covid-19 pandemic and its aftershocks. During the pandemic's first wave, central government sought to impose decisions about the management of Covid testing and the 'track and trace' system of infection control. Yet even the prime minister's strategist, Dominic Cummings, compared the government's response to a supermarket trolley swerving from one side of the aisle to the other (Mazey and Richardson, 2021). The policy tasks at hand were too complex for the centre to navigate alone. Increasingly, central government relied on other tiers of government to manage the pandemic (Diamond and Laffin, 2022).

Moreover, in a climate of increasingly 'frenetic' policymaking shaped by rapidly rising mortality rates, it became apparent that the Scottish, Welsh and Northern Ireland governments did not always agree with Whitehall's approach to managing the virus. Growing resistance required the UK executive to reformulate its Covid strategy, acknowledging the reality of devolved governance and the importance of inter-governmental relations (Diamond and Laffin, 2022). City-region mayors, notably the mayor of Greater Manchester, Andy Burnham, questioned Whitehall's approach, highlighting in particular the inadequacy of economic support during lockdowns. The case highlights the extent to which the UK executive's power is qualified by multi-level governance. The evolution of the multi-level polity makes it necessary to revisit key tenets of the core executive framework.

Of course, there are limits to how far power has actually been devolved in the UK. The executive is able to thwart sub-regional autonomy (Kenny and Sheldon, 2021). Sceptics argue that UK devolution is a façade. Not only has the delegation of legislative responsibility been constrained: Wales, for example, has limited fiscal autonomy, while the UK government recently overruled the Scottish Government's proposed legislation on trans rights. Westminster retains the right to abolish the devolved institutions if it so chooses, underlining the primacy of parliamentary sovereignty. The UK has no written constitution to formally protect the political and legislative autonomy of the devolved institutions and local authorities (Keating, 2017). Local councils such as Croydon in South London were recently placed in 'special measures' unilaterally by the department in Whitehall. Moreover, the executive can override ministers in the devolved governments if it so chooses.

That said, optimists about the long-term fate of UK devolution insist that a Rubicon has been crossed. For all the imperfections of devolution, the process of decentralising power has unleashed potent countervailing forces in UK politics. The momentum away from the Westminster model towards decentralisation and sub-national autonomy appears unstoppable according to some commentators (Kenny and Sheldon, 2021). There are those who believe the devolution process has put Scotland on an inevitable path towards independence, threatening to break up the UK. While the ultimate destination of UK devolution is unknown, its role in undermining the unitary state and the Westminster model is beyond question.

The consequence for the core executive is that ministers must learn to operate in an increasingly multi-level polity. Past governments sought to promote improved inter-governmental coordination between Whitehall and the devolved administrations, notably in creating bodies such as the Joint Ministerial Council (JMC). The management of the Covid-19 pandemic highlighted the importance of functional inter-governmental relations and conflict resolution mechanisms. To deal with crises effectively, the core executive has to abandon the pretence that it can govern from the centre alone, investing in the institutions of multi-level governance and shaping a political culture that acknowledges growing pluralism and the dispersal of power in the UK.

Challenge to the core executive (3): Individual citizens

The core executive offered a sophisticated conception of how power operates in the UK polity at the centre. Nevertheless, as we have seen, the framework focused almost entirely on institutions and actors within central government. It had relatively little to say about the relationship between the executive and citizens. As such, the core executive approach is increasingly anachronistic. This section seeks to bring citizens back into our understanding of how central government operates.

It is important to recognise the myriad ways in which the core executive communicates with citizens. The communications capability of Number 10 Downing Street and Whitehall departments has expanded dramatically over the last 30 years. Modern politics has become more personalised, focused on the 'political celebrity' of the prime minister who aims, 'to dominate government-centric political communications' (Heffernan, 2006: 582). Following the election of the New Labour government in 1997, there was a major expansion in the capacities of the Downing Street communications operation under Tony Blair's chief spokesman, Alastair Campbell. As Heffernan (2006) notes, communicating through the media directly to citizens remains an important power resource at the prime minister's disposal.

Moreover, relations with citizens help to shape the perceived legitimacy of the executive's policy agenda. Central government's ability to achieve its policy goals increasingly relies on governance tools such as 'co-production', in which citizens become directly involved in the delivery of public services. Achieving improvements in national educational performance, for example, depends on the cooperation of parents, who spend more time with their children than teachers. Similarly, in healthcare, the most important advances in improving outcomes relate to changes in individual behaviour and lifestyles, notably smoking cessation alongside alterations in diet and exercise. During the initial stages of the Covid-19 pandemic, the executive was required to communicate directly through press conferences in 10 Downing Street, persuading citizens to comply with rules on social mixing and self-isolation.

Consequently, government policies rely on altering the behaviour of citizens while changing their adherence to social norms. Such approaches stem from the belief that 'government can protect its citizens by influencing their behaviour for their own and society's good' (Gregory, 2020: 372). In 2010, David Cameron established the Behavioural Insights Team (BIT) or 'Nudge Unit' in 10 Downing Street. The Unit's aim was 'to inject a new and more realistic understanding of human behaviour across UK government' (Halpern, 2015: iv). It was believed that 'small changes in processes ... led to significant shifts in outcomes' in the courts, collection of taxes, and issuing motor vehicle fines (Halpern, 2015: iv), and as such the deployment of behavioural change was championed by Cameron as prime minister. He argued that it would be possible to cut costs while making government more efficient by reshaping citizens' behaviour.

Meanwhile, there are more opportunities than ever for citizens to communicate directly with central government, notably the prime minister, using social media platforms and filing online petitions on the Downing Street website. Since the 1970s, the UK has developed a more active citizenry alongside interest groups that demand policy changes while using powerful communications channels (Mazey and Richardson, 2021). The internet has the capacity to empower the individual at the expense of civil society, even if the evidence suggests that new technologies have relatively little impact on existing power structures and political arrangements (Wright, 2015: 414). The launch of e-petitions in UK government has been a major innovation in modern democracy. From 2006 to 2015, for example, more than 33,000 petitions were published on the Downing Street website with over 12 million signatures; 3,258 of these petitions received official government responses (Wright, 2015: 418).

As Wright (2015) noted, actors in the core executive disagree about the long-term impact of innovations in e-democracy. There are ministers who dismiss e-petitions as inconsequential initiatives that have a negligible effect on policy outcomes. Others claim that e-petitions are a 'pernicious' development since they give a false impression of political influence that is likely to disillusion citizens even further; worse, they encourage governments to overreact to populist pressures on issues such as crime and immigration (Wright, 2015). Most surveys indicate that citizens perceive that petitions make very little impact on public policy, while those who did submit them were dissatisfied with the 'dismissive' and 'superficial' responses they received from government departments. Overall, the perception is that 'governments don't know how to listen'. Despite that, citizens continue to engage with such processes (Wright, 2016: 855).

There is little evidence that the centre has become more open and responsive to citizens, endorsing a pluralist view of power. The core executive retains the capacity to define the policy agenda, marginalising issues that are judged to be 'too difficult' while reinforcing power inequalities. Moreover, as Hay and Stoker (2009) elaborate, such developments have taken place within the context of an 'anti-political culture' characterised by disenchantment with the political class and major changes, 'in the relationship between government and citizens'. Successive governments have maintained the dominance of 'national and local representative institutions' while permitting citizens limited access to the 'variety of new engagement mechanisms' (Hay and Stoker, 2009: 327).

Hay and Stoker are sceptical that such mechanisms have much impact given that so many politicians seek to exploit the anti-politics mood; ministers have reinforced anti-politics sentiment by removing key decisions from democratic decision-making and handing them to technocrats (notably in setting interest rates where power was transferred from the Treasury to the independent Monetary Policy Committee of the Bank of England in 1997). Many institutions from banks to NHS hospitals are overseen by independent regulators on behalf of politicians. As a result, government is more distant from citizens who struggle to navigate policymaking systems of inordinate complexity: there are over 20 separate public bodies and arms-length agencies in the NHS alone.

Challenge to the core executive (4): The dysfunctional centre

The original core executive approach assumed that central government was characterised by reciprocity, cooperation and mutual dependency. This assumption appears less plausible given the increasingly dysfunctional nature of UK government at the centre. The growing instability is driven by conflict between civil servants and ministers which has intensified over the last three decades. The increasing discord was fuelled by the growth of outside appointees and political advisers (HM Government, 2017). Appointees do not necessarily lead to the politicisation of Whitehall, yet advisers inevitably reshape the culture of government. Appointees marginalise and undermine civil servants, contesting their monopoly over policy advice (Grube, 2015). Political staff are becoming a 'critical mass' within Whitehall, while bureaucrats are treated as, 'an obstacle to be overcome' (Bakvis and Jarvis, 2012: 16; Grube, 2015). Secretaries of state are supported by junior ministers, parliamentary private secretaries, political advisers, temporary appointees and outside experts (Rutter, 2013). This vast ministerial 'entourage' can block civil service advice from reaching politicians. The paradox is that outsiders brought into government to make policymaking more efficient and responsive end up making the process more convoluted and confused.

The core executive approach assumes that actors and institutions cooperate with one another to achieve their policy goals. The rejection of a zero-sum view of power was an important and valuable conceptual shift. Nevertheless, the last decade of UK government indicates that 'court politics' at the centre has become more chaotic and dysfunctional as traditional hierarchies persist. For example, there is evidence that ministers sought to sideline civil servants who questioned their preferred policy direction. Policy-active ministers have come to depend on politically appointed advisers, think tanks and ad hoc external experts (Grube, 2015). The 'deliberation deficit' and the failure to properly test policy proposals led to a litany of failures and blunders to which the UK appears unusually exposed (King and Crewe, 2013).

Need to know: The role of think tanks

Think-tanks are increasingly important institutions in UK politics and policymaking. There are many different types. Some think tanks are non-partisan independent bodies such as

(Continued)

the Institute for Fiscal Studies (IFS) that monitors the tax and spending plans of central government. Other think tanks are more aligned ideologically on left/right grounds. They provide policy ideas helping to shape the political agenda of government. Think tanks more commonly associated with the centre-right include the Institute of Economic Affairs (IEA) and Policy Exchange, both of which influenced the reform ideas of the short-lived Truss government in 2022.

Similarly, there have been disagreements over policy implementation between the core executive and NGOs, civil society and frontline organisations beyond central government. Conflict between actors at the centre is considerable while the scope for cooperation is more limited than was once believed. As such, dispensing with the zero-sum view of power may be premature. While power in the core executive approach is conceived as fluid and contingent, Lukes' (1974) 'multi-dimensional' view of power concluded that actors with privileged access to resources can still dominate decision-making. The 'three faces of power' according to Lukes (1974) are the power to take decisions; the power to keep issues off the agenda ('non-decisions'); and the power to shape prevailing values and beliefs. Ministers in UK government can, if they choose, subordinate officials and coerce sub-regional tiers of government to do what the centre determines. As such, an alternative perspective on power, drawing on Lukes, questions the core executive emphasis on the fluidity of power and resource exchange.

Over the last decade, UK officials were compelled to confront a 'perfect storm' of austerity, declining administrative capacity, covert politicisation, and fragmentation in the UK polity (Pyper, 2020). The dominant theme has been the growth of 'organised chaos' and turbulence in policymaking. Too often, governments have ended up introducing 'placebo policies' that gave the impression of action but are merely concerned with deflecting unwelcome public and media attention (Mazey and Richardson, 2021). Recent housing policies in England have been criticised as placebo-style measures. Such policies seek to highlight that government is acting on an issue of public concern, yet in practice little substantive progress is made because obstacles such as the availability of land and restrictions on 'green belt' construction around cities are never addressed. Across the policy landscape, Whitehall was becoming less effective while the civil service was increasingly demoralised. Grube's (2015) concept of 'megaphone bureaucracy' highlighted that officials were more likely to speak out in opposition to government initiatives. Tensions grew in the aftermath of the UK's decision to leave the EU in 2016: ministers feared that the civil service did not believe in EU withdrawal and was attempting to sabotage the process. Senior officials were openly attacked by Conservative MPs. As a result, civil servants no longer trusted ministers to defend them.

Whitehall was dispirited by the growth of politically embarrassing fiascos. Wilkinson's (2011) study of the Department for Environment, Food and Rural Affairs (Defra) found policymaking increasingly 'anarchic'. Crewe and King (2013: 5) insist that policy blunders were 'rooted in poorly designed policymaking and delivery structures'. Mistakes arose because there was 'less time and space for reflection on, and consideration of, evidence' (Crewe and King, 2013: 5). External actors were prone to tell ministers merely what they wanted to hear

(House of Commons, 2013). Outside appointees and consultants together with political advisers were able to control the flow of information to ministers. As a result, the policymaking process became increasingly convoluted and byzantine. Notable failures included the Troubled Families Programme and the Universal Credit welfare policy (Crewe and King, 2013).

When Iain Duncan Smith was appointed secretary of state at the Department for Work and Pensions (DWP) in 2010, his plans for Universal Credit had been developed in opposition drawing on the expertise of the independent think tank the Centre for Social Justice (CSJ). It was said that as a result, officials played little role in shaping the policy (Rutter, 2013). This meant that Universal Credit was not fully stress-tested prior to implementation. Delivery problems identified by frontline staff were largely ignored. Officials were reluctant to tell ministers that their proposals were flawed (Aucoin, 2012).

Similarly, the introduction of the Troubled Families Programme (TFP) by the coalition government in 2011 created major problems. Cairney (2018) believes that TFP was an example of 'policy-based evidence-making' rather than evidence-based policy. The programme relied on questionable assumptions 'about who the "troubled families" are, what causes their behaviour, and how to stop it'. Civil servants were not allowed to stress-test those assumptions prior to implementation (Cairney, 2018: 5). Ministers came into government with 'an ideational policy portfolio … [and] their own strong priorities on what policy change is needed' (Richardson, 2018: 12). In relation to evidence-based policy in Whitehall, there are unresolved questions about who determines what constitutes credible and legitimate evidence in the policymaking process.

As a result, UK central government increasingly resembled a 'microwave not slow cooker' policy environment where proposals were agreed without adequate scrutiny. A 'them and us' culture was emerging between ministers and civil servants that weakened the central state's governing capacity. The 'close, co-operative relationship' between ministers and officials was eroding (Tiernan, 2011). Consequently, policymaking became less effective. Of course, such changes are not particular to Britain. A breakdown in resource dependency has been observed elsewhere in the Anglophone countries (Craft and Halligan, 2020). In European states, notably Denmark, there is evidence of growing politicisation within the permanent bureaucracy alongside the emergence of personalised court politics (Rhodes and Salomonsen, 2021). Even in Germany, widely seen as the policymaking 'powerhouse' of the European Union (EU), there are concerns that policy capacities have diminished and that German governments can only make incremental changes to existing institutional arrangements (Mazey and Richardson, 2021).

Contemporary observers of UK central government have concluded that 'the core executive approach overlooked the possibility that the best term to describe the British system was not prime ministerial or presidential, but dysfunctional' (Garnett, 2021: 228). The concept of the core executive was well placed to explain the post-1997 Blair era that emphasised 'joining up' and coordination of government agencies to address major policy challenges from social exclusion to teenage pregnancy. Yet empirical alterations invalidated the model after 2010, as the Cameron administration sought to reform the operating structure of central government while transforming the bureaucracy (HM Government, 2012). The May, Johnson, Truss and Sunak governments have shown little sign of reversing course.

In outlining the core executive approach, Smith (1999: 106) noted: 'The analysis of ministerial–civil service relations has been framed in terms of who has power ... such a criterion oversimplifies these relationships'. Yet the interaction between ministers and officials is no longer centred on reciprocity and mutual dependency. The core executive is an ideal-type model that tells ministers and officials *how* to behave (Garnett, 2021). If both sides work collaboratively, it is believed the outcome will be better policymaking. Yet over the last decade, Whitehall reforms have depleted reciprocity, notably by centralising decision making and encouraging ministers to look to the prime minister's office rather than departments, while marginalising civil servants (Diamond, 2018). Ministers now rely less on officials. The evidence indicates that a shift has occurred towards a more unstable and conflictual model where the 'public service bargain' between ministers and officials has been depleted. In understanding UK executive and bureaucratic politics, it is necessary to revisit the main assumptions of the core executive approach.

Conclusion

Our understanding of how the UK core executive operates has improved markedly in the last 30 years. The zero-sum view of power has been discarded in favour of a model that emphasises the pluralistic nature of power relations in the state, and the dependence of actors on a wide array of policy delivery networks beyond central government. Yet despite a period of constitutional innovation in UK politics over recent decades, citizens, non-government organisations, policy networks and devolved bodies still struggle to meaningfully influence the executive's agenda. Power remains unequal and asymmetric rather than dispersed, as pluralist accounts implied. Richards and Smith (2016: 510) have remarked: 'In practice, the centripetal tendency in the British system, of power being drawn back to the centre, has not disappeared.'

Nonetheless, Dunleavy and Rhodes (1991: 108) observed more than 30 years ago that UK governments are compelled 'to appreciate the limits upon central government capabilities to push through unilaterally changes in policy implementation within current state structures'. The executive's authority is 'incomplete' while it cannot readily overcome systematic resistance from sub-regional actors and civil society. The centre is prone to miscalculation and error in policymaking. Recent studies underlined the problems of 'group-think' where a small elite cadre has excessive influence over the policy process (King and Crewe, 2013).

Moreover, the UK state has become more focused on performance and delivery, yet ministers are compelled to acknowledge that the executive's control of implementation is necessarily limited. There is relatively little that can be achieved by command-and-control from the centre. As such, the centre's power to enact policy change is limited, particularly in complex fields of social and environmental policy. Ministers and central departments simply do not know enough about the realities on the ground. The centre seeks to exert ever greater control over the performance of public services and the state, yet Whitehall's ability to shape outcomes remains patchy and inconsistent.

In summary, analysis of the UK core executive invites us to address a core paradox, namely that while the dominant image remains the concentration of power at the centre, the capacity of the executive to achieve substantive policy change diminished sharply over the last 30 years. The goal of securing improvements in public services leads the executive and prime ministers to intervene more. Yet in practice, they control *less*. Increasingly, policy problems are identified that are inherently complex, manifested differently across the UK. Consequently, the policy effectiveness of central government in Britain is diminishing. The evidence suggests that a well-functioning policymaking system entails a plurality of voices and ideas.

Taken in the round, the UK state was once believed to be a model for other countries to emulate. As noted elsewhere, 'The Westminster parliamentary system is both a political heritage and a concept. Across the Commonwealth, the Westminster system as a political heritage was either 'implanted' by the colonial rulers or 'transplanted' by the settlers of British ancestry' (Chowdhury, 2020: 45). Yet the UK executive no longer provides a governing framework that other countries can or should replicate. Despite the growth of a more plural and fragmented polity, the degeneration of UK government in recent decades, caught between governing frenetically from the centre and acknowledging the reality of power dispersal and policy heterogeneity, has been striking. Rebuilding state capacity and coherence in an era of 'perma-crisis' will not be straightforward.

Key take-home points

- We can best understand the workings of the UK core executive by adopting a pluralistic and networked view of power rather than a zero-sum model.
- The paradox of the UK executive is that while the centre's image of being dominant and all powerful is still pervasive, there are limits to the capacity of central government to affect policy change in a complex polity.
- Given the declining quality of UK governance in recent decades, the image of Britain's 'Rolls-Royce' machinery of government has eroded. Britain's executive is no longer considered a model for other countries to emulate.

Annotated reading list

The role and powers of the prime minister have been examined extensively over the last 20 years.

Richards, D. (2011) Changing patterns of executive governance. In R. Heffernan, P. Cowley and C. Hay (eds), *Developments in British Politics*. Basingstoke: Palgrave Macmillan, pp. 29–50.

This chapter provides a helpful summary. The following consider the premierships of Tony Blair, David Cameron, Theresa May, the role of the cabinet in UK politics and the civil service respectively.

Diamond, P. (2019) *The End of Whitehall? Government by Permanent Campaign*. Basingstoke: Palgrave Macmillan.

Fawcett, P. and Rhodes, R. (2007) Central government. In A. Seldon (ed.), *The Blair Years, 1997–2007*. Cambridge: Cambridge University Press.

Kavanagh, D. (2007) The Blair premiership. In A. Seldon (ed.), *The Blair Years, 1997–2007*. Cambridge: Cambridge University Press.

Marsh, D., Richards, D. and Smith, M.J. (2002) Reassessing the role of departmental cabinet ministers. *Public Administration*, 78(2), 305–326.

Pyper, R. and Burnham, J. (2011) The British civil service: Perspectives on 'decline' and 'modernisation'. *British Journal of Politics and International Relations*, 13(2) (2011), 189–205.

Seldon, A. and Snowdon, P. (eds) (2016) *Cameron at 10: The Verdict*. London: William Collins.

Seldon, A, (2019) *May at 10*. London: Biteback.

Websites

The 10 Downing Street website provides transcripts of the Prime Minister's speeches and daily press briefings. www.gov.uk/government/organisations/prime-ministers-office-10-downing-street

The Cabinet Office website has detailed information on the *Ministerial Code*, cabinet committees and the civil service. www.cabinet-office.gov.uk

The civil service website and the companion site to Martin Stanley's (2021) *How to Be a Civil Servant* (London: Richborne Publishing) cover the organisation and its recent reform. www.civilservice.gov.uk *and* www.civilservant.org.uk

Part III
Big questions

12 An economy for all?.. 247
13 UK environment and climate change politics.. 273
14 Britain in the world.. 293

12
An economy for all?

Kate Alexander-Shaw

Image 12.1 The Bank of England, in London © Photo by aslysun on Shutterstock

Learning objectives

After reading this chapter, you should be able to:

- Have an overview of some key trends in the UK economy today
- Understand the different economic policy models that have been applied by successive UK governments in recent decades
- Explore how politics and economics interact, the extent to which politics can change economic outcomes, and why there may be constraints on it doing so

Introduction

This chapter takes a critical look at Britain's economy and the policy models that have shaped it into what it is today. It considers what balance of interests is reflected in the current state of the UK economy, how economic and political resources are distributed, and the extent to which the United Kingdom can claim to have an economy for all.

But before we begin, a preliminary question: what exactly *is* the economy? There is, after all, no single object that we can point to that constitutes the economy of a country. Rather, when we speak about 'the economy' we are referring to economic activity: a broad category that has to do with the distribution of material resources in a particular place (usually a nation-state). Sometimes the economy gets boiled down to a single indicator: for example, when journalists ask if the economy is doing well, they are often asking: is output, or gross domestic product (GDP), growing? More often, however, we must take an overview of a selection of economic indicators from GDP growth to employment rates, productivity and more. Out of the landscape of potentially relevant data we must construct an account of the economy as a whole, deciding what we consider most important and leaving out other dimensions. This chapter is no exception; it attempts to provide a fairly balanced overview of key economic trends in the United Kingdom, but such overviews are always selective.

Because of this, a key aim of this chapter is to equip you with the tools and the confidence to think about the economy for yourself: to ask what is missing from this and other such accounts, and to go looking for more information to fill in the gaps. For the UK, the Office for National Statistics is the key source for most economic data. For international comparisons, the website of the Organisation for Economic Cooperation and Development (OECD) has an interactive databank that can be used to put UK trends in their wider context. You should explore these tools and get to know what they offer; when it comes to understanding the economy, data are powerful.

But of course, we cannot only grasp the importance of economic policy at the level of statistical trends. Vital as such measures are, it is equally important to ground our analyses in an awareness that the economy is not just an abstract concept; economics touches the lives of every person and household in the country. The opportunities available to us, the resources we possess and the way those resources are distributed throughout society: this is what political economy is all about. Analysing the economy requires both good data and good questions that place economic trends in the context of people's lived experience. With that in mind, we will begin with a case study.

Case study: Home ownership in the UK's political economy

In 1977, newlyweds Dave and Suzanne (not their real names) bought their first home, a small terraced house in a town in the west of England, for £8,300. Their deposit was 5 per cent of the purchase price, around £400. Their earnings, in non-graduate jobs, were around £200 per month, so their annual income in the year they bought their home was around 30 per cent of the price of the property.

Over the years that followed, home ownership would significantly shape Dave and Suzanne's economic fortunes. Their house increased in value as the economy heated up in the early 1980s, and they sold it for several times what they had paid. As their family grew, they continued moving up the property ladder, taking advantage of the easier availability of mortgage credit to borrow larger amounts. This did not always work out in their favour: in the early 1990s mortgage interest rates increased sharply; at risk of repossession, they sold their home at a loss and downsized. But after that, 30 years of uninterrupted house price growth saw them accumulate significant housing equity and eventually pay off their mortgage in full. Now approaching retirement, their housing wealth will help them live comfortably after they stop working, and perhaps pay for their care needs in old age.

The terraced house they had bought in 1977 was sold again in 2021, for just over £370,000. For the property to be as affordable in 2021 as it was for Dave and Suzanne in 1977, the new owners would have needed earnings of £111,000 per year.

This case study is not intended to be perfectly representative of housing trends in this period – for example, growth in the value of this particular property was above the national average. However, it illustrates some of the key structural changes in the UK's housing market since the 1970s. House prices grew faster than earnings, making home ownership less and less affordable for first-time buyers. That affordability squeeze was mitigated by the expanded availability of mortgage finance after it was liberalised in the 1980s, and by cheap mortgage credit in the low-interest-rate years of the early 21st century. Even so, the rising cost of home ownership has contributed to two other trends: a widening wealth gap between homeowners and renters, and a generation gap between older cohorts, for whom home ownership has been an engine of prosperity, and younger generations who are less likely to be able to buy a home. This inter-generational inequality tends to reinforce intra-generational inequality, as access to inherited housing wealth becomes a key factor in younger households becoming homeowners and accumulating property wealth over their lifetimes.

The take-away is that the economic fortunes of individuals and households are created in a wider structural context. The income and wealth available to us are not simply products of our individual choices; they rely substantially on the economic landscape in which our choices are made. This context changes significantly over time, and between places.

The UK economy today

By any measure, the United Kingdom is one of the richest countries in the world. UK GDP is the sixth largest globally; after adjusting for the cost of living (known as purchasing power parity) the UK is ninth in the world. Life expectancy for UK citizens is over 80 years on average; households' disposable income is higher than the average for an OECD country, and employment rates are high by international standards. Despite this, opinion polls show that for almost a decade, UK citizens have become steadily more pessimistic about the state of the national economy. While the UK remains an objectively wealthy nation by global standards, for many people it does not feel like it.

In that context, some recent commentary has raised the spectre of economic decline (Resolution Foundation, 2022). Since the financial crisis of the late-2000s growth in the UK economy has been sluggish, averaging just 2 per cent per year in the 2010s. Wages have stagnated in real terms, putting pressure on households' standard of living – gradually at first, and then more sharply with the post-pandemic return of inflation. In the same period, working hours have increased by 11 per cent, more than in comparable countries, as UK citizens have taken on more work to compensate for flat wage growth. On top of all this, the economic consequences of the UK leaving the European Union are complex, uncertain and still unfolding, a situation made particularly difficult to interpret by the arrival of a global pandemic in the same year Brexit was enacted. To begin to understand the implications of these conflicting signals we need to consider the shape of the UK economy: how wealth, income and economic output are distributed.

It should be noted that throughout most of the chapter, data is presented up to 2019 and does not incorporate the Covid-19 period. This is not to deny the importance of the pandemic, which was not only a public health crisis but also a severe economic shock. However, the unusual nature of that shock means that it can be distorting of the longer-running trends we are interested in. For this reason, the pandemic years are occasionally excluded from the analysis.

Economic activity, jobs and industries

The UK, like many other advanced economies, has undergone a set of interlinked structural transformations in recent decades. Technological changes, the expansion of education (particularly higher education), changing patterns of consumption and increasing global market integration have all had an impact on the balance of activity across sectors in the economy. Most significantly, there has been a shift away from manufacturing and towards a service-based economy (Figure 12.1). In the 1970s, a quarter of all jobs in the UK were in the manufacturing sector; by 2019 this had dropped to 8 per cent. Service sectors including retail, professional services, health and education have all grown since the 1970s, and employment across all service sectors has risen from 64 to 84 per cent of total jobs.

A key feature of the UK economy is the uneven distribution of economic activity around the country. Output is concentrated particularly in London and the south-east of England,

An economy for all? • 251

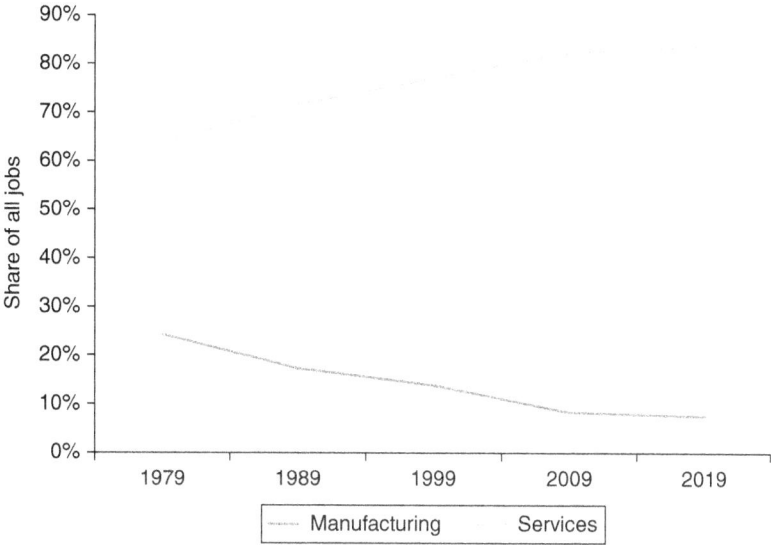

Figure 12.1 Services and manufacturing as a share of all jobs

Source: Office for National Statistics (2023), Workforce jobs by industry, https://www.ons.gov.uk/employmentandlabourmarket/peopleinwork/employmentandemployeetypes/datasets/workforcejobsbyindustryjobs02

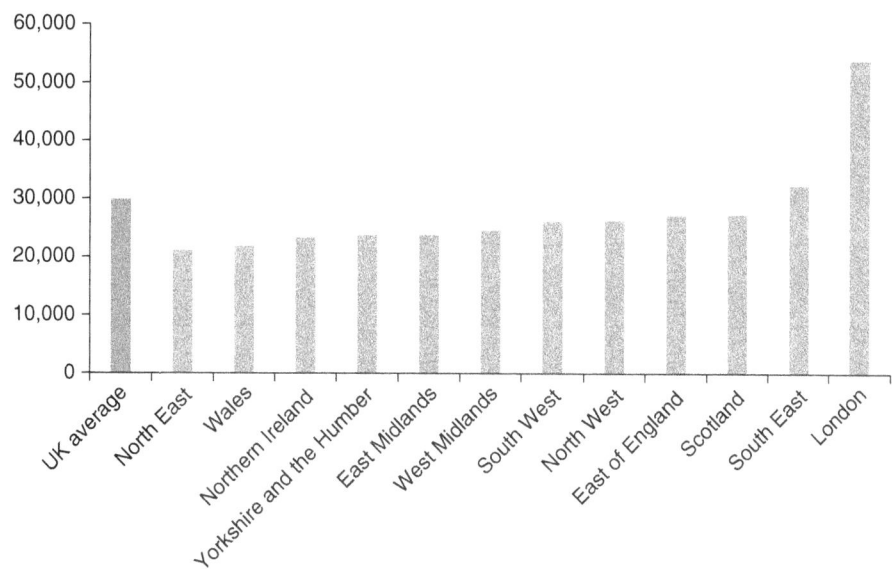

Figure 12.2 Regional gross value added (GVA)

Source: Office for National Statistics (2023), Regional gross value added (balanced), data for 2019 https://www.ons.gov.uk/economy/grossvalueaddedgva/datasets/nominalregionalgrossvalueaddedbalancedperheadandincomecomponents

which together account for almost 40 per cent of the total. Only those two regions have higher-than-average gross value added (GVA) output per person, and indeed London is an outlier within the UK, with output per head at almost £54,000 in 2019, two-thirds higher than the next richest region, the south-east (Figure 12.2). London is in many ways not comparable with other regions of the UK, being a wholly urban area with a younger population than the other regions. However, its dramatically higher output also reflects the predominance of the financial sector within the capital's economy. Excluding London, average output per head ranges from just over £21,000 in the north-east of England to just over £32,000 in the south- east.

Unemployment in the UK is low by international standards, at around 4 per cent of working age people compared with an OECD average of 5.4 per cent. This level of unemployment is also low by historic standards for the UK, despite having risen in the aftermath of the global financial crisis towards the end of the first decade of the 2000s (Figure 12.3). However, rates of unemployment vary across the UK, ranging from 2.3 per cent in Northern Ireland to 6.2 per cent in the north-east of England (Office for National Statistics, Labour Force survey, data for September–November 2019). Compared with other countries, particularly in continental Europe, the UK has flexible labour markets that allow firms to hire and fire workers more readily than elsewhere; as a result unemployment tends to rise sharply during economic downturns, but also to recover fairly quickly. Underneath those headline trends, however, the picture is more complex; strong employment data can mask underlying issues such as under-employment (when people cannot work as many hours as they would like) and precarious employment, including through zero-hours contracts.

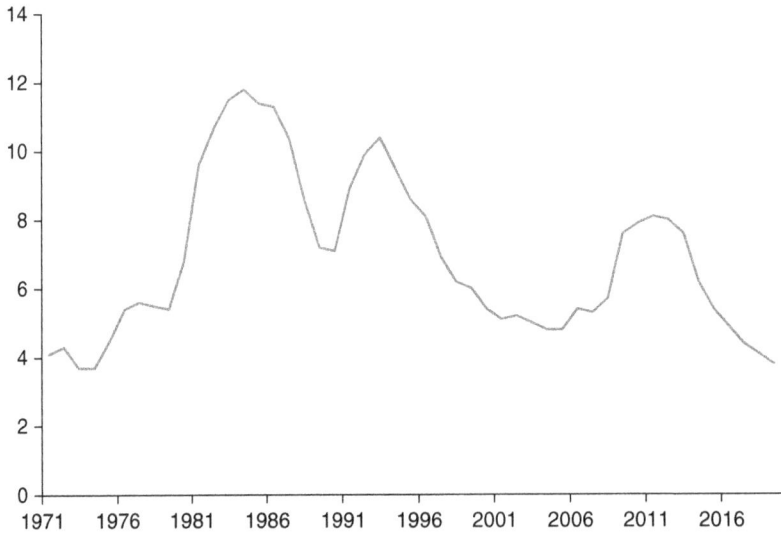

Figure 12.3 Unemployment rate, 1971–2019

Source: Office for National Statistics (2023), Unemployment rate, annual data, seasonally adjusted, https://www.ons.gov.uk/employmentandlabourmarket/peoplenotinwork/unemployment/timeseries/mgsx/lms?referrer=search&searchTerm=mgsx

Income and wealth

Figure 12.4 represents the distribution of household disposable income in the UK in 2022, when the median income (after taxes and transfers) was £32,300 per year. On the horizontal axis, the population is divided up into household income brackets of £1,000. On the vertical axis, the height of the column represents the number of individuals in each income bracket (e.g. the highest column shows 1.7 million people living in a household with an income between £27,000 and £28,000 per year. The distribution is positively skewed, meaning that there is a greater range of values in the top half of the distribution, where relatively few people report very high earnings, than in the bottom half of the distribution where many people are clustered at similar household incomes. In 2022 approximately 70 per cent of people in the UK had a household income of less than £44,000 per year, and 90 per cent earned less than £66,000. One in ten people had annual household incomes under £14,500.

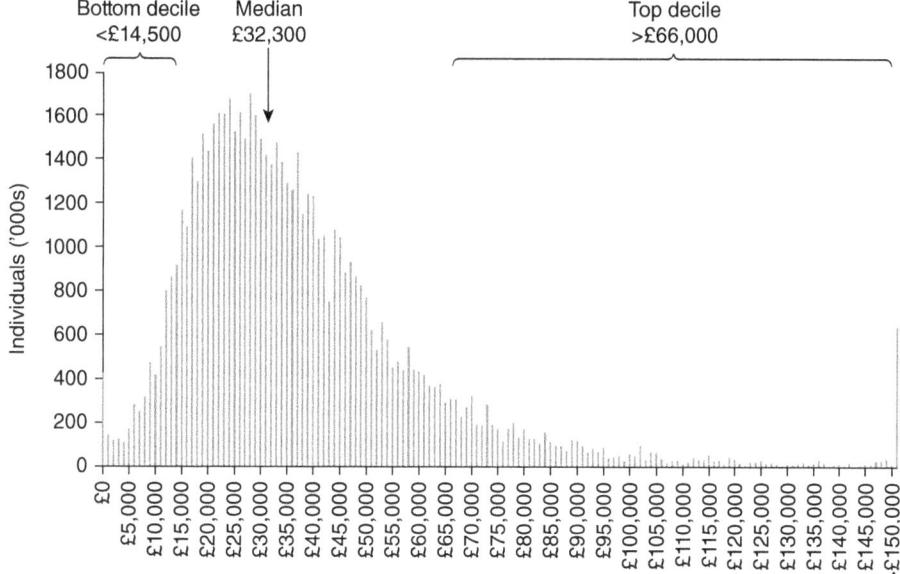

Figure 12.4 Distribution of incomes in the UK, 2022

Source: Office for National Statistics (2023), Distribution of UK household disposable income, financial year ending 2022,

https://www.ons.gov.uk/peoplepopulationandcommunity/personalandhouseholdfinances/incomeandwealth/adhocs/1406distributionofukhouseholddisposableincomefinancialyearending2022

Spotlight on research: Understanding income data

Income data can be presented in a number of different ways. The ONS distinguishes between original income (earnings and other income before taxes and transfers, such as benefits) and disposable income (after taxes and transfers). Note that 'disposable', in this technical sense, does not mean money left to spend each month; unless specifically stated, it does not take account of outgoings such as housing costs.

(Continued)

Household income data is also generally *equivalised* – that is, adjusted for the composition of the household. This allows for comparisons across different types of households, recognising that the income requirements of, for example, a family with several children are different from those of a single person living alone.

The shape of the income distribution in the UK is not unusual: most developed countries have a similar skew, with a smaller number of high earners at the top of the scale, and the great majority of households compressed around the median. However, incomes in the UK are more unequal than in many comparable nations. Figure 12.5 shows that amongst the member countries of the OECD – mostly wealthier nations with developed economies – the UK has one of the highest rates of income inequality, and the highest of any European country in the group. This relatively high inequality is substantially driven by very high incomes at the top of the distribution, which in turn reflect certain distinctive features of the UK economic mix, particularly the influence of the UK's large financial services sector where the pay of top earners has been pulling away from earnings in the rest of the economy (Hopkin and Alexander Shaw, 2016). In this regard, the distribution of incomes in the UK more closely resembles the United States than nearer neighbours in Europe.

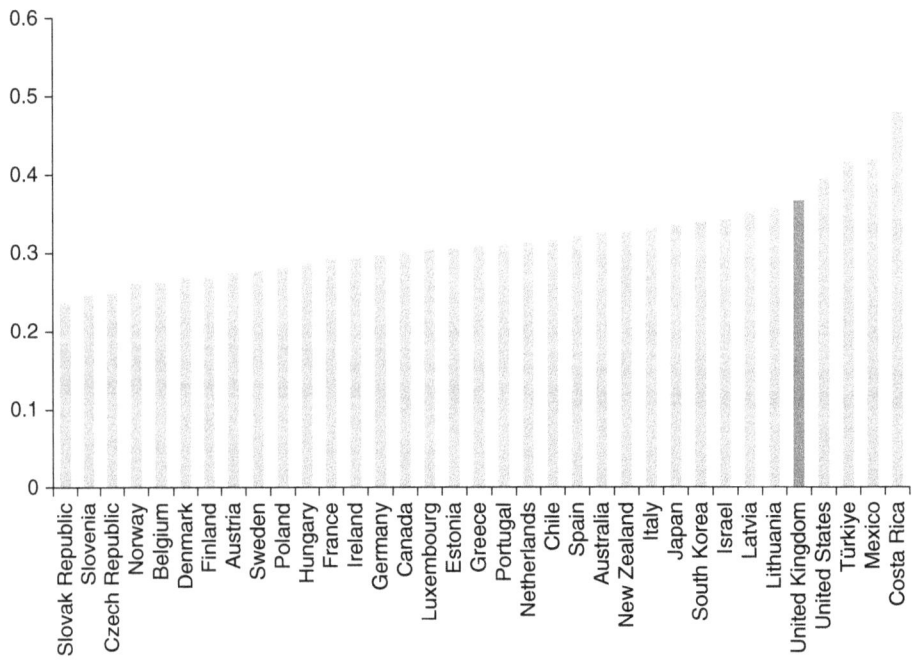

Figure 12.5 Income inequality in the OECD, Gini coefficient

Source: OECD (2023), "Income distribution", OECD Social and Welfare Statistics (database), https://doi.org/10.1787/data-00654-en

Spotlight on research: Measuring inequality

One of the most commonly used measures of inequality is the 'Gini coefficient', named after its inventor, Corrado Gini. This is a statistical measure that represents, in a single value, the dispersion of incomes in a population, usually a country. The value of the coefficient is always between 0 and 1, which represent the logical ends of the scale: a value of zero would imply no inequality, because all incomes are precisely equal; a value of 1 would represent perfect inequality, where one unit in the population has 100 per cent of the income. In practice, countries will always fall somewhere in between; the key point is that a higher Gini reflects a more unequal society in which the income distribution is wider.

Other measures are available and capture different dimensions of inequality. For example, the Gini coefficient looks only at income inequality and leaves out asset wealth. Alternative measures of income inequality include the 90:10 ratio, which compares how wide the gap is between people at the 10th percentile in the population with those at the 90th percentile (thus leaving out the more extreme tail values). Depending on the analytical context, different measures will be suitable for different purposes. Nonetheless, the Gini is an important and widely used indicator and is particularly useful for making comparisons across countries.

Income is not the only way in which economic resources are distributed in an economy; it is also important to consider distributions of wealth. Whereas income data reflect earnings in a given year, wealth data reflect households' stock of certain kinds of assets, including property (real estate) and pensions, which accumulate over time. The distribution of these assets across different groups in society is so uneven that averages are not particularly meaningful here, and it makes more sense to look at the wealth holdings of segments of the population. The Office for National Statistics estimated in 2020 that the bottom half of the wealth distribution in Great Britain – half of the population – collectively owned just 6 per cent of all wealth, while the wealthiest 10 per cent of individuals held 50 per cent of the wealth (Figure 12.6). Even these figures may be an underestimate, since wealth data are based on surveys that struggle to capture a reliable picture of the very richest households.

Putting data in context

Many of the trends described above are not unique to the UK. For example, Britain is far from the only country to have gone through a process of de-industrialisation, or to have faced the challenges of globalisation and inequality. Most developed countries have moved towards service-based economies in recent decades, finding themselves better placed to compete in industries that favour high skills and education, and less able to compete with the low production costs of manufacturers in developing countries. At the same time, citizens in the rich democracies have become less tolerant of the environmental consequences of manufacturing and extractive industries; an economic model based on importing goods while exporting services has the advantage of moving such environmental externalities somewhere else. Take mining, for example: in the 1980s, the collapse of the coal mining industry was a watershed

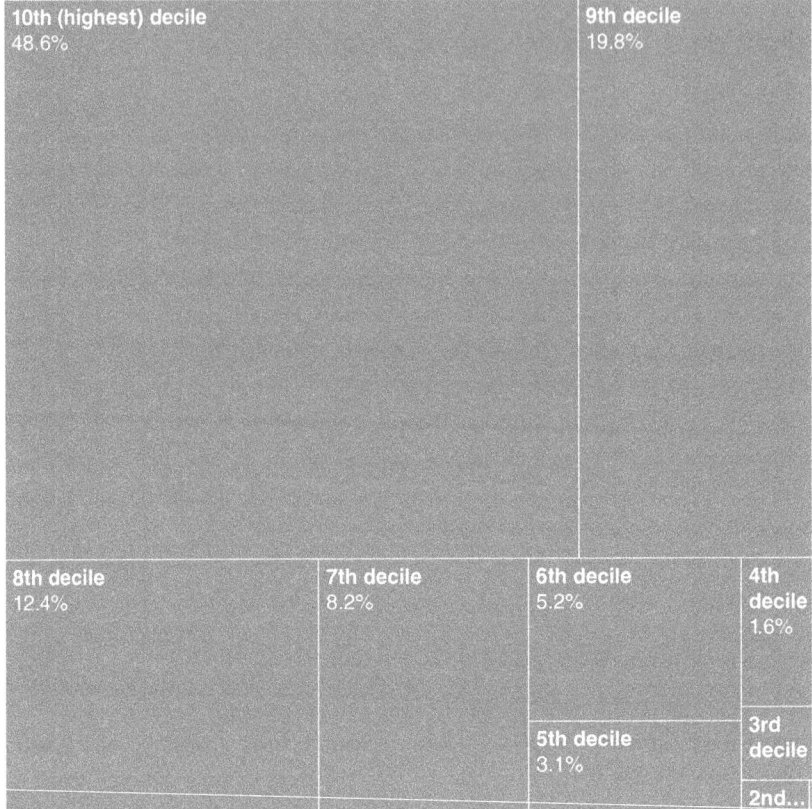

Figure 12.6 Wealth shares by population decile

Source: Office for National Statistics (2022) Distribution of individual total wealth by characteristic in Great Britain: April 2018 to March 2020, https://www.ons.gov.uk/peoplepopulationandcommunity/personalandhouseholdfinances/incomeandwealth/bulletins/distributionofindividualtotalwealthbycharacteristicingreatbritain/april2018tomarch2020

moment in the UK's transition to a service-based economy. Strike action in defence of coal mining was equivalent to more than 30,000 working days, and during the strikes approximately 11,000 people were arrested. In the 2020s, by contrast, extractive industries face an uphill battle for even minimal public support. The controversy around shale gas exploration (often known as fracking) shows how difficult it would be for the government of a rich democracy to move their economic mix back towards extractive industries; in the UK as elsewhere, economic transformations are not easily reversed. Markets change, as does public opinion.

However, focusing primarily on macroeconomic trends can lead us to underestimate the extent to which economic policy makes a difference. The next section takes a tour of the economic policy models that have been applied by successive British governments, looking at how they have sought to organise the relationship between the state and the economy, and between public institutions and private markets. This is how a political economy perspective differs from a purely economic account of change: it returns continually to a simple question: what is the difference that politics has made, or could make, to economic outcomes?

Economic policy in the UK: The difference that politics makes

Postwar Keynesianism

After the destruction of the Second World War, economic policy in the UK was concerned with rebuilding the economy, alongside the development of new welfare state institutions. In the postwar decades economic policy was highly interventionist by modern standards, based on a conviction that reconstruction could not be achieved through laissez-faire policies that relied on markets and private actors to produce the necessary investment. The Attlee government of the late 1940s is remembered for having built the National Health Service, but it also oversaw a radical reorganisation of the economic life of the UK, via a series of nationalisations including the railways, the Bank of England, and industries such as coal and steel. Some of these interventions were made possible by the extraordinary powers taken by governments during wartime, based on the explicit argument that in times of crisis, private interests must be subordinated to the common good. However, the managed economy of the postwar period was also rooted in the intellectual currents of the day, and particularly the thinking of economist John Maynard Keynes, whose theories implied a vital role for the state in stabilising the economy across economic cycles. According to Keynesian theory, economies can get stuck in periods of depression and excess unemployment. Rather than assuming that the market could get itself out of such a slump, Keynesian economics favoured counter-cyclical fiscal policy – that is, the government using its spending power to stimulate demand and increase economic output during downturns. As well as calling on the state to intervene in the economic cycle, postwar Keynesianism favoured a 'mixed economy' with a substantial role for public ownership of economic assets, and public management of strategically important parts of the economy.

By the 1970s however, this postwar consensus was coming under pressure, both in the UK and in the wider world. Since 1944 the monetary policies of the rich economies had been coordinated under the Bretton Woods system, named after the New Hampshire town in which it was originally negotiated. These arrangements were aimed at combining trade openness and economic cooperation between nations with currency stability through a system of coordinated exchange rates. Currencies including the British pound were pegged (with some flexibility) in relation to the US dollar, which was in turn pegged to gold at a fixed rate of convertibility (see Eichengreen, 2013). This coordination had been a key means of stabilising the world economy through the postwar reconstruction period, but over time changes in the relative competitiveness of member countries' economies made it increasingly difficult to sustain a system in which currencies could only adjust through negotiation between governments. The United States, faced with an overvalued dollar and growing demands on its gold reserves, suspended dollar convertibility in 1971, and the fixed exchange rate system collapsed for good in 1973. It was replaced by a system of floating exchange rates that increased the flexibility of the world financial system, but also exposed countries to new currency risk.

Through the 1970s, political instability in the Middle East contributed to spikes in the price of oil, affecting manufacturing and households alike. The UK entered a period of so-called stagflation, with falling growth and rising inflation simultaneously. With these global economic currents affecting the value of people's wages, pay bargaining by the trades unions became increasingly combative, and industrial action rose across the decade. In 1973, strikes by coal miners led to the imposition of a three-day week for some businesses to conserve energy. The upheavals of the 1970s reached a peak in 1978–1979, when the government's attempts to stick to a 5 per cent pay cap for the public sector triggered a further wave of industrial action, including symbolically potent strikes by gravediggers and refuse collectors. The press dubbed it the 'winter of discontent', conjuring the image of a nation in chaos and criticising the Labour government of the day for underestimating the crisis (Hay, 2010). The economic developments of the 1970s would have been challenging for any government, but they posed particularly serious challenges for Keynesian policy and its faith in government's ability to steer the ship. By 1979 a turning point was approaching, and a radically different economic policy paradigm was waiting in the wings.

The 1980s: The UK's neoliberal revolution

In 1979, the Conservative party returned to power under Margaret Thatcher and embarked on what would become a radical overhaul of UK economic policy. Where the postwar consensus had favoured interventionist economic management, the Thatcher government saw such interventions as being at the root of the economic turmoil of the 1970s. Instead, the incoming government believed in the productive power of free markets, with the new prime minister pledging to help the country 'shake off the self-doubt induced by decades of dependence on the state as master, not as servant' (Margaret Thatcher Foundation, 2023a). In this new paradigm, government intervention was thought to introduce inefficiency, stifling enterprise and growth; if the UK was to prosper again, a radically new relationship between government and market – indeed, between government and individual citizens – would be necessary.

Thatcher's economic model deployed a combination of lower taxes, deregulation and privatisation intended to unleash the full potential of the economy (Gamble, 2021). Income taxes were cut in the first year of the Conservative government, bringing the top rate down from 83 per cent to 60 per cent, and to 40 per cent by the end of the 1980s. Over the course of that decade the government's belief in private enterprise saw it enact a wave of privatisations, from public utilities including British Telecom to flagship companies like British Airways and Rolls Royce. Deregulation of the banking sector opened up a new era of financialised capitalism, establishing the City of London as a global financial centre and making it a keystone of the UK's economic model ever since (Vinen, 2009). The Thatcher government's faith in private ownership also extended into social policy: for example, the new 'right to buy' initiative enabled council tenants to buy their homes at a discounted price, and proved extremely popular, with over a million sales in the 1980s. The common thread throughout was the pursuit of market-led prosperity, breaking the perceived dependence of both businesses and individuals on the state.

Alongside these economic reforms, the government was determined to confront what they saw as an over-powerful union movement standing in the way of British prosperity. Across several rounds of legislation the Thatcher government acted to curtail industrial action, imposing new restrictions on the conduct of ballots, changing the law on picketing and banning secondary actions (strikes in support of other industrial actions). These reforms of labour rights were accompanied by aggressive policing strategies against protesting workers intended as a show of government strength against unions, which were decried as the 'enemy within' (Margaret Thatcher Foundation, 2023b). This anti-union push was very substantially successful. After the defeat of the miners' strike in 1984–1985, both union membership and industrial action reduced dramatically, effectively removing strikes from the political landscape in the UK through the 1990s and 2000s (Figure 12.7). After the industrial unrest of the 1970s this was a stunning reversal and a structural change in the balance of the UK's political economy.

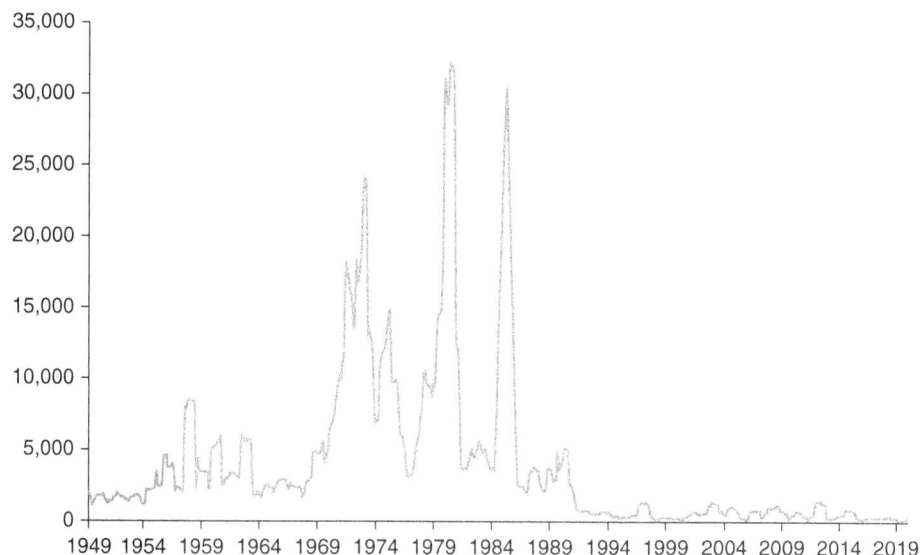

Figure 12.7 Industrial action, 1949–2019 (Total working days, '000s)

Source: Office for National Statistics (2023), Labour disputes in the UK, https://www.ons.gov.uk/employmentandlabourmarket/peopleinwork/workplacedisputesandworkingconditions/datasets/labdlabourdisputesintheuk

The new paradigm adopted by the Thatcher government has often been referred to as 'neoliberal', since it combined classical liberalism's mistrust of state power with a new suite of economic and monetary policies responding specifically to the economic problems of the day. Neoliberalism was by no means just a British invention; in the United States, the Reagan administration was enacting its own pro-market revolution, and the US president would be a key political and ideological ally for Thatcher. The UK was, however, one of the most enthusiastic adopters of neoliberal principles, and the effects on Britain's economy were profound. Through the 1970s GDP growth had been extremely volatile, and the economy shrank in the first two years of the Thatcher government. After that however, the 1980s saw an economic upturn in the UK, with growth peaking at over 5 per cent in 1987–1988. At the same time, unemployment rocketed from under 4 per cent in the mid-1970s to almost 12 per cent in 1984, particularly for men previously in full-time employment (Blanchflower and Freeman, 1993). The very rapid de-industrialisation of the UK, especially in the north of England, Wales and Scotland, alongside the reduced power of the unions, contributed to a sharp rise in income inequality (Figure 12.8), taking the country from being roughly as equal as Germany, to inequality levels closer to the USA (Hopkin and Alexander Shaw, 2016). For some, the Thatcher years had brought a welcome revival after the turmoil of the 1970s; self-employment increased in the 1980s, as did rates of home ownership and female participation in the labour market. But for households and communities left out of the boom it was a time of enormous upheaval and loss.

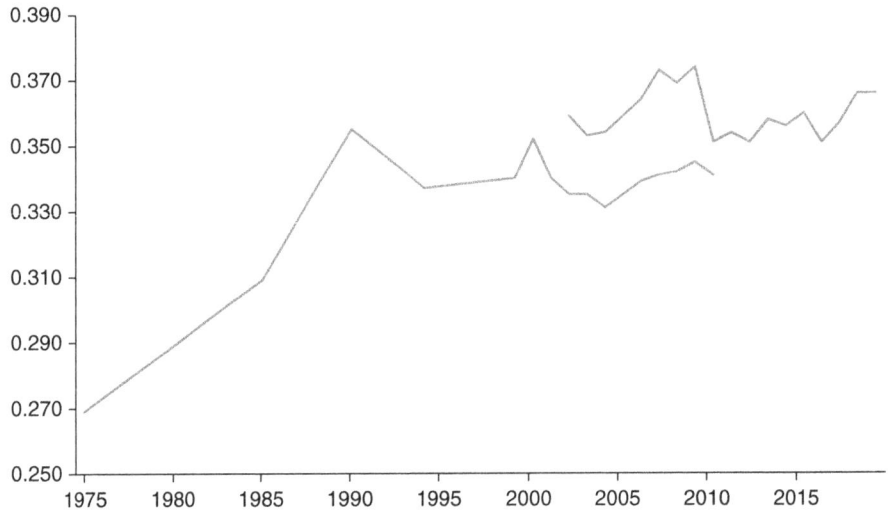

Figure 12.8 Income inequality in the UK, Gini coefficient, 1975–2019

Source: OECD (2023), "Income distribution", OECD Social and Welfare Statistics (database), https://doi.org/10.1787/data-00654-en. Note that methodological changes in 2012 mean that the time series is not continuous.

By the mid-1990s the UK's neoliberal transformation was well advanced, but the downsides of the new economic model were increasingly evident. Long-term unemployment was high, while the Conservatives' preference for private enterprise over public provision had left some key public services in a poor state. The economic boom of the 1980s had given way to a period of recession in the early 1990s, when unemployment once again increased. This time the economic pain was not confined to former industrial areas, but also affected many of the lower middle-class homeowners that had been a key part of the Conservatives' electoral coalition. Thatcher resigned in 1990 amid public protests against proposals to reform local taxation, while the Conservative party was at war with itself over the UK's relationship with the European Community, an issue that would soon escalate with important consequences for the economy.

In 1990 the UK had joined the European Exchange Rate Mechanism (ERM), which meant committing to maintain an exchange rate within a certain range of other European currencies. UK politicians had long been split over whether to tie the British pound to European currencies in this way; monetary and political integration with the EU were key internal battlegrounds for the Conservative party, creating deep rifts within the Thatcher government. The UK had declined to join the ERM at its inception in 1979, but in 1990 the government believed ERM membership offered potential benefits in terms of controlling inflation and stabilising exchange rates, and that the time was now right to join (Johnson, 1994). However, keeping the pound within the criteria for ERM membership soon proved difficult, and as the UK economy slowed down in the early 1990s the currency peg became a barrier to restoring competitiveness. By 1992, the strain was such that some investors believed that UK membership of the ERM could not be sustained, triggering a wave of currency speculation that threatened a full-blown crisis for the pound. The Bank of England and the Treasury were forced to intervene, buying Sterling in the currency markets and raising interest rates to prop up the value of the pound. On 16 September 1992, (dubbed 'Black Wednesday' in the press), it became clear that these actions had failed and the UK was forced to withdraw from the ERM altogether. In the immediate term, leaving the ERM resolved the crisis, but the episode nonetheless had important consequences. Materially, the instability of the ERM crisis had hit households in the pocket: in a country where many homeowners had variable-rate mortgages, the pain of higher interest rates had been quickly transmitted into people's personal finances. Politically, the crisis was a disaster for the government, inflicting serious damage on the Conservative party's reputation for sound economic management.

New Labour's 'third way' economics

In 1997 the Labour party returned to power determined to capitalise on the Conservatives' missteps and become the party of economic competence in the eyes of the public. However, the political economy of New Labour was not only a response to the weaknesses of Thatcherism; it also saw itself as responding to the failures of postwar social democracy, and as offering a centrist 'third way' between these two poles. With that goal in mind, Labour made it clear from the outset that there would be no return to postwar economic planning. Under the leadership of the economically liberal Tony Blair the party had rebranded itself as 'New Labour', symbolically detaching itself from the party's socialist traditions and adopting a relentlessly modernist rhetoric of forward progress (Finlayson, 2003). This rebranding had been cemented in 1995 when Labour scrapped Clause 4 of the party constitution, replacing a commitment to 'the common ownership of the means of production, distribution and exchange' – that is, socialism – with a blander aspiration towards 'a community in which power, wealth and opportunity are in the hands of the many, not the few'.

For New Labour, economic change was to be pursued through supply-side reform of the economy: that is, policies to create the conditions for growth rather than to directly stimulate it. For example, public spending could support the provision of education and skills in the workforce, but industrial policy to directly support companies would be an intervention too far. On tax and spending, New Labour were quick to rule out any increase in rates of income tax or national insurance, including higher rates of tax for top earners. New Labour would be the party of aspiration, not overt redistribution, with one cabinet minister stating that the government was 'intensely relaxed about people getting filthy rich, as long as they pay their taxes' (Mandelson, 2010: 265). Market outcomes would, for the most part, be allowed to run: a business-friendly environment should keep growth going and tax receipts coming in, and that being so, the government would be able to afford to invest in better public services. This approach has been criticised as a 'politics of accommodation' (Hay, 1999) in which the preferences of certain kinds of firms were built into government policy, based on a belief that investment would otherwise move elsewhere.

While the question of higher or more progressive taxes was off the table, New Labour were prepared to make some redistributive moves on public spending. The introduction of a new system of tax credits helped target support towards low-income households, and particularly towards lone parents, as a means of tackling child poverty (see Sloman, 2019). Economic reforms such as the introduction of a minimum wage also helped raise household incomes in the lower part of the distribution. As a consequence, and despite ongoing income growth for the highest earners, the Gini coefficient stopped climbing, remaining high but stable over the New Labour period. To some extent, inequality was stabilising because the big economic shifts of the Thatcher revolution turn had now taken their course, but policy also played an important role, particularly in providing more generous support for low-income families.

The policies of the New Labour era should be placed in their wider context since political choices in one country are never made in a vacuum. The ideology of the New Labour era borrowed liberally from policy trends in other countries, particularly the Clinton-era Democratic party in the United States. Like Blair, Clinton was a 'third way' politician, rhetorically splitting the difference between the 'new right' politics of the 1980s and the leftwing ideas of the 1960s and 1970s. Third way rhetoric aimed to project a pragmatic centrism, as in Blair's manifesto claim that 'New Labour is a party of ideas and ideals but not of outdated ideology. What counts is what works' (Labour Party, 1997). Third-way economic policy was built on a belief that the old tensions – between capital and labour, inflation and jobs, economic stability and social justice – were yesterday's battles. In this analysis, it was assumed that pursuing low inflation and steady growth would deliver benefits to everyone, not just the better off. Tax revenues from a buoyant economy could be spent on raising the living standards of the poorest, but only once a pro-business, pro-globalisation environment had been credibly established. In such a context, the success of the City of London was viewed as a national asset, rather than a source of inequality or risk: if a world-beating finance industry meant that some people were paid very high salaries, this was a price worth paying for the GDP growth, and tax revenues, generated by the banking sector. For a decade, this growth model appeared to be delivering on its promises, as the UK experienced a long period of steady, unbroken growth, far removed from the volatile business cycles of the past. However, this 'great moderation' (Bernanke, 2004) could not last forever.

In 2008 the long economic boom of the 1990s and 2000s came to an abrupt end, with the arrival of a global financial crisis. Trouble had been brewing in international markets since 2007, as losses on risky loans in America's sub-prime mortgage markets began to emerge. But while these sub-prime losses were to be the catalyst, they were not of themselves the crisis; they spiralled into a global financial meltdown for two connected reasons. First, it represented a previously unsuspected liability of uncertain size, making the risk attached to sub-prime impossible to price, and generating huge uncertainty in the market. Second, the losses had been distributed throughout the financial system through complex derivatives that bundled good debt with bad, making a mockery of the credit ratings attached to them and further undermining confidence. It was not the dollar amount of the sub-prime losses that caused the crash, but the uncertainty they had injected into a deeply interconnected financial system that required trillions of dollars in liquidity to keep the show on the road every day (see Tooze, 2019). Through 2008, the financial sector underwent a system-wide contraction in liquidity that brought down firms including the US investment bank Lehman Brothers and the insurance giant AIG, and threatened a wave of further insolvencies with serious implications for the wider economy, particularly in the UK with its huge banking industry.

This was by no means the first financial crisis the world had ever seen (Reinhart and Rogoff, 2009), but it was turbo-charged by the complexity and interconnectedness of 21st century finance. For the political economy of the UK, the crash contained some important lessons. First, the nature of the crisis exposed the flaws of the economic orthodoxy of both the neoliberal and the third way periods, which had assumed that unfettered markets would be functional and self-correcting. For 30 years it had been an article of faith that the source of economic instability was generally government interference, so the events of 2008 were profoundly contradictory of that paradigm. This lesson would not be easy to learn; neoliberal ideas were deeply embedded in the UK and elsewhere, and the policy model they supported would not disappear overnight (see Crouch, 2011). Second, the global financial crisis generated economic policy reversals that would have been previously unthinkable, and once again placed the role of the state at centre stage. In the UK, fearing that the whole banking system was at risk, the government undertook drastic measures, including taking public stakes in some private banks (effectively nationalising them), and compelling others to accept government bailouts. The era of finance-led growth was suddenly over, and with it the era of government non-intervention in the market. Going into the 2010s, there was little doubt that economic policy would be more interventionist than before; the question was what interventions would be pursued, and how the costs of the crisis would be distributed across the economy, and across society.

Economic policy after the crash: Austerity and Brexit

The financial crisis of the late 2000s ushered in a period of significant upheaval in UK politics. Labour lost the 2010 general election but no other party held a parliamentary majority, so the UK was governed by a coalition for the first time since the Second World War. One of the consequences of the financial crisis had been a sharp increase in public debt, thanks to the combined effect of rising spending (particularly on unemployment benefits), falling tax receipts and slowing growth. The new Conservative–Liberal Democrat government argued that this debt, and the annual budget deficit (the amount the government spends less the amount of revenues it collects), posed a threat to the UK's economic stability, stating from the outset that 'tackling the deficit is our first priority'. The UK, they argued, had been living beyond its means for too long and needed to 'ensure, like every solvent household in the country, that what we buy we can afford ... tackling this budget deficit is unavoidable' (HC Deb 20 Oct 2010, c.949).

Image 12.2 Terraced housing in the North of England

© Photo by Clare Louise Jackson on Shutterstock

Critics of austerity argued that this analogy to household debt was misplaced because governments, unlike households, can roll over their debt into the future, while cutting government spending during an economic downturn would depress growth even further (Blyth, 2013). Nonetheless, the coalition government held firm and enacted a programme of austerity measures that reduced overall public expenditure from 47 per cent of GDP to 42 per cent in just five years, and to 40 per cent by the end of the decade. Large cuts to public spending were the main component, as well as real-terms public sector pay cuts and an increase in the rate of value-added tax (VAT). And this was not austerity by stealth: the coalition repeatedly made the case that painful adjustments were necessary to repair the public finances, and the public proved surprisingly open to those arguments. While austerity measures were often individually controversial, focus groups showed that the simple message behind austerity – that reducing public borrowing was the responsible choice – resonated with many people. At a time when people had just seen an economic boom based on easy credit end badly, the pain of spending cuts could be rationalised as 'reaping what we sowed' (Stanley, 2014). In 2015, the Conservatives regained a slim majority in parliament, but their Liberal Democrat coalition partners, whose popularity among students had evaporated when they voted to increase the tuition fee cap to £9,000 per year, were all but wiped out.

In 2016, the UK economy underwent another shock when the public voted, by a slim majority of 52 per cent to 48 per cent, to leave the European Union. As well as remaking the UK's political relationship with the EU, Brexit reversed the trajectory of four decades of economic integration with Europe, making it one of the most important turning points for UK economic policy in generations. But while the referendum set in train a process of political decoupling, it left nearly all the big economic questions unanswered. Such uncertainty is an inherent feature of referendums, which reduce complex political questions to a simple binary: change or continuity? A vote for Leave could represent many kinds of potential change while Remain implied a vote for the status quo.

Given that, it is not surprising that the Remain vote was strongest in London, the epicentre of UK prosperity. Across the nations and regions of the UK only London, Scotland and Northern Ireland returned a majority for remaining in the EU; a majority in Wales and the rest of England voted to leave. Support for Brexit was strongest among older, less educated and poorer voters (Hobolt, 2016), and in the communities that had benefited least from the UK's pro-globalisation economic policies (Carreras et al., 2019). Even so, the heterogeneity of the Leave coalition defies simple explanation in economic terms. While the Leave vote included many households in economically depressed places, it also had strong support in prosperous parts of southern England (Surridge et al., 2021). Focus group evidence suggests that what these economically dissimilar voters had in common was the hope of a reinvigorated local economy outside the EU, and a willingness to risk change on the basis that the status quo was not good enough (Gartzou-Katsouyanni et al., 2021). Across all these dimensions, the Brexit vote exposed the complexity of the interaction between people's economic situation and their political preferences.

Through all these phases of policymaking, the underlying question that governments face is consistent: how should we organise the relationship between the state and the market? The way that each generation answers this question depends on their assessment of past policy models and their shortcomings. The next phase of economic policymaking will contend with immediate problems such as inflation and the rising cost of living, alongside longer-term challenges such as decarbonising the economy and adapting to new technologies such as artificial intelligence. The choices governments make in response to those challenges will, as always, be informed by their view of the proper role of government in the economy: what it can – or should – do to effect change.

Towards an economy for all: Thinking about economic change

The guiding theme of this textbook is a *pluralist* perspective on the UK today. In this perspective, we operate with an awareness that society is composed of different groups, interests and movements; it is the interaction between these many voices that shapes the country as it exists today, and as it might exist in future. This means focusing not only on the most powerful but on the broader set of actors that make up UK society, including some that are often marginalised.

But how can we best apply this approach to the politics of the economy? We have already seen that economic resources are not equally distributed; furthermore, the political resources with which actors may shape the economy are concentrated in certain institutions, and out of reach to the majority of people. The very language of economic policy can be opaque and off-putting to ordinary citizens, limiting public involvement in the politics of the economy. When applying a pluralist perspective to the economy we must be careful not to understate the structural asymmetries that underpin it, or to overstate the agency of individuals and social movements to effect economic change. More so than many of the policy areas discussed in this book, economic policy is subject to powerful structural constraints that are not easily overcome. In this context, can we meaningfully talk about the economy in pluralist terms? This section confronts this problem by considering how the economy could be different, as well as discussing the barriers to change. We do this by considering three different sets of constraints on economic policy in the UK – institutional, economic and political.

Institutional barriers: Economic policy centralisation in the UK

Economic policy in the UK is made, for the most part, by central government. Fiscal policy (tax and spending) is particularly centralised; local councils have only very limited tax-raising powers, relying on central grants for the majority of their funding, and with limited control over how council tax and business rates are levied. For the devolved nations, tax policy is mostly reserved to Westminster. The Scottish government has gradually assumed greater fiscal autonomy, particularly over income tax, but continues to get around half of its funding from block grants which are determined by spending decisions made by the UK government. Wales has similarly moved towards some devolution of income taxes, but to a lesser degree than in Scotland. The Northern Ireland Assembly has some limited power to cut corporation tax but this option has not yet been exercised. Meanwhile monetary policy for the whole of the UK is reserved to the central bank. Overall, the long-standing centralisation of UK governance ensures that power over economic policy is concentrated in two institutions in London: the Treasury and the Bank of England.

Labour prime minister Harold Wilson has been credited with the observation that 'whichever party is in office the Treasury is in power'. Indeed, a distinctive feature of the UK is that unlike in many European countries there is no separate ministry of the economy, with control of both the public finances and of economic strategy sitting in a single department. Critics of the department have argued that it habitually inclines towards fiscal and monetary conservatism, suspicion of deficit spending, and a preference for lower taxation and inflation control over other economic objectives such as full employment (see Berry, 2021). In this account, the Treasury is an institutional barrier to the kind of activist Keynesianism that was prevalent in the mid-20th century, and to change generally. It is debatable whether the 'Treasury view' is fixed to this extent; for example, in times of crisis such as the 2008 banking crash or the Covid-19 pandemic, the Treasury played a role in devising policies that imply an expansive role for the state in stabilising the economy. In between crises, however, the department's historic role in controlling the nation's purse strings, and guarding the stability of its currency, may make it wary of certain kinds of policy change.

To the extent that the Treasury possesses a settled view of optimal economic policy, this will also reflect wider currents in economic thinking. The role of economists as experts has attracted new scrutiny since the 2010s, not least given the failure of mainstream economics to predict the global financial crisis. Student-led organisations such as Rethinking Economics have called for a shake-up in the way that economics is taught in universities, and for the inclusion of heterodox theories that question standard assumptions about rational actors and naturally self-equilibrating markets (Fischer et al., 2018). This crisis of expertise has not been confined to academic circles. In the run-up to the Brexit referendum in 2016, one government minister was asked why he was recommending leaving the EU despite the expert consensus that it would be bad for the UK economy. His answer: that the public had 'had enough of experts' (Sky News, 2016); essentially, that given the damaged credibility of the economics profession, voters could reasonably reject the economic case for Remain. Debates about the influence of the Treasury may be seen as an extension of these broader debates about the status of economic experts, and the ultimate question of what space is left for democratic choices around economic policy.

Monetary policy provides another example of this tension. The Bank of England (which, despite its name, is the central bank for the whole of the UK) was made formally independent of government in 1997, tasked with keeping inflation within a target range. The New Labour government had backed independence on the basis that central bankers, unlike politicians, did not have to worry about re-election and so could take the unpopular decisions necessary to keep inflation down. Where government ministers might hesitate to raise interest rates in an election year because it would affect things like the cost of voters' mortgages, central bankers could ignore the electoral cycle and focus only on controlling inflation. However, by removing interest-rate decisions from the political arena, central bank independence does not only remove political short-termism; it also institutionalises one set of policy judgements for the long run. In doing so it removes the option of certain alternatives – for example, allowing some inflation to run, or holding back rate rises to avoid depressing growth during a recession. Rethinking UK monetary policy would mean reinventing the Bank's mandate around a different balance of priorities; in such ways the design of institutions can become a key parameter in the political economy.

Economic barriers: The constraining power of markets

A second key set of constraints on economic policy come from private markets. As we have seen, governments differ significantly in their approach to economic policy, but all are subject in some way to structural constraints in the economic system itself. Economist and political scientist Charles Lindblom (1982) famously dubbed this constraint 'the market as prison': the tendency of firms to withdraw investment if they feel that the policy environment is unfavourable. Crucially, this withdrawal of capital does not imply any kind of coordination on the part of the private sector; individual firms, separately pursuing their own interests, can add up to a structural constraint on governments that might like to raise taxes, regulate business activity or otherwise intervene to shape or restrain the market. To this extent, states are sometimes seen as structurally dependent on capital, obliged to accommodate its preferences, though the extent of this constraint is hotly debated (Przeworski and Wallerstein, 1988). In practice, it can be difficult to predict the threshold at which government policy might trigger disinvestment and firms may have incentives to exaggerate the risk, but even a perceived threat of capital flight can be enough to constrain policy.

The government also has to worry about the reaction of financial markets to its policies. Because of this, policymakers must continually make judgements on the likely reaction of market actors to their policy choices, introducing a degree of uncertainty and risk to all economic policy decisions. The UK government found this out to its cost in 2022 when budget announcements under then prime minister Liz Truss caused a volatile reaction in financial markets, increasing the amount of interest the UK had to pay on its borrowing and threatening to destabilise the pound. The result was the resignation of both chancellor and prime minister and the reversal of nearly all the policy measures that had been announced. The episode served to illustrate that rapid changes in economic policy can be destabilising unless handled very carefully.

Political barriers: The puzzle of redistribution and the median voter

Another useful way to think about the politics of the economy is to examine the tension between voters' economic interests and policy outcomes. After all, the presence of economic inequality in democratic societies poses a theoretical puzzle to political science. Based on the foundational work of economist Anthony Downs (1957), formal theories of electoral competition assume that political candidates will maximise their share of the vote by satisfying the preferences of as many voters as possible. Simple electoral maths should then favour policies that would benefit a majority of voters at the expense of a minority. In democracies like the UK, where voting rights are universal but income is unequally distributed, there should always be a mathematical majority for policies that would redistribute resources from the richest citizens to the rest. This is the puzzle of the median voter – since the income distribution is skewed, the median voter will have a below-average income, so more people would benefit from redistributive policy than would pay for it. Logically, if politicians were chasing the median voter, this would leave top earners as a minority interest group in a weak position.

In practice, this 'median voter theory' does not capture the world we live in. In fact, societies with higher inequality, such as the United Kingdom and United States, tend to have *less* redistributive welfare states, taxing less as a proportion of the economy and spending less on welfare programmes compared with more equal countries. However, thinking about *why* the world does not fulfil median voter theory's logical predictions is a useful way into thinking about the tensions facing economic policymakers, and about the barriers to economic policy change. To understand why median voter theory's predictions are not realised, we need to scrutinise the assumptions the theory is based on.

First, the Downsian model of political competition makes a simple assumption that voters are able to calculate their own best interests, so if voters are uninformed or misguided, this assumption fails. This is quite a plausible problem in matters of economic policy, where voters may not be able to accurately identify their own position on income distribution, and so cannot judge whether they would be winners or losers from changes to tax and public spending. Second, for median voters' interests to prevail, voters must not only perceive their interests but reliably turn out to vote for them. If citizens do not turn out at election time, the democratic mechanism cannot operate and median voter theory breaks down. This is a particularly serious problem if turnout is uneven across social groups, as we know it tends to be – for example, election-day turnout is often lowest among younger cohorts and lower socioeconomic groups. The electorate may contain a majority who would benefit from redistributive spending, but if poorer voters are systematically less likely to vote, the electoral maths will not favour redistribution to the same extent.

Third, median voter theory assumes that voters are thinking about their interests on one particular dimension – in this example, income redistribution – and that they have a shared and objective assessment of what policy should be on that dimension. In practice of course, voter preferences are more complex and multifaceted than this. On economic policy, citizens' views on policy do not always reduce to simple calculations of self-interest but connect to people's sense of what is fair, what is practically achievable, and what is congruent with their sense of identity and community. If voters do not believe that redistribution is morally justified, if they believe themselves to be on the path to becoming richer and would prefer lower taxes when they get there, if they do not approve of, or identify with, other groups who would benefit from public spending, they may withdraw support from redistributive policies even if they would benefit from them. Indeed, voters may not be thinking about economic policy at all; elections are fought on many issues at once, and the low-income median voter may have completely different priorities on polling day.

Finally, there is a fundamental assumption in median voter theories that voters' preferences exist prior to politics, and that politicians' role is always to observe and respond to them. Both parts of that assumption are questionable. Politicians may be policy-seeking rather than vote-seeking, pursuing what they consider the best policy even if it departs from their voters' preferences. The Liberal Democrats' reversal on student tuition fees in 2010 is a vivid example, though it also shows how politically costly policy-seeking can be (Butler, 2021) And, crucially, the assumption of extant voter preferences leaves little space for the ways in which politics may lead and shape public opinion. Political campaigns offer powerful narratives that cultivate support for some kinds of policy and place others out of bounds; economic change may require years of groundwork to mould opinion and generate (or undermine) public support for particular policies. The agenda-setting role of the media has long been recognised as critical in this regard (McCombs and Shaw, 1972), and the landscape of mediating institutions has now expanded to include print, broadcast, online and social media. Of course, not all voices are equally well positioned to lead the discourse or shape public opinion. But to assume that voters' preferences are stable, rational and prior to the political messaging they receive is to disregard the power of political communication and the channels through which it proceeds.

Conclusion

When thinking about economic policy, in the UK or anywhere else, the underlying question recurs: how much scope is there for governments to change anything? Economic models are complex, interconnected and structurally embedded in the ways our economies are organised. Despite this, the choices of successive governments do make a difference to economic outcomes, sometimes in the short term, and sometimes over a much longer horizon. Not every country experiences globalisation, or deindustrialisation, or technological advances in the same way because the political economy of each country has been shaped by the policy legacies of many years. Who controls the economic policy agenda, and which economic ideas they choose to mobilise, are therefore vitally important questions. Cultivating a critical perspective that asks which ideas are driving policy and which are excluded, whose interests those ideas serve and whose they neglect or obscure is an essential step in interrogating the economic conditions of the day and fitting them into a longer-run view of the political economy. As economist J. K. Galbraith (1998) knew, the conventional wisdom can generate complacency, leading us to interpret events according to what sits most comfortably with our interests and prior positions. The message of this chapter has been that a political economy perspective must retain a live curiosity about the economy and its interaction with our politics. Economics is everywhere and always political; combining good data with good questions must always be worthwhile.

Key take-home points

- The UK is one of the world's largest economies but is characterised by relatively high income inequality and by regional imbalances.
- The economic trends we observe in the UK (and elsewhere) are not apolitical phenomena; they have been significantly shaped by the economic policy models applied by successive governments.
- While the choices of governments matter a great deal, reshaping the economy is not easy; there are important economic, institutional and political barriers to change, and especially to change that would redistribute economic and political resources.

Annotated reading list

Blyth, M. (2013) *Austerity: The History of a Dangerous Idea*. Oxford: Oxford University Press.

Essential reading, not just on the merits (or otherwise) of austerity in fiscal policy but also on the processes by which economic ideas gain, and retain, their power as policy models. For a precis of the argument, see this Youtube clip in which the author lays it all out: www.youtube.com/watch?v=go2bVGi0ReE

Hopkin, J. and Shaw, A.K. (2016) Organized combat or structural advantage? The politics of inequality and the winner-take-all economy in the United Kingdom. *Politics & Society*, 44(3), 345–371.

For more background on inequality trends in the UK, you could start with this article by Jonathan Hopkin and me, which sets out to understand how the UK ended up with such an unequal society after the 1980s. We take Jacob Hacker and Paul Pierson's classic book *Winner-Take-All Politics*, which looks at the politics of inequality in the United States, and apply it to the UK, finding both similarities and important differences between the two countries.

Resolution Foundation (2022) *Stagnation Nation: Navigating a Route to a Fairer and More Prosperous Britain: The Interim Report of the Economy 2030 Inquiry*. Resolution Foundation and Centre for Economic Performance, LSE. https://economy2030.resolutionfoundation.org/wp-content/uploads/2022/07/Stagnation_nation_interim_report.pdf

A timely and important, if sobering, report on the state of the UK economy today, and the prospects for renewal. The Economy 2030 Inquiry brings together respected think tank the Resolution Foundation with academics from the LSE's Centre for Economic Performance, funded by the Nuffield Foundation; this is the interim report. Find out more about the Inquiry at https://economy2030.resolutionfoundation.org/about

13
UK environment and climate change politics

Clare Saunders

Image 13.1 Cows grazing on green pasture. Grazing for conservation or environmental villains due to methane production? © Photo by Dmitry Naumov on Shutterstock

Learning objectives

After reading this chapter, you should be able to:

- Explore the ways in which UK environment and climate politics is a dynamic assemblage through the case study of veganism and the related animal movement. The case study illustrates three key themes in UK environmental politics.
- Understand why a range of differentiated environmental organisations exist and how political and lifestyle activism interact as part of an environmentalist assemblage with rhizomatic power.
- Examine the pathways through which environmental knowledge is constructed, assembled, contested and sometimes used to inform UK environmental policy.
- Through the lens of pluralism, you will learn about the range of related political views held between and among vegans and environmentalists.
- You will explore how these energy flows that shape environmental knowledge construction assemble, and how contestation challenges and shapes representative institutions, organisations and individual citizens.

Introduction

Despite decades of government and organisational efforts, and high levels of public concern – in 2022 around three-quarters of the population of Great Britain aged 16 and over reported being worried about climate change (ONS, 2022) – the world still finds itself facing the terrifying duo of environmental and climate crises. Environmental Performance Index scores for the UK find the country performing in the bottom quartile (the 25% least well performing countries) of 180 countries for several measures of ecosystem vitality and ecosystem services, for fisheries, for carbon dioxide from land cover, for greenhouse gasses per capita and for nitrogen dioxide pollution (Environmental Performance Index, 2022). In 2022 it was reported that only 14 per cent of English rivers have good ecological status due to pollution and poor regulatory practice (UK Parliament, 2022b).

Why are environmental problems so difficult to solve? Arguably, and as we illustrate in this chapter through the lens of veganism, it's because the issues of environment and climate change are incredibly complex and entangled assemblages that overlap with many other regulatory arenas. These entanglements are deeply embedded into the country's current socioeconomic arrangements and practices. In turn, these filter through to, and are propped up by, citizens' lifestyles in feedback loops. Additionally, it is an unfortunate fact that, under successive Conservative governments, the environment – despite rhetoric to the contrary – ends up playing third fiddle after the economy and immigration (e.g. see Carter and Clements, 2015, on David Cameron's poor record at delivering his promised 'Greenest Government Ever'). In any government preoccupied with the rebound from the Covid-19 pandemic, in the context of the Russian war on Ukraine and the rising cost of living, the environment is bound to slide down the agenda yet further, while environmental issues are exacerbated by these intersecting issues.

In the UK, the environment and climate change are governed and disputed by a series of global conventions, the Europeanisation of policy (only slowly being dismantled despite Brexit), UK policymakers across multiple departments, executive agencies and other public bodies, devolved UK policymakers (England, Wales and Northern Ireland), unitary authorities or district/borough and local councils, scientific institutions, local practices, international NGOs, activists, citizens groups, consumers' associations, businesses, scientific institutions, our everyday lives and more. All UK government departments are required to adhere to sustainable procurement guidelines, and many have remits directly related to environmental issues, most notably the Department for Food and Rural Affairs (DEFRA), the Department for Transport (DfT) and the Department for Business, Energy and Industrial Strategy (BEIS). The fact that the environment cuts across the work of different departments begins to illustrate the ways in which the environment and climate change are crosscutting issues (see Need to know below).

Not only does the politics of the environment and climate take place in a broad set of overlapping arenas, the thematic areas of environment and climate change also encompass a dizzying range of issues. These include business practices, town and country planning (i.e. plans for and the building of new homes and other infrastructure), transport systems, nature conservation, food production and consumption, waste management, energy production and usage and the management and remedying of water, land and air pollution. Even that is not an exhaustive list. Put differently, environmental politics crops up almost everywhere!

If environmental politics is everywhere, then climate change politics also surrounds us. Much of what we do as humans requires the input of energy or resources derived from fossil fuels that contribute to the accumulation of greenhouse gases in the atmosphere; many modes of transport, the food we eat and the clothes we wear have carbon embedded in them. Indeed transport and food production are considered hefty contributors to greenhouse gas emissions. In 2020, transport contributed 24 per cent of the UK's domestic greenhouse gas emissions and agriculture contributed 12 per cent (not including the processing, packaging, transport and refrigeration and freezing of food products and the management of post-consumer waste).

We can also understand the ubiquity of environmental politics as a *practice* by thinking through the variety of ways one could engage in environmental politics. For example, one could: be a country delegate at an international climate conference; be a minister for Environment Food and Rural Affairs; be a member of the Civil Service Environment Network; provide evidence as an academic to inform a select committee; lobby the government for change; participate in a march, demonstration, rally or vigil; engage in civil disobedience to directly stop unwanted pollution; oppose an application for planning permission; provide wildlife habitat in your private garden; change your lifestyle to have minimal impact on Earth's systems … and the list goes on.

Need to know: Roles and responsibilities of key UK government departments, executive agencies and other public bodies on the environment

- **Department for Environment, Food and Rural Affairs:** A government department responsible for 'improving and protecting the environment' as well supporting 'our world-leading food, farming and fishing industries' (Defra website).

(Continued)

- **Department for Transport**: A government department that supports the development of a transport network that allows UK citizens and goods to travel smoothly around the country. Note that between 1997 and 2001, Transport was merged with Environment in the Department of the Environment, Transport and the Regions.
- **Department for Business, Energy and Industrial Strategy**: An important government department that focuses on developing the economy, ensuring the UK is a scientific powerhouse and in developing energy security based on more sustainable energy produced in the UK itself. Note that between 2008 and 2016, the Energy remit was held by a Department of Energy and Climate Change.
- **Office of Gas and Electricity Markets (Ofgem)**: A non-ministerial department that regulates the companies that provide the country with gas and electricity to help control prices. It acts in the public interest and helps the energy industry to achieve environmental improvements.
- **Food Standards Agency**: A non-ministerial department that aims to ensure that people can buy and eat safe, healthier and more sustainable food.
- **Forestry Commission**: A non-ministerial department that seeks to improve the environmental and societal value of woodlands.
- **Water Services Authority**: A non-ministerial department known as Ofwat, which regulates drinking water and sewage in England and Wales.
- **Animal and Plant Health Authority**: An executive agency that seeks to look after the economy and environment by safeguarding animal and plant health.
- **Committee on Climate Change**: An independent, but statutory, committee that was established as part of the UK Climate Change Act (2008). It provides the UK government with guidance on progress and suggestions to help it reach its aspired target of net zero greenhouse gas emissions by 2050.
- **National Park Authorities**: They exist for each of the 15 national parks in the UK and manage these sites for environmental protection, biodiversity management and public enjoyment.
- **Natural England**: A non-departmental public body, sponsored by Defra, which advises the government on the natural environment.
- **Environment Agency**: An executive non-departmental public body, also sponsored by Defra. It helps enforce regulations related to air, land and water pollution, and assists with flood prevention and management.
- **Office for Environmental Protection**: A public body that works to improve the environment by ensuring that the government and other public authorities are accountable for policies and actions affecting the environment.
- **National Infrastructure Commission**: Provides the government with impartial advice to help it develop sustainable and useful long-term infrastructure projects.
- **Natural Capital Committee**: Advises government on the state of English natural capital (the 'goods' provided to us by natural systems that we rely on for survival), and on the implementation of its 25 Year Environment Plan.
- **Environmental Audit Committee**: A cross-party group that seeks to assess the extent to which government departments are succeeding at delivering environmental protection and sustainable development.

- **Behavioural Insights Team:** Formerly the Nudge Unit, now exists independently of government, but continues to provide advice on encouraging behaviour change (including pro-environmental).

For a full list of UK government departments, executive agencies and other public bodies, see www.gov.uk/government/organisations

Focusing the chapter

The intertwinement of environmental issues and climate change within so many spheres of governance and with so many different aspects of our lives represents a packed assemblage. To cover it comprehensively would require an encyclopaedic volume. To focus the chapter, we will explore veganism as an illustrative running case because it talks well to the general approach of this book in focusing *beyond Westminster* using a Deleuzian assemblages approach (see Chapter 1). The ways in which veganism and vegan advocacy function in the UK allow us to examine not only the responses of governmental institutions (especially Defra), but also a range of campaign groups (e.g. The Vegan Society and related organisations in the animal movement) and individuals that operate in overlapping spheres in interacting ways.

The rest of the chapter explores three key themes. First, it explores the emergence of veganism as a political movement in the UK, comparing it with broader environmental movements and exploring the impacts it has had on people's lifestyles and government policy. Common with related environmental movements, splinter groups form, groups professionalise, new factions emerge and outcomes are multifarious and oftentimes hard to pin down, characteristic of rhizomatic power (see Chapter 1). The different contributions of individuals and organisations in the animal movement have allowed for the emergence and persistence of a variety of different organisations working to attain similar but differentiated goals. The existence of a differentiated field is interpreted through the lens of *organisational ecology*. This framework helps to explain how so many different types of organisations manage to co-exist within a social and political context that is competitive for support from the public.

Second, it considers the ways in which environmental and moral concerns are constructed and explores the challenges that UK policymakers face when having to sift through competing scientific reports to inform policy. Science is used politically in ways that allow for contestation and recontestation, often with the bounds of public acceptability forming an important part of the political debate. You will learn about the concept of *bounded rationality* (Simon, 1947), which illuminates how the broad array of information available on environmental issues can be confusing for policy-makers. Indeed, the findings of different studies can imply different optimal policy outputs.

Third, we take up the theme of post-politics, a term used to explain how political causes become depoliticised through mainstreaming and corporate takeover. We do this through considering some of the narratives that challenge the way veganism has developed in the UK as a political cause. This discussion shows how environmental and animal movements leak into debates related to political economy, feminism and social justice, and how post-politics undermines pluralism.

The dynamic nature of political and lifestyle activism: From splinter groups to government interlocuters

Many mainstream environmental NGOs that are now so central to UK environmental governance – like Friends of the Earth – emerged as radical groups, disenchanted with their more moderate forebears. Formerly radical environmental NGOs in Britain have become semi-institutionalised; put differently, they used to struggle to get through the doors of Westminster but now find them ajar (Rootes, 2013). The situation is similar with The Vegan Society. It emerged as a splinter group from the Vegetarian Society, concerned that the Vegetarian Society was not going far enough to reduce the harm of *all* forms of animal exploitation caused by human diets. In turn, the Vegetarian Society was concerned that espousing a vegan diet would reduce its appeal to broad swathes of the public because of its more drastic divergence from conventional UK diets (Wrenn, 2019).

Initially, veganism focused on food and drink products only (Cross, 2013) but eventually broadened out to all consumables. According to the Vegan Society, veganism is 'a philosophy and way of living which seeks to exclude – as far as is possible and practicable – all forms of exploitation of, and cruelty to, animals for food, clothing or other purpose' (Vegan Society n.d.-a). The Vegan Society's definition of veganism is perhaps purposively vague in recognising the limits on the possibility and practicality of its key aspiration. For example, many supposedly vegan food products rely, in their production, on destroying agricultural pests. The encompassing nature of the modern definition of veganism allows it to be linked with a variety of other political causes including anti-speciesism, anti-racism, feminism (Adams, 2010a[1990]), environmentalism and health (Wrenn, 2019), but is also linked with punk, and its emphasis on morality ties it to many forms of spirituality and religious movements (Cherry, 2021). We return to discuss some controversies around veganism in the section on pluralism in UK environmental politics. For now, we situate veganism within a broader animal and environmental assemblage, illustrating the variety of tactics and foci of animal movements and their rhizomatic power.

Organisations within the animal and related environmental movement are diverse. They are sometimes more and sometimes less connected with flows of information and energy to environmental movements. They form dynamic assemblages that I refer to in some of my other work as 'environmental networks' (Saunders, 2014).

Similar to environmental organisations writ large, there are two key ways to categorise the different types of animal organisations in the UK animal movement: by their action repertoires and by their foci. In relation to action repertoires, Munro (2005) identifies four classes of tactics employed by the animal movement: persuasion (e.g. petitions, leaflets, poems and bearing witness), protest (e.g. demonstrations, theatrical events and media stunts), non-cooperation (e.g. civil disobedience, legal obstructions and ethical vegetarianism/veganism) and intervention (animal rescue, sit-ins and blockades). Persuasion in the animal movement often uses what Jasper and Poulsen (1995) call 'moral shocks', which draw on highly emotive pictures and text to point out the maltreatment of animals in dominant industrial food systems and laboratories. Many-a-time have I seen moral shock imagery on the back of public lavatory doors in the UK. In this way, environmental politics invades even our most private public spaces! The jury is out on whether moral shocks are effective for recruitment to environmental and animal activism. They might work better for those already ideologically inclined to caring about animals but are likely to fail among members of society more broadly for whom animals are decentred by the tendency to treat animals as a missing referent – as if meat and other products from dead animals were not once sentient creatures (Adams, 2010a; Arcari et al., 2021; Wrenn, 2013). It is important to note that most of the actions engaged in by animal movement activists in the UK are non-violent. This contrasts with dominant media representations of activists that often disproportionately emphasise threatening behaviour like letter bombing and arson attacks (Munro, 2005).

In the 2020s, and into the foreseeable future, we must also add to Munro's (2005) schemata information and communications technology (ICT) based strategies. These continue to be important to animal activism but were central to vegan advocacy and awareness raising during the Covid-19 lock-downs in 2020 and 2021. Vegan Outreach, for example, formed in the early 1990s as an educational initiative espousing the benefits of veganism to young people at schools and colleges. During the pandemic, it significantly altered its tactics to reach out to people through ICT strategies. Operational across multiple countries, Vegan Outreach's *10 Weeks to Vegan* guided action plan has over a quarter of a million people signing up to it each year. Between January and November 2022, 350,000 people across the world signed up. The Vegan Society, similarly, has a VeGuide app, which assists people to make vegan consumer choices. Such online tools provide a variety of services to vegans from helping them to become aware of background issues to developing vegan product literacy and shaping identities (Lawo et al., 2020).

In relation to foci, Munro (2012), in a different article, identifies the following strands of animal activism: animal welfare, animal liberation, animal rights and radical animal liberation. Animal welfare is concerned with ensuring that domesticated animals are kept in humane conditions (e.g. Royal Society for the Protection of Birds and Compassion in World Farming). Animal liberation seeks to set animals free from human domination (e.g. British Society for the Abolition of Vivisection). Animal rights views animals as sentient beings (e.g. PETA). And radical animal liberation seeks no compromise in defence of animals (e.g. Animal Liberation Front). To this list, I would also add animal rescue and promoting veganism. Animal rescue locates, rehomes and looks after mistreated and unwanted animals. Archetypal examples of animal rescue organisations are the Donkey Sanctuary and Hillside Animal Sanctuary. The promotion of veganism, by pro-vegan organisations like the Vegan Society, is multifaceted: raising awareness, helping people convert to and remain committed to veganism and lobbying for change at the government level. It is worth pointing out that these are not mutually exclusive categories: there is overlap between and among these wings of the animal movement, which together make a complex network – or assemblage – of organisations. It is also the case that vegetarianism and veganism intersect, although perhaps less in the animal welfare wing.

Each of these foci are often related to particular strategies (see Table 13.1). To understand why so many different types of animal organisations exist, see Theory box below.

Table 13.1 Animal movement foci and strategies

Foci	Strategies	Organisational example
Vegan diet	Promoting vegan diet	Vegan Society
Animal welfare	Awareness-raising Lobbying Legal tactics	Compassion in World Farming (CiWF)
Animal liberation	Unconventional legal tactics Bearing witness Civil disobedience	British Society for the Abolition of Vivisection
Animal rights	Disruption Radical Militant (but non-violent)	People for the Ethical Treatment of Animals
Radical animal liberation movement	Illegal Violent Terrorist/extremist	Animal Liberation Front
Animal rescue	Finding and caring for animals abused by humans in service or science	Hillside Animal Sanctuary

(Based on Munro, 2012)

Theory box: Organisational ecology

Why do so many different types of animal and environmental organisations exist? And how do they manage to maintain themselves when competition for members and volunteers is high? To help answer these questions, we can turn to organisational ecology. Organisational ecology draws on population ecology (from neoclassical biosciences) to argue that organisations are affected by other organisations that exist in the organisational landscape (Hannan and Freeman, 1977, 1989). They survive by carefully crafting out a niche for themselves. This involves differentiating themselves from other similar organisations so that they have something uniquely marketable to 'sell' to potential supporters. Niches are developed through sets of interacting processes among organisational fields related to target markets, issue foci, ideologies and organisational forms. Along the way, organisations collaborate, conflict and compete. One can tell that an organisation has found its niche when it is able to sustain itself or grow. Organisations that do not have niches will find themselves in direct competition with other organisations and may struggle to survive due to competition for resources, or confusion among the public over who-does-which types of action.

The organisational ecology of the animal movement illustrates the tensions that arise in UK environmental movement organisations as old groups mature, professionalise and sometimes become tamer, and new groups emerge to form the vanguard. The Vegan Society has developed from a radical anti-speciesism organisation to a professionalised NGO concerned with its survival. It has to maintain its reputation to be able to influence governments as well as to pay for its premises and staff. Its professionalism has allowed it to broaden is public appeal, but, in so-doing, it risks upsetting its grassroots supporters. It has tried to distance itself from the broader animal movement so as not to attract negative attention from police, counter-terrorists and counter-movements (Wrenn, 2019).

Compassion in World Farming (CiWF) has faced similar issues. It was established by a British farmer in 1967 who was disgusted with the ways in which animals were treated in (then newly emerging) intensive agricultural systems. It works on undercover investigations, lobbying and campaigning and directly influencing businesses to reduce the suffering of animals in farming systems. It is perhaps most famous for its involvement in campaigns against the live export of calves, especially at the port of Brightlingsea, which it considered to be cruel and barbaric (McLeod, 1988). Like the Vegan Society, it is a professional NGO that seeks to maintain its reputation so as not to jeopardise the support it receives from the public. CiWF has also been keen not to be associated with more radical protests that have used force – and sometimes violence – to prevent the live exports of animals (see Case studies below).

Case studies: Real-life stories and the politics of the everyday

Jill Phipps (1964–1995) sadly passed away in her early thirties while doing service for animals. She is often hailed as a courageous animal activist, even a martyr. She died in the most tragic of circumstances.

Jill had a long history of animal rights activism – she was a fervent rescuer of dogs and attended her first demonstration against the fur trade with her mother, aged only 11. She continued to attend protests with her friends and family. Indeed, personal networks are a known predictor of engagement in activism, particularly in the riskier forms of activism in which Jill engaged as she grew older (Saunders, 2022). Aged 21, she participated in a protest that involved sabotaging the property of a company that was damaging animals by testing its products on them. She only narrowly escaped arrest. She continued to attend protests against vivisection and hunt saboteur meetings. On her 31st birthday, she was involved in a demonstration against Phoenix Aviation, an airline company that exported live calves by air out of Coventry airport. Masked protesters later smashed the windows of the CEO's home property. It was not known if Jill was one of these protesters. On the tragic day, not long after, she was so committed to stopping live exports that she put her body in front of an articulated lorry in the freight yard at Coventry airport. Perhaps the driver didn't see her? Perhaps it was the fault of the police that she was not noticed? She unfortunately ended up crushed under the wheels of a lorry in the freight yard, proclaimed dead on the arrival of paramedics. Due to a lack of evidence, the lorry driver was not found guilty of manslaughter (Vallely, 1995).

Her story is one of commitment and sorrow, with huge ramifications for her friends, family, fellow activists and the wider animal movement. RIP Jill Phipps.

It is also worth briefly drawing attention to Animal Rising, which was initially a splinter group of Extinction Rebellion that has veganism at the centre of its attention and which directly challenges the industrial meat complex. It formed out of disillusionment with Extinction

Image 13.2 Extinction Rebellion activists march for animal justice (London, 28 August 2021).

© Photo by BradleyStearn on Shutterstock

Rebellion's initial exclusion of these issues (Arcari et al., 2021). It has routinely engaged in civil disobedience and sabotage of industrial outlets and offices that it sees driving unsustainable food production and consumption.

The animal rights assemblage has been successful in maintaining itself: like rhizomes that are hard to destroy, new grassroots organisations have emerged, while more mature elements of the assemblage have institutionalised. In 1944, when the Vegan Society was established, few had heard of the notion of veganism, and political institutions in the UK barely recognised animal rights as a concern. Fast forward to the present time, and we can see a significant shift in public awareness and acceptance of veganism. Vegan products and dishes are, these days, readily available in shops and serveries throughout the UK. Although some have acclaimed that there has been a mainstreaming of veganism, whose popularity has increased dramatically in recent years (Sexton et al., 2022), it is estimated that fewer than 4 per cent of the UK population are vegans (YouGov, 2022). Dominant discourse in the UK is still somewhat vegaphobic (Cole and Morgan, 2011). The politics of environmental veganism are felt acutely in everyday life through the ridiculing of vegans, characterising them as overly sensitive, ascetic or hostile and belittling the relative ease of veganism for those committed. Non-vegans might denigrate vegans as a means to feel alright about their own, arguably less ethical, practices, to obtain cognitive dissonance and to preserve their own identities (De Groeve and Rosenfeld, 2021).

Moreover, there have been major changes in the Vegan Society's ability to access, to be heard by, and to collaborate with UK representative institutions. Select committees, and departmental consultations associated with government departments, allow the Vegan Society to put evidence forward to inquiries on cross-cutting issues.

In general, it is very difficult to ascertain the outcomes of social movements (Roth and Saunders, 2023, Chapter 7). This is because there could be multiple other factors that have influenced a government's policy decisions. However, it is possible to trace lines of argument from the Vegan Society and other vegan advocacy through to the UK government's *National Food Strategy* (Defra, 2021). The *Strategy* emphasises that 'substantial shifts [away from meat] are required if we are to reduce the environmental and health impacts of our consumption, while supporting the high standards of food, farming and animal welfare that the public expects' (Defra, 2021: 202). Among the recommendations is the importance of investing in alternative meat-free proteins, which it estimates would create an additional 10,000 manufacturing jobs and the retention of 6,500 jobs in agriculture (Defra, 2021).

The Vegan Society's contribution to Defra's *Health and Harmony* inquiry (2018) was one of 43,356 consultation responses. The Vegan Society's arguments about the need to move beyond animal exploitation were lost among a sea of voices, with dominant policy approaches remaining, in the Vegan Society's view, rather tokenistic in relation to animal health and welfare (n.d.-b). In 2017, the All-Party Parliamentary Group on Vegetarianism and Veganism was founded consisting of one independent MP, three from the Labour party and one from the Conservative party who share an interest in vegetarianism and veganism, including 'catering, public health, environmental issues and animal rights' (UK Parliament, 2022c). This group is sponsored by the Vegan Society, which coordinated a Veganuary Parliamentary Reception at Westminster Hall in January 2023. One of the group's recent meetings has been on climate friendly and plant-based catering, aiming to normalise vegan catering, which ties in with work to this effect being undertaken by the Behavioural Insights Team. Group members write individual and group letters to secretaries of state (for Health and Social Care, and for Environment, Food and Rural Affairs), sharing insights and lobbying for change. But this group is one of many select committees that are all clamouring for attention from policy-makers. How do UK environmental policy-makers decide which issues to focus on and how to solve them? Scientific evidence plays a major role in shaping such decisions. But which scientific evidence is used? And is it always objectively shaping policy?

Policy-makers' dilemma: The scientific construction of environmental knowledge

Environmental problems are real. We can often see, smell, hear or touch the problems and implement programmes of work to redress them with measurable differences. However, it is important to recognise that humans' understandings of problems and solutions are, at least to some extent, *socially constructed* from the so-called facts that we have available to us and the way we set up, shape and approach those facts.

Inevitably, in their seeking of evidence, or their setting up of inquiries, UK environmental and climate policymakers are guided by their pre-existing assumptions and extant knowledge. They will also have their finger on the pulse of public opinion and media discourse and will be influenced by other actors such as think tanks, interest groups, their own political party and rival political parties, trade unions and industry. Policymakers will most probably not sign up to journal articles to proactively discover relevant (social) science, but will find information through parliamentary briefings, policy briefings, the mass media, social media channels, responses to select committee inquiries and government/departmental inquiries or through other forms of lobbying. They may, therefore, see and be receptive to only a relatively limited array of evidence before making decisions.

Despite scientific consensus on anthropogenic climate change, it is important to recognise the complexity of environmental knowledge, and the challenges that this brings to UK policymakers. Nobody has comprehensive knowledge and there is no such thing as 100 per cent objective measurement of environmental problems. Indeed, there is perhaps no such thing as a rational UK environmental policymaker who can pick an optimal policy solution based on the evidence available. In the environmental politics literature (Connelly et al., 2012), this problem is referred to using the concept of bounded rationality (Simon, 1945). Decision-makers have individual and organisational 'bounds' that limit both their knowledge and their capacity. It is simply not possible for anyone to achieve objective rationality because of the trillions of pieces of formal and informal evidence that would need to be assembled and assimilated to reach such a state. Simon (1945: 79) stated that 'even an approximation to objective rationality is hard to conceive'. Historically, UK environmental policymakers have filtered information, expressing preference for hard science over richer and more contextualised qualitative evidence, often benefiting economies and technological entrepreneurs and negatively affecting communities (Grove-White, 1999).

Even supposedly objective science is based on subjective decisions. The scientific discipline(s) drawn upon to construct a scientific study shapes the ways scientists frame problems, the instruments they use to measure them, the definition and operationalisation of key concepts and variables, the analytical choices that scientists make and the decisions they make in the presentation of results. As Pinch (1990) wrote: 'Physics, mathematics and biology can and have been shown to be treatable as socially constructed bodies of knowledge ... Scientists (like jazz pianists, cordon bleu cooks or lawyers) are specialists who are encultured into a body of practices and skills' (Pinch, 1990: 295).

Science has also been criticised for producing generalising arguments that do not fit specific localised situations. Wynne (1992), for example, famously critiqued the way the Ministry of Agriculture Farming and Food (now reorganised into Defra) drew on a particular type of environmental evidence to advise sheep farmers in Cumbria, Wales how to manage their livestock in the aftermath of radioactive fallout from the Chernobyl nuclear disaster in 1986. Farmers themselves, familiar with their own land, would probably have been able to manage the situation more appropriately using their own deeply situated lay knowledge.

Many vegans in the UK, as well as the UK-based animal and environmental NGOs that provide networks of support for them, argue that veganism has a significant role to play in helping reduce global greenhouse gas emissions. At face value, data on the proportion of greenhouse gas emissions deriving from animal farming makes a strong and convincing case for veganism. As Pendergrast (2016: 107) writes, 'growing awareness of the environmental consequences of consuming animal products, in addition to mainstream recognition of animal rights and health benefits, has played a significant role in the rising interest in veganism'. The vegan movement's turn to environmentalism may have helped veganism to recruit new supporters, but it has not always been popular among vegans themselves. Wrenn's (2019) analysis of copies of *The Vegan* (the Vegan Society's newsletter) reports a letter from a member published in 2005 complaining about the distraction of 'unrelated radicalism' (Wrenn, 2019: 201).

Today, the Vegan Society claims that 'one of the most effective things an individual can do to lower their carbon footprint is to avoid all animal products' (Vegan Society n.d.-c). Its website refers to issues with cow flatulence that produces methane gas and air pollution, and with animal feed (grain and soya) production that drives deforestation and habitat loss and requires vast amounts of land and water. A key issue with meat production is that protein, water and energy get lost in the food cycle because animals consume magnitudes more of these than they produce. There are, therefore, significant land and energy efficiencies to be gained from humans consuming grains rather than feeding grains to cattle.

The information presented on the Vegan Society's website at the time of writing draws heavily on scientific evidence presented in the Food and Agriculture Organisation of the UN's (FAO) report on *Tackling Climate Change through Livestock* report (Gerber et al., 2013). It uses this source to highlight these concerns in the context of rapidly rising meat consumption throughout the world, which is on course to double from 2013 levels by 2050. A report like this, from a renowned organisation like the FAO, has been important in legitimising the Vegan Society's environmental claims about a vegan diet. It was preceded by the FAO's well-reported *Livestock's Long Shadow* report in 2006 (FAO, 2006), which catapulted the relationship between meat and climate change into the public realm in the early noughties. The 2006 report boldly highlighted the significant effects of livestock on land degradation, atmosphere, climate, water and species diversity, concluding that 'The livestock sector emerges as one of the top two or three most significant contributors to the most serious environmental problems ... [and] the impact is so significant that it needs to be addressed with urgency' (FAO, 2006: xx).

Back in the early 2000s, I remember doing a crude greenhouse gas calculator assessment for my food consumption with a fellow Friends of the Earth activist. As a vegan, my scores came out incredibly low. My fellow activists' carbon footprint from food was through the roof, but the only meat she ate was her own extensively reared and incredibly local lamb. I was left feeling smug, but she, perhaps quite rightly, questioned some of the assumptions behind the greenhouse gas calculator.

Some studies have estimated that a vegan diet can reduce overall emissions from food by a particular amount. For example, Berners-Lee et al. (2012) estimated this to be 26 per cent, and Green et al. (2015) estimated it to be 40 per cent. However, without a full understanding of what a vegan diet consists of – to my knowledge no-one has yet conducted a robust study of what UK vegans actually eat (i.e. how much is processed, frozen or imported) – it is not possible to accurately pinpoint specific percentages in this way. The balance of evidence currently available seems to suggest, though, that a vegan diet could make a significant contribution to reductions in greenhouse gas emissions. A systematic review of 63 studies examining the effects of different types of diets on the environment found that vegan, vegetarian and then pescetarian diets respectively were generally the least damaging to the environment. But it wasn't all positive. A vegan diet was found to have higher rates of water usage than several other diet categories (Aleksandrowicz et al., 2016).

There are many other valid counterarguments to vegans' claims about the negative effects of meat eating in relation to farmers' livelihoods and lifestyles and the environmental externalities of alternatives to meat. My local farm shop in Cornwall (nominally in the UK, despite historical and ongoing struggles for independence), produces organic beef, and the farmer is adamant about the value of low intensity agriculture for maintaining his land. The fertility of his soil depends heavily on the organic and locally produced fertiliser that his cows produce to feed his fruit and vegetable crops. Indeed, one might quite logically draw attention to the negative externalities of chemical-based fertilisers in the absence of silage in a resource-challenged context.

The environmental journalist George Monbiot has further raised UK public awareness of the environmental effects of meat-based diets and the need for more sustainable alternatives (Monbiot, 2022). His book *Regenesis* (2023), which elucidates a host of worrying issues with livestock production and proposes a shift to human consumption of grain and laboratory-created meat instead, is already being acclaimed a new *Silent Spring*, Rachel Carson's (1962) book, which pointed out the devastating ecological effects of the pesticide DDT (full name dichlorodiphenyltrichloroethane), and has often been hailed an important forebear of the modern (i.e. post-1970s) environmental movement.

Yet *Regenesis*' claims are highly contested in UK environmental politics discourse, not least because public appeal for veganism is low and many people, including vegans themselves, are sceptical about laboratory-produced meat. In the Summer of 2022, the *Guardian* published a series of letters from farmers in response to Monbiot's arguments. Farmer Simon Fairlie from Charmouth, Dorset, who farms Jersey cows, pointed out that the meta-study Monbiot had cited to illustrate a negative relationship between grazing and biodiversity also referred, elsewhere, to grazing having 'a positive effect on plant diversity' and that in some environments grazing is 'a required management technique to support native biodiversity'. An ecological assessment of the biological diversity of his own grazing lands showed tens of species of plants, and a great variety of insects, birds and mammals. To stop grazing, he argued, would result in the land being converted to bramble and bracken in the short term and tree coverage in the long term. To him, mixed grazing and the resultant biologically diverse land is preferable to ubiquitous forest cover (Fairlee, 2022). Indeed, the well-known custodian of the UK countryside, the National Trust, continues with high levels of success to use livestock grazing to maintain upland heaths, calcareous grasslands and lowland/coastal heaths (Hearn, 1995). It is perhaps important to point out that not all forms of livestock farming have identical and generalisable effects on the environment.

Exploring the benefits to the environment of small amounts of restorative animal-based agriculture is a relatively new scientific field, perhaps struggling to get attention given the political salience of the 'meat is bad for the environment' storyline in the UK. Regenerative pastoral (livestock) farming, it is claimed by some, can, in the right amounts as part of a mixed cropping system, help to regenerate degraded farmland, and lock in carbon, even achieving carbon neutrality (e.g. see Rowntree et al., 2020). Doubtless, critics will find ways to socially deconstruct this branch of science just as vegans' arguments about the environmental impacts of meat eating can be deconstructed by other alternative scientific findings. The 'Spotlight on research' below further illustrates how pastoral beef farmers can be represented variously from being 'conservation heroes' through to 'climate villains' (Hallgren et al., 2020).

Spotlight on research: Farmers – heroes or villains?

In their chapter 'Conservation hero and climate villain binary identies of Swedish farmers' in the *Routledge Handbook of Ecocultural Identity*, Hallgren and colleagues (2020) discuss the ways in which farmers are generally represented as either 'conservation heroes', responsible for helping the ecological diversity of semi-natural pastures, or as 'climate villains', responsible for the destruction of the environment via the production of vast amounts of greenhouse gas emissions. The 'hero' image views semi-natural pasture farmers as moral actors who have unique knowledge about the landscape and nature and use this to benefit the environment and society more broadly. According to this image, they produce healthier good quality meat compared to imported or intensely farmed meat, ensure the preservation of beautiful landscapes (to which grazing contributes) and also assure animal welfare. This trope is supported by some important Swedish nature conservation organisations that present semi-natural pasture farmers as important contributors to biodiversity and the preservation of endangered key species. Moreover, farming is seen as a vulnerable livelihood – one that involves long hours and low pay – and it is engaged in for love of the land and animals more than for profit.

The alternative 'villain' trope tends to blame *meat* rather than farmers for environmental damage but implies that farmers are driving climate change and that their activities are generally immoral. This way of conceiving of semi-natural pasture farmers may conflate them with mass/intensive livestock farming. This approach has been given credence by the FAO (2006) report, media attention and advocacy from the environmental, vegetarian and vegan lobbies.

Which label is the right one? What do you think? And why?

Post-politics and the undermining of pluralism

Several UK governments have committed themselves to the delivery of sustainable development, just as the current Conservative government has committed itself to reducing greenhouse gas emissions from meat production. But are these commitments genuine? Many commentators have written about the rhetoric–reality gap in UK sustainable development policy (Revell, 2005). Sustainable development is often considered to be a guise for business as usual painted with a green tinge. Is commitment to reducing greenhouse gases by reducing demand for meat similarly tokenistic? We explore these arguments in this section through the lenses of pluralism and post-politics.

UK climate–environment–food politics extends beyond science, movements and political institutions. There are also entanglements with the political economy. Perhaps vegetarian and vegan lobbying is not responsible for the UK's recent policy emphasis on non-meat alternative proteins to protect the environment. Instead, this emphasis might simply be reflecting economic opportunism. What has been noted in UK environment–food policy documents themselves is the relative success of meat-free proteins used in US food systems, including the Impossible Burger that appears 'bloody' like the real thing and now accounts for 10 per cent of McDonald's burger sales in the US (Defra, 2021: 124). Corporate veganism, referred to as 'Big Veganism' by Sexton et al. (2022), illustrates the ethical dilemmas in the political economy of veganism. Big Veganism has trade-offs. Although widespread availability of vegan products through fast food outlets and supermarkets is useful for converting more people to a life less dependent on animal exploitation and greenhouse-gas-intensive meat, it goes against the ethos of many vegans who oppose large-scale industrial agriculture. It feeds the corporate giants in ways that are exploitative to consumers *and* arable farmers by relying on high-tech processes that produce food of little tested and sometimes-dubious nutritional quality, while undercutting farmers and paying staff low wages to provide cheap food to customers.

In the UK in the 1980s, vegans needed to make their own plant-based milk alternatives from soya beans. In the early 1990s, the purchase of vegan milk alternatives required shopping in (mostly independent) alternative health food stores. In the 2020s, one can find a variety of plant-based milks in all the major supermarkets. One could question the extent to which Big Veganism is an effective political alternative in the modern world where food giants are continuing to corner markets, undercut farmers and prop up the most intensive and least environmentally and animal friendly forms of agriculture.

This underlies a broader picture in environmental politics. Generally, environmental issues that are easy to solve within dominant social, political and economic systems are fixable much more readily than those that require drastic changes to ways of doing things. It is, perhaps, for this reason that the Montreal Protocol (1987) to phase out CFCs and other ozone-depleting chemicals was easy for countries to agree on and to enact. It required a shift in the gases used in refrigeration and in aerosols rather than their complete phasing out. It had little impact on our overall way of life. By contrast, action on climate change has been more difficult to secure (and agree on across nations), perhaps because of its complexity (Connelly et al., 2012). Likewise, we might expect a complete shift in the UK away from exploitative agricultural systems to be more difficult to get traction for than investment in plant-based protein products that can sit within otherwise existing exploitative models of food production.

There are, therefore, resonances between Giraud's (2021) concept of post-veganism and what Blühdorn (2007) calls post-environmentalism. The concern captured by both of these concepts is that once quite radical narratives that had the potential to drastically alter and improve our relationships with animals and the environment have been co-opted into mainstream ways doing things. There is plenty of evidence to suggest that this is happening in the forms of UK environmental politics that surround our every day lives. The label 'plant-based' is thought to co-opt vegan narratives and practices, moving them away from the countercultures involved in securing, sharing and transforming relatively cheap unprocessed staple foods sourced from plants. As hinted at earlier, the term 'sustainable development' has similarly been somewhat diluted to justify, rather than fundamentally alter, business as usual (Saunders, forthcoming).

Post-politics also comes to recognise the ways in which pluralism is undermined rather than strengthened in the UK environmental assemblage. A vegan magazine selling the diet through standardised forms of sexual objectification of women undermines feminist and queer politics (Wright, 2015), just as environmental magazines that feature mostly white people undermine decolonial and anti-racist projects (Yarborough and Thomas, 2010).

Carol Adams, author of *The Sexual Politics of Meat* (1990), pointed out how meat is sexualised in Western society. Her multifaceted argument can be boiled down to several key points. First, barbecues and steak houses, she argued, had become places of male fraternity. Having blood on one's hands and being in charge of or standing around the barbecue are seen as especially male things to do. The female's role is to serve the meat, or to be otherwise servile to it. Second, she argued that the animals used to produce meat are often a 'missing referent' (note how we talk of beef not cows), which has allowed suffering to be overlooked or even mocked. Third, she argued that meat was part of an animal–industrial complex that exploits feminised protein (think of eggs and milk). Fourth, she was particularly critical of the way in which People for the Ethical Treatment of Animals (PETA) sexualised women, exploiting them and presenting them as if they themselves are animals. To be a vegetarian (or vegan) was thus, for her, intrinsically linked to opposing the patriarchy.

The sexualisation of meat has continued into the 21st century (Adams, 2010a, 2010b). More recently, PETA has used body-perfect models, with their body parts marked 'loin, round, rib, chuck, et cetera' (Adams, 2010b: 306), to encourage people to become vegetarian by stressing the sentience of animals through their biological similarities to humans, using the message that 'All Animals Have the Same Parts'. In a second rendition a Filipina model was used, perhaps responsive to concerns about racial representation. However, this does not escape the sexualisation of women that has been opposed by the UK women's liberation movement since its inception. For Adams (2010b: 306), such practice 'sadly confirms how intractable and interconnected oppressions are.' In accepting heterosexual (semi?) pornographic images of white women for the cause of animal rights, moral violence is performed to people of colour, to women and to those who identify as queer. This is problematised in a post-politics frame through its justification of several dominant, but harmful, ways of doing things. These are objectifying the perfect body, justifying the sexualisation of women, entrenching classical (but unrealistic) ideals of beauty – with damaging effects on many women's mental and physical health – and assuming and therefore promoting notions of white supremacy and heterosexuality, all of which sideline others' important alternative stories at the sharp end of UK politics.

Conclusion

Environmental politics is everywhere! It is in what we buy, how we dress and what we eat. It is not only in our lifestyles, but also embedded into the political economy of the country. It is carried through people, through groups and organisations, through norms, through socio-politics and through institutions. These actors influence one another in an environmental assemblage, which is dynamic and evolving, but always developing new rhizomatic structures in the shape of grassroots activism and lifestyles. Circulating through this system are a variety of forms of knowledge, some of which are deeply contextualised, others of which are highly generalised (many are a mixture). The ways in which forms of environmental knowledge 'stick' to key decision-makers is dependent on policymakers' own understandings and preferences for particular ways of measuring and understanding the environment. As vegan–environmental discourses (like sustainable development discourses before them) gain traction in public and policy spheres, we can begin to reveal a post-political scene, one in which the contradictions of dominant systems are revealed by attempts to mainstream environmental challenges. In response, new forms of activism will appear. Like rhizomes they will be difficult to erase, and environmental politics continues to evolve dynamically.

Key take-home points

- Environmental and climate politics in the UK is a packed assemblage with complex and dynamic links among contexts, actors, institutions and knowledge.
- Environmental organisations in the UK often mature and institutionalise, encouraging new and more radical groups to emerge.
- Environmental knowledge in the UK is complex and contested, and policymakers are more likely to favour established or generalised knowledge bases.
- The success of the UK environmental movement is hard to measure. Environmental discourses can become mainstreamed and shape policy, but their radical edge can be lost in the process.
- Post-politics reveals tensions that dominant approaches to environmental and animal issues cause, leading to upsets between and among different movements (environmental, queer, gender, sex).

Annotated reading list

Giraud, E.H. (2021) *Veganism: Politics, Practice and Theory*. London: Bloomsbury Academic Press.

This is a comprehensive resource on the political roots and consequences of veganism. It contributes to literatures on politics, social movements, counter-cultures and food studies. It provides a thorough exploration of the different ways in which veganism is expressed: identity, food, diet, agriculture, labour, cruelty-free and more. The history of veganism and the organisations supporting it are explained, revealing similarities with the ways in which environmental movement organisations evolve. The book particularly explores the entanglements of human and non-human exploitation. The term 'intersectional veganism' is coined to shed light on the ways in which vegan politics talks to other pressing political concerns including environmentalism, (anti-)racism, speciesism and sexism. Although the author carefully positions herself as a vegan, the book is not simply pro-vegan. Importantly, it includes a scathing critique of post-veganism, otherwise known as 'the rise of plant-based capitalism'. This important discussion reveals the problems with the appropriation of veganism as a commodity created and sold by large agricultural companies, which replicate structural problems with existing food systems. Food systems that exploit people, environments, technologies and genes to create cheap plant-based alternatives to meat are a far cry from the grassroots vegan movement that focuses on cheap, natural, equitable and shared food. In this way, the book warns of the dangers of lifestyle activism being co-opted by the very sources it initially sought to resist.

Blüdhorn, I. (2000) *Post-Ecologist Politics: Social Theory and the Abdication of the Ecologist Paradigm*. Winwick: The White Horse Press.

This seminal work in the development of green political theory offers a trenchant critique of hopeful forms of thinking through and resisting environmental change. Many green political theorists, like the social movements they may support, and like the grassroots vegan activism we explore in this chapter, seek to change the fundamental basis of society to encourage it to become more environmentally friendly. For Blüdhorn, this is a pipe dream and is non-attainable, not least because environmental movements are, in his view, at best supported by a minority and gently smiled upon as benevolent. He argues that environmental change is constant, and that the forces of capitalism, guided by technocentrism (i.e. a belief that technology can save us), will inevitably corrupt attempts to genuinely put humans in tune with ecological systems. (We see elements of this happening in the shift towards Big Veganism). This results in a favouritism among policymakers and many members of the public towards an approach known as ecological modernisation – that is, a belief that society, technology and environment sit in a mutually reinforcing win–win–win triangle. Technologically oriented capitalism and the cultures that accompany it are, according to Blüdhorn, impossible to disentangle, rendering the challenge one of coming to terms with humans' out-of-step relationship to the environment, rather than attempting but failing to change it. For many, this represents a defeatist and unwelcome contribution to the literature on environmental politics, but Blüdhorn also has a scary sense of realism. His arguments help explain why capitalist systems keep winning over the environment, and why it has been difficult to institute effective environmental policies in Western democracies to date.

14
Britain in the world

Ben Whitham

Image 14.1 British military personnel speaking at a training centre for the Afghan Armed Forces, Kabul, Afghanistan, c.2008 © Photo by Rob Leyland on Shutterstock

Learning objectives

By the end of this chapter you should be able to:

- Understand the significance of the Brexit referendum and the contested foreign policy narrative of 'Global Britain'
- Understand the contentious relationship between public opinion and British foreign policy
- Understand Britain's historical and contemporary role(s) and status in the world, and the extent to which these have or have not been shaped by pluralistic influences
- Discuss key controversies of British foreign policy in the Middle East
- Discuss Britain and 'Anglo-America' as assemblages in the world

Chapter overview

The UK's politics do not begin or end at its territorial borders – and in any case, these borders have not been static throughout history. This chapter explores British politics by considering how they are enmeshed in the wider world. From 'internal colonialism' and the formation of Great Britain and the UK, through the British Empire, to post-Brexit foreign policy entanglements and controversies, the chapter will show what it means to think of the UK as an 'assemblage': not a neatly defined, territorially bounded sovereign actor, but rather a messy, sometimes blurred, and often violent constellation of political, economic and military power in the world.

Introduction

The Brexit referendum and its aftermath

In June 2016, the UK held a national referendum – a popular vote in which the entire electorate was entitled to participate – on an issue of foreign policy: whether the country should remain a member of the European Union (EU), or leave.

A total of 33.6 million people voted in the 'Brexit' referendum, amounting to 72.2 per cent of the British electorate. Of those who voted, 17.4 million (52%) voted for the UK to leave, while 16.1 million (48%) voted for the UK to remain in the EU (Electoral Commission, 2016). In the hours after the referendum results were announced, the prime minister of the UK's Conservative party government, David Cameron, delivered a speech in which he confirmed: 'The British people have voted to leave the European Union and their will must be respected' (Cameron, 2016).

In practice, it would be three-and-a-half years before the UK finalised its exit from the EU, on 31 January 2020. Even then, a specially negotiated treaty (the Withdrawal Agreement) between the UK and EU provided for a transition period in which the UK would continue to pay into the EU budget and retain EU laws. At the time of writing, in 2023, technical and legal issues – especially in relation to the Withdrawal Agreement's Northern Ireland Protocol – remain unresolved.

Why was the Brexit referendum such a remarkable, pivotal moment in British political history? There are several reasons that are commonly discussed:

- First, the referendum's outcome came as a shock to many, including political scientists and public opinion pollsters who specialise in predicting the outcome of votes. Up to the eve of the referendum, most of the major public opinion polling companies were publishing results that suggested a small but decisive majority for remaining in the EU (YouGov, 2016; Ipsos, 2016).
- Second, the leaders of both major political parties (Conservative and Labour) and many of the smaller political parties holding seats in parliament (including the Scottish National Party, the Liberal Democrats, and the Green Party) had all preferred and promoted a 'remain' vote. Cameron's Conservative government, which had made calling a referendum one of its key 2015 general election pledges, went so far as to post a leaflet to every household in the country entitled 'Why the Government believes that voting to remain in the European Union is the best decision for the UK', setting out evidence in support of a remain position (HM Government, 2016).
- Third – and of no small relevance to understanding the surprise of some at the outcome – the referendum seemed to act as a cypher for a whole host of broader social and political issues and tensions. In particular, 'leave' voters often cited immigration concerns (something right-wing politicians and news media had focused on heavily in the preceding years) as a key factor in their decision. Issues of race and racism, social class, welfare entitlements, unemployment, healthcare and social housing were all reported to be among the factors that leave voters were animated by. Some have suggested that a form of 'imperial nostalgia', encouraged by the leave campaign's 'taking back control' sloganeering, was at play in the vote. Theresa May characterised this, and political commentator David Goodhart made the same argument at length (Goodhart, 2017), as being a vote for British national identity and against a 'rootless' cosmopolitanism populated by 'citizens of nowhere'.
- Fourth, the referendum's campaigns and outcome stoked national conversations about elite political and economic power, the financing of political campaigns, foreign interference and cyber security, manipulation of public opinion, and the rise of a new transnational right-wing movement that connected pro-Brexit figures like Nigel Farage (then of the UK Independence Party) to the movement that swept Donald J. Trump to power as 45th president of the United States later in 2016, including a resurgent far-right. These issues remain particularly prominent in UK politics today, both in the so-called 'culture wars' between right-wing, left-wing, and centrist or liberal political values, and in the increasingly heavy influence of the Conservative Party's most right-wing fringe over its legislative and policy agenda.

Pluralism, the public and British foreign policy

A fifth, less widely-discussed reason to view the Brexit referendum as an unusual and important moment, is its very nature as a popular vote on a foreign policy issue. Foreign policy has been defined as '*a set of actions or rules governing the actions of an independent political authority deployed in the international environment*' (Morin and Paquin, 2018: 3 [emphasis in original]). The generic form of 'independent political authority' on the world stage is commonly taken to be the nation-state, and the foreign policies of such states can therefore be loosely defined as the sets of actions (and/or rules governing those actions) they pursue outside of their own territorial borders. Foreign policies therefore cover a huge range of urgent and contentious political issues, from trade and development aid to climate change and war, and of course membership of treaty-based international organisations like NATO and the EU. In this sense, that there should be a major national debate – and even a referendum – on a foreign policy question might not seem all that surprising. But historically, foreign policy has not been an area of pluralist politics and democratic scrutiny.

As the British historian and influential 'realist' theorist of international relations (IR) E.H. Carr noted in 1939: 'Down to 1914, the conduct of international relations was the concern of persons professionally engaged in it. In democratic countries, foreign policy was traditionally regarded as outside the scope of party politics' (Carr, 2016: 62 [1939]). While the two world wars helped to dispel the view that foreign policy was the sole domain of professional diplomatic and military 'experts', leading to the rise of public diplomacy in the 20th century, public opinion on foreign affairs remains a controversial and complex issue. The so-called 'Almond-Lippmann' consensus, developed in the 1950s, suggested that the general public's 'characteristic response to questions of foreign policy is one of indifference' (Almond, 1950: 53), while on those occasions where public opinion is more animated, it 'has been destructively wrong at the critical junctures' (Lippmann, 1955: 20). Sometimes called 'mood theory', this thesis posited that the great mass of ordinary people in a society are too ill-informed, and too fickle or emotional, to be involved in the grave matter of foreign policy decision-making.

Need to know: Public diplomacy

The Second World War – arguably a result of failed diplomacy after the First World War – cost millions of lives. In its aftermath, there was a turn against secrecy, and diplomacy became increasingly open, especially through high-level summits attended by journalists and NGOs as well as state representatives.

The British public's vote to leave the EU could be viewed as a validation of the Almond-Lippmann thesis. The leave vote was encouraged by pro-Brexit politicians like Nigel Farage and Michael Gove who denounced 'experts' and said that the public had 'had enough' of them, and Boris Johnson, who frequently made unsubstantiated claims that leaving the EU would actually improve life in Britain – including a vastly better-funded National Health Service (NHS). This popular pro-Brexit 'mood' ignored not only the guidance of all major political parties and the government itself but also the formally neutral civil servants of HM Treasury, which announced in April 2016 that 'a vote to leave would mean Britain would be permanently poorer' (HM Treasury, 2016). So why was the leave campaign successful? What vision of Britain did it offer that appealed to or shaped public opinion?

One key motif that emerged during the leave campaign, and which remains prominent in post-Brexit political discourse, is that of 'Global Britain'. The pro-Brexit movement, both before and after the referendum, promoted the idea that exiting the EU – leaving behind its supranational legal frameworks and collective approach to migration, security, trade and the world economy – would effectively 'free Britain up' to attain (or rather reclaim) its status as a dominant, independent, global power in world order. After David Cameron resigned as prime minister in 2016, having effectively lost the referendum, his successor Theresa May delivered a speech to the Conservative Party conference on what she called 'Global Britain, our ambitious vision for Britain after Brexit' (May, 2016). A few weeks later, Boris Johnson – who would ultimately replace May as prime minister when her failure to complete the Brexit process (and loss of many Conservative seats in an ill-judged snap election) brought her down – gave a speech at the Royal Institute of International Affairs at Chatham House, a key British foreign policy think tank. Johnson claimed that 'people around the world are looking for a lead from Britain' and argued that, in a post-Brexit context: 'We are a protagonist – a global Britain running a truly global foreign policy' (Johnson, 2016). This was the vision of Britain in the world that the leave campaign proposed: a strong sovereign actor, freed from the constraints of collective action imposed by EU membership, engaging once more (as in its imperial age) at the level of the global rather than the regional.

To what extent does this vision of 'Global Britain' reflect the realities of the contemporary, post-Brexit role and status of the UK in the world? And how is this vision connected to Britain's imperial past and postcolonial present? What does the Brexit referendum tell us about pluralism in British foreign policymaking? Are the institutions of, and debates on, British foreign policy becoming more pluralistic and, if so, is this desirable? This chapter aims to address these questions and the overlapping issues they represent. First, we explore Britain's role(s) and place(s) in the world, in historical and contemporary context. Next, some of the key institutions, trends and controversies in British foreign policymaking are presented to shed light on the shifting character of Britain as a foreign policy actor. Finally, the conclusion considers how we might (re-)frame Britain in the world as an 'assemblage' rather than an actor.

Spotlight on research: Global Britain – Empire's 'still-beating heart'?

Oliver Turner's (2019) article 'Global Britain and the narrative of empire' aims to 'bring focus and substance to debates about the meanings and applications of Global Britain since 2016' (727). Turner does so by first defining Global Britain as a foreign policy narrative, and then analysing its efficacy, domestically and internationally.

For Turner, narratives 'convey stories about the world and the actors within it'. He finds that the Global Britain narrative constructed by the Foreign and Commonwealth Office (see below) is a 'narrative of empire'. This does not mean that it is an explicit injunction to restore the British Empire. Rather, it offers a kind of autobiography of 'who' Britain is to be in the world: 'a familiar, soothing story about the UK as a nation with truly global attributes and

(Continued)

aspirations' (Turner, 2019: 729), which can put the whole world into the service of its own national interest. Global Britain is intended as a 'painkiller' to follow Brexit, as the Commonwealth was to the Empire. But empire remains its 'still-beating heart [...] giving its bombastic rhetoric logic and meaning' (ibid.).

Though the Global Britain narrative may be 'seductive and comforting' to some, Turner finds it is flawed and unlikely to be efficacious for three reasons. First, as a 'painkiller', it is really a domestic narrative, unlikely to find external buy-in; second, it is fundamentally 'regressive' – oriented towards a past that no longer exists; third, and most important, it fails as a foreign policy narrative because its bombastic framing 'fundamentally contradicts the understandings and preferences of international partners about what the modern day UK represents' (Turner, 2019: 731).

In this article, the imperial narrative of Global Britain is doomed to failure because it asserts a form of national identity and global power that simply does not fit the world Britain is in – a world where regionalisation and cooperation, rather than narrow national interest and unilateralism, would better serve such a 'middle' power.

Britain's role(s) and place(s) in the world

From an imperial to a postcolonial power

From at least the late 18th century – when Britain's empire stretched all the way from India to its east, to North America to its west – it was often described as an empire upon which 'the sun never sets'. But this empire had begun much closer to home. English conquest and colonisation of the Cornish, the Welsh, the Scots and the Irish was a product of 'Anglo-Saxon chauvinism, the earliest form of English nationalism' (Robinson, 1983: 34). This 'internal' form of colonial racism, casting Celts and others in the British Isles as inferior to the Anglo-Saxon English, constituted the model that would ultimately be extended to the peoples of Africa, Asia, the Americas, and Oceania (Robinson, 1983: 2). By the early 20th century, the British Empire had become the largest empire in history in terms of the territory and population it included (Taagepera, 1997). As its major settler-colonies – including Australia and the 13 colonies that would become the Eastern part of the USA – broke away, the empire shrank. And in the 19th and 20th centuries, a series of uprisings and independence movements across its other imperial 'possessions' – particularly India's independence in 1947 – effectively brought the British Empire to an end.

Chapter 3 offers a fuller account of Britain's global imperial and colonial history, but the empire, its end, and the transformations of British politics and society in its postcolonial era, provide essential context for critically exploring discourses of 'Global Britain' today. The British body politic was transformed in the postwar and post-imperial era by the migration of people from its former colonies in Asia, Africa and the Caribbean. Many in Britain's white-racialised majority had benefited from, and/or supported its imperial foreign policies. The 'wages of whiteness' (Roediger, 2022) cut across the country's deep class divides, since the spoils of empire paid for much of Britain's domestic grandeur (Koram, 2022; Sanghera, 2021) and even underwrote the establishment of its welfare state (see Bhambra, 2022) – itself a postwar settlement of antagonisms between capital and labour in the UK (Harvey, 2005). Therefore, while racism best served Britain's ruling class, functioning to 'divide and rule' the global proletariat, active working-class racism was an essential and ever-present component of Britain's imperial history (Virdee, 2014). Britain had never been homogenously 'white' (Kaufmann, 2017; Otele, 2020), but its increasingly multicultural, racially and religiously diverse, postcolonial character altered its cultural, political and economic dynamics. The presence of diasporic communities of colour within Britain complicated the often-racist narratives that had traditionally justified a colonising, extractive foreign policy agenda. In the context of the 'postcolonial political' (Hesse and Sayyid, 2006), interactions between Britain's people and its foreign policymakers would take on new tensions and dimensions.

Need to know: A history of violence – Britain or the UK in the World?

Why does this chapter refer to 'Britain' rather than 'the UK' in the world? There are good reasons to use Britain rather than UK in some instances, two of which are especially pertinent to this chapter. First is the specific history of *power* and *violence* that the use of Britain and British evokes. The United Kingdom of Great Britain and Northern Ireland (usually abbreviated to UK) has only existed as a territorial sovereign state in its current form for a century and is the product of violent *English* conquest. The 1707 and 1800 Acts of Union that founded 'Great Britain' and preceded the modern UK resulted from English invasions and counter-insurgencies in Scotland and Ireland. Today's UK was born in 1922, when most of the island of Ireland won its independence from the British through armed struggle and formed the Irish Free State (later the Republic of Ireland). Furthermore, throughout this period and well after the formation of today's UK, the *British Empire* was the pertinent sovereign entity when discussing the political assemblage that is the focus of this book. A second, related, reason for referring to Britain is that the term is often preferred by political actors, even for formal policy initiatives such as 'Global Britain'. It is therefore not only in historical context that we can understand Britain to be the pertinent location of power and politics. English political actors and those with an interest in Westminster remaining the locus of sovereign power may be more predisposed to use 'British', and to popularise the notion that Britishness and Englishness are essentially interchangeable since Britain – and by extension the UK – is itself the (forcible) creation of the English. Debates over Scottish independence in recent years show that the integrity and unity of the UK as a sovereign entity in the world are not settled.

The rise of international organisation

The end of the Second World War, the collapse of Britain's empire, and the onset of the process of decolonisation coincided with an era of unprecedented international organisation, in which it often played a key role. In 1944, shortly before the end of the war, Britain was one of the key powers represented at the Bretton Woods conference, which paved the way for the establishment of the international financial institutions: the International Monetary Fund (IMF), the World Bank, and later the World Trade Organization (WTO). The failed League of Nations experiment of the inter-war years was replaced by the United Nations (UN), of which Britain was one of the 50 founding members, at a conference in the USA in 1945. The UN would grow to become by far the largest international organisation ever created, in terms of state membership, bureaucracy and scope. Today it has 193 member states, hundreds of thousands of employees around the world (including more than 6,000 at its New York City headquarters), and dozens of large agencies and 'organs' comprising the total 'UN system', from the General Assembly and the Security Council to the World Health Organization and the UN Development Programme.

While Britain had lost the majority of its empire by the end of the 1950s, this formal sovereign power arrangement of Britain in the world was arguably replaced by a new, subtler but no less material form of global power. This transformation was characterised by the Ghanaian politician and pan-Africanist intellectual Kwame Nkrumah as the emergence of 'neo-colonialism' (Nkrumah, 1970), and was deeply connected to the rise of international organisation in the second half of the 20th century. Though the international organisations mentioned above were explicitly concerned with supporting peace and economic development, their critics came to see them as extensions of broadly 'Western' (or 'Global North'), and specifically Anglo-American, imperial power into the postcolonial age. In the late 20th century, following the postwar reconstruction of Europe, institutions like the IMF and World Bank, for instance, turned to facilitating loans from Global North former colonising powers including the UK to 'developing', formerly colonised countries in the 'Global South'. Such loans often came with conditionalities that were beneficial to UK, US, and other Global North states and businesses, such as requiring the privatisation of recipient countries' essential utilities and 'opening-up' of their resources and markets to foreign investment. Meera Sabaratnam and Mark Laffey call the international order that emerged in this period a system of 'complex indebtedness' (Sabaratnam and Laffey, 2023). In Nkrumah's terms, the formerly colonised state has 'all the outward trappings of international sovereignty', but the international financial system means that in truth its economy – and consequently also its politics, which are constrained by that economic base – are 'directed from outside' (Nkrumah, 1970: ix).

Britain was also a key founding member the North Atlantic Treaty Organization (NATO). Another important treaty-based international organisation to emerge in the aftermath of the Second World War, NATO is a military alliance proclaiming 'collective security' for its members, and bringing many European states under what is sometimes called the 'nuclear umbrella' of the USA. NATO was originally intended to deter Soviet expansion and became a focal point of the Western, capitalist 'side' of the Cold War. In the post-Cold War era, its role has been less clear, and its participation in some interventions – the Afghanistan War, for example – has been viewed by critics as neo-imperialist state violence (Chomsky, 2008).

Britain's role in these international financial, political and military organisations – and in the nascent European Union, which also had its roots in the postwar settlement and decolonisation, but which Britain would not join until 1973 – was never one of hegemonic dominance. It was no minor power, either. Its imperialism had provided it with a major economy on the global stage, and it was one of the first generation of nuclear weapons states. But within these organisations, Britain had to contend and negotiate with a range of other states, and often to accept multilateral compromise solutions. As economic globalisation and the technological revolution transformed the world in the 1970s and 1980s, the UK effectively 'hitched its wagon' to regionalist and multilateralist international organisations and to its 'special relationship' with the USA – though, as we will see, these two sets of commitments would come into conflict.

Need to know: Hegemony

In international politics, a hegemonic power is one that is able to strongly influence or control the policies and decisions of other states. This may be achieved through a concentration of military, economic, and/or political power with the hegemonic state. Hegemons may be regional or global (the USA is often seen as having attained, if only briefly, the status of a global hegemon after the collapse of the Soviet Union and before the resurgence of China).

The post-Cold War era

The most significant British foreign policy decision in the immediate post-Cold War era was joining the Gulf War against Iraq in 1991. This was the first major armed conflict Britain had embarked upon since its fight with Argentina over the Falkland Islands almost a decade earlier. It was also to be an intervention of a much greater scale, and with repercussions that arguably continue to play out to the present day. In justifying the UK's involvement in the war to parliament, John Major, the Conservative prime minister, emphasised the multilateral nature of the intervention. Major pointed to UN Security Council resolution 678, which authorised the use of force to end Iraq's invasion of neighbouring Kuwait, and to the 'exhaustive diplomatic efforts through the UN, the European Community, Arab Governments and others' that had not resolved the situation, and said that the war was launched with the 'greatest reluctance' and with 'no quarrel with the people of Iraq', but only with the country's leader, Saddam Hussein.

The USA played the leading role in the Gulf War, committing significantly more troops and resources. This was a key moment in establishing what is sometimes called the 'unipolar' world order, as the collapse of the USSR and of the Cold War's American–Soviet dynamics of 'bipolarity' left the USA as the world's sole superpower – a state of unparalleled economic, military and political power and influence. The USA would go on to establish itself as what some called the 'world police' in this new global context, in many cases with the UK at its side. While the language of multilateralism was everywhere, and the USA, UK and other allied states, invoked the UN, NATO and other international organisations, there was a widespread perception of a 'US-led' world order – the 'new world order' that President George H.W. Bush had said the 1991 Gulf War inaugurated (Nye, 1992).

Need to know: Unipolarity, bipolarity, multipolarity

World order is often characterised as having 'poles' of concentrated power. The 19th century, for instance, where many 'superpowers' existed, is seen as a multipolar era. The Cold War period of the 20th century is seen as a bipolar world order, since the USA and USSR became the two key superpowers, while other states fell into their orbit (Britain was 'attracted' to the US-led 'pole'). And in the post-Cold War period, an initial period of unipolarity (or American 'global hegemony') has more recently given way to a new multipolarity as a result of China's and Russia's resurgence as major powers in world politics.

The military interventions of the early 1990s seemingly set the pattern for Britain's role in the world for years to come. If America was the sheriff of the 'world policing' military interventions of the 1990s and 2000s, then the UK was its most loyal deputy. In 1999, against the backdrop of a major NATO bombing campaign – the alliance's intervention in the Kosovo War – Tony Blair famously described a 'new doctrine of international community'. This doctrine married an emphasis on political and economic 'global governance' (efforts at steering the forces of globalisation) to an interventionist, policing-style approach to conflict and security. The declaration of a 'war on terror' by President George W. Bush Jr. in response to the 9/11 attacks of 2001, meanwhile, saw the UK again acting as the USA's closest military ally, participating in a series of controversial conflicts and interventions under this banner (see discussion below), some of which continue to shape British foreign policy into the 2020s.

Theory box: Whose foreign policy?

Traditionally, theories of international relations (IR) tended to treat states as unitary and rational actors interacting within a 'states system', and to view their internal workings as 'black boxes' of limited relevance to understanding outcomes at the international level. In the 1950s, a subfield of IR emerged that challenged this view: foreign policy analysis (FPA).

FPA theories suggest that if we want to explain how and why particular things happen in world politics, we need to take a more fine-grained approach, beginning from a subnational level of analysis. How do presidents, prime ministers and ministers of foreign affairs make decisions on matters of foreign policy? What roles do their personal psychology and characteristics play? To what extent are foreign policy decision-making processes constrained (or enabled) by bureaucrats – the career civil servants, diplomats and expert advisors who serve permanently, irrespective of the government of the day – and constitutional powers or mandates? And how do pressures from public opinion, media, political party agendas and ideologies affect foreign policy decisions?

FPA scholarship, which has really flourished in the post-Cold War era with the mainstreaming of 'constructivist' IR theory, and its emphasis on exploring the social construction of world politics, has addressed all of these questions and more. But it has tended to retain a focus on 'elite' political decision-making, even when it does look at public opinion. The focus on elites in foreign policymaking is reflective of the fact that, as noted above, foreign policy was traditionally regarded as a specialised field sitting beyond the reach of democratic accountability, as a matter of pure national interest. In a highly pluralist system, many actors would have a say in UK foreign policy, including the general public. In practice, foreign policy decisions tend to be more effectively influenced by more powerful institutional actors.

However, the view that the leaders of states would necessarily make decisions that are in the interest of their populations has become increasingly hard to sustain. From wars to international trade deals, there are good reasons to suspect that politicians tend to make foreign policy decisions that benefit (or are perceived to benefit) themselves, their own socioeconomic class or ethnic grouping, big businesses and other powerful international actors, but perhaps less so the wider population. Whereas FPA theories traditionally focused on questions of power in terms of the 'pulling and hauling' (Allison, 1969) among members of the political elite, recent work in the field has begun to foreground questions of race, gender and class. The rise of the 'feminist foreign policy' agenda is one prominent example of this shift. A feminist approach to foreign policy decision-making – foregrounding the rights of women, and other issues of gender and sexuality, as well as a more conciliatory approach to international relations and a 'human' approach to security – has not only been advocated by FPA thinkers (e.g. Achilleos-Sarll et al., 2023), but has also been formally adopted as a national foreign policy approach in countries including Canada and Sweden. Such shifts suggest an increasingly pluralist approach to both the analysis and the practice of foreign policymaking. Meanwhile increased scrutiny and contestation of foreign policy decision-making – especially in the age of global social media – make the image of the state-as-actor less relevant, while the image of an assemblage of state and non-state actors and processes can better illustrate how decisions are made.

Institutions, trends and controversies in British foreign policy

The development and roles of Britain's foreign policy institutions

For the British Empire to be as phenomenally profitable as it was, it required careful administration to ensure the effective and efficient exploitation of the colonised peoples, lands and resources that fell under its imperial control. In addition to a vast and complex bureaucracy across the colonised countries themselves, central government resources were directed at the running of the empire. The first Colonial Office was established in 1768, under the government of William Pitt the Elder, with a central mission of reasserting control over the North American settler-colonies, which were soon to break away and establish their independence. This new government department itself absorbed the duties of older bodies, including the

Commissioners for Trade and Plantations. In 1801 the Colonial Office merged with the War Office (today's Ministry of Defence), but in 1854 – at the very height of Britain's 'imperial century' – the two were separated, with a new Colonial Office being established under the Secretary of State for the Colonies (and former Home Secretary), George Grey. This second Colonial Office existed until 1966, when it was renamed the Commonwealth Office as the British Empire collapsed. The Commonwealth is the special post-imperial arrangement between Britain and its former colonies, sometimes characterised as 'Empire 2.0' (Turner, 2019). Just two years later, the Commonwealth Office was itself merged into the Foreign Office, which had held a general foreign affairs remit since 1782, forming the Foreign and Commonwealth Office (FCO) in 1968. In 2020 the Conservative government abolished the Department for International Development that had been established by Tony Blair's Labour government in 1997 to administrate the UK's (then-expanding) aid and development programmes. Its responsibilities were absorbed by the FCO, which was renamed the Foreign, Commonwealth and Development Office (FCDO).

The FCDO is a ministry of foreign affairs in the tradition first established by France's Cardinal Richelieu in the 17th century. It is populated by career bureaucrats – civil servants – working to research, develop and implement government policy, and to coordinate and support the UK's diplomatic service in other countries. But its history in entities like the Colonial Office lends it a distinctly British flavour. Its central mission has included the maintenance and extension of various forms of British power around the world, from administrating the Commonwealth to leading British propaganda initiatives. The BBC's World Service radio and online news service, for example – which started life as the BBC Empire Service in 1932 – has always been funded by the Foreign Office. In the context of the Cold War, it was seen as a strategically important propaganda outlet for winning over the people of the communist Eastern Bloc to the politics and culture of Western, capitalist liberal democracies. In the post-Cold War context, the core of this mission remains intact, albeit in a more general sense. In 2021, for instance, the BBC's director general announced that 'The Foreign, Commonwealth & Development Office (FCDO) will be providing £94.4m to help the BBC World Service build on their great work upholding global democracy', and noting '£8m in additional investment to tackle disinformation and further improve the BBC's digital offer to audiences around the world' (Davie, 2021). The World Service, which boasted the same year 'an all-time record audience of 351m, in 42 languages including English', thus remains a well-funded component of the British state's effort at projecting what the international relations theorist Joseph Nye calls 'soft power' (Nye, 1990), on a global level.

The Secretary of State for Foreign Affairs, or Foreign Secretary, is the minister with ultimate responsibility for the FCDO and for British foreign policy and diplomacy – though the prime minister will also often be involved in significant foreign policy decisions and may lead or attend diplomatic meetings (particularly in the form of 'summit diplomacy') on big issues including security and, more recently, the environment. The British foreign secretary is considered to hold one of the four 'great offices of state', along with the prime minister, chancellor, and home secretary. This is an indication of the role's perceived significance and prestige; it is widely understood that because foreign policy pertains to matters of war and peace, and to the fundamental claim of the state to provide 'security' to its people, it should be treated as one of the most important policy areas.

Case study: The machinery and landscape of the British foreign policymaking assemblage

In the UK, as in many other states, foreign policymaking is principally the domain of the executive branch of government. This means that the cabinet of government ministers (officially 'secretaries of state', in the case of most policy portfolios), appointed and led by the prime minister, can pursue foreign policies of its choosing, with limited scrutiny and control exerted by the other key 'branches' of government: the legislature (parliament) and judiciary. While the secretary of state for Foreign, Commonwealth and Development Affairs (foreign secretary) is the cabinet minister with specific responsibility for overseeing foreign policy, major initiatives and decisions on foreign policy may also originate with the cabinet itself, or with the prime minister as the UK's official head of government. Such initiatives are also subject to the constitutional convention of cabinet collective responsibility, meaning that dissenting ministers would be expected to resign rather than refuse to support a cabinet decision on a foreign policy issue. More 'everyday' forms of foreign policy decision-making, and the implementation of the government's decisions, is largely left to those formally politically neutral civil servants executing government policy. The 17,300 civil servants (as of June 2023) working for the Foreign, Commonwealth and Development Office (FCDO) and its Diplomatic Service, in the UK and overseas, are in the main responsible for executing the foreign policies of the government, but executive and advisory functions may also be fulfilled by, for example, the armed forces, senior military officials at the Ministry of Defence, or by officials from other government departments with relevant knowledge or powers on a given foreign policy issue. Important though they are, all of these formal, constitutional arrangements for the design and implementation of British foreign policy exist within a wider assemblage of actors, institutions, powers and processes. This landscape includes less formal, or informal, actors and powers. Lobbying, for example, happens across many policy areas in the UK, and is comparatively lightly regulated. This means that organisations and individuals – especially those representing business interests, but also political campaigners such as NGOs and charities – can and do seek to influence government into pursuing particular foreign policies. The major corporations of the British defence industry for example – the manufacturers of military aircraft, weapons and munitions – may have an interest in the state pursuing certain kinds of military intervention overseas. Human rights campaigners, on the other hand, may attempt to press government to avoid armed conflict, or to prevent arms sales to regimes with questionable records on respect for human rights. Whether any given institutional or individual lobbyist, or coalition of lobbyists, is able to successfully shape foreign policy outcomes will be determined by a number of factors. For businesses, for instance, their relative size and contribution to the national economy, and therefore to the perceived 'national interest', will likely play a role, while campaign groups will likely find more influence when their political arguments are aligned to the politics or aims of the governing party of the day. As discussed earlier, public opinion can also have a significant impact on the machinery of foreign policymaking, as of course can the foreign policy initiatives, decisions and actions of other states, and of international organisations – all of which may constitute constraining or enabling conditions for the UK's own foreign policymaking.

Controversies and contestation in 21st-century British foreign policy

Though this chapter began with a discussion of Brexit, as a key British foreign policy controversy of recent years, it is – as was emphasised above – an unusual, if not unique, case. To understand Britain in the world today, especially as an 'assemblage', it is worth considering some of its more typical foreign policy entanglements and controversies. Britain's role in the Middle East and North Africa (MENA) region has been a long-standing source of controversy and contestation. Until relatively recently, Britain's role in the Middle East was under-explored in histories of empire, in part because Britain's imperial 'possessions' in the region were 'acquired by subterfuge; ruled (for the most part) by proxy; abandoned in confusion' (Darwin, 1999: 159). Yet from the 1917 Balfour Declaration supporting the 'establishment in [then British-controlled] Palestine of a national home for the Jewish people' to the 1956 Suez Crisis, in which Britain invaded Egypt to regain control of a key shipping lane (and former colonial possession) following its nationalisation by President Nasser, British foreign policy has been at the very centre of several long-standing crises in the MENA region. This trend has continued through the post-Cold War era, from the 1991 Gulf War discussed above, to the ongoing and extensive programme of British airstrikes in Syria and Iraq under the banner of the 'fight against Daesh [the so-called 'Islamic State in Iraq and Syria'/ISIS]' (Ministry of Defence, 2023). We now turn to three examples of 21st-century British foreign policy controversies in the Middle East that help shed light on its contemporary role in the region, as an 'assemblage' that escapes the narrow definition of Britain as a state actor.

The invasion of Iraq

Public interest in British foreign policy reached fever pitch in the early 21st century. The declaration of the 'Global War on Terrorism' (GWoT) by US President George W. Bush following the attacks on the World Trade Centre and the Pentagon in 2001 marked the beginning of a controversial new foreign policy agenda in the UK too. British prime minister Tony Blair pledged to support the US in its new mission and followed it into major armed conflicts in Afghanistan and Iraq. While Bush initially benefited from what foreign policy analysts call a 'rally around the flag effect' on post-9/11 public opinion (Morin and Paquin, 2018: 177), the GWoT was to become increasingly controversial and contested. The 2003 invasion of Iraq, which had no discernible connection to the 9/11 attacks, was especially controversial. In the UK, it is widely viewed as a turning point in the previously positive public opinion of Blair. On the eve of the invasion, public opinion was 52 per cent against war, and Britain saw the largest political demonstration in its history, with from 750,000 to 2 million people marching in London on 15 February 2003. Several cabinet ministers and many of the governing Labour party's backbench MPs also opposed war. Blair decided to join the US-led coalition in invading Iraq anyway, and the UK made the second largest commitment of troops and equipment throughout the conflict. Major controversies included: the lack of a clear UN Security Council mandate for the use of force, despite Bush and Blair's claims to the contrary; a potentially spurious pretext in relation to weapons of mass destruction (WMD) in Iraq that were never found; the use of torture and controversial counterinsurgency methods in the prosecution of the conflict; the perception that the real motivation was control of Iraq's vast oil reserves; the ultimate failure of the invasion in producing a more 'stable' Iraq; and its setting of the scene for the rise of ISIS. Blair was personally associated with several controversies, including the 'sexing-up' of a dossier of evidence of WMD in an effort to win over the British public, and his 2002 memo to Bush, declassified in 2016 as part of the UK's public inquiry into the war, which began 'I will be with you, whatever', at a time when Blair's public stance in Britain was that no decision to join a US invasion had yet been made. The Iraq War, and Britain's key supporting role in it, is today often understood to have played a role in longer-term destabilisation of the region and 'radicalisation' of people around the world in opposition to Western states and their foreign policies. This includes the rise of 'Islamist' militancy and terrorist attacks inside the UK, such as the 2005 London bombings, and the ISIS-inspired attacks in London and Manchester in 2017, among many others.

The bombing of Syria

In 2013, as social revolutions and civil wars rocked the MENA region in the wake of the 2011 'Arab Spring', and mindful of the role the Iraq invasion played in ultimately turning public opinion against his predecessor Tony Blair, prime minister David Cameron called a parliamentary vote on the government's plan to join a possible military intervention against Syria after the state's reported use of chemical weapons against rebels and civilians. Cameron's government narrowly lost the vote and initially committed not to join any intervention. However, a fresh vote in 2015, as ISIS reached its peak amid the breakdown of the state monopoly on violence – controlling huge swaths of territory and brutally ruling populations in Syria and Iraq – authorised UK involvement in airstrikes against targets in Syria (such strikes were still taking place in Iraq, as they had been since 2003). A significant parliamentary majority supported the airstrikes, which continue to take place on a regular basis as recently as 2022, including many opposition MPs – Labour MP Hilary Benn made the most quoted speech in the debate on the issue, describing ISIS as 'fascists'. But this ostensible plurality of support is troubled by tensions between the public and the politicians. For example, the Labour MP Stella Creasy voted in favour of the airstrikes, despite widespread criticism from her constituents and local party members in Waltham Forest – a borough where one in five people identify as Muslim, and at a historical juncture where Britain's military interventions were viewed by critics as disproportionately targeting majority-Muslim countries. Creasy stood by her decision at a later public meeting on the grounds that ISIS could not be negotiated with and military force was therefore essential. Controversies in relation to this intervention include: the fact that, though ISIS has been largely eradicated from the region, it has only expanded elsewhere, in Africa and South Asia, while the Assad regime remains in power in Syria, and a bloody civil war continues without an end in sight; the further normalisation of the use of drone strikes to carry out extrajudicial killings by the UK against those it deems 'terrorists', without a legal requirement to present evidence against them or any efforts to detain or prosecute them – today the Ministry of Defence publishes a monthly list of the 'terrorists' it has killed by drone strike in Syria and Iraq (MoD, 2023).

The arming of Saudi Arabia

Anna Stavrianakis argues that: 'About once a decade, an arms trade scandal punctures public consciousness and generates debate about British foreign policy' (Stavrianakis, 2018: 92). These scandals, Stavrianakis points out, include the so-called 'Arms to Iraq' case under the Conservative government in the early 1990s, and the use of British weapons in atrocities in East Timor later that decade during the New Labour government. From 2015, she notes, there has been a degree of scandal and public scrutiny in relation to the UK's arms trade with Saudi Arabia, and the latter's war in neighbouring Yemen. The 'Al-Yamamah' deal is a long-term arms-for-oil trade agreement between the UK and Saudi Arabia. It has long been a controversial deal and was subject to a criminal investigation into corruption by the UK's Serious Fraud Office in the 2000s, which was stopped by an intervention from the prime minister on 'national interest' grounds (itself generating further controversy). In 2010, the UK's main contractor in the deal, BAE Systems, pleaded guilty to corruption-related charges in an American court. But controversy around Britain's arming of Saudi Arabia has been heightened in recent years by the latter country's war in Yemen. When civil war broke out in Yemen in 2014, between government forces and the Houthi rebel group, Saudi Arabia intervened to support the embattled government forces. This intervention is sometimes viewed as a 'proxy' conflict between Sunni Muslim-dominated Saudi Arabia and Shia-Muslim dominated Iran (which may have provided material support to the Houthi). Controversies of British foreign policy in relation to its arming of Saudi Arabia in this context include: the further enflaming of Sunni–Shia tensions in the Middle East; the use of British-made weapons against Yemeni civilians, and their role in causing a major humanitarian crisis in the country, which in 2022 the UN declared 'remains the world's worst humanitarian crisis', with six million displaced people and more than 23 million 'in dire need of humanitarian assistance' (UNHCR, 2022). Britain's position on the issue was clarified by then prime minister Theresa May on a visit to Saudi Arabia (accompanied by corporate arms dealers) in 2017, when she was asked by journalists about the 'May doctrine' of foreign policy in relation to UK–Saudi arms deals and the unfolding crisis in Yemen. May effectively dismissed criticisms of the arms deals, responding: 'Well, the May doctrine of foreign policy is that everything we do is in our British national interest' (BBC News, 4 April 2017).

Image 14.2 A Royal Air Force 'Reaper' drone on display at RAF Fairford air base, UK, in July 13, 2018.

© Photo by VanderWolf Images on Shutterstock

These three cases amount to only a small sample of Britain's foreign policy controversies in the 21st century to date, but they usefully illustrate some of the enduring dynamics and social tensions in the pluralist politics of Britain in the world in general, and Britain in the Middle East in particular. The pursuit of 'national interest' above all, and a willingness to set aside public opinion in the name of specific strategic alliances, and especially support for the USA as a global power, have all characterised Britain's role in the world in recent decades, limiting the plurality of voices that hold sway even as those voices grow louder in the age of global social media. Britain has long exceeded its national territorial borders. Britain is 'in the world' as an assemblage of material things, such as the aircraft and munitions Saudi Arabia uses to wage war in Yemen; of events and processes, from the Balfour Declaration to the Iraq invasion; and of people as political actors, from prime ministers to journalists and the general public. When we say that 'Britain' or 'the UK' did, does or will do something in the world, this richer image of the assemblage is more accurate and fulsome than traditional state-as-actor metaphors, which assume a bounded and unitary entity making and carrying out singular 'decisions'.

What about the good stuff?

This chapter, in keeping with the thrust of this book, has presented a 'critical' account of Britain in the world. That is to say, it has proceeded from the premise that Britain's presence and activity in the world, as a nation-state or an 'assemblage' (see Conclusion below), has often been a source of socioeconomic tension, injustice, violence and exploitation. Yet this is a controversial, and perhaps still marginal, stance. The politicians of the country's biggest political parties, the bureaucrats of the FCDO, the diplomats, soldiers, many business leaders, and a good proportion of the general public, would likely support the view that Britain has been mainly or wholly a force for good in the world. From industrialisation in its colonies (railways in India being perhaps the most cliched example), to its postcolonial policies on foreign aid – whether humanitarian, as in the case of the 2023 Turkey earthquake response, or military, as in the case of Russia's 2022 invasion of Ukraine – and its 'democracy promotion' activities, many examples could be found to support such a position.

And yet any view of Britain as a benevolent force in the world requires us to set aside the fact that the very same politicians, diplomats, military leaders and so on, have reliably (and across party political divides and governments) also couched Britain's role in the world as pursuing its 'national interest'. Liberalism – in the broadest sense of the rights-based individualist political order that underpins 'liberal democracy' as a state model – proceeds from the view that in their international relations, states like the UK can indirectly or unintentionally benefit other states and societies, through the very pursuit of their own national self-interest. This is what Immanuel Kant called the 'unsocial sociability' of international politics (Kant, 1983: 31). On this view, British foreign policy initiatives aim to make a world better-suited to serving the country's material interests (accumulating wealth, power and security), and in doing so they change other societies for the better. From colonisation to humanitarian intervention, this macro-level liberal foreign policy narrative has claimed that even the most violent military interventions, occupations and expropriations of other societies can be beneficial to them, as they are remoulded in the image of the UK itself (understood as a stable and desirable political and economic order). As students of UK politics, we should at the very least hold this exceptionalist narrative – that Britain is always or usually on the 'right side of history' in its interactions with the wider world – at a critical distance.

Britain as assemblage-in-the world, or Anglo-America?

As Joanie Willett noted in Chapter 1, we can usefully understand UK politics through the concept of the 'assemblage'. This applies also to Britain's role(s) and place(s) in the world. These are constituted through assemblages of foreign policies and the social elites and institutions that create and contest them, on the one hand, and the publics (in the UK and elsewhere) whose interests such policies are supposed to represent or curtail, on the other. From the British Empire to post-Brexit 'Global Britain', Britain in the world is a complex and contested, messy social, political and economic entity. Britain in the world is itself a sort of assemblage – not an immutable 'seamless totality' characterised by a 'transcendent essence' (DeLanda, 2016), however much politicians find it useful to portray it as such, but rather an always-emergent, shifting, contested social constellation of power interacting and overlapping with other such constellations to produce world politics.

Though the assemblage is a popular way to characterise such social formations today, it is not without precedent. The geographer Doreen Massey, in her critique of popular top–down conceptualisations of globalisation, argued that 'places' in general, including countries like the UK, should not be thought of as 'areas with boundaries around' but rather as 'articulated moments in networks of social relations' (Massey, 1991: 29). Massey's call for a politically progressive 'global sense of place' offers a way of thinking about Britain in the world that this chapter has sought to bring to the fore. On this view, our understanding of what Britain is as a political entity – and especially of what 'Global Britain' is, was, or might be – depends upon 'a sense of place, an understanding of "its character", which can *only* be constructed by linking that place to places beyond' (Massey, 1991: 29 [emphasis added]).

To close this chapter with a final provocation: perhaps 'Britain' does not exist in the world at all – at least as a singular entity or 'actor'. As the discussion and examples in the chapter have shown, Britain has – at least since the end of the Second World War and the end of empire – often acted in tandem with the USA, its vastly larger (economically and militarily) and more powerful ally. It has also followed American economic, cultural and political trends (often by contrast to wider European norms). In thinking of Britain as an assemblage in the world, we might reconceptualise it as part of a wider global assemblage: Anglo-America. 'Led by the British Empire until the beginning and by the United States since the middle of the twentieth century, Anglo-America has been at the very center of world politics', argues Peter J. Katzenstein (2012: 1). It is at once a 'civilizational identity' and a powerful global force, which has been able to dominate and steer the wider imagined community of 'the West'. But even if we accept this analysis, it raises many new questions today. In the post-Trump, post-Brexit age – an era of resurgent nationalisms and parochialisms in Anglo-America – and with an ascendant China and broader Global South challenge to the authority of 'the West', will Anglo-America, and its British component, matter very much in the world of the near future?

Conclusion

This chapter began with an exploration of Brexit as a contemporary case study in the relationship between political pluralism, foreign policymaking, and Britain's place in the wider world. Although the Brexit referendum ostensibly concerned an issue of foreign policy – membership of a treaty-based, inter-governmental, international organisation – the discussion here has shown how it exceeds this narrow framing. Brexit was (and perhaps still is, since it remains a 'live' political problem) also about migration and immigration, race and racism, social policy, healthcare and welfare, and imperial nostalgia, to name but a few issues motivating voters and animating political arguments on the referendum.

This chapter has sought to demonstrate that, from the history of the British Empire to Brexit and beyond, issues of foreign policy – how the British state acts and exists beyond its territorially defined borders – have always been messily and inextricably intertwined with social issues within those borders. In fact, borders themselves are a messy social construction (with direct material effects), produced, policed and sometimes challenged through struggles between and across British state and society, and their interactions with other states and societies. The assemblage of Britain-in-the-world is an always-emergent constellation of power, rather than a neatly bounded foreign policy 'actor'.

Key take-home points

- The UK itself emerged out of a history of 'internal' violence and conquest by the English, and its status as a coherent and unified territorial space remains unsettled.
- While foreign policy has largely been treated as a sensitive political decision-making arena, firewalled from pluralist influences, the politics of Brexit illustrate how public opinion can impact and interact with foreign policy.
- The post-Brexit foreign policy narrative of 'Global Britain' is contested and controversial, viewed by some as a form of imperial 'nostalgia'.
- From the British Empire to postwar international order, and 21st century UK foreign policymaking in the Middle East, Britain can be viewed as a controversial and often violent power in the world.
- To the extent that the UK exists as an assemblage in the world, it is often found bound to the USA in a civilisational identity sometimes called 'Anglo-America'.

Annotated reading list

Alden, C. and Aran, A. (2012) *Foreign Policy Analysis: New Approaches.* Abingdon: Routledge.

Several good textbooks on foreign policy analysis emerged in the early 21st century, but Alden and Aran's is helpful for extending the themes in this chapter in that it is specifically oriented toward new and non-traditional approaches in the field. Our understanding of Britain as a foreign policy actor (or assemblage) in which pluralism and contestation shape outcomes requires such an orientation in a field that traditionally focused largely on elite politics.

Ali, N. (2023) *The Violence of Britishness: Racism, Borders and the Conditions of Citizenship*. London: Pluto Press.

A critical account of the UK's postcolonial order, exploring the intersections of its 'Prevent' counter-radicalisation strategy in the wake of the 2005 London bombings with what its then home secretary Theresa May would call the 'hostile environment' for undocumented migrants and former imperial subjects.

Katzenstein, P.J. (ed.) (2012) *Anglo-America and its Discontents: Civilizational Identities beyond West and East*. Abingdon: Routledge.
Vucetic, S. (2011) *The Anglosphere: A Genealogy of a Racialized Identity in International Relations*. Stanford: Stanford University Press.

Two useful books for thinking about Britain's historical and contemporary entanglements with wider civilisational or racial identities, and how these have shaped, constrained and enabled its interaction with the wider world. Arguably, Britain in the world cannot be understood without understanding Britain in Anglo-America, in the Anglosphere or in 'the West'.

Koram, K. (2022) *Uncommon Wealth: Britain and the Aftermath of Empire*. London: John Murray.

This book offers a critical account of post-imperial Britain-in-the-world and the Commonwealth that replaced empire. Koram unpicks the post-Brexit vision of 'Global Britain', highlighting the cracks in an extremely unequal country, as well as the impacts its colonisation and decolonisation of other societies have had on the world.

Vucetic, S. (2021) *Greatness and Decline: National Identity and British Foreign Policy*. Montreal and Kingston: McGill-Queen's University Press.

Vucetic explores British 'exceptionalism' in foreign policy: the centrality to British national identity (among the masses as well as political elites) of visions of British 'greatness' and aspirations to 'world leading' status. He also highlights some of the tensions encountered by this exceptionalism at times of relative material decline, and intellectual 'declinism', in the UK.

References

Abdul, G. (2023) Who is Richard Sharp and why is he quitting the BBC? *The Guardian*, 28 April 2023.

Achilleos-Sarll, C., Thomson, J., Haastrup, T., Färber, K., Cohn, C. and Kirby, P. (2023) The past, present, and future(s) of feminist foreign policy. *International Studies Review*, 25(1), 1–29.

Ackers, P. (2020) Industrial relations and the limits of the state: Can a left Labour government resurrect comprehensive sectoral collective bargaining and restore trade union power? *The Political Quarterly*, 91(1), 173–181.

Adams, C.J. (2010a[1990]) *The Sexual Politics of Meat: A Feminist-Vegetarian Critical Theory*. New York: Continuum.

Adams, C.J. (2010b) Why feminist-vegan now? *Feminism and Psychology*, 20(2), 302–317.

Adcock, R. & Vail, M. (2012) Beyond pluralism? corporatism, globalization, and the dilemmas of democratic governance. In M. Bevir (ed.), *Modern Pluralism: Anglo-American Debates since 1880*. Cambridge: Cambridge University Press.

Ahmed, S. (2004) *The Cultural Politics of Emotion*. Edinburgh: Edinburgh University Press.

Akala (2018) *Natives: Race and Class in the Ruins of Empire*. London: Two Roads.

Albertazzi, D. (2016) Going, going,… not quite gone yet? 'Bossi's Lega' and the survival of the mass party. *Contemporary Italian Politics*, 8(2), 115–130.

Albertazzi, D. and van Kessel, S. (2021) Right-wing populist party organisation across Europe: The survival of the mass party? Introduction to the thematic issue. *Politics and Governance*, 9(4), 224–227.

Aleksandrowicz, L., Green, R., Joy, E.J. and Smith, P. (2016) The impacts of dietary change on greenhouse gas emissions, land use, water use and health: A systematic review. *PLOS ONE*, 11(11), e0165797.

Almond, G.A. (1950) *The American People and Foreign Policy*. New York: Harcourt, Brace and Company.

Allan, S. (2010) *News Culture*, 3rd edn. Maidenhead: McGraw-Hill/Open University Press.

Allen, P. (2016) Review of The House of Commons: An Anthropology of MPs at Work by Emma Crewe. *Parliamentary Affairs*, 69(4), 947–950.

Allison, G.T. (1969) Conceptual models and the Cuban Missile Crisis. *The American Political Science Review*, 63(3), 689–718.

Anderson, L. (2017) *Deviance: Social Constructions and Blurred Boundaries*. Berkeley, CA: University of California Press.

Anderson, B. (1983, 1991) *Imagined Communities: Reflections on the Origin and Spread of Nationalism*. London: Verso.

Anitha, S., Pearson, R. and McDowell, L. (2018) From Grunwick to Gate Gourmet: South Asian women's industrial activism and the role of trade unions. *Revue Française de Civilisation Britannique*, XXIII-1. https://journals.openedition.org/rfcb/1790

Antonucci, L., Horvath, L., Kutiyski, Y. et al. (2017) The malaise of the squeezed middle: Challenging the narrative of the 'left behind' Brexiter. *Competition & Change*, 21(3), 211–229.

All Party Parliamentary Group (APPG) on British Muslims (2019) *Islamophobia Defined*. https://static1.squarespace.com/static/599c3d2febbd1a90cffdd8a9/t/5bfd1ea3352f531a6170ceee/1543315109493/Islamophobia+Defined.pdf

APSE (2021) Local By Default: APSE Local Government Commission 2030 Report.

Arcari, P., Probyn-Rapsey, F. and Singer, H. (2021) Where species don't meet: Invisibilized animals, urban nature and city limits. *Environment and Planning E: Nature and Space*, 4(3), 940–965.

Archer, L., Müller, H. Jones, L., Ma, H., Gleave, R., Cerqueira, A., Hamilton, T. and Shennan-Farpón, Y. (2022) Towards fairer conservation: Perspectives and ideas from early-career researchers. *People and Nature*, 22(4), 612–626.

Ares, E. and Bolton, P. (2020) The rise of climate change activism? *House of Commons Library Insight*. https://commonslibrary.parliament.uk/the-rise-of-climate-change-activism

Arian, A. and Shamir, M. (1983) The primarily political functions of the left-right continuum. *Comparative Politics*, 15(2), 139–158.

Ashcroft, R. and Bevir, M. (2016) Pluralism, national identity and citizenship: Britain after Brexit. *The Political Quarterly*, 87(3), 355–359.

Ashcroft, R. and Bevir, M. (2021) Brexit and the myth of British national identity. *British Politics*, 16, 117–132.

Asher, K. and Ramamurthy, P. (2020) Rethinking decolonial and postcolonial knowledge beyond regions to imagine transnational solidarity. *Hypatia*, 35, 542–547.

Atterton, J. (2007) The 'Strength of Weak Ties:' Social networking by business owners in the Highlands and Islands of Scotland. *Sociologia Ruralis*, 47(3), 228–245.

Aucoin, P. (2012) New political governance in Westminster systems: Impartial public administration and management performance at risk. *Governance*, 25(2), 177–199.

Bagehot, W. (2001) *The English Constitution* (Cambridge Texts in the History of Political Thought) (P. Smith, Ed.). Cambridge: Cambridge University Press.

Bajpai, O., Dutta, V., Singh, R., Chaudhary, L. and Pandey, J. (2020) Tree community assemblage and abiotic variables in tropical moist deciduous forest of Himalayan Terai eco-region. *Proceedings of the National Academy of Sciences, India Section B*, 20200101, 1–11.

Bakvis, H. and Jarvis, M.D. (2012) (eds) From New Public Management to New Political Governance: Essays in Honour of Peter Aucoin. Montreal: McGill-Queen's University Press.

Bale, T., Webb, P. and Poletti, M. (2019) Footsoldiers: Political party membership in the 21st century. Abingdon: Routledge.

Ball, J., Hauck, J., Holland, R., Lovegrove, A., Snaddon, J., Taylor, G. and Peh, K.S.H. (2022) Improving governance outcomes for water quality: Insights from participatory network analysis for chalk stream catchments in England. *People and Nature*, 4(5), 1352–1368.

Bally, C. (2007) Rammohan Roy and the advent of constitutional liberalism in India, 1800–1830. *Modern Intellectual History*, 4(1), 25–41.

Barlow, P. and Paun, A. (2013) *Civil Service Accountability to Parliament*. London: Institute for Government.

Barnett, S. and Gaber, I. (2001) *Westminster Tales: The Twenty-First-Century Crisis in Political Journalism*. London: Continuum.

Barnett, S. and Petley, J. (2021) Why Ofcom must find its backbone. *British Journalism Review*, 32(1), 29–36.

Barnett, N., Giovannini, A. and Griggs, S. (2021) *Local Government in England – 40 Years of Decline*. Unlock Democracy. https://static1.squarespace.com/static/5bd057c434c4e2d8eb0434e6/t/60796c249a89215efe3cd382/1618570303662/Local+Government+in+England+-+40+Years+of+Decline.pdf

Bartlett, J., Bennett, S., Birnie, R. and Wibberley, S. (2013) *Virtually Members: The Facebook and Twitter Followers of UK Political Parties*. London: Demos. https://demos.co.uk/research/virtually-members

Bartolini, S. and Mair, P. (1990) Identity, Competition, and Electoral Availability: The Stabilisation of European Electorates 1885–1985. Cambridge: Cambridge University Press.

Bates, S., Kerr, P. and Serban, R. (2018) Questioning the government. In C. Leston-Bandeira & L. Thompson (eds), *Exploring Parliament*. Oxford: Oxford University Press, pp. 174–186.

Bates, S.R., Kerr, P., Byrne, C. and Stanley, L. (2014) Questions to the prime minister: A comparative study of PMQs from Thatcher to Cameron. *Parliamentary Affairs*, 67(2), 253–280.

Bayliss, D., Olsen, W. and Walthery, P. (2017) Well-being during recession in the UK. *Applied Research in Quality of Life*, 12(2), 369–387.

BBC 2023a About the BBC www.bbc.com/aboutthebbc/governance/mission

BBC, 2023b Editorial guidelines. Guidance: Impartiality. www.bbc.co.uk/editorialguidelines/guidance/impartiality

BBC News (25 June 2014) Phone-hacking trial explained. www.bbc.co.uk/news/uk-24894403

BBC News (14 September 2014) Scottish independence: Crowd protests against 'BBC bias'. www.bbc.co.uk/news/uk-scotland-29196912

BBC News (15 February 2015a) Sunday Herald sees sales rise after backing independence. www.bbc.co.uk/news/uk-scotland-scotland-business-31624118

BBC News (19 July 2015b) Mhairi Black's maiden speech tops 10m online views. www.bbc.co.uk/news/uk-scotland-scotland-politics-33585087

BBC News (4 April 2017) Theresa May defends UK ties with Saudi Arabia. www.bbc.co.uk/news/uk-politics-39485083

BBC News (30 April 2018) Amber Rudd resigns as home secretary. www.bbc.co.uk/news/uk-politics-43944988

BBC News (14 June 2022) SNP MP Patrick Grady faces Commons suspension for sexual misconduct. www.bbc.co.uk/news/uk-politics-61798663

BBC News (20 October 2022) MPs allege bullying during chaotic fracking vote. www.bbc.co.uk/news/uk-politics-63322533

Beach Guardian (2022) Engage, educate, empower against plastic pollution. www.beachguardian.org

Beckers, K., Walgrave, S. and Van den Bulck, H. (2018) Opinion balance in vox pop television news. *Journalism Studies*, 19(2), 284–296.

Beech, M. and Hickson, K. (2014) Blue or purple? Reflections on the future of the Labour Party. *Political Studies Review*, 12(1), 75–87.

Beetham, D. (2006) Parliament and Democracy in the Twenty-First Century. Geneva: Inter-Parliamentary Union.

BEIS/ONS Department for Business Energy & Industrial Strategy (2022) *Trade Union Membership, UK 1995–2021: Statistical Bulletin.* https://assets.publishing.service.gov.uk/government/uploads/system/uploads/attachment_data/file/1077904/Trade_Union_Membership_UK_1995-2021_statistical_bulletin.pdf

Bell, A. and Hindmoor, A. (2009) *Rethinking Governance.* Oxford: Oxford University Press.

Bennett, J. (2010) *Vibrant Matter.* Durham: Duke University Press.

Bennett, S., Moon, D.S., Pearce, N. & Whiting, S. (2021) Labouring under a delusion? Scotland's national questions and the crisis of the Scottish Labour Party. *Territory, Politics, Governance,* 9(5), 656–674.

Bennie, L., Mitchell, J. and Johns, R. (2021) Parties, movements and the 2014 Scottish independence referendum: Explaining the post-referendum party membership surges. *Party Politics,* 27(6), 1184–1197.

Benton, M. and Russell, M. (2013) Assessing the impact of parliamentary oversight committees: The select committees in the British House of Commons. *Parliamentary Affairs,* 66(4), 772–797.

Bergson, H. (2004 [1908]) *Matter and Memory.* Mineola, NY: Dover Publications.

Bernanke, B. (2004) The great moderation. Remarks by Governor Ben S. Bernanke at the meetings of the Eastern Economic Association, Washington, DC, 20 February 2004. www.federalreserve.gov/boarddocs/speeches/2004/20040220/default.htm

Berners-Lee, M., Hoolohan, C., Cammack, H. and Hewitt, C.N. (2012) The relative greenhouse gas emissions of realistic dietary choices. *Energy Policy,* 43, 184–190.

Berry, C. (2021) *Understanding the Treasury: A Learning Resource for Undergraduate Students in Political Science and Economics.* Manchester Metropolitan University. www.mmu.ac.uk/sites/default/files/2021-11/Understanding%20the%20Treasury.pdf

Berry, C. and Giovannini, A. (eds) (2018) *Developing England's North: The Political Economy of the Northern Powerhouse.* London: Palgrave.

Besley, N. and Goldsmith, T. (2019) *How Parliament Works* (Eighth Edition). London: Routledge.

Bevir, M. (2012a) *Governance: A Very Short Introduction.* Oxford: Oxford Academic.

Bevir, M. (2012b) A history of modern pluralism. In M. Bevir (ed.), *Modern Pluralism: Anglo-American Debates since 1880.* Cambridge: Cambridge University Press.

Bezanson, K. (2006) The neo-liberal state and social reproduction. In K. Bezanson and M. Luxton (eds), *Social Reproduction.* Montreal: McGill's–Queen's University Press, pp. 173–214.

Bezanson, K. and Luxton, M. (eds) (2006) *Social Reproduction.* Montreal: McGill's–Queen's University Press.

Bhambra, G.K. (2014) Postcolonial and Decolonial Dialogues. *Postcolonial Studies,* 17(2), 115–121.

Bhambra, G.K. (2022) Relations of extraction, relations of redistribution: Empire, nation, and the construction of the British welfare state. *British Journal of Sociology,* 73(1), 4–15.

Bhattacharya, T. (ed.) (2017) *Social Reproduction Theory.* London: Pluto.

Billig, M. (1995) *Banal Nationalism.* London: Sage.

Binder, M. (2021) Enhancing democracy: Can civic engagement foster political participation? *Social Science Quarterly,* 102(1), 47–68.

Birch, A.H. (1964) *Representative and Responsible Government: An Essay on the British Constitution.* London: Allen and Unwin.

Blanchflower, D.G. and Freeman, R.B. (1993) Did the Thatcher reforms change British labour performance? NBER Working Paper 4384, National Bureau of Economic Research. https://ssrn.com/abstract=227031

Blinder, S. and Allen, W. (2016) Constructing immigrants: Portrayals of migrant groups in British national newspapers, 2010–2012. *International Migration Review*, 50, 3–40.

Blondel, J. (1970) Legislative behaviour: Some steps towards cross-national measurement. *Government and Opposition*, 5, 67–85.

Bloodworth, J. (2019) Hired: Six Months Undercover in Low-Wage Britain. London: Atlantic.

Blühdorn, I. (2007) Sustaining the unsustainable: Symbolic politics and the politics of simulation. *Environmental Politics*, 16(2), 257–275.

Blyth, M. (2013) *Austerity: The History of a Dangerous Idea*. Oxford: Oxford University Press.

Bogdanor, V. (2001) *Devolution in the United Kingdom*. Oxford: Oxford University Press.

Bogdanor, V., Khaitan, T. & Vogenauer, S. (2007) Should Britain Have a Written Constitution? *The Political Quarterly*, 78(4), 499–517.

Boler, M. and Davis, E. (2018) The affective politics of the post-truth era: Feeling rules and network subjectivity. *Emotion, Space, and Society*, 27, 75–85.

Bolton, P. (2023) *Higher Education Student Numbers*. House of Commons Library. https://researchbriefings.files.parliament.uk/documents/CBP-7857/CBP-7857.pdf

Bonefeld, W. (2016) Science, hegemony and action. *Journal of Social Sciences*, 12(2), 19–41.

Boo, K. (2016) On not 'giving voice to the voiceless'. www.pulitzer.org/article/not-giving-voice-voiceless

Booth, O., Butler, C., Jeffery, D. and Roe-Crines, A. (2023) Selecting Sunak: Conservative MPs' nomination preferences in the (second) British Conservative Party leadership election. *Parliamentary Affairs*. https://doi.org/10.1093/pa/gsad010

Boucek, F. (2009) Rethinking factionalism: Typologies, intra-party dynamics and three faces of factionalism. *Party Politics*, 15(4), 455–485.

Boyer, K., Dermott, E. and MacLeavy, J. (2017) Regendering care in the aftermath of recession? *Dialogues in Human Geography*, 7(1), 56–73.

Brittain, V. (2004 [1933]) A Testament to Youth: An Autobiographical Study of the Years 1900–1925. London: Virago.

Bryant, C. (2010) English identities and interests and the governance of Britain. *Parliamentary Affairs*, 63(2), 250–265.

Brookes, R.L.J. and Wahl-Jorgensen, K. (2004) The media representation of public opinion: British television news coverage of the 2001 general election. *Media, Culture & Society*, 26(1), 63–80.

Brüggemann, M., Engesser, S., Büchel, F., Humprecht, E. and Castro, L. (2014) Hallin and Mancini revisited: Four empirical types of western media systems. *Journal of Communication*, 64(6), 1037–1065.

Bryant, C. (2003) These Englands, or Where Does Devolution Leave the English? *Nations and Nationalisms*, 9(3), 393–412.

Bryant, C. (2008) Devolution, equity and the English question. *Nations and Nationalisms*, 14(4), 664–683.

Bryant, C.J. (2019) We can't keep meating like this: Attitudes towards vegetarian and vegan diets in the United Kingdom. *Sustainability*, 11(23), 6844.

Bulpitt, J. (2008) *Territory and Power in the United Kingdom*. Colchester: ECPR Press.

Burke, M., Ockwell, D. and Whitmarsh, L. (2018) Participatory arts and affective engagement with climate change: The missing link in achieving climate compatible behaviour change. *Global Environmental Change*, 49, 95–105.

Burnett, A. and Nunes, R. (2021) Flatpack democracy: Power and politics at the boundaries of transition. *Environmental Policy and Governance,* 31(3) 223–236.

Burton-Cartledge, P. (2012) *Is there bias on BBC Question Time?* www.newstatesman.com/politics/2012/11/there-bias-bbc-question-time

Butler, C. (2021) When are governing parties more likely to respond to public opinion? The strange case of the Liberal Democrats and tuition fees. *British Politics*, 16, 336–354.

Butler, D. and Stokes, D. (1974) *Political Change in Britain*. London: Macmillan.

Cairney, P. (2007) A 'multiple lenses' approach to policy change: The case of tobacco policy in the UK. *British Politics*, 2, 45–68.

Cairney, P. (2014) The territorialisation of interest representation in Scotland: Did devolution produce a new form of group–government relations. *Territory, Politics, Governance*, 2(3), 303–321.

Cairney, P. (2018) The UK government's imaginative use of evidence to make policy. *British Politics*, 14(1), 1–22.

Cameron, D. (2016) EU referendum outcome: PM statement, 24 June 2016. www.gov.uk/government/speeches/eu-referendum-outcome-pm-statement-24-june-2016

Campbell, A., Converse, P., Miller, W. and Stokes, D. (1960) *The American Voter*. New York: John Wiley & Sons.

Campbell, R. (2012) What do we really know about women voters? Gender, elections and public opinion. *Political Quarterly*, 83(4), 703–710.

Campbell, R. and Shorrocks, R. (2021) Finally rising with the tide? Gender and the vote in the 2019 British elections. *Journal of Elections, Public Opinion and Parties*, 31(4), 488–507.

Carlson, M. (2009) Dueling, dancing, or dominating? Journalists and their sources. *Sociology Compass*, 3, 526–542.

Carr, E.H. (2016 [1939]) *The Twenty Years' Crisis*. London: Palgrave Macmillan.

Carreras, M., Carreras, Y.I. & Bowler, S. (2019) Long-term economic distress, cultural backlash, and support for Brexit. *Comparative Political Studies*, 52(9), 1396–1424.

Carson, R. (1962) *Silent Spring*. Boston: Houghton Mifflin.

Carter, N. and Clements, B. (2015) From 'greenest government ever' to 'get rid of all the green crap'. *British Politics*, 10(2), 204–225.

Caygill, T. (2019) Legislation under review: An assessment of post-legislative scrutiny recommendations in the UK. *Journal of Legislative Studies*, 25(2), 295–313.

Caygill, T. and Griffiths, A. (2018) Parliament and petitions. In C. Leston-Bandeira and L. Thompson (eds), *Exploring Parliament*. Oxford: Oxford University Press, pp. 322–332.

Celis, K. and Childs, S. (2020) *Feminist Democratic Representation*. Oxford: Oxford University Press.

Chambers, S. and Carver, T. (2008) William E. Connolly: Democracy, Pluralism, and Political Theory. Abingdon: Routledge.

Cherry, E. (2006) Veganism as a cultural movement: A relational approach. *Social Movement Studies*, 5(2), 155–170.

Cherry, E. (2015) I was a teenage vegan: Motivation and maintenance of lifestyle movements. *Sociological Inquiry*, 85(1), 55–74.

Cherry, E. (2021) Vegan studies in sociology. In *The Routledge Handbook of Vegan Studies*. Abingdon: Routledge, pp. 150–160.

Childs, S. (2016) *The Good Parliament*. Bristol: University of Bristol.
Chomsky, N. (2008) Humanitarian imperialism: The new doctrine of imperial right, *Monthly Review*, 60(4), 22–50.
Chomsky, N. and Herman, E. (1995) Manufacturing Consent: The Political Economy of the Mass Media. London: Vintage.
Chowdhury, M.J.A. (2020) Eastminster adaptations in the Westminster model: The confusing case of Bangladesh. www.dhakalawreview.org/blog/2020/02/eastminster-adaptations-in-the-westminster-model-the-confusing-case-of-bangladesh-4488
Churchill, W. (1947) Speech in the House of Commons (11 November), published in 206–07 The Official Report, House of Commons (5th Series), 11 November 1947, vol. 444.
Clark, T. (2018) From *The Silent Watchdog* to the Lost Watchdog: The decline of the UK regional press coverage of local government over 40 Years. *Media History*, 27(2), 177–196.
Clarke, H., Sanders, D., Stewart, M. and Whiteley, P. (2004) *Political Choice in Britain*. Oxford: Oxford University Press.
Clarke, S. (1992) The global accumulation of capital and the periodisation of the capitalist state form. In W. Bonefeld, R. Gunn and K. Psychopedis (eds), *Open Marxism I: Dialectics and History*. London: Pluto, pp. 133–179.
Clements, B.E.N. and Field, C.D. (2014) Public opinion toward homosexuality and gay rights in Great Britain. *The Public Opinion Quarterly*, 78(2), 523–547.
Clough, P. (2010) The affective turn: Political economy, biomedia and bodies. *Theory, Culture & Society*, 25(1). https://doi.org/10.1177/0263276407085156
Coates, S. (2023) 'Westminster Accounts: Speakers call for overhaul of All-Party Parliamentary Groups. *Sky News*. https://news.sky.com/story/westminster-accounts-speakers-call-for-overhaul-of-all-party-parliamentary-groups-12795326
Cochrane, A. (2022) Veganism as political solidarity: Beyond 'ethical veganism'. *Journal of Social Philosophy*, 54(1), 59–76.
Cockburn, C. (1983) Brothers: Male Dominance and Technological Change. London: Pluto.
Cockett, R. (1994) *Thinking the Unthinkable*. London: Harper Collins.
Cole, M. and Morgan, K. (2011) 'Vegaphobia: Derogatory discourse of veganism and the reproduction of speciesism in UK national papers. *British Journal of Sociology*, 62(1), 134–153.
Coley, D., Howard, M. and Winter, M. (2011) Food miles: Time for a re-think. *British Food Journal*, 113(7), 919–934.
Colley, L. (1992) *Britons: Forging the Nation*. New Haven, CT: Yale University Press.
Colley, L. (2009) *Britons: Forging the Nation 1707–1837*. New Haven, CT: Yale University Press.
Colley, L. (2014) *Acts of Union and Disunion*. London: Profile Books.
Collins, I. (2018) Allegations of bias on BBC Question Time. https://iaincollins.medium.com/bias-in-bbc-question-time-66f77ecc11ec
Collins, P.H. (2000 [1990]). Black Feminist Thought: Knowledge, Consciousness and the Politics of Empowerment, 2nd edn. London: Routledge.
Conboy, M. (2011) *Journalism in Britain: A Historical Introduction*. London: Sage.
Connelly, J., Smith, G., Benson, D. and Saunders, C. (2012) *Politics and the environment: from theory to practice*. Routledge.
Connolly, W. (1991) Identity/Difference: Democratic Negotiations of Political Paradox. New York: Cornell University Press.

Connolly, W. (1995) *The Ethos of Pluralization: Volume 1*. Minneapolis, MN: University of Minnesota Press.
Connolly, W. (2002) *Neuropolitics: Thinking, Culture, Speed*. Minneapolis, MN: University of Minnesota Press.
Connolly, W. (2005) *Pluralism*. Durham: Duke University Press.
Connolly, W. (2008) *Capitalism and Christianity: American Style*. Durham, NC: Duke University Press.
Connolly, W. (2017) *Facing the Planetary: Entangled Humanism and the Politics of Swarming*. Durham, NC: Duke University Press.
Considine, M. (2002) The end of the line? Accountable governance in the age of networks, partnerships, and joined up services. *Governance*, 15(1), 21–40.
Constitution Unit (n.d.) *What is a Constitution?* Constitution Unit Explainers, available from: https://www.ucl.ac.uk/constitution-unit/explainers/what-constitution
Converse, P. (1964) The nature of belief systems in mass publics. In D. Apter (ed.), *Ideology and Discontent*. New York: Free Press, pp. 206–261.
Cottle, S. (1998) Ulrich Beck, 'risk society' and the media: A catastrophic view? *European Journal of Communication*, 13(1), 5–32.
Cottle, S. (2003) News, Public Relations and Power. London: Sage.
Council of Europe (1985) *European Charter of Local Self-Government*. www.coe.int/en/web/conventions/full-list?module=treaty-detail&treatynum=122
Cracknell, R. and Tunnicliffe, R. (2022) Social background of MPs 1979–2019. House of Commons Library Briefing paper, 15 February 2022, number 7483.
Craft, J. and Halligan, J. (2020) Advising Governments in the Westminster Tradition: Policy Advisory Systems in Australia, Britain, Canada and New Zealand. Cambridge: Cambridge University Press.
Crenshaw, K. (1991) Mapping the margins: Intersectionality, identity politics, and violence against women of color. *Stanford Law Review*, 43(6), 1241–1299.
Crerar, P. (2023) Nadhim Zahawi sacked as Tory party chair over tax affairs. www.theguardian.com/uk-news/2023/jan/29/nadhim-zahawi-sacked-tory-party-chair-tax-affairs-rishi-sunak
Cressey, P. and MacInnes, J. (1980) Voting for Ford: Industrial democracy and the control of labour. *Capital & Class*, 11, 5–37.
Crewe, E. (2015) The House of Commons: An Anthropoloy of MPs at Work. London: Bloomsbury.
Crewe, I. and King, A. (2013) *The Blunders of Our Governments*. London: One World Publications.
Cromby, J. & Willis, M. (2014) Nudging into subjectification: Governmentality and psychometrics. *Critical Social Policy*, 2, 241–259.
Cross, L. (2013) Veganism defined (1951). *Gentle World*, 7 August. https://gentleworld.org/veganism-defined-written-by-leslie-cross-1951
Crouch, C. (2011) The Strange Non-Death of Neoliberalism. Cambridge: Polity.
Cruddas, J. (2021a) *The Dignity of Labour*. Cambridge: Polity.
Cruddas, J. (2021b) The Labour Party and the future of work II: Policy, productivity and technology. *Renewal*, 10 June. https://renewal.org.uk/labour-and-the-future-of-work-2
Cruddas, J., Thompson, P., Pitts, F.H. & Ingold, J. (2021) Labour's political strategy: Age, assets and the politics of work. *Labourlist*, 2 August. https://labourlist.org/2021/08/labours-political-strategy-age-assets-and-the-politics-of-work

Curran, J. and Seaton, J. (2003) *Power without Responsibility: Press, Broadcasting and the Internet in Britain*. London: Routledge.

Curran, J., Gaber, I. and Petley, J. (2005) *Culture Wars: The Media and the British Left*. Edinburgh: Edinburgh University Press.

Curran, J., Gaber, I. and Petley, J. (2018) *Culture Wars: The Media and the British Left*. London: Routledge.

Curry, O.S. (2019) What's wrong with moral foundations theory, and how to get moral psychology right. *Behavioral Scientist*, 26 March. https://behavioralscientist.org/whats-wrong-with-moral-foundations-theory-and-how-to-get-moral-psychology-right

Curtis, C. (2022) Meet the 'Wands' – the voters who could decide the next UK election. *The Guardian*, 6 July 2022. www.theguardian.com/commentisfree/2022/jul/06/wands-voters-next-uk-election-marginal-seats-electorate

Cutts, D., Goodwin, M. and Milazzo, C. (2017) Defeat of the People's Army? The 2015 British general election and the UK Independence Party (UKIP). *Electoral Studies*, 48, 70–83.

Cutts, D., Goodwin, M., Heath, O. and Surridge, P. (2020) Brexit, the 2019 general election and the realignment of British politics. *The Political Quarterly*, 91, 7–23.

Dahl, R. (1957) The Concept of Power. *Behavioural Science*, 2(3), 201–215.

Dahl, R. (1978) Pluralism revisited. *Comparative Politics*, 10(2), 191–203.

Dalton, R.J. and Weldon, S.A. (2005) Public images of political parties: A necessary evil? *West European Politics*, 28(5), 931–951.

Dalton, R.J., Farrell, D.M. and McAllister, I. (2011) *Political Parties and Democratic Linkage: How Parties Organize Democracy*. Oxford: Oxford University Press.

Dandoy, R. (2010) Ethno-regionalist parties in Europe: A typology. *Perspectives on Federalism*, 2(2), 194–220.

Darabont, F. (Creator) (2010–2022) *The Walking Dead* [Motion Picture]. Retrieved from https://www.imdb.com/title/tt1520211/

Darwin, J. (1999) An Undeclared Empire: The British in the Middle East, 1918–1939. In R.D. King and R.W. Kilson (eds), *The Statecraft of British Imperialism: Essays in Honour of Wm. Roger Louis*. London: Frank Cass.

Datts, M. and Gerl, K. (2023) Intra-party communication in the digital era – an empirical case study of party delegates from the German Greens. *German Politics*. https://doi.org/10.1080/09644008.2023.2168649

Davidson, T. and Berezin, M. (2018) Britain first and the UK Independence Party: Social media and movement–party dynamics. *Mobilization: An International Quarterly*, 23(4), 485–510.

Davie, T. (2021) BBC World Service to receive continued additional funding from Foreign, Commonwealth & Development Office. www.bbc.com/mediacentre/2021/world-service-funding

Davies, J. (2022) Black Lives Matter in London, June 2020: Patrick Hutchinson, instant celebrity, and changing discourses of race and class in British media. *Celebrity Studies*, 13(2), 261–269.

Davies, N. (2009) *Flat Earth News*. London: Chatto & Windus.

Davis, S. (2007) Government to put graphic warnings on tobacco products. *British Medical Journal*, 335(7618), 468–469.

De Groeve, B. and Rosenfeld, D.L. (2021) Morally admirable or moralistically deplorable? A theoretical framework for understanding character judgments of vegan advocates. *Appetite*, 168, 105693.

Deacon, B. (2007) *Cornwall: A Concise History*. Cardiff: University of Wales Press.

DEFRA (2018) Health and Harmony Inquiry. Available at: https://assets.publishing.service.gov.uk/media/5a952ad9e5274a5b849d3ad1/future-farming-environment-consult-document.pdf. (Last accessed 28 November 2023).

DEFRA (2021) National Food Strategy. Available at: https://www.gov.uk/government/publications/national-food-strategy-for-england. (Last accessed 28 November 2023).

Dekavalla, M. and Jelen-Sanchez, A. (2017) Whose voices are heard in the news? A study of sources in television coverage of the Scottish independence referendum. *British Politics*, 12, 449–472.

Delanda, M. (2016) *Assemblage Theory*. Edinburgh: Edinburgh University Press.

Deleuze, G. and Guattari, F. (2004) *A Thousand Plateaus*. London: Continuum.

Diamond, P. (2014) Governing Britain: Power, Politics and the Prime Minister. London: IB Tauris.

Diamond, P. (2018) *The End of Whitehall*. Basingstoke: Macmillan.

Diamond, P. and Laffin, M. (2022) The United Kingdom and the pandemic: Problems of central control and coordination. *Local Government Studies*, 48, 2, 211–231.

Dinerstein, A.C. (2002) Regaining materiality: Unemployment and the invisible subjectivity of labour. In A.C. Dinerstein and M. Neary (eds), *The Labour Debate: An Investigation into the Theory and Reality of Capitalist Work*. Aldershot: Ashgate, 203–225.

Dinerstein, A.C. and Pitts, F.H. (2018) From post-work to post-capitalism? Discussing the basic income and struggles for alternative forms of social reproduction. *Journal of Labor and Society*, 21(4), 471–491.

Dommett, K., Kefford, G. and Power, S. (2021a) The digital ecosystem: The new politics of party organization in parliamentary democracies. *Party Politics*, 27(5), 847–857.

Dommett, K., Fitzpatrick, J., Mosca, L. and Gerbaudo, P. (2021b) Are digital parties the future of party organization? A symposium on *The Digital Party: Political Organisation and Online Democracy* by Paolo Gerbaudo. *Italian Political Science Review/Rivista Italiana di Scienza Politica*, 51(1), 136–149.

Dorey, P. (2017) Jeremy Corbyn confounds his critics: Explaining the Labour party's remarkable resurgence in the 2017 election. *British Politics*, 12, 308–334.

Dorey, P. (2020) The Core Executive. In M. Garnett, *The Handbook of British Politics and Society*, London: Routledge, pp. 15–32.

Dorling, D. and Tomlinson, S. (2020) *Rule Britannia: Brexit and the End of Empire*. Hull: Biteback Publishing.

Downs, A. (1957) An economic theory of political action in a democracy. *Journal of Political Economy*, 5(2), 135–150.

Duffy, B. (2022) Britain's descent into culture wars has been rapid, but it needn't be terminal. *The Conversation*, 12 May. https://theconversation.com/britains-descent-into-culture-wars-has-been-rapid-but-it-neednt-be-terminal-182885

Duménil, G. and Lévy, D. (2005) The neoliberal (counter-) revolution. In A. Saad-Filho and D. Johnston (eds), *Neoliberalism: A Critical Reader*. London: Pluto Press, 9–19.

Dunleavy, P. and Margetts, H. (2001) From majoritarian to pluralist democracy? Electoral reform in Britain since 1997. *Journal of Theoretical Politics*, 13(3), 295–319.

Dunleavy, P. and Rhodes, R.A.W. (1989) Government beyond Whitehall. In H.M. Drucker, A. Gamble and G. Peele (eds), *Developments in British Politics 2*. Basingstoke: Macmillan.

Dunleavy, P. and Rhodes, R.A.W. (1990) Core executive studies in Britain. *Public Administration*, 68, 3–28.

Durose, C., Richardson, L., Combs, R., Eason, C. and Gains, F. (2013) Acceptable difference: Diversity, representation and pathways to UK politics. *Parliamentary Affairs*, 66(2), 246–267.

Durrheim, K., Okuyan, M., Twali, M., García-Sánchez, E., Pereira, A., Portice, J.S., Gur, T., Wiener-Blotner, O. and Keil, T.F. (2018) How racism discourse can mobilize right-wing populism: The construction of identity and alliance in reactions to UKIP's Brexit 'Breaking Point' campaign. *Journal of Community & Applied Social Psychology*, 28(6), 385–405.

Easat-Daas, A. (2020) Muslim Women's Political Participation in France and Belgium. Basingstoke: Palgrave Macmillan.

Edge, M. (2022) Re-Examining the UK Newspaper Industry. London: Routledge.

Eichengreen, B. (2013) The rise and fall of the Bretton Woods system. In R.E. Parker and R.M. Whaples (eds), *Routledge Handbook of Major Events in Economic History*. Abingdon: Routledge.

Eldridge, J., Kitzinger, J. and Williams, K. (1997) *The Mass Media and Power in Modern Britain*. Oxford: Oxford University Press.

Electoral Commission (2016) Results and turnout at the EU referendum. www.electoralcommission.org.uk/who-we-are-and-what-we-do/elections-and-referendums/past-elections-and-referendums/eu-referendum/results-and-turnout-eu-referendum

Elgie, R. (2011) Core executive studies two decades on. *Public Administration*, 89(1), 64–77.

Elias, A. & Tronconi, F. (2011) From Protest to Power: Autonomist Parties and the Challenges of Political Representation. Vienna: Braumüller.

Elkins, C. (2022) Legacy of Violence: A History of the British Empire. New York: Knopf.

Elliards, X. (2023) Scottish Labour brand SNP's Kate Forbes a 'tartan Tory' in attack ad. *The National*, 15 March. www.thenational.scot/news/23389383.scottish-labour-brand-snps-kate-forbes-tartan-tory-attack-ad

Elstub, S., Farrell, D.M., Carrick, J. & Mockler, P. (2021) *Evaluation of Climate Assembly UK*. Newcastle: Newcastle University.

Environmental Performance Index (2022) 2022 EPI results. Available at: https://epi.yale.edu/epi-results/2022/component/epi (Last accessed 28/11/2023).

Ernst & Young (2023) *Navigating through Turbulence*. https://assets.ey.com/content/dam/ey-sites/ey-com/en_uk/news/2023/6/uk-and-scotland-attractiveness-survey-2023.pdf

Evans, E. (2015) The Politics of Third Wave Feminisms: Neoliberalism, Intersectionality, and the State in Britain and the US. London: Palgrave Macmillan.

Evans, G. and Mellon, J. (2020) The re-shaping of class voting. British Election Study, 6 March. www.britishelectionstudy.com/bes-findings/the-re-shaping-of-class-voting-in-the-2019-election-by-geoffrey-evans-and-jonathan-mellon

Evans, G. and Menon, A. (2017) *Brexit and British Politics*. Cambridge: Polity Press.

Evans, G., Heath, A. and Lalljee, M. (1996) Measuring left–right and libertarian–authoritarian values in the British electorate. *British Journal of Political Science*, 47(1), 94–112.

Evans, P. and Silk, P. (2023) *A New Structure for Interparliamentary Relations in a Devolved Great Britain and Northern Ireland*. London: Study of Parliament Group. https://studyofparliamentgroup.org/study-of-parliament-group-papers

Evans, R. (2020) The history wars. *New Statesman*, 17 June 2020. www.newstatesman.com/longreads/2020/06/history-wars

Fairlie, S. (2022) Organic food production may be key to saving our land, online resource, available at: https://www.theguardian.com/environment/2022/may/15/organic-food-production-may-be-key-to-saving-our-land (Last accessed 28 November 2023).

Fairlie, S. (2022) How lifestock grazing is benefiting the planet. *Letters: Guardian.* www.theguardian.com/environment/2022/aug/21/how-livestock-grazing-is-benefiting-the-planet#_=_

Fanon, F. (2004 [1961]) *The Wretched of the Earth.* New York: Grove Press.

FAO (2006) *Livestock's Long Shadow: Environmental Issues and Options.* www.fao.org/3/a0701e/a0701e.pdf

Farquharson, C., Rasul, I. and Sibieta, L. (2020) *Key Workers: Key Facts and Questions.* London: Institute for Fiscal Studies.

Faucher-King, F. & Treille, E. (2003) Managing intra-party democracy: Comparing the French Socialist and British Labour party conferences. *French Politics*, 1(1), 61–82.

Fawcett, P. (2014) Critical encounters with decentred theory: Tradition, metagovernance, and parrhēsia as story-telling. In N. Turnbull (ed.), *Interpreting Governance, High Politics and Public Policy: Essays Commemorating Interpreting British Governance.* London: Routledge.

Featherstone, S. (2009) Englishness. Twentieth Century Popular Culture and the Forming of English Identity. Edinburgh: Edinburgh University Press.

Feldman, S. (1988) Structure and consistency in public opinion: The role of core beliefs and values. *American Journal of Political Science*, 32(2), 416–440.

Fella, S., Uberoi, E. and Cracknell, R. (2019) *European Parliament Elections 2019: Results and Analysis.* https://commonslibrary.parliament.uk/research-briefings/cbp-8600

Fenwick, J. (2022) 55 Tufton Street: The other black door shaping British politics, BBC News, 26 September 2022. www.bbc.co.uk/news/uk-politics-63039558

Feola, M. (2016) Fear and loathing in democratic times: Affect, citizenship, and agency. *Political Studies*, 64, 53–69.

Ferguson, N. (2004) Empire: How Britain Made the Modern World. London: Penguin.

Ferguson, S. (2017) Children, childhood and capitalism. In T. Bhattacharya (ed.), *Social Reproduction Theory.* London: Pluto, pp. 68–93.

Ferriter, D. (2019) The Border: The Legacy of a Century of Anglo-Irish Politics. London: Profile Books.

Fieldhouse, E. and Bailey, J. (2023) A new electoral map? Brexit, realignment and the changing geography of party support in England. *Political Geography*, 102. https://doi.org/10.1016/j.polgeo.2023.102862

Fieldhouse, E.A., Evans, G., Green, J., Mellon, J. and Prosser, C. (2021) Volatility, realignment and electoral shocks: Brexit and the UK general election of 2019. SSRN: https://ssrn.com/abstract=3764477 or http://dx.doi.org/10.2139/ssrn.3764477

Fieldhouse, E., Green, J., Evans, G., Mellon, J., Prosser, C., Schmitt, H. and van der Eijk, C. (2019) *Electoral Shocks: The Volatile Voter in a Turbulent World.* Oxford: Oxford University Press.

Fieldhouse, E., Green, J., Evans, G., Prosser, C., de Geus, R., Bailey, J., Schmitt, H., van der Eijk, C. and Mellon, J. (2022) British Election Study, 2019: Post-Election Random Probability Survey [data collection]. UK Data Service. SN: 8875, DOI: 10.5255/UKDA-SN-8875-1

Fielding, S. and Geddes, A. (1998) The British Labour Party and 'ethnic entryism': Participation, integration and the party context. *Journal of Ethnic and Migration Studies*, 24(1), 57–72.

Finlayson, A. (2003) *Making Sense of New Labour.* London: Lawrence & Wishart.

Fischer, L., Hasell, J., Proctor, J.C., Uwakwe, D., Ward-Perkins, Z. and Watson, C. (eds) (2018) *Rethinking Economics: An Introduction to Pluralist Economics.* Abingdon: Routledge.

Fish, J., King, A. and Almack, K. (2018) Queerying activism through the lens of the sociology of everyday life. *The Sociological Review*, 66(6), 1194–1208.

Fisher, J., Fieldhouse, E. and Cutts, D. (2014) Members are not the only fruit: Volunteer activity in British political parties at the 2010 general election. *The British Journal of Politics and International Relations*, 16(1), 75–95.

Flinders, M. (2010) Explaining majoritarian modification: The politics of electoral reform in the United Kingdom and British Columbia. *International Political Science Review*, 31(1), 41–58.

Flinders, M. and Lowery, G. (2023) Period politics and policy change: The taxation of menstrual products in the United Kingdom, 1996–2021. *Contemporary British History*, 37(2), 238–265.

Foley, M. (2000) *The British Presidency*. Manchester: Manchester University Press.

Ford, R., Bale, T., Jennings, W. and Surridge, P. (2021) *The British General Election of 2019*. London: Palgrave MacMillan.

Ford, R. and Goodwin, M. (2014) Understanding UKIP: Identity, social change and the left behind. *The Political Quarterly*, 85(3), 277–284.

Foucault, M. (1995) Discipline & Punish: The Birth of the Prison. New York: Vintage Books.

Foucault, M. (1998) The History of Sexuality 1: The Will to Knowledge. London: Penguin.

Foucault, M. (2004) *Society Must be Defended*. London: Penguin Books.

Foulkes, D., Jones, J.B. and Wilford, R.A. (1983) *The Welsh Veto: The Wales Act 1978 and the Referendum*. Cardiff: University of Wales Press.

Fox, R. and Korris, M. (2010) Making Better Law: Reform of the Legislative Process from Policy to Act. London: Hansard Society.

Francis, P. (2021) Black Lives Matter. How the UK movement struggled to be heard in the 2010s. https://theconversation.com/black-lives-matter-how-the-uk-movement-struggled-to-be-heard-in-the-2010s-161763

Fraser, N. (2016) Contradictions of capital and care. *New Left Review*, 100, 99–117.

Freeden, M. and Stears, M. (eds) (2013) *The Oxford Handbook of Political Ideologies*. Oxford: Oxford University Press.

Freise, M. and Hallman, T. (eds) (2014) Modernising Democracy: Associations and Associating in the 21st Century, London: Springer.

Friends of the Earth (2020) Ban on plastic straws, stirrers, and cotton buds begins. https://friendsoftheearth.uk/sustainable-living/ban-plastic-straws-stirrers-and-cotton-buds-begins

Fung, A. (2003) Recipes for public spheres: Eight institutional design choices and their consequences. *The Journal of Political Philosophy*, 11(3), 338–367.

Gabriel, D. (2016) Blogging while black, British and female: A critical study on discursive activism. *Information, Communication and Society*, 19(11), 1622–1635.

Gailmard, S. (2014) Accountability and principal–agent theory. In M. Bovens, R. Goodin and T. Schillemans (eds), *The Oxford Handbook of Public Accountability*. Oxford: Oxford University Press, pp. 90–105.

Galbraith, J.K. (1998) *The Affluent Society* (Fortieth anniversary edition). London: Penguin.

Galligan, Y. (2013) Gender and politics in Northern Ireland: The representation gap revisited. *Irish Political Studies*, 28(3), 413–433.

Galtung, J. and Ruge, M. (1965) The structure of foreign news: The presentation of the Congo, Cuba and Cyprus crises in four Norwegian newspapers. *Journal of International Peace Research*, 2, 64–90.

Gamble, A. (2021) Thatcherism and Conservative politics (1983) in *After Brexit and Other Essays*. Bristol: Bristol University Press.

Gans, H. (1980) Deciding What's News. A Study of CBS Evening News. New York: Vintage.

Garner, S. (2010) The entitled nation: How people make themselves white in contemporary England. *Sens Public*. http://sens-public.org/IMG/pdf/SensPublic_SGarner_entitled_nation.pdf

Garnett, M. (2021) The British Prime Minister in an Age of Upheaval. London: Routledge.

Gartzou-Katsouyanni, K., Kiefel, M. and Olivas Osuna, J.J. (2021) 'Voting for your pocketbook, but against your pocketbook? A study of Brexit at the local level. *Politics & Society*, 50(1), 3–43.

Geddes, M. (2017) Committee hearings of the UK Parliament: Who gives evidence and does this matter? *Parliamentary Affairs*, 71(2), 283–304.

Geddes, M. (2020) Dramas at Westminster: Select Committees and the Quest for Accountability. Manchester: Manchester University Press.

Geddes, M. (2023) Good Evidence: How Do Select Committees Use Evidence to Support Their Work? Edinburgh: Edinburgh University.

Gentleman, A. (2019) The Windrush Betrayal: Exposing the Hostile Environment. London: Guardian Faber.

Gerbaudo, P. (2018) *The Digital Party: Political Organisation and Online Democracy*. London: Pluto Press.

Gerbaudo, P., Marogna, F. and Alzetta, C. (2019) When 'positive posting' attracts voters: User engagement and emotions in the 2017 UK election campaign on Facebook. *Social Media + Society*, 5(4).

Gerber, P.J., Steinfeld, H., Henderson, B., Mottet, A., Opio, C., Dijkman, J., Falcucci, A. and Tempio, G. (2013) Tackling climate change through livestock – A global assessment of emissions and mitigation opportunities. *Food and Agriculture Organization of the United Nations* (FAO), Rome.

Gewin, V. (2021) A new study on regenerative grazing complicates climate optimism. *Civil Eats*, 6 January. https://civileats.com/2021/01/06/a-new-study-on-regenerative-grazing-complicates-climate-optimism

Gibernau, M. (1996) Nationalisms: The Nation-State and Nationalism in the Twentieth Century. Oxford: Polity Press.

Gibson, R. and Ward, S. (1999) Party democracy on-line: UK parties and new ICTs. *Information, Communication & Society*, 2(3), 340–367.

Gilroy, P. (2002) *Aint No Black in the Union Jack* Abingdon: Routledge Classic.

Gingrich, J. (2019) Did state responses to automation matter for voters? *Research & Politics*, 6(1), 2053168019832745.

Giovannini, A. (2016) Towards a 'new English regionalism' in the North? The case of Yorkshire first. *The Political Quarterly*, 87(4), 590–600.

Giovannini, A. (2018) The uneven governance of devolution deals in Yorkshire. In C. Berry and A. Giovannini (eds), *Developing England's North: The Political Economy of the Northern Powerhouse*. London: Palgrave.

Giovannini, A. (2021a) Levelling Up. In *Brexit and Beyond*. UK in a Changing Europe. https://ukandeu.ac.uk/research-papers/brexit-and-beyond

Giovannini, A. (2021b) The 2021 Metro Mayor elections: localism rebooted? *The Political Quarterly*, 92(3), 474–485.

Giovannini, A. (2022) The 'evolution' of devolution: Assessing Labour's legacy in England. In M. Gordon and A. Tucker (eds), *The New Labour Constitution Twenty Years On*. Oxford: Hart Publishing.

Giovannini, A. and Rose, J. (2020) England: The North–South Divide. In M. Garnett (ed.) *The Routledge Handbook of British Politics and Society*. Abingdon: Routledge, pp. 215–227.

Giovannini, A. and Vampa, D. (2020) Towards a new era of regionalism in Italy? A comparative perspective on autonomy referendums. *Territory, Politics, Governance*, 8(4), 579–597.

Giraud, E.H. (2021 *Veganism: Politics, Practice and Theory*. London: Bloomsbury Academic Press.

Giupponi, G. and Machin, S. (2022) *Labour Market Inequality*. London: Institute for Fiscal Studies. https://ifs.org.uk/inequality/labour-market-inequality

Glasser, T. (n.d.) *Objectivity precludes responsibility*. www.columbia.edu/itc/journalism/j6075/edit/readings/glasser.html

Goffman, E. (1956) *The Presentation of the Self in Everyday Life*. Edinburgh: University of Edinburgh.

Golding, W. (1997 [1954]) *Lord of the Flies*. London: Faber & Faber.

Goodhart, D. (2017) *The Road to Somewhere*. London: Hurst.

Goodwin, B. (2016) *Using Political Ideas*. Chichester: Wiley.

Goodwin, M. (2023) Value, Voice and Virtue: The New British Politics. Milton Keynes: Penguin Books.

Gottleib, J. and Toye, R. (2013) The Aftermath of Suffrage: Women, Gender, and Politics in Britain 1918–1945. London: Palgrave Macmillian.

Graham, J., Haidt, J. and Nosek, B.A. (2009) Liberals and conservatives rely on different sets of moral foundations. *Journal of Personality and Social Psychology*, 96(5), 1029–1046.

Graham, J., Haidt, J., Koleva, S., Motyl, M., Iyer, R., Wojcik, S.P. and Ditto, P.H. (2013) Moral foundations theory: The pragmatic validity of moral pluralism. In P. Devine and A. Plant (eds), *Advances in Experimental Social Psychology*. Cambridge, MA: Academic Press, pp. 55–130.

Grant, W. (2000) Pressure Groups and British Politics. Basingstoke: Macmillan.

Green, R., Milner, J., Dangour, A.D., Haines, A., Chalabi, Z., Markandya, A., Spadaro, J. and Wilkinson, P. (2015) The potential to reduce greenhouse gas emissions in the UK through healthy and realistic dietary change. *Climatic Change*, 129, 253–265.

Greenebaum, J. (2012) Veganism, identity and the quest for authenticity. *Food, Culture and Society*, 15(1), 129–144.

Greenslade, R. (2020) Why our newspapers might not survive the contagion of coronavirus. *The Guardian*, 12 April.

Gregory, A. (2020) The fundamentals of measurement and evaluation of cmmunication. In V. Luoma-aho and M.-J. Canel (eds), *The Handbook of Public Sector Communication*. Hoboken, NJ: Wiley Blackwell, 367–382.

Grove-White, R. (1996) 'Environmental knowledge & public policy needs: on humanising the research agenda' in S. Lash, B. Szernsynski and B. Wynne (eds), *Risk, Environment and Modernity*, London: Sage, pp. 269–286.

Grube, D. (2015) Responsibility to be enthusiastic? Public servants and the public face of 'promiscuous' partisanship. *Governance*, 28(3), 305–320.

Gunn, R. (1987) Notes on 'class'. *Common Sense* 2, 15–25.

Gutmann, A (ed.) (1998) *Freedom of Association*. Princeton: Princeton University Press.

Hackett, R. (2005) Is there a democratic deficit? In S. Allan (ed.), *Journalism: Critical Issues*. Maidenhead: Oxford University Press, pp. 85–97.

Hackney, F., Saunders, C., Hill, K. and Willett, J. (2021) Changing the world not just our wardrobes: A senibility for sustainable clothing, care, and quiet activism. In E. Paulicelli and M. Veronica (eds.), *Routledge Companion to Fashion Studies*. Abingdon: Routledge, pp. 111–121.

Haddon, C. (2022) Calling a general election. Institute for Government. www.instituteforgovernment.org.uk/explainer/calling-general-election

Haenfler, R. (2019) Changing the world one virgin at a time: Pledgers, lifestyle movements, and social change. *Social Movement Studies*, 18(4), 425–443.

Hagglund, M. (2019) *This Life*. New York: Anchor Books.

Haidt, J. (2012) *The Righteous Mind: Why Good People are Divided by Politics and Religion*. New York: Pantheon Books.

Hallgren, L. Bergeå, H.L. and Källström, H.N. (2020) Conservation hero and climate villain binary identies of Swedish farmers. In T. Milstein and J. Castro-Sotomayor (eds), *Routledge Handbook of Ecocultural Identity*. London: Routledge, Chapter 4.

Hall, S. (2017) *Gramsci and Us*. London: Verso.

Hall, S., Critcher, C., Jefferson, T., Clarke, J. and Roberts, B. (2013 [1978]) The social production of news. In *Policing the Crisis*. London: Red Globe Press, pp. 56–80.

Hallin, D. and Mancini, P. (2004) *Comparing Media Systems: Three Models of Media and Politics*. Cambridge: Cambridge University Press.

Halpern, D. (2015) *Inside the Nudge Unit: How Small Changes Can Make a Big Difference*. London: Random House.

Hambleton, R. and Sweeting, D. (2004) U.S.-style leadership for English local government? *Public Administration Review*, 64(4), 474–488.

Hampton, M. (2008) The fourth estate ideal in journalism history. In S. Allan (ed.), *The Routledge Companion to News and Journalism*. London: Routledge.

Hannan, K. and Freeman, J. (1977) The population ecology of organisations. *American Journal of Sociology*, 82, 929–964.

Hannan, K. and Freeman, J. (1989) *Organizational Ecology*. Cambridge: Cambridge University Press.

Hansard Society (2014) *Tuned in or Turned off? Public Attitudes to Prime Minister's Questions*. London: Hansard Society. http://doc.ukdataservice.ac.uk/doc/7577/mrdoc/pdf/7577_tuned_in_or_turned_off_public_attitudes_to_pmqs_2014.pdf

Harcup, T. (2022) *Journalism: Principles and Practice*. London: Sage.

Harcup, T. and O'Neill, D. (2001) What is news? Galtung and Ruge revisited. *Journalism Studies*, 2(2), 261–280.

Harcup, T. and O'Neill, D. (2017) What is news? News values revisited (again). *Journalism Studies*, 18(12), 1470–1488.

Harmel, R. (2018) The how's and why's of party manifestos: Some guidance for a cross-national research agenda. *Party Politics*, 24(3), 229–239.

Harte, D., Howells, R. and Williams, A. (2018) *Hyperlocal Journalism: The Decline of Local Newspapers and the Rise of Online Community News*. London: Routledge.

Harvey, D. (2005) A Brief History of Neoliberalism. Oxford: OUP.

Harvey, F. (2019) Plastic straws, cotton buds, and drink stirrers to be banned in Britain. *The Guardian*, www.theguardian.com/environment/2019/may/22/england-plastic-straws-ban

Hay, C. (1999) The political economy of New Labour: Labouring under false pretences? Manchester: Manchester University Press.

Hay, C. (2007) *Why We Hate Politics*. Cambridge: Polity Press.

Hay, C. (2010) Chronicle of a death foretold: The Winter of Discontent and the construction of the crisis of British Keynesianism. *Parliamentary Affairs*, 63(3), 446–470.

Hay, C. and Stoker, G. (2009) Revitalising politics: Have we lost the plot? *Representation*, 45(3), 225–236.

Hayes, G., Doherty, B. & Cammiss, S. (2022) We attended the trial of the Colston four: Here's why their acquittal should be celebrated. https://theconversation.com/we-attended-the-trial-of-the-colston-four-heres-why-their-acquittal-should-be-celebrated-174481

Haywood, A. (2000) *Key Concepts in Politics*. Basingstoke: Palgrave.

Hazell, R. (ed.) (2006) *The English Question*. Manchester: Manchester University Press.

HC Deb 20 Oct 2010, c.949.

HC Deb 16 Sept 2015, c.1038.

HC Deb 16 Jan 2020, c.1268.

Hearn, K.A. (1995) Stock grazing of semi-natural habitats on National Trust land. *Biological Journal of the Linnean Society*, 56(suppl_1), 25–37.

Heath, O. (2015) Policy representation, social representation and class voting in Britain. *British Journal of Political Science*, 45(1), 173–193.

Heath, O. (2018) Policy alienation, social alienation and working-class abstention in Britain, 1964–2010. *British Journal of Political Science*, 48(4), 1053–1073.

Hechter, M. (1975) *Internal Colonialism: The Celtic Fringe in British National Development, 1536–1966*. London: Routledge and Kegan Paul.

Hechter, M. and Opp, K.D. (2001) *Social Norms*. New York: Russell-Sage Foundation.

Heery, E. (2016) British industrial relations pluralism in the era of neoliberalism. *Journal of Industrial Relations*, 58(1), 3–24.

Heffernan, R. (2003) Prime ministerial predominance: Core executive politics in the UK. *The British Journal of Politics and International Relations*, 5(3), 347–372.

Heffernan, R. (2006) The prime minister and the news media: Political communication as a leadership resource. *Parliamentary Affairs*, 59(4), 582–598.

Heidar, K. (2006) Party membership and participation. In R.S. Katz and W.J. Crotty (eds), *Handbook of Party Politics*. London: Sage Publications, pp. 301–315.

Heinisch, R. and Mazzoleni, O. (2016) *Understanding Populist Party Organisation: The Radical Right in Western Europe*. London: Palgrave Macmillan.

Henderson, A. and Wyn Jones, R. (2021) *Englishness: The Political Force Transforming Britain*. Oxford: Oxford University Press.

Henn, M. and Foard, N. (2012) Young people, political participation and trust in Britain. *Parliamentary Affairs*, 65(1), 47–67.

Hepburn, E. (2009) Introduction: Re-conceptualizing sub-state mobilization. *Regional and Federal Studies*, 19(4–5), 477–499.

Hesse, B. and Sayyid, S. (2006) Narrating the postcolonial political and the immigrant imaginary. In N. Ali, V.S. Kalra and S. Sayyid (eds), *A Postcolonial People: South Asians in Britain*. London: C. Hurst & Co..

Hester, M. (1996) Patriarchal reconstruction and witch hunting. In J. Barry, M. Hester and G. Roberts (eds), *Witchcraft in Early Modern Europe*. Cambridge: Cambridge University Press, pp. 288–306.

Heywood, A. (2015) Key Concepts in Politics and International Relations. London: Palgrave.

Hix, S. and Marsh, M. (2007) Punishment or protest? Understanding European Parliament elections. *The Journal of Politics*, 69(2), 495–510.

HM Government (2012) *The Civil Service Reform Plan*. London: HM Government.

HM Government (2016) Why the government believes that voting to remain in the European Union is the best decision for the UK. https://assets.publishing.service.gov.uk/government/uploads/system/uploads/attachment_data/file/515068/why-the-government-believes-that-voting-to-remain-in-the-european-union-is-the-best-decision-for-the-uk.pdf

HM Government (2017) *Special Adviser Numbers*. London: HM Government.

HM Treasury (2016) HM Treasury analysis shows leaving EU would cost British households £4,300 per year. www.gov.uk/government/news/hm-treasury-analysis-shows-leaving-eu-would-cost-british-households-4300-per-year

Hobbes, T. (1985 [1651]) *Leviathan*. London: Penguin Books.

Hobolt, S.B. (2016) The Brexit vote: A divided nation, a divided continent. *Journal of European Public Policy*, 23(9), 1259–1277.

Hobolt, S.B., Leeper, T.J. and Tilley, J. (2021) Divided by the vote: Affective polarization in the wake of the Brexit referendum. *British Journal of Political Science*, 51(4), 1476–1493.

Hobsbawm, E. and Ranger, T. (2014) *The Invention of Tradition*. Cambridge: Cambridge University Press.

Hobsbawm, E. (1999) Industry and Empire: From 1750 to the Present Day. London: Penguin Books.

Holden, C. and Hawkins, B. (2013) 'Whisky gloss': The alcohol industry, devolution and policy communities in Scotland. *Public Policy and Administration*, 28(3), 253–273.

Hooghe, L. and Marks, G. (2003) Unraveling the Central State, but How? Types of Multi-level Governance. *American Political Science Review*, 97(2), 233–243.

Hooghe, L. and Marks, G. (2018) Cleavage theory meets Europe's crises: Lipset, Rokkan, and the transnational cleavage. *Journal of European Public Policy*, 25(1), 109–135.

Hopkin, J. and Alexander Shaw, K. (2016) Organized combat or structural advantage? The politics of inequality and the winner-take-all economy in the United Kingdom. *Politics & Society*, 44(3), 345–371.

Hopkins, A. (2018) MSP calls for UK-wide plastic straw ban. *The Spirits Business*. www.thespiritsbusiness.com/2018/01/msp-calls-for-uk-wide-plastic-straw-ban

House of Commons (2013) Public Administration and Constitutional Affairs Select Committee Second Report: Public Engagement in Policy-Making. London: House of Commons.

House of Commons (2015) Parliament and politics: Key issues for the 2015 Parliament. www.parliament.uk/business/publications/research/key-issues-parliament-2015/parliament-politics

House of Commons (2021) *Standing Orders*. 2 December 2021. HC 804 2019–2021. https://publications.parliament.uk/pa/cm5802/cmstords/so_804_2021/so-804_02122021v2.pdf

House of Commons Reform Committee (2009) *Rebuilding the House*. 12 November 2009. HC 1117. 2008–2009. https://publications.parliament.uk/pa/cm200809/cmselect/cmrefhoc/1117/1117.pdf

House of Lords Library (2022) House of Lords data dashboard: Current membership of the House. https://lordslibrary.parliament.uk/house-of-lords-data-dashboard-membership-of-the-house

Huntington, S.P. (1993) The clash of civilisations? *Foreign Affairs*, 72, 22–49.

Hurth, V. (2010) Creating sustainable identities: The significance of the Ffnancially affluent self. *Sustainable Development*, 18(3), 123–134.

Husband, G. and Ireland, A. (2022) Contextualising further education governance in Northern Ireland: History, policy and practice. *Post-Compulsory Education*, 27(3), 351–372.

Inglehart, R. (1981) Post-materialism in an environment of insecurity. *American Political Science Review*, 75(4), 880–900.

Institute for Government (2022) *Neighbourhood Services under Strain: How a Decade of Cuts and Rising Demand for Social Care Affected Local Services*. www.instituteforgovernment.org.uk/publications/neighbourhood-services

Inversi, C., Cefaliello, A. and Dundon, T. (2020) #HereToDeliver: Valuing food delivery workers in the future. *Policy@Manchester*, 25 June. https://blog.policy.manchester.ac.uk/health/2020/06/heretodeliver-valuing-food-delivery-workers-in-the-future

Ipsos (2016) Ipsos EU Referendum Prediction Poll. www.ipsos.com/en-uk/ipsos-eu-referendum-prediction-poll

Ipsos (2022) Ipsos Veracity Index 2022. www.ipsos.com/en-uk/ipsos-veracity-index-2022

Jasper, J.M. and Poulsen, J.D. (1995) Recruiting strangers and friends: Moral shocks and social networks in animal rights and anti-nuclear protests. *Social Problems*, 42(4), 493–512.

Jeffery, C. and Wincott, D. (2006) Devolution in the United Kingdom: Statehood and citizenship in transition. *Publius: The Journal of Federalism*, 36(1), 3–18.

Jeffery, D., Heppell, T., Hayton, R. and Crines, A. (2018) The Conservative Party leadership election of 2016: An analysis of the voting motivations of Conservative parliamentarians. *Parliamentary Affairs*, 71(2), 263–282.

Jennings, W. (2009) The public thermostat, political responsiveness and error-correction: Border control and asylum in Britain, 1994–2007. *British Journal of Political Science*, 39(4), 847–870.

Jennings, W. and John, P. (2009) The dynamics of political attention: Public opinion and the Queen's Speech in the United Kingdom. *American Journal of Political Science*, 53(4), 838–854.

Jennings, W. and Stoker, G. (2016) The bifurcation of politics: Two Englands. *The Political Quarterly*, 87(3), 372–382.

John, P. (2013) Experimentation, behaviour change and public policy. *The Political Quarterly*, 84(2), 238–246.

Johns, R. & Mitchell, J. (2016) *Takeover: Explaining the Extraordinary Rise of the SNP*. London: Biteback Publishing.

Johns, R. (2019) Slippery polls: Why public opinion is so difficult to measure. In P. Cowley and R. Ford (eds), *Sex, Lies and Politics: The Secret Influences That Drive Our Political Choices*. London: Biteback Publishing, p. 6.

Johnson, B. (2016) *Global Britain: UK Foreign Policy in the Era of Brexit*. www.chathamhouse.org/sites/default/files/events/special/2016-12-02-Boris-Johnson.pdf

Johnson, C. (1994) The UK and the Exchange Rate Mechanism. In C. Johnson and S. Collignon (eds), *The Monetary Economics of Europe: Causes of the EMS Crisis*. Rutherford: Fairleigh Dickinson University Press.

Johnson, M. (2022) Doing the right thing? An insitutional perspective on responsible restructuring in UK government. *Human Resource Management*, 1, 76–91.

Johnston, N. (2022) *Who Can Vote in UK Elections?* Research Briefing cbp-8985. House of Commons Library. https://commonslibrary.parliament.uk/research-briefings/cbp-8985

Judge, D. and Partos, R. (2018) MPs and their constituencies'. In C. Leston-Bandeira and L. Thompson (eds), Exploring Parliament. Oxford: Oxford University Press, pp. 264–273.

Kant, I. (1983) *Perpetual Peace and Other Essays*, Cambridge: Hackett.

Katz, B. and Nowak, J. (2018) *The New Localism: How Cities Can Thrive in the Age of Populism.* Washington, DC: Brookings Institution Press.

Katz, R.S. and Mair, P. (1993) The evolution of party organizations in Europe: The three faces of party organization. *American Review of Politics*, 14, 593–617.

Katzenstein, P.J. (ed.) (2012) Anglo-America and its Discontents: Civilizational Identities beyond West and East. Abingdon: Routledge.

Kaufmann, M. (2017) Black Tudors: The Untold Story. London: Oneworld.

Keating, M. (1999) Plurinational Democracy: Stateless Nations in a Post-Sovereignty Era. Oxford: Oxford University Press.

Keating, M. (2005) Asymmetrical government: Multi-national states in an integrating Europe. *Publius: The Journal of Federalism*, 29(1), 71–86.

Keating, M. (2017) Brexit and devolution in the United Kingdom. *Politics and Governance*, 5(2), 1–3.

Keating, M. (2021) State and Nation in the United Kingdom: The Fractured Union. Oxford: Oxford University Press.

Kelly, R. and White, I. (2016) All-women shortlists. House of Commons Library Briefing Paper, 7 March 2016. Number 5057. https://commonslibrary.parliament.uk/research-briefings/sn05057

Kelso, A. (2009) *Parliamentary Reform at Westminster.* Manchester: Manchester University Press.

Kenny, M. (2014) *The Politics of English Nationhood.* Oxford: Oxford University Press.

Kenny, M. (2016) The Politicisation of Englishness: towards a framework for political analysis. *Political Studies Review*, 14, 325–334.

Kenny, M. and Sheldon, J. (2021) When planets collide: The British Conservative Party and the discordant goals of delivering Brexit and preserving the domestic union, 2016–2019. *Political Studies*, 69(4), 965–984.

Kipling, R. (1899) *Internet Modern History Sourcebook. Rudyard Kipling: The White Man's Burden, 1899.* https://sourcebooks.fordham.edu/mod/kipling.asp

Kitschelt, H.P. (1988) Left-libertarian parties: Explaining innovation in competitive party systems. *World Politics*, 40(2), 194–234.

Koram, K. (2022) Uncommon Wealth: Britain and the Aftermath of Empire. London: John Murray.

Kriesi, H. (1998) The transformation of cleavage politics: The 1997 Stein Rokkan lecture. *European Journal of Political Research*, 33(2), 165–185.

Krook, M.L. (2018) Westminster too: On sexual harassment in British politics. *The Political Quarterly*, 89(1), 65–72.

Kulig, E. (10 March 2023) The strange lives of Parliamentary staffers. *Politics.co.uk*. www.politics.co.uk/comment/2023/03/10/the-strange-lives-of-parliamentary-staffers

Kumar, K. (2009) *The Making of English National Identity.* Cambridge: Cambridge University Press.

Labour Party (1997) 'New Labour: Because Britain deserves better.' Manifesto of the Labour Party. http://www.labour-party.org.uk/manifestos/1997/1997-labour-manifesto.shtml

Labour Party (2021) *Employment Rights: Green Paper.* https://labour.org.uk/wp-content/uploads/2022/09/Employment-Rights-Green-Paper.pdf

Ladner, A., Keuffer, N. and Bastianen, A. (2021) *Local Autonomy Index in the EU, Council of Europe and OECD countries (1990–2020).* Release 2.0. Brussels: European Commission.

Lassman, P. (2011) *Pluralism*. Cambridge: Polity.
Latour, B. (2005) Reassembling the Social: An Introduction to Actor Network Theory. Oxford: Oxford University Press.
Law, I., Easat-Daas, A., Merali, A. and Sayyid, S. (eds) (2020) *Countering Islamophobia in Europe*. Basingstoke: Palgrave Macmillan.
Lawo, D., Esau, M., Engelbutzeder, P. and Stevens, G. (2020) Going vegan: The role(s) of ICTs in vegan practice transformation. *Sustainability*, 12, 5184.
Lawson, T. (2014) Memorialising colonial genocide in Britain: The case of Tasmania. *Journal of Genocide Research*, 16(4), 441–461.
Lemke, T. (2021) *The Government of Things: Foucault and the New Materialisms*. New York: New York University Press.
Leston-Bandeira, C. and Thompson, L. (2017) Integrating the view of the public into the formal legislative process: Public reading stage in the UK House of Commons. *The Journal of Legislative Studies*, 23(4), 508–528.
Levy, A. (2014) *Small Island*. London: Tinder Press.
Levy, J. (2010) Public Bill Committees: An assessment scrutiny sought; scrutiny gained. *Parliamentary Affairs*, 63(3), 534–544.
Lewis, H. (2021) Fox news gets a British accent. *The Atlantic*, 16 June.
Lewis, J., Williams, A. and Franklin, B. (2008) A compromised fourth estate? *Journalism Studies*, 9(1), 1–20.
Lijphart, A. (2012) Patterns of Democracy: Government Forms and Performance in Thirty-Six Countries. Yale University Press.
Lilly, A., White, H., Shepley, P., Sargeant, J., Osei, K. & Olajugba, S. (2021) *Parliamentary Monitor 2021*. London: Institute for Government. Available at: www.instituteforgovernment.org.uk/sites/default/files/publications/parliamentary-monitor-2021.pdf
Lind, M. (2020) *New Class War*. New York: Atlantic.
Lindblom, C.E. (1959) The Science of "Muddling Through." *Public Administration Review*, 19(2), 79–88.
Lindblom, C.E. (1982) The Market as Prison. *The Journal of Politics*, 44(2), 324–336.
Ling, T. (2002) Delivering joined-Up government in the UK: Dimensions, issues and problems. *Public Administration*, 80(1), 615–656.
Lippmann (1955) *Essays in the Public Philosophy*. Boston, MA: Little, Brown.
Lipset, S.M. and Rokkan, S. (1967) Cleavage structures, party systems and voter alignments: An introduction. In S.M. Lipset and S. Rokkan (eds), *Party Systems and Voter Alignments: Cross-National Perspectives*. New York: Free Press, pp. 1–64.
Locke, J. (1988 [1689]) *Two Treatises of Government*. Cambridge: Cambridge University Press.
Lombardozzi, L. (2020) Gender inequality, social reproduction and the universal basic income. *The Political Quarterly*, 91(2), 317–323.
Lombardozzi, L. (2023) The andro-white marketization of volunteer and community services: A case study of London's social reproduction crisis. *Geoforum*, 140, 103697.
Lombardozzi, L. and Pitts, F.H. (2020) Social form, social reproduction and social policy: Basic income, basic services, basic infrastructure. *Capital & Class*, 44(4), 573–594.
Lovenduski, J. (2005) *Feminizing Politics*. London: Wiley.
Lucas, K., Brooks, M., Darnton, A. and Elster-Jones, J. (2008) Promoting pro-environmental behaviour: Existing evidence and policy implications. *Environmental Science and Policy*, 11, 456–466.

Lucio, M.M. and McBride, J. (2020) Recognising the value and significance of cleaning work in a context of crisis. *Policy@Manchester*, 10 June. https://blog.policy.manchester.ac.uk/posts/2020/06/recognising-the-value-and-significance-of-cleaning-work-in-a-context-of-crisis

Lukes, S. (1974, 2021) *Power: A Radical View*, 3rd edn. London: Macmillian.

Lynch, P. (2013) *SNP: The History of the Scottish National Party*, 2nd edn. Cardiff: Welsh Academic Press.

Lynch, P. (2019) *Aye or Nae*. Cardiff: Welsh Academic Press.

MacFadyen, P. (2017) Flatpack Democracy: A DIY Guide to Creating Independent Politics. Bath: Eco-Logic Books.

Mac Sweeney, N. (2023) The West: A New History of an Old Idea. WH Allen.

Mackay, F. and McAllister, L. (2012) Feminising British politics: Six lessons from devolution in Scotland and Wales. *The Political Quarterly*, 83(4), 730–734.

Mair, P. and Katz, R. (2002) The ascendancy of the party in public office: Party organizational change in twentieth-century democracies. *Political Parties*, 24, 113–136.

Mair, P. and Mudde, C. (1998) The party family and its study. *Annual Review of Political Science*, 1(1), 211–229.

Mandelson, P. (2010) The Third Man: Life at the heart of New Labour. HarperPress.

March, J.G. and Olsen, J.P. (1984) The new institutionalism: Organisational factors in political life. *American Political Science Review*, 78(2), 738–749.

March, J.G. and Olsen, J.P. (1989) *Rediscovering Institutions*. New York: Free Press.

Margaret Thatcher Foundation (2023a) Speech to Conservative Party Conference, 12th October 1979. https://www.margaretthatcher.org/document/104147

Margaret Thatcher Foundation (2023b) Speech to 1922 Committee ("the enemy within"), 19th July 1984. https://www.margaretthatcher.org/document/105563

Margolis, M., Resnick, D. and Tu, C.C. (1997) Campaigning on the Internet: Parties and candidates on the World Wide Web in the 1996 primary season. *Harvard International Journal of Press/Politics*, 2(1), 59–78.

Marinetto, M. (2003) Governing beyond the centre: A critique of the Anglo-governance school. *Political Studies*, 51(3), 592–608.

Marks, G. and Wilson, C.J. (2000) The past in the present: A cleavage theory of party response to European integration. *British Journal of Political Science*, 30(3), 433–459.

Marmor, A. (2009) *Social Conventions: From Language to Law*. Princeton, NJ: Princeton Monographs in Philosophy.

Marr, A. (2005) *My Trade*. London: Picador.

Martin, R., Pike, A., Tyler, P. and Gardiner, B. (2016) Spatially rebalancing the UK economy: Towards a new policy model. *Regional Studies*, 50(2), 342–357.

Martiniello, M. (ed.) (2005) *Political Participation, Mobilisation and Representation of Immigrants and Their Offspring in Europe*. Malmö, Sweden: School of International Migration and Ethnic Relations, Malmö University.

Martinson, J. (2018) Pale, male and posh: The media is still in a class of its own. *The Guardian*, 18 April.

Marx, K. (1976) *Capital*, Vol. I. London: Penguin.

Marx, K. (1990 [1867]) *Das Kapital*. Capital: Penguin Books.

Massetti, E. (2018) Left-wing regionalist populism in the 'Celtic' peripheries: Plaid Cymru and the Scottish National Party's anti-austerity challenge against the British elites. *Comparative European Politics*, 16, 937–953.

Massey, D. (1991) A global sense of place. *Marxism Today*, June, pp. 24–29.

May, T. (2016) Britain after Brexit. A vision of a Global Britain. May's Conference speech: full text. https://conservativehome.com/2016/10/02/britain-after-brexit-a-vision-of-a-global-britain-theresa-mays-conservative-conference-speech-full-text

Mayhew, K., Deer, C. and Mehak, D. (2004) The move to mass higher education in the UK: Many questions and some answers. *Oxford Review of Education*, 30(1), 65–82.

Mazey, S. and Richardson, J. (2021) Governments stuff up all the time: Why expect Aotearoa New Zealand to be different. In *Policy-Making under Pressure: Rethinking the Policy Process in Aotearoa New Zealand*. Albany, Auckland: Aotearoa Books, pp. 21–39.

McAdam, D. and Tarrow, S. (2010) Ballots and barricades: On the reciprocal relationship between elections and social movements. *Perspectives on Politics*, 8(2), 529–542.

McAngus, C. (2016) Party elites and the search for credibility: Plaid Cymru and the SNP as new parties of government. *The British Journal of Politics and International Relations*, 18(3), 634–649.

McCann, P. (2020) Perceptions of regional inequality and the geography of discontent: insights from the UK. *Regional Studies*, 54(2), 256–267.

McCombs, M.E. and Shaw, D.L. (1972) The agenda-setting function of mass media. *Public Opinion Quarterly*, 36(2), 176–187.

McDonnell, A. and Curtis, C. (2019) How Britain voted in the 2019 general election. YouGov. https://yougov.co.uk/politics/articles/26925-how-britain-voted-2019-general-election?redirect_from=%2Ftopics%2Fpolitics%2Farticles-reports%2F2019%2F12%2F17%2Fhow-britain-voted-2019-general-election

McDowell-Naylor, D., Cushion, S. and Thomas, R. (2022) The role of alternative online political media in the 2019 general election. In D. Wring, R. Mortimore and S. Atkinson (eds), *Political Communication in Britain*. London: Palgrave Macmillan, pp. 149–166.

McKittrick, D. and McVea, D. (2012) Making Sense of the Troubles. A History of the Northern Ireland Conflict. London: Viking.

McGarvey, D. (2018) Poverty Safari: Understanding the Anger of Britain's Underclass. London: Picador.

McGarvey, N. (2020) Local government. In M. Keating (ed.), *The Oxford Handbook of Scottish Politics*. Oxford: Oxford University Press.

McLeod, R. (1988) Calf exports at Brightlingsea. *Parliamentary Affairs*, 51(3), 345–352.

Media Reform Coalition (2021) *Who Owns the UK Media?* London: Media Reform Coalition.

Memmi, A. (2003 [1974]) *Portrait of the Colonizer: Portrait of the Colonized*. Translated from the French by H. Greenfield. London: Earthscan.

Mezey, M. (1979) *Comparative Legislatures*. Durham: Duke University Press.

Milburn, K. (2019) *Generation Left*. Cambridge: Polity.

Mill, J.S. (1997 [1868]) *The Subjection of Women*. Mineola, NY: Dover Publications.

Mill, J.S. (2008 [1859]) *On Liberty and Other Essays*, 3rd edn. Oxford: Oxford University Press.

Miller, W. (1981) The End of British Politics? Scots and English Political Behaviour in the Seventies. Oxford: Oxford University Press.

Mills, C. (1997) *The Racial Contract*. London: Cornell University Press.

Mills, C. (2009) Rousseau, the master's tools, and anti-contractarian contractarianism. *The CLR James Journal*, 15(1), 92–112.

Mills, C. (2017) *Black Rights/White Wrongs: The Critique of Racial Liberalism*. Oxford: Oxford University Press.

Mills, C. (2022) The wretched of Middle-earth: An Orkish manifesto. *The Southern Journal of Philosophy*, 1(60), 105–135.

Ministry of Defence (2023) Update: Air strikes against Daesh. www.gov.uk/government/news/update-air-strikes-against-daesh

Mitchell, J. (2006) Evolution and devolution: Citizenship, institutions, and public policy, *Publius: The Journal of Federalism*, 36(1), 153–168.

Mitchell, J. (2009) *Devolution in the UK*. Manchester: Manchester University Press.

Mitchell, J. (2010) The Westminster model and the state of unions. *Parliamentary Affairs*, 63(1), 85–88.

Modood, T. (2000) Anti-essentialism, multiculturalism, and the 'recognition' of religious groups. In W. Norman and W. Kymlica (eds), *Citizenship in Diverse Societies*. Oxford: Oxford University Press, pp. 175–196.

Modood, T. (2005) A defence of multiculturalism. *Surroundings*, 29, 62–71.

Monbiot, G. (2022) Unholy cow. *The Guardian*, 16 August.

Monbiot, G. (2023) *Regenesis: Feeding the World without Devouring the Planet*. London: Penguin.

Montpetit, É. (2016) *In Defense of Pluralism: Policy Disagreement and Its Media Coverage*. Cambridge: Cambridge University Press.

Morgan, K. (2002) The English question: Regional perspectives on a fractured nation. *Regional Studies*, 36(7), 797–810.

Morin, J.-F. and Paquin, J. (2018) *Foreign Policy Analysis: A Toolbox*, London: Palgrave Macmillan.

Mosey, R. (2016) This has been a sour and tawdry EU campaign – and broadcasters must take some responsibility. www.newstatesman.com/politics/2016/06/has-been-sour-and-tawdry-eu-campaign-and-broadcasters-must-take-some

Moxham, R. (2003) *A Brief History of Tea: Addiction, Exploitation, and Empire*. London: Constable & Robinson.

Mudde, C. (2004) The populist zeitgeist. *Government and Opposition*, 39(4), 541–563.

Munro, L. (2005) Strategies, action repertoires and DIY activism in the animal rights movement. *Social Movement Studies*, 4(1), 75–94.

Munro, L. (2012) The animal rights movement in theory and practice: A review of the sociological literature. *Sociology Compass*, 6(2), 166–181.

Murray, C.R.G. and Armstrong, M.A. (2022) A mobile phone in one hand and Erskine May in the other: The European Research Group's parliamentary revolution. *Parliamentary Affairs*, 75(3), 536–557.

Murray, R. (2016) The political representation of ethnic minority women in France. *Parliamentary Affairs*, 69, 586–602.

Nairn, T. (1977) The Break-Up of Britain. London: Verso.

Nasar, S. (2020) Remembering Edward Colston: Histories of slavery, memory, and black globality. *Women's History Review*, 29(7), 1218–1225.

Newman, N. (2022) *Reuters Institute Digital News Report 2022*. https://reutersinstitute.politics.ox.ac.uk/digital-news-report/2022/united-kingdom

Nkrumah, K. (1970) Neo-Colonialism, the Last Stage of Imperialism, London: Panaf Books.

Norman, W. and Kymlica, W. (2000) Citizenship in culturally diverse societies: Issues, contexts, concepts. In W. Kymlica and W. Norman (eds), *Citizenship in Diverse Societies*. Oxford: Oxford University Press, pp. 1–42.

Norris, P. (1999a) Introduction: The growth of critical citizens. In P. Norris (ed.), *Critical Citizens: Global Support for Democratic Governance*. Oxford: Oxford University Press, pp. 1–28.

Norris, P. (1999b) Gender: A gender-generation gap? In G. Evans and P. Norris (eds), *Critical Elections: British Parties and Voters in Long-Term Perspective*. London: Sage, pp. 177–180.

Norton, P. (1990) Parliament and policy in Britain: The House of Commons as a policy influencer. In P. Norton (ed.), *Legislatures*. Oxford: Oxford University Press, pp. 177–180.

Norton, P. (2013) *Parliament in British Politics*, 2nd edn. Basingstoke: Palgrave Macmillan.

Nurse, A. (2020) Andy Burnham's standoff with London was always about more than just lockdown money. *The Conversation*, 23 October. https://theconversation.com/andy-burnhams-standoff-with-london-was-always-about-more-than-just-lockdown-money-148594

Nye, J.S. (1990) Soft power. *Foreign Policy*, 80, 153–171.

Nye, J.S. (1992) What new world order? *Foreign Affairs*, 71(2), 83–96.

Ó Beacháin, D. (2018) *From Partition to Brexit: The Irish Government and Northern Ireland*. Manchester: Manchester University Press.

O'Donnel, A. (2017) Shame is always a revolution: The politics of affect in the thought of Gilles Deleuze. *Deleuze Studies*, 11(1), 1–24.

OBV (Operation Black Vote) (2019) *BAME Local Political Representation Audit 2019*. www.obv.org.uk/sites/default/files/images/pdf/BAME-LOCAL-POLITICAL-REPRESENTATION-AUDIT-FINAL.pdf

OECD (2019) *Negotiating Our Way Up: Collective Bargaining in a Changing World of Work*. Geneva: OECD. www.oecd-ilibrary.org/employment/negotiating-our-way-up_1fd2da34-en

OFCOM (2023) Guidance notes. Section five: Due impartiality and due accuracy and undue prominence of views and opinions. www.ofcom.org.uk/tv-radio-and-on-demand/broadcast-codes/broadcast-code/section-five-due-impartiality-accuracy

Office of the Parliamentary Commissioner for Standards (2023) Register of All-Party Parliamentary Groups. https://publications.parliament.uk/pa/cm/cmallparty/230111/register-230111.pdf

O'Neill, D. and O'Connor, C. (2008) The passive journalist: How sources dominate the local news. *Journalism Practice*, 2(3), 487–500.

ONS (2019) HI00 Regional labour market: Headline Labour Force Survey indicators for all regions. www.ons.gov.uk/employmentandlabourmarket/peopleinwork/employmentandemployeetypes/datasets/headlinelabourforcesurveyindicatorsforallregionshi00

ONS (2022) Worries about climate change, Great Britain: September to October 2022. Section 6. www.ons.gov.uk/peoplepopulationandcommunity/wellbeing/articles/worriesaboutclimatechangegreatbritain/septembertooctober2022#:~:text=During%20the%20latest%20period%2C%2074,6%20to%2017%20October%202021

Oreskes, N. and Conway, E. (2010) *Merchants of Doubt*. London: Bloomsbury Press.

Otele, O. (2020) *African Europeans: An Untold History*. London: C. Hurst & Co..

O'Toole, T., DeHanas, D.N., Modood, T., Meer, N. and Jones, S.H. (2013) *Taking Part: Muslim Participation in Contemporary Governance*. University of Bristol, Bristol. www.bristol.ac.uk/media-library/sites/ethnicity/migrated/documents/mpcgreport.pdf

Page, R. (2015) *Stigma*. London: Psychology Press.

Pakes, A. and Pitts, F.H. (2022) Fair pay agreements: How Labour can help people get on at work – not just get even. *Progressive Britain*. www.progressivebritain.org/fair-pay-agreements-how-labour-can-help-people-get-on-at-work-not-just-get-even

Panitch, L. (1986) Working-Class Politics in Crisis: Essays on Labour and the State. London: Verso.

Parekh, B. (2008) *A New Politics of Identity*. London: Palgrave Macmillian.

Parsons, C. (2022) White supremacy in retreat? Past histories and contemporary racisms in the public pedagogies of Britain and America. *Whiteness and Education*, 7(1), 93–110.

Pateman, C. & Mills, C. (2007) *Contract and Domination*. Cambridge: Polity.

Pattie, C. and Johnston, R. (2016) Resourcing the constituency campaign in the UK. *Party Politics*, 22(2), 203–214.

Paun, R. (2022) An immigrant's tale. *British Future*. www.britishfuture.org/an-immigrants-tale

Paun, A., Sargeant, J., Nicholson, E. & Rycroft, L. (2018) Sewel convention. Institute for Government. www.instituteforgovernment.org.uk/explainer/sewel-convention

Paun, A., Wilson, J. & Hall, D. (2019) Local government. Institute for Government: Explainer. www.instituteforgovernment.org.uk/explainer/local-government#footnoteref1_xm4xxfw

Peattie, K. & Peattie, S. (2009) Social marketing: A pathway to consumption reduction? *Journal of Business Research*, 62, 260–298.

Peele, G. (2018) Enoch Powell and the Conservative Party: Reflections on an ambiguous legacy. *Political Quarterly*, 89(3), 377–384.

Pendergrast, N. (2016) Environmental concerns and the mainstreaming of veganism. In T. Raphaely and D. Marinova (eds), *Impact of Meat Consumption on Health and Environmental Sustainability*. Hershey, PA: IGI Global, pp. 106–122. www.igi-global.com/book/impact-meat-consumption-health-environmental/134810

Pettitt, R. (2013) Party conferences are far from perfect, but our democracy would be worse off without them. Democratic Audit Blog. www.democraticaudit.com/2013/09/16/party-conferences-are-not-perfect-but-our-democracy-would-not-be-better-off-without-them/

Pierre, J. and Peters, G. (2020) *Governance, Politics, and The State*. London: Red Globe Press.

Pierson, P. (2000) Increasing returns, path dependence and the study of politics. *American Political Science Review*, 94(2), 251–267.

Pinch, T. (1990) The culture of scientists and disciplinary rhetoric. *European Journal of Education*, 25(3), 295–304.

Pirie, M. (2012) Think Tank: The Story of the Adam Smith Institute. London: Biteback.

Pitkin, H. (1967) The Concept of Representation. Berkleley, CA: University of California Press.

Pitts, F.H. (2022a) Marx in Management & Organisation Studies: Rethinking Value, Labour and Class Struggles. Abingdon: Routledge.

Pitts, F.H. (2022b) Contemporary class composition analysis: The politics of production and the autonomy of the political. *Capital & Class*. https://doi.org/10.1177/03098168221139284

Pitts, F.H. (2022c) The politics of work and the politics of value. *Futures of Work*, 23, 26 May. https://futuresofwork.co.uk/2022/05/26/the-politics-of-work-and-the-politics-of-value

Pitts, F.H., Lombardozzi, L. and Warner, N. (2017) *Beyond Basic Income: Overcoming the Crisis of Social Democracy?* Brussels: Foundation for European Progressive Studies.

Pitts F.H., Thompson, P., Cruddas, J. and Ingold, J. (2022) Culture wars and class wars. *Renewal: Journal of Social Democracy*, 30(3), 80–94.

Poguntke, T., Scarrow, S.E., Webb, P.D., Allern, E.H., Aylott, N., Van Biezen, I., Calossi, E. and Verge, T. (2016) Party rules, party resources and the politics of parliamentary democracies: How parties organize in the 21st century. *Party Politics*, 22(6), 661–678.

Polsby, N. (1975) Legislatures. In F.I. Greenstein and N. Polsby (eds), *Handbook of Political Science* (Vol. V). Reading: Addison-Wesley Press, pp. 277–296.

Pomerantsev, P. (2016) Why we're post-fact. *Granta*, 20 July.

Ponsford, D. (2021) Four men own Britain's news media. Is that a problem for democracy? *New Statesman*, 12 February 2021.

Pressman, J.L. and Wildavsky, A. (1984) Implementation: How Great Expectations in Washington Are Dashed in Oakland; Or, Why It's Amazing That Federal Programs Work at All, This Being a Saga of the Economic Development Administration as Told by Two Sympathetic Observers Who Seek to Build Morals on a Foundation. Berkeley, CA: University of California Press.

Price, J. (2017) Can the ferret be a watchdog? Understanding the launch, growth and prospects of a digital, investigative journalism start-up. *Digital Journalism*, 5(10), 1336–1350.

Prichard, C. and Mir, R. (2010) Organizing value. *Organization*, 17(5), 507–515.

Przeworski, A. and Wallerstein, M. (1988) Structural dependence of the state on capital. *The American Political Science Review*, 82(1), 11–29.

Pulzer, P. (1967) Political Representation and Elections in Britain. London: Allen and Unwin.

Putnam, R. (2000) Bowling Alone: The Collapse and Revival of American Community. London: Simon Schuster.

Pyper, R. (2020) Debate: The British civil service: Contextualising development challenges. *Public Money & Management*, 40(8), 555–557.

Raikes, L., Giovannini, A. and Getzer, B. (2019) *Divided and Connected: Regional Inequalities in the North, the UK and the Developed World*. London: IPPR. www.ippr.org/publications/state-of-the-north-2019

Rawls, J. (1999 [1971]) *A Theory of Justice*. Cambridge, MA: Belknap Press.

RICS (2023) About RICS. www.rics.org/about-rics

Reinhart, C.M. and Rogoff, K.S. (2009) *This Time Is Different: Eight Centuries of Financial Folly*. Princeton, NJ: Princeton University Press.

Resolution Foundation (2022) Stagnation Nation: Navigating a Route to a Fairer and More Prosperous Britain: The Interim Report of the Economy 2030 Inquiry. Resolution Foundation and Centre for Economic Performance, LSE. https://economy2030.resolutionfoundation.org/wp-content/uploads/2022/07/Stagnation_nation_interim_report.pdf

Revell, A. (2005) Ecological modernization in the UK: rhetoric or reality? *European Environment*, 15(6), 344–361.

Rhodes, A. (2019) Movement-led electoral communication: Extinction Rebellion and party policy in the media. In E. Thorsen, D. Jackson and D. Lilleker (eds), *UK Election Analysis 2019: Media, Voters and Campaign*. The Centre for Comparative Politics and Media Research, Bournemouth University, p. 77.

Rhodes, R.A.W. (2007) Understanding governance: Ten years on. *Organization Studies*, 28, 1243–1264.

Rhodes, R.A.W. and Salomonsen, H. (2021) Duopoly, court politics and the Danish core executive. *Public Administration*, 99(1), 72–86.

Richards, D. and Smith, M. (2015) Devolution in England, the British political tradition and the absence of consultation, consensus and consideration. *Representation*, 51(4), 385–401.

Richards, D. and Smith, M. (2016) The Westminster model and the 'indivisibility of the political and economic elite': A convenient myth whose time is up? *Governance*, 29(4), 499–516.

Richardson, J. (2018) The changing British policy style: From governance to government? *British Politics*, 13(1), 215–233.

Rivers Trust [The] (2021) *State of Our Rivers: We're Fighting for the Future of Our Rivers. Will You Join Us?* https://theriverstrust.org/key-issues/state-of-our-rivers

Robinson, C. (1983) *Black Marxism: The Making of the Black Radical Tradition.* London: Zed Press.

Roediger, D.R. (2022) *The Wages of Whiteness: Race and the Making of the American Working Class.* London: Verso.

Roe-Crines, A., Heppell, T. and Jeffery, D. (2021) Theresa May and the Conservative Party leadership confidence motion of 2018: Analysing the voting behaviour of Conservative parliamentarians. *British Politics*, 16, 317–335.

Rokkan, S. and Urwin, D. (1982) The Politics of Territorial Identity: Studies in European Regionalism. London: Sage.

Rootes, C. (2013) *The environmental movement in Great Britain.* In: Environmental Movements around the world: Shades of Green in Politics and Culture. Praeger, Santa Barbara CA, Denver CO and Oxford. pp. 45–67.

Rose, R. (1982) Understanding the United Kingdom. London: Longman.

Rose, R. and Shephard, M. (2016) The long and the short of the SNP breakthrough. In P. Cowley and D. Kavanagh (eds), *The British General Election of 2015.* London: Palgrave Macmillan.

Ross Arguedas, A, Robertson, C., Fletcher, R. and Nielsen, R. (2022) *Echo Chambers, Filter Bubbles, and Polarisation: A Literature Review.* Oxford: Reuters Institute for the Study of Journalism. https://reutersinstitute.politics.ox.ac.uk/sites/default/files/2022-01/Echo_Chambers_Filter_Bubbles_and_Polarisation_A_Literature_Review.pdf

Roth, S. and Saunders, C. (2023) *Organising for Change: Social Change Makers and Social Change Organisations*, Bristol: Bristol University Press.

Rowlinson, M. and Hassard, J. (1994) Economics, politics and labour process theory. *Capital & Class*, 18, 65–97.

Rowntree, J.E., Stanley, P.L., Maciel, I.C., Thorbecke, M., Rosenzweig, S.T., Hancock, D.W., Guzman, A. and Raven, M.R. (2020) Ecosystem impacts and productive capacity of a multi-species pastured livestock system. *Frontiers in Sustainable Food Systems*, 4, p. 232.

Rowse, A.L. (1941) *Tudor Cornwall.* London: Jonathan Cape.

Ruiz, P. (2022) Covid publics and Black Lives Matter: Posts, placards, and posters. *Javnost – The Public*, 29(2), 165–178.

Russell, M. (2013) The Contemporary House of Lords: Westminster Bicameralism Revived. Oxford: Oxford University Press.

Russell, M., Gover, D. and Wollter, K. (2016) Does the executive dominate the Westminster legislative process? Six reasons for doubt. *Parliamentary Affairs*, 69(2), 286–308.

Rutter, J. (2013) *Opening-Up Policymaking.* London: Institute for Government.

Sabaratnam, M. and Laffey, M. (2023) Complex indebtedness: Justice and the crisis of liberal order. *International Affairs*, 99(1), 161–180.

Said, E. (1978, 2003) *Orientalism.* London: Routledge.

Saini, R. and Begum, N. (2020) Demarcation and definition: Explicating the meaning and scope of 'decolonisation' in the social and political sciences. *The Political Quarterly*, 91(1), 217–221.

Sanders, A. and Shorrocks, R. (2019) All in this together? Austerity and the gender-age gap in the 2015 and 2017 British general elections. *The British Journal of Politics and International Relations*, 21(4), 667–688.

Sandford, M. (2022) *Local Government in England: Structures*. House of Commons Library Briefing 07104 https://researchbriefings.files.parliament.uk/documents/SN07104/SN07104.pdf

Sandford, M. (2023a) *Directly Elected Mayors*. House of Commons Library Briefing 05000. https://researchbriefings.files.parliament.uk/documents/SN05000/SN05000.pdf

Sandford, M. (2023b) *Devolution to Local Government in England*. House of Commons Library Briefing 07029. https://researchbriefings.files.parliament.uk/documents/SN07029/SN07029.pdf

Sanghera, S. (2021) Empireland: How Imperialism Has Shaped Modern Britain. London: Penguin.

Sartori, G. (1976) *Parties and Party Systems: A Framework for Analysis*. Cambridge: Cambridge University Press.

Saunders, C. (2014) Environmental Networks and Social Movement Theory. London: Bloomsbury Academic.

Saunders, C. (forthcoming) Environmental movements and environmental political theory in the Anthropocene. In M. Wisseburg and A. Machin (eds), *Edward Elgar Handbook of Environmental Political Theory in the Anthropocene*. London: Edward Elgar.

Saunders, C. (2022) Social networks and recruitment for environmental movements. In M. Grasso and M. Giugni (eds), *Routledge Handbook of Environmental Movements*. London: Routledge.

Scarparo, S. (2008) Accountability in the UK devolved parliament and assemblies. In M. Ezzamel, N. Hyndman, I. Lapsley and A. Johnsen (eds), *Accounting in Politics: Devolution and democratic accountability*. London: Routledge, pp. 38–44.

Scarrow, S. (2015) Beyond Party Members: Changing Approaches to Partisan Mobilization. Oxford: Oxford University Press.

Schmitter, P. (1974) Still the century of corporatism? *Review of Politics*, 36(1), 85–131.

Scott, J. and Wills, J. (2017) The geography of the political party: Lessons from the British Labour Party's experiment with community organising, 2010 to 2015. *Political Geography*, 60, 121–131.

Scottish Constitutional Convention (1995) *Scotland's Parliament, Scotland's Right*. Scottish Constitutional Convention Final Report, available at: https://www.parliament.scot/-/media/files/history/scotlands-parliament-scotlands-right.pdf

Sexton, A.E., Garnett, T. and Lorimer, J. (2022) Vegan food geographies and rise of Big Veganism. *Progress in Human Geography*, 46(2), 605–628.

Seyd, P. and Whiteley, P. (2004) British party members: An overview. *Party Politics*, 10(4), 355–366.

Shilliam, R. (2018) *Race and the Undeserving Poor: From Abolition to Brexit*. Newcastle: Agenda Publishing.

Shipman, T. (2017) *All Out War*. London: Allen Lane.

Showunmi, V. and Tomlin, C. (2022) *Understanding and Managing Sophisticated and Everyday Racism: Implications for Education and Work*. Lanham, MD: Lexington Books.

Sijstermans, J. (2021) The Vlaams Belang: A mass party of the 21st century. *Politics and Governance*, 9(4), 275–285.

Sijstermans, J. (2023) Explainer: Replacing Scotland's First Minister. UK in a Changing Europe blog. https://ukandeu.ac.uk/explainers/replacing-scotlands-first-minister

Silk, P. (2018) Devolution and the UK Parliament. In A. Horne and G. Drewry (eds), *Parliament and the Law*, 2nd edn. Oxford: Hart Publishing, pp. 181–206.

Simon, H. (1985) Human nature and politics: The dialogue of psychology with political science. *American Political Science Review*, 52(2), 290–310.

Simon, H.A. (1947) *Administrative Behavior: A Study of Decision-Making Processes in Administrative Organization*. New York: Macmillan.

Sloam, J. (2007) Rebooting democracy: Youth participation in politics in the UK. *Parliamentary Affairs*, 60(4), 548–567.

Sloman, P. (2019) Transfer State: The Idea of a Guaranteed Income and the Politics of Redistribution in Modern Britain. Oxford: Oxford University Press.

Sky News (2016) Michael Gove – 'EU: In Or Out?'. Streamed live on 3rd June 2016. www.youtube.com/watch?v=t8D8AoC-5i8

Smith, J., Davies, S., Feng, H., Gan, C., Grépin, K., Harman, S., Herten-Crabb, A., Morgan, R., Vandan, N. and Wenham, C. (2021) More than a public health crisis: A feminist political economic analysis of Covid-19. *Global Public Health*, 16(8–9), 1364–1380.

Smith, M. (1999) *The Core Executive*, Basingstoke: Palgrave Macmillan.

Smith, M. (2014) A crisis of political parties. In D. Richards, M. Smith and C. Hay (eds), *Institutional Crisis in 21st-Century Britain*. London: Palgrave Macmillan, pp. 101–124.

Smookler, J. (2006) Making a difference? The effectiveness of pre-legislative scrutiny. *Parliamentary Affairs*, 59(3), 522–535.

Sneider, M., Iseke, A. and Pull, K. (2021) The gender pay gap in European executive boards: The role of executives' pathway into the board. *International Journal of Human Resource Management*, 32(14), 2952–2974.

Sobolewska, M. and Begum, N. (2020) *Ethnic Minority Representation in UK Local Government*. https://documents.manchester.ac.uk/display.aspx?DocID=49921

Sobolewska, M. and Ford, R. (2020) Brexitland: Identity, Diversity and the Reshaping of British Politics. Cambridge: Cambridge University Press.

Sorensen, E. and Torfing, J. (2007) *Theories of Democratic Network Governance*. Basingstoke: Palgrave Macmillian.

Sorenson, E. and Torfing, J. (2017) Metagoverning collaborative innovation in governance networks. *American Journal of Public Administration*, 47(7), 829–839.

Soroka, S.N. and Wlezien, C. (2009) *Degrees of Democracy: Politics, Public Opinion, and Policy*. Cambridge: Cambridge University Press.

Spence, L.K. (2020) Ella Baker and the challenge of black rule. *Contemporary Political Theory*, 19(4), 551–572.

Spencer, D.A. (2000) Braverman and the contribution of labour process analysis to the critique of capitalist production – twenty-five years on. *Work, Employment and Society*, 14(2), 223–243.

Spinoza, B. (1996) [1677] *Ethics*, London: Penguin Classics.

Spivak, G.C. (1988) Can the subaltern speak? In C. Nelson and L. Grossberg (eds), *Marxism and the Interpretaion of Culture*. London: Macmillan.

Stanley, L. (2014) 'We're reaping what we sowed': Everyday crisis narratives and acquiescence to the age of austerity. *New Political Economy*, 19(6), 895–917.

Stavrianakis, A. (2018) When 'anxious scrutiny' of arms exports facilitates humanitarian disaster. *The Political Quarterly*, 89(1), 92–99.

Steenvoorden, E. and Harteveld, E. (2018) The appeal of nostalgia: The influence of societal pessimism on support for populist radical right parties. *West European Politics*, 41(1), 28–52.

Stephenson, P. (2012) *European Union Legislation on the Welfare of Farm Animals*. CiWF report. www.ciwf.org.uk/media/3818623/eu-law-on-the-welfare-of-farm-animals.pdf

Stevano, S., Mezzadri, A., Lombardozzi, L. and Bargawi, H. (2021) Hidden abodes in plain sight: The social reproduction of households and labour in the Covid-19 pandemic. *Feminist Economics*, 27(1–2), 271–287.

Stoker, G. (1998) Governance as theory: Five prepositions. *International Social Science Journal*, 50(155), 17–28.

Stoker, G. (2006) *Why Politics Matters: Making Democracy Work*. Basingstoke: Palgrave Macmillan.

Stokes, S.C. (1999) Political parties and democracy. *Annual Review of Political Science*, 2(1), 243–267.

Surridge, P. (2018) Brexit, British politics, and the left-right divide. *Political Insight*, 9(4), 4–7.

Surridge, P. (2021) *Brexit, British politics and values*. UK in a Changing Europe. https://ukandeu.ac.uk/long-read/brexit-british-politics-and-values

Surridge, P., Wager, A. and Wincott, D. (2021) *Comfortable Leavers: The Expectations and Hopes of the Overlooked Brexit Voters*. UK In A Changing Europe. https://ukandeu.ac.uk/wp-content/uploads/2021/04/Comfortable-Leavers-1.pdf

Sutton Trust [The] and the Social Mobility Commission (2019) *Elitist Britain 2019: The Educational Backgrounds of Britain's Leading People*. www.suttontrust.com/research-paper/elitist-britain-2019

Taagepera, R. (1997) Expansion and Contraction Patterns of Large Polities: Context for Russia. *International Studies Quarterly*, 41(3), 475–504.

Tatari, E. and Mencutek, Z. (2015) Strategic intersectionality and political representation: Female Muslim councilors in London. *Journal of Women, Politics & Policy*, 36(4), 415–439.

Thelen, K. and Steinmo, S. (1992) Historical Institutionalism in comparative politics. In S. Steinmo, K. Thelen and F. Longstreth (eds), *Structuring Politics: Historical Institutionalism in Comparative Analysis*. Cambridge: Cambridge University Press, pp. 1–32.

Thomas, P. and Frier, S. (2018) Campaigning to change law and policy. In C. Leston-Bandeira and L. Thompson (eds), *Exploring Parliament*. Oxford: Oxford University Press, pp. 111–121.

Thompson, K. (1995) Media and Modernity: A Social Theory of the Media. London: Polity.

Thompson, L. (2013) More of the same or a [eriod of change? The impact of Bill Committees in the twenty-first century House of Commons. *Parliamentary Affairs*, 66(3), 459–479.

Thompson, L. (2014) Evidence taking under the microscope: Has oral evidence affected the scrutiny of legislation in House of Commons committees? *British Politics*, 9, 385–400.

Thompson, P. (1989) *The Nature of Work*. London: Macmillan.

Thompson, P. (1990) Crawling from the wreckage. In D. Knights and H. Willmott (eds), *Labour Process Theory*. London: MacMillan, pp. 95–124.

Thompson, P. and Smith, C. (2001) Follow the red brick road. *International Studies of Management and Organization*, 30, 40–67.

Thompson, P., Pitts, F.H., Ingold, J. and Cruddas, J. (2022) Class composition, Labour's strategy and the politics of work. *Political Quarterly*, 93(1), 142–149.

Thomson, J. (2019) *Abortion Law and Political Institutions: Explaining Policy Resistance*. London: Palgrave Macmillan.

Tiernan, A. (2011) Advising Australian federal governments: Assessing the evolving capacity and role of the Australian public service. *Australian Journal of Public Administration*, 70(4), 335–346.

Tinline, P. (2022) *The Death of Consensus*. London: Hurst.

Tocqueville, A. (2003) [1835/1840] *Democracy in America*. London: Penguin Classics.

Tolson, A. (2019) 'Out is out and that's it the people have spoken': Uses of vox pops in UK TV news coverage of the Brexit referendum. *Critical Discourse Studies*, 16(4), 420–431.

Tomaney, J. and Pike, A. (2020) Levelling up? *The Political Quarterly*, 91(1), 43–48.

Tonge, J. (2020) Beyond Unionism versus Nationalism: The rise of the Alliance Party of Northern Ireland. *The Political Quarterly*, 91(2), 461–466.

Tooze, A. (2019) *Crashed: How a Decade of Financial Crises Changed the World*. London: Penguin Random House.

Torrance, D. (ed.) (2020) Ruth Davidson's Conservatives: The Scottish Tory Party, 2011–19. Edinburgh: Edinburgh University Press.

Torrance, D. (2022a) *Introduction to Devolution in the United Kingdom*. House of Commons Library, Research briefing CBP 8599. https://researchbriefings.files.parliament.uk/documents/CBP-8599/CBP-8599.pdf

Torrance, D. (2022b) *The Anglo-Irish Treaty 1921*. House of Commons Library, Research briefing CBP 9260. https://commonslibrary.parliament.uk/research-briefings/cbp-9260

Torrance, D. (2023) *Devolution in Wales: 'A process, not an event'*. House of Commons Library, Research briefing CBP 8318. https://commonslibrary.parliament.uk/research-briefings/cbp-8318

Tsang, A. (2018) McDonalds to switch to paper straws in Britain. *New York Times*, 15 June. www.nytimes.com/2018/06/15/business/mcdonalds-plastic-straws-britain.html

Tuchman, G. (1972) Objectivity as strategic ritual: An examination of newsmen's notions of objectivity. *American Journal of Sociology*, 77(4), 660–679.

Turner, O. (2019) Global Britain and the narrative of empire. *The Political Quarterly*, 90(4), 727–734.

Tversky, A. and Kahneman, D. (1974) Judgment under uncertainty: Heuristics and biases. *Science*, 185(4157), 1124–1131.

Uberoi, E. and Burton, M. (2023) *Ethnic Diversity in Politics and Everyday Life*. House of Commons Library, Research briefing 01156 https://researchbriefings.files.parliament.uk/documents/SN01156/SN01156.pdf

UK Parliament (2020) Climate Assembly UK. www.parliament.uk/get-involved/committees/climate-assembly-uk

UK Parliament (2022a) 'Chemical cocktail' of sewage, slurry and plastic polluting English rivers puts public health and nature at risk. https://committees.parliament.uk/committee/62/environmental-audit-committee/news/160246/chemical-cocktail-of-sewage-slurry-and-plastic-polluting-english-rivers-puts-public-health-and-nature-at-risk/#:~:text=Only%2014%25%20of%20English%20rivers,of%20health%20for%20chemical%20contamination

UK Parliament (2022b) Launch of the Interparliamentary Forum. www.parliament.uk/business/news/2022/february-2022/launch-of-the-interparliamentary-forum

UK Parliament (2022c) Register of All-Party Parliamentary Groups (as at November 2022). https://publications.parliament.uk/pa/cm/cmallparty/221130/vegetarianism-and-veganism.htm

UK Parliament (2023) Churchill and the Commons Chamber. www.parliament.uk/about/living-heritage/building/palace/architecture/palacestructure/churchill

UK 2070 Commission (2020) *Make No Little Plans – Acting At Scale For A Fairer And Stronger Future*. Final Report of the UK2070 Commission https://uk2070.org.uk/wp-content/uploads/2022/06/UK2070-FINAL-REPORT-Copy.pdf

UNHCR (2022) Yemen crisis explained. www.unrefugees.org/news/yemen-crisis-explained

Vallely, P. (1995) For what cause did Gill Phipps die? *Independent*, 3 February 1995. www.independent.co.uk/news/uk/for-what-cause-did-jill-phipps-die-1571300.html

Van Cappellen, P., Rice, E., Catalino, L. and Federickson, B. (2018) Positive affective processes underlie positive health behaviour change. *Psychology and Health*, 33(1), 77–97.

Van Ingen, E. and Van Der Meer, T.W.G. (2015) Schools or pools of democracy? A longitudinal test of the relation between civic participation and political socialization. *Political Behavior*. 38, 83–103.

Vegan Society (n.d.-a) Key facts. www.vegansociety.com/about-us/further-information/key-facts

Vegan Society (n.d.-b) How we influence policy. Available at: https://www.vegansociety.com/get-involved/our-work-policy-makers/how-we-influence-policy (last accessed 28 November 2023)

Vegan Society (n.d.-c) 'Why go vegan?'. Available at: https://www.vegansociety.com/go-vegan/why-go-vegan (last accessed 28 November 2023).

Vestergren, S. and Uysal, M.S. (2021) Beyond the choice of what you put in your mouth: A systematic mapping review of veganism and vegan identity. *Frontiers in Psychology*, 13. https://doi.org/10.3389/fpsyg.2022.848434

Vidal, D. and Bourtel, K. (2005) *Le mal-être Arabe: Enfants de la colonisation*. Marseille: Éditions Agone.

Virdee, S. (2014) *Racism, Class and the Racialized Outsider*. Basingstoke: Palgrave Macmillan.

Vinen, R. (2009) *Thatcher's Britain: The Politics and Social Upheaval of the Thatcher Era*. London: Simon & Schuster.

Watts, D. (2007) *Pressure Groups*. Edinburgh: Edinburgh University Press.

Watts, J. and Bale, T. (2019) Populism as an intra-party phenomenon: The British Labour party under Jeremy Corbyn. *The British Journal of Politics and International Relations*, 21(1), 99–115.

Webb, J., Johns, M., Roscoe, E., Giovannini, A., Qureshi, A. and Baldini, R. (2022) *State of the North 2021/22: Powering Northern Excellence*. IPPR North Report https://www.ippr.org/files/2022-01/1642509678_sotn-2021-22-jan-22.pdf

Webb, P.D. (1995) Are British political parties in decline? *Party Politics*, 1(3), 299–322.

West, J., Saunders, C. and Willett, J. (2021) A bottom up approach to slowing fashion: Tailored solutions for consumers, *Journal of Cleaner Production*, 296, 126387.

Wheaton, B. (2006) Identity, politics, and the beach: Environmental activism in surfers against sewage. *Leisure Studies*, 3, 279–302.

Whiteley, P., Larsen, E., Goodwin, M. and Clarke, H. (2021) Party activism in the populist radical right: The case of the UK Independence Party. *Party Politics*, 27(4), 644–655.

Whitten, L.C. and Phinnemore, D. (2023) *Implementing the Windsor Framework*. UK in a Changing Europe Explainer. https://ukandeu.ac.uk/explainers/implementing-the-windsor-framework/

Wieviorka, M. (1998) 'Is multiculturalism the solution? *Ethnic and Racial Studies*, 21(5), 881–910.

Wilkinson, K. (2011) Organised chaos: An interpretative approach to evidence-based policy-making in Defra. *Political Studies*, 9(4), 915–944.

Willett, J. (2021) *Affective Assemblages and Local Economies*. Lanham, MD: Rowman and Littlefield.

Willett, J. and Cruxon, J. (2019) Towards a participatory representative democracy? UK parish councils and community engagement with British Politics. *British Politics*, 14(3), 311–327.

Willett, J. and Giovannini, A. (2014) The uneven path of UK devolution: Top–down vs bottom–up regionalism in England – Cornwall and the North-East compared. *Political Studies*, 62(2), 343–360.

Willett, J., Saunders, C., Hackney, F. and Hill, K. (2022) The affective economy and fast fashion: Materiality, embodied learning and developing a sensibility for sustainable clothing. *Journal of Material Culture*, 27(3), 219–237.

Willett, J., Tidy, R., Tregidga, G. and Passmore, P. (2019) Why did Cornwall vote for Brexit: Assessing the implications for EU structural funding programmes. *Environment and Planning C*, 37(8), 1343–1360.

Williams, A. (2019) *Political Hegemony and Social Complexity: Mechanisms of Power after Gramsci*. Basingstoke: Palgrave Macmillian.

Wills, J. (2016) *Locating Localism: Statecraft, Citizenship and Democracy*. Bristol: Policy Press.

Wills, J. (2023) Bridging the gaps between *demos* and *kratos*: Broad-based community organising and political institutional infrastructure in London, UK. *Analysis of Urban Change, Theory, Action*. https://doi.org/10.1080/13604813.2023.2209446

Wilson, D. & Game. C. (2011) *Local Government in the United Kingdom*, 5th edn. Basingstoke: Palgrave Macmillan.

Wilson, G.K. & Barker, A. (2003) Bureaucrats and politicians in Britain. *Governance*, 16(3), 349–372.

Winton, A. and Howcroft, D. (2020) What Covid-19 tells us about the value of human labour. *Policy@Manchester*, 7 April. https://blog.policy.manchester.ac.uk/posts/2020/04/what-covid-19-tells-us-about-the-value-of-human-labour

Wollestonecraft, M. (2009 [1792]) A Vindication of the Rights of Women and a Vindication of the Rights of Men. Oxford: Oxford University Press.

Woodcock, J. and Graham, M. (2019) *The Gig Economy: A Critical Introduction*. Cambridge: Polity.

Wrenn, C.L. (2013) Resonance of moral shocks in abolitionist animal rights advocacy: Overcoming contextual constraints. *Society and Animals*, 21, 379–394.

Wrenn, C.L. (2019) The Vegan Society and social movement professionalization, 1944–2017. *Food and Foodways*, 27(3), 190–210.

Wright, S. (2015) Populism and Downing Street e-petitions: Connective action, hybridity, and the changing nature of organizing. *Political Communication*, 32(3), 414–433.

Wright, S. (2016) 'Success' and online political participation: The case of Downing Street e-petitions. *Information, Communication & Society*, 19(6), 843–857.

Wynne, B. (1992) Misunderstood misunderstanding: Social identities and public uptake of science. *Public Understanding of Science*, 1, 281–304.

Yarborough, A. & Thomas, S. (2010) Women of color in critical animal studies. [Themed issue] *Journal for Critical Animal Studies*, 8(3).

Yeates, N. (2012) Global Care Chains. *Global Networks*, 12(2), 135–154.

YouGov (2016) YouGov's eve-of-vote poll: Remain leads by two. https://yougov.de/politics/articles/15766-final-eve-poll-poll

YouGov (2022) Meet Britain's vegans and vegetarians, online resource. Available at: https://yougov.co.uk/society/articles/40517-meet-britains-vegans-and-vegetarians. (Last accessed 28 November 2023).

Yusoff, K. (2018) *A Billion Black Anthropocenes or None*. Minneapolis, MN: University of Minnesota Press.

Zanoni, P. (2019) Labor market inclusion through predatory capitalism? In S. Vallas & A. Kovalainen (eds), *Work and Labor in the Digital Age*. Bingley: Emerald Publishing, pp. 145–164.

Zechner, M. and Hansen, B.R. (2015) Building power in a crisis of social reproduction. *Roar*. https://roarmag.org/magazine/building-power-crisis-social-reproduction

Index

Page numbers in *italics* refer to figures; page numbers in **bold** refer to tables.

activism
   environment and climate politics and, 154, 156, 278–283, **280**. *See also* veganism
   LGBTQ+ communities and, 108
   political parties and, 142–144
   women's suffrage and, 8–9
Acts of Union (1707), 36, 42, 125, 299
Acts of Union (1800), 36, 43, 299
Adam Smith Institute (ASI), 195
Adams, C., 288–289
additional member system, 180, **181**
adjournment debates, 212
administrative devolution, 42, 117, 129–130. *See also* devolution
affect and affective economy, 100, 107–108, 110, 111
age and generations, 75–76, 175–176, *176*, 249
agenda setting (non-decision-making) power, 22
Ahmed, S., 107–108
Akala, 59, 63, 65
Alden, C., 311–312
Ali, N., 312
All-Party Parliamentary Group on British Muslims, 59
All-Party Parliamentary Group on Vegetarianism and Veganism, 283
All Party Parliamentary Groups (APPGs), 59, 106, 222–223, 283
Allen, P., 148
Allison, G.T., 303
Almond, G., 296
Almond-Lippmann consensus, 296
alternative vote system, 180, **181**
Amnon A., 311–312
anarchism, 10
Anderson, B., 5, 51
Anglo-America, 310
Anglo-Irish Treaty (1921), 43–44
Animal and Plant Health Authority, 276
animal liberation, 279–280, **280**
animal rescue, 279–280, **280**
animal rights activism, 279–282, **280**. *See also* veganism
Animal Rising, 281–282
animal welfare, 279–280, **280**
Arab Spring, 307
Argentina, 301

Arian, A., 151
Arms to Iraq case, 308
arms trade. *See* defence industry
Ashcroft, R., 26, 29–30, 31, 109
assemblage(s)
   concept of, 9, 20–21, 27–28, 30
   Anglo-America as, 310
   environment and climate politics and, 277–278, 282
   foreign policy and, 305, 306–311
   governance as, 99–101
   political change and, 109–111
   UK as multi-national state and, 34, 38, 39, 50
Astor, N., 23
asymmetric devolution, 117–118
Attenborough, D., 100, 107
austerity, 263–264

Backbench Business Committee, 211–212, 213
BAE Systems, 308
Bagehot, W., 46
Bakvis, H., 239
Bale, T., 182
Balfour Declaration (1917), 306
Bank of England, 239, 257, 261, 266, 267
Barker, A., 233
Barnett, N., 137
Barnett, S., 193
Basque region, 4
Bates, S., 210
Beach Guardian, 102
Beaumont, C., 114
Beetham, D., 210
Begum, N., 67
Behavioural Insights Team (BIT), 109, 238, 277, 283
Belfast Agreement (1998), 44, 131–132
Bell, A., 235
Benn, H., 307
Bennett, J., 20
Benton, M., 214
Bergson, H., 107
Berners-Lee, M., 285
Bevir, M., 26, 29–30, 31, 109
Bezanson, K., 81
Bhabha, H., 56
Bhambra, G.K., 56

Big Society, 235–236
Big Veganism, 287–288
Billig, M., 51
Binder, M., 112–113
bipolarity, 301–302
Black Lives Matter (BLM) movement, 18, 19–20, 21, 23, 28
Black, M., 147
Blair, T.
   foreign policy and, 302, 304, 306–307
   New Labour and, 171
   'third way' economics and, 261–263
   See also Labour government (1997–2010)
Bloodworth, J., 86
Blüdhorn, I., 290–291
Blue Labour, 151
Blühdorn, I., 288
Blyth, M., 270
Bogdanor, V., 43
Bonefeld, W., 80
Boo, K., 191
Breitbart News, 199
Bretton Woods conference (1944), 257–258, 300
Brexit, 148, 149, 222, 240, 264–265, 294. *See also* Brexit referendum (2016)
Brexit Party, 173–174, *175*, *176*
Brexit referendum (2016)
   overview of, 6–7
   British general election (2019) and, 75, 170, 172–174, 176–178
   economy and, 264–265, 266–267
   foreign policy and, 294–298
   nationalisma nd, 39
   news media and, 200–201
   Northern Ireland and, 50, 131–132
   pluralism and, 21, 26, 29–30
   political change and, 109
   political parties and, 141, 153, 156, 295
   Scotland and, 128
Brexitland, 178
The Bristol Cable, 199
Britain First (BF), 156
Britain, V., 8
British, use of term, 38
British Broadcasting Corporation (BBC), 192–194, 195, 200, 304
British Election Study (BES), 164–166, **166**, 167–168, 171–172
British Empire. *See* colonialism
British general election (2019)
   overview of, 4, 168–171, *169–170*, 178–179
   European Parliament election (2019) and, 173–174, *175*
   place–class identity and, 170–172
   social characteristics and, 174–178, *176–178*
   structural inequalities and, 75
   values and, 173, *174*

British Islamic Medical Association (BIMA), 68
British political tradition (BPT), 226
Britishness, 38–39
broadcast journalism, 192–195. *See also* British Broadcasting Corporation (BBC)
bullying, 155–156
Bulpitt, J., 116
Burke, E., 188
Burnham, A., 152, 236
Bush, G.H.W., 301
Bush, G.W., 302, 306–307
Butler, D., 167–168

Cabinet Office. *See* core executive
Cairney, P., 227–228, 241
Cameron, D.
   Behavioural Insights Team and, 109, 238
   Big Society and, 235–236
   Brexit referendum (2016) and, 294, 295, 297
   devolution and, 127, 134
   foreign policy and, 307
   Prime Minister's Questions (PMQs) and, 210–211
   See also Coalition government (2010–2015)
Campbell, A., 167, 237
Canary, 199
caring labour, 80–81, 84–85, 86–87, 92
Carlson, M., 191
Carlyle, T., 188
Carr, E.H., 296
Carson, R., 286
Catalonia, 4, 125
Catholicism, 43–44, 130–131
Celis, K., 218
Centre for Social Justice (CSJ), 241
centre–periphery cleavage, 124–133, 151–152
Change UK, 148
Channel 4, 193
Cheung, A., 137
Chewing Gum Task Force, 123
Childs, S., 218, 219, 220
Chomsky, N., 190, 192
Chowdhury, M.J.A., 243
Church of Scotland, 125
Churchill, W., 163, 206
civil war, 60–61
Clark, T., 197
Clarke, S., 88
class. *See* social class
climate activism, 154, 156. *See also* Extinction Rebellion (XR); veganism
Climate Assembly UK, 214
climate change, 98, 214, 274, 285. *See also* environment and climate politics
Climate Change Act (2008), 276
Clinton, B., 262
clothing industry, 110–111
Coalition government (2010–2015)

core executive and, 231, 241
devolution and, 127, 134
economy and, 263–264
news media and, 196–197
See also Cameron, D.
collective bargaining, 89
Colley, L., 4, 51
Collins, P.H., 64
Colls, R., 39
Colonial Office, 303–304
colonialism
overview of, 7–8, 13–14, 55–56
Brexit referendum (2016) and, 297
Britain's role(s) and place(s) in the world and, 298–303
foreign policy institutions and, 303–304
pluralism and, 18–19, 28
reading list, 71
social contract theory and, 54, 60–64, 69–70
combined authorities (CAs), 134
Commissioners for Trade and Plantations, 303–304
Committee for Womens Suffrage, 104
Committee on Climate Change, 276
Commonwealth Office, 304
Compassion in World Farming (CiWF), 281
complex government, 227–228
Conboy, M., 187, 189, 197
Connolly, W., 20, 27–28, 29, 31, 100–101, 107, 108, 188
consensus democracies, 46–47
conservatism, 9–10
Conservative and Unionist Party (Tories)
overview of, 140, 141, 150
Brexit referendum (2016) and, 295
British general election (2019) and, 4, 169, *170*, 175–178, *176*
bullying in, 155–156
electoral system and, 154–155
European Parliament election (2019) and, *175*
evolution of, 153
minority representation in, 67
news media and, 194, 197, 202
place–class identity and, 171–172
political competition and, 151
public opinion and, 164
social characteristics and, 175–178, *176*
social movements and, 156
structural inequalities and, 75
three faces of parties and, 143, 144, 145, 148
See also Coalition government (2010–2015)
Conservative government (1979–97)
core executive and, 233
devolution and, 126, 129
foreign policy and, 297, 308
Greater London Council and, 48–49
neoliberalism and, 76, 82–83, 258–261, *259–260*

Conservative government (2015–)
core executive and, 231–232
foreign policy and, 304, 308
political change and, 111
See also specific prime ministers
consociationalism, 149
Constitution Unit, 46
constitutions, 45–50, 118
Converse, P., 161, 162, 164, 165, 166–167
Corbyn, J., 145, 199, 210–211
core executive
overview of, 47, 226–234, *230*, 242–243
devolution and, 227, 229, 234, 236–237
dysfunctional nature of, 227, 239–242
individual citizens and, 227, 237–239
pluralism and, 227, 229, 238, 242
policy networks and, 227, 234–236
Cornwall, 37, 133
Corsica, 4
Coulson, A., 196–197
Council of Europe, 120
COVID-19 pandemic
core executive and, 236, 237–238
economy and, 250
news media and, 189, 196, 202
structural inequalities and, 77–78, 84–85, 86–89
Cowley, P., 182
Creasy, S., 307
Crenshaw, K., 69, 71
Crerar, P., 189, 202
Crewe, E., 148, 158, 212
Crewe, I., 240–241
Crossman, R., 228
Cruddas, J., 89, 90
cultural change, 109–111
cultural norms, 99, 103–111
culture wars, 6, 29–30
Cummings, D., 231, 236
Curran, J., 6

Dahl, R., 21–22, 26, 229
Dalton, R.J., 152
Darabont, F., 61
Davidson, R., 148
Deacon, B., 39
dealignment, 150, 169–170
death of consensus, 78
debates, 211–212
decision-making power, 22
decolonisation, 11, 299–300. *See also* colonialism
defence industry, 305, 308–309
Delanda, M., 20
Deleuze, G., 20, 22, 27, 107, 111
democracy
news media and, 186–190
parties' role in, 154–155
political parties and, 144

racism and, 18–19
social capital and, 112
See also direct democracy; e-democracy; liberal democracy; social democracy
Democratic Unionist Party (DUP), 131, 132, 141, 153
Denham, A., 144
Denmark, 241
Denver, D., 183
Department for Business, Energy and Industrial Strategy (BEIS), 275, 276
Department for Environment, Food and Rural Affairs (Defra), 102, 240–241, 275, 282–283
Department for International Development, 304
Department for Transport (DfT), 123, 275, 276
Department for Work and Pensions (DWP), 241
Desai, J., 69
descriptive representation, 218–220
devolution
  overview of, 42, 44, 116–118, 123–125, 136
  constitutional settlement and, 49–50
  core executive and, 227, 229, 234, 236–237
  education and, 123
  England and, 117, 133–136, *135*
  local government and, 120–123
  Northern Ireland and, 44–45, 117, 130–133
  political parties and, 152
  reading list, 137
  Scotland and, 3, 44–45, 117, 125–128
  UK as multi-national state and, 38–39, 44–45, 50
  UK Parliament and, 44–45, 221–222
  Wales and, 3, 42, 117, 128–130
digital news, 191–192, 197–199. *See also* social media
digital parties, 143–144
diplomacy, 296
Diplomatic Service, 305
direct democracy, 199–200. *See also* referendums
disabilities, 75
diversity, 28, 29–30. *See also* pluralism
Donelan, M., 193
Dooley, S., 111
Dorling, D., 109
Downs, A., 268–269
Dunleavy, P., 229, 242
Durose, C., 22

e-democracy, 238
Easat-Daas, A., 59
echo chambers, 199
economic activity, 248, 250–252, *251–252*
Economic and Social Research Council (ESRC), 173
economic libertarianism, 10
economy
  overview of, 248–249
  austerity and, 263–264
  Brexit and, 264–265, 266–267
  current state of, 250–257, *251–254*, *256*
  neoliberalism and, 258–261, *259–260*
  pluralism and, 265–270
  postwar Keynesianism and, 257–258
  reading list, 270–271
  'third way' economics and, 261–263
education, 1, 123, *177*, 178, 250
Edward VI, 207
Egypt, 306
elections
  overview of, 13, 160, 181
  reading list, 182–183
  voting behaviour and, 166–168
  See also British general election (2019); referendums
Electoral Reform Society (ERS), 154
electoral systems
  overview of, 180, **180–181**
  additional member system, 180, **181**
  alternative vote system, 180, **181**
  first-past-the-post (FPTP) system, 143, 154, 180, **180**, 195
  single transferable vote system, 131, 180, **181**
Elstub, S., 214
England
  devolution and, 117, 133–136, *135*
  economic activity in, 250–252
  formation of UK and, 41–45
  local government in, 12, 118–123, *122*
  Union Flag and, 36–38, *37*
English Question, 133–135
Englishness, 38–39
entryism, 68
Environment Act (2022), 106
Environment Agency, 102, 276
environment and climate politics
  overview of, 274–278, 289–290
  activism and, 154, 156, 278–283, **280**. *See also* veganism
  assemblage(s) and, 277–278, 282
  environmental knowledge and, 283–287
  governance and, 119
  political change and, 98
  post-politics and, 287–289
  reading list, 290–291
  select committees and, 214
  See also Extinction Rebellion (XR); veganism
Environmental Audit Committee, 102, 111, 276
environmental knowledge, 283–287
Environmental Performance Index, 274
Equality Act (2010), 8, 9
essentialism, 59, 60
ethno-regionalist political parties, 152
European Exchange Rate Mechanism (ERM), 261

European Free Alliance, 4
European Parliament election (2019), 173–174, *175*
European Research Group (ERG), 145, 148
European Union (EU), 300–301. *See also* Brexit; European Parliament election (2019)
Evans, G., 171–172, 200–201
Evans, P., 222
Evans, R., 7–8
executive devolution, 117. *See also* devolution
executive power
   overview of, 226–228
   cabinet versus prime ministerial government debate and, 226, 228–229
   foreign policy and, 305
   fusion of powers system and, 208–209
   reading list, 243–244
   separation of powers systems and, 25, 208–209
   UK as multi-national state and, 44–45
   See also core executive
Extinction Rebellion (XR), 154, 156, 281–282

factions, 145
fair pay agreements (FPAs), 78, 91
Fairlie, S., 286
Fanon, F., 56, 71
Farage, N., 172, 295, 296
Fawcett, P., 235
Featherstone, S., 133
federalism, 50, 118
feminism, 10, 19–20
feminist foreign policy, 303
feminist institutionalism, 132–133
The Ferret, 198–199
Fieldhouse, E., 183
Final Straw campaign, 100
first-past-the-post (FPTP) system, 143, 154, 180, **180**, 195
fiscal devolution, 117, 236, 266. *See also* devolution
Fish, J., 108, 110
Fisher, J., 145
Five Star Movement, 143–144
flags, 35–38, *37*, 140
Flatpack Democracy, 103
Flinders, M., 51–52, 104
Floyd, J., 64
Food and Agriculture Organisation (FAO), 285, 287
Food Standards Agency, 276
Forbes, K., 100, 144, 151
Ford, R., 109, 178, 182, 183
Foreign and Commonwealth Office (FCO), 304
Foreign, Commonwealth and Development Office (FCDO), 304–305. *See also* core executive
Foreign Office, 304

foreign policy
   overview of, 294
   Brexit referendum (2016) and, 294–298
   Britain's role(s) and place(s) in the world and, 298–303
   controversies and contestation in, 306–309
   institutions and, 303–305
   reading list, 311–312
foreign policy analysis (FPA), 302–303
Foreign Secretary (Secretary of State for Foreign Affairs), 304–305
Forestry Commission, 276
Foucault, M., 22, 60
fourth estate, 188–190. *See also* news media
Fox, R., 215
France, 4, 66, 304
Francis, P., 18
Freeden, M. & Stears, M., 9
Frier, S., 222–223
fusion of powers systems, 208–209

Gabriel, D., 108, 110, 114
Galbraith, J.K., 270
Galligan, Y., 22
Galtung, J., 195
Gans, H., 191
Garner, S., 58
Garnett, M., 241
GB News, 193
Geddes, M., 213, 224
gender and gender inequality
   British general election (2019) and, 176–177, *177*
   feminist institutionalism and, 132–133
   foreign policy and, 303
   political representation and, 23–24
   representation and, 218–219
   sexual objectification of women and, 288–289
   structural inequalities and, 8–9, 74–79, 80–88, *86*
   women's suffrage and, 8–9
general elections, 178–180, **179**, **180–181**. *See also* British general election (2019)
generations. *See* age and generations
Gentleman, A., 189, 202, 203
Gerbaudo, P., 143–144
Gerber, P.J., 285
Germany, 118, 241
gig economy, 86
Gilroy, P., 8, 18, 21, 29
Gini coefficient, 255, 262
Giraud, E.H., 288, 290–291
Gladstone, W.E., 42
Glasser, T., 195
Global Britain, 297–299, 310
Global South, 300
Global War on Terrorism (GWoT), 306–307

Goffman, E., 68
Golding, W., 61
Goldsmith, Z., 156
Goodhart, D., 295
Goodman, C., 196–197
Goodwin, B., 9
Goodwin, M., 109
Gove, M., 190, 296
governance, 28–29, 99–104, 119
government, 28–29, 100, 102–103, 119, 305. *See also* executive power; scrutiny of government; *specific governments*
Government of Wales Act (2006), 148–149
Gramsci, A., 56, 106
Greater London Council, 48–49
green parties, 144
Green Party of England and Wales
    overview of, 141
    Brexit referendum (2016) and, 295
    British general election (2019) and, 173–174, *176*
    European Parliament election (2019) and, 173–174, *175*
    evolution of, 153
    social characteristics and, *176*
    three faces of parties and, 144
Green, R., 285
green theories, 10
Greenslade, R., 196
Gregory, A., 238
Grey, G., 304
Grube, D., 240
Guattari, F., 20, 22, 27, 107, 111
Guido Fawkes, 199
Gulf War (1991), 301, 306–307

Haenfler, R., 105
Haidt, J., 161–162
Hall, S., 190–191
Hallgren, L., 286–287
Halpern, D., 238
Hammond, P., 231–232
Hampton, M., 188
Hansard Society, 210
Hansen, B.R., 80–81, 83
Harcup, T., 188, 195, 196
Harmel, R., 147
Hay, C., 220, 238–239
Hayward, K., 137
Health and Harmony (Defra, 2018), 283
Hechter, M., 4
Heffernan, R., 237
hegemony, 106, 301
Henderson, A., 39
Herman, E., 190, 192
Hester, M., 8
Hindmoor, A., 235
historical institutionalism, 207–208

Hobbes, T., 60–62
Hobhouse, E., 8
home ownership, 75–76, 249
Home Rule, 43
Hooghe, L., 150
Hopkin, J., 270
House of Commons
    overview of, 206–207
    devolution and, 221–222
    first-past-the-post (FPTP) system and, 143, 154, 180, **180**, 195
    legislative scrutiny and, 214–216, **215**
    representation and, 218–220
    scrutiny of government and, 210–214, *213*
House of Lords
    overview of, 206–207
    electoral system and, **181**
    legislative scrutiny and, 216–217
    parliamentarians in, 149
    proposed abolition of, 50
    representation and, 219–220
    scrutiny of government and, 211, 212, 214
Hurth, V., 110

iconic activism, 108
ideological power, 22
IMPRESS, 198
income, 253–254, *253–254*
income inequality, 255, 260, *260*, 262, 268
Independent Press Standards Organisation (IPSO), 196–197
inequality. *See* gender and gender inequality; income inequality; structural inequalities
Inglehart, R., 150
Institute for Fiscal Studies (IFS), 89, 239–240
Institute of Economic Affairs (IEA), 195, 240
institutions, 11. *See also specific insitutions*
internal colonialism, 4, 44
internal diversity, 35
Internal Market Bill, 222
International Association of Oil and Gas Producers, 102
International Monetary Fund (IMF), 300
international organisation, 299–302. *See also specific organisations*
intersectionality, 66, 69, 80–88
intra-party democracy (IPD), 144
Ipsos, 160, 198
Iran, 308
Iraq, 301, 306–307
Ireland
    formation of UK and, 41, 43–44
    Union Flag and, 36–38, *37*
    See also Northern Ireland; Republic of Ireland
Irish Free State, 43–44
Irish War of Independence, 43–44
Islam and Muslims, 58, 59, 67–68, 308
Islamophobia, 59

Israel, 46
Italy, 4, 46, 48, 118, 125, 143–144
ITV News, 193

James I of England, 42
Japan, 35
Jarvis, M.D., 239
Jasper, J.M., 278–279
Jennings, W., 163, 172, 175
Johns, R., 164, 183
Johnson, B.
  Brexit referendum (2016) and, 75, 172, 296
  core executive and, 231, 232
  COVID-19 pandemic and, 189, 190, 236
  foreign policy and, 297
  news media and, 189, 190, 191–192
Joint Ministerial Council (JMC), 237
Jones, G., 228
judiciary, 25, 208–209, 305

Kahneman, D., 161
Kant, I., 60, 309
Katz, R.S., 142, 146, 147
Katzenstein, P.J., 310, 312
Keating, M., 51
Keynes, J.M., 257–258
Kilbrandon Commission (Royal Commission on the Constitution), 49, 126
King, A., 240–241
Kingdom of Great Britain, 42–43
Kipling, R., 55
Kitschelt, H.P., 150
Koram, K., 312
Korris, M., 215
Kosovo War (1999), 302
Kriesi, H., 150
Kuenssberg, L., 198
Kulig, E., 147
Kwarteng, K., 232
Kymlica, W., 26

Labour government (1974–1979), 258
Labour government (1997–2010)
  arms trade and, 308
  core executive and, 237
  devolution and, 134
  foreign policy and, 304, 306–307
  scrutiny of government and, 212–213
  'third way' economics and, 261–263
Labour Party
  overview of, 141, 150
  Brexit referendum (2016) and, 295
  British general election (2019) and, 4, 169, 170, 170, 175–178, 176
  centre–periphery cleavage and, 133
  electoral system and, 154–155
  European Parliament election (2019) and, 175
  evolution of, 153
  fair pay agreements (FPAs) and, 91
  foreign policy and, 307
  minority representation in, 67
  news media and, 194, 197
  place–class identity and, 171–172
  political competition and, 151
  public opinion and, 164
  representation and, 218
  Scotland and, 125–127
  social characteristics and, 175–178, 176
  structural inequalities and, 75–76
  three faces of parties and, 142–143, 144, 145, 149
  Wales and, 129, 130
labour power, 79–80, 88
Laffey, M., 300
Lancaster, B., 39
Latour, B., 21
Laws in Wales Acts (1535 and 1542), 41
League of Nations, 300
left–right dimension, 151
legislative consent motions (LCMs), 221–222
legislative devolution, 117. *See also* devolution
legislative power, 25, 208–209. *See also* legislatures
legislative scrutiny, 214–217, **215**
legislatures
  foreign policy and, 305
  parliamentarians and, 147–150
  See also Northern Ireland Assembly; Scottish Parliament; UK Parliament; Welsh Parliament (Senedd Cymru)
Leston-Bandeira, C., 224
Leveson Inquiry, 190, 196–197, 198
Levy, A., 8, 215
Lewis, J., 203
LGBTQ+ communities, 19–20, 56–57, 108
liberal democracy, 19–20, 24–28, 309–310
Liberal Democrats (Lib Dems)
  overview of, 141
  Brexit referendum (2016) and, 295
  British general election (2019) and, 169, 170, 173–174, 176
  economy and, 264, 269
  European Parliament election (2019) and, 173–174, 175
  evolution of, 153
  minority representation in, 67
  social characteristics and, 176
  as 'third party,' 150
  three faces of parties and, 143, 145, 149
  See also Coalition government (2010–2015)
Liberal Party, 150
liberalism, 10. *See also* neoliberalism
life expectancy, 250
Lijphart, A., 46–47
Lind, M., 90
Lindblom, C., 267

line of flight, 111
Lippmann, W., 296
Lipset, S.M., 124–125, 149–150, 152
local governance, 102–103
local government
    overview of, 11–12, 116, 118–123, *122*
    core executive and, 236
    devolution and, 120–123
    electoral system and, **180–181**
    governance and, 102–103
Local Government Act (1985), 48–49
Localism Act (2011), 103
Locke, J., 25–26, 62
Lombardozzi, L., 93
London Assembly, **181**
low politics, 116
Lowenduski, J., 133
Lowery, G., 104
Lukes, S., 22, 240
Luxton, M., 81
Lynch, P., 200

Mackay, F., 132
Mair, P., 142, 146, 147
Major, J., 301
majoritarian democracies, 46–47
March, J.G., 207–208
markets, 267–269
Markievicz, C., 23
Marks, G., 150, 152
Marmor, A., 104
Marr, A., 188–189
Martiniello, M., 59
Marx, K., 79–80
Massey, D., 310
Maude, F., 233
May, T., 111, 148, 231–232, 295, 297, 308
mayors, 121, **180**, 236
McAllister, L., 132
McKay Commission, 221
Mebyon Kernow, 37, 133, 152
median voter theory, 268–269
megaphone bureaucracy, 240
Mellon, J., 171–172, 200–201
Memmi, A., 55–56, 57, 59
meta-governance, 235
micropolitics, 108–109
Middle East and North Africa (MENA) region, 258, 301, 306–309
migration, 107–108
Miliband, E., 151
Mill, J.S., 8, 26, 60
Miller, W., 167
Mills, C., 62–63, 71
Ministry of Agriculture Farming and Food, 284
minority representation, 54–55, 65–69, 70, 219
Mitchell, J., 39, 40–41, 42, 44, 148
Modood, T., 26, 29, 58

Momentum, 145
Monbiot, G., 286
monetary policy, 267
Montreal Protocol (1987), 288
mood theory, 296
Moral Foundations Theory (MFT), 161–162, 164
moral pluralism, 24–26
moral shocks, 278–279
Morin, J.-F., 295–296
Mosey, R., 195
Moxham, R., 19
Mulcaire, G., 196–197
multi-level governance, 234, 236–237
multi-national states
    overview of, 4–5, 34–35
    UK as, 3–5, 34–39, *37*, 50
multi-speed membership, 146
multiculturalism, 28, 29, 57–58
multipolarity, 302
Munro, L., 278, 279
Muslim Arts and Culture Festival (MAC Fest), 68
myth of return, 57

Nairn, T., 4
Nasser, G.A., 306
nation-states, 3, 5–7, 34–35, 61
National Food Strategy (Defra, 2021), 282–283
national identities, 5–7, 38–39, 42–44
National Infrastructure Commission, 276
national park authorities, 276
nationalism, 10
nations, 34–35. *See also* multi-national states
Natural Capital Committee, 276
Natural England, 102, 276
natural environment, 20. *See also* environment and climate politics
Natural Resources Wales, 102
NatureScot, 102
neo-colonialism, 300
neoliberalism, 76–77, 82–83, 258–261, *259–260*
Net Zero Wales, 98
Netherlands, 4
New Labour, 171. *See also* Blair, T.; Labour government (1997–2010)
New York Times (newspaper), 100
New Zealand, 46, 78, 91
Newman, N., 198
news media
    overview of, 13, 186–190
    broadcast journalism and, 192–195
    echo chambers and, 199
    as extension of corporate and state power, 190–192
    pluralism and, 186–187, 197, 198–199, 201–202
    print journalism and, 196–197
    reading list, 203
    referendums and, 199–201

See also social media
news values, 195–196
Nkrumah, K., 300
non-decision-making (agenda setting) power, 22
Norman W., 26
normative behaviourism, 64
Norris, P., 220
North Atlantic Treaty Organization (NATO), 300, 302
Northcote-Trevelyan Report (1854), 233
Northern Ireland
  Brexit referendum (2016) and, 50, 131–132
  calls for reunification of Ireland and, 49–50
  devolution and, 44–45, 117, 130–133
  economic activity in, 252
  fiscal autonomy in, 266
  formation of UK and, 44
  governance in, 102
  local government in, 118–123, *122*
  minority representation in, 66
Northern Ireland Assembly
  overview of, 12, 44–45, 130–131, 132
  electoral system and, **181**
  eligible voters in, **179**, 180
  political parties and, 148–149
Northern Ireland Environment Agency, 102
Norton, P., 206, 209, 212, 221
Novara Media, 199

objectivity, 194–195
Ofcom, 192, 193
Office for Environmental Protection, 276
Office for National Statistics (ONS), 248, 253
Office of Gas and Electricity Markets (Ofgem), 276
Olsen, J.P., 207–208
O'Neill, D., 195, 196
Operation Black Vote, 65
opposition days, 211–212
oral questions, 210–211
Organisation for Economic Cooperation and Development (OECD), 91, 248
organisational ecology, 280
Orientalism, 57
Osborne, G., 190

Paine, T., 25
Pankhurst, E., 104
Paquin, J., 295–296
Parekh, B., 29
parliamentarians, 147–150
parliamentary questions, 210–211
parliaments, 12. *See also* legislatures
partisan identification, 166–168
party conferences, 144
party families, 155–156
Pateman, C., 71
Paun, R., 19

Pendergrast, N., 284
People for the Ethical Treatment of Animals (PETA), 289
performativity, 68
Peston, R., 198
petitions, 220–221
Petitions Committee, 220–221
Petley, J., 193
Phipps, J., 281
Pierson, P., 208
Pinch, T., 284
Pirate parties, 143–144
Pirie, M., 195
Pitkin, H., 218
Pitt, W. the Elder, 303–304
Pitts, F.H., 93
place–class identity, 170–172
placebo policies, 240
Plaid Cymru, 128–129, 130, 141, 152, 156–157, 169–170
plastic pollution, 100, 101, 107
pluralism
  concept of, 19–20, 24–28, 30
  overview of, 1–2, 13–14
  assemblages and, 20–21, 27–28, 30
  core executive and, 227, 229, 238, 242
  devolution and, 49–50
  diversity and, 28, 29–30
  economy and, 265–270
  environment and climate politics and, 287–289
  foreign policy and, 295–298, 303
  governance and, 28–29
  multiculturalism and, 28, 29
  news media and, 186–187, 197, 198–199, 201–202
  political change and, 107, 109
  political parties and, 150–151
  political representation and, 22–24, 54–55, 65–69, 70, 219
  power and, 20, 21–22
  reading list, 31–32
  structural inequalities and, 78–79, 88–93, *92*
  UK as multi-national state and, 35
  UK Parliament and, 23–24, 210–214, 218–220, 221–222
Policy Exchange, 240
policy networks, 227, 234–236
political activism, 105–107
political behaviour, 64–65
political change
  overview of, 98–99, 113–114
  cultural norms and, 99, 103–111
  governance and, 99–104
  reading list, 114
  social capital and, 99, 111–113
political cleavage theory, 124–133, 149–150, 151–152

political competition, 150–152
political participation
  concept of, 59
  minority representation and, 54–55, 65–69, 70, 219
  postwar migrants and, 54, 63–65, 70
  racism and, 59–60
  social contract theory and, 54, 60–64, 69–70
political parties
  overview of, 12, 140–141
  Brexit referendum (2016) and, 141, 153, 156, 295
  political competition and, 150–152
  reading list, 158
  three faces of the, 141–150
  (waning?) importance of, 152–157
  See also specific parties
political pluralism, 22–24
political representation
  pluralism and, 22–24, 54–55, 65–69, 70, 219
  UK Parliament and, 218–220
Political Studies Association, 101
Pomerantsev, P., 198
populism, 10, 21, 75, 156–157
post-environmentalism, 288
post-legislative scrutiny, 217
post-politics, 287–289
post-structuralism, 22
post-veganism, 288
postcolonialism, 56–57, 298–303. *See also* colonialism
Poulsen, J.D., 278–279
Powell, E., 19, 21
power
  news media and, 187–192
  pluralism and, 20, 21–22
  political change and, 100–102
  social contract theory and, 54, 60–64, 69–70
pre-legislative scrutiny, 217
predistribution, 78–79, 88–91
Press Complaints Commission, 197
Pressman, J.L., 235
pressure groups, 101–102, 105–107, 110–111
Price, J., 198
Prime Minister's Questions (PMQs), 150, 210–211
principal–agent theory, 209
print journalism, 196–197
production, 77
proportional representation, 154–155
Protect Our Waves All Party Parliamentary Group (APPG), 106
Protestantism, 43–44, 130–131. *See also* Church of Scotland
public bill committees, 215–216
public diplomacy, 296
public opinion, 160–166, *165*, **166**, 269, 296–298, 305

Pulzer, P., 168
purchasing power parity, 250
The Purple Book (Labour Party), 151
Putnam, R., 27, 28, 32, 112

race and racism
  concepts of, 58–60
  colonialism and, 7–8, 55–56
  foreign policy and, 299, 303
  impact on democracy of, 18–19
  political participation and, 59–60
  structural inequalities and, 74–79, 80–88, *86*
  UK assemblage and, 21
racial contract theory, 62–63, 69–70
racialisation, 59
radical animal liberation movement, 279–280, **280**
Raikes, L., 137
Reagan, R., 76, 259–260
referendums, 13, 154–155, 160, 166–168, 199–201. *See also* Brexit referendum (2016); Scottish independence referendum (2014)
Reform of the House of Commons Committee, 212–213
Regional Development Agencies, 134
regional inequalities, 5
religion, 43–44, 125, 130–131
Republic of Ireland, 36, 43–44, 49–50, 131
resistance, 22
Resolution Foundation, 271
resonance machines, 100, 108
rhizomes, 20, 22, 30. *See also* assemblage(s)
Rhodes, R.A.W., 229, 242
Richards, D., 234, 243
Richelieu, Cardinal, 304
right-wing populism, 21, 75
Rivers Trust, 102
Robinson, C., 298
Rokkan, S., 39–40, 124–125, 149–150, 152
Rose, R., 38
Rousseau, J.-J., 25
Rowse, A.L., 41
Royal Commission on the Constitution (Kilbrandon Commission), 49, 126
Royal Institution of Chartered Surveyors (RICS), 101–102
Rudd, A., 189
Ruge, M., 195
Russell, D., 39
Russell, M., 51–52, 214, 217

Sabaratnam, M., 300
Said, E., 56, 57
Salisbury–Addison Convention, 216
Sandford, M., 137
Sanghera, S., 7–8
Sartori, G., 154, 155
Sartre, J.-P., 55, 56

Saudi Arabia, 308–309
Scarrow, S., 145–146
Scotland
  Brexit referendum (2016) and, 128, 131
  devolution and, 3, 44–45, 117, 125–128
  fiscal autonomy in, 266
  formation of UK and, 41, 42–43
  governance in, 102
  local government in, 118–123, *122*
  minority representation in, 66
  Union Flag and, 36–38, *37*
  See also Scottish independence referendum (2014)
Scotland Act (1978), 126
Scotland Act (1997), 127
Scotland Act (2016), 221–222
Scott, J., 142–143
Scottish Constitutional Convention, 126
Scottish Environment Protection Agency, 102
Scottish independence referendum (2014)
  overview of, 3, 49–50, 140–141, 151–152
  devolution and, 127
  news media and, 199–201
  political parties and, 3, 140–141, 148, 151–152, 170, 199–200
Scottish National Party (SNP)
  overview of, 125–127, 141
  Brexit referendum (2016) and, 295
  British general election (2019) and, 169–170, *170*, *176*
  bullying in, 156
  European Parliament election (2019) and, *175*
  evolution of, 153
  political competition and, 151–152
  populism and, 156–157
  referendum on independence (2014) and, 3, 140–141, 148, 151–152, 170, 199–200
  social characteristics and, *176*
  as 'third party,' 150, 169–170
  three faces of parties and, 144, 147, 148, 149
Scottish Office, 125
Scottish Parliament, 12, 44–45, 127, 148–149, **179**, 180, **181**
scrutiny of government, 209–214, *213*
Secretary of State for Foreign Affairs (Foreign Secretary), 304–305
Secretary of State for the Colonies, 304
select committees, 212–214, *213*
Senedd and Elections (Wales) Act (2020), 130
Senedd Cymru (Welsh Parliament), 12, 129, 148–149, **179**, 180, **181**
separation of powers systems, 25, 208–209
Serban, R., 51–52
service-based economy, 250
Sewel Convention, 221–222
Sexton, A.E., 287–288
sexual objectification of women, 288–289
Shamir, M., 151

Sharp, R., 190
Shaw, A.K., 270
Shilliam, R., 8, 18
Silk, P., 222
Simon, H.A., 284
single transferable vote system, 131, 180, **181**
Sinn Féin, 131, 141, 149, 152
Sky News, 193, 223
Sloam, J., 157
Slovenia, 4
Smith, I.D., 241
Smith, M., 232, 234, 242
smoking, 105
Sobolewska, M., 67, 178, 183
social capital, 99, 111–113
social characteristics, 174–178, *176*
social class
  British general election (2019) and, 170–172
  foreign policy and, 303
  partisan identification and, 166–168
  political representation and, 23–24
  structural inequalities and, 74–88, *86*
social contract theory, 54, 60–64, 69–70
social democracy, 10
social media, 143, 147, 153–154, 192, 197–198. *See also* digital news
Social Mobility Commission, 23
social movements, 154, 156. *See also* activism
social reproduction theory, 77–88, 93
Sorenson, E., 235
Spain, 4, 48, 118, 125
Spence, L.K., 64
Spinoza, B., 107
Spivak, G.C., 56
state-building processes, 39–45
state of nature, 61–62
stateless nations, 35
states, 34–35. *See also* multi-national states; nation-states
Stavrianakis, A., 308
Stevano S., 94
Stoker, G., 172, 175, 220, 238–239
Stokes, D.E., 167–168
Stokes, S.C., 152
Stormont. *See* Northern Ireland Assembly
strategic rituals, 194–195
structural inequalities
  overview of, 8–9, 13–14, 74–79
  fair pay agreements (FPAs) and, 78, 91
  pluralism and, 78–79, 88–93, *92*
  predistribution and, 78–79, 88–91
  reading list, 93–94
Study of Parliament Group, 222
Sturgeon, N., 140
sub-state nationalist parties, 152
substantive representation, 218–220
Suez Crisis (1956), 306
Suffragettes, 104

Sufi Islam, 308
Sunak, R., 65, 66, 202
Sunni Islam, 308
Surfers Against Sewage (SAS), 105–106, 112
Surridge, P., 151
sustainable development, 110–111, 287–289
Sutton Trust, 23
Syria, 306, 307

Thatcher, M.
  core executive and, 233
  devolution and, 126, 129
  neoliberalism and, 258–261, *259–260*
thermostatic model of public opinion, 163–164
think tanks, 195, 239–240
third parties, 150, 169–170
'third way' economics, 261–263
Thomas, P., 222–223
Thompson, L., 158, 215–216, 224
Thompson, P., 79, 94
Thomson, J., 114
Times (newspaper), 192
Tocqueville, A. de, 26, 112
tokenism, 67–68
Tolson, A., 201
Tomlinson, S., 109
Torfing, J., 235
trade unions, 54–55, 69, 85–86, 89, 93
Treasury, 232, 261, 266–267, 296. *See also* core executive
Troubled Families Programme (TFP), 241
Troubles, 44, 130
Trump, D., 194, 295
Truss, L., 155, 232, 240
Tuchman, G., 194–195
Turner, O., 297–298
Tversky, A., 161

UK in a Changing Europe, 173
UK Independence Party (UKIP)
  Brexit referendum (2016) and, 141, 153, 156, 172, 295
  political change and, 109
  structural inequalities and, 75
  three faces of parties and, 143
UK Parliament
  overview of, 12, 206–209, 223
  eligible voters in, **179**, 180
  external relations and, 220–223
  fusion of powers system and, 208–209
  historical roots of, 42–43, 44–45, 206–207
  legislative scrutiny and, 214–217, **215**
  parliamentarians and, 148–149
  reading list, 224
  representation and, 218–220
  scrutiny of government and, 209–214, *213*
  See also House of Commons; House of Lords
Ulster, 43

unemployment, 252, *252*
Union Flag, 36–38, *37*
Union of the Crowns (1603), 42
union states, 39–40, 44–45
unipolarity, 301–302
unitary states, 39–40, 44–45
United Kingdom of Great Britain and Northern Ireland (UK)
  overview of, 2–3
  vs. Britain, 299
  constitutional settlement of, 45–50
  historical roots of, 39–45
  institutions in, 11. *See also specific insitutions*
  as multi-national state, 3–5, 34–39, *37*, 50
  reading list, 51–52
  See also colonialism; devolution
United Nations (UN), 300, 301, 308
United Nations Climate Conferences (COP meetings), 98
United States
  Bretton Woods system and, 257–258
  Gulf War (1991) and, 301, 306–307
  neoliberalism and, 259–260
  neoliberalism in, 76
  separation of powers system in, 208–209
  'third way' economics and, 262–263
universal basic income, 87–88
Universal Credit welfare policy, 241
Urban Wastewater Treatment Directive (1991), 105–106
Urwin, D., 39–40
utilitarianism, 26

valence, 173–174
valorisation, 77
value–attitude gap, 109–110
values, 173, *173*
Vegan Outreach, 279
Vegan Society, 278, 280–281, 282–283, 284–285
veganism
  overview of, 274, 277, 289–290
  activism and, 278–283, **280**
  environmental knowledge and, 284–286
  post-politics and, 287–289
Vegetarian Society, 278
Veracity Index, 197–198
voting behaviour, 166–168. *See also* British general election (2019)
Vucetic, S., 312

Wales
  devolution and, 3, 42, 44–45, 117, 128–130. *See also* Welsh Parliament (Senedd Cymru)
  fiscal autonomy in, 236, 266
  formation of UK and, 41–42
  governance in, 102
  local government in, 118–123, *122*

minority representation in, 66
political change in, 98
Union Flag and, 36–38, *37*
Wales Act (1978), 129
Wales Act (2006), 129
Wales Act (2014), 129–130
Wales Act (2017), 130, 221–222
War Office, 304
Warsi, S., 65
Water Services Authority, 276
Watts, D., 217
wealth, 253–254, *253–254*. *See also* income inequality
Webb, P., 154, 182
Welsh nationalism, 128
Welsh Office, 42, 128
Welsh Parliament (Senedd Cymru), 12, 129, 148–149, **179**, 180, **181**
Wessex Regionalists, 37
Westminster model, 46–50, 226, 229, 234. *See also* core executive
Westminster Palace (Houses of Parliament), 150, 206–207. *See also* UK Parliament
Westphalia, Treaty of (1648), 34–35
Wheaton, B., 106
Whitehall departments. *See* core executive; *specific departments*
Wildavsky, A., 235
Wildlife Fund for Nature, 101
Wilkinson, K., 240

Willett, J., 310
Wills, J., 142–143
Wilson, C.G., 152
Wilson, G.K., 233
Wilson, H., 266
Windrush generation, 8, 54, 57–58, 65, 189, 202
winter of discontent, 258
Withdrawal Agreement, 294
Wollestonecraft, M., 8, 104
Wollstonecraft, M., 25
women. *See* gender and gender inequality
women's suffrage, 8–9, 104
World Bank, 300
World Trade Organization (WTO), 300
Wrenn, C.L., 284
Wright Reforms, 211–213
Wright, S., 238
written questions, 211
Wyn Jones, R., 39
Wynne, B., 284

Yemen, 308–309
Yes Scotland campaign, 141. *See also* Scottish independence referendum (2014)
Yorkshire, 37, *37*, 133
Yorkshire Party, 37, 133, 152
Yousaf, H., 65, 144

Zahawi, N., 189
Zechner, M., 80–81, 83

www.ingramcontent.com/pod-product-compliance
Lightning Source LLC
Chambersburg PA
CBHW080213040426
42333CB00044B/2643